AUSTRALIAN FISHING NETWORK

AUSTRALIAN
FISH
GUIDE

REVISED AND EXPANDED
3rd EDITION

by Frank Prokop

Published and distributed by
Australian Fishing Network
48 Centre Way, Croydon South, Victoria 3136
Telephone: (03) 9761 4044 Facsimile: (03) 9761 4055
Email: sales@afn.com.au
Website: www.afn.com.au

ISBN 9781865 131078

First published 2000, Reprinted 2001, 2002. Revised 2nd Edition 2002, Reprinted 2004.

Revised and Expanded 3rd Edition 2006, Reprinted 2008

Illustrations by Trevor Hawkins
Rig illustrations by Geoff Wilson

INTRODUCTION

There are many books describing the species that are caught by recreational anglers in Australia. Some of these books are good and some are not so good, but they are either written for scientists or beginners. There is a need for a book which describes fish in language that most anglers can understand and apply in the field or later when they are admiring their prize.

This book provides the information on the species that are regularly taken including their identification and range and some helpful fishing information. This book will be a useful addition to the bookshelves of the keen and occasional recreational fisher in Australia. It is hoped that those who care enough to buy a book of this kind will follow a few simple rules to ensure that future fishing is available. These include:

taking only as many fish as you need, irrespective of the bag limits;

taking ice and ensuring that the catch is edible and able to be used;

if fishing for the table, killing them as soon as possible;

if releasing them, giving fish the best chance for future capture and

placing all litter including discarded fishing line and empty bait packets into garbage bins.

If today's recreational fishers follow these simple rules quality recreational fishing will continue to be available. There has been an enormous improvement in the attitude and approach of recreational fishers since the late 1980s. Government and the community are increasingly recognising the importance of recreational fishing and making adjustments to commercial fishing to ensure that sufficient fish are available for recreational fishing. We all need to do our part by ensuring that there are enough fish available to reproduce, as poor environmental conditions for recruitment can occur at any time.

This edition is larger and contains information on more fish and how to catch them. The format has also been improved.

I would like to thank the anglers of Australia for their support of the *Australian Fish Guide*. Please enjoy the book.

Frank Prokop

AUTHOR: FRANK PROKOP

FISH ILLUSTRATIONS: TREVOR HAWKINS

RIG ILLUSTRATIONS: GEOFF WILSON

EDITORS: STEPHEN BOOTH
BILL CLASSON

DEDICATION

This book is dedicated to every parent, friend or grandparent who has taken a child fishing. These children are our future and by knowing about the fish that are available, and how to catch them, they can help to ensure that quality fishing is available for their own children (who can torment them on their first fishing trips).

Enjoy every day as if it might be your last and take the time to tell those who are near to you that you love them.

Finally, give the 'last cast' just a few more seconds. You are always only one hit away from a memorable trip.

ACKNOWLEDGEMENT

For the third edition it is fitting that I acknowledge the people who made the Australian Fish Guide one of the most popular fishing books in Australia.

Firstly to Bill Classon for having the vision to see the book as it would look when finished and the patience to allow me to write it at my own pace.

To Trevor Hawkins for the superb illustrations and for drawing a cunjevoi, even if it is not a real challenge to Trevor's considerable talents. To Geoff Wilson whose rigs and drawings have made this book extra special.

To all the people at AFN over the years for your unfailing good cheer and understanding my tiny scribbles in the margins when making edits. All of you are friends and special people - including my mate Jim Harmon!

To people like Steve Newman who patiently explains the differences between trevally and cod species so that I have a hope of passing on some way of identifying fish which doesn't involve a full autopsy.

To my family for allowing me to have the space and time to write the fishnig books.

To my my surgeons, Stephen Archer and Professor David Morris, and my GP Saint Robert Turnbull - for without their surgical skills and support I would have struggled more in battling Cancer.

Finally to all those who have bought my books over the years and given me positive feedback. Thanks to you all.

CONTENTS

POISONOUS - DO NOT EAT

CAUTION - MAY CAUSE CIGUATERA POISONING

ARCHER FISH

Scientific name *Toxotes chatareus*. Also known as Rifle fish.

Range The archer fish is found from the northern end of 80-Mile beach south of Broome around the top end to the Townsville area. The similar Gulf archer fish *Toxotes jaculatrix* is found in streams of the Gulf of Carpentaria.

Description A deep bodied fish of tropical freshwater regions. The dorsal fin is set well back, which enables the fish to sit parallel to the surface where it watches for insect life in overhanging branches which it shoots down with a spurt of water from its mouth. They have several large spots on the body and a large, upturned mouth which makes identification relatively easy. While the archer fish may grow to around a kilogram and 30 cm, they are commonly encountered at much smaller sizes.

Fishing Archer fish are avid takers of lures and flies, often hitting large lures intended for barramundi. They are good fun on light spinning or fly tackle and will take all standard trout flies or lures in larger sizes. Small archer fish make good live baits for barramundi but they are more attractive as aquarium fish, where their water spouting habits make them immensely popular with local kids. Fair eating quality.

BASS, AUSTRALIAN

Scientific name *Macquaria novemaculeata*. Also known as Bass, Australian perch.

Range From Fraser Island and the Mary River and coastal drainages as far as the Gippsland lakes system in Victoria. The range of Australian bass has been considerably expanded through stockings and the fish can be found in a number of impoundments in Queensland, NSW and Victoria.

Description The Australian bass is a handsome fish which can reach more than 4 kg in impoundments, but any fish from the rivers over 2.4 kg is an extremely noteworthy capture. Males are smaller than females and a large male will be up to 1.5 kilograms. The Australian bass is easily confused with the similar estuary perch. Even experts can confuse the two species, but they can be most easily separated by the forehead profile which is straight or slightly rounded in the bass and is concave or slightly indented in the estuary perch. Estuary perch prefer tidal waters or the lower reaches of coastal rivers. Australian bass are more common in the northern part of the range with estuary perch becoming increasingly common in southern NSW and Victoria. Australian bass must have salt water to breed and the increased construction of weirs and dams on coastal streams has had a significant impact on bass numbers.

Fishing The Australian bass is arguably the best light tackle sportfish of temperate waters in Australia. They have a close affinity for structure and will dash out from their snag to grab a lure, bait or fly and madly dash back into cover, busting off the unwary. While not as powerful as mangrove jacks of tropical waters, they are spectacular sport in their own right. Australian bass can be extremely aggressive, feeding on fish, shrimps, prawns, insects, lizards and small snakes that may fall into the water. Australian bass are more active at dusk, dawn or at night. Fishing on a summer's evening is almost unbeatable, with surface lures or popping bugs on a fly rod producing spectacular strikes at dusk and well into the night. Many lures work well and bass anglers are have massive collections of surface lures, shallow divers, deep divers, soft plastics, spinnerbaits and special lures in every conceivable pattern and colour. Bass can also be taken trolling in dams very close to cover or in rivers along rock walls or under overhanging branches where casting is very difficult. In many instances, casts with lure or fly have to be within 30 cm of cover to get a strike. Very slowly working the lure near cover will bring a bass out for a look and when the retrieve is commenced, a slashing strike can result. Many baits work well for bass, with live baits being best. A live shrimp or prawn drifted under a quill float will almost guarantee a response from any bass, but this includes very small fish which may be gut hooked if the hook is set too late. Live fish such as poddy mullet also work well, as do grasshoppers, worms and live cicadas during summer. Although Australian bass make excellent eating, almost all fish are now returned by increasingly enlightened anglers, but it must be stressed that fish in dams will not breed, even if they have very full ovaries.

ARCHER FISH

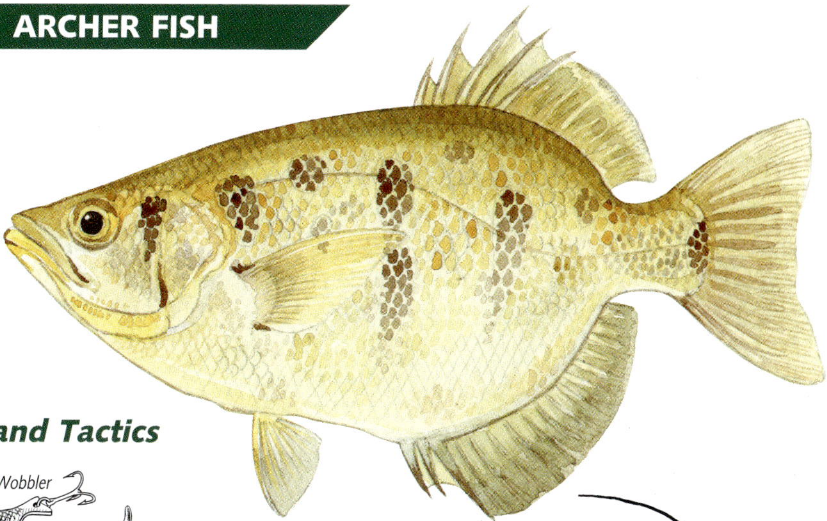

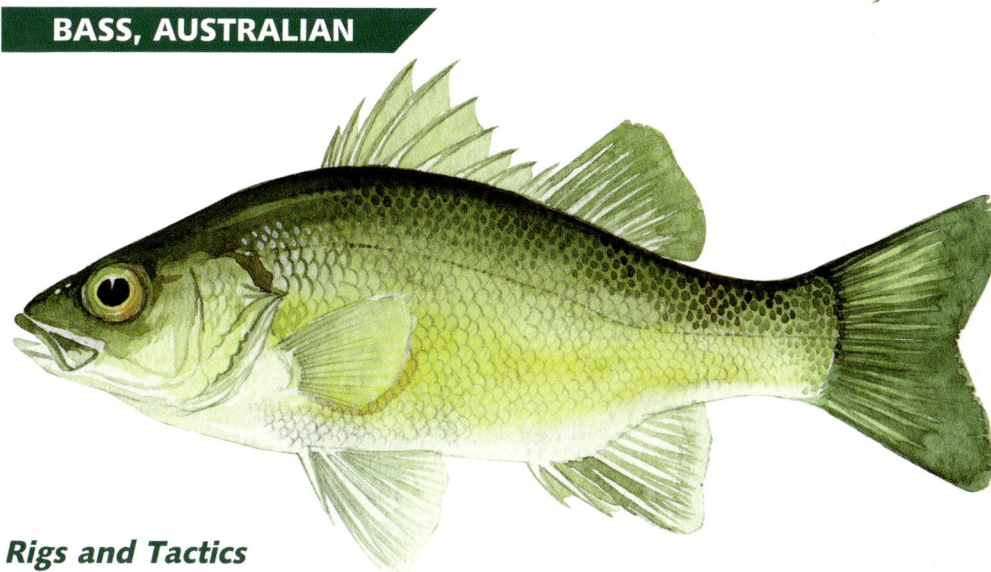

Rigs and Tactics

Wonder Wobbler
Mr Twister
24 kg trace
Minnow Lure
Fly fishing is successful

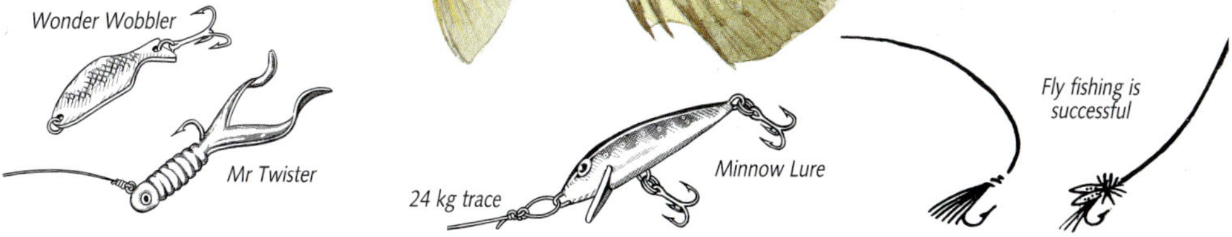

BASS, AUSTRALIAN

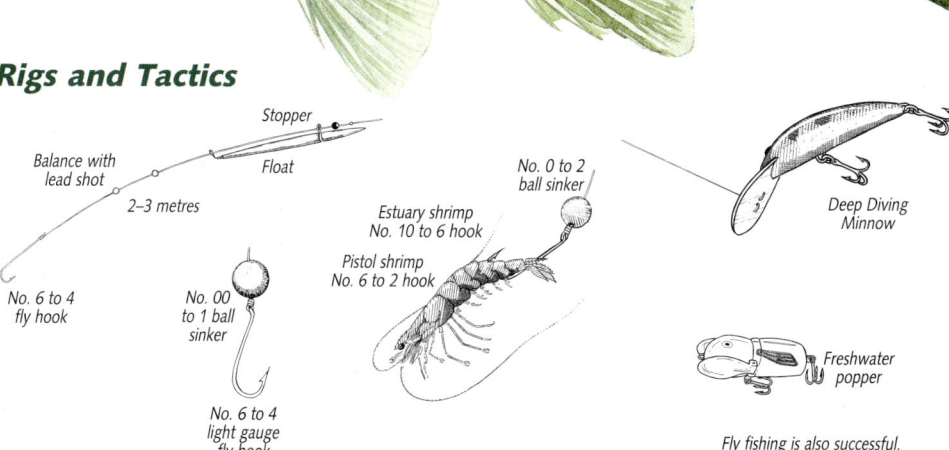

Rigs and Tactics

Stopper
Balance with lead shot
Float
2–3 metres
No. 6 to 4 fly hook
No. 00 to 1 ball sinker
No. 6 to 4 light gauge fly hook
No. 0 to 2 ball sinker
Estuary shrimp No. 10 to 6 hook
Pistol shrimp No. 6 to 2 hook
Deep Diving Minnow
Freshwater popper

Fly fishing is also successful.

CARP

Scientific name *Cyprinus carpio*. Also known as European carp, Euro, common carp, koi, blubber lips, mud sucker. Lightly scaled individuals known as mirror carp and those with no or very few scales are known as leather carp.

Range Introduced into Australia in 1872, the carp did not have a significant impact until the so-called Boolara strain escaped into Lake Hawthorn near Mildura in 1964. Since then the carp has spread widely throughout the Murray-Darling drainage and coastal systems along the east coast and recently Tasmanaia. A recent report from the Peel-Harvey system near Mandurah Western Australia indicates that the spread may not yet be complete. Introductions are likely to continue through escaped koi carp from farm dams or poorly designed garden ponds. Carp are also introduced by foolish but well intentioned people who release their pets into waterways when they grow too large or the family goes on holidays.

Description The carp has a relatively small, downward pointing mouth surrounded by two pairs of barbels, with the second pair more prominent. The first spines in the dorsal and anal fins are strongly serrated. Scales may be present, in rows and of a larger size, or almost entirely absent. The decorative koi is a variety of carp and, if released, can breed to wild strain fish capable of much more rapid growth and reproduction. Carp can hybridise with common goldfish (*Carassius auratus*).

Fishing Although much maligned, the carp is a powerful fighting fish, especially on light line. Carp are here to stay and in many urban areas provide fishing where little or none was previously available. They can reach 10 kg or more but are more common at 2 – 5 kilograms. Carp can be taken on a wide variety of bait rigs, but coarse fishing techniques elevate carp to a much higher level. The use of coarse fishing gear, rigs and baits such as corn kernels and maggots can account for big bags of carp. Carp take wet flies well and occasionally take lures intended for trout. Carp should not be returned to the water but should not just be left on the banks to rot. Carp are poor eating, although some people do enjoy them, in spite of their frequent muddy taste and large number of Y shaped bones.

CATFISH, EEL-TAILED

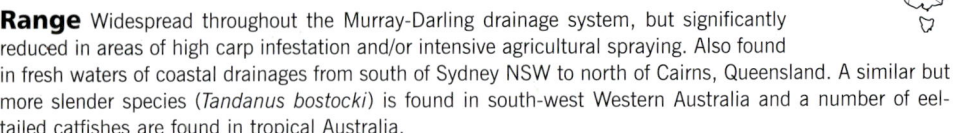

Scientific name *Tandanus tandanus*. Also known as Tandan, freshwater jewfish, dewfish, freshwater catfish, kenaru, cattie, tandan catfish.

Range Widespread throughout the Murray-Darling drainage system, but significantly reduced in areas of high carp infestation and/or intensive agricultural spraying. Also found in fresh waters of coastal drainages from south of Sydney NSW to north of Cairns, Queensland. A similar but more slender species (*Tandanus bostocki*) is found in south-west Western Australia and a number of eel-tailed catfishes are found in tropical Australia.

Description A fascinating largely nocturnal species with smooth skin and a robust eel-like tail. The eel-tailed catfishes' intimidating looks mask a terrific eating and hard fighting fish. The eel-tailed catfish possesses stout and poisonous spines on the dorsal and pectoral fins. The poison is stronger in juvenile catfish for, as the fish grows, the channel along the spine where the poison passes grows over and the spikes become less dangerous in animals over about 20 centimetres. However, the small fish hide in weeds during the day and can spike unwary waders. Immerse the wound in hot water and seek medical advice If swelling or persistent pain cause continued discomfort. These catfish do not possess a true stomach, merely a modification of the intestine. The testes look like fancy scalloping edging and catfish mate in large excavated nests of up to a metre in diameter which they aggressively defend.

Fishing The eel-tailed catfish is a nocturnal feeder, so fishing after dark is by far the best. These catfish take worms, shrimps, yabbies, prawns and insect larvae. A small running sinker rig will produce the best results and, as the fish roam widely after dark, fishing in shallow water near the edge of drop-offs can be extremely productive. A berley of crushed garden snails laid out on dusk can attract large numbers of catfish. Fish with snails or worms for best results. Eel-tailed catfish will occasionally take lures during nesting and invariably fool the angler into thinking they have hooked a large cod. Catfish fight hard but dirty and will dive into nearby sticks or rocks to break you off. Excellent eating.

CARP

Rigs and Tactics

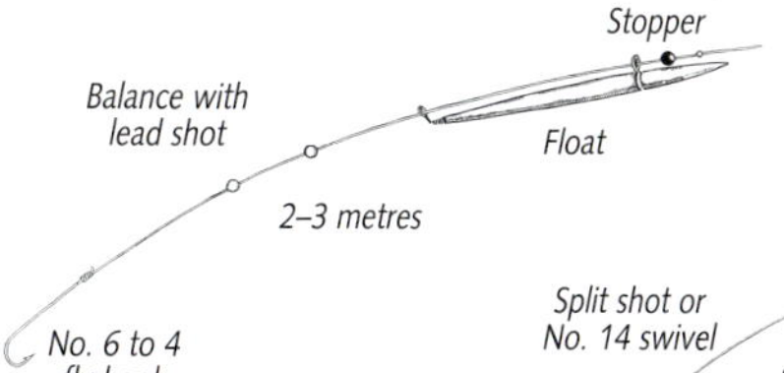

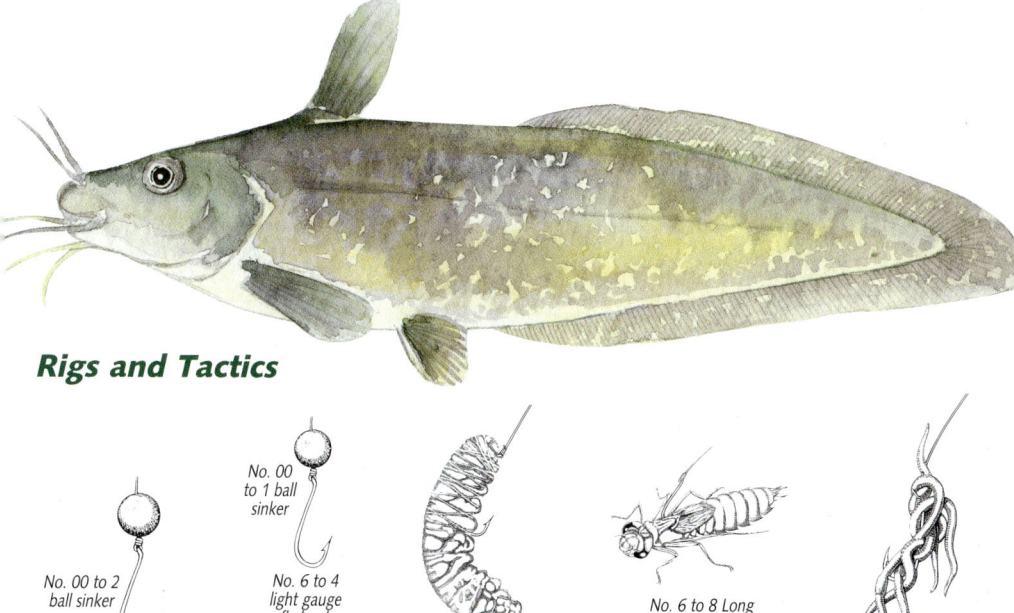

No. 00 to 1 ball sinker

No. 6 to 4 light gauge fly hook

No. 6 to 4 Baitholder hook

Balance with lead shot

2–3 metres

No. 6 to 4 fly hook

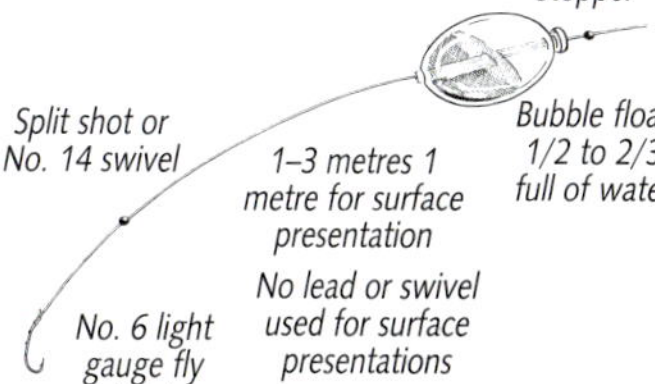

Stopper

Float

Split shot or No. 14 swivel

No. 6 light gauge fly hook

1–3 metres 1 metre for surface presentation

No lead or swivel used for surface presentations

Stopper

Bubble float 1/2 to 2/3 full of water

CATFISH, EEL TAILED

Rigs and Tactics

No. 00 to 2 ball sinker

No. 4 to 1 Suicide or baitholder hook

No. 00 to 1 ball sinker

No. 6 to 4 light gauge fly hook

Attach grub to hook with hosiery elastic (bait mate)

No. 6 to 8 Long shank baitholder

No. 6 to 4 Baitholder hook

COD, EASTERN FRESHWATER

Scientific name *Maccullochella ikei*. Also known as Clarence River cod, Eastern cod, East coast cod, cod.

Range Richmond and Clarence River systems. Stocked fish replaced extinction in Richmond system in recent years. Endangered species. The recovery of Eastern Freshwater cod is largely due to Dr Stuart Rowland.

Description Closely related to the Murray cod but distinguished by range and Eastern Freshwater cod possess long leading filaments on ventral fin. Eastern Freshwater cod are more lightly built than Murray cod, especially near the tail and have heavier mottling patterns.

Fishing Classic ambush feeder living near cover in deep holes in beautiful clear streams. Takes diving and surface lures and large live baits. The fight is strong and there is inevitably a surge when the boat or angler is first sighted and the danger realised. This species is totally protected and if accidently taken must be returned immediately to the water.

COD, MURRAY

Scientific name *Maccullochella peelii peelii*. Also known as Cod, goodoo, green fish, codfish, ponde.

Range Once common throughout the Murray-Darling basin except for at high altitude, numbers have become progressively reduced. Recent closed seasons, bag limits and further controls on set lines coupled with increased community and public stockings have seen cod fishing improve in a number of areas in recent years. Murray cod have been introduced into other waters including Lake Grassmere in Western Australia.

Description The Murray cod is the largest Australian freshwater fish, reaching 1.8 m and 113 kilograms. Cod grow an average of 1 kg per year in rivers and 2 kg per year in larger dams. Has prominent mottling on body, reducing towards a white or cream belly. Fin borders except pectoral fins are white. Differs from similar trout cod in having lower jaw equal or longer than upper jaw , more prominent mottling and heavier tail wrist. Murray cod also prefer more sluggish water than trout cod.

Fishing Murray cod are the largest predator in many inland waters. They take large lures, especially deep divers cast to snags or drop-offs in larger, slower rivers or dams. Murray cod are now a legitimate target for keen fly fishers. Murray cod reward patience, as a lure repeatedly cast to cod holding cover, or to a following fish will often eventually evoke a strike. As Murray cod are ambush feeders, large or flashy lures often work best. Murray cod are best known for taking a wide range of baits including live fish (where permitted), bardi grubs, yabbies, worms, ox heart and even scorched starlings. Murray cod are very good eating, especially under 10 kilograms. Anglers should only take as many cod as they need.

COD, MARY RIVER

Scientific name *Maccullochella peeli mariensis*. Also known as Cod, Queensland freshwater cod.

Range The Mary River cod is considered to found only in the Mary River system, but the status of the now extinct Brisbane River cod is unknown. Has now been stocked into several Queensland impoundments.

Description Similar to Eastern Freshwater cod, but more closely related to the Murray cod. Easily separated by the limited range.

Fishing Takes lures and baits within its limited range. This species is at risk and should be returned regardless of the prevailing regulations.

COD, EASTERN FRESHWATER

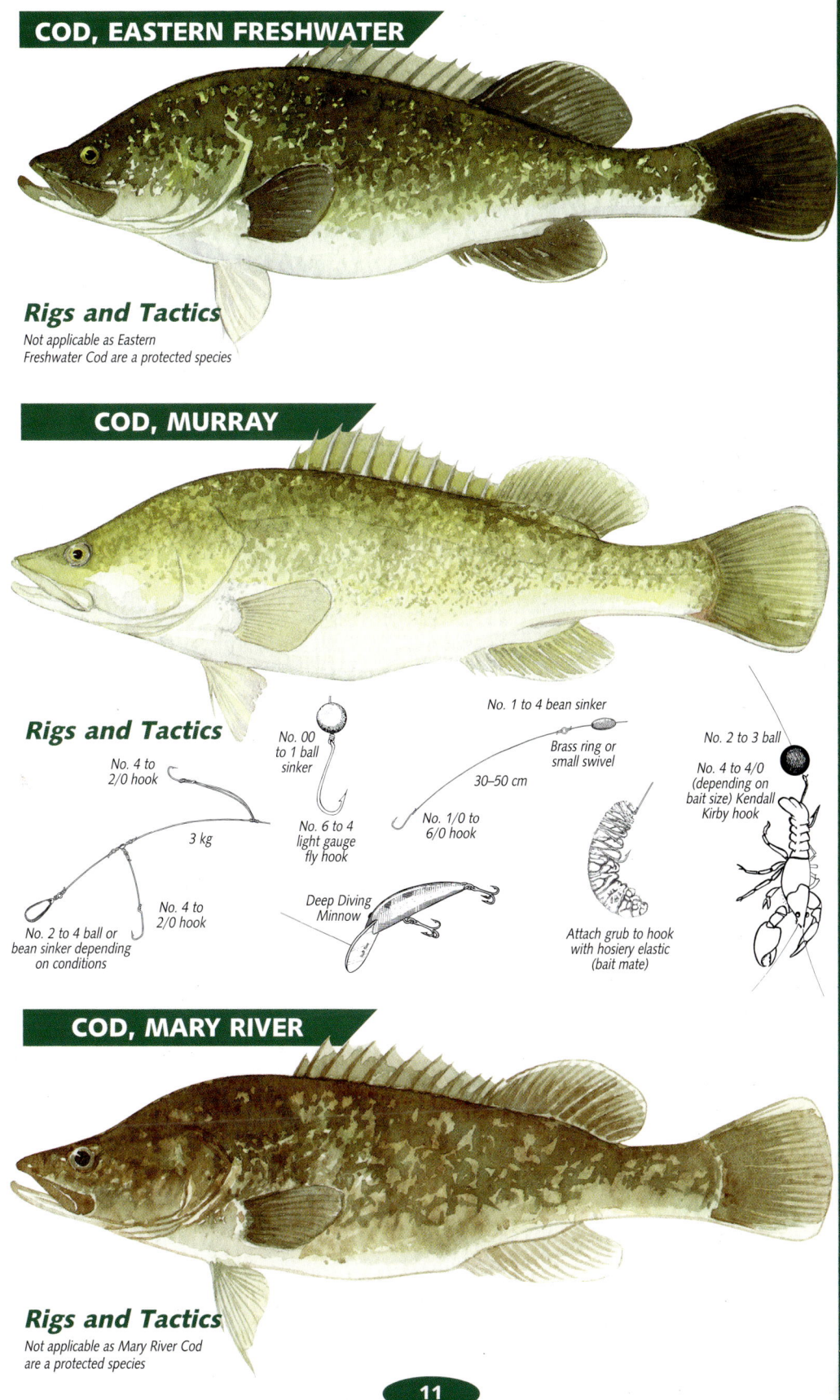

Rigs and Tactics

Not applicable as Eastern Freshwater Cod are a protected species

COD, MURRAY

Rigs and Tactics

No. 4 to 2/0 hook

3 kg

No. 4 to 2/0 hook

No. 2 to 4 ball or bean sinker depending on conditions

No. 00 to 1 ball sinker

No. 6 to 4 light gauge fly hook

No. 1 to 4 bean sinker

Brass ring or small swivel

30–50 cm

No. 1/0 to 6/0 hook

Deep Diving Minnow

Attach grub to hook with hosiery elastic (bait mate)

No. 2 to 3 ball

No. 4 to 4/0 (depending on bait size) Kendall Kirby hook

COD, MARY RIVER

Rigs and Tactics

Not applicable as Mary River Cod are a protected species

COD, SLEEPY

Scientific name *Oxyeleotris lineolatus* Also known as Sleeper.

Range Fitzroy River system northwards including tropical fresh water through central Queensland to Ord River in Western Australia.

Description This is a sluggish, fresh water, bottom dwelling species that reaches 3 kg and 48 centimetres. This species looks like a large but inactive gudgeon, with a large mouth, two separate dorsal fins and a lower jaw that protrudes beyond the upper jaw. This species has been touted as a potential aquaculture species due to its placid nature but this has not yet been proven commercially.

Fishing This hardy species can be taken on baits of shrimps, cherabin, worms, live fish and even prawns. The sleepy cod can be taken on jigs flies and slowly worked lures on occasion. The sluggish nature of this fish makes it poor sport and leads to many a claim of a snag at first, but this is compensated for by its excellent eating qualities.

COD, TROUT

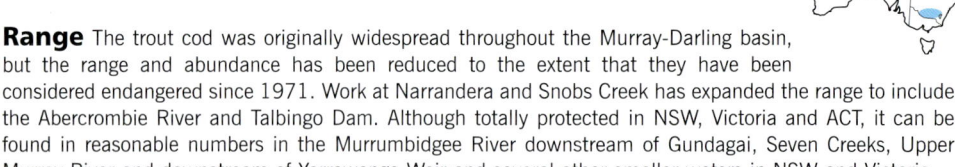

Scientific name *Maccullochella macquariensis.* Also known as Blue nose cod, bluenose, rock cod, blue cod.

Range The trout cod was originally widespread throughout the Murray-Darling basin, but the range and abundance has been reduced to the extent that they have been considered endangered since 1971. Work at Narrandera and Snobs Creek has expanded the range to include the Abercrombie River and Talbingo Dam. Although totally protected in NSW, Victoria and ACT, it can be found in reasonable numbers in the Murrumbidgee River downstream of Gundagai, Seven Creeks, Upper Murray River and downstream of Yarrawonga Weir and several other smaller waters in NSW and Victoria.

Description The trout cod is capable of reaching 16 kg and 800 mm but much more common at 1 – 2 kilograms. A handsome aggressive fish which puts up a terrific fight for its size, the trout cod has a slate grey to greenish blue colour and dashed markings. Trout cod, particularly juveniles have a prominent stripe through the eye and an overhanging upper jaw. The tail wrist is much narrower than in Murray cod.

Fishing Trout cod are aggressive and feed on yabbies, bardi grubs and scrub worms. They will also take a wide variety of lures and seem to have a special preference for the colour blue. All trout cod must be immediately returned to the water.

EEL, LONG-FINNED

Scientific name *Anguilla reinhardtii.* Also known as Freshwater eel, eel, spotted eel.

Range From Cape York south to Melbourne Victoria and northern and eastern Tasmania. These eels now use the Snowy Mountains scheme to be recorded from the Murray and Murrumbidgee Rivers.

Description Eels are fascinating animals which are often loathed but play an important part in culling older or sick fish, birds or anything else they can catch. Australian eels are thought to spawn in the Coral Sea. Juvenile eels as elvers migrate great distances up rivers and can travel overland over wet grass and can negotiate large dams walls. Long-finned eels can spend more than 10 years in fresh waters until the urge to move downstream takes the adult eels. The long-finned eel is much larger than the short-finned eel (*Anguilla australis*) and has the dorsal fin extending well forward of the anal fin. The head is broad and the lips fleshy. Colour varies with the environment but, except when migrating to the sea, is brown or olive-green with a lighter belly.

Fishing The long-finned eel is often taken while fishing for other fish. They fight extremely hard and can be mean enough to try to bite the hand which tries to unhook it. The long-finned eel can demonstrate knot tying tricks when hooked. These eels are opportunistic feeders and can take live baits larger than the 10% of the body length which legend believes applies. Worms, grubs, live fish or cut baits will take eels, but liver and beef heart are irresistible. Long-finned eels can reach over 2 m and 20 kg, although divers claim much larger sizes in some dams. Eels make good eating, especially when smoked, although many Australians are strongly prejudiced against them. Large eels gain a top price in China, whereas smaller eels are more popular in Japan.

COD, SLEEPY

Rigs and Tactics

No. 2 to 2/0 hook

No. 1 to 3 bean sinker

No. 00 to 1 ball sinker

No. 6 to 4 light gauge fly hook

No. 0 to 2 ball sinker

Estuary shrimp No. 10 to 6 hook

Pistol shrimp No. 6 to 2 hook

No. 6 to 4 Baitholder hook

COD, TROUT

Rigs and Tactics

Not applicable as Trout Cod are a protected species

EEL, LONG FINNED

Rigs and Tactics

No. 4 to 2/0 hook

3 kg

No. 4 to 2/0 hook

No. 2 to 4 ball or bean sinker depending on conditions

Attach grub to hook with hosiery elastic (bait mate)

No. 1/0 to 6/0 hook

30–50 cm

No. 1 to 4 bean sinker

Brass ring or small swivel

No. 2 to 3 ball

No. 4 to 4/0 (depending on bait size) Kendall Kirby hook

GRAYLING, AUSTRALIAN

Scientific name *Prototroctes maraena.* Also known as Grayling, cucumber fish.

Range Grose River near Sydney to the Hopkins River in Victoria and Tasmania in coastal streams.

Description The grayling is a relatively small species which has been greatly affected by the damming of coastal rivers. The Australian grayling is a pretty fish with a distinctive cucumber odour and an adipose fin. The dorsal fin is set well behind the pelvic fins. This species reaches 33 cm but is much more common at 15 to 20 centimetres. The grayling spawns in brackish waters and spends its life in clean fresh water, feeding on insects and occasionally plant matter.

Fishing This species is rarely taken by recreational anglers. Due to its small size and recognition of its vulnerable status it is not targeted. Grayling will take small dry flies and worms on very small hooks drifted through the fast water and into the heads of pools. They fight well for their size. The grayling was regarded by early pioneers as an excellent table fish but would not be eaten today. The Australian grayling is totally protected in NSW.

GRUNTER, LEATHERY

Scientific name *Scortum hilli.* Also known as Green-hide jack, Hill's grunter.

Range Found in the Dawson and Fitzroy River systems of Central Queensland.

Description A relatively small species reaching only around a kilogram in weight. It has a number of irregular dark blotches over its body which may be absent in some specimens. It has a heavier build than many freshwater grunter and the teeth are tiny and in continuous bands.

Fishing A strong fighter but very poor eating. The leathery grunter can school up during a fresh and will readily take baits such as mussels, shrimps and worms. Standard light line bottom rigs with a small running sinker work best.

GRUNTER, SOOTY

Scientific name *Hephaestus fuliginosus.* Also known as Black bream, purple grunter, sooty.

Range From the Kimberley region of Western Australia around the top end to central Queensland. This species has been stocked into a number of Queensland impoundments where they have demonstrated exceptional growth and provide quality sport.

Description In the wild, sooty grunter can reach 4 kg and 50 cm, but in stocked impoundments such as Tinaroo Dam they can be considerably larger than this. This species has a reasonably large mouth and the lips may be blubbery in some specimens. Colour can be extremely variable, from light brown to black. Sooty grunter can be omnivorous and will on occasion eat green algae.

Fishing The sooty grunter prefers faster water in rivers and can inhabit mid-stream snags in riffles. In dams these fish are found around cover, especially fallen timber. Sooty grunter will readily take live shrimp or cherabin, worms or grubs. They will readily take a variety of lures including diving lures, spinner baits, bladed spinners, jigs, soft plastics and flies. Sooty grunter fight well without jumping and are undervalued as a sport fish by many anglers, partly because they are reasonably common in many areas. Sooty grunter are a fair to poor food fish which can be weedy tasting. Species such as barramundi which occur in the same areas are much better fare.

GRAYLING, AUSTRALIAN

Rigs and Tactics

No. 6 to 8 Long shank baitholder

Fly fishing is successful

No. 6 to 4 Baitholder hook

GRUNTER, LEATHERY

Rigs and Tactics

Minnow Lure

24 kg trace

No. 1/0 to 6/0 hook

No. 1 to 4 bean sinker

Brass ring or small swivel

30–50 cm

Fly fishing can also be successful.

Wonder Wobbler

Mr Twister

No. 0 to 2 ball sinker

Estuary shrimp No. 10 to 6 hook

Pistol shrimp No. 6 to 2 hook

GRUNTER, SOOTY

Rigs and Tactics

Minnow Lure

24 kg trace

No. 1/0 to 6/0 hook

No. 1 to 4 bean sinker

Brass ring or small swivel

30–50 cm

Fly fishing can also be successful.

Wonder Wobbler

Mr Twister

No. 0 to 2 ball sinker

Estuary shrimp No. 10 to 6 hook

Pistol shrimp No. 6 to 2 hook

LUNGFISH, AUSTRALIAN

Scientific name *Neoceratodus forsteri*. Also known as Queensland lungfish, lungfish, ceratodus.

Range Originally found only in the Burnett and Mary Rivers, the Australian lungfish has now been introduced into the Brisbane River, Albert River, Coomera River and Enoggera Reservoir. They have been introduced into other southern Queensland waters, but their status is uncertain.

Description The Australian lungfish is the most primitive of Australia's freshwater fish, which has remained unchanged for over 100 million years. The head is large and the eye very small. The body is brown and covered in large scales. The pectoral fins are large and paddle-like as are the well set back pelvic fins. The tail is extremely fleshy and though broad, is eel-like. The Australian lungfish possesses a single lung and can gulp air from the surface of oxygen poor waters, but unlike the African and American lungfish, it cannot survive completely out of water for extended periods.

Fishing The lungfish is omnivorous, eating weed on occasion and can be accidentally taken on worms, frogs or shrimp. They are sluggish fighters and as they are totally protected, should be immediately returned to the water.

MULLET, FRESHWATER

Scientific name *Myxus petardi*. Also known as Pinkeye mullet, pinkeye.

Range Burnett River in Queensland and southwards as far as the Georges River near Sydney.

Description A streamlined mullet with a limited range and a preference for spending large amounts of time either in fresh water or near the upper tidal limits. The freshwater mullet can grow to 80 cm and more than 7 kg, but is more commonly encountered at 30 – 40 centimetres. The name 'pinkeye' comes from the fact that the eye often appears bloodshot when taken by commercial fishermen in nets. The eye itself is large and is generally yellow, yellow-brown or orange tinged and lacks the fatty eyelid which is found on sea mullet. The upper body profile is straight and the mouth is at the front of the head. The freshwater mullet has fine teeth on the tongue. The tail is moderately forked.

Fishing The freshwater mullet is largely herbivorous and so can be difficult to catch. Best bets are using maggots, bread or small pieces of worm or prawn. Berley greatly assists the acceptance of baits. Freshwater mullet can occasionally be taken on small wet or dry flies. The freshwater mullet makes good eating, but they need to be cleaned quickly as they can have a muddy or iodine taint if they have been feeding on bottom sediment or weed. Freshwater mullet, like all mullet species have oily flesh which lends itself very well to smoking or as a cut flesh bait for other species.

PERCH, JUNGLE

Scientific name *Kuhlia rupestris*. Also known as Rock flagtail.

Range Burdekin River and other eastern Cape York streams down to Fraser Island in Queensland.

Description A handsome fish which can be distinguished by its preference for clean clear freshwater coastal streams. The body and base of the caudal fin is liberally speckled with dark spots. The lobes of the tail fin are generally white. The mouth is large and can take large baits and lures. This species has been severely reduced in range and number due to decreasing water quality in its streams.The jungle perch is a relatively small species, reaching 2.4 kg but frequently caught above 0.5 kilograms.

Fishing A true recreational fishing prize, the jungle perch takes a variety of small lures readily. They can also be taken on fly, but the remote nature and often overgrown of their preferred habitat makes fly presentation difficult. Baits such as frogs, grasshoppers and worms also work well. While this species is reputed to be good eating, the jungle perch is vulnerable to overfishing and all fish should be carefully released.

LUNGFISH, AUSTRALIAN

Rigs and Tactics

Not applicable as Australian Lungfish are a protected species

MULTI, FRESHWATER

Rigs and Tactics

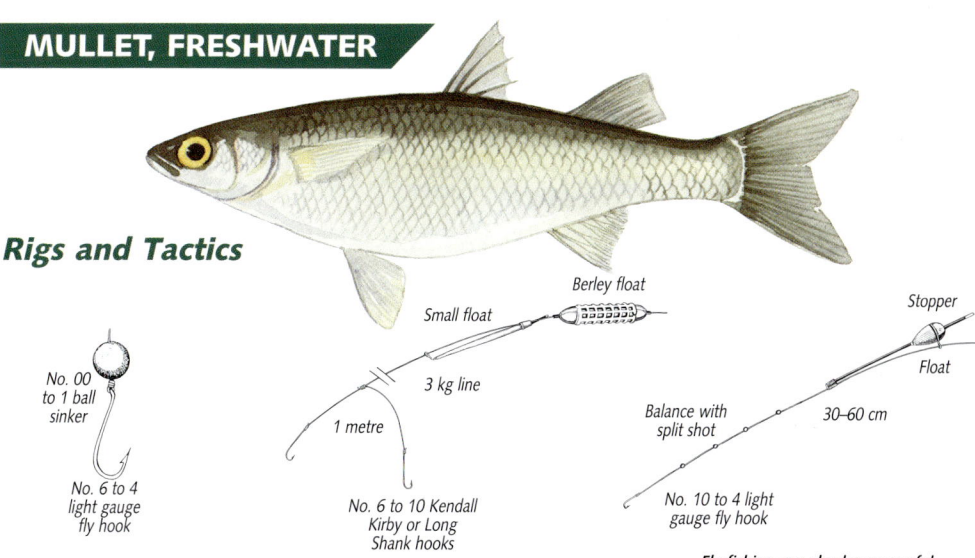

No. 00
to 1 ball
sinker

No. 6 to 4
light gauge
fly hook

Small float

Berley float

3 kg line

1 metre

No. 6 to 10 Kendall
Kirby or Long
Shank hooks

Stopper

Float

Balance with
split shot

30–60 cm

No. 10 to 4 light
gauge fly hook

Fly fishing can also be successful.

PERCH, JUNGLE

Rigs and Tactics

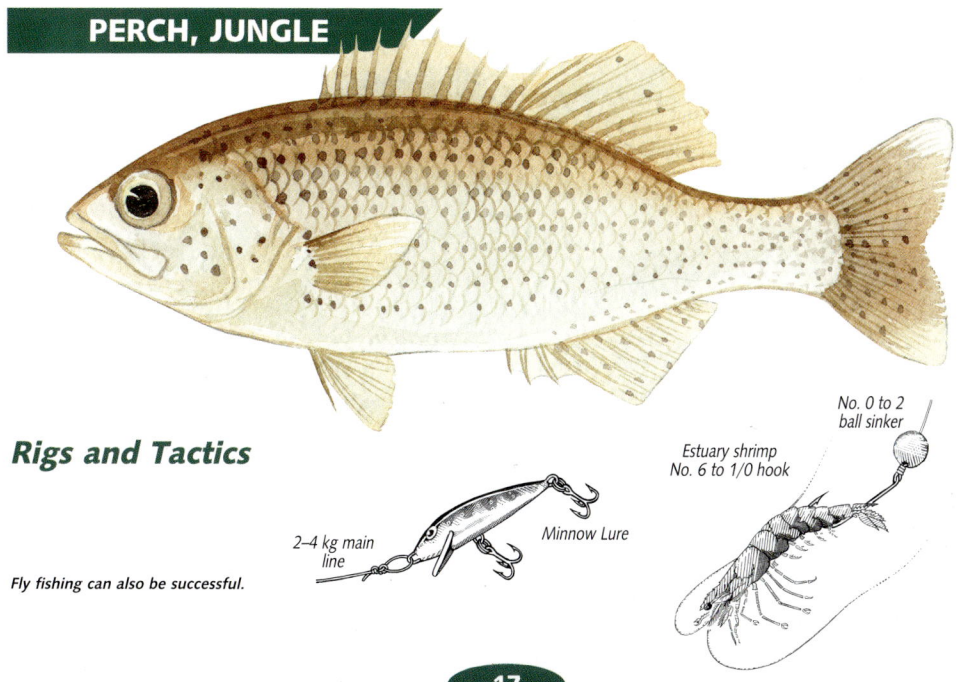

2–4 kg main
line

Minnow Lure

Estuary shrimp
No. 6 to 1/0 hook

No. 0 to 2
ball sinker

Fly fishing can also be successful.

PERCH, GOLDEN

Scientific name *Macquaria ambigua*. Also known as Golden, callop, yellowbelly, Murray perch.

Range Wide distribution throughout the Murray-Darling basin. Separate genetic stocks are thought to be found in the Dawson-Fitzroy system and the Bulloo and Lake Eyre internal drainage systems. Golden perch have had their range substantially increased through stockings into areas outside its normal range. These stockings have been spectacularly successful. They have also been introduced into Western Australia, central Queensland and western South Australia. Golden perch cannot reproduce in farm dams or impoundments.

Description The golden perch is a deep bodied fish which becomes more heavily set as it gets larger. Fish over 5 kg resemble a football, with a tail and a small moderately tapered head with a distinctly concave forehead. The lower jaw extends slightly beyond the upper jaw. The colour varies with the water quality, ranging from pale green to almost cream out of very muddy western waters to deep green and with obvious golden overtones, particularly in the throat and belly region. There are two distinctive extended filaments on the ventral fins. Golden perch are most commonly encountered in the 1 – 2 kg range especially in rivers. However, the extremely successful stocking in Queensland, New South Wales and to a lesser extent Victorian impoundments has seen a huge increase in the number of 5 – 10 kg fish being caught with the odd fish to 15 kg being reported.

Fishing The natural rivers where golden perch were once extremely common no longer ever run clear through poor land use and de-snagging. In these rivers, golden perch are almost exclusively a bait proposition, except in the upper reaches or near barrages where lures can be used. Baits include worms, yabbies, shrimps, bardi and wood grubs, frogs (where legal) and less common baits such as kangaroo meat or liver. However, fishing for golden perch has exploded in popularity in impoundments. Bait fishing includes bobbing with yabbies near drowned timber or sight fishing with shrimps or live fish to cruising fish on the edge of weed beds, along rock walls or on drop-offs near points where this species positions itself to ambush prey. Lure fishing is now the most popular method of fishing for golden perch. Golden perch often follow lures, so a slight pause near the end of the retrieve will often entice a strike and working the rod while trolling is similarly more successful.

PERCH, MACQUARIE

Scientific name *Macquaria australasica*. Also known as Mountain perch, white eye perch, silvereye, macca, mountain perch, Murray bream, black perch, Macquaries.

Range Increasingly restricted due to decreasing water quality and competition with species such as redfin, the Macquarie perch is now found only in the cooler upper reaches of streams in the Murray-Darling system. It is likely that there is a separate and smaller sub-species found in coastal streams from the Sydney water supply south to the Shoalhaven system plus the Yarra system in Victoria. Macquarie perch can do well in dams such as Dartmouth, Wyangala, Burrinjuck, Tallowa and Cataract.

Description Macquarie perch are a distinctly perch-like fish reaching 3.5 kg but are commonly caught at half a kilogram. The Tallowa Dam and Kangaroo River population is rarely seen at even this size and many fish are around 15 to 20 centimetres. Although colouration can vary from black to blue-grey to light grey and piebald, the Macquarie perch has a distinctive white iris around the eye in all but black specimens. The mouth is relatively small and the lips are fairly obvious without being blubbery. The pectoral fins have two extended white filaments which readily separates them from Australian bass in Tallowa Dam.

Fishing The Macquarie perch is a somewhat timid biter and is extremely curious, often repeatedly following small minnow lures, spinners or flies. They can be taken by lure or fly, but most Macquarie perch are taken on worms, with mudeyes, yabbies and wood grubs also working. In some streams Macquarie perch will be caught on crickets and grasshoppers. A lightly weighted bottom rig or a vertical jigging bait rig in impoundments will take the most fish. In dams, fish around the base of drowned timber, especially if there is a gravel bottom (such as a drowned road) nearby, while in rivers, the edges of drop-offs or near deep snags or rock walls are best. Macquarie perch are more active at night or at dusk and dawn. Macquarie perch are excellent eating but they are totally protected in many areas and care should be taken to preserve these magnificent fish.

PERCH, GOLDEN

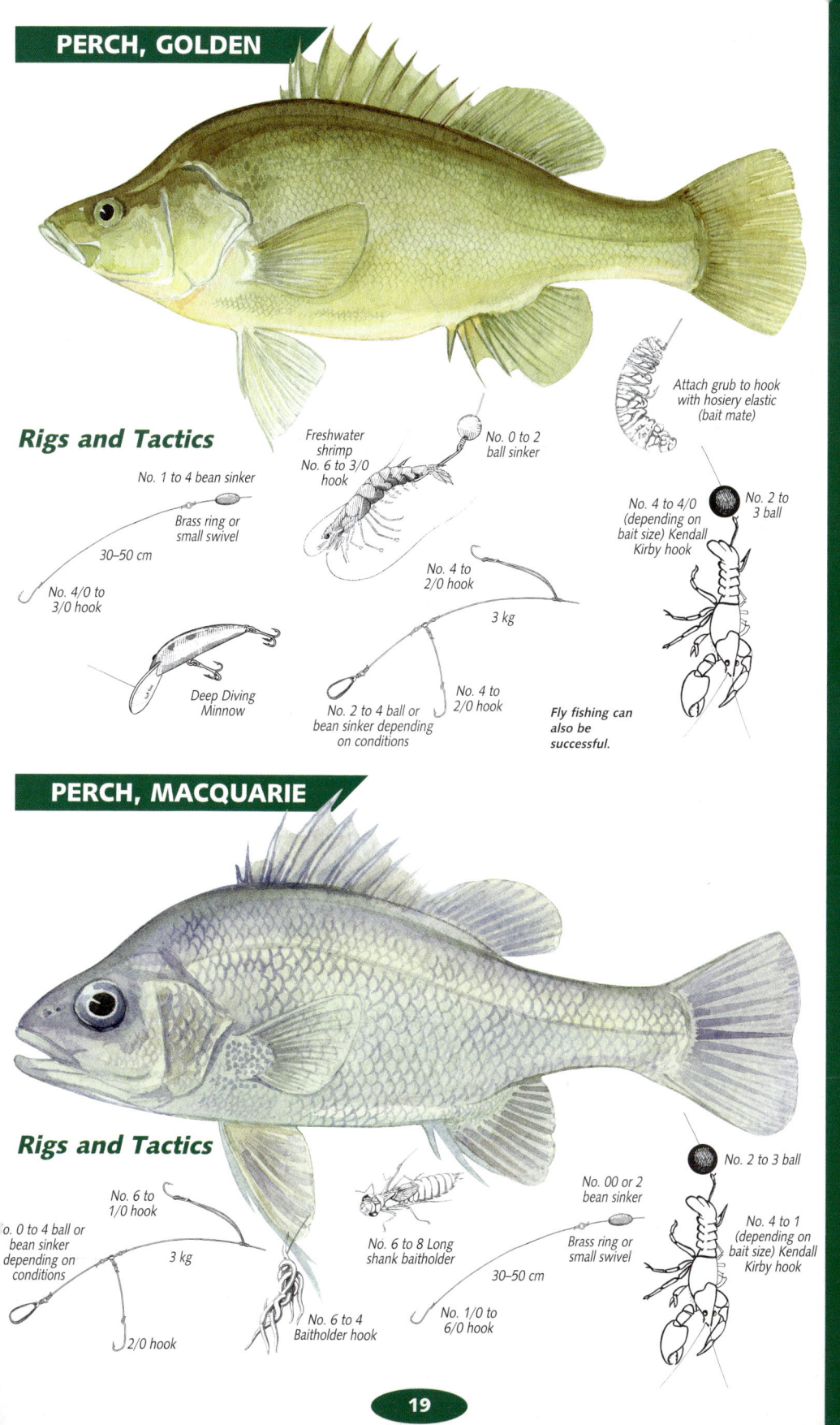

Rigs and Tactics

No. 1 to 4 bean sinker

Brass ring or small swivel

30–50 cm

No. 4/0 to 3/0 hook

Deep Diving Minnow

Freshwater shrimp
No. 6 to 3/0 hook

No. 0 to 2 ball sinker

No. 4 to 2/0 hook

3 kg

No. 2 to 4 ball or bean sinker depending on conditions

No. 4 to 2/0 hook

Attach grub to hook with hosiery elastic (bait mate)

No. 4 to 4/0 (depending on bait size) Kendall Kirby hook

No. 2 to 3 ball

Fly fishing can also be successful.

PERCH, MACQUARIE

Rigs and Tactics

No. 6 to 1/0 hook

o. 0 to 4 ball or bean sinker depending on conditions

3 kg

2/0 hook

No. 6 to 8 Long shank baitholder

No. 6 to 4 Baitholder hook

No. 00 or 2 bean sinker

Brass ring or small swivel

30–50 cm

No. 1/0 to 6/0 hook

No. 2 to 3 ball

No. 4 to 1 (depending on bait size) Kendall Kirby hook

PERCH, SILVER

Scientific name *Bidyanus bidyanus*. Also known as grunter, black bream, bidyan, Murray perch, tcheri, freshwater bream, silver.

Range Widespread but patchy distribution throughout the Murray-Darling basin except the cooler headwaters of streams. The silver perch has suffered a significant decline in number and range. Silver perch are now considered threatened in many Murray-Darling basin rivers where they were once as common as carp are now. The range is being extended by aquaculture ventures, escapees and stocking in Queensland Dams. Silver perch are common in Cataract Dam near Sydney which is unfortunately closed to angling. Silver perch breed in Cataract Dam and Burrinjuck Dam.

Description The silver perch is a fine freshwater fish species, reaching 8 kg but most frequently encountered at between 0.3 kg and 1 kg, especially in impoundments. Larger silver perch frequently become omnivorous or almost entirely vegetarian, full of the green slimy weed which can seriously affect lure and bait fishing at some times of the year. The silver perch has a small head and small mouth, but they take large lures on occasions. As the fish grows, its head appears smaller than its body, especially in dams where fast growth rates leave a heavier body in larger fish. The rear margin of the small scales is dark grey or deep brown which gives a cross hatched appearance. The fish may grunt on capture but this is not as loud or as common as in other species. In dams especially, silver perch form schools of similar sized fish, with smaller schools of large fish.

Fishing Silver perch are becoming increasingly rare in rivers. Silver perch are totally protected in SA and in NSW silver perch may only be taken from stocked impoundments. Quite easy to breed in hatcheries, large numbers have been stocked into dams throughout south-eastern Australia. Silver perch prefer faster water and can be taken in or downstream of rapids or broken water. Best baits are worms, peeled yabby tail, shrimps and a variety of smaller grubs. More exotic baits like snails, ox heart and chicken breast will also take fish on occasion. Silver perch can sometimes be found schooled near sunken timber where bobbing with worm or small yabby baits will pick up silvers and other species. Silver perch will take lures, but their small mouth means that small lures are best. In rivers or shallow waters silver perch love Celta or other spinner type lures, while small minnows like the Mann's 5+, McGrath minnow, small Legend Lure and small Halco Laser lures work well. Silver perch fight well and are a good eating fish, although larger specimens can be dry and may have a slight weed taint.

REDFIN

Scientific name *Perca fluviatilis* Also known as English perch, European perch, redfin perch, reddie.

Range An introduced species with a wide distribution in temperate waters ranging from around Pindari Dam in northern NSW, throughout southern NSW and Victoria, Tasmania, southern South Australia and the south-west of Western Australia. Redfin are found in some coastal drainages in a few dams.

Description The redfin has prominent scales and five to six prominent vertical stripes which may extend nearly to the belly. These stripes are less prominent in larger fish. The dorsal fin is set well forward and when erect, resembles a small 'sail'. The ventral and anal fins are often very bright red or orange, often with a tinge of white at the ends. The tail fin can also be bright orange, or orange-yellow. Redfin are often found around drowned timber, at drop-offs near points, or on submerged islands. Redfin prefer cooler water and in summer, the largest fish are almost always below the thermocline in dams or large river holes. Redfin are aggressive and prolific breeders. In impoundments they can stunt out, producing thousands of mature fish as small as 15 cm who consume everything and continue to reproduce. In other areas, they can reach 3 kg and provide excellent sport with a variety of techniques.

Fishing In dams, one of the most successful techniques is to anchor among drowned timber and bob with bait or lures. With bait, a small ball sinker runs to the top of the hook which is baited with yabby, worm, cricket, grub or shrimp. Lures like the Baltic Bobber or the Buzz Bomb also work well. In any case, the bait is lowered to the bottom and vertically jigged between 30 cm and a metre or so before being dropped to the bottom. Drifting baits near drowned timber in large holes in rivers or near drop-offs in rivers or dams is very succesful. Redfin are aggressive lure takers, with bladed, Celta type lures, diving lures and small Rapala minnows taking many fish.

PERCH, SILVER

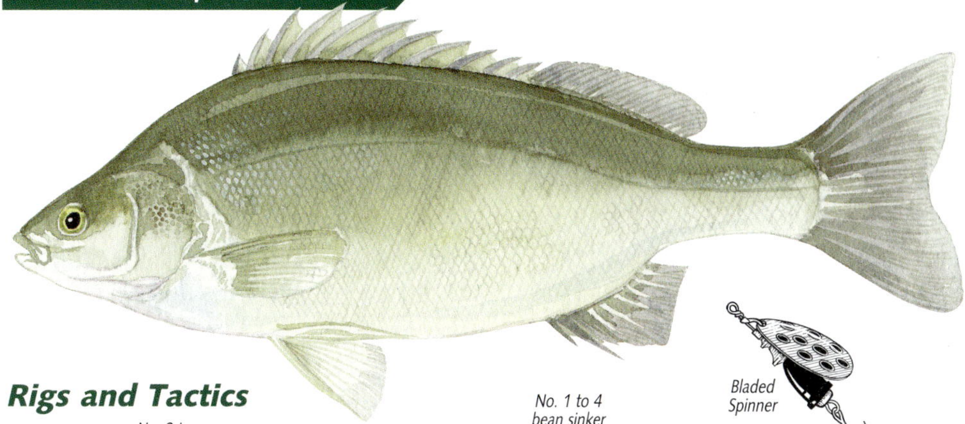

Rigs and Tactics

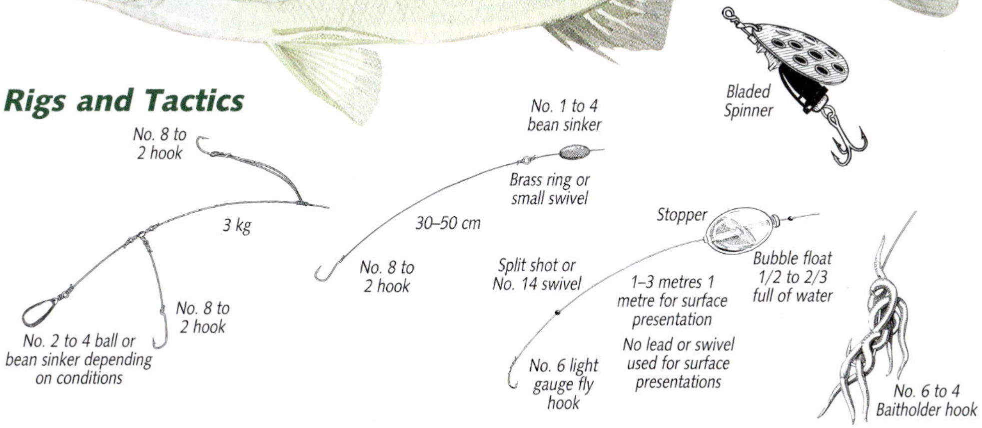
Bladed Spinner
No. 8 to 2 hook
3 kg
No. 8 to 2 hook
No. 2 to 4 ball or bean sinker depending on conditions
No. 1 to 4 bean sinker
Brass ring or small swivel
30–50 cm
No. 8 to 2 hook
Stopper
Bubble float 1/2 to 2/3 full of water
Split shot or No. 14 swivel
1–3 metres 1 metre for surface presentation
No lead or swivel used for surface presentations
No. 6 light gauge fly hook
No. 6 to 4 Baitholder hook

REDFIN

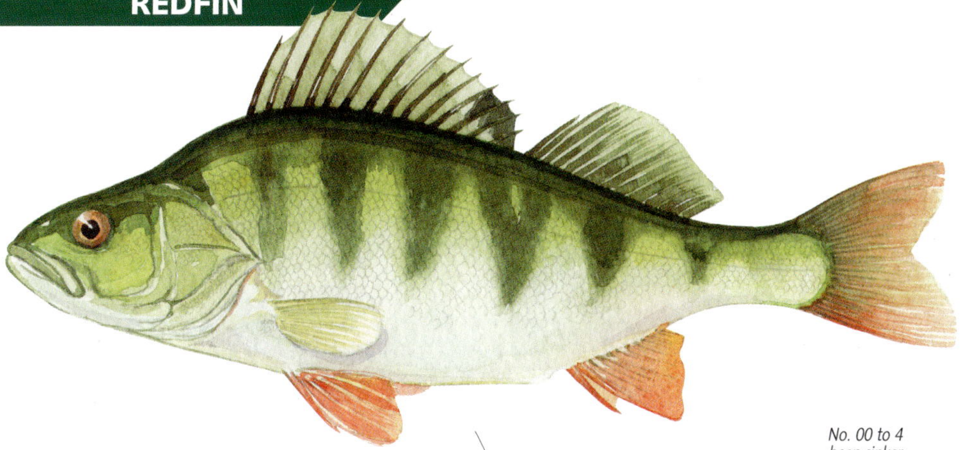

Rigs and Tactics

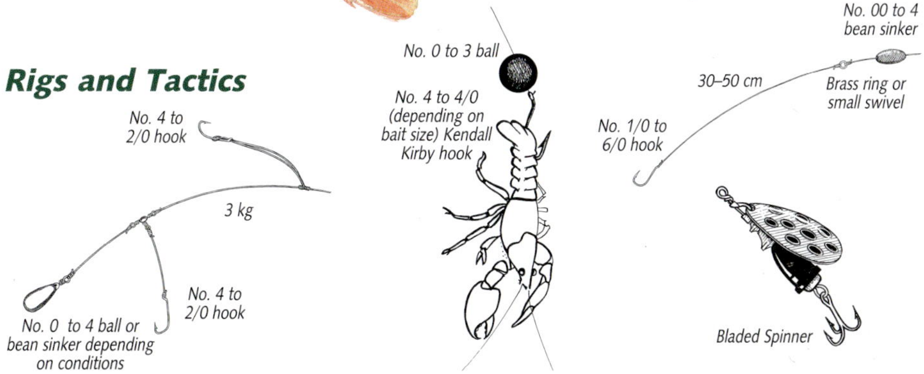
No. 4 to 2/0 hook
3 kg
No. 4 to 2/0 hook
No. 0 to 4 ball or bean sinker depending on conditions
No. 0 to 3 ball
No. 4 to 4/0 (depending on bait size) Kendall Kirby hook
No. 00 to 4 bean sinker
30–50 cm
Brass ring or small swivel
No. 1/0 to 6/0 hook
Bladed Spinner

RIVER BLACKFISH

Scientific name *Gadopsis marmoratus*. Also known as Blackfish, marble cod, slippery, slimy.

Range There are now several species of river blackfish recognised including a larger species *Gadopsis bispinosis*, the two spined river blackfish. The distribution of the river blackfish is patchy and becoming increasingly rare in many areas. River blackfish exist in a variety of locations including in the Abercrombie River, lower Murrumbidgee River and are relatively common in Dunn's Swamp near Rylestone in NSW with a wider distribution in Victoria.

Description The river blackfish is a small elongated native freshwater fish species which is easily identified by the pelvic fins which are reduced to two rays, each of which is divided and finger-like near the end. The dorsal fin is very long and the tail fin is obviously rounded. The mouth is fairly large and the lower jaw is shorter than the upper jaw. This species has a distinctive marbled colouring and fish may vary in colour from almost black, to olive or light brown and there may be obvious purple overtones. The scales are small and the body feels very slimy, giving rise to several alternate common names. River blackfish do not appear to cohabit well with trout and prefer very snaggy waters. They are mainly nocturnal, laying up during the day in cover like hollow logs, which they also use to lay their eggs. The river blackfish can reach over 35 cm, although the two-spined species (which has obvious golden overtones) can reach nearly 5 kg in remote areas.

Fishing River blackfish are much more active at night and are a bait fishing proposition, although they have been taken on wet flies and nymphs on occasion. River blackfish are fished with lightly weighted or unweighted rigs, but the line needs to be strong enough for the snaggy country these fish prefer. Coarse fishermen often take river blackfish from waters where they are not commonly encountered. The best bait by far is worms, with shrimps, maggots and mudeyes taking fish. This species will frequently swallow the hook, so setting the hook quickly, or leaving the hook in gut hooked fish is recommended. River blackfish are quite rare so if possible, they should be returned to the water. River blackfish are quite small but have been regarded as a quality food fish in past times.

SALMON, ATLANTIC

Scientific name *Salmo salar*. Also known as Salmon.

Range The Atlantic salmon has a very restricted range in the wild in Australia, limited to areas where they are regularly stocked. In NSW Atlantic salmon are found in Jindabyne and Burrinjuck Dams. Experimental stockings below Hume, Burrinjuck and Wyangala Dams have failed. They are caught in reasonable numbers in Tasmania as escapees from the increasing aquaculture industry.

Description The Atlantic salmon is a generally silvery fish that can have relatively few spots on its body and is often confused even by experienced anglers with silvery, lake coloured brown trout. The most obvious difference (other than location) is that the Atlantic salmon has a tail that while not clearly forked, is obviously indented. The brown trout is frequently called square tail and has a straight tail profile. The caudal peduncle (wrist of tail) is longer than for the similar brown trout. Atlantic salmon need very cold clean water which is basically unavailable in Australia. In Europe and North America they are the prince of fish but here they are quite slender, with a tendency towards being decidedly skinny and undernourished in NSW, while some smelt feeders in Tasmania can be more robust. In NSW fish over a kilogram, other than released broodfish are rare, while in Tasmania the size is frequently determined by the size at escape from fish farms.

Fishing Heralded by Donald Francois of NSW Fisheries on its introduction as the saviour of freshwater fishing, the Atlantic salmon has been a disastrous experiment for recreational anglers, although it has created a sizeable aquaculture industry in Tasmania. It is only a matter of time before NSW Fisheries stops stocking this species which provides its best fishing in Lake Jindabyne for a few days after older broodstock are released. Atlantic salmon are taken on standard trout lures and flies while fishing for other species. They prefer fish as food and smelt or gudgeon patterns work best in Tasmania. Atlantic salmon from sea cages taste devine, but specimens from Burrinjuck Dam taste very ordinary.

RIVER BLACKFISH

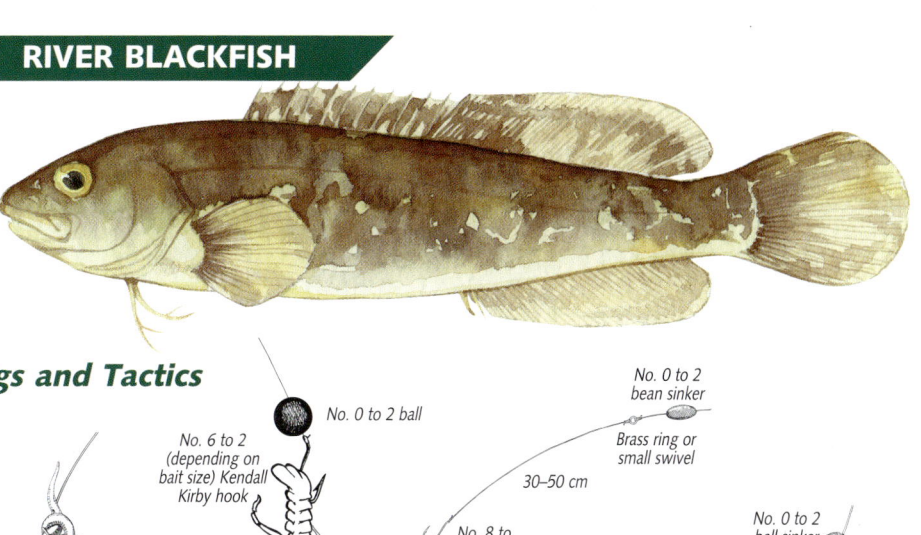

Rigs and Tactics

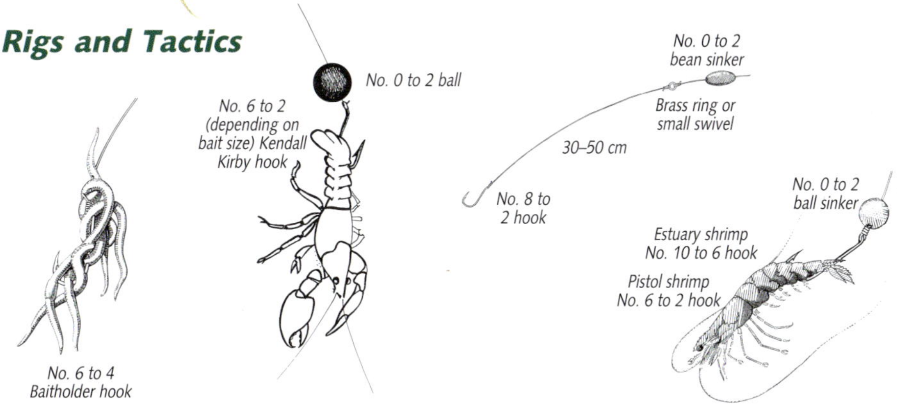

No. 0 to 2 ball

No. 6 to 2 (depending on bait size) Kendall Kirby hook

No. 6 to 4 Baitholder hook

No. 0 to 2 bean sinker

Brass ring or small swivel

30–50 cm

No. 8 to 2 hook

No. 0 to 2 ball sinker

Estuary shrimp No. 10 to 6 hook

Pistol shrimp No. 6 to 2 hook

SALMON, ATLANTIC

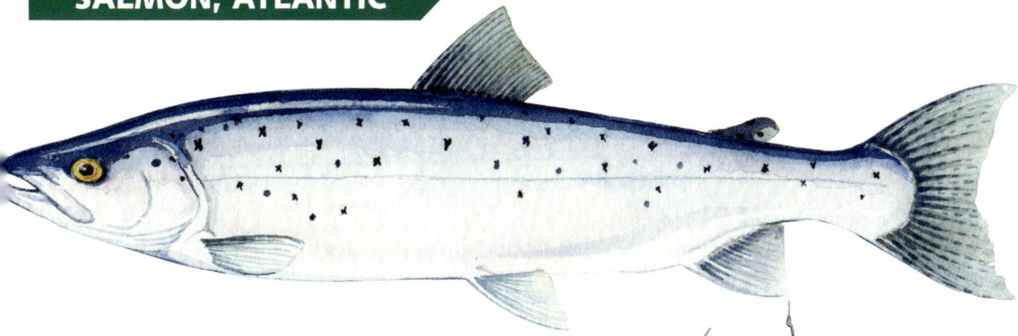

Rigs and Tactics

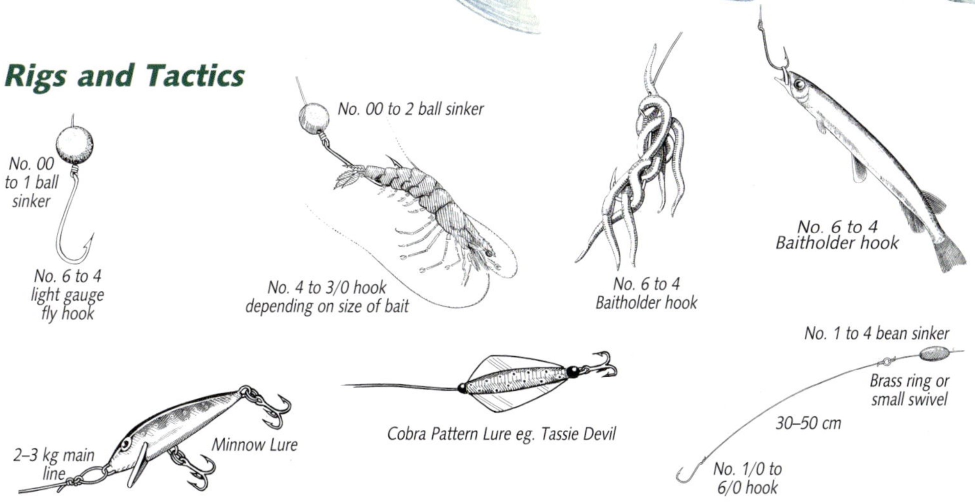

No. 00 to 1 ball sinker

No. 6 to 4 light gauge fly hook

No. 00 to 2 ball sinker

No. 4 to 3/0 hook depending on size of bait

No. 6 to 4 Baitholder hook

No. 6 to 4 Baitholder hook

2–3 kg main line

Minnow Lure

Cobra Pattern Lure eg. Tassie Devil

No. 1 to 4 bean sinker

Brass ring or small swivel

30–50 cm

No. 1/0 to 6/0 hook

Fly fishing can also be successful.

23

SALMON, CHINOOK

Scientific name *Oncorhynchus tshawytscha.* Also known as Quinnat salmon, king salmon.

Range Chinook salmon are produced in Victoria for stocking into waters there. The best fisheries are in Lakes Purrumbete and Bullen Merri. They are also released into Toolondo Reservoir and Albert Lakes in Victoria. The Chinook salmon in Australia does not reproduce naturally and must be stocked.

Description The chinook salmon is a handsome fish with silver sides and a rather more pointed head than other trout and salmon species, with mature males developing a distinctive hooked jaw. The mouth around the teeth in the lower jaw is distinctly grey-black which clearly identifies this species. Chinook salmon can reach 9 kg, but growth and survival is dependent upon water conditions and availability of forage species like galaxiids and pygmy perch.

Fishing Controversy dogs the stocking program for this important species due to stocking rates, size and times. Chinook salmon feed mainly on fish and can be taken by casting or trolling classical trout lures, or with live minnows or even dead smelt or whitebait. Fishing is best in spring when the fish are found in shallower water and accessible with a broader range of methods. Later in the season, trolling with lead lines or downriggers or vertical jigging around baitfish which show on a depth sounder produces fish. A very good fighting fish and excellent eating

---

SARATOGA, GULF

Scientific name *Scleropages jardinii.* Also known as Northern saratoga, northern spotted barramundi, bony tongue.

Range This species has an extensive but patchy distribution from the Jardine River in the Gulf of Carpentaria to the Adelaide River east of Darwin. Aquaculture production of this species has seen the range extended, particularly as saratoga are being increasingly recognised as a quality recreational angling species.

Description A primitive species obviously designed for feeding close to the surface, the gulf saratoga has a relatively straight dorsal profile. The gulf saratoga has a large upturned mouth which extends beyond the back edge of the large eye whereas in the southern saratoga the jaw extends to the middle of the eye. A single small barbel is found under the lower lip. The dorsal fin is set well back and commences well behind the anal fin. The pectoral fins are large and set low down on the body but unlike the southern saratoga do not reach the base of the pelvic fins. The dorsal, anal and tail fins are dark with many small red spots and the scales have curved red bars compared to the southern saratoga which has vertical bars on the scales. The gulf saratoga prefers clear streams and faster flowing upper reaches of streams but can adapt to impoundments.

Fishing The gulf saratoga is a surface and midwater feeder which will consume insects, small fish and crustaceans. While the gulf saratoga will take small lightly weighted baits such as cherabin, shrimps and small frogs, they are most highly regarded as lure and fly targets. The gulf saratoga is a fantastic fish on the fly, taking deceiver and Dalhberg diver flies. Gulf saratoga will also take minnow and spinner lures. Surface lures such as jerk baits, prop lures and chuggers work very well. The bony mouth can make setting the hook difficult and many lures are thrown on the jump. As saratoga are mouth breeders, there will be times in the spring/early summer when the females who carry the eggs will not feed. The gulf saratoga can reach 90 cm and more than 17 kg, but most fish caught are between 50 and 65 cm in length. The saratoga is a very poor table fish and should be released to provide sport for the future.

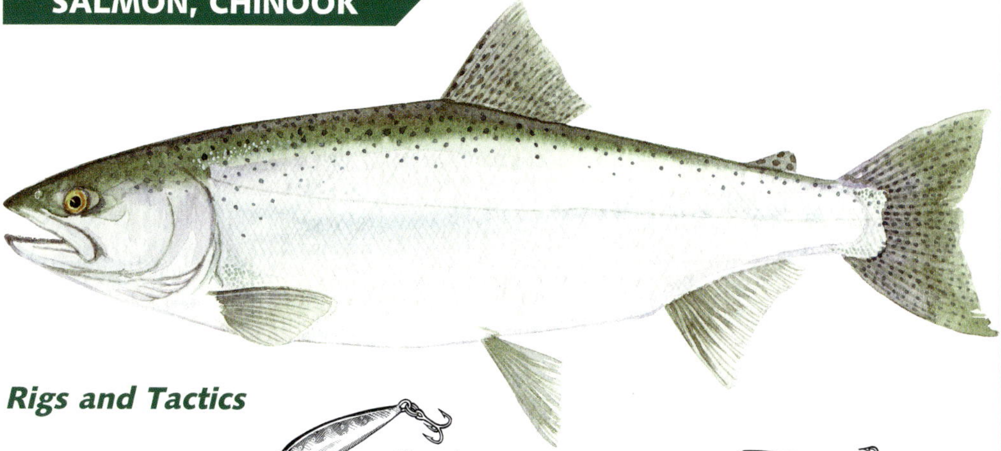

Rigs and Tactics

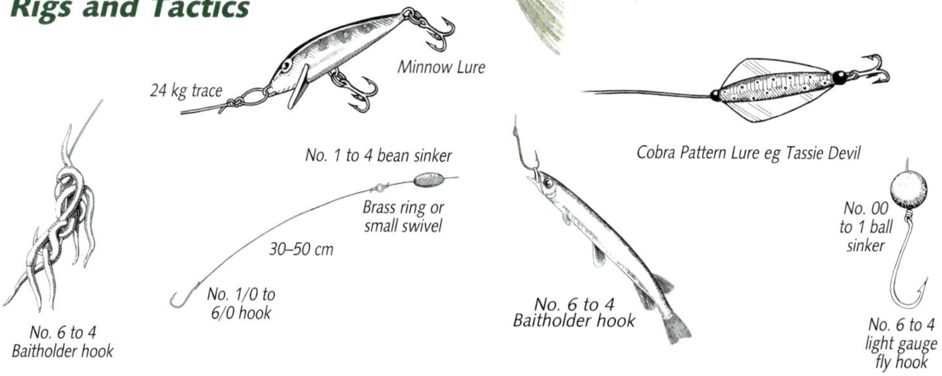

24 kg trace

Minnow Lure

No. 1 to 4 bean sinker

Brass ring or
small swivel

30–50 cm

No. 1/0 to
6/0 hook

*No. 6 to 4
Baitholder hook*

Cobra Pattern Lure eg Tassie Devil

No. 6 to 4
Baitholder hook

No. 00
to 1 ball
sinker

No. 6 to 4
light gauge
fly hook

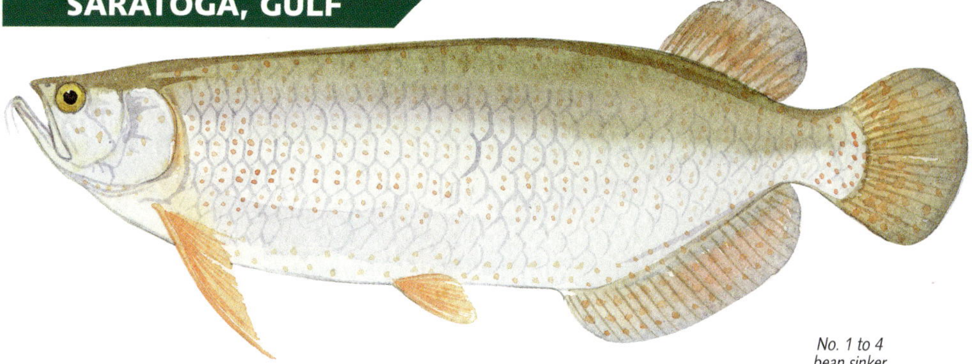

Rigs and Tactics

No. 00 to 2 ball sinker

*Freshwater
popper*

No. 1 to 4
bean sinker

Brass ring or
small swivel

30–50 cm

No. 1/0 to
6/0 hook

*Fly fishing is
successful*

No. 4 to 3/0 hook
depending on size of bait

24 kg trace

Minnow Lure

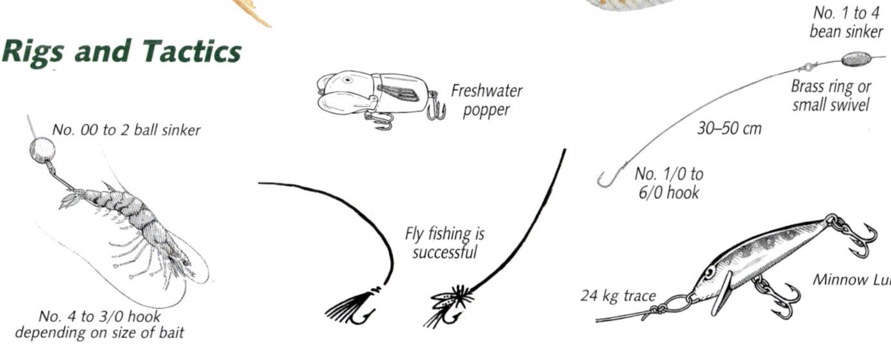

SARATOGA, SOUTHERN

Scientific name *Scleropages leichardti.* Also known as spotted barramundi, spotted saratoga, Dawson river salmon.

Range Native to the Fitzroy River system in southern Queensland, it is now captured in the Mary, Dawson, Burnett, Burdekin, Brisbane and Noosa Systems as well as a number of impoundments in south-east Queensland.

Description The southern saratoga is similar to the gulf saratoga, but the mouth is slightly smaller and the large scales carry two or more red spots which form a vertical streak. The protruding lower jaw carries two small barbels near the lower lip. The pectoral fins are large and extend to the start of the small pelvic fins. The southern saratoga is much lighter through the body than the gulf saratoga and consequently weighs much less for the same length. The saratogas belong to a family commonly known as the bony tongue fishes, which means that the bony mouth can be difficult to set a hook into. The southern saratoga naturally inhabits fairly turbid streams, but they adapt well to impoundments and provide additional sport for keen lure and fly fishers.

Fishing The southern saratoga is becoming an increasingly prized species for specimen fly anglers who value the challenge of spotting and landing this fish. They will rise readily to large surface flies such as the Dahlberg diver and fight hard and spectacularly. Saratoga will also take lures very well, especially surface lures or shallow running lures. Live frogs and unweighted shrimps cast near cruising fish are successful. The saratoga is very poor eating and is much more highly regarded as a sport fish. The very small number of eggs (only 70 to 200) produced by a female means that each fish is valuable and should be carefully looked after.

TENCH

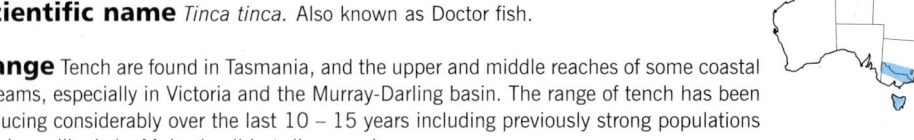

Scientific name *Tinca tinca.* Also known as Doctor fish.

Range Tench are found in Tasmania, and the upper and middle reaches of some coastal streams, especially in Victoria and the Murray-Darling basin. The range of tench has been reducing considerably over the last 10 – 15 years including previously strong populations in places like Lake Mulwala all but disappearing.

Description Tench are an introduced freshwater fish with a fairly thick body with a blunt snout, small red or orange eye and a single barbel at each corner of the mouth. The single dorsal fin is small and high on the back and the tail fin is broad, only slightly forked and rounded at the ends of the lobes. The tench is frequently an attractive olive or golden colour but the body is covered with a fairly thick mucous. In Australia, the tench can reach more than 9 kg and 72 cm but is rarely found above 2 kilograms. Tench prefer slow stretches of water and especially those with shade cover and generous weed growth. Tench appear to be suffering displacement by European carp.

Fishing The tench is one of the most prized species by coarse anglers. Although some tench can be sluggish, others give a powerful fight and they are an attractive fish straight out of the water. Tench are taken with standard coarse fishing methods, including paternoster rigs, feeders and float rigs. Berley, where legal, works well to aggregate fish and increase catches. Best baits include maggots, worms, shrimp, mudeye, corn and luncheon meat. Tench have a fairly small mouth and can be timid biters at times so light and finely tuned gear brings best results. Although a relative of the carp, tench do very little damage to the environment. Tench are poor eating and where legal, the majority are released.

SARATOGA, SOUTHERN

Rigs and Tactics

Fly fishing is successful

No weight to 2 ball sinker

No. 4 to 3/0 hook depending on size of bait

Minnow Lure

Freshwater popper

TENCH

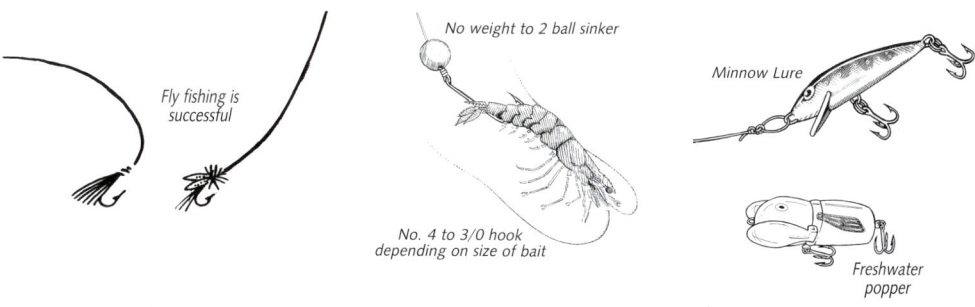

Rigs and Tactics

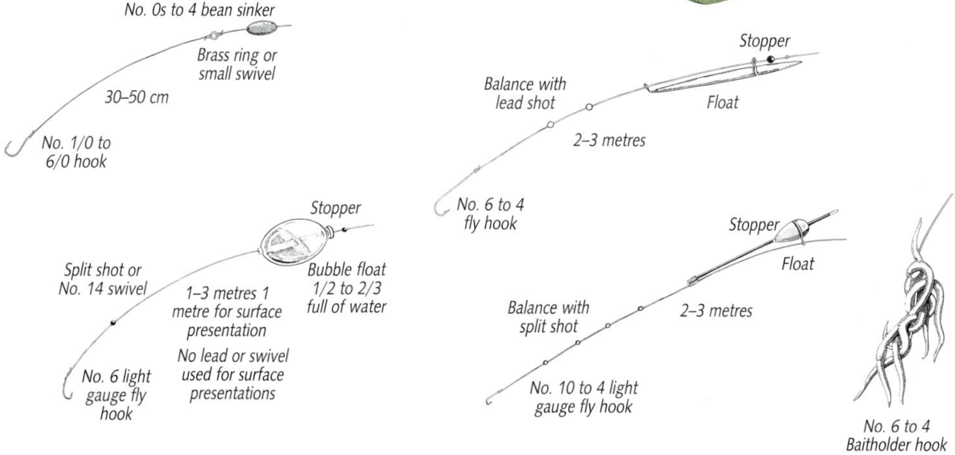

No. 0s to 4 bean sinker

Brass ring or small swivel

30–50 cm

No. 1/0 to 6/0 hook

Stopper

Balance with lead shot

Float

2–3 metres

No. 6 to 4 fly hook

Split shot or No. 14 swivel

Stopper

1–3 metres 1 metre for surface presentation

Bubble float 1/2 to 2/3 full of water

No lead or swivel used for surface presentations

No. 6 light gauge fly hook

Stopper

Float

Balance with split shot

2–3 metres

No. 10 to 4 light gauge fly hook

No. 6 to 4 Baitholder hook

TROUT, BROWN

Scientific name *Salmo trutta.* Also known as Brownie, sea trout, Loch Leven trout.

Range This European native has a wide distribution in cooler waters in Australia. Brown trout are found in upper and occasionally mid reaches of streams in NSW, Victoria, Tasmania, South Australia and south-west Western Australia. There is an increasing fishery for sea run brown trout in Tasmania, although they are also occasionally taken in Victorian coastal streams and the Blackwood estuary in Western Australia.

Description The brown trout is a handsome fish which can exhibit wide colour variations, partly dependent upon the environment in which the fish is found. Sea run fish and some lake dwelling fish are silver in colour with a few spots on the body. River fish in particular can have a beautiful golden sheen and large black spots on the upper body. There are frequently beautiful red spots, surrounded by a white halo below the lateral line which may be mixed with black spots. In all fish, the dorsal fins has some spots but the tail fin has none or a few very faint spots. The tail fin is either square or very slightly indented, whereas the Atlantic salmon has an obvious indent or fork to the tail. The adipose fin is obvious and may be lobe-like in larger fish. The mouth is large and the jaws become hooked to a degree in males during spawning. Brown trout can grow quickly, especially where food is plentiful such as in dams when new ground is being inundated, or for sea run fish feeding on whitebait or other fish. The brown trout can reach 25 kg overseas, but in Australia they have been recorded to 14 kilograms.

Fishing Many books have been specifically written about fishing for this challenging and rewarding species. Brown trout are generally the most highly regarded Australian trout species, due to their large size and the skill which is needed to entice these fish to strike. Brown trout take a variety of foods which may include other trout, minnows, insect larvae, terrestrial insects, snails and worms. Brown trout are specifically targeted by a huge number of recreational fishers, wherever they occur. Brown trout can be taken throughout the day, but the best times are dawn, dusk and at night. Night time is often the best in heavily fished waters, where a few wily, large, and often cannibalistic specimens can often be found. Many brown trout are taken on fly, with nymphs, streamers, wet flies and dry flies all taking fish. Many brown trout feed heavily on yabbies or snails and imitations of these can be very productive. Brown trout generally prefer the slower waters of pools or the tails of pools in streams or deeper waters of lakes, moving into feeding stations during peak periods. Brown trout are more difficult to entice to take flies than rainbow trout and their strong dogged fight makes them a rewarding capture. Brown trout are also taken on a wide variety of lures, with favourites including lead head jigs, spoons, bladed lures like the Celta, and minnow or yabby lures. Large brown trout can become cannibalistic, so the spotted dog colour pattern in a 5 – 7 cm minnow lure works well. As brown trout are often tight to cover, accurate casting is required and may result in lost lures. It is important to work the lure or fly close to cover, or near the bottom where many brown trout take the majority of their food. Trolling lures by themselves or with cowbells or lead lines can cover lots of territory and pick up active fish. Lures should work near the thermocline, along drop-offs or close to other cover. When fish are found at a certain depth, different lures should be tried to maximise catches. Brown trout take a variety of baits, with mudeyes, yabbies, minnows, grubs and worms being most successful. Brown trout will also take maggots, garden snails, corn, cheese, marshmallows and dog food on at least some occasions. There are two basic bait rigs. The first is the classic bubble float (or quill) rig which is used mainly with mudeye or where legal, live minnow baits. However, worms and even yabbies fished under a float close to the bottom can do well especially if there are also carp or other bottom feeders in the area. The other bait rig is the bottom rig, with the least amount of weight you can use being favoured. A long trace and a sliding sinker works well as does a paternoster rig in rivers with a moderate flow. If possible, brown trout should be allowed to move a short distance with the bait before setting the hook. Brown trout are very good eating although like all trout there are some fine bones to be navigated. The general rule with brown trout is that they taste better out of colder and cleaner water.

Lake Brown Trout
or Sea Run Brown Trout

River Brown Trout

Western Lakes Brown Trout

Rigs and Tactics

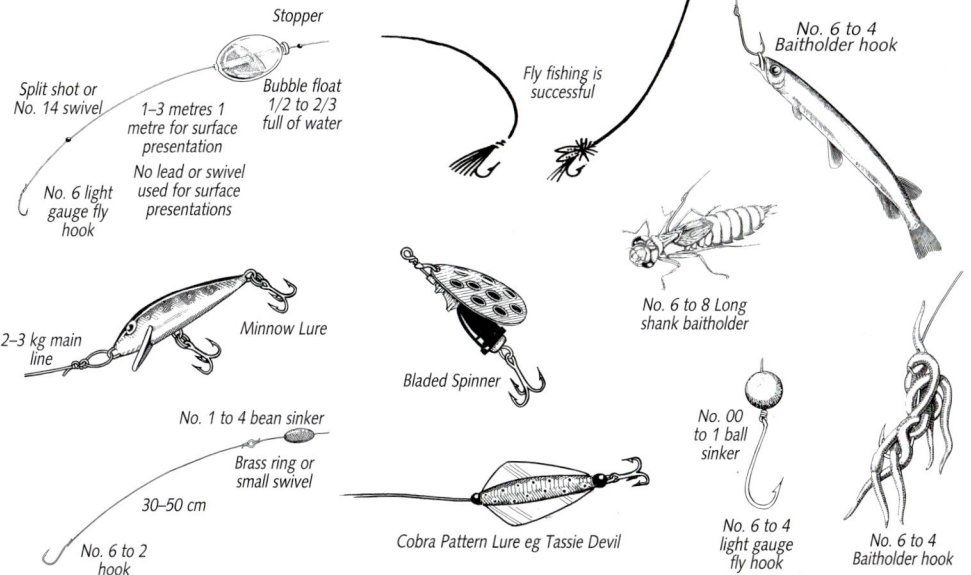

Stopper

Split shot or
No. 14 swivel

1–3 metres 1
metre for surface
presentation

Bubble float
1/2 to 2/3
full of water

No. 6 light
gauge fly
hook

No lead or swivel
used for surface
presentations

Fly fishing is
successful

No. 6 to 4
Baitholder hook

2–3 kg main
line

Minnow Lure

Bladed Spinner

No. 6 to 8 Long
shank baitholder

No. 1 to 4 bean sinker

Brass ring or
small swivel

30–50 cm

No. 6 to 2
hook

Cobra Pattern Lure eg Tassie Devil

No. 00
to 1 ball
sinker

No. 6 to 4
light gauge
fly hook

No. 6 to 4
Baitholder hook

TROUT, BROOK

Scientific name *Salvelinus fontinalis*. Also known as Brookie, brook char, char.

Range A species of char with a very strong preference for clear cold water which severely limits the available waters in Australia. The brook trout is found in Lake Jindabyne, Three Mile Dam and a few small creeks around Jindabyne and the Upper Snowy Mountains. They are found in a few locations in Tasmania, notably Clarence Lagoon and had been introduced with minimal success in a few streams in South Australia.

Description The brook trout is a stunningly attractive species. The ventral and anal fins are bright orange with a black line and then a white leading edge. The markings on the dark upper body are either dots or irregular small lines of cream or off white. The dorsal fin has wavy colouration. The males in spawning condition develop a markedly hooked jaw and even brighter colours. The mouth is large, extending well behind the back edge of the eye. The tail is large and moderately indented or lightly forked. The brook trout can reach around 4 kg in Australia, but the largest fish are generally released brood stock from the hatcheries. These fish do extremely well in hatcheries but do not adapt nearly as well to the wild where they are generally out-competed by other trout species. Any wild caught brook trout is a prize in Australia.

Fishing The brook trout will feed on minnows, flies and insects and may be taken with natural baits and artificials of all these. Dry flies, wet flies and nymphs work best and these hard fighting fish are a real challenge on the fly. Brook trout will take lead head jigs and small minnow lures. Brook trout prefer small and pristine streams and presentation is important due partly to the nature of the lies in these streams. In impoundments, brook trout favour creek or river mouths and may be taken with standard casting or trolling methods. The brook trout is excellent eating, frequently having bright orange flesh, but due to their rarity, most anglers release these fish after a photograph is taken. The long term future for the brook trout in Australia is not good and they may ultimately disappear from wild waters.

TROUT, RAINBOW

Scientific name *Oncorhynchus mykiss*. (formerly *Salmo gairdnerii*) Also known as rainbow, 'bow, Steelhead.

Range Rainbow trout are found from Spring Creek in southern Queensland, through cooler waters at higher elevation across NSW and Victoria. Rainbow trout are found in Tasmania, in the hills of South Australia and south-western Western Australia as far north as Lake Leschenaultia east of Perth. Australia does not possess the prolific runs of 'Steelhead' rainbow trout found in the species' native North America, but some sea run fish are taken in Tasmanian estuaries. Rainbow trout have recently been reclassified in recognition to its relationship with the Pacific salmon such as the Chinook or Quinnat salmon.

Description Rainbow trout possess the fleshy adipose fin of all salmonids behind the dorsal fin. The tail may be slightly forked but characteristically rainbow trout have spots over the entire tail and all of the body except the belly. A pink stripe along the body ranges from very pale in sea run and lake fish to crimson in river fish and those on their spawning run. Male rainbows develop a hooked lower jaw as spawning approaches. Females retain a more rounded head.

Fishing Rainbow trout are generally easier to catch than brown trout but usually fight harder and often jump spectacularly. Rainbow trout are more mobile and will feed more freely in mid to shallow depths. This means that methods such as trolling are more successful, but rainbow trout can selectively feed on daphnia (water fleas) which can make them more difficult to catch. Rainbow trout prefer faster water in streams than brown trout and will often take up station at the head of pools. Rainbow trout can be taken on fly, lure or bait. They take dry flies, wets, nymphs and streamer flies. Rainbow trout can be taken on bright colours and gaudy streamer flies can work well. All standard trout lures work well for rainbow trout, with spinner blade lures like the Celta, Tasmanian devil type lures, leadhead jigs and small minnow lures like the Rapala CD5 and Halco Laser Pro 45 among the most consistent producers. Rainbow trout take all baits. A lightly weighted worm in streams or fairly close to the bank takes fish as do mudeyes fished under a bubble float or trolled with Cowbell trolling blades. Yabbies, grubs and live fish (where legal) take good catches. Rainbow trout make good or excellent eating, especially when taken from cold water and the flesh is bright orange. There are a wide variety of excellent recipes for rainbow trout, but a freshly caught fish wrapped in foil with the gut cavity filled with onion, tomato, butter and lemon pepper certainly takes some beating.

Female

Male

Rigs and Tactics

Minnow Lure

2–3 kg main line

No. 1 to 4 bean sinker

Brass ring or small swivel

30–50 cm

No. 4 to 10 hook

No. 6 to 4 Baitholder hook

Cobra Pattern Lure eg Tassie Devil

Fly fishing is successful

No. 6 to 4 Baitholder hook

Lake

River

Rigs and Tactics

Minnow Lure

2–3 kg main line

No. 1 to 4 bean sinker

Brass ring or small swivel

30–50 cm

No. 4 to 10 hook

No lead or swivel used for surface presentations

Split shot or No. 14 swivel

1–3 metres 1 metre for surface presentation

No. 6 light gauge fly hook

Stopper

Bubble float 1/2 to 2/3 full of water

Bladed Spinner

Cobra Pattern Lure eg Tassie Devil

Fly fishing is successful

No. 6 to 4 Baitholder hook

TROUT, TIGER

Scientific name *no name*. Cross between brook trout and brown trout Also known as Tiger, Hybrid trout.

Range The tiger trout is a sterile hybrid of the brook and brown trout. It is found only in waters where it is regularly stocked. It is considered particularly suitable for deep clear lakes where limited spawning streams is a disadvantage for rainbow trout. Tasmania is currently experimenting with this hybrid.

Description The tiger trout is a handsome fish possessing many of the body markings of the attractive brook trout, with many prominent scribbling markings but in a looser pattern than for the brook trout. The ventral and anal fins may have similar white margins as for brook trout. The tiger trout is still largely a small scale experimental species. The sizes and adaptability to the wild is still being assessed.

Fishing Standard trout fishing techniques for impoundments where these fish are found will produce results. The tiger trout is considered good eating.

TUPONG

Scientific name *Pseudaphritis urvillii*. Also known as Congolli, freshwater flathead, marble fish, sand trout.

Range Bega in southern NSW and coastal drainages around to South Australia and including the Murray-Darling basin, also Tasmania .

Description The tupong is a predatory freshwater or estuarine species generally found among snags or bottom debris of larger pools. The tupong is related to the icefishes of Antarctica. The tupong can reach 36 cm but is more commonly seen at 15 to 20 centimetres. The tupong can be identified by the two separate dorsal fins, the second dorsal fin is long and extends almost to the tail. The anal fin is also long. The tail is square. There may be dark blotches on the backs and sides but there is a dark stripe along the body below the lateral line. The eye is yellow and set high on the head.

Fishing A classic ambush feeder that may bury itself in the sand and erupt to eat insects, shrimp or small fish. Best baits are shrimp, worms or mudeyes fished with a light sinker and a long leader. Tupong may take flies or small jigs or lures on occasions. Tupong have suffered a decrease in range and abundance and should he returned where possible. They are fair eating and are aggressive as aquarium fish.

TROUT, TIGER

Rigs and Tactics

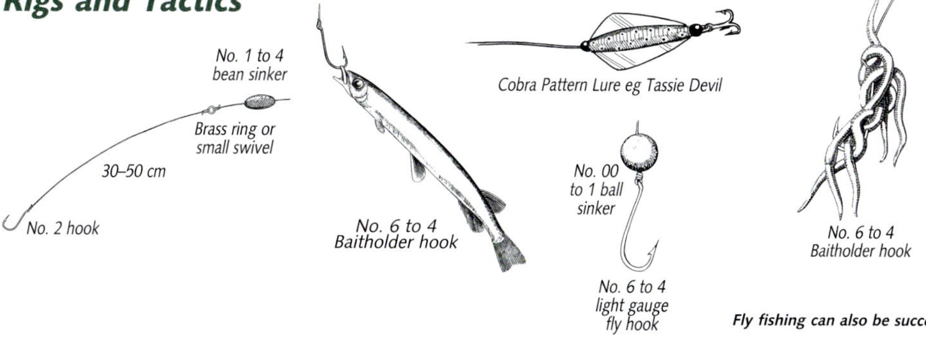

No. 1 to 4
bean sinker

Brass ring or
small swivel

30–50 cm

No. 2 hook

No. 6 to 4
Baitholder hook

Cobra Pattern Lure eg Tassie Devil

No. 00
to 1 ball
sinker

No. 6 to 4
light gauge
fly hook

No. 6 to 4
Baitholder hook

Fly fishing can also be successful.

TUPONG

Rigs and Tactics

No. 00 to
2 ball
sinker

No. 6 to 1
Suicide or
baitholder hook

No. 6 to
2 hook

3 kg

No. 2 to 4 ball or
bean sinker depending
on conditions

No. 4 to
2/0 hook

No. 1 to 4
bean sinker

Brass ring or
small swivel

30–50 cm

No. 6 to
2 hook

No. 6 to 4
Baitholder hook

BONY BREAM

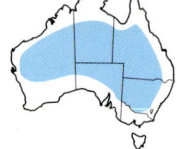

Scientific name *Nematalosa erebi.* Also known as Melon fish, pyberry and tukari.

Range Found throughout fresh waters around Australia except in the south-east coastal and south-west coastal drainages and in Tasmania. An extremely important forage species throughout its range.

Description The bony bream has a deep compressed body with scale-less head and small toothless mouth. The mucous (slime) has an odour similar to jam melons. Scales are easily shed during handling but the bony bream possesses sharp serrated ridge on dorsal and ventral surfaces. The last ray on the single dorsal fin is elongated.

Fishing Can form vast shoals in shallow waters, especially after floods which stimulate spawning but this fish is rarely caught by angling. The bony bream may be occasionally caught with coarse fishing hair rigs and tiny baits. Bony bream don't stay alive well as a live bait but make a passable dead bait for fish such as Murray cod.

CHERABIN

Scientific name *Machrobracium rosenbergii* Also known as cherubin, cherrabin, freshwater prawn

Range Throughout tropical Australia.

Description A large freshwater and upper estuarine shrimp that is capable of reaching around 300 grams. The cherabin can be a deep translucent blue to a brown depending on the clarity of the water. Cherabin have a characteristic pair of very long, slender but remarkably flexible nippers that can be a dark brown or almost black. The nippers do not look like they can do much damage, but they can really give a painful nip. There is a similar species (*Machrobrachium australiense*) which is found in the Murray Darling drainage which reaches around 12 cm in body length and which is often brown or translucent in colour.

Fishing The cherabin is considered to be excellent eating and although it is an absolutely first rate live bait and almost as good a dead bait, many do not make it into the bait bucket and are consumed in their own right. Cherabin are taken in throw nets and can be berleyed up with small bits of meat or unscented soap flakes. Cherabin can be taken in bait traps or an old paint tin with holes in it and a piece of meat hung in the neck of the tin set in a deeper hole. One of the best baits is a piece of Sunlight or other unscented soap which works surprisingly well. Cherabin can also be taken with a scoop net and a torch at night when they are much more active.

GALAXIA SPECIES

Scientific name *Family Galaxiidae.* Also known as Minnows, Native trout, galaxias, trout minnow, jollytail, whitebait of Tasmania and New Zealand.

Range A total of 20 species are found in Australia. Many species such as the Peddar galaxias, Swan galaxias and Clarence galaxias are found in very isolated populations in Tasmania. The Common jollytail or spotted minnow (*Galaxias maculatus*) has an extensive range from southern Queensland through southern waters and Tasmania to Albany in Western Australia. These important forage species are found in cooler fresh waters from southern Queensland to central Western Australia. Most species require estuarine waters to spawn and the upstream migration of juveniles results in tasty whitebait in Tasmania and New Zealand.

Description Galaxiids are small tubular fish easily identified by the single dorsal fin set well back on the body and above the anal fin. There is no adipose fin. The head is small and relatively pointed. Many of these species are very pretty.

Fishing With the exception of whitebait fishing in some coastal streams of Tasmania and the taking of these fish as minnows by kids, these species are not a fishing target. However, galaxiids make terrific live bait (where permitted) for trout, redfin and other fish. Hook them lightly near the dorsal fin and fish them under a light float or partly filled bubble to take any nearby predators. Trout and other species' predation is implicated in the reduced range for several galaxiid species.

BONY BREAM

Rigs and Tactics

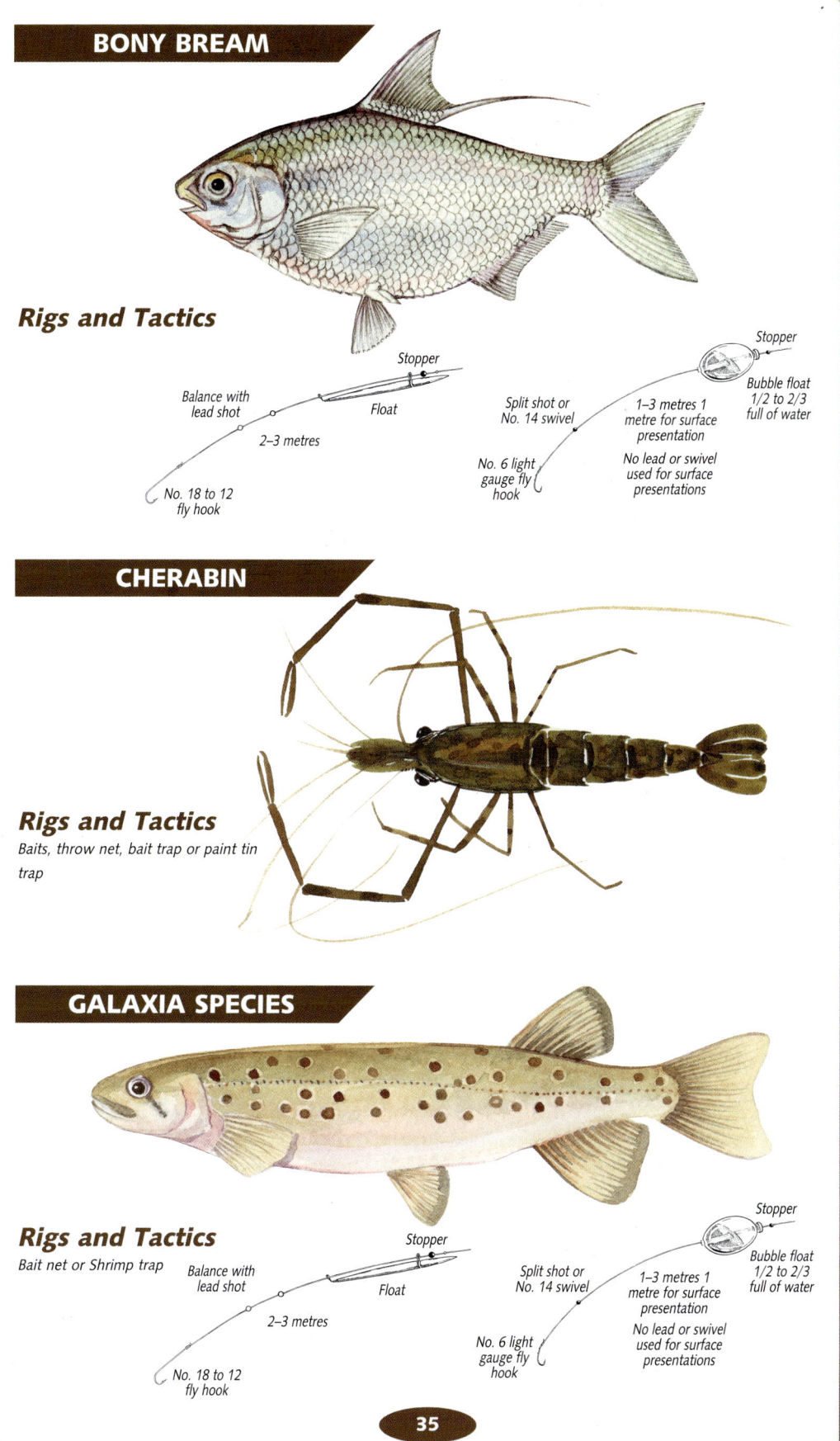

Stopper

Balance with
lead shot

Float

2–3 metres

No. 18 to 12
fly hook

Split shot or
No. 14 swivel

No. 6 light
gauge fly
hook

1–3 metres 1
metre for surface
presentation

No lead or swivel
used for surface
presentations

Stopper

Bubble float
1/2 to 2/3
full of water

CHERABIN

Rigs and Tactics

Baits, throw net, bait trap or paint tin
trap

GALAXIA SPECIES

Rigs and Tactics

Bait net or Shrimp trap

Stopper

Balance with
lead shot

Float

2–3 metres

No. 18 to 12
fly hook

Split shot or
No. 14 swivel

No. 6 light
gauge fly
hook

1–3 metres 1
metre for surface
presentation

No lead or swivel
used for surface
presentations

Stopper

Bubble float
1/2 to 2/3
full of water

GOLDFISH

Scientific name *Carassius auratus*. Also known as golden carp, crucian carp.

Range Introduced into most waters of Australia, with many introductions through aquarists releasing fish or escaped bait from irresponsible anglers. Common in many waters and capable of hybridising with common carp.

Description The goldfish can reach 3 kilograms. This is a far cry from the deformed animals frequently sold in aquarium shops but which can breed wild strain goldfish as offspring. The goldfish has a straight lateral line and has no barbels near its mouth.

Fishing Goldfish in the larger sizes fight well and are good sport. Light lines and baits of worms, maggots, corn or bread crusts take these fish. Rigs used in coarse fishing can take surprising numbers from urban ponds. Goldfish have many wishbone shaped bones and are considered very poor eating by all but the most dedicated fans. All goldfish should be humanely killed and under no circumstances should any aquarium fish be released into the wild.

GUDGEON

Scientific name *Family Gobiidae*, subfamilies *Eleotridinae* and *Butinae*. There are numerous names for the 40 – 50 freshwater species around Australia.

Range Found throughout Australian fresh water, gudgeon are an extremely important forage species. The blind gudgeon is only found in caves of North-west Cape, Western Australia while the big-headed gudgeon has a wide range and can be found from the Burdekin River in northern Queensland to west of Port Lincoln in South Australia and including Tasmania.

Description Gudgeons are a very diverse group containing several beautiful aquarium species such as the Empire gudgeon and Purple spotted gudgeon. All species lack a lateral line, have two dorsal fins with 2 – 8 spines in the first dorsal and have separate ventral fins. In several species the male and female have different colouration or body shape.

Fishing With the exception of the sleepy cod which can reach 48 cm and 3 kg and the snakehead gudgeon from around the Daintree region which can grow to 40 cm, the gudgeons are important forage species which are better known as bait than as targets in their own right. The sleepy cod is reasonable eating but its sluggish nature means that it is poorly regarded as a sport fish. Gudgeons can be taken on worms, maggots or other baits, with the hook size tailored to the size of the species being sought. Where allowed, gudgeons make an excellent and hardy live bait, with the big-headed gudgeon particularly effective.

GUDGEON, WESTERN CARP

Scientific name *Hypseleotris klunzingeri* Also known as carp gudgeon

Range From the Mary River in southern Queensland and in coastal streams and rivers as far south as the Hunter River. In this part of its range it can also be found with the similar firetail gudgeon (*Hypeleotris galii*). The western carp gudgeon is also found in the Murray-Darling drainage.

Description A small and common forage species which grows to 6.5 cm but is often seen at 2.5 to 5 centimetres. The males develop a more prominent sloped forehead and are darker in colour than the females. This species is generally a fairly drab olive colour and lacks the bright orange tail and dorsal fin fringe of the fire tail gudgeon, although there may be an orange or purplish tint to the dorsal fin. The scales appear quite prominent but lack the obvious cross hatching pattern of juvenile silver perch. The western carp gudgeon is very common in farm dams and are often reported as juvenile golden and silver perch or proof that breeding of these larger natives has taken place. In many impoundments, the western carp gudgeon is an important forage species but they are also extremely important as fodder for cormorants which predate upon them heavily. They are most common on the edges of weeds or in shallow bays.

Fishing The western carp gudgeon has a small mouth and is not taken by recreational anglers with normal techniques. They can be taken in scoop nets, especially when berley of crushed worms or maggots are used or the net is worked along the edges of weed beds. This species is quite small and is rarely used as bait.

GOLDFISH

Rigs and Tactics

Stopper
Balance with lead shot
Float
2–3 metres
No. 18 to 12 fly hook
No. 0 or 1 bean sinker
Brass ring or small swivel
30–50 cm
No. 16 to 1 hook
Stopper
Bubble float 1/2 to 2/3 full of water
Split shot or No. 14 swivel
1–3 metres 1 metre for surface presentation
No lead or swivel used for surface presentations
No. 6 light gauge fly hook

GUDGEON

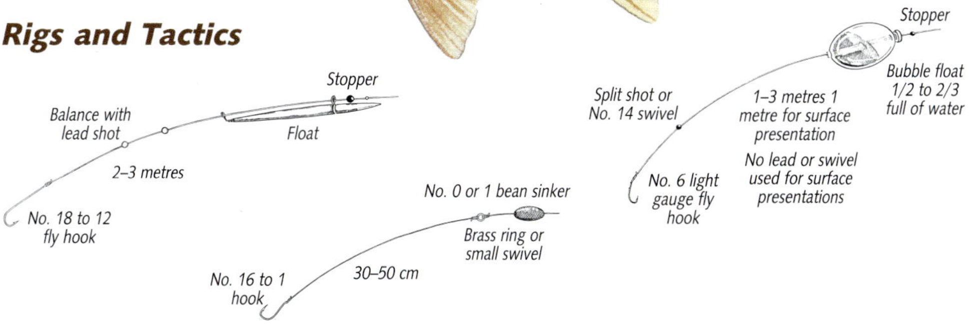

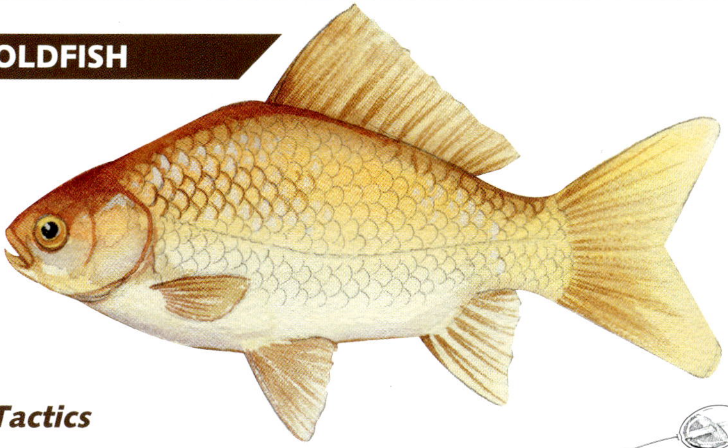

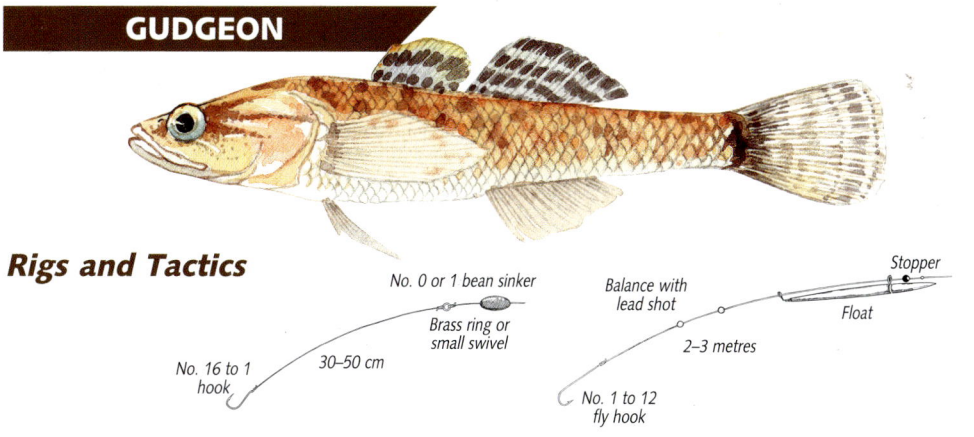

Rigs and Tactics

No. 0 or 1 bean sinker
Brass ring or small swivel
30–50 cm
No. 16 to 1 hook
Balance with lead shot
Stopper
Float
2–3 metres
No. 1 to 12 fly hook

GUDGEON, WESTERN CARP

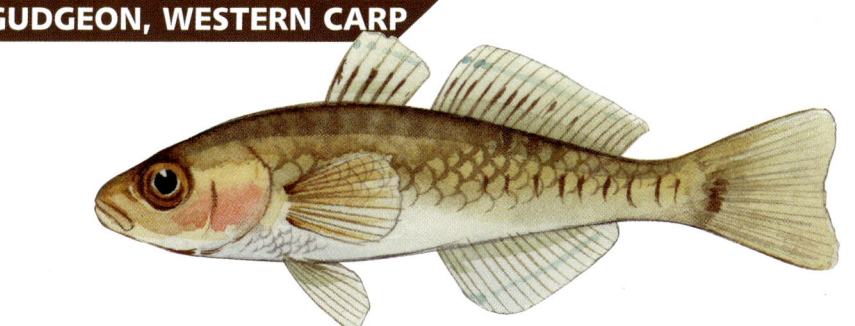

Rigs and Tactics

Used as bait.

GUDGEON, FLATHEAD

Scientific name *Philypnodon grandiceps* Also known as big-headed gudgeon, freshwater gudgeon

Range From the Burdekin River system in Queensland south-wards and including Tasmania although rare there and along the south coast as far as the Gulf of Vincent in South Australia. This species is found throughout the Murray-Darling basin and can be found in dams, rivers or estuaries.

Description A small but important forage species, the flathead gudgeon can be a common part of the diets of native fish or trout. The flathead gudgeon can reach 12 cm but is more commonly seen as 5 – 9 centimetres. The flathead gudgeon has a large head with a very large mouth for its size. There are two separate dorsal fins, which separates the gudgeons from the galaxiid minnows. The pectoral fins are large and are used to hold the fish in position. There can be a black spot at the base of the large, rounded tail fin. The colour is generally tan to chocolate brown, with a cream coloured belly. The orange eggs can be clearly seen in the belly of females as they approach breeding season.

Fishing The flathead gudgeon is a bait fish and is not generally targeted, but they can be caught on a line. Their large mouth means that larger specimens can actually take a worm bait meant for larger fish and they can frustrate coarse anglers fishing with a single maggot. The flathead gudgeon will eat the bait and then stay in the same spot, as flathead can do in the marine environment which can be frustrating. In places where they are legally able to be used as bait, this fish are hardy and make an excellent bait. They can be taken on a small wet fly or nymph, or a worm bait on a size 14 to 18 hook. They can also be taken in a net that has been fitted with curtain mesh which is more robust than cheesecloth. Berley with crushed worms, snails or maggots will bring in good numbers or they can be taken by pushing the net into the edges of weed beds or under rocks. Flathead gudgeon are more active at night. The best rig to use is a bubble float or light stick float weighted to a fair degree so that there isn't too much resistance. Use a swivel and a 30 – 45 cm trace. Set the float so that the bait sits at around the thermocline (the layer of colder water) which is often around 1.2 to 1.8 m deep. These fish can also be drift fished or even rigged dead to troll behind cowbells instead of mudeyes or worms. Note that using live fish for bait is illegal in some states. The flathead gudgeon is not a good aquarium species as they are aggressive to other fish, especially at night and they are prone to fungal diseases. They prefer fresh or live food.

HERRING, FRESHWATER

Scientific name *Potamalosa richmondia*. Also known as Nepean herring.

Range Found in the freshwater or upper estuarine reaches of coastal rivers from the Noosa River in Southern Queensland to the Hawkesbury River in NSW.

Description The freshwater herring is an attractive silvery fish with the characteristic ventral scutes (serrations) of the true herrings. The body is slender, although some large females can develop a more robust profile. The head is scaleless and bears a superficial resemblance to the pilchard but the freshwater herring can reach 32 centimetres.

Fishing This species is one of the best training species for fly fishers available. They are forgiving of sloppy presentation and will take dry and wet flies. The same fish will often rise repeatedly to the same fly and once hooked they are scrappy fighters who jump nicely. Freshwater herring have many fine bones but these can be consumed after the fish is cooked. Freshwater herring bruise easily and the scales can be easily dislodged so care must be taken if releasing these fish.

GUDGEON, FLATHEAD

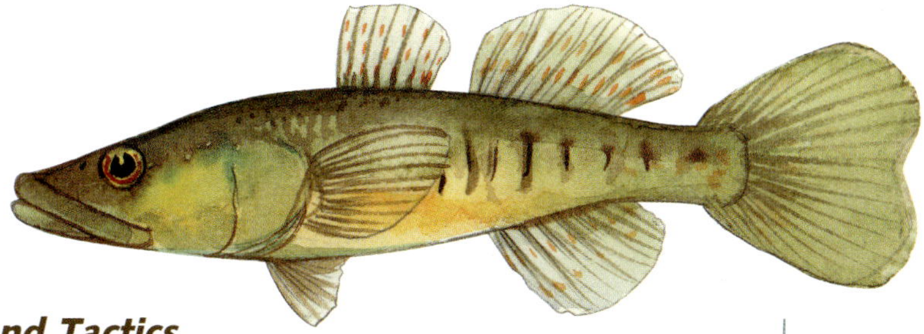

Rigs and Tactics

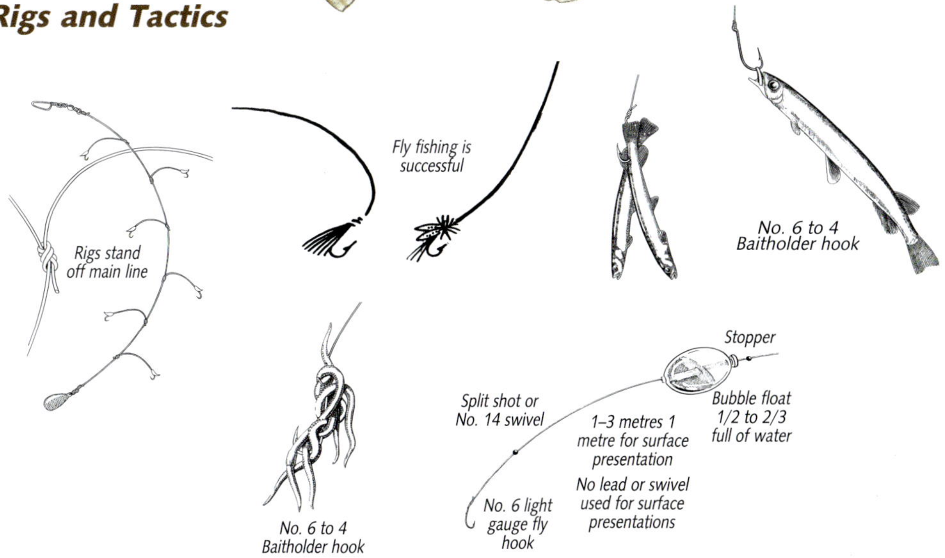

Rigs stand off main line
Fly fishing is successful
No. 6 to 4 Baitholder hook
No. 6 to 4 Baitholder hook
Stopper
Bubble float 1/2 to 2/3 full of water
Split shot or No. 14 swivel
1–3 metres 1 metre for surface presentation
No lead or swivel used for surface presentations
No. 6 light gauge fly hook

HERRING, FRESHWATER

Rigs and Tactics

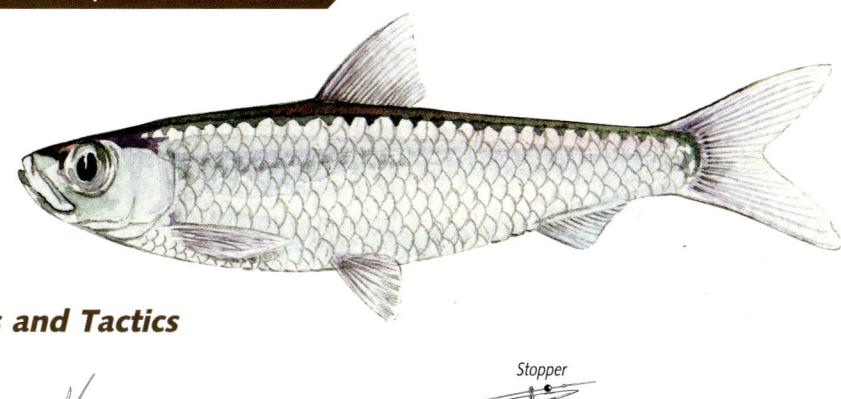

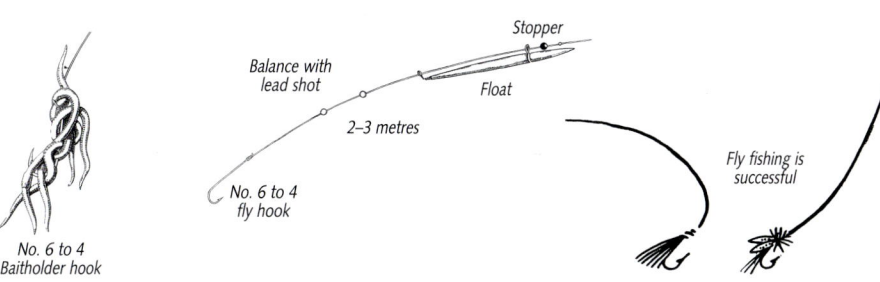

No. 6 to 4 Baitholder hook
Balance with lead shot
Stopper
Float
2–3 metres
No. 6 to 4 fly hook
Fly fishing is successful

MARRON

Scientific name *Cherax.* Also known as Freshwater crayfish.

Range The marron is found naturally only in the south-west of Western Australia. Its range in Western Australia has been extended through introductions to near Geraldton in the north and to near Esperance in the south. However, the inland range of marron in WA is now being rapidly reduced by increased salinity and loss of habitat. Marron have been introduced into the eastern states for aquaculture especially Kangaroo Isalnd in South Australia and escapees may be found near these sites. The rare hairy marron's is found in the Margaret River catchment.

Description The marron is a large freshwater crustacean, reaching nearly 2 kg and a total length of over 38 centimetres. Marron can be identified by the fairly light claws and the five distinct keels on the head and two spines on the tail fan. Marron are generally a dark brown, although large marron that moult less frequently can have quite dirty shells. Marron can be separated from the other native Western Australian crustaceans. Koonacs have heavier claws and more closely resemble yabbies but have four less obvious head keels. Gilgies have heavier claws than marron and lack the serrations on the outside of the claws. Gilgies only grow to 12 cm and have a mottled colour.

Fishing Fishing is now restricted to a fairly short summer season of around eight weeks. Marron are taken with two hoop drop nets which are fitted with heavy bottom grids to allow undersize marron to escape, wire scoop nets or with a bushman's snare. Best baits for hoop netting are fish flesh, heart, liver or any red meat. The snare is a piece of heavy wire is looped onto the end of a pole or fishing rod. The snare is placed behind a marron which is attracted to shallow water by chicken laying pellets. A light is shone on the head of the marron and has it backing into the wire. A deft flick of the wrist and the kicking marron is carried to the shore. Snaring marron is easily the most challenging and enjoyable crustacean fishing in Australia. Marron are glorious eating. They are magnificent eaten fresh and have a very large tail which is full of delicious meat.

MURRAY CRAYFISH

Scientific name *Euastacus armatus.* Also known as Spiny crayfish, whiteclaw.

Range Found in the some tributaries of the Murray-Darling Basin including the Murray River, Murrumbidgee River, upper Abercrombie River, Glenelg River and some impoundments such as Blowering, Jounama and Talbingo.

Description The Murray crayfish is a striking example of the spiny freshwater crayfish which can grow to over 2 kilograms. Apart from the fact that the spiny crayfish is found in freshwater, it is easily differentiated from the marine lobsters by the presence of the two strong claws. These claws are white or off-white in the Murray crayfish. The tail is armed with prominent spines which are also white. There are several other east coast spiny crayfish and the giant Tasmanian species, all of which are confined to specific ranges.

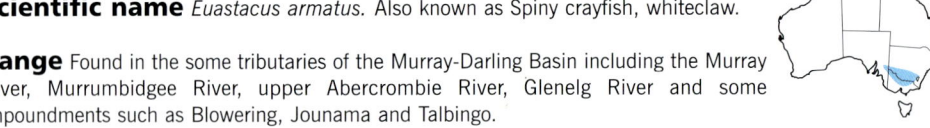

Fishing The Murray crayfish is most active during cooler water temperatures. The construction of large dams has had a significant impact on the activity of these animals. Murray crayfish were once most active during the cooler months of winter and during spring floods caused by snow melt. Irrigation discharges peak in middle to late summer, have extended the period of activity of Murray crayfish, especially in the Murray and Murrumbidgee Rivers. Murray crayfish are taken in two hoop drop nets set near snags and deeper muddy banks. Baits used include carp, ox heart, liver, rabbit, chicken and pilchard. All berried females must be returned immediately and bag and size limits are strictly enforced. Murray crayfish numbers have become significantly reduced; in the lower Murray through increased salinity and increased use of agricultural chemicals and in other areas through these factors and over fishing. Murray crayfish are magnificent eating and there is little better than eating freshly caught crays boiled in a tin on the banks of the river. Unfortunately, the Murray crayfish has a relatively small tail which contains less meat than their size might suggest. Many large crays are preserved and mounted for displays. Inject the cray with a dilute solution of formalin over a few days and inject glycerin directly into the joints of the claws and legs to prevent them from becoming brittle with age.

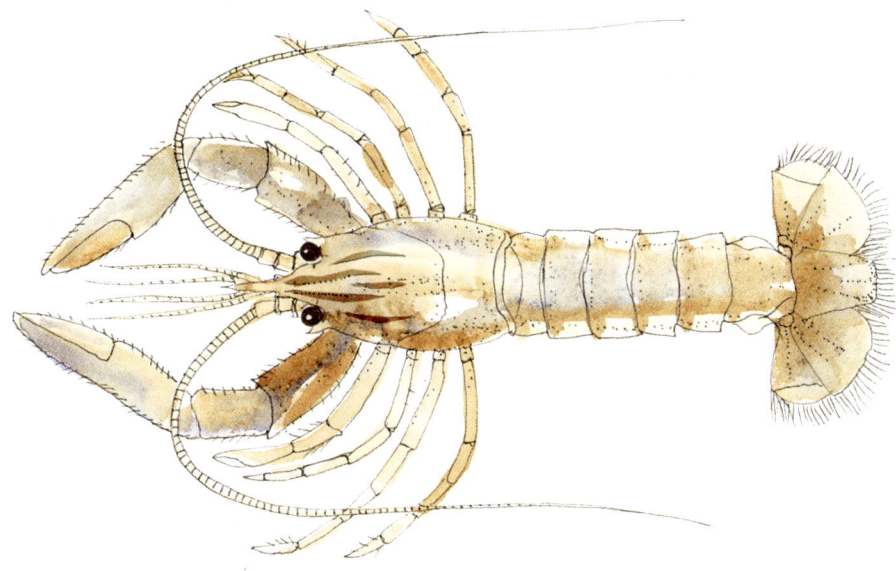

Rigs and Tactics

Rigs: Baited yabby pot

MURRAY CRAYFISH

Rigs and Tactics

Rigs: Baited yabby pot

MOSQUITO FISH

Scientific name *Gambusia affinis.* Also known as Gambusia, eastern gambusia, gambies, Starling's perch.

Range Now found in virtually all permanent waters in Australia other than Tasmania through well meaning but ultimately irresponsible introductions from 1925 in Sydney and especially from World War II onwards to control mosquitoes.

Description The mosquito fish is a small species, females reach 6 cm with males no larger than 3.5 centimetres. The mosquito fish is a live bearer, giving birth to miniature live young. The mosquito fish is a less colourful and flamboyant relative of the common guppy. The larger female has a prominent black spot at the rear of the abdomen where the young develop. The males have a large and prominent first anal ray which is called a gonopodium and is used to internally fertilise the eggs within the female. Under good conditions young mosquito fish can reach maturity within two months. Mosquito fish can rapidly build up populations, leading to large schools of these voracious fish which regrettably prefer foods other than mosquito larvae when alternatives are available.

Fishing This species is not a recreational fishing target species and is best known as food for native aquarium species. Under no circumstances should mosquito fish be released alive into any water. Mosquito fish have the nasty habit of nipping fins of other fish and eating their eggs.

MOUTH ALMIGHTY

Scientific name *Glossamia aprion.* Also known as Northern mouthbreeder, gobbleguts.

Range Fitzroy River system in Western Australia and coastal river systems around the Top End to northern NSW around Coffs Harbour. Ranges from fresh water to tidal waters.

Description An aggressive and very game species, the mouth almighty will try to eat any live food which is smaller than it is. The mouth almighty can reach 20 cm and 600 g but is commonly much smaller than that size. The mouth almighty has a pointed snout and a large mouth which extends behind the very large eye. A dark bar extends from the shoulder through the eye. The base colour may vary but is a shade of brown and can change rapidly when the fish is frightened. The mouth almighty is a mouth brooder, with the male taking up the eggs and holding them until they hatch.

Fishing The mouth almighty is a solitary animal which prefers still, weedy areas and as a result is not often encountered by anglers. They can be taken on worms, live shrimp and small live fish. Mouth almighty are occasionally taken on lures. Mouth almighty make an interesting aquarium fish but don't readily take dead food and will consume or harass other fish.

NIGHTFISH

Scientific name *Bostockia porosa* Also known as Western cod

Range Native to the south-west of Western Australia from the Moore River to near Albany

Description Clearly the runt of the Australian cod family, the nightfish tells you much about the natural freshwater environment of Western Australia outside of the tropics. Whereas its big cousin the Murray cod can reach 1.8 m and more than 100 kg, the nightfish can reach 16 cm and is often seen as an adult at 8 – 10 centimetres. The nightfish is, as its name suggests, most active after dark. It is clearly related to the Murray cod and a visitor from the east can get excited by the juvenile cod. Unfortunately, the natural environment of the Western Australian streams can be unkind and only smaller fish can survive the long and hot, dry summers. The nightfish has the prominent rounded tail and low spiny dorsal fin with a more lobed soft and longer soft dorsal. The dorsal, anal and tail fins are heavily mottled. It lacks the extended first rays on the ventral fins of the other cod species.

Fishing The nightfish is most commonly targeted by recreational fishers as a first rate live bait for redfin perch. They can be taken on small hooks baited with worm or maggot and fished near timber in small but permanent streams and especially those with few trout or redfin. They are often caught with the western galaxiid minnow which is also used as bait.

MOSQUITO FISH

Rigs and Tactics

Scoop net or bait trap

Fly fishing is
successful

MOUTH ALMIGHTY

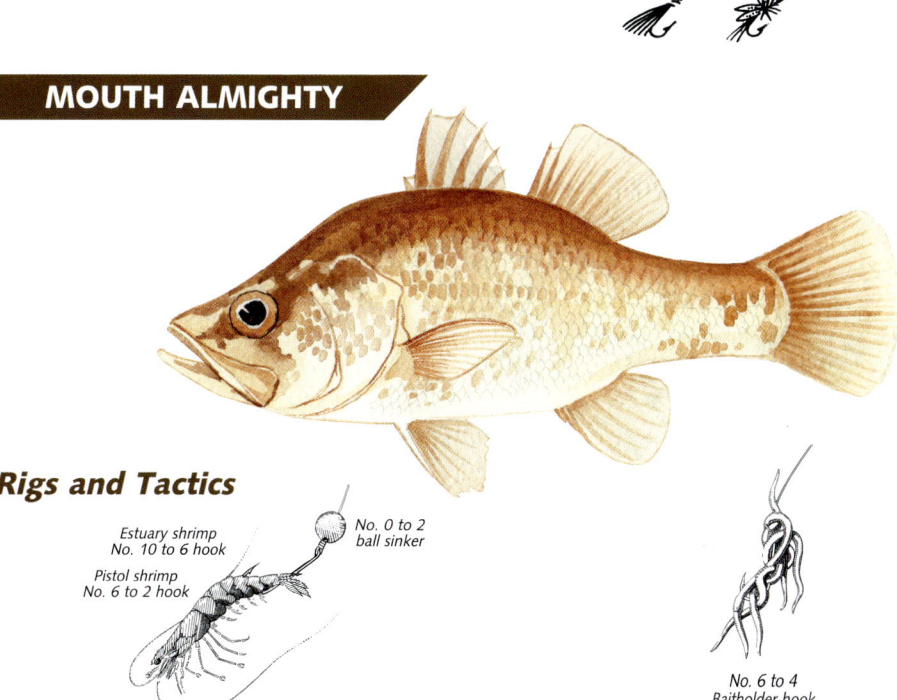

Rigs and Tactics

Estuary shrimp
No. 10 to 6 hook

Pistol shrimp
No. 6 to 2 hook

No. 0 to 2
ball sinker

No. 6 to 4
Baitholder hook

NIGHTFISH

Rigs and Tactics

No. 8 to 12 long
shank hook

Small split
shot

Small slices of
fish bait

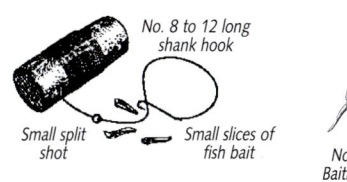

No. 16 to 14
Baitholder hook

PERCH, PYGMY

Scientific name *Nannoperca australis.* Also known as Southern pygmy perch

Range The pygmy perch has a wide range including fresh water from the southern part of NSW coastal streams to the South Australian Gulf and including the southern portion of the Murray Darling basin. The pygmy perch is also found in the north of Tasmania and on King and Flinders Islands.

Description The pygmy perch is a small forage or aquarium species which reaches 8 cm in length but rarely longer than 6.5 centimetres. The pygmy perch is rarely locally abundant and is found in weedy, slow flowing waters or lakes. The single dorsal has 7 – 9 rays with the first soft rays longer than the last dorsal spines. Black or dark brown blotches are found in irregular rows along the flanks. Generally the body colour is drab, except in breeding season around September-October when the males in particular develop bright red fins with black margins.

Fishing The pygmy perch is a favourite food of many larger predators including trout, redfin and other native fish. They may be caught on tiny hooks baited with worm or more commonly in scoop nets with fine mesh. Where legal pygmy perch make an excellent live bait. They are also an excellent aquarium species.

PERCH, SPANGLED

Scientific name *Leiopotherapon unicolor.* Also known as Spangled, jewel perch, bobby cod, nicky.

Range One of the most widespread of all freshwater fishes, being found in fresh coastal and inland waters from northern Western Australia and around the top end, including the harsh inland drainages of central Australia and the Murray-Darling system north of Condobolin. They are extremely hardy, tolerating very hot water with little oxygen and increasing salinity up to full seawater, but contrary to many local legends, they cannot survive by burrowing in mud.

Description The spangled perch is a small, aggressive schooling fish with characteristic pattern of rusty or golden brown spots over a generally brown or silvery body. The spangled perch can reach 600 g, but in some waters, hordes of fish of 50 – 200 g will consume any baits in the vicinity.

Fishing They will take baits of worms, grubs, maggots, shrimps, small yabbies, peeled yabby tail and small fish. Spangled perch will also take small lures such as micro jigs. Their fairly large mouth and strong appetite means that they can take baits intended for larger fish. Where legal, spangled perch make a hardy live bait for other species.

RAINBOW FISH

Scientific name *Family Melanotaeniidae.* Family includes: Blue-eyes, sunfish, rainbow fish.

Range A common group of small freshwater species most common in warmer tropical waters and only reaching around 3 – 15 cm in length. Although a few blue-eye species can be found in brackish or estuarine mangrove areas, most rainbow fishes require good quality fresh water.

Description Some of Australia's most colourful native aquarium species are included in the rainbow fish group, including the attractive honey blue-eye (*Pseudomugil mellis*) and the bright rainbow fishes. The group is recognised by a pointed and flattened snout, large scales, two closely set dorsal fins, the second of which is long and extends to the wrist of the tail and no scales between the pelvic base and the anus on the belly. The anal fin is also long and there is a membrane which joins the pelvic fin to the body of the fish. This group of fishes become more brightly coloured at spawning time, with males much more colourful than females.

Fishing These species are best known as aquarium species. They can be taken in cast nets from tropical creeks and the largest rainbow fish species make an acceptable live bait. The mouth is small and they are not an angling target species. Rainbow fish are too small to be considered as food fish, but if captured or purchased can provide hours of enjoyment in an aquarium as they mix well with other types of fish and most species are quite hardy.

PERCH, PYGMY

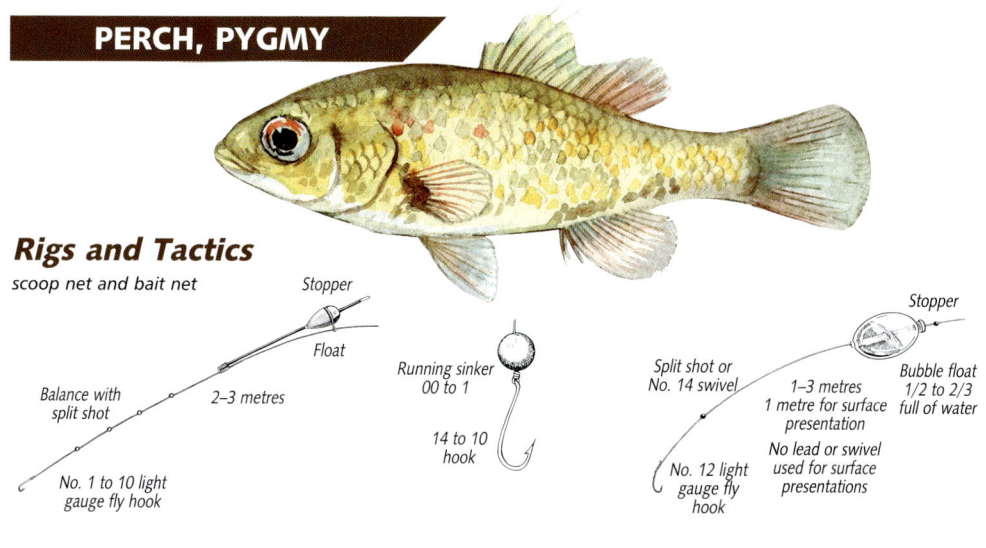

Rigs and Tactics

scoop net and bait net

Stopper

Float

Balance with
split shot

2–3 metres

No. 1 to 10 light
gauge fly hook

Running sinker
00 to 1

14 to 10
hook

Split shot or
No. 14 swivel

1–3 metres
1 metre for surface
presentation

Stopper

Bubble float
1/2 to 2/3
full of water

No lead or swivel
used for surface
presentations

No. 12 light
gauge fly
hook

PERCH, SPANGLED

Rigs and Tactics

No. 1 to 4 bean sinker

Brass ring or
small swivel

30–50 cm

No. 8 to
1/0 hook

No. 8 to
1/0 hook

3 kg

No. 8 to
1/0 hook

No. 2 to 4 ball or
bean sinker depending
on conditions

No. 6 to 4
Baitholder hook

RAINBOW FISH

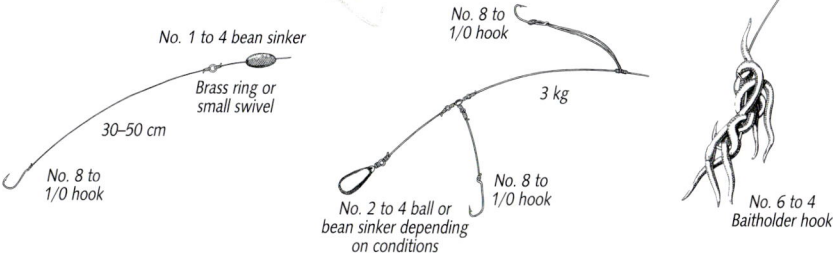

Rigs and Tactics

Cast net

ROACH

Scientific name *Rutilus rutilus.*

Range The roach is an introduced species from Europe and has a disjointed range being found in a number of streams in Victoria.

Description The roach is a less damaging member of the carp family. Ironically, roach numbers, like tench appear to be impacted upon by competition with larger carp. The roach can reach 45 cm and 2 kg but is commonly found at smaller sizes. The roach has a small head and mouth and lacks barbels. The forehead profile is smooth and lacks the prominently indented nostrils of the goldfish. The scales are also finer than in the goldfish. The roach has a short and high dorsal fin. The fins other than the dorsal fin are orange to red. The eye is also red.

Fishing The roach is a highly prized species by coarse fishermen in Europe and here in Australia due to its scrappy fight and the challenge of finding and hooking these fish. The roach prefers slow moving water in larger holes, especially those with overgrown banks. The roach is taken with a variety of light coarse fishing tackle, with small baits such as maggot, worm, bread, casters and shrimp fished under a light float working very well. Berley with bread, maggots or chopped worms helps to bring roach which may form schools to the angler. The fight is strong but clean. Roach are not regarded as a food fish but in some areas it may be illegal to release them alive back into waterways.

SHRIMP, FRESHWATER

Scientific name *Machrobrachium australiense* Also known as Murray shrimp, long-claw shrimp

Range Throughout the Murray Darling basin

Description A similar but smaller species to the cherabin of tropical waters. The claws are also long, up to twice the total body length. The claws look lightweight, but can inflict a nasty nip. The body is translucent and this large freshwater shrimp can reach around 12 cm but is often seen at around 5 – 7 centimetres. There are many other small shrimps in freshwater but they lack the long claws and do not generally get bigger than 2 centimetres. The freshwater shrimp is easily separated from the yabbies and its relatives by the rostrum or head spike which is like that on prawns. The body is also much more prawn-like and the legs are much lighter in build.

Fishing The freshwater shrimp can be scooped up around weeds during the day, or on the flats after dark with a torch and scoop net. Freshwater shrimp are more commonly taken in shrimp traps. These are now commercially available, or an old paint tin with a bait of heart, spleen, hock or especially unscented soap like Sunlight works well. The freshwater shrimp makes an excellent live bait for all native fish. They are especially deadly for silver perch and Macquarie perch that can be fairly difficult propositions at times. They can be bobbed for golden perch and redfin or fished under a float for trout and bass. Larger freshwater shrimp make very good eating.

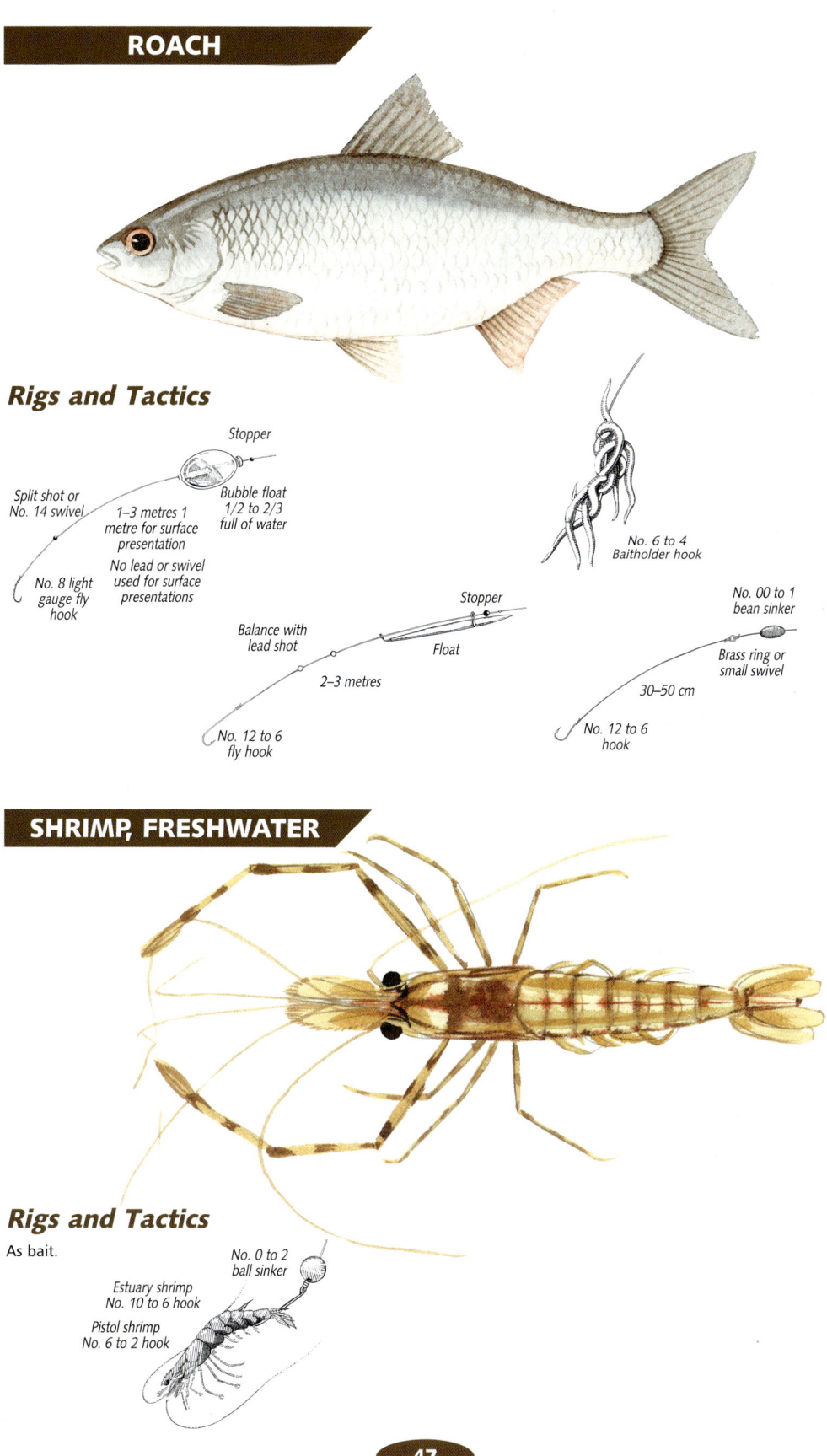

Rigs and Tactics

Stopper

Split shot or
No. 14 swivel

1–3 metres 1
metre for surface
presentation

Bubble float
1/2 to 2/3
full of water

No. 8 light
gauge fly
hook

No lead or swivel
used for surface
presentations

No. 6 to 4
Baitholder hook

Balance with
lead shot

Stopper

Float

No. 00 to 1
bean sinker

2–3 metres

No. 12 to 6
fly hook

No. 12 to 6
hook

30–50 cm

Brass ring or
small swivel

SHRIMP, FRESHWATER

Rigs and Tactics

As bait.

No. 0 to 2
ball sinker

Estuary shrimp
No. 10 to 6 hook

Pistol shrimp
No. 6 to 2 hook

SMELT, AUSTRALIAN

Scientific name *Retropinna semoni.*

Range Fitzroy River system in Queensland and throughout coastal drainage systems also the Murray-Darling system and the Lake Eyre internal drainage. A stocking into Tasmania in the 1960s has not resulted in a wide distribution. A similar but smaller species, the Tasmanian smelt (*Retropinna tasmanica*) is found in much of Tasmania.

Description A small but extremely important schooling forage species throughout the south-east, the smelt reaches 10 centimetres. The smelt is relatively translucent with the internal organs and skeleton obvious. Larger specimens have an olive upper colour and lighter belly colour. There may be a silver stripe running down the middle of the body. An adipose fin and lack of fin pigmentation are typical.

Fishing The smelt is not taken by recreational anglers except in scoop nets. They do not handle well, losing scales and stressing to death. As a result, they make a poor live bait, but are a good dead bait or trolled for trout and salmon. Given the importance of smelt as forage fish in many dams, especially for trout, it is surprising that smelt imitation lures are not used more widely.

TILAPIA, SPOTTED

Scientific name *Tilapia mariae.* Also known as Black mangrove cichlid, Niger cichlid.

Range Restricted range but the tilapias are widely available in aquarium shops and releases are inevitable. The tilapia are part of the cichlid family, with the convict, Jack Dempsey and Mozambique cichlids different species which are all causing problems in Queensland waters. Tilapia are common in the Chapman River near Geraldton Western Australia and in the Morwell area of Victoria, especially the cooling pond of Hazelwood power station.

Description The spotted tilapia has up to 8 or 9 dark spots on the sides, which become less in number and prominence as the fish approaches the maximum size of 30 centimetres. The eye is a deep red. The dorsal fin is long with 15 or 16 spines joined to 12 to 15 rays. The posterior lobe extends nearly to the rounded tail. The anal fin is also long and gives the fish a decided triple tail appearance. The ventral fins are also quite long. The spotted tilapia lays its eggs on vegetation or submerged logs and both parents guard the eggs and juveniles until they are around 2.5 centimetres.

Fishing Tilapia feed largely on plankton and vegetation, although they will take small baits such as maggots or corn, fished with coarse fishing rigs and tackle. While tilapia fight well, they should all be killed and if any tilapia or cichlids are recorded from waters where they have never been seen, it should be reported to the authorities. Tilapia are a pest and responsible recreational anglers should express their concern about the easy access to these species for aquarists or aquaculturists and the subsequent release or escape and impact on wild environments.

SMELT, AUSTRALIAN

Rigs and Tactics

Scoop net and bait trap

TILAPIA, SPOTTED

Rigs and Tactics

No tilapia should ever be returned alive to the water.

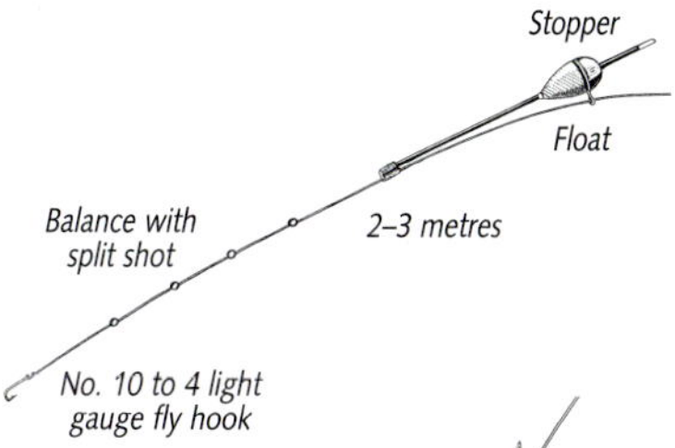

Stopper

Float

Balance with
split shot

2–3 metres

No. 10 to 4 light
gauge fly hook

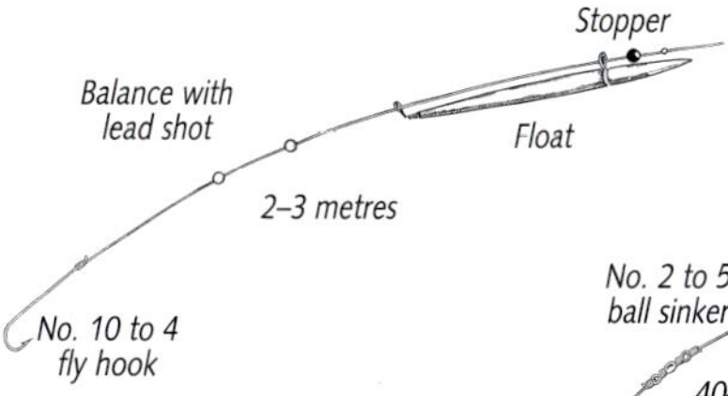

Stopper

Float

Balance with
lead shot

2–3 metres

No. 10 to 4
fly hook

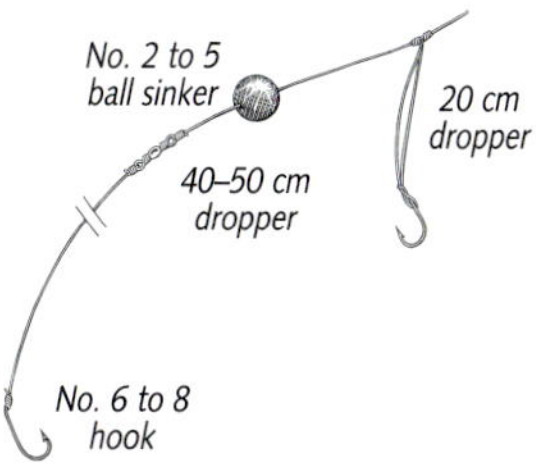

No. 2 to 5
ball sinker

40–50 cm
dropper

20 cm
dropper

No. 6 to 8
hook

No. 6 to 4
Baitholder hook

YABBY

Scientific name *Cherax destructor* Another similar species *Cherax albidus* is believed to be found in Western Australia and some other waters. Also known as Yabbie, freshwater yabbie, freshwater crayfish, crawbob, lobby.

Range Found in most suitable waters in Australia due to escapees from fishing bait, aquaculture facilities or deliberate introductions. The yabby is found in virtually all waters where the temperature does not exceed around 32 degrees Celsius. In northern waters the redclaw (*Cherax quadricarinatus*) becomes more common. The taxonomy of yabbies is regularly reviewed and new species may be described.

Description The yabby is a medium sized freshwater crayfish growing to around 25 cm total length. The scientific name destructor comes from the habit of the yabby of digging burrows near the banks of waters in which it is found. This can lead to danger for stock which may trip in the burrows or from bank slumping. Yabbies will also take cover in logs, rocks or artificial cover such as onion bags, cut branches, cans, besser blocks or PVC pipes. Yabbies can be easily identified by the smooth shell with only two small ridges behind the eyes which do not extend to the joint in the carapace. The claws are relatively large and are generally blue-green with a lattice of lighter colour especially on the outside of the claws. There is a distinctive red mark on the inside of the main pincer. The tail is reasonably large and provides high quality flesh. Out of clear water, yabbies can be a bright blue while out of muddy water they rend to be grey-blue, or grey but they can tend to brown.

Fishing Large yabbies prefer still waters and are more active at night in clear water. Yabbies can be caught with a variety of methods with the most pleasurable being with a piece of meat tied to a string. The meat is tossed into a muddy dam and when a yabby is felt, it is slowly pulled to the bank. The yabby is either scoop netted or grabbed by enthusiastic youngsters. Yabbies can be gathered by scoop netting yabbies in the shallows, by getting them out of logs, cans or other hides or more commonly with opera house style nets. These nets are currently illegal in Western Australia. Yabbies are magnificent eating, although some can have a slightly muddy taste which is improved if the vein is removed. Yabbies cooked in a kerosene tin on the edge of the dam is heaven to many inland farming families. Small yabbies make excellent bait for all freshwater fish, but live yabbies have the habit of crawling into timber or rocks where they are safe from predators. Peeled yabby tail works extremely well for most fish, including in salt water.

Rigs and Tactics

Rigs: Baited yabby pot

ELEPHANT FISH

Scientific name *Callorhynchus milii*. Also known as Elephant shark, ghost shark, whitefish, plownose chimera.

Range A cool water fish found from Esperance in Western Australia to Jervis Bay in NSW. It can be found in deeper water most of the year, with females entering shallow bays in summer to lay their eggs.

Description The elephant fish is a unique species easily recognised by the fleshy nose which is used to find food in sandy or lightly silted bottoms. The pectoral fins are large and used like a ray for navigation. The eggs are spindle shaped, about 20 cm long and take 8 months to hatch. Unlike most sharks, the elephant fish has a single gill slit. It has a prominent dorsal spine like a Port Jackson shark and can inflict a painful wound if not handled carefully.

Fishing Until recently, these fish were shunned due to their ugly appearance. However, the flesh is white and firm and good eating and they are being increasingly targeted in southern bays and inlets in summer. Light bottom rigs get maximum sport from these fish. However it is important to realise that the summer fishery targets spawning fish and the take of these fish should be limited to ensure that they are not over-exploited.

RAY, EAGLE

Scientific name *Aetobatus narinari*. Also known as Spotted eagle ray, duckbill ray, flying ray, white-spotted eagle ray.

Range Around all Australia.

Description The eagle ray has a shining brown-black top of the body with a large number of white spots on the back half of the body. The eagle ray has an unusual bulging head with a long and tapering snout which is flattened rather like a duck's bill. The teeth are shaped like a chevron and are used for crushing oysters, pipis and other molluscs. The tail is very long and thin and is around 4 times the width of the body. The eagle ray has 2 – 6 barbed spines at the base of the tail. The eagle ray is a very large species, reaching a width of around 3.5 m, but it is commonly seen at around 1.8 metres.

Fishing The eagle ray is commonly seen jumping or cruising in shallow water or near the surface in ocean waters. The flaps often break the water as the eagle ray moves along, giving the impression of two sharks travelling together. Like most stingrays, the eagle ray is not specifically targeted by recreational anglers. The eagle ray's ability to swerve and rapidly change direction makes the fight of the eagle ray more interesting than the usual dour, physical slog of most other rays. The eagle ray bites best on mollusc baits including pipi, cockle or mussel. They are also taken on squid and cuttlefish baits. Like all rays, the mouth is under the body and the bait should be right on the bottom. As the barbs are close to the body, and the spiracles are large for gripping the eagle ray, this is one of the less dangerous rays. The flesh is of good quality and is under-rated as a food fish.

ELEPHANT FISH

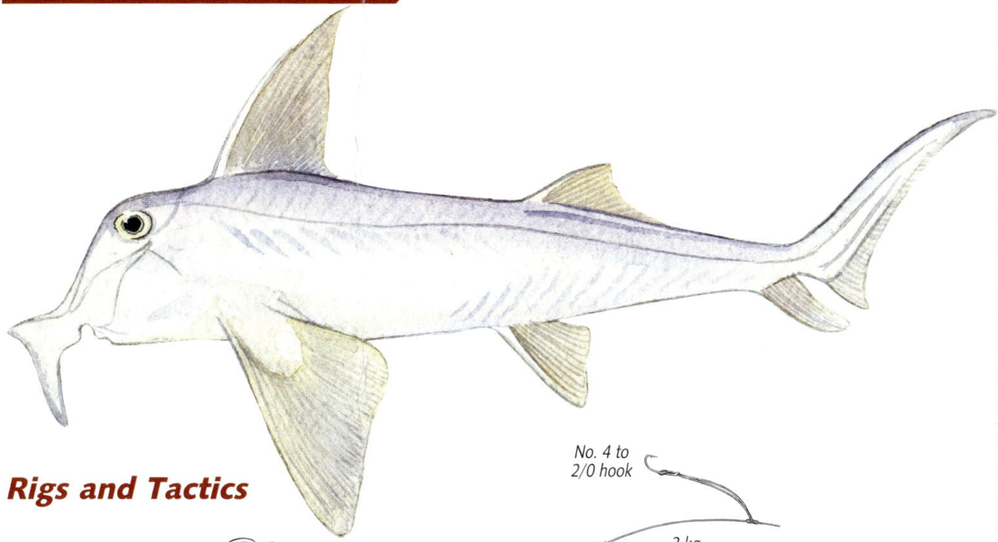

Rigs and Tactics

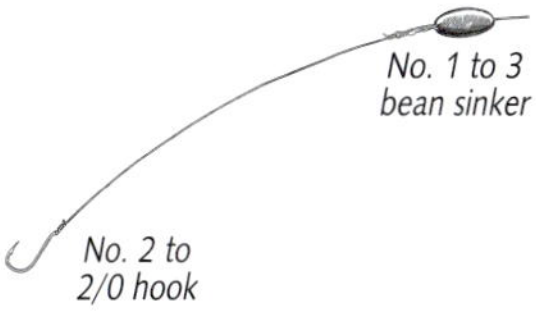

No. 1 to 3
bean sinker

No. 2 to
2/0 hook

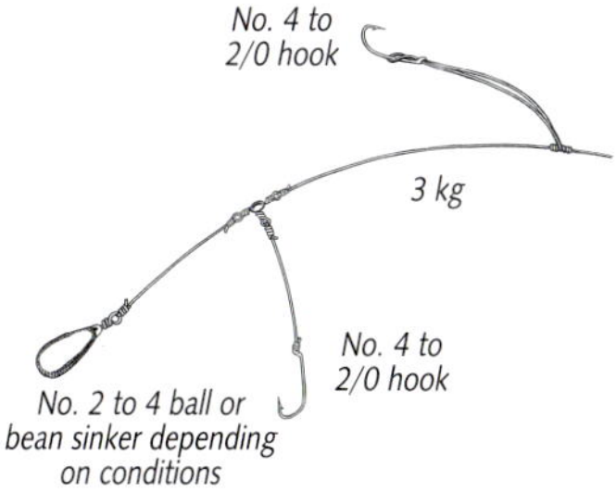

No. 4 to
2/0 hook

3 kg

No. 4 to
2/0 hook

No. 2 to 4 ball or
bean sinker depending
on conditions

RAY, EAGLE

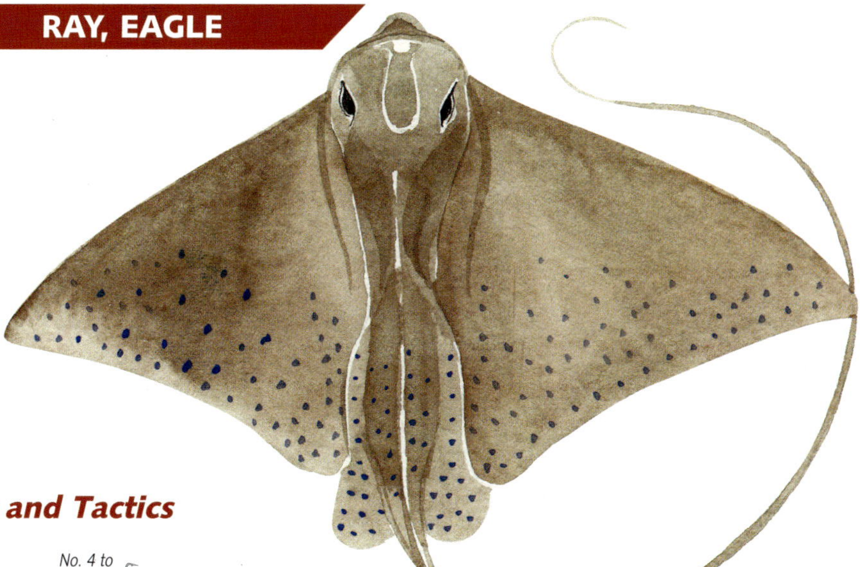

Rigs and Tactics

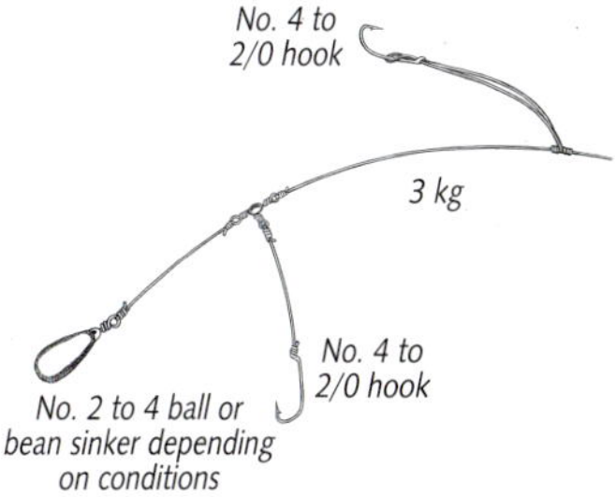

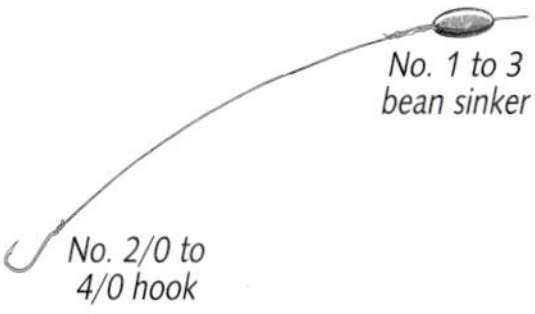

No. 4 to
2/0 hook

3 kg

No. 4 to
2/0 hook

No. 2 to 4 ball or
bean sinker depending
on conditions

No. 1 to 3
bean sinker

No. 2/0 to
4/0 hook

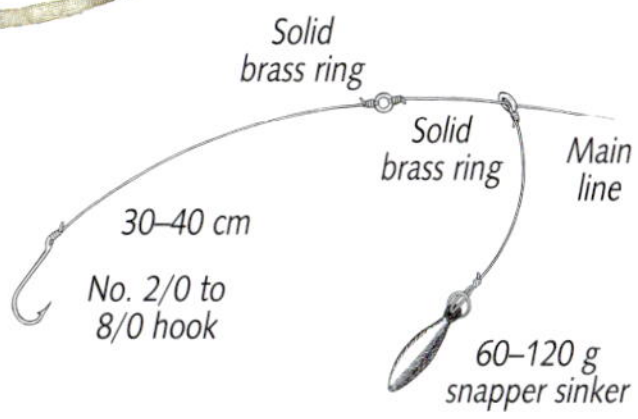

Solid
brass ring

Solid
brass ring

Main
line

30–40 cm

No. 2/0 to
8/0 hook

60–120 g
snapper sinker

RAY, FIDDLER

Scientific name *Trygonorhina fasciata* Also known as magpie ray, southern fiddler ray

Range Lancelin in Western Australia and southern waters, but only northern Tasmania and to around the Gold Coast in southern Queensland, although rarely found further north.

Description A beautifully marked species, the fiddler ray is actually rarely taken by line fishermen but is often seen in shallow sandy bays throughout its range and can be part of the by-catch of prawn trawlers. The fiddler ray has a brown body covered in a pattern of blue bars often edged in black. The fiddler ray grows to 1.2 m and has a round head region, small flaps and a long tail region. The head shape differs from the shovelnose rays which have a triangular head shape.

Fishing While rarely taken by recreational fishers, the fiddler ray makes quite good eating. It is taken when fishing for species such as bream, whiting or flathead in shallow bays on baits such as prawn, pipi, beach worm and occasionally squid or fish baits.

RAY, LONGTAIL

Scientific name *Himantura uarnak*. Also known as Coachwhip ray, longtail stingray, mangrove ray.

Range Dampier Archipelago in north-west Western Australia and tropical waters into northern New South Wales.

Description The longtail ray is one of the larger rays measuring up to 2 m across the disc and with a whip-like tail that is two to three times the width of the body. One or two spines are set fairly close to the body but can be dangerous if not handled carefully. Two separate colour varieties are recognised, one with small black spots and one with a meshwork pattern of rosettes across the back. There are brown blotches near the margins of the otherwise white underside. The longtail ray is found near sandy beaches, sandy flats near reefs and shallow mangrove estuaries where they can be found in large numbers. The habit of remaining partly buried on tidal flats can lead to them being accidentally stepped on. It is for this reason that a shuffling walk is recommended when walking in tidal mangrove creeks and associated flats.

Fishing The longtail ray is not a targeted species and needs to be carefully handled to avoid being hit by the spines. This species is often encountered when fishing for bream and flathead in northern waters and as it can reach more than 50 kg, often results in the loss of rigs and other gear when using light outfits. The longtail ray is not highly regarded as a food fish, but like all stingrays, the flaps make good eating if handled well. If someone were to be pierced with a stingray spine, first aid is important as the wound can easily become septic and the venom in many cases can increase the pain. To denature (cook) the protein in the venom, immerse the affected area in hot water but not so hot that it scalds. Medical assistance should always be sought as a sting ray wound can easily become badly infected and should be treated as very serious.

RAY, MANTA

Scientific name *Manta birostris*. Also known as Devil ray, devil fish, Flying devil fish, Ox ray, Diamond fish, Eregoodoo, Munguna

Range Rottnest Island in Western Australia and tropical waters to Newcastle in NSW but more common in warmer waters.

Description The magnificent manta ray is easily distinguished by its large size and the presence of a pair of large horn-like flippers on the head which the manta ray uses to push plankton into its cavernous mouth. The manta ray is black or dark grey on the top and white or off white on the underside. The tail is short. The manta ray can be 6 metres across the wings and weigh more than 2 tonnes. It is found in inshore waters. Manta rays can often be seen leaping and seeming to glide over the surface. Scientists are unsure whether this behaviour is related to removing parasites or some other purpose. Groups of smaller manta rays can sometimes be found together.

Fishing The manta ray is a plankton feeder and therefore cannot be caught on a line. In spite of this manta rays are extremely important to recreational fishers for two important reasons. Firstly, sighting a manta ray makes a fishing trip truly memorable. A large manta ray broaching is a truly remarkable sight and one that lasts a very long time. Secondly, manta rays are frequently accompanied by 'escorts' in the form of large cobia, queenfish or trevally. Remoras are usually present. A popper, diving or slice type lure cast near a cruising manta ray will often tempt extremely large sportsfish that can be otherwise difficult to locate. Take special care not to cast too close to the manta as they will bolt with remarkable speed and foul hooking a manta ray is irresponsible.

RAY, FIDDLER

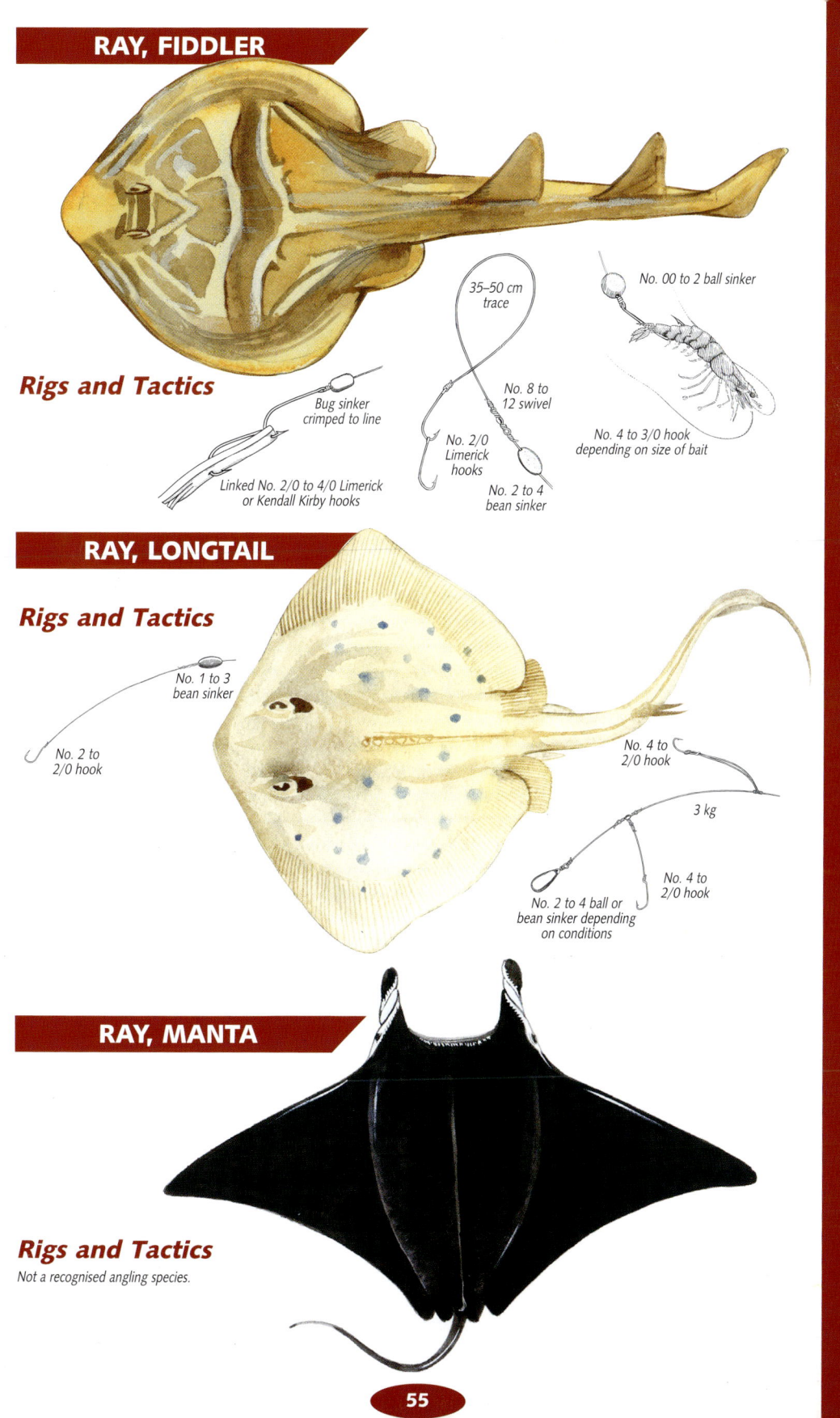

Rigs and Tactics

Bug sinker
crimped to line

Linked No. 2/0 to 4/0 Limerick
or Kendall Kirby hooks

35–50 cm
trace

No. 8 to
12 swivel

No. 2/0
Limerick
hooks

No. 2 to 4
bean sinker

No. 00 to 2 ball sinker

No. 4 to 3/0 hook
depending on size of bait

RAY, LONGTAIL

Rigs and Tactics

No. 1 to 3
bean sinker

No. 2 to
2/0 hook

No. 4 to
2/0 hook

3 kg

No. 2 to 4 ball or
bean sinker depending
on conditions

No. 4 to
2/0 hook

RAY, MANTA

Rigs and Tactics

Not a recognised angling species.

RAY, SHOVELNOSE

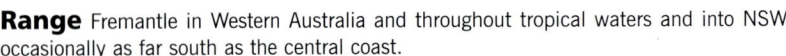

Scientific name *Rhynchobatus djiddensis.* Also known as White-spotted shovelnose ray, fiddler, shovelnose shark, white-spotted guitarfish.

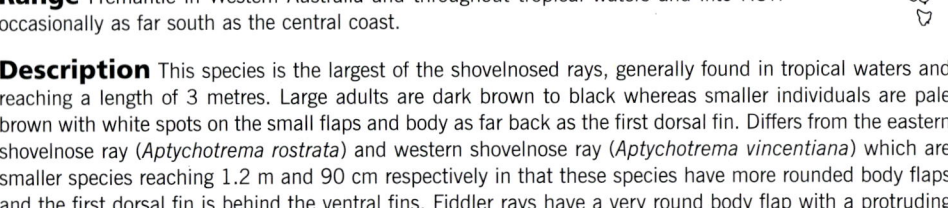

Range Fremantle in Western Australia and throughout tropical waters and into NSW occasionally as far south as the central coast.

Description This species is the largest of the shovelnosed rays, generally found in tropical waters and reaching a length of 3 metres. Large adults are dark brown to black whereas smaller individuals are pale brown with white spots on the small flaps and body as far back as the first dorsal fin. Differs from the eastern shovelnose ray (*Aptychotrema rostrata*) and western shovelnose ray (*Aptychotrema vincentiana*) which are smaller species reaching 1.2 m and 90 cm respectively in that these species have more rounded body flaps and the first dorsal fin is behind the ventral fins. Fiddler rays have a very round body flap with a protruding shark-like tail. None of these species have spines, or sharp teeth, and are not dangerous.

Fishing Many anglers will remember encounters with shovelnose rays, as this species is often encountered when fishing beaches and near shallow reefs for other species. Mulloway anglers in particular often catch shovelnose rays and the first dogged run of the ray feels much like the first strong run of a decent mulloway. Great disappointment is experienced as the realisation gradually dawns, often because of the duration of the fight, that it is not a large mulloway on the line. Shovelnose rays feed primarily on molluscs and many are taken on pipi baits. They are opportunistic and will eat most baits including pilchards, whole fish, prawns and many others. Like sting rays, shovelnose rays' mouth is under the head, so lifting the bait off the bottom will significantly reduce the number of rays which are encountered.
Although not highly regarded as food, shovelnose rays are good eating.

SAWFISH, GREEN

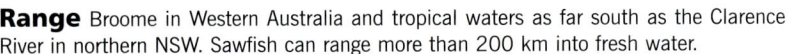

Scientific name *Pristis zijsron.* Also known as Sawfish.

Range Broome in Western Australia and tropical waters as far south as the Clarence River in northern NSW. Sawfish can range more than 200 km into fresh water.

Description The green sawfish is capable of reaching more than 7 m in total with a characteristic saw protruding from the upper jaw. This species has teeth along the entire length of the saw. A cartilaginous relative of the sharks and rays, the young are born live with a gelatinous covering over the already developed saw to protect the mother during birth.

Fishing The green sawfish prefers muddy bottoms and can cause excitement if a boat passes over it in shallow water. Sawfish are a scourge to net fishermen and can cause great damage to nets, boats or unwary fishermen. Sawfish are rarely taken by recreational fishers, generally on cut flesh baits. All saw sharks are now totally protected in Western Australia.

SHARK, BLACK-TIPPED REEF

Scientific name *Carcharhinus melanopterus* Also known as blacktip, reef shark

Range Shark Bay in Western Australian and throughout tropical waters as far south as the southern end of the Great Barrier Reef in Queensland.

Description A small but easily identified whaler species reaching around 1.8 metres. The black-tipped reef shark has an obvious black tip to all of its fins, including both lobes of the tail. This is the only species with a black tip to the dorsal fin. The black-tipped reef shark is found on reef country and is an active hunter. They will move up onto very shallow on a rising tide searching for food with their dorsal fins and even their backs scything through the water. They often travel in groups and can be quite disconcerting for swimmers or divers. They are considered to be one of the least dangerous of the whaler species, but caution should always be exercised, especially in groups of fish or where blood is in the water.

Fishing The black-tipped reef shark is not targeted and is taken as an incidental capture. Like all whaler sharks, they have teeth capable of cutting through anything other than strong wire trace. This species is often blamed for fish stealing, but their small size and less aggressive nature means that it is often a case of mistaken identity. The black-tipped reef shark prefers cut baits but can be taken on live baits, squid, pilchards or other whole fish. Like the other whalers, the black-tipped reef shark makes quite good eating but is often overlooked for the more highly regarded reef species from the same areas.

RAY, SHOVELNOSE

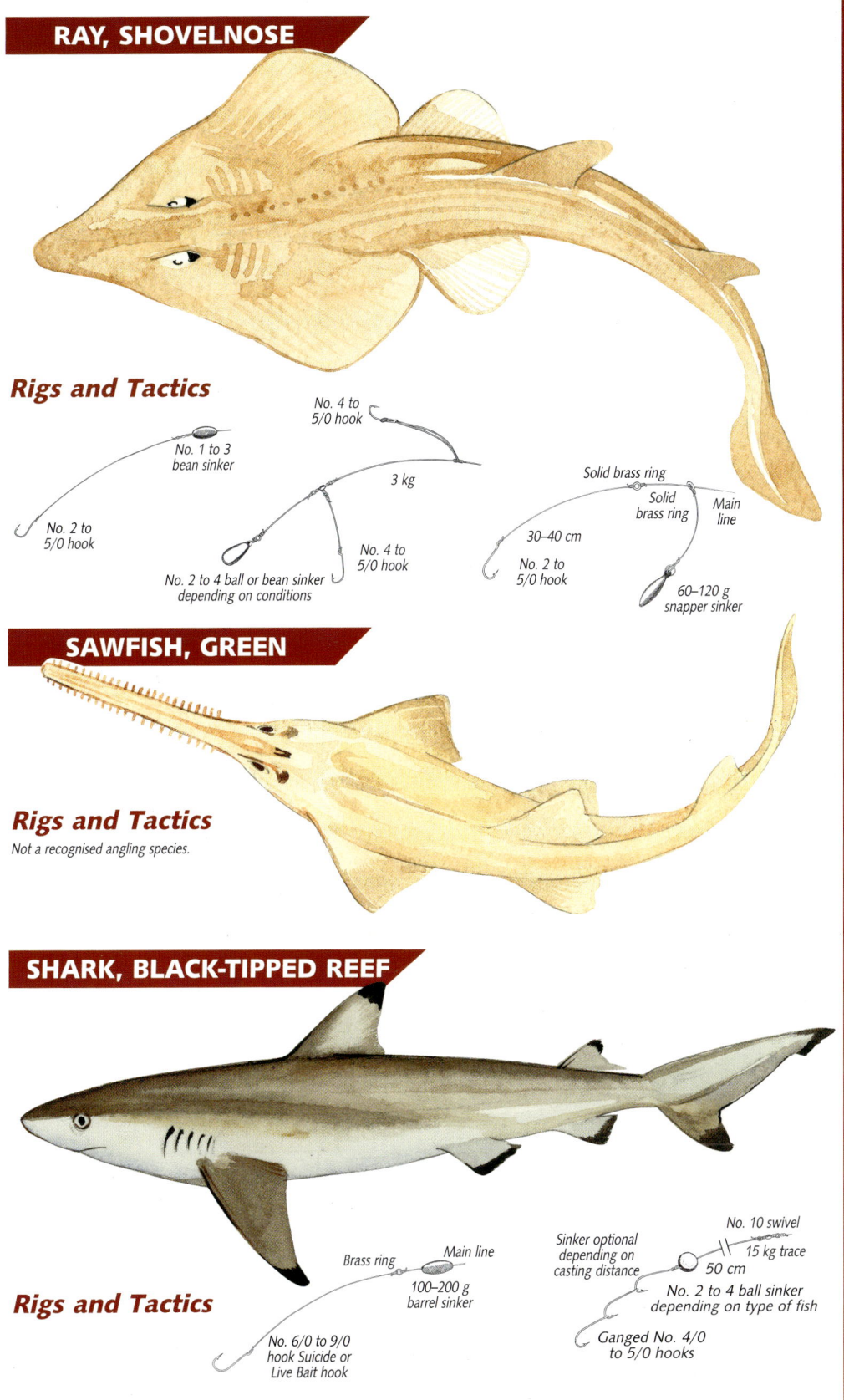

Rigs and Tactics

No. 4 to 5/0 hook

No. 1 to 3 bean sinker

No. 2 to 5/0 hook

3 kg

No. 4 to 5/0 hook

No. 2 to 4 ball or bean sinker depending on conditions

Solid brass ring

Solid brass ring

Main line

30–40 cm

No. 2 to 5/0 hook

60–120 g snapper sinker

SAWFISH, GREEN

Rigs and Tactics

Not a recognised angling species.

SHARK, BLACK-TIPPED REEF

Rigs and Tactics

Brass ring

Main line

100–200 g barrel sinker

No. 6/0 to 9/0 hook Suicide or Live Bait hook

Sinker optional depending on casting distance

No. 10 swivel

15 kg trace

50 cm

No. 2 to 4 ball sinker depending on type of fish

Ganged No. 4/0 to 5/0 hooks

SHARK, BLACK WHALER

Scientific name *Carcharinus obscurus*. Also known as Whaler, common whaler, river shark, river whaler, dusky shark.

Range Albany in Western Australia and around the top end to at least Sydney. Sketchy reports from the Northern Territory and a single report from South Australia means the distribution could be wider.

Description A very dangerous species which is often found in areas frequented by people. The black whaler is common in inshore waters and may move up coastal rivers to pure freshwater. The black whaler is responsible for a large number of attacks, some of which have been fatal. Small specimens to 2 m and probably lost, have been known to bite swimmers in places like the Gold Coast canals. The black whaler can reach more than 5.5 m but is most common at up to 3 m where they frequently steal fish from anglers lines. The upper teeth of black whaler are distinctly triangular and broad with moderate serrations. A ridge of skin runs along the back between the two dorsal fins.

Fishing The black whaler is not a very discerning feeder, although they do enjoy stealing quality table fish from angler's lines. They can also follow schools of mullet well into fresh water, herding them into shallows or below the falls at places like the Clarence River where several sharks can work together to gorge themselves. Any live or dead fish will take these sharks. In estuaries, they can be taken on crab or prawn baits, providing a momentary buzz before biting through the line. Moderate lines and a wire trace are necessary. While these sharks can be a pest, killing them just to get them out of the water is unnecessary as they play an important role in the aquatic ecosystem. Black whalers are good eating, but like all sharks they should be refrigerated as soon as possible as they can develop an ammonia taste if not well treated.

SHARK, BLUE

Scientific name *Prionace glauca*. Also known as Blue whaler, great blue shark.

Range Circum-Australia but rarely seen in tropical waters or close to land.

Description The blue shark is a striking blue colour which inhabits oceanic waters. Similar in appearance to the mako but the blue shark has much larger pectoral fins which are floppy and scythe-like, smaller gill slits and the teeth are triangular and serrated. When at the surface, both the dorsal fin and top lobe of the tail of the blue shark breaks the surface, but the blue shark can also be caught at great depth. The blue shark can grow to 3.8 m and nearly 200 kilograms.

Fishing Being an oceanic species, the blue shark is most commonly encountered by game fishermen. The blue shark is also commonly caught on long lines by commercial fishermen. The blue shark can be taken on live baits, whole fish, cut baits or squid and at a wide variety of depths. The blue shark can be annoying for those specialist anglers who fish for the ultimate prize, broadbill swordfish, taking deeply fished cyalume lit baits. The blue shark will not jump and though regarded as dangerous, is not often encountered by divers and swimmers.

SHARK, BRONZE WHALER

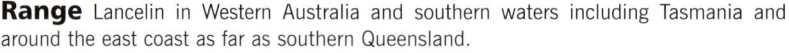

Scientific name *Carcharhinus brachyurus*. Also known as Copper shark, cocktail shark.

Range Lancelin in Western Australia and southern waters including Tasmania and around the east coast as far as southern Queensland.

Description A fairly common shark of offshore waters, but which occasionally enters large embayments. The bronze whaler is dangerous and has been responsible for several fatalities in Australia. The bronze whaler is very similar to the black or whaler shark but the bronze whaler generally has a bronze or coppery colour, which fades to grey after death. The upper teeth are narrow and slightly concave on this species. The bronze whaler lacks the distinctive skin ridge running between the two dorsal fins which is present on the black whaler. The bronze whaler reaches 3.25 m and more than 200 kilograms.

Fishing The bronze whaler can be taken with a variety of live or dead fish baits, large cut baits and squid. Bronze whalers are attracted by berley and can be found around boats, usually showing up as catch rates improve. The fight of the bronze whaler is strong and dogged, in common with many sharks. A wire or steel trace is essential. The bronze whaler makes good eating and smaller specimens are often used by fish and chip shops.

SHARK, BLACK WHALER

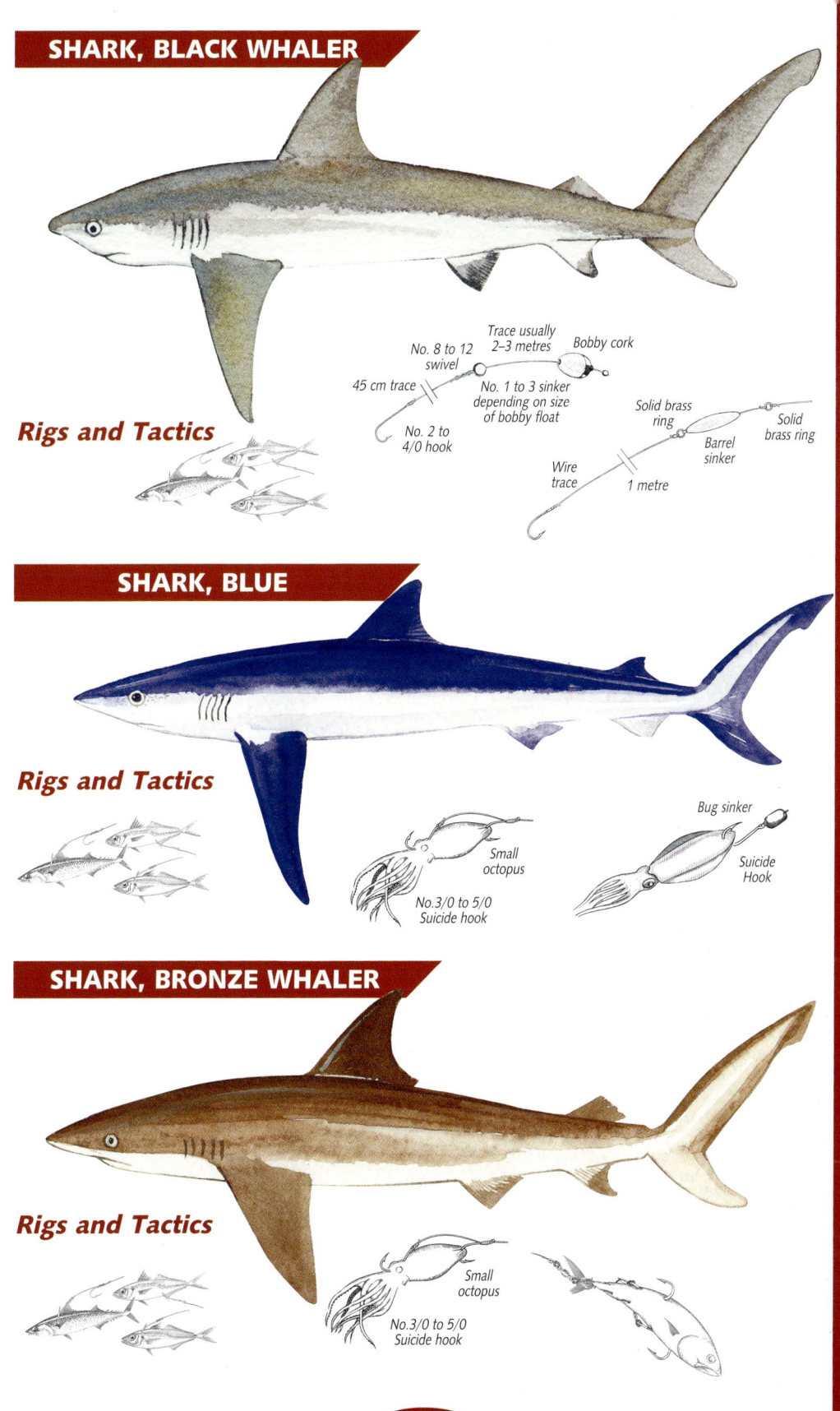

Rigs and Tactics

No. 8 to 12 swivel

Trace usually 2–3 metres

Bobby cork

45 cm trace

No. 1 to 3 sinker depending on size of bobby float

No. 2 to 4/0 hook

Solid brass ring

Barrel sinker

Solid brass ring

Wire trace

1 metre

SHARK, BLUE

Rigs and Tactics

Small octopus

No.3/0 to 5/0 Suicide hook

Bug sinker

Suicide Hook

SHARK, BRONZE WHALER

Rigs and Tactics

Small octopus

No.3/0 to 5/0 Suicide hook

SHARK, BULL

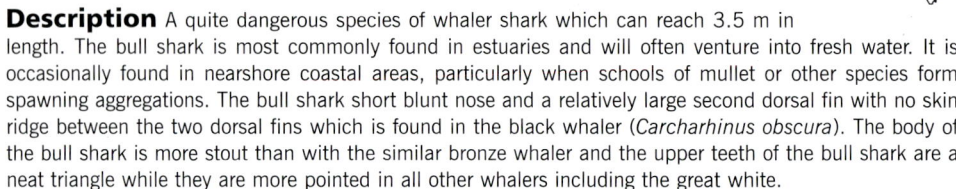

Scientific name *Carcharhinus leucas* Also known as river whaler, estuary whaler, Swan River whaler.

Range Perth Western Australia and northern waters to as far south as Sydney in NSW.

Description A quite dangerous species of whaler shark which can reach 3.5 m in length. The bull shark is most commonly found in estuaries and will often venture into fresh water. It is occasionally found in nearshore coastal areas, particularly when schools of mullet or other species form spawning aggregations. The bull shark short blunt nose and a relatively large second dorsal fin with no skin ridge between the two dorsal fins which is found in the black whaler (*Carcharhinus obscura*). The body of the bull shark is more stout than with the similar bronze whaler and the upper teeth of the bull shark are a neat triangle while they are more pointed in all other whalers including the great white.

Fishing The bull shark is considered by some authors to be the third most dangerous species of shark after the great white and the tiger shark. It feeds in murky estuarine waters and probably hones in on the splashes of swimmers to a greater extent. Although large bull sharks can be responsible for fatal attacks such as the 1923 attack in the Swan River in Perth, smaller sharks can inflict a fair bit of damage without necessarily killing the victim. Bull sharks are taken with standard shark methods, large hook, long wire trace and a bait of live fish, cut bait or bait such as ox heart. They will bite off rigs intended for mulloway and when hooked put up a dogged fight. The bull shark is not highly regarded as a food fish.

SHARK, GREY NURSE

Scientific name *Carcharias taurus.* Also known as Grey nurse.

Range Shark Bay in Western Australia and southern waters but rarely in Tasmania, and around the east coast as far as Mooloolaba in Queensland.

Description Easily recognised by the two similar sized dorsal fins and the rows of long fang-like teeth which have two small cusps near the base. This species is familiar to many as it is often kept in larger aquariums where its impressive teeth and relatively placid nature make it an ideal attraction for viewers and divers. The grey nurse shark can exceed 3.5 m, but they look considerably larger in aquariums.

Fishing Grey nurse sharks feed on schools of fish and may be taken with standard shark fishing baits and rigs. Their territorial nature, ability to be found close to shore in some places and their tendency to hang virtually motionless has made them susceptible to fishermen but especially spearfishermen. In spite of their fearsome appearance, the grey nurse shark has only been confirmed in one unprovoked attack, making them one of the most 'companionable' species. The Commonwealth has recently protected grey nurse sharks, while they have been protected in NSW for many years. Controversial grey nurse sanctuaries have been imposed on the east coast following intense and emotive lobbying by green groups.

SHARK, GUMMY

Scientific name *Mustelus antarcticus.* Also known as Sweet William.

Range Shark Bay in Western Australia and southern waters, including Tasmania to southern Queensland.

Description The gummy shark is a small, harmless shark reaching only 1.75 metres. The teeth in both jaws are smooth and flattened and arranged in a flat pavement-like pattern. The gummy shark looks similar to the school shark, but the school shark's teeth are sharp and triangular and the tail fin has a broad and deeply notched upper lobe, giving a double tail appearance. The upper body of the gummy shark is covered with small white spots which are less apparent in larger fish.

Fishing The gummy shark is frequently taken by anglers on deeper water snapper grounds with standard snapper baits and rigs. The gummy shark is more common on deeper water grounds and is a commercial fishing target which has been seriously overfished in many southern waters. The gummy shark can move into shallow water on occasion. The best baits for gummy shark are squid, cuttlefish, octopus, pilchard and any fresh fish baits. They are most often taken on the bottom hook of a snapper paternoster rig. The gummy shark makes excellent eating and is highly regarded.

SHARK, BULL SHARK

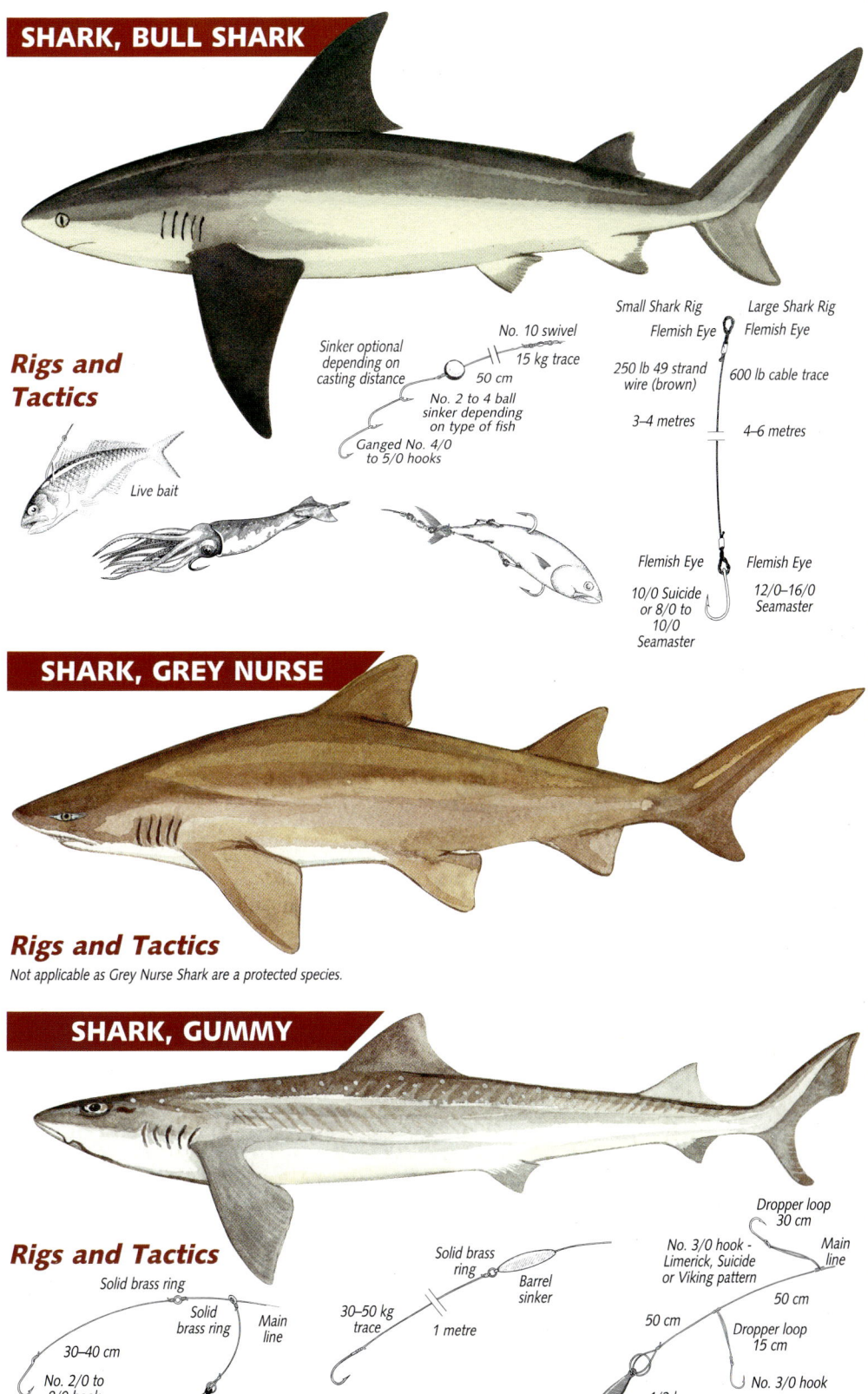

Rigs and Tactics

Live bait

Sinker optional
depending on
casting distance

No. 10 swivel
15 kg trace
50 cm

No. 2 to 4 ball
sinker depending
on type of fish

Ganged No. 4/0
to 5/0 hooks

Small Shark Rig
Flemish Eye

250 lb 49 strand
wire (brown)

3–4 metres

Flemish Eye

10/0 Suicide
or 8/0 to
10/0
Seamaster

Large Shark Rig
Flemish Eye

600 lb cable trace

4–6 metres

Flemish Eye

12/0–16/0
Seamaster

SHARK, GREY NURSE

Rigs and Tactics

Not applicable as Grey Nurse Shark are a protected species.

SHARK, GUMMY

Rigs and Tactics

Solid brass ring

Solid
brass ring

Main
line

30–40 cm

No. 2/0 to
8/0 hook

60–120 g
snapper sinker

Solid brass
ring

Barrel
sinker

30–50 kg
trace

1 metre

Dropper loop
30 cm

No. 3/0 hook -
Limerick, Suicide
or Viking pattern

Main
line

50 cm

50 cm

Dropper loop
15 cm

No. 3/0 hook

1/2 kg
snapper sinker

SHARK, HAMMERHEAD

Scientific name *Sphyrna lewini*. Also known as Scalloped hammerhead shark.

Range Circum-Australia but more common in northern waters, while a close relative, the smooth-headed hammerhead (*Sphyrna zygaena*) is more common in southern waters.

Description There is absolutely no mistaking the hammerhead shark, whose distinctive, broad head is unique. The scalloped hammerhead shark can reach 6 m but is more common at around 3 metres. This species has a distinctive groove at the front edge of the hammer, which extends to the nostrils, which are near the eyes. They are common offshore, but can enter bays and inlets. The smooth headed hammerhead lacks the distinctive groove or notch and reaches around 4 m in the colder water it prefers.

Fishing Small specimens can be found cruising on the surface, while larger hammerhead often find boats catching other fish, or take large baits set for sharks or other gamefish. The hammerhead shark can fight strongly and at larger sizes can be a formidible foe. The hammerhead has been involved in few attacks in Australia but should be treated with caution. It is considered reasonable eating.

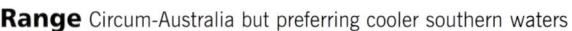

SHARK, MAKO

Scientific name *Isurus oxyrinchus*. Also known as Shortfin mako, blue pointer, mackerel shark, jumping shark.

Range Circum-Australia but preferring cooler southern waters

Description The mako shark is a sleek, beautifully streamlined close relative of the great white. The mako differs from the great white in being more streamlined and having distinctly pointed and hooked upper teeth as opposed to the distinctly triangular teeth in the great white. The mako is distinctly blue in colour though this fades to grey-blue after death. The pectoral fin is shorter than in the blue shark. The mako prefers deep offshore waters, but can move into more coastal waters where its sleek form and hooked teeth make short work of any hooked fish. If the hooked fish is skull dragged past the mako, it can provoke an attack on the boat, leaving teeth in the hull and very shaken fishermen.

Fishing The mako shark is the most prized shark species for game fishermen. The strong fight and leaps of up to 6 m add to the excitement of taking these fish. Very good quality tackle is required and live or fresh dead fish baits will increase chances of a hook up. The mako responds well to berley, especially near deep water current lines or schools of mackerel. The mako is extremely dangerous for small boat fishermen as they can attack boats, jump into boats while still 'green', causing incredible damage, or even while seemingly dead they can muster energy to trash a small cockpit with slashing teeth and tail. The mako is reasonable eating in small to medium sizes but should be bled and put on ice to prevent a build-up of ammonia in the flesh.

SHARK, HAMMERHEAD

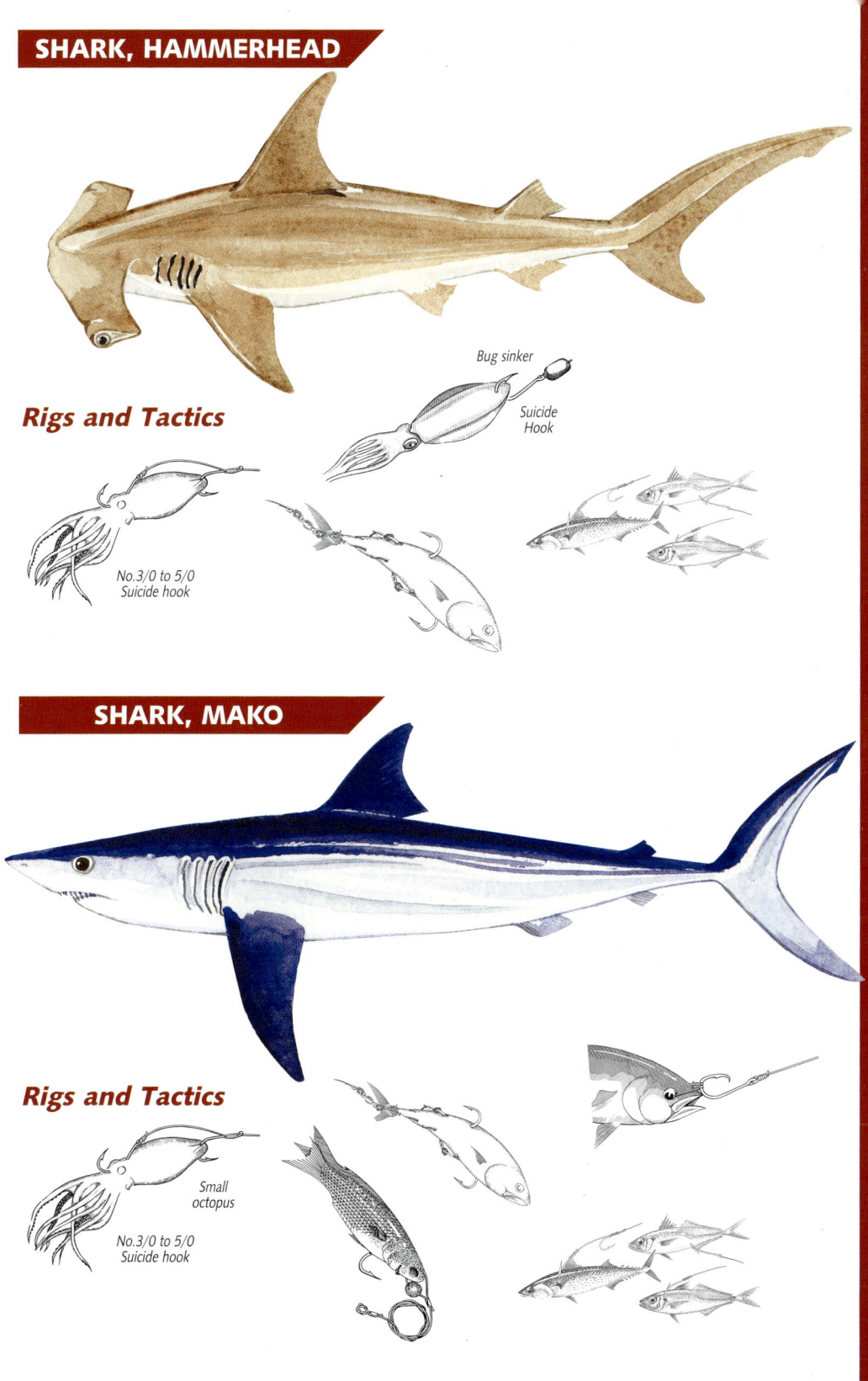

Rigs and Tactics

Bug sinker

Suicide Hook

No.3/0 to 5/0
Suicide hook

SHARK, MAKO

Rigs and Tactics

Small octopus

No.3/0 to 5/0
Suicide hook

SHARK, PORT JACKSON

Scientific name *Heterodontus portusjacksoni.* Also known as Bull shark, horn shark.

Range Abrolhos Islands in Western Australia and southern waters including Tasmania and around to Moreton Bay in Queensland.

Description The Port Jackson shark is a harmless species of inshore reefs and adjacent sand and weed patches which may group together in large numbers. The Port Jackson shark is an extremely primitive species readily identifiable by the bony ridge above the eye and a strong dorsal spine in front of both dorsal fins. The teeth are small and pointed in the front of the jaws with crushing teeth to the rear. The Port Jackson shark lays the distinctive 'Mermaid's purse' egg case which is attached to kelp and is frequently washed up on beaches after storms. The Port Jackson shark can reach 2 m but is more common at around a metre.

Fishing The Port Jackson shark is rarely welcome, especially when they are present in large groups. They give a sluggish fight and are not eaten by many people. They prefer baits of squid, crabs, prawns octopus but will take pilchards and cut baits as well. Contrary to popular belief, the Port Jackson shark, though a living fossil, is not protected as they are quite common. However, they should not be killed and thrown away as they are an important part of the aquatic environment.

SHARK, SCHOOL

Scientific name *Galeorhinus galeus.* Also known as Snapper shark, eastern school shark, greyboy, grey shark, soupfin shark, tope.

Range Rottnest Island in Western Australia and southern waters including Tasmania and around the east coast as far as southern Queensland.

Description The school shark is a very slow growing, small and harmless species which is common in cool southern waters. It is more common in offshore areas, where it forms the basis of a substantial, but overfished commercial fishery. Juveniles may occasionally be found in coastal bays. This species is readily identified by the tail fin shape, which has the upper lobe broad and deeply notched, giving the appearance of a double tail. The dorsal fin is set well forward and is closer to the commencement of the pectoral than the ventral fins. Both jaws carry sharp, triangular teeth of similar size which immediately separates the school shark from the gummy shark with its smooth and flattened teeth. The school shark can reach 2 m and 60 kg but is commonly much smaller. School sharks can live more than 40 years and a tagged fish had grown only 18 cm in over 35 years at liberty.

Fishing The school shark is frequently taken with gummy sharks and other cool water reef species on the deeper reefs of southern waters. Standard snapper rigs and baits of fish flesh, squid and cuttlefish will take the majority of school sharks. A trace is recommended as the school shark can easily bite through monofilament lines. Smaller specimens can be taken on similar shallower reefs in larger bays and estuaries. The school shark is excellent eating but should be kept cool as, like all sharks, a build up of ammonia can accumulate in the flesh if the fish is not well handled.

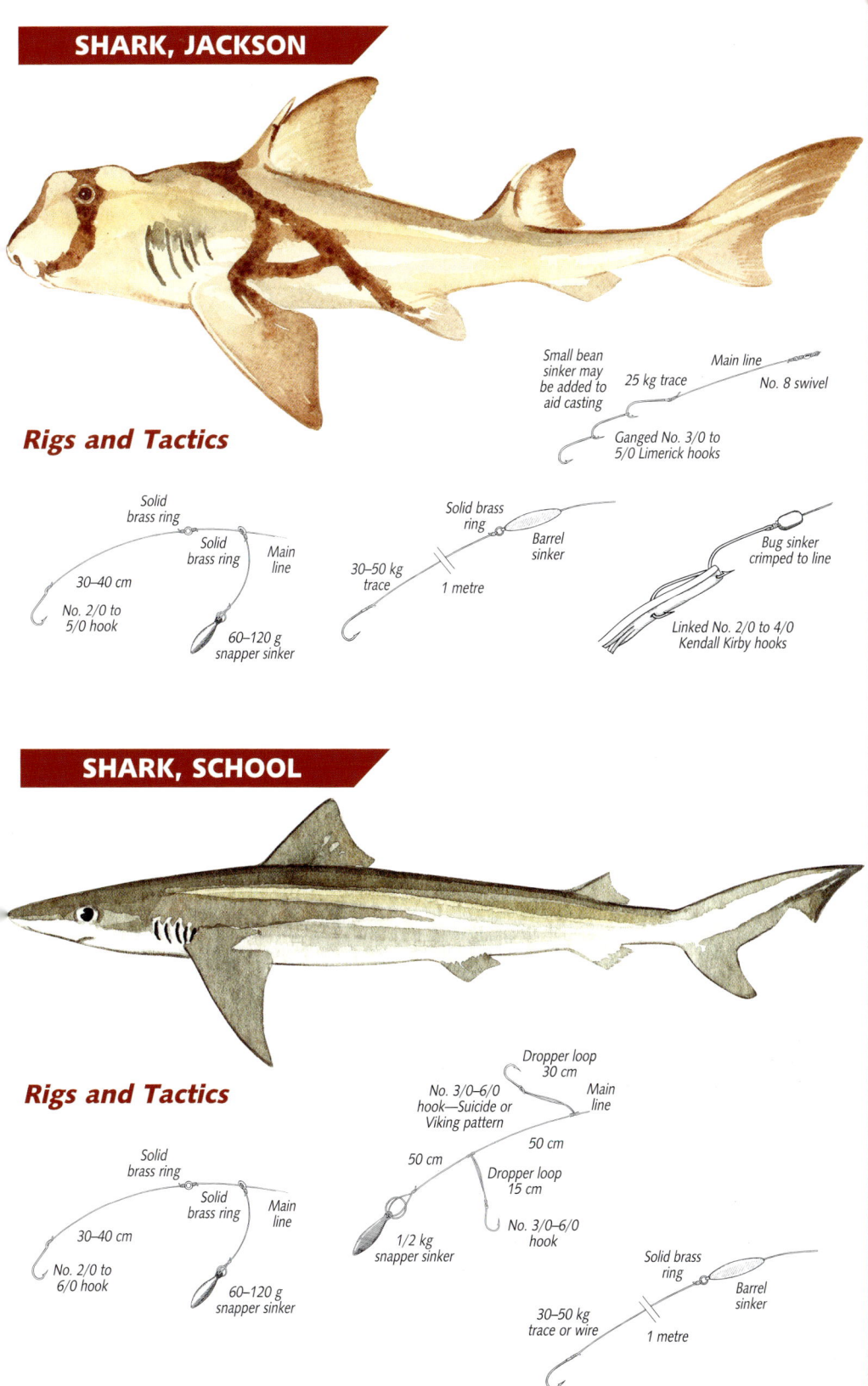

SHARK, JACKSON

Rigs and Tactics

Small bean sinker may be added to aid casting

25 kg trace

Main line

No. 8 swivel

Ganged No. 3/0 to 5/0 Limerick hooks

Solid brass ring

Solid brass ring

Main line

30–40 cm

No. 2/0 to 5/0 hook

60–120 g snapper sinker

Solid brass ring

Barrel sinker

30–50 kg trace

1 metre

Bug sinker crimped to line

Linked No. 2/0 to 4/0 Kendall Kirby hooks

SHARK, SCHOOL

Rigs and Tactics

Solid brass ring

Solid brass ring

Main line

30–40 cm

No. 2/0 to 6/0 hook

60–120 g snapper sinker

Dropper loop 30 cm

Main line

No. 3/0–6/0 hook—Suicide or Viking pattern

50 cm

50 cm

Dropper loop 15 cm

1/2 kg snapper sinker

No. 3/0–6/0 hook

Solid brass ring

Barrel sinker

30–50 kg trace or wire

1 metre

SHARK, SEVEN GILLED

Scientific name *Notorynchus cepedianus*. Also known as Cow shark, ground shark, Tasmanian tiger shark, broad-snouted shark, broadnose seven gill shark.

Range West of Esperance and southern waters including Tasmania around to Sydney in NSW.

Description The seven gilled shark is a primitive species easily identified by its single dorsal fin, set well back and the seven gill slits. The head is also broad and the mouth has an unusual upper lip. The colour is grey with scattered darker grey and white spots. The seven gill shark reaches 4.5 m and is frequently seen at 3 metres. Although the seven gill shark has never been confirmed in an attack on humans, it is considered dangerous to swimmers and divers due to its size and the fact that it can turn up in bays and estuaries.

Fishing The seven gill shark is rarely targeted by fishermen. It can be taken on standard shark baits and rigs in nearshore coastal waters. It makes reasonable eating.

SHARK, SPOTTED WOBBEGONG

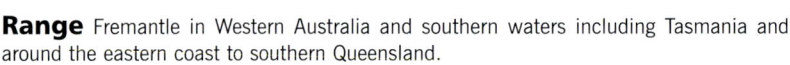

Scientific name *Orectolobus maculatus*. Also known as Common catshark, tassel shark.

Range Fremantle in Western Australia and southern waters including Tasmania and around the eastern coast to southern Queensland.

Description The spotted wobbegong shark inhabits coastal and estuarine reefs of cooler waters, being most common in NSW. Wobbegongs are easily identified by the numerous fleshy tentacle-like appendages around the front of the rounded head. This species is identified by two wart-like protrusions above each eye and the large pale-edged spots which resemble eyes on the dorsal surface. The spotted wobbegong can reach 3.2 m and is harmless except when disturbed by divers. There have been some instances where large wobbegongs have felt trapped in small caves by divers and attacked. There was an attack at Shellharbour in NSW, where a silver face mask attracted a bite requiring numerous stitches.

Fishing The wobbegong is frequently taken by spearfishermen as it lies virtually motionless during the day, either in caves or lairs near inshore reefs. Wobbegongs are taken by anglers fishing from shore or boats on inshore reefs. As they are sometimes taken by anglers more used to Port Jackson sharks, they can bite unwary anglers as they unhook this species. Wobbegongs will take squid, fish or cut baits, using either standard rock fishing or shallow reef rigs such as two hook paternoster rigs or running sinker rigs. Wobbegongs give a strong fight and make good eating.

SHARK, THRESHER

Scientific name *Alopias vulpinus*. Also known as Fox shark.

Range Circum-Australia

Description The thresher shark is easily identified by the extremely long tail fin which is thrashed around to stun victims in schools of fish. The head is sharp pointed and the eye a striking black colour. The thresher shark prefers oceanic waters but can occasionally be found in deeper water bays. It can reach more than 6 m and more than 225 kilograms.

Fishing The thresher shark is considered a worthy gamefishing opponent and if mouth hooked can exhibit high jumps and fast jinking runs. The thresher shark can be hooked in the tail, especially with lures and live baits, as the thresher shark uses its tail to knock prey around. The thresher shark will take standard shark baits and rigs, however a longer trace is recommended as the tail can abrade the line during a prolonged battle. The thresher shark is considered dangerous, as although it has not attacked humans, it has attacked several boats in a similar manner to mako sharks. The thresher shark makes reasonable eating, especially in small and medium sizes.

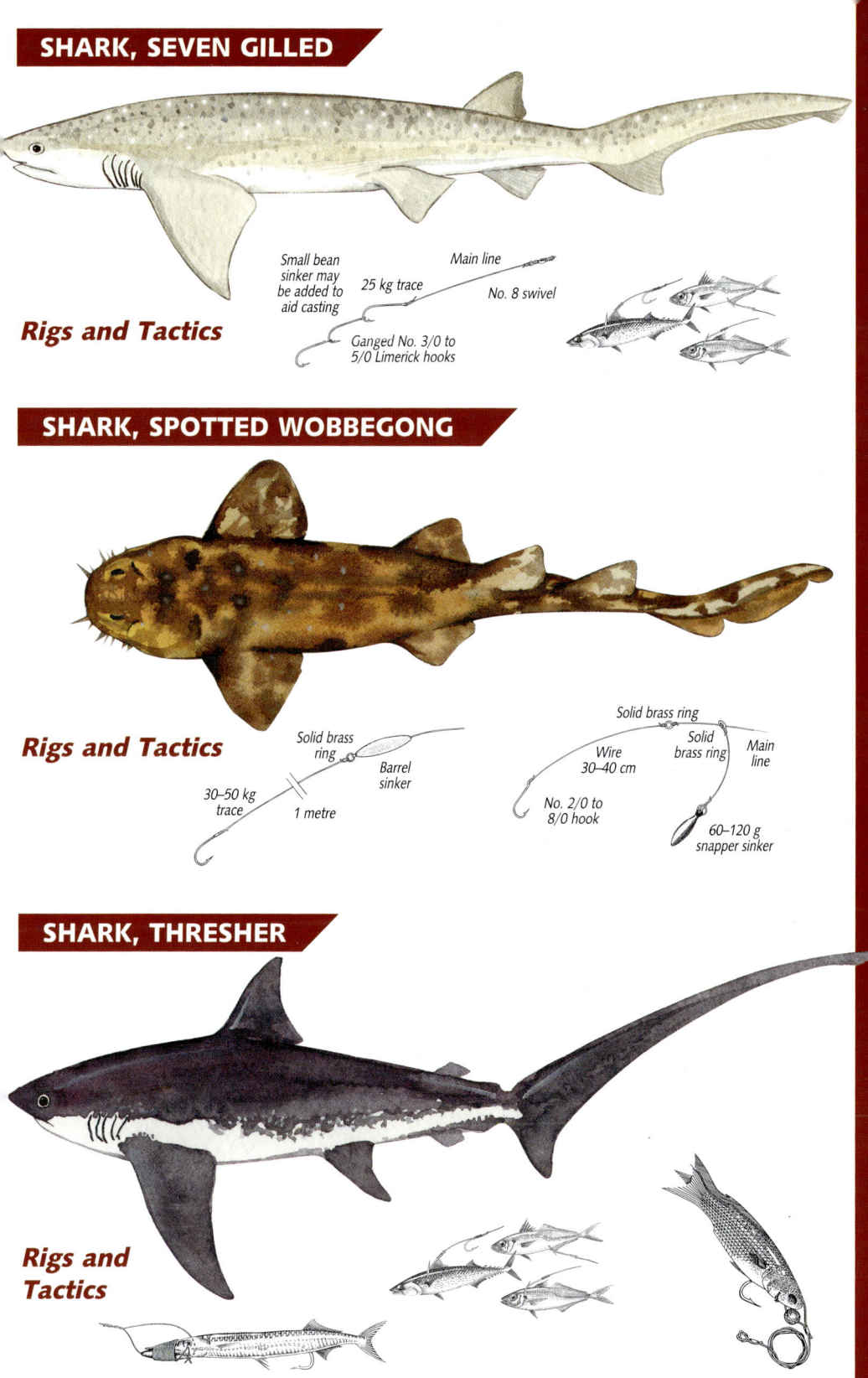

SHARK, SEVEN GILLED

Rigs and Tactics

Small bean sinker may be added to aid casting

25 kg trace

Main line

No. 8 swivel

Ganged No. 3/0 to 5/0 Limerick hooks

SHARK, SPOTTED WOBBEGONG

Rigs and Tactics

Solid brass ring

Barrel sinker

30–50 kg trace

1 metre

Solid brass ring

Wire 30–40 cm

Solid brass ring

Main line

No. 2/0 to 8/0 hook

60–120 g snapper sinker

SHARK, THRESHER

Rigs and Tactics

SHARK, TIGER

Scientific name *Galeocerdo cuvier.*

Range Circum-Australia but more common in warmer waters.

Description A large and extremely dangerous species of shark. The tiger shark can be found well offshore and can venture into the surf zone on occasions, especially during breeding season. The characteristic colour pattern of the tiger shark is a tiger-like series of bars on the upper body. The teeth are unusually shaped, being large and pointed backwards, with strong serrations, especially on the back edge. Although the colouring and shape are distinctive, a dive charter at Ningaloo Reef, with a boat load of tourists, attempted to dive with a tiger shark they thought was a whale shark. The shark, like many when well fed and not threatened, was docile and there was no real incident. The tiger shark can reach nearly 6.5 m and more than 600 kilograms.

Fishing The tiger shark is a famous visitor to the old whaling stations of Australia, where large numbers of tigers, with a few great whites would attack whale carcasses waiting to be flensed. Tiger sharks are attracted by berley and are taken with very large dead baits, especially those with oily or bloody flesh. The tiger shark is a powerful and dogged opponent and is sought by some specialist gamefishermen. Taking any large shark from small boats requires enormous preparation and should not be attempted by any inexperienced angler. The tiger shark is a large and opportunistic feeder which will attack humans and should be treated with extreme caution. If sharks are not being targeted and a large tiger shark shows up – move.

SHARK, WHALE

Scientific name *Rhiniodon typhus.* Also known as Rhinodon shark

Range Shark Bay in Western Australia northwards and across the top of Australia on occasions. Most commonly seen at Ningaloo Reef, especially during March and April, forming the basis of a considerable tourism industry.

Description The world's largest fish. Believed to reach 18 metres in length but most animals seen in Western Australia are young males 8-11 metres in length with some as long as 12-13 metres sighted. Grey colour with distinctive pattern of white spots about the size of a pool ball and white or lighter coloured bars. Researchers have identified individual animals from their markings.

Fishing The whale shark has been totally protected in Western Australia for many years and no-one would contemplate killing one of these majestic animals. They have been taken in some Indonesian villages who use the entire animal and evoke outrage from Chardonnay conservationists and conservation managers who milk every cent possible from the tourism industry, even though these are fish which should be managed by fisheries managers. If encountered, whale sharks often have cobia, tuna or mahi mahi in attendance. Care should be taken when approaching these animals as protection zones exist.

SHARK, TIGER

Rigs and Tactics

SHARK, WHALE

Rigs and Tactics

Not applicable as Whale Shark are a protected species.

SHARK, WHITETIP

Scientific name *Triaendon obesus*. Also known as White-tipped reef shark, whitetip

Range Point Quobba in Western Australia and northern waters to Mackay in Queensland, although some specimens may be found further south.

Description A common species found close around tropical reefs. The whitetip shark is often seen resting in caves or on the bottom. It is similar to the silvertip shark (*Carcharhinus albimarginatus*) which has a white tip to the pectoral fin as well as the dorsal and tail fin. The whitetip shark grows to more than two metres while the silvertip shark reaches more than 3 metres. The whitetip has a short and rounded snout. It is a live bearer and is considered harmless. Although it can also enter feeding aggregations, it is smaller and less aggressive than most of the other reef sharks. The whitetip is often encountered by divers who photograph and talk about the meeting which is likely to be more stressful to the shark.

Fishing The whitetip shark is a smaller and relatively sluggish fish. It will take fish live, whole and cut baits and squid or octopus baits. It is rarely targeted and although the teeth are not dangerous, they can bite off standard reef rigs. The whitetip shark is not highly regarded as an eating or sporting fish.

SHARK, WHITE POINTER

Scientific name *Carcharodon carcharias*. Also known as Great white shark, white shark, white death.

Range Circum-Australia but preferring cooler southern waters.

Description The white pointer shark is a large and extremely dangerous species and the star of the Jaws movies which has lead to the misguided destruction of many harmless sharks. However, the white pointer is responsible for more attacks on humans than any other species. The white pointer is a heavy set species, reaching 6.4 m and more than 1200 kilograms. As in most shark species, males are smaller and easily identified by the claspers which assist in copulation. The white pointer shark has a conical snout, long gill slits and extremely sharp, serrated triangular teeth. The colour is generally grey to dark grey above with a white belly. The white pointer prefers oceanic waters and does not often move close inshore, except to breed or to follow seal colonies when pups are produced. They are more commonly found inshore along the south coast or Tasmania.

Fishing The white pointer is now totally protected, although some are still taken by commercial fishermen. There are special procedures for the few fish which are hooked by recreational fishers. White pointers were viewed as the ultimate capture for game fishermen, with many young recreational fishers being aware of Bob Dyer's 1062 kg fish from Moreton Island and Alf Dean's 1208 kg fish in 1960 from South Australia, which has been regarded as the Mecca of white pointer shark fishermen.

SHARK, WHITETIP

Rigs and Tactics

Small
octopus

No.3/0 to 5/0
Suicide hook

SHARK, WHITE POINTER

Rigs and Tactics

Not applicable as White Pointer Shark are a protected species.

SKATE, MELBOURNE

Scientific name *Raja whitleyi*. Also known as Whitley's skate, great skate.

Range Western part of South Australia and southern waters to near Gosford in NSW.

Description All skates lack the venomous spines of the stingrays and stingarees. This species is the largest, reaching 50 kg and 1.7 metres. The Melbourne skate is common in shallow coastal waters but is most commonly caught in trawls. The upper surface is brownish-grey and flecked with white. The undersurface of the triangular snout is a similar colour. In the smaller thornback skate (*Raja lemprieri*) which is common in Tasmania, the underside of the snout is black. The upper surface is covered with sharp denticles with the largest on either side of the midline whereas the thornback skate has a row of prominent spines along the backbone.

Fishing Baits must be fished on the bottom with standard bottom fishing rigs over sand or other soft bottom. Baits include squid, prawns, cut fish or worm baits. In common with all dorsally compressed species, skates put up an extremely powerful, if unspectacular fight. They can sit on the bottom until the frustrated angler breaks the line. Skates are very good eating, with the wings being very tasty and passable 'mock' scallops can be made with a round cookie cutter.

STINGAREE, COMMON

Scientific name *Trygonoptera testaceous*

Range Around the Gulf of St Vincent in South Australia and east including the east coast to Brisbane in Queensland.

Description The stingarees are easily separated from the stingrays by having a tail fin on a relatively short tail rather than a whip like tail ending in a point. The common stingaree reaches 75 cm which makes it a real challenge on bream gear. It is found in coastal waters or estuaries where it favours areas of sand and reef. It is most common in NSW waters. The common stingaree has no spots or bands on its dorsal surface which is sandy-brown to a deep chocolate brown. The bottom or ventral surface is white or creamy white and has a brown margin. There are one or two spines which are serrated and venomous. A sting requires medical attention and is very prone to deep infection.

Fishing The common stingaree is not a target species but is taken in reasonable numbers by anglers fishing for bream, flathead or mulloway. The common stingaree is most active at night and can move into quite shallow water. Like all the ray species, the common stingaree puts up an extremely strong, dogged and unspectacular fight. They may burrow into the sand and not be able to be dislodged, especially if the angler is using light line. The common stingaree is an opportunistic feeder and can be taken on most baits if presented on the bottom. The common stingaree is not generally regarded as a food fish.

STINGRAY, BLACK

Scientific name *Dasyatis thetidis*. Also known as Black stingaree

Range Shark Bay in Western Australia southwards and temperate waters around to Coffs Harbour. More common from Fremantle to Sydney.

Description A large species of stingray reaching 180 cm across the back and around 4 metres in total length and weight of more than 160 kilograms. The black stingray is found over sand or mud bottoms at the back of beaches and occasionally in larger estuaries. Is blue-grey to black on the top with short tubercules on the top of the head and over the middle of the back. There are two spines on the thick tail which can be very dangerous, especially if the stingray is trodden upon.

Fishing The large size of the black stingray means that it is a real challenge when line fishing. They can be hooked when fishing for mulloway, tailor or salmon from the beach or while drift fishing for flathead, snapper or even whiting on sand or mud patches. The extreme power and rhythmic beat of the 'wings' is characteristic. If a large black stingray chooses to bury itself in the sand, capture is virtually impossible, even with heavy gear. Black stingrays will take most fish or squid baits but is not specifically targeted. Stingrays are underestimated as a food fish.

SKATE, MELBOURNE

Rigs and Tactics

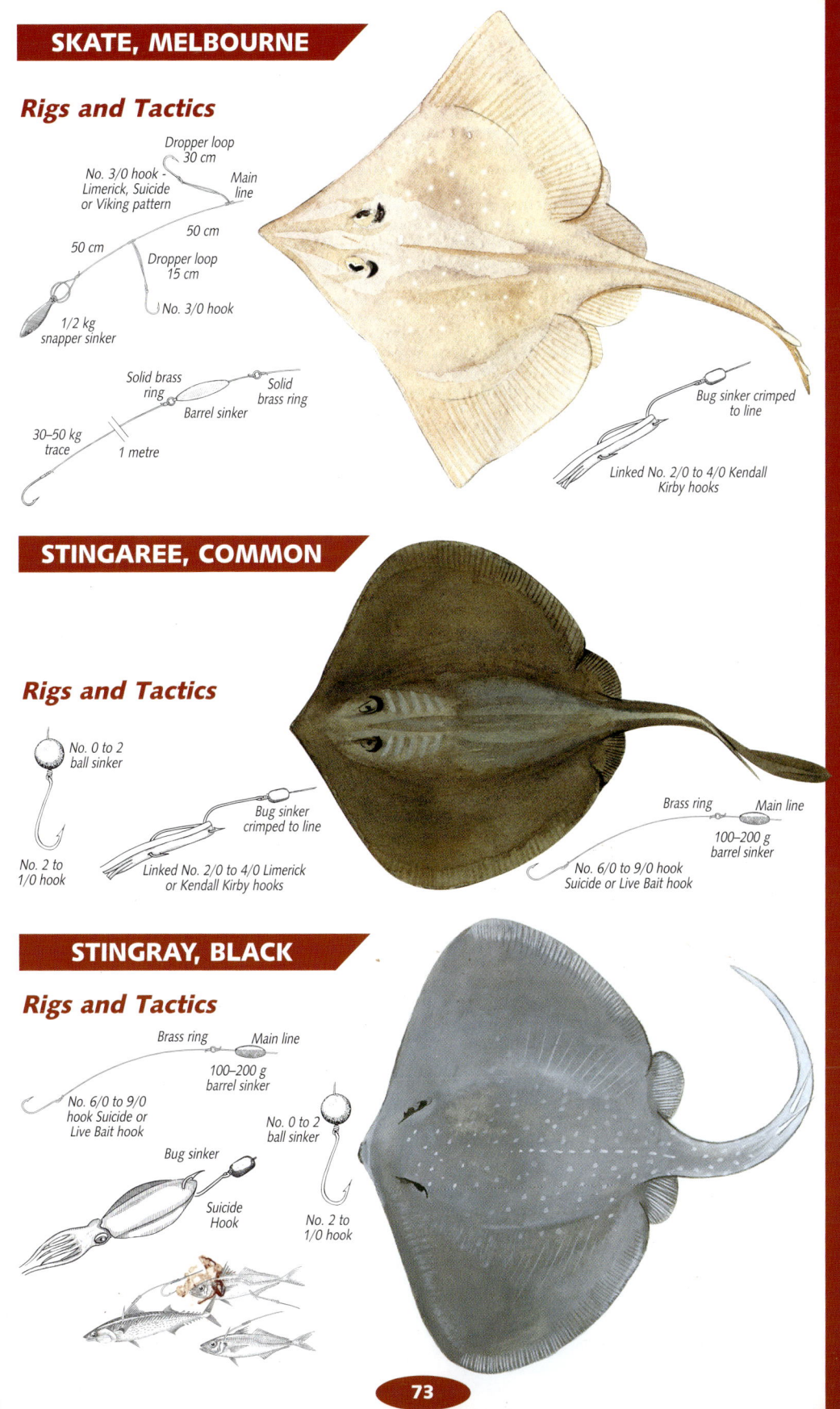

Dropper loop 30 cm
No. 3/0 hook Limerick, Suicide or Viking pattern
Main line
50 cm
50 cm
Dropper loop 15 cm
No. 3/0 hook
1/2 kg snapper sinker

Solid brass ring
Barrel sinker
Solid brass ring
30–50 kg trace
1 metre

Bug sinker crimped to line
Linked No. 2/0 to 4/0 Kendall Kirby hooks

STINGAREE, COMMON

Rigs and Tactics

No. 0 to 2 ball sinker
No. 2 to 1/0 hook
Bug sinker crimped to line
Linked No. 2/0 to 4/0 Limerick or Kendall Kirby hooks

Brass ring
Main line
100–200 g barrel sinker
No. 6/0 to 9/0 hook Suicide or Live Bait hook

STINGRAY, BLACK

Rigs and Tactics

Brass ring
Main line
100–200 g barrel sinker
No. 6/0 to 9/0 hook Suicide or Live Bait hook
No. 0 to 2 ball sinker
Bug sinker
Suicide Hook
No. 2 to 1/0 hook

73

STINGRAY, COACHWHIP

Scientific name *Himantura toshi*. Also known as Black-spotted stingray, coachwhip ray, long-tailed ray, wulura.

Range Dampier Archipelago in Western Australia northwards and to around Coffs Harbour NSW.

Description A relatively large species, although reported maximum sizes vary from 75 cm to 1.5 metres. The tail is long and whip-like. The tail generally has two spines and has 30 or more dark to bluish black rings or marks. The colour can vary on the back and may include spots, waves or scribbles or few markings over a brown background. The coachwhip ray gives birth to live young with a small capsule which covers the spines to prevent them from damaging the mother at birth.

Fishing The coachwhip ray feeds predominantly on molluscs on the intertidal sand and mud-flats. It can be taken in deeper holes at low tide when fishing for other species such as bream or whiting. The coachwhip ray is quite timid and will move away from wading anglers. The spines are quite dangerous and extreme caution should be exercised when handling most stingrays. The barbs are serrated and can break off in the wound or cause enormous damage when tearing back out of the wound. There may be poison glands, or at least the slime causes inflammation, bleeding and infections.

STINGRAY, COWTAIL

Scientific name *Dasyatis sephen*. Also known as Fantail ray, Cowtail ray, Banana-tail ray, Weralli, Guergunna.

Range Onslo in Western Australia and northern waters to Coffs Harbour in northern NSW.

Description A coastal species with a long and particularly dangerous tail, which is capable is attacking someone with its one or two spines even while holding the ray by the normally safe eye sockets. The cowtail ray can reach 65 cm across the body disc. The long tail is twice as long as the body is wide and has a distinctive skin flap along part of the tail past the spines, but the end of the tail is whip-like. The snout ends in a small point. The black or dark brown upper surface is covered with small granules and there are one or two tubercules on a midline of the back.

Fishing The cowtail ray feeds primarily on shellfish such as cockles, oysters and turban shells. It can be taken on pipi, cockle, prawn or squid baits and less often on fish baits. This species is not targeted and due to the length and flexibility of its tail should never be attempted to be landed. As soon as the distinctive tail flap is sighted, the line should be cut.

STINGRAY, SMOOTH

Scientific name *Dasyatis brevicaudata* Also known as giant stingray, short-tail stingray.

Range Shark Bay in Western Australia and southwards throughout cooler waters including Tasmania and as far north as the Noosa River in southern Queensland.

Description This is the largest species of stingray in the world, reaching 4.3 m in length with a 2.1 m disc width and a weight of 340 kilograms. The smooth stingray is found in coastal and estuarine waters and favours sandy bottoms, especially those near reef and weed but can be found at depths of up to 70 metres. The smooth stingray lacks any ridges or scales along its back which gives this species its name. There is usually a series of white spots on the dorsal surface along the sides of the head. There are one or two tail spines which can be up to 37 cm long and there is one fold of skin on the lower surface of the tail.

Fishing Large smooth stingrays are almost unstoppable on standard fishing tackle. They are not considered a target species except by those who would rather wrestle a big stingray than pay a gym membership. They will take a wide variety of baits intended for other species and if the bait is on the bottom, there is a chance that a stingray will take it. They have a special fondness for roe sacs as a bait. The smooth ray is not generally considered as a food fish, but in the smaller sizes their flaps make good eating.

STINGRAY, COACHWHIP

Rigs and Tactics

Not a recognised angling species.

STINGRAY, COWTAIL

Rigs and Tactics

Not a recognised angling species.

STINGRAY, SMOOTH

Rigs and Tactics

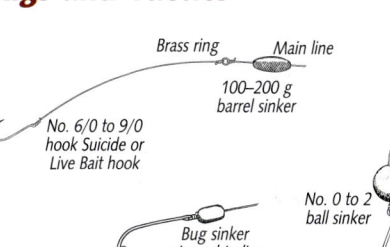

Brass ring   Main line

100–200 g
barrel sinker

No. 6/0 to 9/0
hook Suicide or
Live Bait hook

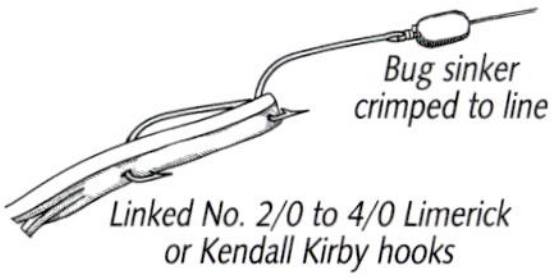

Bug sinker
crimped to line

Linked No. 2/0 to 4/0 Limerick
or Kendall Kirby hooks

No. 0 to 2
ball sinker

No. 2 to
1/0 hook

75

BARRAMUNDI

Scientific name *Lates calcarifer.* Also known as Barra, giant perch.

Range The barramundi range extends from the Mary River in Queensland around the top end to Shark Bay in Western Australia, although the barramundi is most famous as a northern Australia species.

Description The barramundi is a special fish which is as beautiful in reality as it is in the dreams of so many anglers. It has a small head with a large mouth and large eyes which glow bright red in torch light or at certain angles in daylight. Barramundi have large scales and a particularly powerful tail. Coupled with their thick shoulders, barramundi can put up a good fight although not all fish will exhibit the famous gill arching leaps when hooked. The barramundi can be a brilliant silver colour for sea run fish, ranging to a very dark, chocolate brown colour for fish in billabongs at the end of the dry season or those grown in aquaculture facilities. Small barra and those in aquaria exhibit a characteristic light stripe down the forehead between the eyes which becomes more pronounced when the fish is excited. Barramundi in Australia change sex as they grow older (interestingly barramundi in Thailand do not change sex). All fish start out as males and, after spawning once or twice, become female for the rest of their lives. It is therefore impossible to catch a granddaddy barra as it would certainly be female. This sex change is more related to age than size, but barramundi over 8 kg are almost certainly all female. This fact, coupled with the need to spawn in estuaries, makes barramundi vulnerable to overfishing and makes management of the species particularly difficult.

Fishing There are few thrills in fishing in Australia to match the thumping strike of a large saltwater barramundi on a well cast lure or fly. Barramundi are taken in some of the most beautiful country in Australia and, as top predators which are susceptible to commercial and recreational overfishing, the more remote the area, the better your chances of really large specimens. Barramundi are classical ambush feeders and require some stream craft to be most successful. In tidal reaches, look for places which congregate food, especially on a dropping tide such as eddies or draining creek mouths. In freshwater, look for cover and cast close to or beyond likely looking snags, drop-offs or rock bars. Baitcast or trolled diving minnow lures have been the most successful for barramundi for many years, but a supply of rattling spot lures, soft plastic jigs and spinnerbaits can be deadly. Even when there is little or no surface activity, barramundi can make a spectacular slashing strike at a surface lure. With many American made lures, change the hooks, as a large barramundi can be lost through straightening light gauge hooks designed for smaller fish. More and more anglers are fishing for barramundi with the fly. Flies such as Dahlberg Divers and Deceiver patterns work very well and have the advantage of being able to be repeatedly placed very near to cover while drifting along a shore, teasing barra to strike. Many barramundi are taken on live bait. A common rig is to fish a live fish on the bottom of a large hole. However, a live cherabin or fish under a float and drifted past a likely snag can entice even the most reluctant fish to strike. The Northern Territory and Western Australia have strict rules for the taking of barramundi. The only way that quality fishing can be maintained is to increase commercial closed waters and recreational fishers should take only the fish which are absolutely necessary.

BONEFISH

Scientific name *Albula neoguinaica.* Also known as Ladyfish, ghost of the flats.

Range Shark Bay in Western Australia around the top end to Port Hacking in NSW, also Lord Howe Island.

Description The bonefish is similar in appearance to the sand whiting, with the small, downward pointing mouth and is found in similar habitats. However, the bonefish has a single dorsal fin and grows to a much larger size (4.5 kg although a larger specimen was taken on Lord Howe Island). The more deeply forked tail provides the tremendous power for which this species is renowned.

Fishing The bonefish is not as common in Australian waters as it is in places like Florida. It is most commonly taken by surprised anglers fishing the tidal flats for whiting. Standard whiting gear and baits works well, the bonefish is now being soundly targeted in Australia. If a bonefish can be spotted cruising tidal flats, small leadhead jigs or bead head flies provide some of the best pound for pound sportfishing in the world. The bonefish exhibits blistering runs and stamina that makes the capture extremely memorable. Bonefish are very poor eating due to numerous small bones and should be returned.

BARRAMUNDI

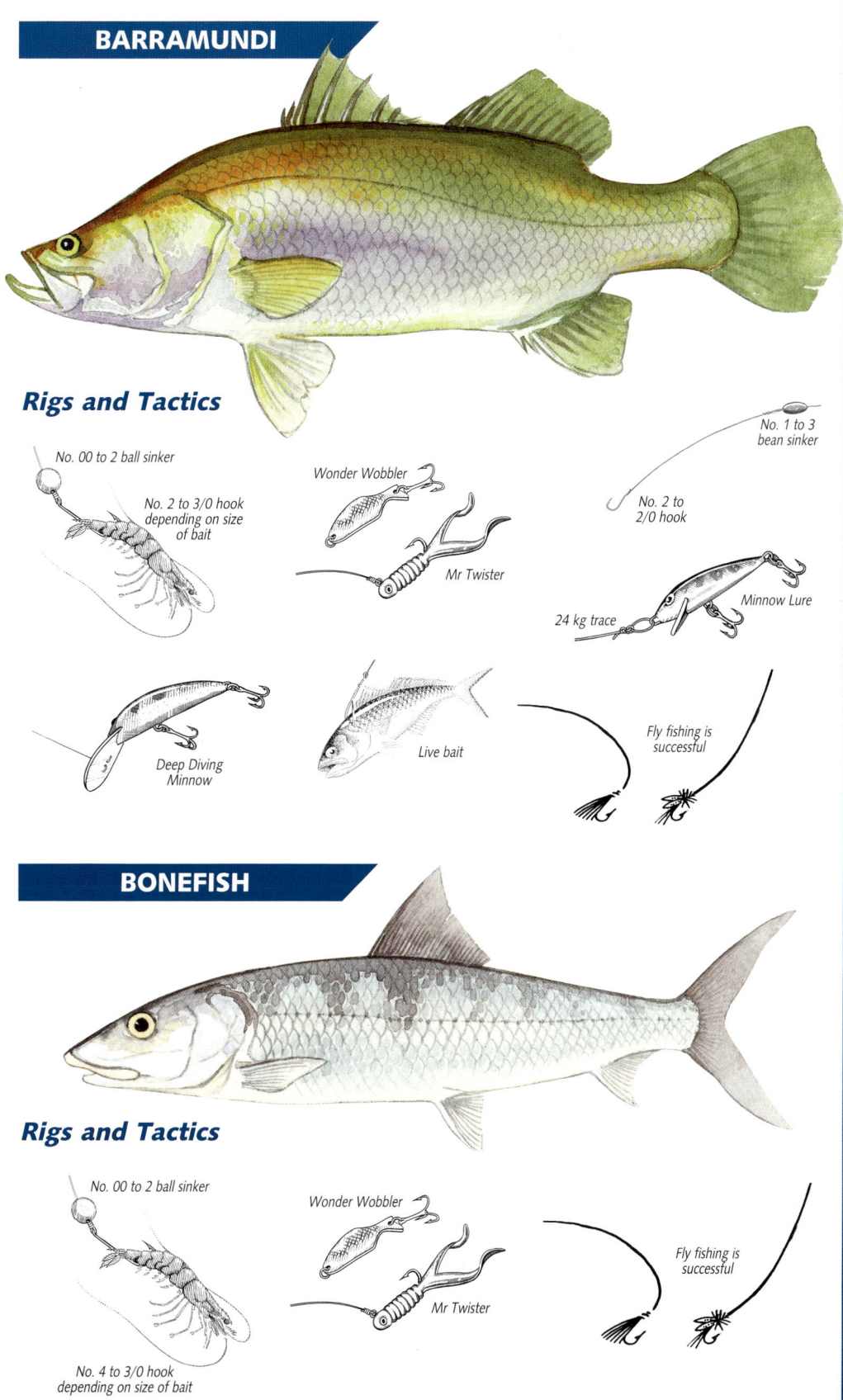

Rigs and Tactics

No. 00 to 2 ball sinker

No. 2 to 3/0 hook
depending on size
of bait

Wonder Wobbler

Mr Twister

No. 1 to 3
bean sinker

No. 2 to
2/0 hook

24 kg trace

Minnow Lure

Deep Diving
Minnow

Live bait

Fly fishing is
successful

BONEFISH

Rigs and Tactics

No. 00 to 2 ball sinker

Wonder Wobbler

Mr Twister

Fly fishing is
successful

No. 4 to 3/0 hook
depending on size of bait

BREAM, BLACK

Scientific name *Acanthopagrus butcheri*. Also known as Bream, blue nosed bream and southern black bream.

Range From Shark Bay in Western Australia and around southern and western coasts to Mallacoota in Victoria and Tasmania.

Description The black bream is a very highly sought after angling species of the estuaries of the southern parts of Australia. It can be found in oceanic waters in the gulf regions of South Australia but not in Western Australia. A recently discovered population in Lake Clifton near Perth can tolerate salinity over double that of sea water. The black bream looks very similar to the yellowfin bream and hybrids have been recorded from the Gippsland lakes in Victoria. The major difference is in fin colour, with the black bream possessing brownish or dusky ventral and anal fins. The mouth is fairly small with rows of peg like teeth and crushing plates on the palate. It reaches a maximum size of around 3.5 kg, but a specimen over 1 kg is highly regarded.

Fishing This is one of the most sought after species in Australia. They are most commonly fished with a light line of 3 – 5 kilograms. Alvey reels on long slow action rods were the most popular but bait running reels on shorter rods are mounting a serious challenge. Bream generally bite best on a rising tide and after dark but many quality fish, including on lures, are taken during the day and in ambush sites on the bottom half of the tide. Bream can be timid biters so as little weight as possible should be used and any sinker must run freely. Best baits are prawn and yabby, although beach, blood and squirt worms, pipi, anchovy or blue sardine and flesh baits also work extremely well. Some anglers make their own special dough baits out of flour and water with added meat, cheese, sugar, fish oils or other secret ingredients. When bream bite, it is important to let them run up to a metre before setting the hook. The bream will then run strongly for the nearest cover and many fish are lost on this initial surge. Many bream are now being taken on lures and is one of the fastest growing forms of lure fishing. Small minnow lures or soft plastics fished close to cover, drop offs or oyster leases can provide fantastic fishing. The black bream makes excellent eating.

BREAM, PIKEY

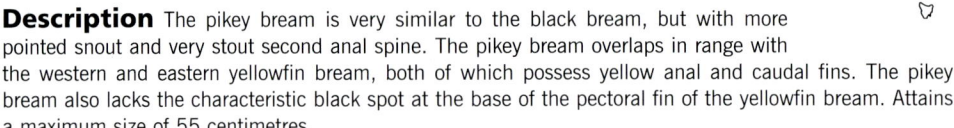

Scientific name *Acanthopagrus berda* Also known as Bream.

Range Onslow in Western Australia around the northern coast to central Queensland.

Description The pikey bream is very similar to the black bream, but with more pointed snout and very stout second anal spine. The pikey bream overlaps in range with the western and eastern yellowfin bream, both of which possess yellow anal and caudal fins. The pikey bream also lacks the characteristic black spot at the base of the pectoral fin of the yellowfin bream. Attains a maximum size of 55 centimetres.

Fishing Similar methods as for the black bream, but more common around jetties, pylons and creek mouths. The pikey bream makes excellent eating but should be bled and chilled after catpure.

BREAM, BLACK

Rigs and Tactics

10 kg trace

Minnow Lure

No. 2 to 5 ball sinker

40–50 cm dropper

20 cm dropper

No. 4 to 2/0 Long Shank, Eastern Estuary or Suicide hook depending on species sought

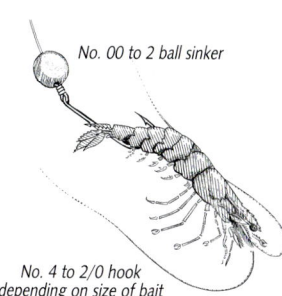

No. 00 to 2 ball sinker

No. 4 to 2/0 hook depending on size of bait

BREAM, PIKEY

Rigs and Tactics

10 kg trace

Minnow Lure

No. 2 to 5 ball sinker

40 to 50 cm dropper

20 cm dropper

No. 4 to 2/0 Long Shank, Eastern Estuary or Suicide hook depending on species sought

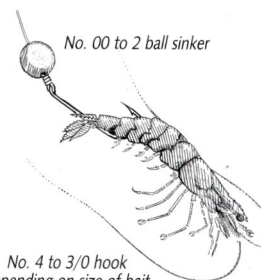

No. 00 to 2 ball sinker

No. 4 to 3/0 hook depending on size of bait

BREAM, YELLOWFIN

Scientific name *Acanthopagrus australis.* Also known as Silver bream, sea bream, surf bream, Eastern black bream.

Range Townsville in Queensland to Lakes Entrance in Victoria.

Description The yellowfin bream is similar to other bream, but with a black spot at the base of the pectoral fin. Also has yellow or yellowish anal and ventral fins. Frequently taken from inshore oceanic waters where the colour is frequently silver, varying to dark olive from estuaries. Lacks the brown horizontal stripes and black stomach cavity lining of the similar tarwhine. Attains a maximum size of 66 cm and 4.4 kg but fish over a kilogram are noteworthy.

Fishing Fantastic fishing for yellowfin bream can be had near the mouths of estuaries in winter when the fish moves downstream to spawn. Estuarine fish can be taken as described for black bream, with oyster leases, rock walls and edges of drop offs being prime spots. Berley works very well when fish are finicky. In ocean waters, bream can be occasionally taken on cabbage weed while fishing for luderick. They are also a prime target when using cunjevoi, often inhabiting the same white water washes as drummer, but often a little further out. Yellowfin bream can be targeted with lightly weighted blue sardines, anchovies or half a pilchard cast into the edge of a good wash. When tailor are feeding, a bait which sinks through the tailor can take some thumping bream. In the surf, pilchards which repeatedly come back with the gut area eaten out by small bites is a sign that bream may be present, especially if fishing the edges of gutters. A half a pilchard rigged on smaller hooks, a pipi or beach worm bait can take these fish. Yellowfin bream are excellent eating although fish taken on weed can have an iodine taint.

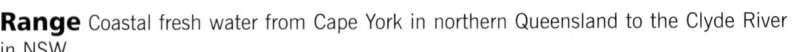

BULLROUT

Scientific name *Notesthes robusta.* Also known as Kroki.

Range Coastal fresh water from Cape York in northern Queensland to the Clyde River in NSW.

Description A superbly camouflaged and extremely dangerous fish with sharp stout spines on the head and gill covers. However, it is the poisonous dorsal spines which deserve the greatest comment. Although a freshwater species, large numbers of bullrouts can be washed into estuaries during freshes where they can be picked up in prawn drag and haul nets. They can grow to 30 cm and are common at 20 cm, packing an even greater punch than the similar but smaller fortescue (whose colour is brown and white as opposed to the mottled brown colours of the bullrout). If stung, soak the affected area in hot but not scalding water to denature (cook) the protein in the toxin. The pain can be intense and local or general painkillers may be necessary.

Fishing Bullrouts are not a target species, but the larger ones are good eating for those brave enough to risk the spines which remain potent after death. Bullrouts can be taken in scoop nets while scooping for shrimp or prawns and their presence is a compelling reason for wearing shoes when wading through weed beds where they frequently lay up during the day. Bullrouts take a variety of baits intended for other species and will occasionally take lures intended for bass.

BREAM, YELLOWFIN

Rigs and Tactics

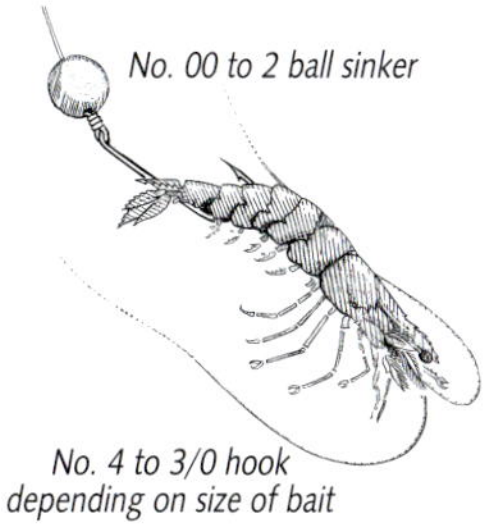

No. 00 to 2 ball sinker

No. 4 to 3/0 hook
depending on size of bait

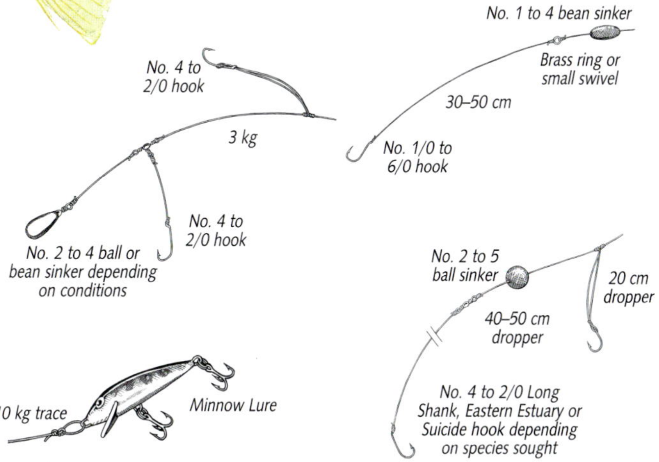

No. 4 to 2/0 hook

3 kg

No. 2 to 4 ball or
bean sinker depending
on conditions

No. 4 to 2/0 hook

10 kg trace   Minnow Lure

No. 1 to 4 bean sinker

Brass ring or
small swivel

30–50 cm

No. 1/0 to
6/0 hook

No. 2 to 5
ball sinker

20 cm
dropper

40–50 cm
dropper

No. 4 to 2/0 Long
Shank, Eastern Estuary or
Suicide hook depending
on species sought

BULLROUT

Rigs and Tactics

Not applicable as Bullrout are not recommended as an angling species

CALE, ROCK

Scientific name *Crinodus lophodon.* Also known as Sea carp, wirrah, weed wirrah, rock cocky, cockatoo fish, cockatoo morwong, marblefish, stinky groper.

Range Byron Bay in NSW to Mallacoota in Victoria.

Description There are three similar species all frequently called sea carp, the southern sea carp (*Aplodactylus arctidens*), western sea carp (*Aplodactylus* sp. that may be the same as the southern sea carp) and the rock cale. These species have a wider range including the entire south coast, a more evenly rounded forehead and can reach 63 centimetres. The rock cale is described here because it is the species most frequently encountered by luderick fishermen. The rock cale has a small head and a hunched back appearance especially in larger specimens. The rock cale can grow to several kilograms but is commonly encountered at between 0.5 and 1.4 kilograms. All fins are covered with pale spots and the body is blotched and may have indistinct vertical bars. The mouth is small, the lips blubbery and the teeth similar to a luderick's and suited for nipping off weed from the rocks. The rock cale is commonly found in the surge zone of the intertidal zone, frequently in large schools. Rock cale may be found near inshore islands where they feed on weed.

Fishing This is an unwelcome species, due to its poor meat quality which is coarse and weed tainted. Spearfishermen who regularly encounter these fish, pass up the shot because they are of little use. The rock cale feeds exclusively on weed and when a school moves in can frustrate luderick fishers. Rock cale are not targeted. They are most commonly taken with luderick float rigs and prefer sea cabbage to string weed. They are occasionally taken on cunjevoi or peeled prawns. They do not fight strongly. Even though the rock cale is not valued, throwing them up the rocks to die is not recommended.

CATFISH, ESTUARY

Scientific name *Cnidoglanis macrocephalus.* Also known as Cobbler.

Range Estuarine and coastal waters from southern Queensland to eastern Victoria and northern Tasmania. Also from western South Australia around to the Abrolhos Islands in Western Australia.

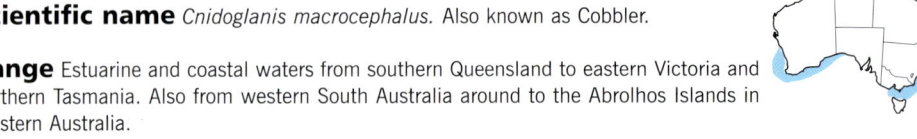

Description A very long eel-tailed species found in muddy or weedy estuaries. They are most commonly caught near washed up weeds or near wood patches. When spawning, cobbler form balls of fish which can be spotted by the muddy water which surrounds them. They make nests in weed and may be significantly affected by weed removal activities. The pectoral and dorsal fins possess a large spine which contains a poison gland. A puncture wound causes a great deal of pain. Treatment is with hot water or compresses to cook the protein. The wound may require hospitalisation or painkilling injections.

Fishing Cobbler are actively fished for in many areas with light bottom rigs and baits of prawn or worms. They are good fighters but must be handled carefully when being unhooked. In some areas, estuary catfish are taken by gidgee or spear in the shallows at night but this method is illegal in many areas and at the very least is not conducive to catch and release fishing. In spite of their appearance, estuary catfish are excellent eating and are highly prized, especially in Western Australia.

CALE, ROCK

Rigs and Tactics

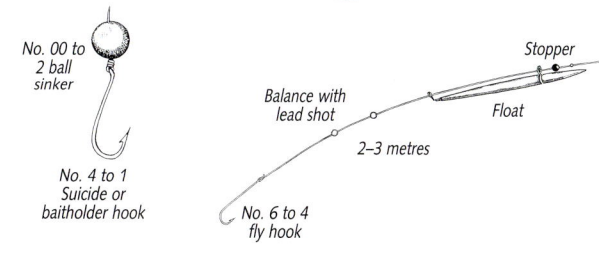

No. 00 to 2 ball sinker

No. 4 to 1 Suicide or baitholder hook

Balance with lead shot

Stopper

Float

2–3 metres

No. 6 to 4 fly hook

CATFISH, ESTUARY

Rigs and Tactics

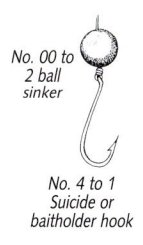

No. 00 to 2 ball sinker

No. 4 to 1 Suicide or baitholder hook

No. 1 to 4 bean sinker

Brass ring or small swivel

30–50 cm

No. 1/0 to 6/0 hook

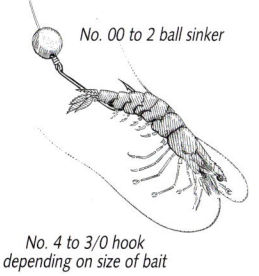

No. 00 to 2 ball sinker

No. 4 to 3/0 hook depending on size of bait

No. 6 to 4 Baitholder hook

CATFISH, FORKTAIL

Scientific name *Arius graeffei.* Also known as Salmon catfish, blue catfish, sea catfish.

Range From Exmouth Gulf in Western Australia northwards around to the Macleay River in northern NSW. The very similar but larger species, the giant salmon catfish is found from the Abrolhos Islands in Western Australia to Moreton Bay in Queensland.

Description These catfish are quite remarkable in that the males hold the large yolky eggs in their mouths until the eggs hatch. The underside of the skull when dried produces a crucifix like structure. The various forktail catfish are difficult to differentiate. The giant salmon catfish (*Arius leptaspis*) grows to over 1.1 m as opposed to 69 cm for the blue catfish. The giant catfish has dorsal and pectoral spines which are the same length. Another similar species is marketed as silver cobbler (*Arius midgleyi*) and reaches weights of 15 kg in Lake Argyle. This species was very rare before the construction of the dam.

Fishing Fork tailed catfish are held in low esteem by many anglers. This is largely as they are often taken while fishing for more prized species like barramundi, queenfish or mangrove jack, taking live baits or creating a false expectation when a lure is hit. Catfish will take baits and lures very well. They have a particular preference for cut baits. Larger forktail catfish fight well and the eating qualities of catfish from clean water is higher than generally believed, as the market acceptance of silver cobbler will attest.

COD, ESTUARY

Scientific name *Epinephelus coioides.* (Frequently misidentified as *Epinephelus malabaricus* or *Epinephelus tauvina*) Also known as Greasy cod, spotted cod, north-west groper, estuary rock cod, gold spotted rock cod, spotted river cod, orange-spotted cod.

Range Rottnest Island in Western Australia around the top end to South West Rocks in NSW, but most common in more tropical waters.

Description The estuary cod is one of the largest and most common cod found in tropical estuaries and coastal reefs reaching a length of over 2 m and 230 kilograms. The estuary cod is olive-green to brown with scattered brown spots. The back has four to six darker blotches which fade with age to uniform brown colour. Similar to Queensland groper but the estuary cod has three opercular spines equal distances apart. The tail is rounded.

Fishing Many states now have maximum size limits to protect larger estuary cod. Fishing is therefore restricted for larger fish which can be taken on rigs as substantial as with baits of whole live mud crab suspended under a 44 gallon drum. Smaller specimens are taken while fishing for standard reef fish with fairly heavy gear. Very large estuary cod can engulf hooked smaller fish in estuaries. Small cod make reasonably good eating.

CATFISH, FORKTAIL

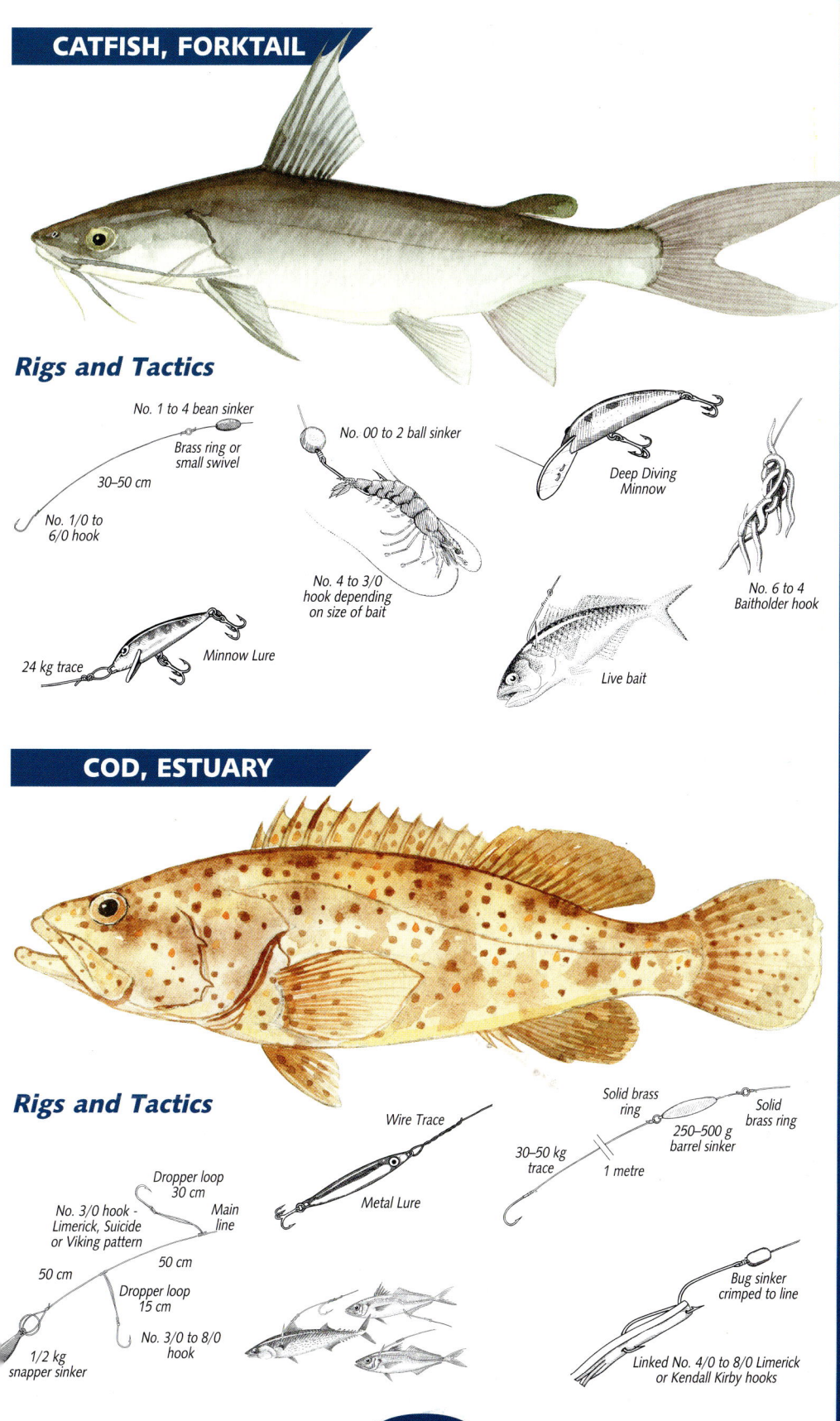

Rigs and Tactics

No. 1 to 4 bean sinker

Brass ring or small swivel

30–50 cm

No. 1/0 to 6/0 hook

24 kg trace

Minnow Lure

No. 00 to 2 ball sinker

No. 4 to 3/0 hook depending on size of bait

Deep Diving Minnow

Live bait

No. 6 to 4 Baitholder hook

COD, ESTUARY

Rigs and Tactics

Wire Trace

Metal Lure

Dropper loop 30 cm

No. 3/0 hook - Limerick, Suicide or Viking pattern

Main line

50 cm

50 cm

Dropper loop 15 cm

No. 3/0 to 8/0 hook

1/2 kg snapper sinker

Solid brass ring

250–500 g barrel sinker

Solid brass ring

30–50 kg trace

1 metre

Bug sinker crimped to line

Linked No. 4/0 to 8/0 Limerick or Kendall Kirby hooks

DART, SNUB-NOSED

Scientific name *Trachinotus blochii*. Also known as Oyster cracker, permit.

Range Ningaloo Reef in Western Australia around the top end as far as Moreton Bay in Queensland, although this is essentially a tropical species.

Description The snub-nosed dart possesses similar characteristics to the swallow-tail dart with elongated sickle shaped dorsal and anal fins. The snub-nosed dart has characteristic orange or yellow colouration of the ventral and anal fins. This fish has quite a small mouth and the nose is rounded. The eye is quite large and close to the mouth. The snub-nosed dart can reach a size of 65 cm and more than 9 kilograms.

Fishing These fish are most often taken on a rising tide in surf zones of ocean beaches on pipi baits, but they can be found in reasonable numbers off oyster leases in some estuaries. In these circumstances snub-nosed dart can use sharp oyster shells to their advantage and a heavier line is required. In surf fishing, standard light surf rigs work best. The snub-nosed dart is excellent eating to match the fantastic sport which these fish provide. The snub-nosed dart is targetted by an increasing number of dedicated fly fishers who rate these shallow water speedsters as world class sportfish.

DART, SWALLOWTAIL

Scientific name *Trachinotus botla*. Also known as Dart, Common Dart, Swallowtail, Southern swallowtail.

Range From Bunbury in Western Australia around the top end to Jervis Bay in NSW but distribution patchy in some tropical waters for this species. Also found with the black spotted dart which is much smaller.

Description From the same family as trevally, the swallowtail dart bears some external similarities and shares the same tenacious side-on fight. Dart are handsome fish with a deeply forked tail. The dorsal fin is set well back on the fish and the first few dorsal and anal rays are elongated. The swallowtail dart has between one and five large spots on the side of the fish. The swallowtail dart is distinguished from the black spotted dart whose spots are smaller than the pupil of the eye. The snub nosed dart has no spots on its sides and a much more blunt, rounded head profile. The swallowtail dart grows to 60 cm but is often caught at smaller sizes. A dart of larger than 1 kg is noteworthy, and their strong fight makes up for their lack of size.

Fishing Swallowtail dart are most frequently caught in the surf but can be taken in sandy bays or sand bars which provide shallow water. They can form small schools, affording fast and furious action. They are generally taken while fishing for whiting or bream and they will take worms, pipis, nippers, and small flesh baits. Blue sardines or whitebait are particularly good bait. Dart will take small lures and leadheaded jigs, where the lighter line allows maximum enjoyment from these tenacious fighters. Dart make good eating but should be bled and kept cool as they can spoil quickly.

DART, SNUB NOSED

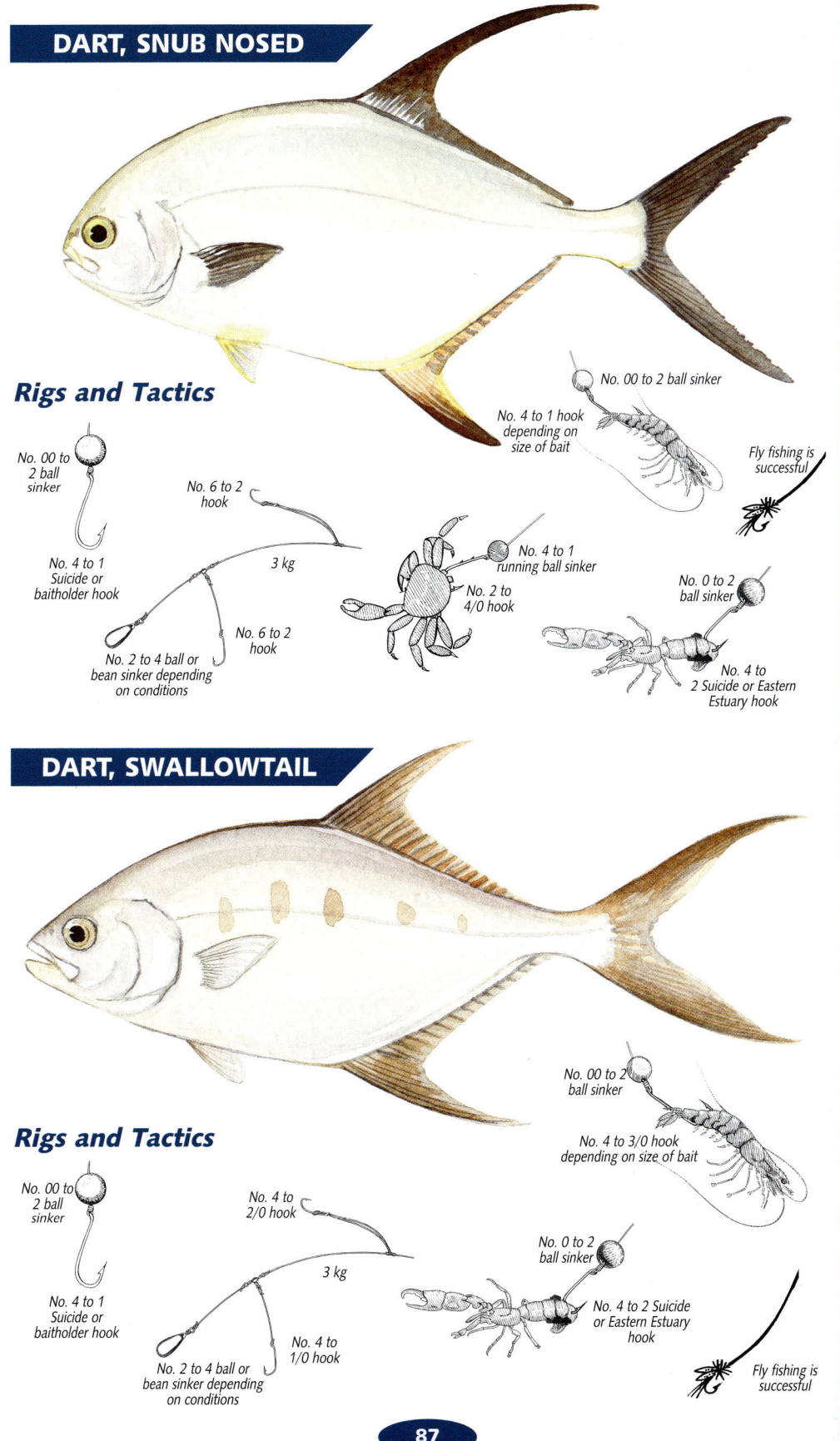

Rigs and Tactics

No. 00 to 2 ball sinker

No. 4 to 1 hook depending on size of bait

Fly fishing is successful

No. 00 to 2 ball sinker

No. 4 to 1 Suicide or baitholder hook

No. 6 to 2 hook

3 kg

No. 6 to 2 hook

No. 2 to 4 ball or bean sinker depending on conditions

No. 4 to 1 running ball sinker

No. 2 to 4/0 hook

No. 0 to 2 ball sinker

No. 4 to 2 Suicide or Eastern Estuary hook

DART, SWALLOWTAIL

Rigs and Tactics

No. 00 to 2 ball sinker

No. 4 to 3/0 hook depending on size of bait

No. 00 to 2 ball sinker

No. 4 to 1 Suicide or baitholder hook

No. 4 to 2/0 hook

3 kg

No. 4 to 1/0 hook

No. 2 to 4 ball or bean sinker depending on conditions

No. 0 to 2 ball sinker

No. 4 to 2 Suicide or Eastern Estuary hook

Fly fishing is successful

DRUMMER, BLACK

Scientific name *Girella elevata.* Also known as Rock blackfish, Eastern rock blackfish, pig, black tank.

Range Noosa Heads in southern Queensland to Wilson's Promontory in Victoria. A similar species, the Western rock blackfish (*Girella tephraeops*) is found from the Recherché Archipelago near Esperance to the Abrolhos Islands off Geraldton in Western Australia. Drummer prefer the white water of surge zones of shorelines or near shore reefs.

Description The black drummer is a deep bodied and incredibly powerful fish. While the black drummer can have mottled colouring in some circumstances, it is often a uniform black colour and never possesses the distinctive vertical stripes of the luderick. The head and mouth is small and the profile rounded. There are 13 spines in the dorsal of the rock blackfish compared with 14 – 16 in the luderick and 11 in the silver drummer.

Fishing This is a strong, dirty fighter who lives close to the rocks and reefs which it will dive into to break off any poorly prepared angler. Black drummer are often encountered by anglers fishing for luderick with delicate gear and light traces which are no match for a large 'pig'. Rock blackfish are often taken on cabbage weed. Cunjevoi and peeled prawn make good bait, but every picker in the area will attack the bait, especially on the edges of the white water. Black drummer can also be taken on bread. With cabbage and bread, berley is an advantage but do not berley so much that the fish can fill up. Other baits include crab portion, abalone gut, and occasionally squid and cuttlefish. Extra strong hooks are recommended. A bobby cork or heavy luderick float, weighted to reduce resistance keeps the bait at the depth that black drummer are found. Lines of 6 – 15 kg are recommended as are extra strong hooks around size 4 – 6. With cunjevoi, a small ball sinker running straight to the hook and cast into the white water will bring results. This rig also works after dark but extra special care must be taken when fishing low rock ledges at night. Small black drummer are good eating if bled and cleaned soon after capture, otherwise a weedy taste can taint the flesh.

DRUMMER, SILVER

Scientific name *Kyphosus sydneyanus.* Also known as Common buffalo bream, Sydney drummer.

Range From Shark Bay in Western Australia around the southern states and Tasmania and along the eastern coast to Point Lookout in southern Queensland.

Description The silver drummer is a large schooling fish growing to 12 kg which offers better sport than eating. These mainly herbivorous fish are found in surge zones and near inshore reefs. They are dusky silver with fairly prominent lengthwise bands. The lips appear more prominent than in rock blackfish and the head is more pointed. The silver drummer can be separated from the similar western buffalo bream (*Kyphosus cornelii*) as the silver drummer has a black or uniformly dusky tail fin which is almost square and the dark, moustache-like line from the upper lip to the eye. The western buffalo bream is poor table fare and is only found from Cape Leeuwin to Shark Bay in Western Australia.

Fishing Silver drummer are fished for with cabbage, bread, cunjevoi and prawns. In Western Australia they are poorly regarded, taking baits such as maggots or blue sardines intended for herring or tailor and may be encountered among schools of the more common western buffalo bream. Silver drummer are caught under floats in the surge zones or on lightly weighted baits fished near inshore reefs. Berley of bread, weed or cunjevoi works well. Silver drummer fight hard but fair and make reasonable eating if bled and cleaned immediately, but larger specimens are definitely more fun to catch than to eat. Rigs are the same as for black drummer, but due to their fair fight, lighter line can be used.

DRUMMER, BLACK

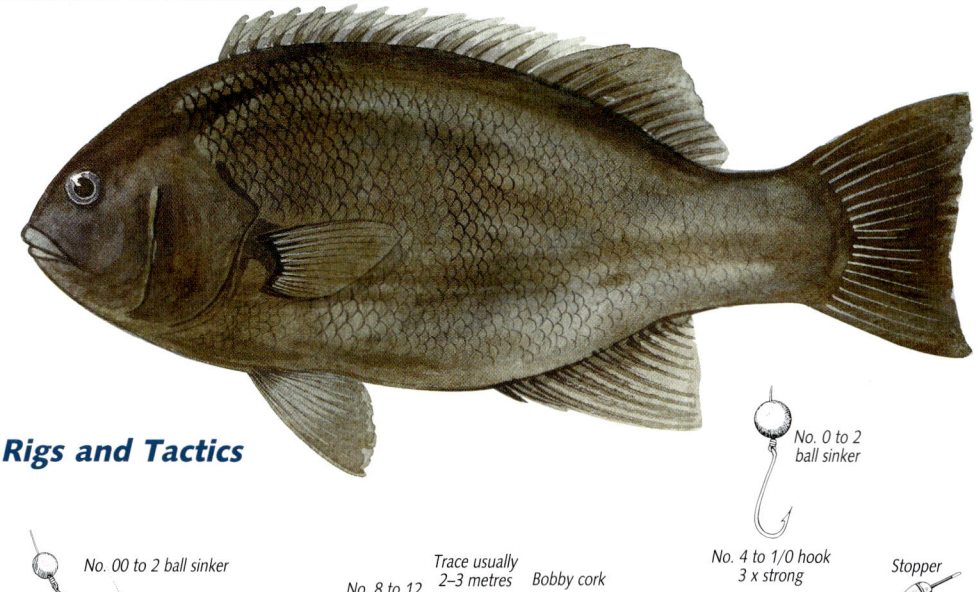

Rigs and Tactics

No. 00 to 2 ball sinker

No. 4 to 3/0 hook
depending on size of bait

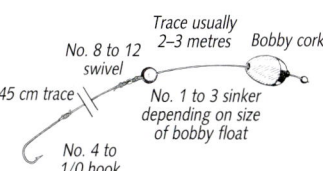

No. 8 to 12
swivel

45 cm trace

No. 4 to
1/0 hook
3 x strong

Trace usually
2–3 metres   Bobby cork

No. 1 to 3 sinker
depending on size
of bobby float

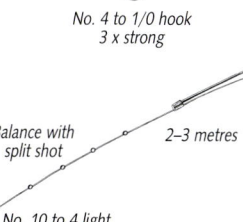

No. 0 to 2
ball sinker

No. 4 to 1/0 hook
3 x strong

Balance with
split shot

Stopper

Float

2–3 metres

No. 10 to 4 light
gauge fly hook

DRUMMER, SILVER

Rigs and Tactics

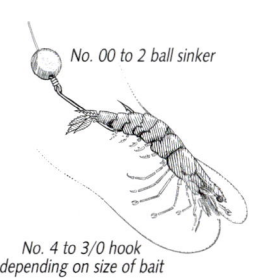

No. 00 to 2 ball sinker

No. 4 to 3/0 hook
depending on size of bait

No. 0 to 2
ball sinker

No. 2 to
1/0 hook

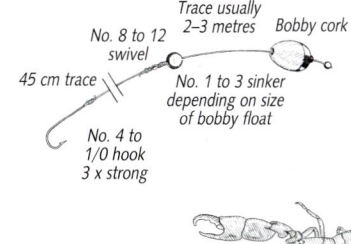

No. 8 to 12
swivel

45 cm trace

No. 4 to
1/0 hook
3 x strong

Trace usually
2–3 metres   Bobby cork

No. 1 to 3 sinker
depending on size
of bobby float

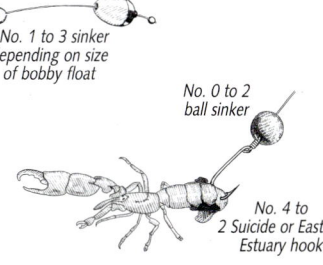

No. 0 to 2
ball sinker

No. 4 to
2 Suicide or Eastern
Estuary hook

EEL, COMMON PIKE

Scientific name *Muraenesox bagio* Also known as pike eel, silver eel.

Range Reported by some authors as coming from northern Western Australia but not reported by Allen. Its range is from eastern Northern Territory and down the east coast as far south as Nowra in NSW.

Description The pike eel is similar to the conger eels, the short finned conger-eel (*Conger wilsoni*) and the Southern conger-eel (*Conger verreauxi*) but the common pike eel has a longer jaw and sharp teeth. The gill opening is set well back form the mouth and just in front of the pectoral fins. The dorsal fin commences in front of the pectoral fins whereas with the congers, the dorsal fin commences behind the pectoral fins. The upper jaw of the common pike eel can be hooked and notched to accommodate some pretty nasty teeth in the front of the lower jaw. The common pike eel grows to 1.5 m and is most commonly found in muddy estuaries or near seagrasses which have a mud or silt/sand bottom nearby. They can be found in quite deep water in these estuaries but are rarely taken from open ocean waters.

Fishing This is one species of fish which can be particularly nasty when captured. They are frequently taken while drifting deeper water in estuaries for flathead, bream or mulloway. A large common pike eel when taken into a boat, will thrash around, rearing onto its tail and lash out with its vicious teeth, biting everything within reach at random. These fish are also extremely hardy and can take a long time to become subdued. A far better tactic is to cut the common pike eel off beside the boat, sacrificing a hook but potentially saving the relationship with all others in the boat. The common pike eel is quite a large species and its impressive fight gives rise to hopes of an extremely large dusky flathead instead of an attacking eel. The common pike eel will take most baits, with live baits, cut baits, pilchard, whitebait, prawns and squid all taking fish. The pike eel is regarded as quite good eating, but very few make it to the table given their unfortunate habit of trying to bite the hand that fed it.

FINGERMARK

Scientific name *Lutjanus johnii*. Also known as Fingermark bream, big scale red, golden snapper.

Range This species is found in northern waters, from the Territory to central Queensland. This fish should not be confused with another species also called Fingermark (*Lutjanus russelli*) which is found over a wider range including Western Australia which is more correctly known as the Moses perch (page 116).

Description The fingermark is a large sea-perch commonly taken from northern inshore and reef waters and estuaries. It has a speckled appearance because of a dark spot on each scale, which gives the appearance of parallel fine stripes. A large black blotch which varies in colour and intensity is located below the soft dorsal rays. Grows to 90 cm and more than 10 kilograms.

Fishing This species has become a renowned deep diving lure taker through the writing of the great Vic McCristal. It can be taken on lures near the mouths of estuaries or rocky outcrops. They also take cut and whole fish baits well and provide excellent sport. Small schools of similar sized fish are frequently encountered. Fingermark are considered excellent eating.

Rigs and Tactics

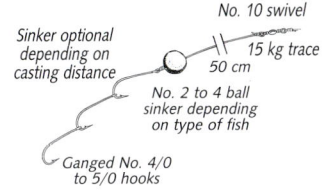

No. 10 swivel

Sinker optional
depending on
casting distance

15 kg trace
50 cm

No. 2 to 4 ball
sinker depending
on type of fish

Ganged No. 4/0
to 5/0 hooks

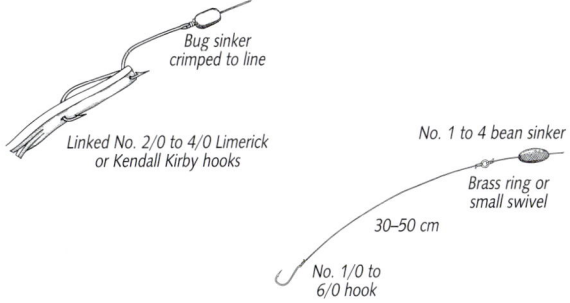

Bug sinker
crimped to line

Linked No. 2/0 to 4/0 Limerick
or Kendall Kirby hooks

No. 1 to 4 bean sinker

Brass ring or
small swivel

30–50 cm

No. 1/0 to
6/0 hook

FINGERMARK

Rigs and Tactics

No. 1 to 4
bean sinker

Brass ring or
small swivel

30–50 cm

No. 1/0 to
5/0 hook

No. 3 to
5/0 hook

10 kg

No. 2 to 4 ball or
bean sinker depending
on conditions

No. 2 to
5/0 hook

No. 4 to 4/0
(depending on
bait size) Kendall
Kirby hook

No. 2 to 3 ball

Deep Diving
Minnow

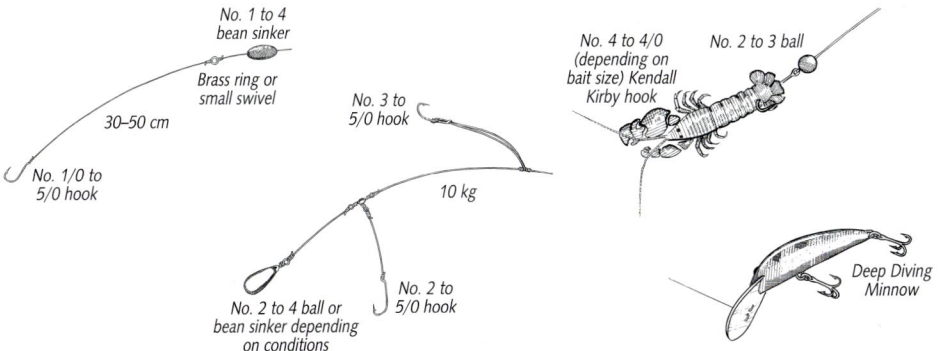

FLATHEAD, BAR-TAIL

Scientific name *Platycephalus endrachtensis*. Also known as Western estuary flathead.

Range Fremantle and northern waters along the top end and as far south as Port Hacking in NSW.

Description The bar-tail flathead is a common species in Western Australian estuaries. It is curiously very common in the Swan River at the southern end of its range. The bar tail flathead can be readily identified by the tail fin which has black and white horizontal stripes on the tail with a yellow blotch at the top of the fin. The similar northern sand flathead which grows to 45 cm has similar tail colouration but no yellow blotch. The bar-tail flathead is found on sand, gravel, light rock and silt bottoms. The bar-tailed flathead is reported as reaching 1 m in length, but in the Swan estuary where it is particularly targeted, any fish above 55 cm is noteworthy and most fish are between 30 and 45 centimetres.

Fishing The bar-tail flathead can be fished with similar methods as for dusky flathead. They will readily take lures such as minnows, jigs and wobblers and they will also take flies well. Bar-tail flathead bite on blue sardines, whitebait, prawns, pipi, squid and crab or pilchard pieces. These should be fished with a light weight on a fairly long trace. A mobile approach works best, fishing the edges of drop-offs especially on a falling tide or on the deeper side during low tide and the early rising tide. Trolling these same areas will also take fish. Bar-tail flathead make very good eating and is a reward for one of casting near sandy drop offs which is the most enjoyable and relaxing forms of fishing.

FLATHEAD, DUSKY

Scientific name *Platycephalus fuscus*. Also known as Estuary flathead, mud flathead, black flathead, flattie, frog and lizard (especially large specimens).

Range Mackay in Queensland to Wilson's Promontory and eastern Bass Strait in Victoria.

Description The dusky flathead is the largest of the 30 species of flathead in Australia, reaching 10 kg and 150 centimetres. Any fish above 5 kg is certainly worth boasting about. The flathead shape is unmistakable, and the dusky flathead also has the sharp opercular (cheek) spines to spike the unwary. The colouration is highly variable from light fawn to black depending on the type of bottom they are found on. The belly ranges from creamy yellow to white. The tail fin features a characteristic dark spot in the top end corner and a patch of blue on the lower half. This is an estuarine or inshore species. This feature plus its large size and good eating make it the ultimate prize for many weekend anglers.

Fishing These are magic fish to target, being common enough to reward the beginner but challenging for the specialist or dedicated angler. Big dusky flathead leave a tell tale indentation in estuarine sand or soft substrate at low tide. They are ambush feeders best fished on a dropping tide in areas where food is concentrated. This includes creek mouths, drop-offs, the sandy side of weed edges and gutters in the surf zone. Dusky flathead can be caught on a rising tide but they can be more finicky and spread out. Trolling the deep edges of drop-offs or flicking baits into these areas works well. Dusky flathead love lures, where the active approach generally brings better results. Diving lures, wobblers and lead head jigs work very well. Trolling diving lures along channel edges takes good numbers of sometimes very large fish and the lure, if weed is not too prevalent, should occasionally touch bottom, putting up a puff of sand. Dusky flathead cannot resist a live poddy mullet or prawn, while cut fish baits, pilchards, whitebait, bluebait, anchovies and prawns all take many fish. It is best to drift or keep the bait moving as they are ambush feeders waiting for the food to come to them. Dusky flathead are very good eating.

FLATHEAD, BAR-TAIL

Rigs and Tactics

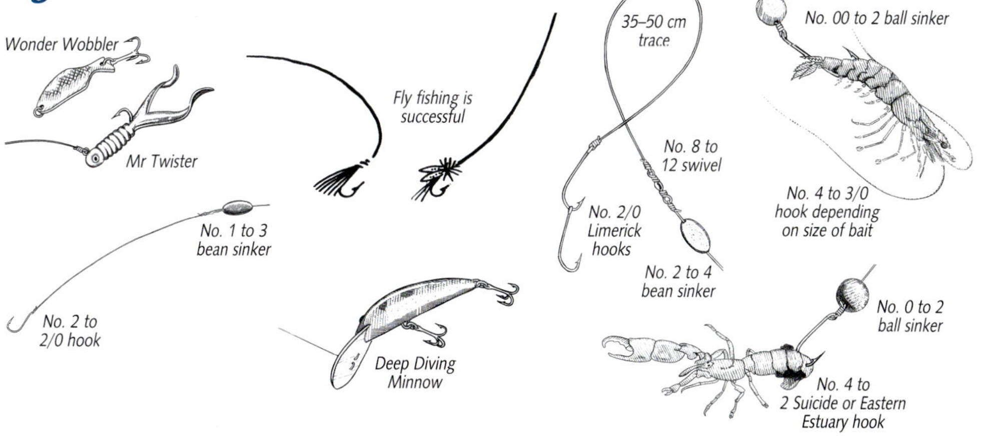

Wonder Wobbler

Mr Twister

No. 1 to 3 bean sinker

No. 2 to 2/0 hook

Fly fishing is successful

Deep Diving Minnow

35–50 cm trace

No. 8 to 12 swivel

No. 2/0 Limerick hooks

No. 2 to 4 bean sinker

No. 00 to 2 ball sinker

No. 4 to 3/0 hook depending on size of bait

No. 0 to 2 ball sinker

No. 4 to 2 Suicide or Eastern Estuary hook

FLATHEAD, DUSKY

Rigs and Tactics

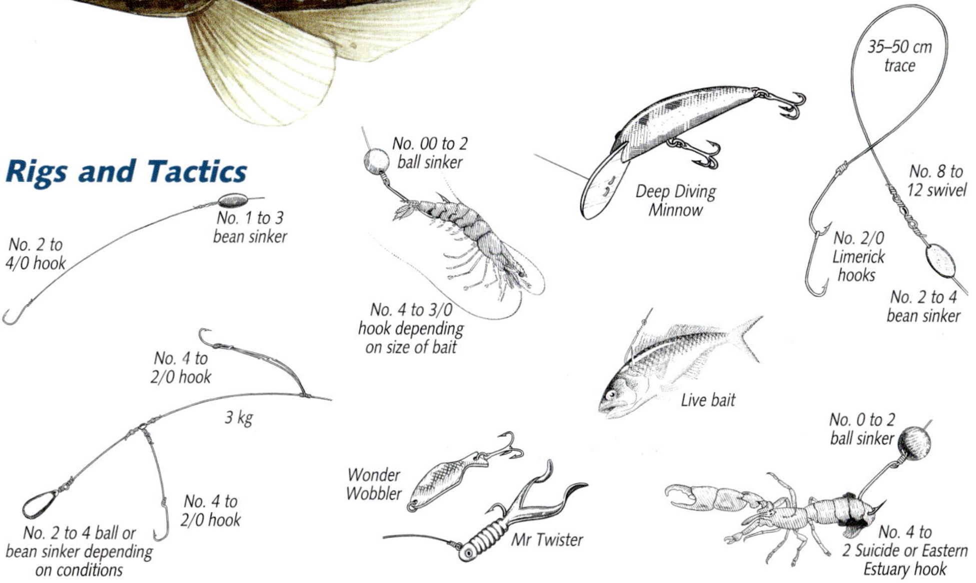

No. 2 to 4/0 hook

No. 1 to 3 bean sinker

No. 00 to 2 ball sinker

Deep Diving Minnow

35–50 cm trace

No. 8 to 12 swivel

No. 2/0 Limerick hooks

No. 2 to 4 bean sinker

No. 4 to 3/0 hook depending on size of bait

No. 4 to 2/0 hook

3 kg

Live bait

No. 0 to 2 ball sinker

No. 2 to 4 ball or bean sinker depending on conditions

No. 4 to 2/0 hook

Wonder Wobbler

Mr Twister

No. 4 to 2 Suicide or Eastern Estuary hook

FLATHEAD, EASTERN BLUE SPOT

Scientific name *Platycephalus caeruleopuntatus.* Also known as Blue-spotted flathead, drift flathead, longnose flathead, red spotted flathead.

Range Southern Queensland around Moreton Bay to central Victoria around Geelong.

Description Flathead identification can be quite difficult, but the Eastern blue spot flathead has three or four black ovals or bars on the lower part of the tail fin. This species is generally found at a length of less than 45 centimetres. The eastern blue spot flathead is a common catch on the sand banks of NSW.

Fishing Recent creel survey work shows that this is the most commonly caught boat species in many parts of central NSW. It is taken while drifting across sand banks ranging from those behind the breakers to deeper drifting grounds in up to 25 fathoms. As with all flathead, catches are better near drop offs, where baitfish are concentrated or near the edge of broken ground. Rigs should be weighted so that they lightly drag across the bottom. Braid lines can be a distinct advantage in deeper water. Best baits are cut baits or pilchard, bluebait, whitebait, prawns and squid. Eastern bluespot flathead are good eating.

FLATHEAD, SAND

Scientific name *Platycephalus arenarius* (Northern sand flathead), *Platycephalus bassensis* (Southern sand flathead) Also known as Northern-flag tailed flathead; Southern - slimy flathead, bay flathead, common flathead, sandy flathead.

Range The northern sand flathead is found from the Northern Territory part of the Gulf of Carpentaria to northern NSW, but can be found as far south as the Central Coast on occasions. The southern sand flathead is found from around Port Macquarie in NSW, but is more common from the NSW south coast to Tasmania and to South Australia. A similar species, the Western sand flathead (*Platycephalus longispinis*) is found from Cape Leeuwin to Carnarvon in Western Australia.

Description The various sand flatheads are generally smaller than the blue-spotted or dusky flathead. The northern sand flathead can reach 45 cm but is more commonly encountered in large numbers at around 30 cm in estuaries or on adjacent beaches. They can be found to a depth of 30 fathoms. They have a distinctive pattern of long, horizontal black stripes on its tail. The southern sand flathead has two or sometimes three squared off black patches on the lower part of the tail fin. This species is reputed to reach over 3 kg but is rarely found over a kilogram.

Fishing These fish are taken with similar methods for other flathead. The northern sand flathead will move upwards a greater distance to take a lure than the other flathead. These fish can be found with other flathead species and can be a pest at smaller sizes, seemingly being all mouth and spines and picking apart baits intended for tailor, bream or large dusky flathead that can all be found in similar areas. They are good eating and are undervalued.

FLATHEAD, EASTERN BLUE SPOT

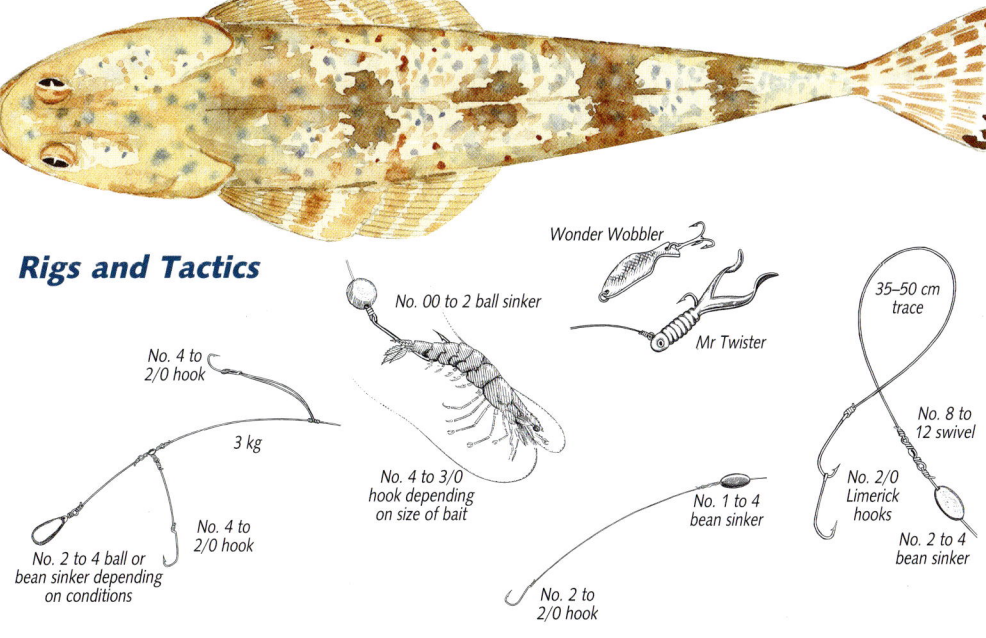

Rigs and Tactics

No. 4 to 2/0 hook

3 kg

No. 4 to 2/0 hook

No. 2 to 4 ball or bean sinker depending on conditions

No. 00 to 2 ball sinker

No. 4 to 3/0 hook depending on size of bait

No. 2 to 2/0 hook

Wonder Wobbler

Mr Twister

No. 1 to 4 bean sinker

35–50 cm trace

No. 8 to 12 swivel

No. 2/0 Limerick hooks

No. 2 to 4 bean sinker

FLATHEAD, SAND

Rigs and Tactics

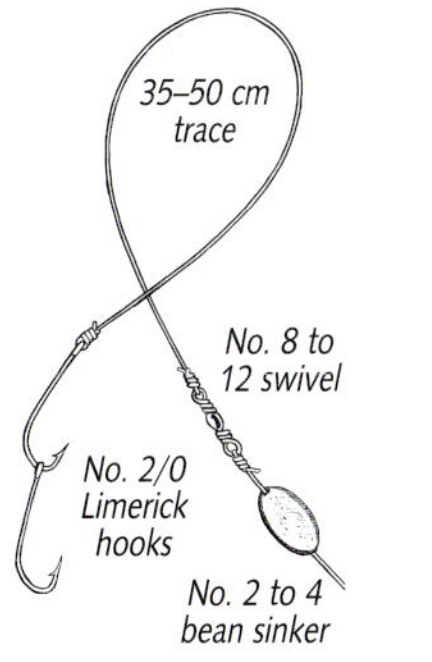

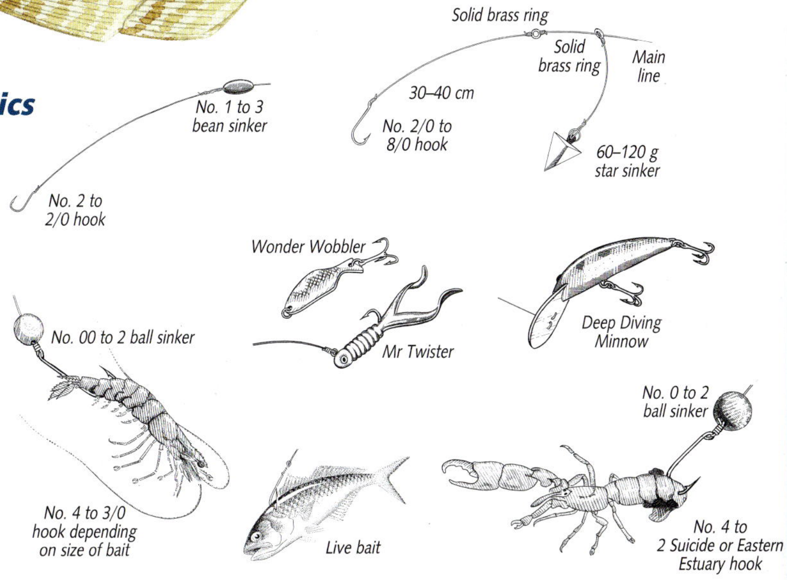

No. 1 to 3 bean sinker

No. 2 to 2/0 hook

35–50 cm trace

No. 8 to 12 swivel

No. 2/0 Limerick hooks

No. 2 to 4 bean sinker

No. 00 to 2 ball sinker

No. 4 to 3/0 hook depending on size of bait

Solid brass ring

Solid brass ring

Main line

30–40 cm

No. 2/0 to 8/0 hook

60–120 g star sinker

Wonder Wobbler

Mr Twister

Deep Diving Minnow

Live bait

No. 0 to 2 ball sinker

No. 4 to 2 Suicide or Eastern Estuary hook

FLATHEAD, SOUTHERN BLUE-SPOTTED

Scientific name *Platycephalus speculator*. Also known as Southern flathead, yank flathead, Castelnau's flathead, southern dusky flathead, bluespot flathead, long nose flathead, shovelnose flathead.

Range From Kalbarri in Western Australia and around the southern part of Australia and Tasmania to the southernmost NSW waters.

Description This flathead can be distinguished on the basis of grey-green spots on the top half of the tail and 3 to 5 large black spots on the lower portion, surrounded by white or off-white. This species also has only one dorsal spine compared with two for many other flathead. The southern blue-spotted flathead can reach a maximum size of nearly 8 kg, although any fish of 3 kg is rare and it is much more common at around a kilogram.

Fishing The southern blue-spot flathead can be found in similar areas to other flatheads, ambushing prey wherever possible. This species can occasionally be found over weed patches or around the edges of weeds. It is not as commonly taken on lures and can be a welcome bonus when fishing for King George whiting or when baits sink through berley fishing for herring and garfish. Like all the flathead, the southern blue-spotted is good eating.

FLATHEAD, TIGER

Scientific name *Neoplatycephalus richardsoni*. Also known as Trawl flathead, king flathead, spiky flathead, toothy flathead.

Range Found from around Sydney in NSW south into Victorian and Tasmanian waters, but they are not found from Western Victoria.

Description Tiger flathead have a somewhat more cylindrical body compared to the obviously compressed form of the other flathead. Tiger flathead colour varies but generally has a reddish-orange or reddish-brown base colour but with brighter orange spots which extend to the tail. The tiger flathead has large teeth on the roof of the mouth. The maximum size is 2.5 kg but they are most often encountered from 0.5 to 1.5 kilograms.

Fishing Tiger flathead are a common trawl species in the south-eastern waters to a depth of 80 fathoms. However, in parts of Victoria and Tasmania they can enter bays, harbours and estuaries. As they are often taken from deep water, heavy handlines or boat rods and typical paternoster rigs with up to four droppers are used. Baits of fish flesh, pilchards, squid or prawns take most fish. In shallower water, live baits prove deadly. Tiger flathead are a highly regarded food fish.

FLOUNDER, GREENBACK

Scientific name *Rhombosolea tapirina*. Also known as Melbourne flounder, southern flounder.

Range Southern NSW and all southern waters including Tasmania to South Australia.

Description The greenback flounder is another right eyed flounder which reaches 0.6 kilograms. It is distinguished from the long snouted flounder by the overall kite-like shape caused by the dorsal and anal fins tapering down to a more triangular shape. The head is also more pointed as it lacks the fleshy snout of the long snouted flounder. This species enters shallow waters on the rising tide at night.

Fishing Where permitted this excellent eating fish is taken by hand spear. Otherwise small lightly weighted baits fished across sand or sand/mud flats at night can take these fish. They are a welcome catch while fishing for other species such as bream and whiting at other times and in deeper water.

FLATHEAD, SOUTHERN BLUE-SPOTTED

Rigs and Tactics

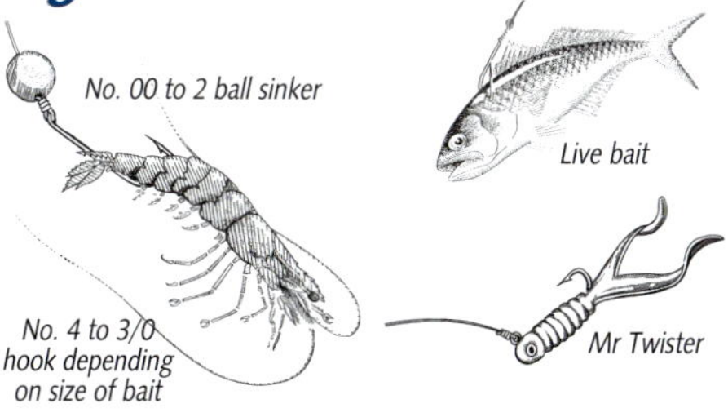

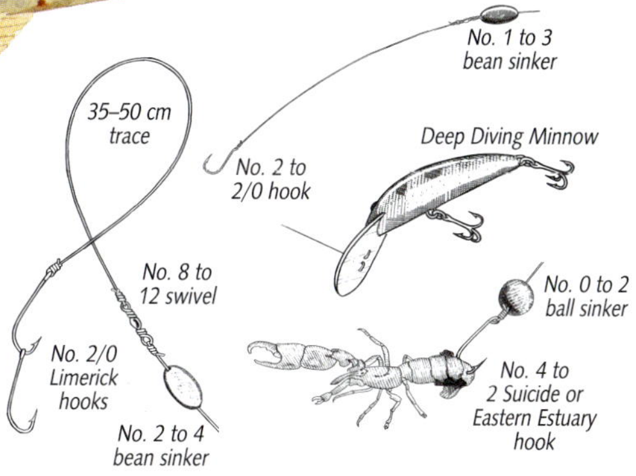

No. 00 to 2 ball sinker

No. 4 to 3/0 hook depending on size of bait

Live bait

Mr Twister

35–50 cm trace

No. 8 to 12 swivel

No. 2/0 Limerick hooks

No. 2 to 4 bean sinker

No. 1 to 3 bean sinker

No. 2 to 2/0 hook

Deep Diving Minnow

No. 0 to 2 ball sinker

No. 4 to 2 Suicide or Eastern Estuary hook

FLATHEAD, TIGER

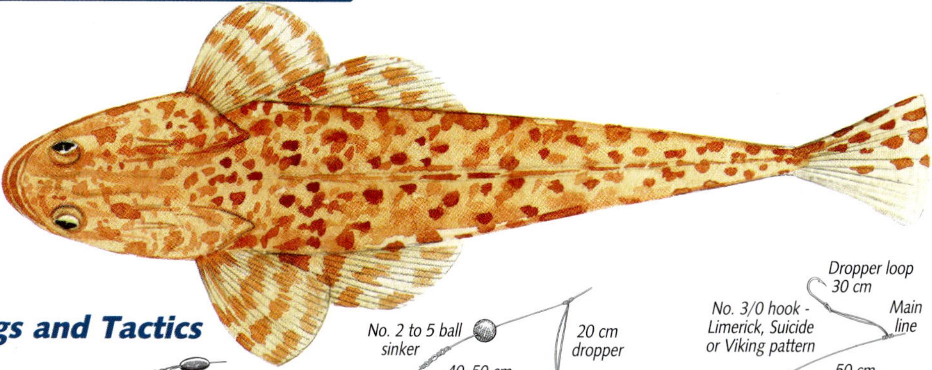

Rigs and Tactics

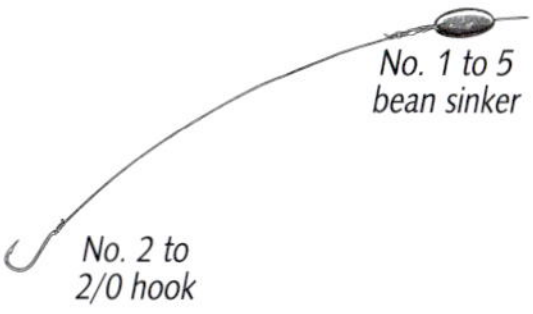

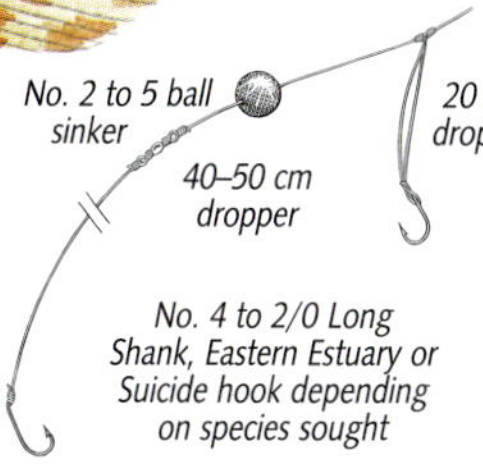

No. 1 to 5 bean sinker

No. 2 to 2/0 hook

No. 2 to 5 ball sinker

40–50 cm dropper

20 cm dropper

No. 4 to 2/0 Long Shank, Eastern Estuary or Suicide hook depending on species sought

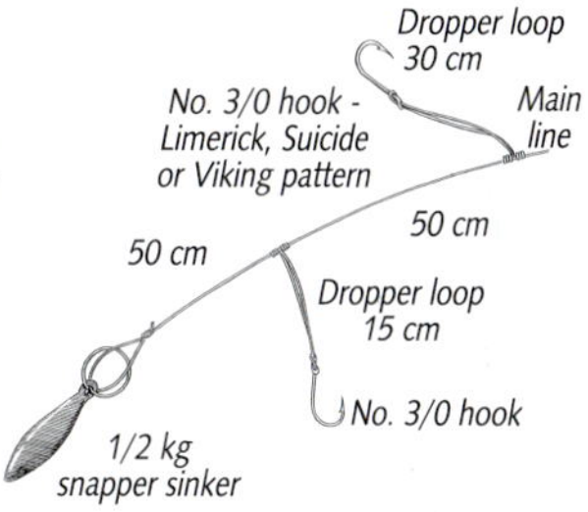

Dropper loop 30 cm

No. 3/0 hook - Limerick, Suicide or Viking pattern

Main line

50 cm

50 cm

Dropper loop 15 cm

No. 3/0 hook

1/2 kg snapper sinker

FLOUNDER, GREENBACK

Rigs and Tactics

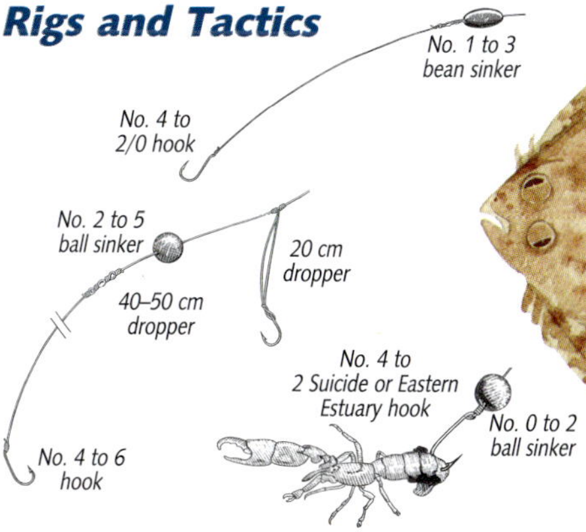

No. 1 to 3 bean sinker

No. 4 to 2/0 hook

No. 2 to 5 ball sinker

40–50 cm dropper

20 cm dropper

No. 4 to 2 Suicide or Eastern Estuary hook

No. 0 to 2 ball sinker

No. 4 to 6 hook

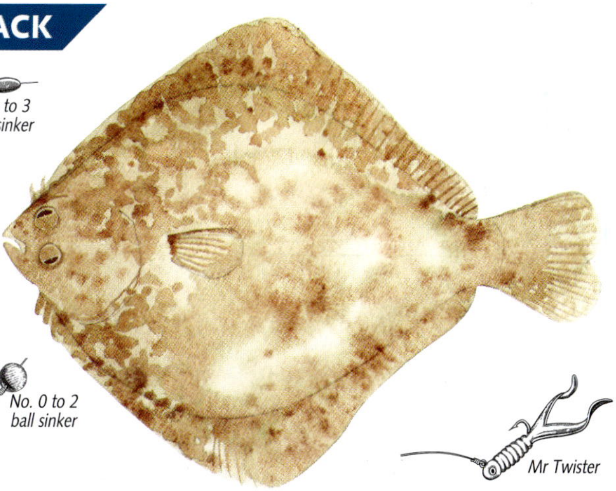

Mr Twister

FLOUNDER, LARGE TOOTHED

Scientific name *Pseudorhombus arsius*. Also known as Flounder.

Range Found in varying numbers throughout Australia, but rare in South Australia and south of Cockburn Sound in Western Australia.

Description The large toothed flounder is a left eyed flounder, i.e. both eyes are on the left side after the right eye migrates around the head during juvenile development. This species has highly variable colouration which can change rapidly, depending on the bottom where it is found. It ranges from the shallow mud and sand banks of estuaries to depths of 35 fathoms. The large toothed flounded possesses large front teeth in its upper and lower jaws. Reaches 50 cm and more than 1 kg but is most common at 30 to 35 centimetres. Flounders have a separate tail which easily distinguishes them from the sole which is another flat fish.

Fishing These flounder are most often a pleasant addition to catches of flathead, bream and whiting. They can take a reasonably large bait and fish flesh, small whole fish and prawns are most often successful. As with other ambush feeders, a more mobile approach and lighter line increases catches. Flounders take small lures readily, with lead head jigs, small minnow lures, wobblers and flies providing great sport. Flounders make excellent eating.

FLOUNDER, LONG-SNOUTED

Scientific name *Ammotretis rostratus*. Also known as Bay flounder, spotted flounder, sole (incorrectly), long-nosed flounder.

Range From Augusta in Western Australia around the southern shores and Tasmania to Port Macquarie in NSW.

Description The long-snouted flounder is a right eyed flounder, with both eyes on the right side. This species has a very rounded head caused by the snout being modified to form a soft, fleshy hook. There are white spots and dots across the body and fins. The square and clearly separate tail ensures that there should be no confusion with the true sole. This species can reach a maximum size of 34 centimetres.

Fishing Taken from coastal waters throughout its range on sand mud and fine gravel bottoms on baits of fish, prawn, nipper and worms. The small mouth means that small or long hooks are an advantage. They are excellent eating and a welcome addition to a mixed bag.

FLOUNDER, SMALL TOOTHED

Scientific name *Pseudorhombus jenynsii*.

Range A generally cooler water species but found from Exmouth Gulf in Western Australia around the southern states but rarely from Tasmania to central Queensland.

Description The small toothed flounder is also left-eyed and similar to the large toothed flounder but does not possess large teeth in the jaws. This species also has five or six prominent eye spots on the body which are an aggregation of small brown spots surrounded by white. Grows to 36 centimetres.

Fishing The small toothed flounder is taken from similar habitats as the other flounders and with similar baits. Flounder can often be taken by drifting or casting to the deeper edges of drop-offs or near the edges of gravel, mud and sand where these fish often lie in wait. Small toothed flounder can also be taken on jigs. Although not a large species, the shape and bone structure lends itself to a tasty and attractive plate presentation.

FLOUNDER, LARGE TOOTHED

Rigs and Tactics

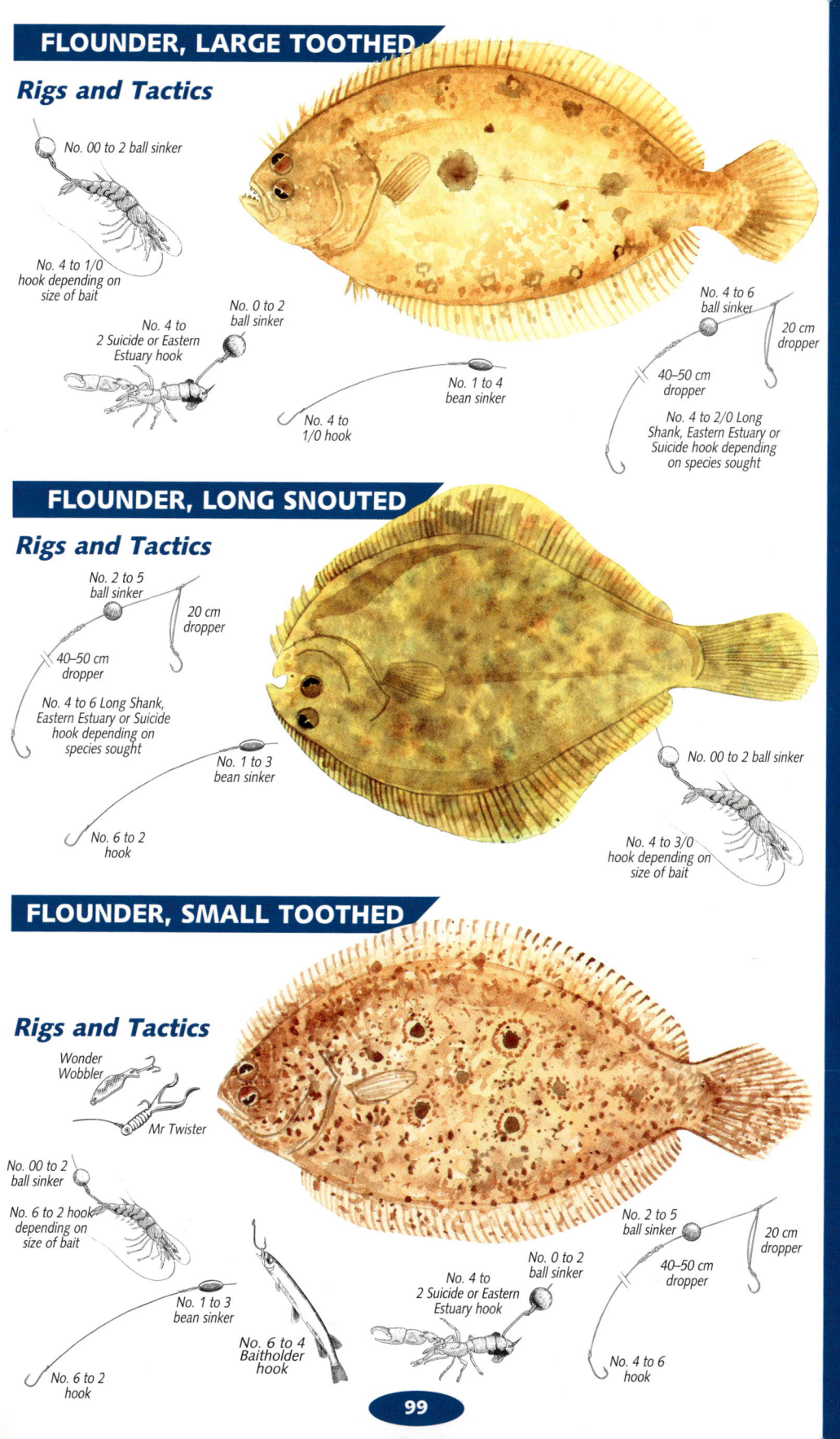

No. 00 to 2 ball sinker

No. 4 to 1/0 hook depending on size of bait

No. 4 to 2 Suicide or Eastern Estuary hook

No. 0 to 2 ball sinker

No. 1 to 4 bean sinker

No. 4 to 1/0 hook

No. 4 to 6 ball sinker

20 cm dropper

40–50 cm dropper

No. 4 to 2/0 Long Shank, Eastern Estuary or Suicide hook depending on species sought

FLOUNDER, LONG SNOUTED

Rigs and Tactics

No. 2 to 5 ball sinker

20 cm dropper

40–50 cm dropper

No. 4 to 6 Long Shank, Eastern Estuary or Suicide hook depending on species sought

No. 1 to 3 bean sinker

No. 6 to 2 hook

No. 00 to 2 ball sinker

No. 4 to 3/0 hook depending on size of bait

FLOUNDER, SMALL TOOTHED

Rigs and Tactics

Wonder Wobbler

Mr Twister

No. 00 to 2 ball sinker

No. 6 to 2 hook depending on size of bait

No. 1 to 3 bean sinker

No. 6 to 2 hook

No. 6 to 4 Baitholder hook

No. 4 to 2 Suicide or Eastern Estuary hook

No. 0 to 2 ball sinker

No. 2 to 5 ball sinker

20 cm dropper

40–50 cm dropper

No. 4 to 6 hook

FORTESCUE, EASTERN

Scientific name *Centropogon australis* Also known as Southern fortescue, fortescue, fortie

Range Hervey Bay in Queensland to Eden in southern NSW. The western fortescue is found from Dampia in Western Australia to Kangaroo Island in South Australia.

Description A small species that packs a definite punch. The reputation of this species far exceeds the 10 cm length that it can reach simply because an encounter can result in a trip to the hospital to treat a puncture wound from the 16 venomous dorsal spines. The fortescue is off white with a number of chocolate brown wide stripes along the body. The tail can also have dark bars. The dorsal spines are prominent and are erect whenever danger threatens. There are also two prominent spines on the preoperculum which, though not poisonous, can inflict a nasty wound and cause concern as the person waits to see if it was a dorsal spine which inflicted the damage. The similar western fortescue (*Centropogon latifrons*) is equally unpopular and is separated by the range and the shorter dorsal spines. This form of close taxonomic inspection is not recommended for amateurs, as even dead specimens can be poisonous.
The similar soldierfish (*Gymnapistes marmoratus*) is found from Fremantle to Sydney in southern water. It is also known as the devilfish or South Australian cobbler. It grows to 23 cm and is scaleless. The soldierfish only has 13 poisonous spines which is little comfort to someone who is stung. All these species are found in estuaries or coastal bays with a preference for weed beds or sponge gardens.

Fishing The Eastern fortescue is often seen by divers but is most commonly encountered by prawn drag netters. This species represents a real risk to those sorting through the weeds, prawns and other debris in the cod-end of a prawn net. To be stung results in an intense pain. Fever and sweating can result. First aid is to immerse the wound in hot water to 'cook' the protein in the venom, immobilise the limb and seek medical attention where pain killer may be applied. Due to its small size, fortescue are rarely taken on a hook, although the larger bullrout can be taken on a variety of baits.

HAIRTAIL

Scientific name *Trichiurus lepturus*. Also known as Ribbonfish, Australian hairtail, largehead hairtail, cutlassfish.

Range Found with a disjointed distribution in deeper estuaries or harbours from Shark Bay in Western Australia to Victoria and South Australia and as far as southern Queensland.

Description The hairtail is a brilliantly silver fish which is strongly compressed and elongated, growing to 2.35 m and a weight of 6 kg, although it is frequently encountered at around 1.5 to 1.8 metres. The hairtail has fearsome fangs which also possess an anti-coagulant, making any cuts bleed profusely. The hairtail has no tail, whereas the similar frostfish (*Lepidopus caudatus*) has a tiny forked tail. The hairtail has no scales, but the brilliant silver skin can be removed by rubbing with a rough cloth. They appear in some estuaries sporadically and in large numbers, but then may not be seen for several more years. The best bets for these fish are in Coal and Candle and Cowan Creeks in the Hawkesbury system and Port Kembla and Newcastle harbours in NSW during autumn and especially winter months, but commercial fishing has had an impact.

Fishing The vast majority of fish are taken at night. The hairtail is a predator which prefers live bait, with yellowtail and slimy mackerel favoured. Hairtail are often taken on dead fish such as garfish, pilchards or fresh cut flesh. Hairtail will strike lures including diving lures and vertically jigged lures or jigs when feeding well but hook-ups are difficult through the teeth. Wire traces or ganged hooks are essential and some anglers use light sticks to assist hairtail finding the bait. As the fish are found in deep holes, setting baits at different depths until fish are found will rapidly locate the optimum depth so all baits can be moved to the same level. The hairtail is excellent to eat with delicate flesh which cooks very quickly.

Rigs and Tactics

Not applicable as Eastern Fortescue are not recommended as an angling species.

HAIRTAIL

Rigs and Tactics

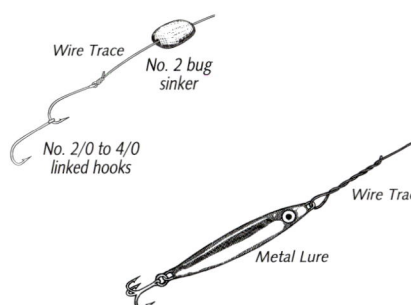

Wire Trace

No. 2 bug sinker

No. 2/0 to 4/0 linked hooks

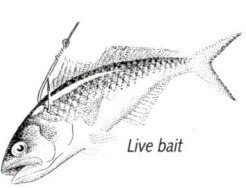

Live bait

Wire Trace

Metal Lure

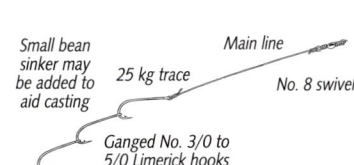

Small bean sinker may be added to aid casting

25 kg trace

Main line

No. 8 swivel

Ganged No. 3/0 to 5/0 Limerick hooks

HERRING, AUSTRALIAN

Scientific name *Arripis georgiana.* Also known as Tommy rough, tommy, ruff, bull herring, Western herring.

Range Taken from Shark Bay in Western Australia along the south coast to the far south coast of NSW but more commonly south of Gippsland Lakes in Victoria and Geraldton in Western Australia.

Description A pretty and highly sought after species, especially in South Australia and Western Australia, the Australian herring is not a 'true' hering from the family Clupidae. Although the Australian herring can reach 40 cm, they are commonly caught at between 22 and 28 centimetres. The herring is similar to the closely related juvenile Australian salmon, but the herring has a larger eye, black tips on the ends of the tail fin lobes and no black blotch at the base of the pectoral fin. The herring's scales feel rough when rubbed towards the head which gives rise to the common name 'ruff', whereas an Australian salmon feels smooth.

Fishing Australian herring specialists can turn angling for these scrappy little fighters to an art form. Standard rigs include a wooden blob (float) whose hole is filled with pollard and pilchard oil, a reasonably long trace and a bait of maggot, prawn, squid or blue bait. When biting freely, Australian herring are taken on pieces of green drinking straw as bait. Herring are an inshore schooling fish which is commonly taken from rock groynes and beaches and are attracted to berley slicks when boat angling, especially inshore around shallow sea grass beds. Best berley includes bread, pollard, finely chopped fish scraps and chip pieces leftover from the local fish and chip shop. Herring are also taken on lures, with Halco wobblers and Tassie Devils or any small lure with red working well. On lures, herring jump as well as their cousins the salmon and although some throw the hooks, they are terrific fun. Herring are also very good eating and far superior to Australian salmon.

HERRING, GIANT

Scientific name *Elops machnata.* Also known as Pincushion-fish.

Range A mainly tropical species, the general range is from Albany in Western Australia around the top end and throughout Queensland to Nowra in NSW, although giant herring have been recorded from South Australia.

Description The giant herring is a beautiful, streamlined fish covered in small scales which are easily dislodged. This species is the largest of the true herrings (Family Clupidae), reaching 1.2 m and 11 kg, although it is frequently encountered at 1 – 4 kilograms. The giant herring has a single dorsal fin with a tiny trailing last ray compared to the tarpon (*page 138*) which has a prominent trailing filament and a much larger eye. The giant herring has a very large upper jaw. The giant herring moves southward with warm currents and is found more commonly in summer and early autumn in more southern areas.

Fishing The giant herring is attracting increasing attention as its qualities as a sports fish are being recognised. Giant herring take trolled or cast lures such as wobblers, spoons and small minnow lures readily and are a challenging proposition on the fly. Giant herring will also take live or fresh fish and prawns. Their spectacular leaps enhance their fight. The giant herring is full of fine bones which make them a very poor table fish. Their loose scales means that they need to be carefully handled to survive release.

HERRING, AUSTRALIAN

Rigs and Tactics

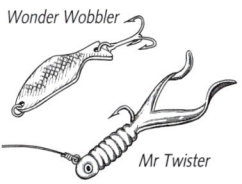

Wonder Wobbler

Mr Twister

3 kg line

1 metre

Small float

Berley float

No. 6 to 10 Kendall
Kirby or Long
Shank hooks

HERRING, GIANT

Rigs and Tactics

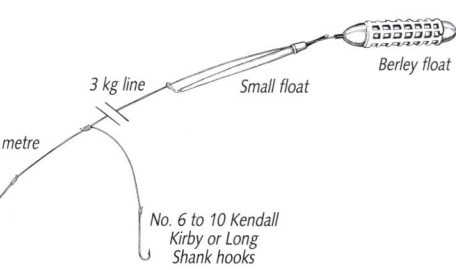

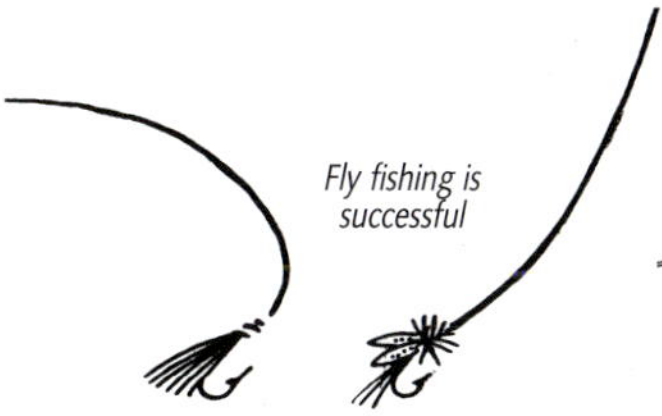

Fly fishing is
successful

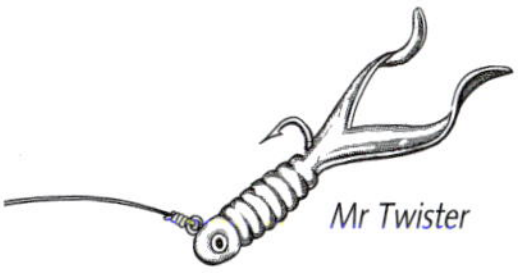

Mr Twister

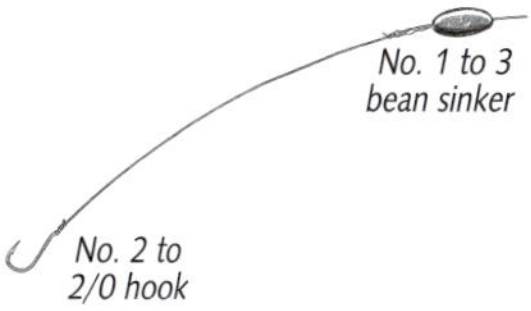

No. 1 to 3
bean sinker

No. 2 to
2/0 hook

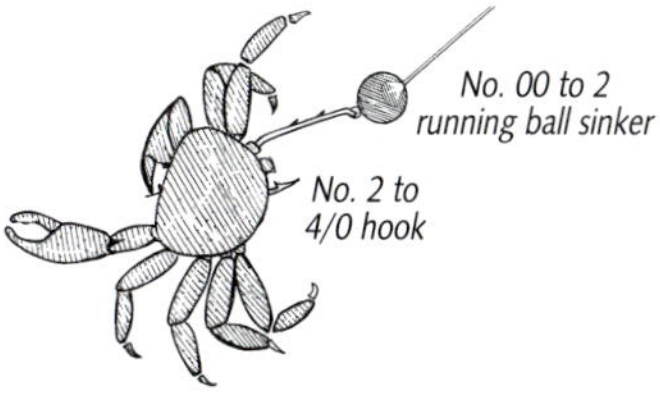

No. 00 to 2
running ball sinker

No. 2 to
4/0 hook

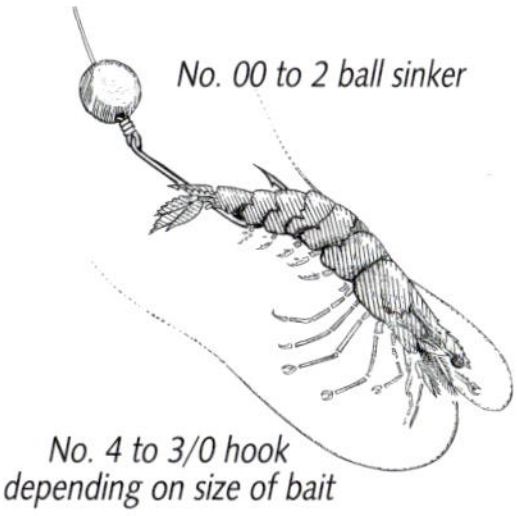

No. 00 to 2 ball sinker

No. 4 to 3/0 hook
depending on size of bait

JAVELIN FISH, SPOTTED

Scientific name *Pomadasys kaakan.* Also known as Spotted grunter-bream, grunter.

Range Shark Bay in Western Australia including northern waters and to around Evans Head in northern NSW, but essentially a tropical species.

Description The spotted javelin fish possesses black spots between the prominent spines of the dorsal fin, although these are much reduced in adult fish. The anal spine is large and prominent, giving rise to the name javelin fish. These fish grind their sharp pharyngeal (throat) teeth which is amplified by the fishes swim bladder. The spotted javelin fish is commonly found at the mouths of mangrove creeks and off rocky foreshores. They can reach 66 cm and 4.5 kilograms.

Fishing The javelin fish feeds on prawns, crabs, worms, small fish and squid and can be taken on all these baits. The javelin fish will often run with the bait before taking it into their mouths. Therefore running sinkers and relatively light line at 4 – 6 kg is an advantage. The javelin fish can be caught on minnow lures and jigs but are rarely fished for specifically in this manner. Javelin fish are a fine table fish which can be frozen at no cost to quality.

JEWFISH, BLACK

Scientific name *Protonibea diacanthus.* Also known as Black jew, Spotted croaker, Spotted jew, Blotched jewfish, black mulloway, northern mulloway.

Range Onslow northwards and northern waters to central Queensland as far as Rockhampton.

Description The black jewfish is a large and prized northern mulloway species, growing to 40 kg and more than 1.5 metres. The range is important as there are few locations where black jewfish and mulloway can be taken together. The black jewfish has two prominent anal spines whereas the mulloway has a small second anal spine. The soft dorsal fin has 22 to 25 rays as opposed to 28 to 31 rays for the smaller and lighter coloured silver jewfish (*Nibea soldado*) of north-eastern waters which also has white ventral fins. The black jewfish has a grey to blackish colour. Young fish have black spots on the back, dorsal and tail fins which fade in adult fish.

Fishing An excellent and highly prized species which frequents inshore reefs and is a famous target at the artificial reefs in Darwin Harbour. The black jewfish has a powerful first run and more stamina than mulloway. The black jewfish is more common in coastal waters, although they will enter estuaries, particularly as juveniles. Rigs are similar to those for mulloway, but their stronger runs and fondness for rough reefs or wrecks leads them to be taken on heavier lines or handlines. Fresh bait definitely improves catches with best being large live baits or fresh cut or whole fish, squid or fresh large prawns. The black jewfish is a prized for its size, tenacity and eating qualities which are excellent.

JAVELIN FISH, SPOTTED

Rigs and Tactics

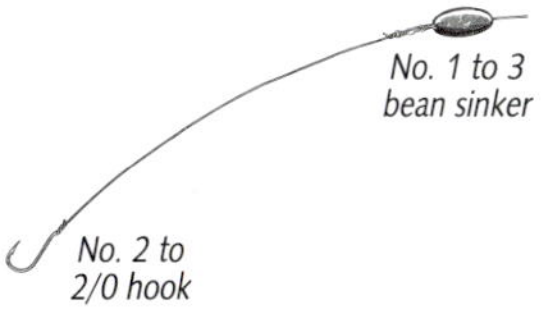

No. 1 to 3
bean sinker

No. 2 to
2/0 hook

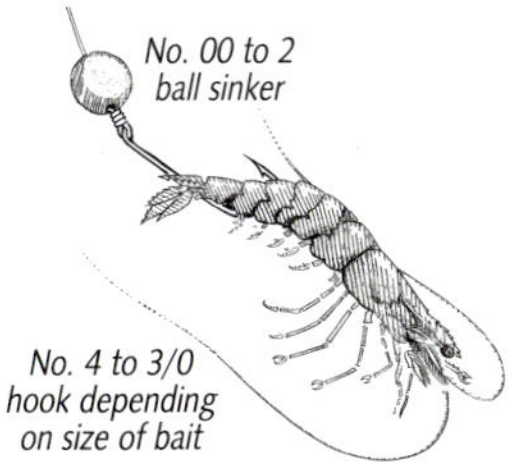

No. 00 to 2
ball sinker

No. 4 to 3/0
hook depending
on size of bait

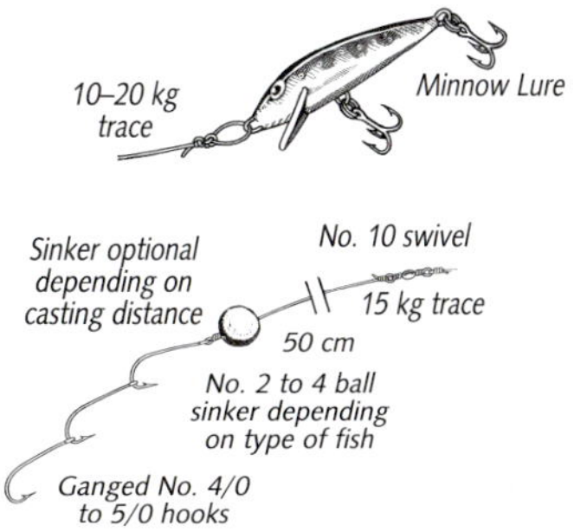

10–20 kg
trace

Minnow Lure

Sinker optional
depending on
casting distance

No. 10 swivel

15 kg trace

50 cm

No. 2 to 4 ball
sinker depending
on type of fish

Ganged No. 4/0
to 5/0 hooks

JEWFISH, BLACK

Rigs and Tactics

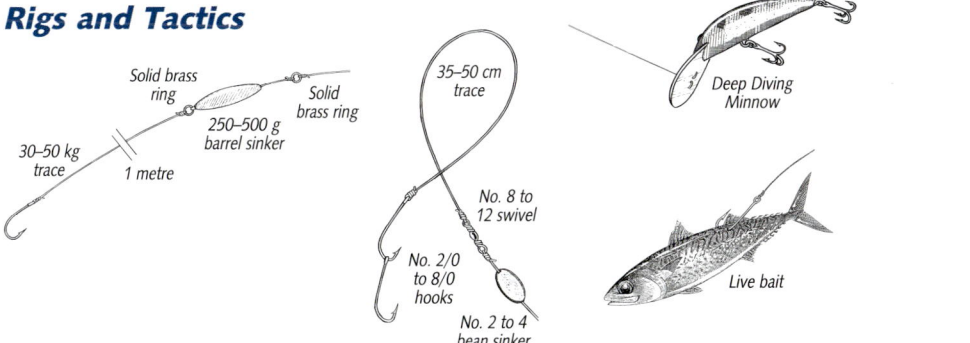

Solid brass
ring

Solid
brass ring

250–500 g
barrel sinker

30–50 kg
trace

1 metre

35–50 cm
trace

Deep Diving
Minnow

No. 8 to
12 swivel

No. 2/0
to 8/0
hooks

No. 2 to 4
bean sinker

Live bait

LEATHERJACKET, FAN-BELLIED

Scientific name *Monocanthus chinensis* Also known as fantail leatherjacket, pouched leatherjacket, pigfish

Range Geographe Bay in Western Australia and northwards through tropical waters and then as far south as Narooma in NSW

Description An unusual species of leatherjacket which reaches 38 centimetres. The fan-bellied leatherjacket prefers areas of seagrass or seagrass adjacent to reefs in larger estuaries and bays. The fan-bellied leatherjacket is easily recognised by the large fan-like pouch on the abdomen. There is a large trailing filament on the top of the tail fin and there are six spines on each side of the wrist of the tail. The back rises up beyond the front spine to the dorsal fin, giving a characteristic triangular shape to the top of the fish. The colour can range from pale brown or yellow brown, through various blotched browns and to nearly black, due largely to the type of habitat in which the fish was taken.

Fishing The fan-bellied leatherjacket is taken on a wide variety of baits and rigs. A small, long shanked hook is recommended due to the small mouth and capacity of leatherjackets to bite off light traces. Using as light a weight as possible will increase bites and hook-ups and enhance the fight of these scrappy fish. The fan-bellied leatherjacket responds to berley and can be considered a pest and a bait stealer. Larger fan-bellied leatherjackets are excellent eating. Smaller fish yield a small but tasty piece of meat when headed and skinned.

LEATHERJACKET, ROUGH

Scientific name *Scobinichthys granulatus*.

Range Shark Bay in Western Australia and southern waters all the way around to Torres Strait in Queensland.

Description This species reaches 34 cm and has no notch for the prominent dorsal spine to lay back into. The rough leather jacket has a large ventral flap, three dark lines across the forehead and dark blotchings over the back and sides. It is common in coastal seagrass beds and adjacent reefs and in estuaries.

Fishing The rough leatherjacket will take prawns, squid, crabs, worms and cut baits. A wire trace or long shank hook can prevent bite-offs. A light line and minimal weight for the conditions can improve the fight of leatherjackets. This species is good eating.

LEATHERJACKET, SIX SPINED

Scientific name *Meuschenia freycineti* Also known as variable leatherjacket

Range Disjointed range from Jurien Bay in Western Australia to Wilson's Promontory, including Tasmania and then from eastern Victoria to Broughton Island in NSW.

Description The six-spined leatherjacket can reach the respectable size of 60 cm, with larger specimens found from the south coast population, although the east coast fish can be more brightly coloured. The six-spined leatherjacket is most easily identified by the prominent scribble pattern in blue or brown on the head and front part of the body. The dorsal and anal fins are yellow in the adult. The tail fin often has a black blotch at its base and a prominent black stripe, especially males. Males often have a yellow and brown blotch on their sides. Females are much less brightly coloured. There are 5 to 8 spines on each side of the wrist of the tail. Adults are usually encountered on coastal reefs whereas juveniles, which often have prominent brown stripes along the sides and less prominent scribbling on the head, are common on seagrass meadows of estuaries and coastal bays.

Fishing Like all leatherjackets, the six-spined leatherjacket has a small mouth and a capacity to pick larger baits intended for the larger reef fish. They show a marked preference for squid or prawn baits but can be taken on a wide variety of baits. A fairly small, long shanked hook is recommended and some anglers use a light wire trace to avoid bite-offs. The difficulty in hooking leatherjackets is more than offset by their excellent eating qualities. They can be headed and the skin peeled off by hand for a very high quality meal.

LEATHERJACKET, FAN-BELLIED

Rigs and Tactics

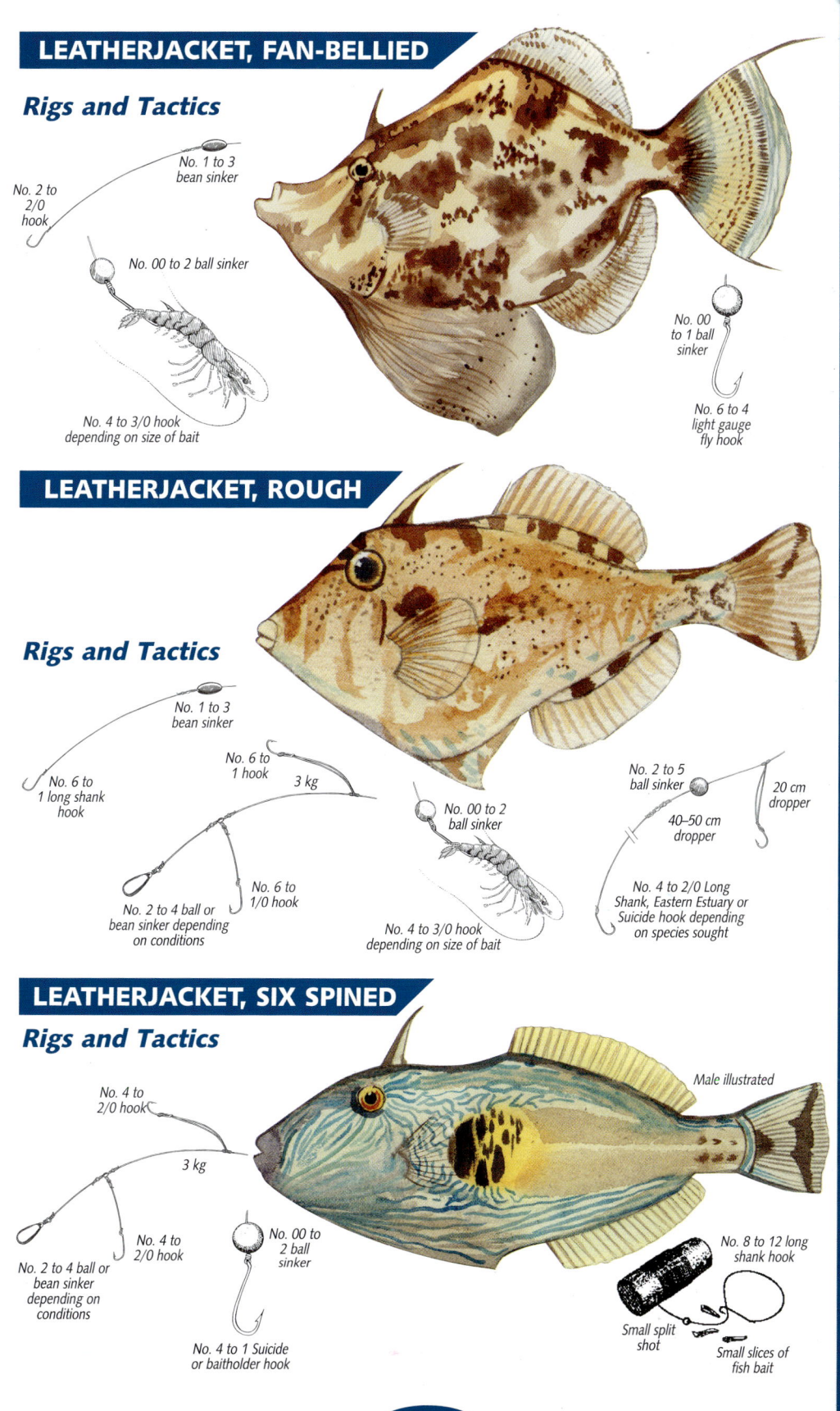

No. 1 to 3
bean sinker

No. 2 to
2/0
hook

No. 00 to 2 ball sinker

No. 4 to 3/0 hook
depending on size of bait

No. 00
to 1 ball
sinker

No. 6 to 4
light gauge
fly hook

LEATHERJACKET, ROUGH

Rigs and Tactics

No. 1 to 3
bean sinker

No. 6 to
1 long shank
hook

No. 6 to
1 hook

3 kg

No. 2 to 4 ball or
bean sinker depending
on conditions

No. 6 to
1/0 hook

No. 00 to 2
ball sinker

No. 4 to 3/0 hook
depending on size of bait

No. 2 to 5
ball sinker

40–50 cm
dropper

20 cm
dropper

No. 4 to 2/0 Long
Shank, Eastern Estuary or
Suicide hook depending
on species sought

LEATHERJACKET, SIX SPINED

Rigs and Tactics

Male illustrated

No. 4 to
2/0 hook

3 kg

No. 4 to
2/0 hook

No. 00 to
2 ball
sinker

No. 2 to 4 ball or
bean sinker
depending on
conditions

No. 4 to 1 Suicide
or baitholder hook

No. 8 to 12 long
shank hook

Small split
shot

Small slices of
fish bait

LONGTOM, SLENDER

Scientific name *Stronylura leiura* Also known as common longtom

Range Albany in Western Australia and around the Western Australian coast, around tropical waters and the east coast to around the Gippsland Lakes in Victoria.

Description The common name is quite apt as the slender longtom is a slender and sleek species. The slender longtom is most easily separated from other longtoms by the bar along the base of the gill cover which can fade after death. The tail fin is square or may be convex. The jaws are elongated and fine and filled with needle sharp teeth. The slender longtom is most commonly found in coastal waters and can be found in large bays and estuaries. This species can reach 110 cm but is most frequently encountered in estuaries at a smaller size.

Fishing Longtoms can provide spectacular sport, jumping wildly when hooked. The very bony jaws make the longtoms hard to hook and keep connected to. They make reasonable eating, but their green bones put many people off. The slender longtom takes a wide variety of lures including poppers, metal slices, jigs and minnow lures and can make a real mess of wooden lures with their teeth. Longtoms will take a variety of baits, with pilchards and cut baits working best. Longtoms can also attack hooked fish.

LONGTOM, STOUT

Scientific name *Tylosurus gavialoides*. Also known as Needlefish, alligator gar.

Range Shark Bay northwards and around the top end to northern NSW around Coffs Harbour.

Description This is a large and widely distributed species of longtom, reaching 1.3 m in length. All longtoms are easily identified by having both jaws extended and full of needle sharp teeth. The stout longtom lacks the keel near the tail of the crocodile longtom (*Tylosurus crocodilus*) which is also slightly more robust. The stout longtom is bright green across the back and upper sides and the pectoral fins have dusky tips. The stout longtom can be found in inshore waters and can attack larger baits intended for mackerel and tuna. Longtoms also jump strongly at lights, making night fishing in some areas very interesting.

Fishing The stout longtom is very game and will attack large and small lures and baits. They are an interesting proposition on fly and lure, but their bony mouths make hooking up very difficult. Any live, whole or cut fish bait will attract longtom, but moving the bait will attract more strikes. Longtom have green or blue green bones and are not highly regarded as food fish. Some care should be exercised when releasing longtom as they have been known to turn rapidly and bite the hand which releases it.

MADO

Scientific name *Atypichthys strigatus*. Also known as Mado sweep.

Range From the Gold Coast southwards to Geelong in Victoria and occasionally in northern Tasmania.

Description The mado is a distinctive fish, white with 6 or 7 prominent brown stripes running lengthwise and extending onto the head. The stripes above the lateral line are most prominent. The pectoral and ventral fins are white but all other fins are bright yellow. The mado can reach 25 cm but is often encountered at 10 – 15 centimetres. They are extremely common around jetties and pylons and rocky outcrops, particularly in more sheltered waters.

Fishing This is frequently the first species caught by budding anglers with a handline on sheltered east coast jetties. They are enthusiastic biters and provide reasonable, if underrated sport and unlimited enjoyment. As mado have a small mouth, a small size 6 – 10 hook baited with fish flesh, prawn, squid, pipi, worm or nearly any small bait will take these fish. Mado react well to any berley and with other species make a colourful school of eager and forgiving targets. Mado are generally better regarded as cat food but many beginning anglers have proudly presented mado to the family for their first personally caught fish feed.

LONGTOM, SLENDER

Rigs and Tactics

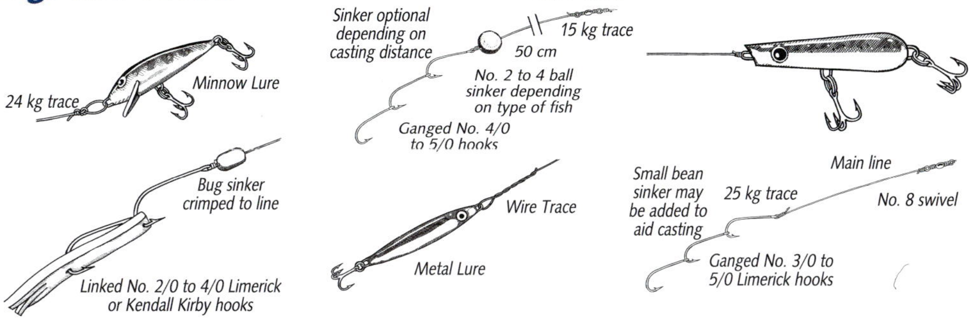

24 kg trace
Minnow Lure

Bug sinker
crimped to line

Linked No. 2/0 to 4/0 Limerick
or Kendall Kirby hooks

Sinker optional
depending on
casting distance

No. 10 swivel

15 kg trace

50 cm

No. 2 to 4 ball
sinker depending
on type of fish

Ganged No. 4/0
to 5/0 hooks

Wire Trace

Metal Lure

Small bean
sinker may
be added to
aid casting

Main line

25 kg trace

No. 8 swivel

Ganged No. 3/0 to
5/0 Limerick hooks

LONGTOM, STOUT

Rigs and Tactics

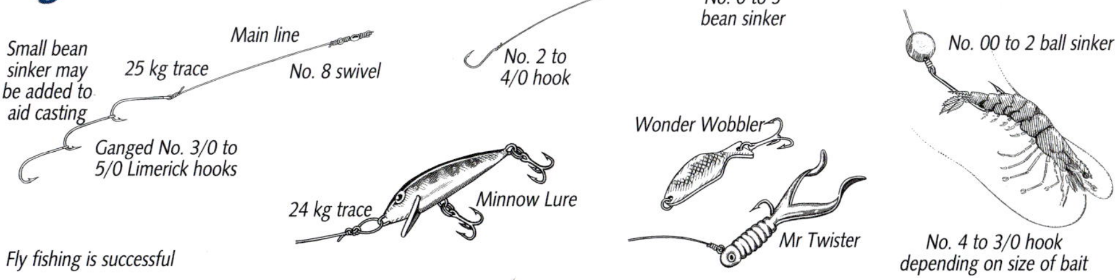

Small bean
sinker may
be added to
aid casting

Main line

25 kg trace

No. 8 swivel

Ganged No. 3/0 to
5/0 Limerick hooks

Fly fishing is successful

24 kg trace
Minnow Lure

Wire trace

No. 0 to 3
bean sinker

No. 2 to
4/0 hook

Wonder Wobbler

Mr Twister

No. 00 to 2 ball sinker

No. 4 to 3/0 hook
depending on size of bait

MADO

Rigs and Tactics

No. 12 to
8 hook

30–50 cm

No. 1 to 4 bean sinker

Brass ring or
small swivel

No. 00 to
2 ball
sinker

No. 12 to 8
Suicide or
baitholder hook

Rigs stand
off main line

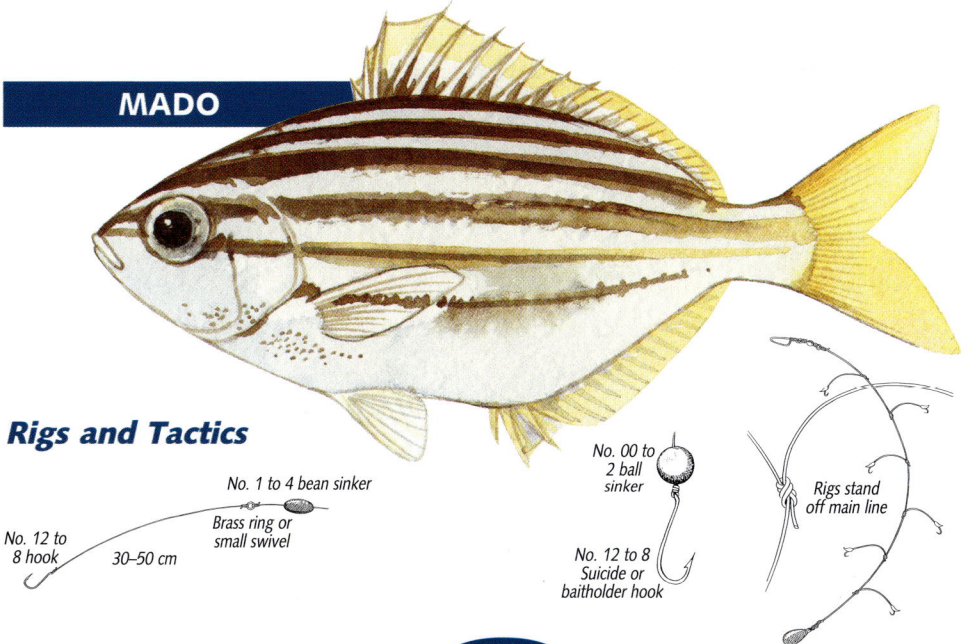

LUDERICK

Scientific name *Girella tricuspidata*. Also known as Blackfish, darkie, bronzie, nigger.

Range Occurs from around Noosa Heads in Queensland around to Adelaide and including Tasmania.

Description A very handsome fish, the luderick has up to 12 narrow vertical dark bars on its upper body. The colour varies from almost black to a pale purplish colour depending on the amount of wash in the area of capture. The tail fin is darker than the body. Luderick are a schooling species, although the largest specimens form much smaller groups. Luderick can reach 70 cm and more than 2 kg but are more common at between 500 and 900 grams. The blackfish can be separated from the similar Zebra fish which has bars which are wider than the spaces between and yellowish fin colouration. The related bluefish (*Girella cyanea*) is only found in NSW and is bright blue with yellow spots. The rock blackfish (black drummer or pig) is often caught in the same oceanic areas as the luderick but lacks the vertical bars. The rock blackfish is a much stronger and dirtier fighting fish.

Fishing There is much mystique associated with fishing for the largely herbivorous luderick. Chasing this species can become addictive and the high skill levels of the best anglers can put off beginners. However, a bit of patience and good observation skills in watching what other anglers are doing and keeping a close eye on wave conditions can bring good rewards. While some quality luderick angling can be had in estuaries, it is fishing from ocean rocks which provides the greatest challenge. A long soft action rod is most important, to quickly pick up slack line during swells and when setting the hook, to cushion the fight of the fish and to assist in washing the fish up when landing it. A centrepin reel is favoured so that line can be paid out quickly during the drift, but many anglers do well with other gear, including threadline outfits. The most effective rig is a well balanced float rig. In heavy swells with lots of white water, use a larger float. In calmer waters or estuaries, a float as light as a porcupine quill or coarse angling float is all that is required. As a rule, the lower the swell, the deeper you fish; up to three metres or so. A light trace (around 3 kg) is important when using a sliding float rig, to prevent the loss of the float to snags, broken off fish or express train drummer which can bust up the more delicate luderick gear. The weight set above and on the trace is such that all but the tip of the float is under the water while fishing. Split shot can be moved around so that the rig does not tangle while casting. Allow the float to fully disappear below the surface before taking up the slack line on a smooth strike action. The two most common baits are string or ribbon weed, which can be found in estuaries and rock pools with sandy substrates, or cabbage (*Ulva latuca*). Cabbage is usually growing right under your feet while fishing for luderick. Use some for berley, either trickled into the water or chopped and mixed with sand. Berley is very important as it attracts nearby schools of luderick and fishing can go from woe to full on very quickly. With cabbage, the best bait is a small tight rosette, with the hook inserted through the nodule at the base of the rosette. A fairly small tidy bright green bait with no faded white edges works best. Wind string weed around the hook so that it puffs out nicely in the water. Work the water close in first, as blackfish can be virtually under your feet. Luderick are rarely taken very far past the edge of the active, fairly turbulent water in the wash zone. Luderick are also taken on rigs designed for rock blackfish, bream and whiting. From the rocks, they will take small cunjevoi baits, but unfortunately, every other fish in the area also picks at the bait. Peeled prawns on a small running sinker rig work well. In estuaries, prawns, worms and nippers (bass yabbies) collect a mixed bag including any luderick in the area. Luderick make good eating if bled and cleaned soon after killing. It is important to gut the fish quickly or the flesh can take on a weed or iodine taint.

Rigs and Tactics

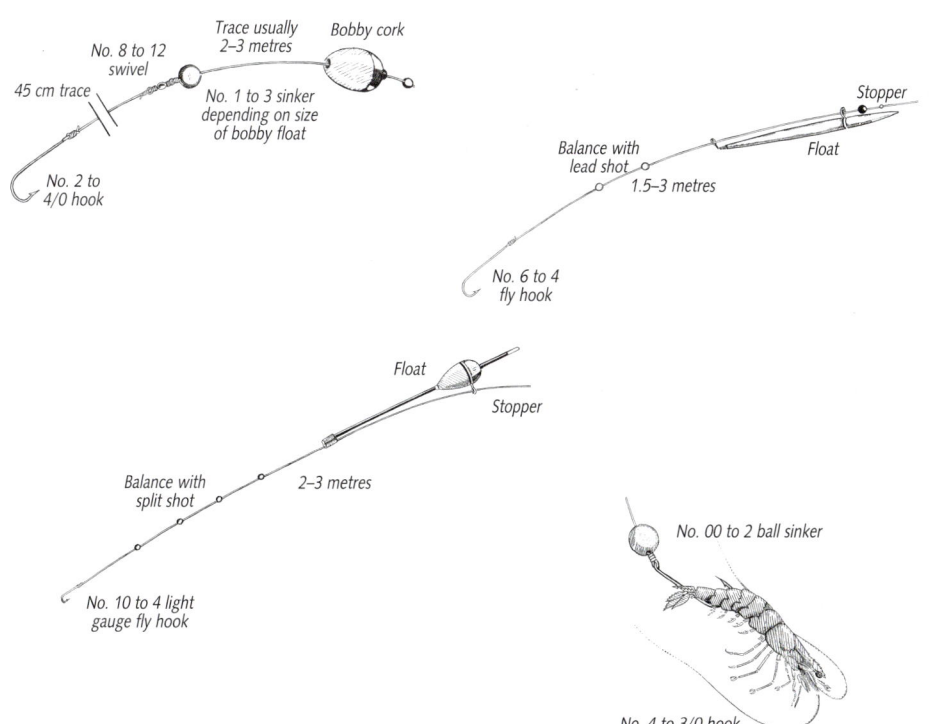

45 cm trace

No. 8 to 12 swivel

Trace usually 2–3 metres

Bobby cork

No. 1 to 3 sinker depending on size of bobby float

No. 2 to 4/0 hook

Stopper

Float

Balance with lead shot

1.5–3 metres

No. 6 to 4 fly hook

Float

Stopper

Balance with split shot

2–3 metres

No. 10 to 4 light gauge fly hook

No. 00 to 2 ball sinker

No. 4 to 3/0 hook depending on size of bait

MANGROVE JACK

Scientific name *Lutjanus argentimaculatus*. Also known as Jacks, red bream, dog bream, red perch, reef red bream, purple sea perch, creek red bream.

Range Exmouth Gulf and tropical waters to around Coffs Harbour in northern NSW.

Description The mangrove jack is best known for its destruction of fishing tackle in tidal creeks, but these tend to be juvenile or small adult fish. The largest specimens are taken on offshore reefs to a depth of 100 metres. Mangrove jack can reach more than 1.2 m and a weight of 15 kg but fish in inshore waters are a real handful at 1 – 3 kilograms. The mangrove jack is often confused with the red bass, which is a much more notorious ciguatera species, especially if caught on reefs. The mangrove jack has a taller dorsal fin, a lack of lengthwise stripes on its side and the absence of black on the fins. Mangrove jacks lack the distinctive pit before the eye of the red bass which is predominantly a coral reef species.

Fishing Mangrove jack are arguably the toughest and dirtiest fighters (pound for pound) in Australian waters. They will dash out and engulf a lure or bait and break off an unwary angler on the nearest snag before they realise the strike has been made. As a result, mangrove jacks require quality, well maintained gear and tight drags. They can destroy cheap equipment as they dive into snags. Mangrove jacks like tough dirty cover although they can be found in deeper holes in tidal waters where they are a bit easier to handle. Diving lures, spinner baits, jigs and flies work well for jacks. They will take cut or whole fish baits, prawns, crabs and especially live baits. The strike is savage and a prelude to the action to come. Mangrove jacks taken on offshore reefs put up a strong fight, but the heavier gear usually used for tropical reef fishing gives a better chance of landing these fish. Mangrove jacks should be handled carefully as their dorsal and opercular spines can create a nasty wound, especially on water softened hands. Jacks can also take a nip at fingers while being unhooked, but are a hardy fish which survives handling well. The mangrove jack is good eating but in offshore waters should be carefully identified as red bass are a dangerous ciguatera species.

MILKFISH

Scientific name *Chanos chanos*. Also known as Moreton bay salmon, salmon herring.

Range Shark Bay in Western Australia northwards and throughout tropical waters to northern NSW.

Description The milkfish is a schooling fish capable of reaching 1.8 m and 15 kg although most commonly seen at 2 – 4 kilograms. The milkfish is a brilliant silvery fish which is distinguished by its very small, toothless mouth which suits its vegetarian diet. It has a large and deeply forked tail which provides enormous power. The scales are not shed as easily as with the giant herring which can also be found in estuaries. Milkfish can also be caught in shallow surf or near coastal reefs.

Fishing Milkfish are occasionally encountered accidentally by anglers fishing for species such as whiting with worm or pipi baits, but their vegetarian diet means that they can frustrate anglers who see a large shoal of large fish which refuse their offerings. Milkfish can provide excellent sport if heavily berleyed with bread and then fished for with a floated piece of crust on a small but strong hook. They can be taken by persistent fly fishers. The first run of the milkfish can strip the gears of cheaper tackle. Milkfish will challenge and delight sportsfishermen. Although milkfish are an aquaculture species in many parts of the world, they are considered poor eating in Australia with many small bones and bland flesh.

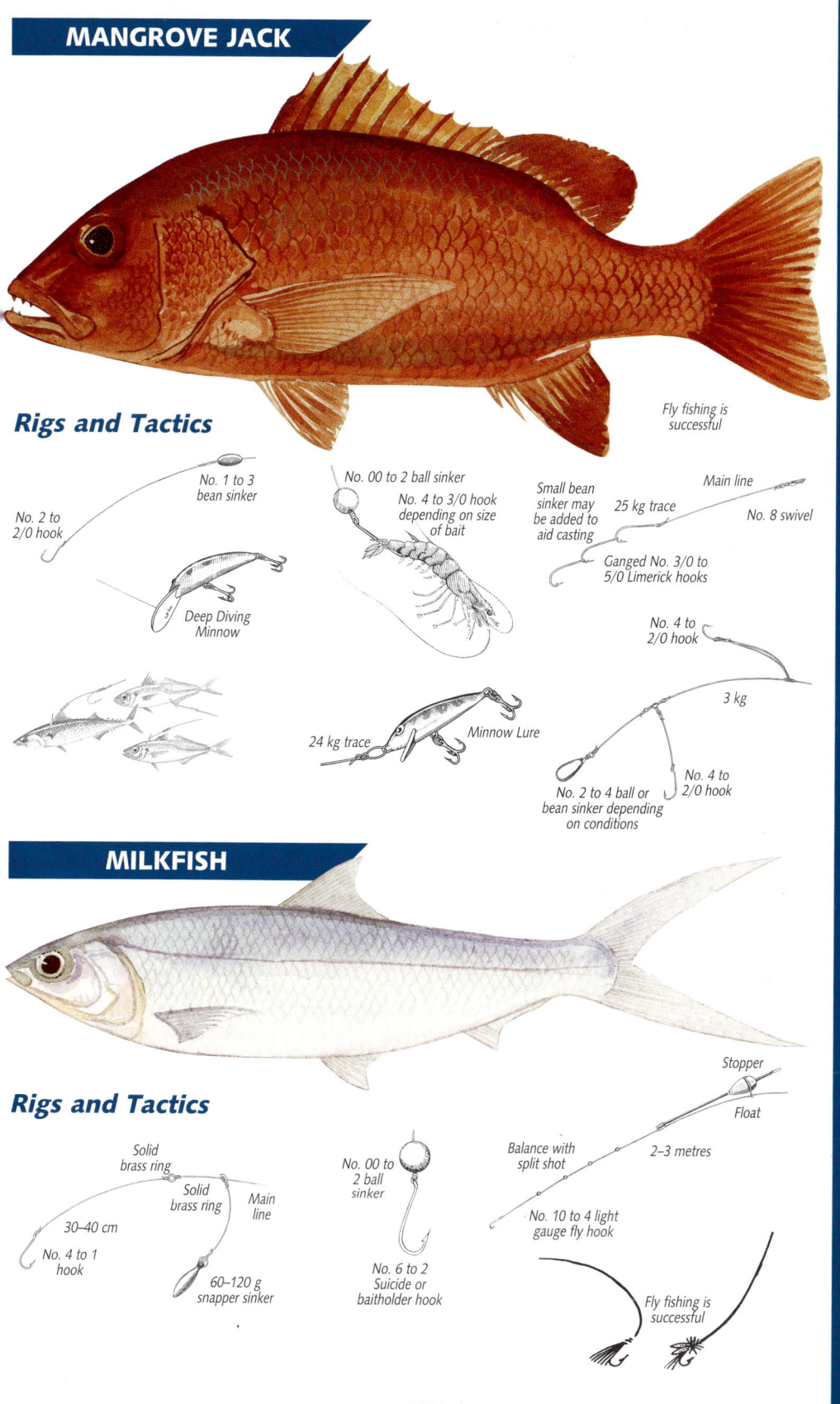

Fly fishing is successful

Rigs and Tactics

No. 1 to 3 bean sinker

No. 2 to 2/0 hook

Deep Diving Minnow

No. 00 to 2 ball sinker

No. 4 to 3/0 hook depending on size of bait

24 kg trace

Minnow Lure

Small bean sinker may be added to aid casting

Main line

25 kg trace

No. 8 swivel

Ganged No. 3/0 to 5/0 Limerick hooks

No. 4 to 2/0 hook

3 kg

No. 2 to 4 ball or bean sinker depending on conditions

No. 4 to 2/0 hook

Rigs and Tactics

Solid brass ring

Solid brass ring

Main line

30–40 cm

No. 4 to 1 hook

60–120 g snapper sinker

No. 00 to 2 ball sinker

No. 6 to 2 Suicide or baitholder hook

Stopper

Float

Balance with split shot

2–3 metres

No. 10 to 4 light gauge fly hook

Fly fishing is successful

MORWONG, DUSKY

Scientific name *Dactylophora nigricans* Also known as Strongfish, butterfish, tillywurti.

Range Lancelin in Western Australia and southern waters including Tasmania to Wilson's Promontory.

Description A large and handsome fish which is easily separated from the other morwongs by longer and more slender body. The dusky morwong can reach 1.2 metres and has the typical morwong mouth with the larger lips and down turned aspect. The pectoral fins have extended rays and the tail fin is prominently forked. Although the dusky morwong is often a slate grey colour, they can be almost silver when on sand and can be mistaken for mulloway from the shore, causing much excitement but no return.

Fishing The dusky morwong is almost never taken by line fishermen as they eat small items and rarely take bait. They are occasionally accidentally hooked on prawn, pipi, squid or worm baits intended for whiting or other species. This species will frequently rest on the bottom and is not easily spooked, making them an easy target for spearfishing. Poor eating.

MULLET, DIAMOND SCALE

Scientific name *Liza vaigiensis.* Also known as Large scale mullet.

Range Exmouth Gulf in Western Australia and around the top end to southern Queensland, occasionally venturing into NSW waters.

Description The diamond scale mullet is a distinctive species by virtue of its square or very slightly indented tail. The rear margin of the scales are black and form a striking diamond shaped pattern which leads to the common name. There are also around five to six broken brown lines on the lower part of the body. The pectoral is dark on all fish and black on juveniles. The diamond scale mullet can reach 55 cm and more than 4.5 kilograms. It can form large schools in estuaries or inshore coastal waters.

Fishing The diamond scale mullet is seldom taken by line but is a common catch in nets where legal. Schools of diamond scale mullet are often seen on intertidal flats. Although an infrequent capture, diamond scale mullet can be taken on small hooks with prawn or worm baits intended for other species. Berleying with bread increases the chances of a hook-up with these powerful fish. Diamond scale mullet are an excellent troll bait for marlin and sailfish. They are very good eating.

MORWONG, DUSKY

Rigs and Tactics

Rarely taken by line fishing.

MULLET, DIAMOND SCALE

Rigs and Tactics

No. 1 to 3
bean sinker

No. 2 to
2/0 hook

MULLET, SAND

Scientific name *Myxus elongatus.* Also known as Tallegalane, black spot mullet, lano.

Range From Cape Naturaliste in Western Australia around southern waters including Tasmania to south Queensland around the Gold Coast. Rare in Western Australia.

Description The sand mullet is a moderately small mullet reaching 41 cm and nudging a kilogram but most commonly encountered around 25 – 30 centimetres. This species has a straight upper profile and pointed head which differs from the sea mullet which has a more rounded snout. The sand mullet generally has a black blotch at the top of the base of the pectoral fin and lacks the obvious fatty eyelid (adipose eyelid) of the sea mullet. The eye colour is yellow-brown or light brown as opposed to the bright yellow of the yellow-eye mullet, but the most obvious difference is that the sand mullet has 9 rays in the anal fin and the yellow-eye mullet 12 rays. The sand mullet is found in bays, lower estuaries and ocean beaches in schools, usually of similar sized fish. They have a strong preference for sandy bottoms.

Fishing The sand mullet will take bread and is particularly susceptible if berleyed up with bread and fished near the surface with a small pinch of dough or bread which is squeezed on the hook. Sand mullet will also take prawns, beach and blood worms, nippers, maggots and occasionally small pieces of skinned squid. The sand mullet will rise to baits so small float rigs work well. A good trick in tidal areas is to use a small float of quill or even cork held against the current with small split shot to a size 12 long shank hook with the bread or dough bait. In estuaries, keep the bait in the finely ground berley trail and allow the fish to hook themselves against the current. Where there is a sandy bottom, very light bottom rigs can produce good mixed bags including mullet. Small prawn pieces can improve your scope for other species, but a smaller hook is recommended for sand mullet. Keeping the bait moving attracts bites and helps to work out when a bread bait may have washed off the hook. Sand mullet are good eating and their slightly oily flesh is ideal for nearly every fish recipe. Mullet also make ideal live, dead or cut bait.

MULLET, SEA

Scientific name *Mugil cephalus.* Also known as Bully mullet, bully, mullet, hard-gut mullet, river mullet. Juveniles referred to as poddy mullet or poddies.

Range Circum-Australia, but sea mullet are most common from southern Queensland to southern NSW, where large schools migrate along the coast in autumn and early winter.

Description The sea mullet is a cylindrical barrel of muscle which is readily identified by the thick, transparent, gelatinous covering over all but the centre of the eyes. They often have several diffuse lateral stripes on the side, but the colour and intensity can vary with the environment. Sea mullet have a distinguishing enlarged and pointed scale behind the top of the pectoral fin. Sea mullet are found from far above the tidal reaches of coastal rivers to reasonable distances offshore, but they are best known for the vast shoals they can form at spawning time on east coast beaches. They are a very large species, reaching 80 cm and over 5 kg, but sea mullet are most commonly encountered at 1 – 2 kilograms.

Fishing Sea mullet are almost exclusively vegetarian and as a result have to be enticed to be taken by recreational anglers, but they are worth the effort. There are few better fighters pound for pound in Australia and on light line, they really sizzle. Sea mullet can be taken on flies and very rarely on accident with small lures but these are challenges beyond all but the most dedicated angler. Sea mullet are best targeted where effluent such as from fruit or vegetable factories, bakeries or flour mills enter the water. Here mullet are trained to take foods such as corn, pineapple or peas and are much easier to catch. In other areas, it may take several days of berley in the same area and tide before sea mullet begin to bite freely. Best baits are dough or bread, prawn or worm pieces, generally fished on or just under the surface. Methods described for sand mullet work well. Patience is required, but well rewarded although in WA they remain almost impossible to catch. Sea mullet are much better eating if taken from ocean beaches where they become hard-gut mullet, not eating but preparing for spawning. Unfortunately in the ocean larger fish are only taken through accidental foul hooking by recreational anglers. Estuarine fish (soft-gut mullet) can taste muddy or weedy and should be cleaned quickly. This poorer taste along with the high by-catch is another reason why commercial gill netting for mullet should be stopped in estuaries.

Rigs and Tactics

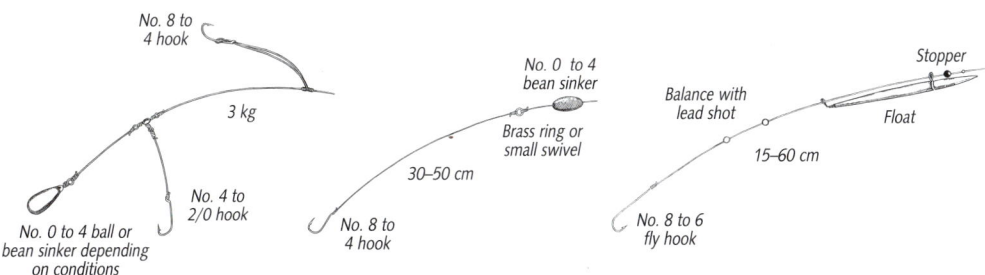

No. 8 to 4 hook

3 kg

No. 4 to 2/0 hook

No. 0 to 4 ball or bean sinker depending on conditions

No. 0 to 4 bean sinker

Brass ring or small swivel

30–50 cm

No. 8 to 4 hook

Balance with lead shot

Stopper

Float

15–60 cm

No. 8 to 6 fly hook

Rigs and Tactics

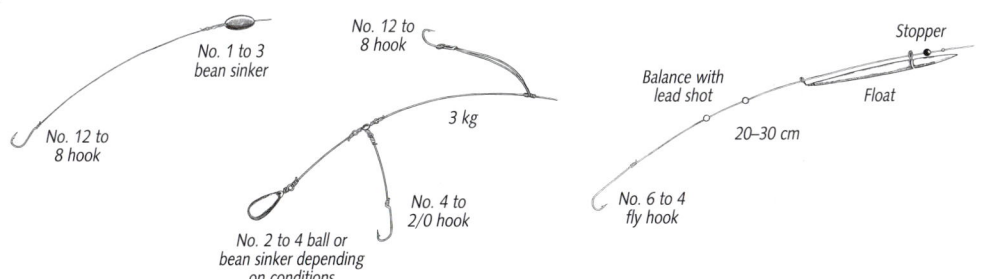

No. 1 to 3 bean sinker

No. 12 to 8 hook

No. 12 to 8 hook

3 kg

No. 4 to 2/0 hook

No. 2 to 4 ball or bean sinker depending on conditions

Balance with lead shot

Stopper

Float

20–30 cm

No. 6 to 4 fly hook

MULLOWAY

Scientific name *Argyrosomus japonicus.* Also known as Jewfish, jew, jewie, butterfish, river kingfish, silver kingfish. Small fish to around 3 kg are generally referred to as soapies due to their rather bland or soapy taste. Fish from 3 – 8 kg are frequently known as Schoolies as they are often encountered in schools which decrease in number as the size increases.

Range Exmouth Gulf in Western Australia around southern waters but extremely rare in Tasmania and along the east coast as far north as Rockhampton.

Description Mulloway are a large and highly prized species found in estuaries, embayments and inshore ocean waters throughout its range. The mulloway can vary in colour from dark bronze to silver and there may be red or purple tinges, but a silver ocean mulloway is a stunning fish. The mulloway has large scales and a generous mouth. A line of silvery spots follows the lateral line in live fish which glows under artificial lights as do the eyes which shine a bright red. A conspicuous black spot is just above the pectoral fin. The tail fin is convex (rounded outwards) and this characteristic differentiates them from the smaller teraglin which has a concave tail and a yellow inside of the mouth. Mulloway differ from the black jewfish which is generally darker with black blotches on the back and has a prominent second anal spine which is short in the mulloway. Mulloway can reach 1.8 m and more than 60 kg, but any fish over 25 kg is worth long term boasting rights for the angler. Mulloway are most commonly caught at 3 – 10 kilograms.

Fishing The mulloway is the largest and most prized species for estuarine and beach fishermen where it is found. A large specimen is generally a test of endurance for the angler with long nights without even a mulloway run, but there is no greater thrill than a large mulloway caught by a dedicated angler. The mulloway can be difficult to hook as they can run reasonable distances before spitting out the bait, just as the angler is preparing to strike. Removing prawn trawling from some NSW estuaries is already paying dividends in better recruitment. The best mulloway fishing is at night although opinions vary on the best moon phases, with many shunning the full moon, while others prefer this time. However, with large mulloway, any night spent using a large, very fresh or live bait gives an advantage for these challenging fish. Soapy or school mulloway can be found in large schools, so if mulloway are located, the action can be quite frantic for a time. A trick of the old time beach fishermen is to rub the next bait on the first mulloway, as they have a distinctive kerosene or faintly cucumber odour and even the largest mulloway often travel in pairs. The theory is that the mulloway scent attracts other fish to the bait which they consume. Mulloway fishing is best near the mouth of tidal rivers or estuaries after heavy rain and on nearby ocean beaches, especially those adjacent to coastal lakes when they break through to the sea. At these times, live mullet or yellowtail, or the famous red and white feather jigs work well. Increasing numbers of fish are being taken on larger diving lures such as Halco Lasers and Mann's Stretch series trolled around bridge pylons, through deep and renowned mulloway holes, or along current lines. A few very dedicated anglers have taken mulloway on flies. Many anglers are disappointed with the fight of mulloway. There is a strong and promising first run followed by a shorter second run. Generally there is a greater chance of losing the fish in a surf zone, to a poor gaff shot or to a lightly hooked fish. Mulloway destined for release need to be quickly returned as they do not handle well. However, the almost legendary status of a large mulloway more than compensates for any disappointment in the fight. Mulloway take baits ranging from fresh fish, especially those with oily flesh, beach worms, live baits, pipi, squid, cuttlefish and less frequently pilchards. The most important attribute of mulloway bait is that it must be very fresh. Best fishing times are from dusk to dawn, although good catches can be made during floods during the day and at some inshore reefs. Rigs should be as light as possible to fit the depth of water or current conditions. A running sinker is essential as mulloway run a long distance before swallowing a bait. Mulloway larger than 3 kg are very good eating and all but the largest fish are very tasty but they can have worms in the flesh. Mulloway are a fast growing species and smaller returned fish will rapidly reach boasting size if handled carefully.

Rigs and Tactics

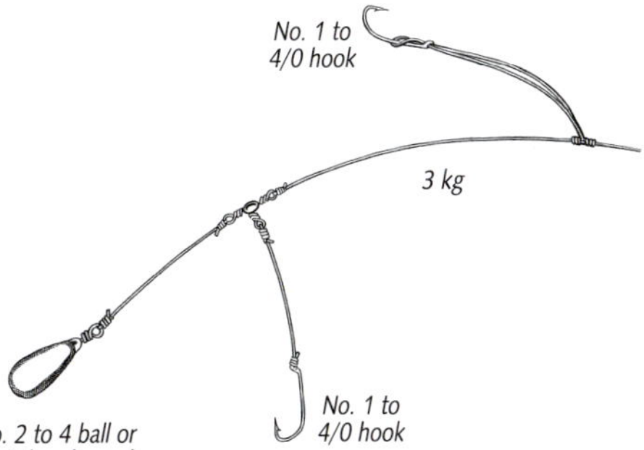

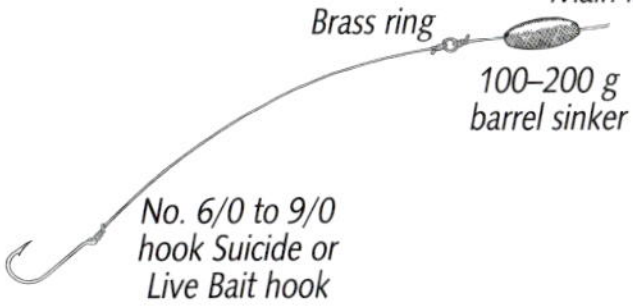

No. 1 to
4/0 hook

3 kg

Solid
brass ring

Solid brass
ring

250–500 g
barrel sinker

30–50 kg
trace

1 metre

No. 2 to 4 ball or
bean sinker depending
on conditions

No. 1 to
4/0 hook

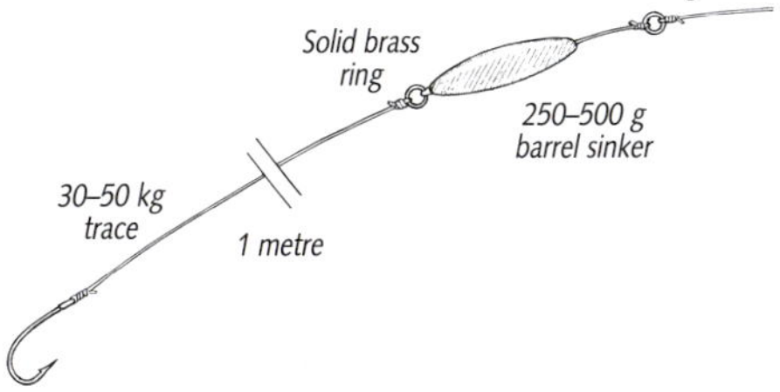

Minnow Lure

Main line

Brass ring

100–200 g
barrel sinker

24 kg trace

No. 6/0 to 9/0
hook Suicide or
Live Bait hook

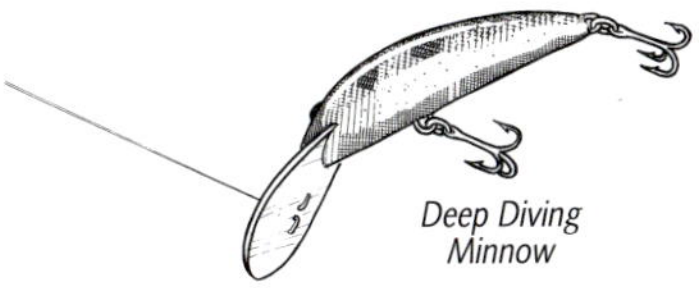

Deep Diving
Minnow

MULLET, YELLOW-EYE

Scientific name *Aldrichetta forsteri*. Also known as Pilch or pilchard, estuary mullet, freshwater mullet, yelloweye.

Range Shark Bay in Western Australia southwards and around southern Australia, including Tasmania to southern NSW.

Description A very common species of southern estuaries and embayments. Yellow-eye mullet also move on or just off beaches near estuaries during winter in Western Australia and early Autumn for east coast stocks. The bright yellow eye, without the gelatinous eye covering, is diagnostic. This species also has small teeth in both jaws and has 12 rays in the anal fin. The yellow-eye mullet grows to 50 cm and more than 1 kg, but is most common at around 25 – 30 centimetres.

Fishing East coast fish are strongly herbivorous and require berley with bread, bran or pollard and use of baits of dough, prawns or worms fished with no weight or under a tiny float. Yellow-eye mullet are most common near weed beds and near the edges of drop-offs. They can also form schools near the mouth of estuaries and embayments. In Western Australia, yellow-eye mullet are much more aggressive feeders and will take a much wider variety of baits, although they can be quite finicky, especially deep within estuaries. During winter on beaches or the mouths of estuaries, yellow-eye mullet readily take blue bait or whitebait as well as prawn, pipi, worms, maggots or small pieces of squid. Berley improves catches. Standard light surf rigs or double hook estuarine rigs works well. Yellow-eye mullet are often very close to shore, so long casts are not always necessary and the cast should be fished right to the shore. Yellow-eye mullet are good eating, especially fish which are taken from beaches or have not been grazing on algae.

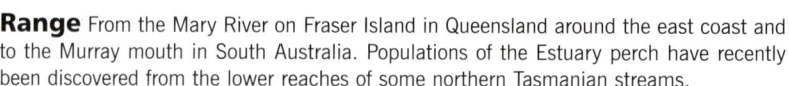

PERCH, ESTUARY

Scientific name *Macquaria colonorum*. Also known as Perch.

Range From the Mary River on Fraser Island in Queensland around the east coast and to the Murray mouth in South Australia. Populations of the Estuary perch have recently been discovered from the lower reaches of some northern Tasmanian streams.

Description The estuary perch is easily confused with Australian bass which can be found in the same areas. Even experienced anglers have difficulty telling the two species apart. The most obvious distinguishing feature is the head profile which is indented or concave in estuary perch and rounded in bass. Estuary perch are very rarely found above the tidal influence of rivers. Estuary perch are also increasingly common in southern waters. Like bass, larger specimens are all female and they must have access to salt water to breed.

Fishing Estuary perch are an excellent fighting and eating fish, but like their cousin the bass, most are returned unhurt today. They are aggressive and can be over-fished by skilled fishers. Estuary perch take surface and deep diving lures and larger flies well, fishing very close to snags and bank-side cover in tidal areas. Accurate casts, within 30 cm of the snag and patience at the beginning of the retrieve gets the best results. Estuary perch are also caught with bait in deep holes in lower tidal reaches during winter spawning aggregations. Estuary perch are particularly partial to a live prawn fished under a float near snags or drop-offs near cumbungi beds. Other popular baits, fished under a float or with minimal weight include live fish, crickets, worms and crabs.

MULLET, YELLOW-EYE

Rigs and Tactics

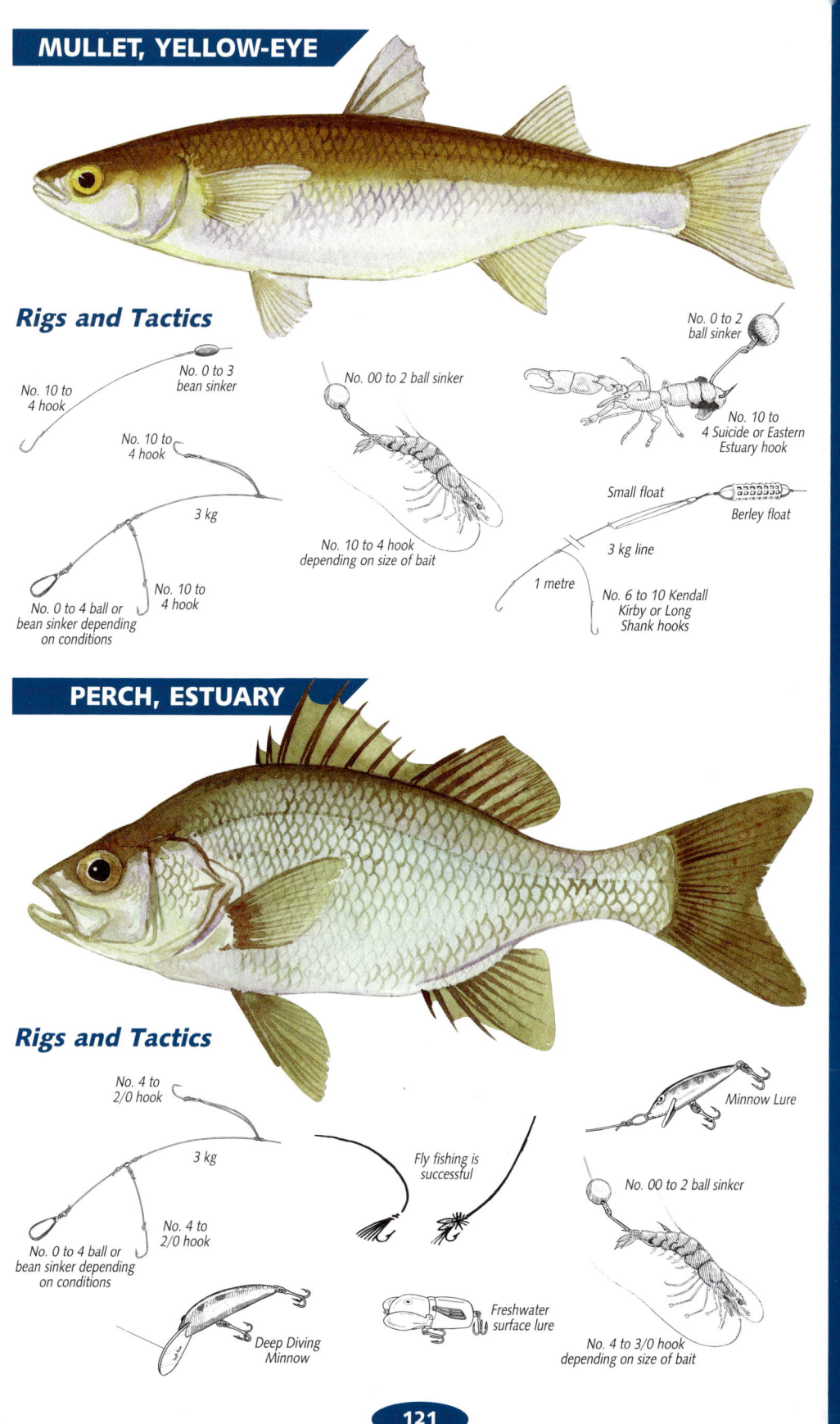

No. 0 to 2
ball sinker

No. 10 to
4 hook

No. 0 to 3
bean sinker

No. 00 to 2 ball sinker

No. 10 to
4 hook

3 kg

No. 0 to 4 ball or
bean sinker depending
on conditions

No. 10 to
4 hook

No. 10 to 4 hook
depending on size of bait

No. 10 to
4 Suicide or Eastern
Estuary hook

Small float

Berley float

3 kg line

1 metre

No. 6 to 10 Kendall
Kirby or Long
Shank hooks

PERCH, ESTUARY

Rigs and Tactics

No. 4 to
2/0 hook

3 kg

No. 0 to 4 ball or
bean sinker depending
on conditions

No. 4 to
2/0 hook

Fly fishing is
successful

Minnow Lure

No. 00 to 2 ball sinker

Deep Diving
Minnow

Freshwater
surface lure

No. 4 to 3/0 hook
depending on size of bait

121

PERCH, MOSES

Scientific name *Lutjanus russelli*. Also known as One spot sea perch, finger-mark (WA).

Range From Shark Bay in Western Australia and tropical waters and as far south as Coffs Harbour in northern NSW.

Description Has a general reddish or pinkish hue, a large mouth with discernible canine teeth and 14 or 15 rays in the dorsal fin. The Moses perch has a distinctive black spot which can be quite pale, below the start of the soft dorsal rays. Most of the black spot is above the obvious lateral line, while the similar black-spot sea perch (*Lutjanus fulviflamma*) has a small black spot, most of which is below the lateral line. The lateral yellow stripes of the black-spot sea perch are not present on the Moses perch. The Moses perch often forms schools of similar sized fish, hanging near coral outcrops and in eddies near reefs. They can be found near drop-offs, on reefs or in depths of up to 80 m, with larger specimens frequently captured from deeper water. The Moses perch reaches 50 cm and nearly 3 kg but is commonly caught at between 25 and 30 centimetres.

Fishing Like many species in this group, the Moses perch can be an aggressive feeder, rising well to minnow lures, feather jigs and even surface poppers cast or trolled to the downstream side of coral outcrops. The school can jostle to be the first to take the lure or bait. Baits include whole or cut fish baits, squid, octopus or prawns. Weights should be kept to a minimum depending on the depth and mood of the fish, as Moses perch will rise to a bait which also puts them further from dangerous coral which they will try to use. In deeper water, lighter weights allow the fish to fight better and keeping the bait just above the bottom will deter some pickers but not Moses perch. The Moses perch is a good eating fish.

PIKE, LONGFINNED

Scientific name *Dinolestes lewini*. Also known as Pike, jack pike, skipjack pike.

Range A coldwater species found from Rottnest Island in Western Australia, but more common south of Geographe Bay and southern waters including Tasmania and along the east coast as far north as Taree.

Description The lonfinned pike is a long slender fish with a large head, large mouth and an underslung jaw extending almost to the front edge of the large eye. This species has two distinct dorsal fins. A prominent and extended anal fin separates this species from the similar striped seapike which also has 2 – 3 brown lateral stripes along its side. The tail and wrist of the tail of the long finned pike are yellow or golden whereas in the striped seapike the tail has a yellow hue, especially near the back edge. The longfinned pike can be confused with the snook, which has the two dorsal fins widely separated and the ventral fin is set well behind the pectoral fin. The snook is a much larger species, reaching more than a metre and over 5 kilograms. The longfinned pike can reach more than 2 kg and 90 cm but is most often encountered at between 40 and 50 centimetres.

Fishing The longfinned pike can form small groups or large schools and in a range of habitats from seagrass meadows to reefs in medium depths but they are most common near shallow reefs or seagrass and near cover such as jetties in shallow water. Longfinned pike take trolled lures well such as chrome spoons, small minnows and jigs. They will also take baits such as fresh cut baits, or whole fish such as pilchards, whitebait or anchovies. Longfinned pike feed better closer to the surface or in midwater, so rigs which use little or no weight or a water filled plastic bubble to aid casting distance will bring the best results. Longfinned pike can be taken from rocks or boat and when a school is located good numbers can be taken. Longfinned pike are not highly regarded as a food fish. Smaller specimens can be used as a live bait for samson fish, kingfish, mulloway or other large predators but must be handled carefully as the scales can shed and the fish do not last as long. Pike makes a good cut bait.

PERCH, MOSES

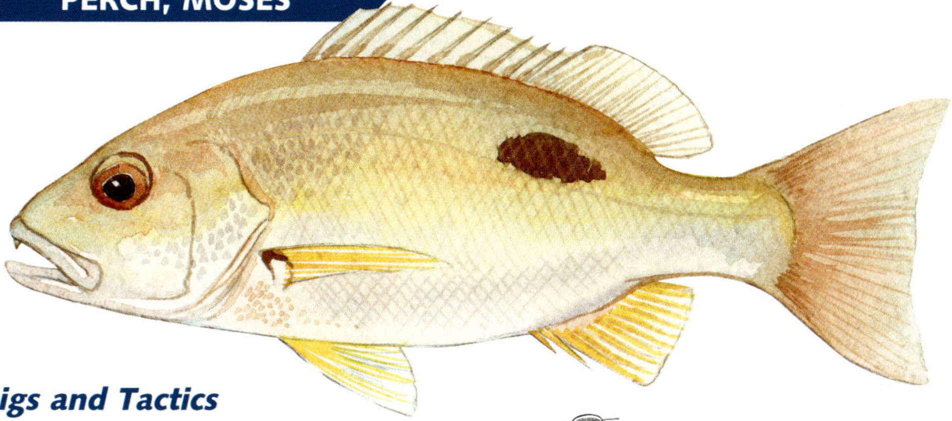

Rigs and Tactics

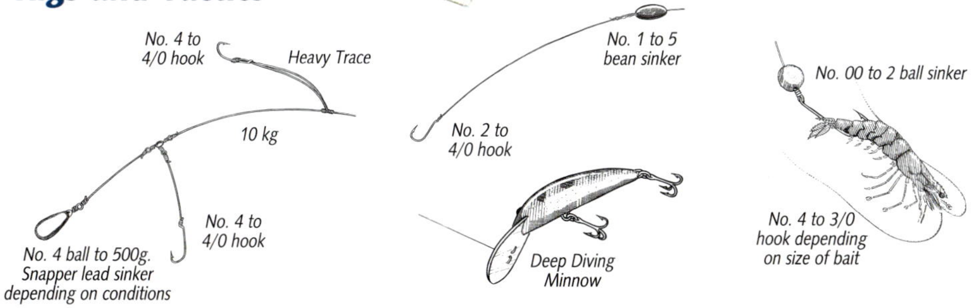

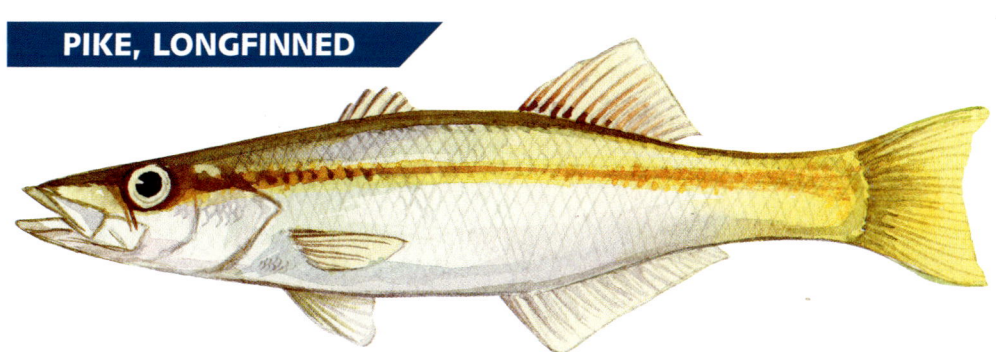

No. 4 to 4/0 hook
Heavy Trace
10 kg
No. 4 to 4/0 hook
No. 4 ball to 500g. Snapper lead sinker depending on conditions
No. 1 to 5 bean sinker
No. 2 to 4/0 hook
Deep Diving Minnow
No. 00 to 2 ball sinker
No. 4 to 3/0 hook depending on size of bait

PIKE, LONGFINNED

Rigs and Tactics

Stopper
No. 10 swivel
Bobby float
No. 2 to 4 ball or bean sinker
No. 3/0 to 5/0 hook gang
Small bean sinker may be added to aid casting
Main line
25 kg trace
No. 8 swivel
Ganged No. 3/0 to 5/0 hooks
Bug sinker crimped to line
Linked No. 2/0 to 4/0 suicide or Kendall Kirby hooks
Wire Trace
Metal Lure

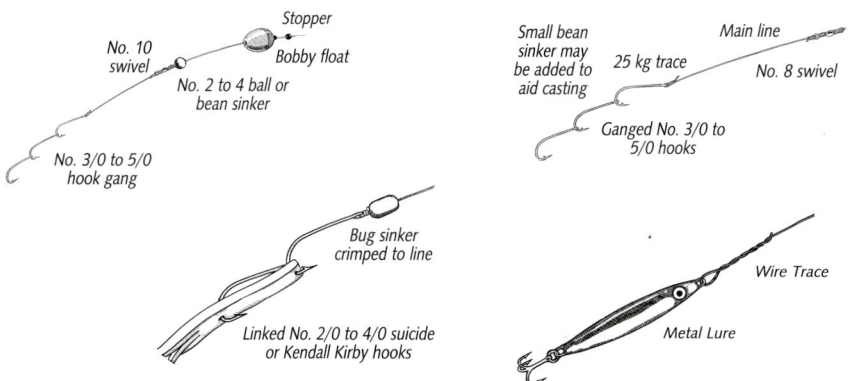

PORCUPINE FISH ☠

Scientific name Family *Diodontidae.* Also known as Burr fish, prickle fish, globe fish.

Range A variety of species are found in inshore areas of Australia, reaching a maximum of 43 cm, but commonly seen at around 20 – 25 centimetres.

Description A very easy group to identify, distinguished by the prominent spines set into the skin and the ability to inflate their bodies with air or water. The spines distinguish porcupine fish from the smooth skinned puffer fish. The similar globe fish group can be distinguished by having the ability to erect their much longer body spines while the body is inflated. The mouth is small but the teeth are fused into two plates which can be capable of cutting fine hooks and easily through line. The dorsal and anal fins are set well back on the body.

Fishing Porcupine fish are not a target fish. They are often taken while fishing for other species in estuaries, bays and in shallow waters such as near sea grass meadows. They can also be a by-catch in prawn dray nets. Porcupine fish will take a wide variety of baits intended for other species, with a special liking for prawns, squid, octopus, nippers and worms. Care should be taken when handling these fish as they can rapidly inflate their bodies and the spines can inflict painful wounds. Porcupine fish are toxic and should never, ever be consumed. The toxins are strongest in the skin, liver and other internal organs but even carefully prepared flesh can result in death.

PUFFERFISH (SEE ALSO TOADFISH) ☠

Scientific name Family *Tetraodontidae* Also known as Toadfish, toad, toado, blowfish, blowie.

Range Circum-Australia, with various species common in inshore waters in different locations.

Description Pufferfish are a group of generally small, smooth skinned species with the ability to inflate their bodies with water or air on capture. The mouth is small and the teeth are fused into plates and separated in the front. Colours vary, with several species brightly coloured. These fish prefer inshore waters where they frequently form large schools. All species are poisonous and should never be consumed or fed to animals. The silver pufferfish, or nor-west blowie (*Lagocephalus sceleratus*) is of particular interest as it can reach a length of nearly a metre. This species can attack divers for no apparent reason and it is capable of biting through hooks or even bones.

Fishing Pufferfish can form vast hordes in shallow water, swarming over any bait and pecking it until it is gone. While pufferfish are almost never targeted, they are frequently captured by young or very inexperienced anglers, some of whom want to keep them. All pufferfish species are highly toxic and should never be consumed, no matter how well they are cleaned. Many pets die after being fed unwanted specimens. Although these fish are not desired and can be despised when schools steal every bait, codes of practice dictate that these fish should either be returned to the water or killed quickly. The only way to avoid pufferfish when they are in plague proportions is to move, fish with a large bait in the hopes that something will remain for more desirable fish, use a large weight to get to the bottom quickly, or use lures, although pufferfish will attack soft plastic and leadhead jigs.

PORCUPINE FISH

Rigs and Tactics

Not applicable as Porcupine Fish are not recommended as an angling species

PUFFERFISH

Rigs and Tactics

Not applicable as Pufferfish are not recommended as an angling species

QUEENFISH

Scientific name *Scomberoides commersonnianus.* Also known as Giant leatherskin, leatherskin, queenie, talang queenfish, skinny, skinnyfish.

Range Exmouth Gulf in Western Australia and through tropical northern waters to Moreton Bay in southern Queensland, but primarily a tropical species.

Description The queenfish is a large, long and laterally (side to side) compressed species which leads to the common name of skinny and a light weight for the length. The mouth is large and extends mouth well beyond the back of the eye whereas other smaller queenfish species have smaller mouths. A series of 5 to 8 oval shaped blotches are found on the sides above the lateral line. The similar but smaller double spotted queenfish (*Scomberoides lysan*) has a double row of spots above and below the lateral line. The queenfish also has a prominent, high and light coloured front part of the dorsal and anal fins. These fish have lance shaped scales which are deeply embedded in a leathery skin. The queenfish can reach 120 cm and more than 11 kilograms. This light weight for the length indicates how skinny the queenfish is when viewed head on.

Fishing Queenfish are found from the upper tidal reaches of tropical rivers to inshore reefs and occasionally near outer reefs which have shallow breaks. Queenfish prefer slightly turbid water with plenty of flow. They are ambush feeders and will lurk near cover such as eddies, rock bars, wharves and creek mouths, especially on a falling tide. Queenfish are spectacular and exciting sportfish, with their slashing strikes and blistering runs, often with aerial displays. Queenfish will take dead baits such as mullet, pilchard, garfish, mudskippers, whiting or fresh prawns and squid. They are also partial to live bait. Queenfish are renowned lure takers, with cast or trolled lures such as sliced chrome lures, spoons, shallow and deep diving minnows, spinner baits and surface lures. Queenfish are excited by escaping baitfish, so a fast, erratic retrieve is most successful. Fly enthusiasts are increasingly targeting queenfish as they are an exciting challenge on light fly gear. Large minnow type flies retrieved through current eddies on a fast strip works best. A heavy monofilament leader is recommended when fishing for queenfish as their jaws and small teeth can damage light traces. The queenfish is an under-rated food fish, mainly because they are often caught in conjunction with barramundi and threadfin salmon which are excellent food fish. Like all tropical fish, the quality of queenfish is improved with immediate bleeding and placing in an ice brine slurry.

SEAPIKE, STRIPED

Scientific name *Sphyraena obtusata* Also known as yellowtail (Qld.), pike

Range Cheynes Beach on the south coast of Western Australia and westwards and the entire west coast and north coast and as far south as Sydney in NSW.

Description A long, slender predator of coastal and estuarine waters with a wide distribution. The striped seapike favours areas of weed and sand but can be frequently encountered around jetties or at the back edges of the wash around nearshore reefs. The teeth of the striped seapike are impressive and can inflict a nasty cut that bleeds profusely, although they do not struggle when being unhooked as much as some other toothy fish. The striped seapike has a prominent brown stripe which runs from the tip of the snout, through the eye and all the way to the base of the bright yellow tail fin. The similar long-finned pike does not have a stripe which extends to the snout. The striped seapike has a much shorter anal fin, being of a similar size to the second dorsal fin whereas with the long-finned pike the anal fin is obviously longer than the second dorsal fin. The striped seapike reaches a length of 55 cm but is often captured at around 30 centimetres.

Fishing The striped seapike is under-rated and often overlooked species which fights with a series of jumps and can bite off the unwary angler. The striped seapike can be considered a nuisance by anglers fishing for tailor and they can make a mess of smaller live baits intended for other species. The striped seapike prefers a bait which is moving and using a jerky retrieve of a shallowly worked bait will bring many more hits than a free drifted bait. They can also be taken on a variety of lures and jigs, although the teeth can damage jig tails or wooden lures. Chrome wonder wobblers can work well. Cut baits and especially those with a white or silver colour seem to work best. Pilchards, squid, whitebait and bluebait are very successful. The striped seapike itself is valued as a live bait for species like kingfish and mackerel. They are quite hardy but can shed their scales and require some careful handling. Striped seapike make a very good cut bait. They are under-rated for their eating qualities which are very good when fresh.

QUEENFISH

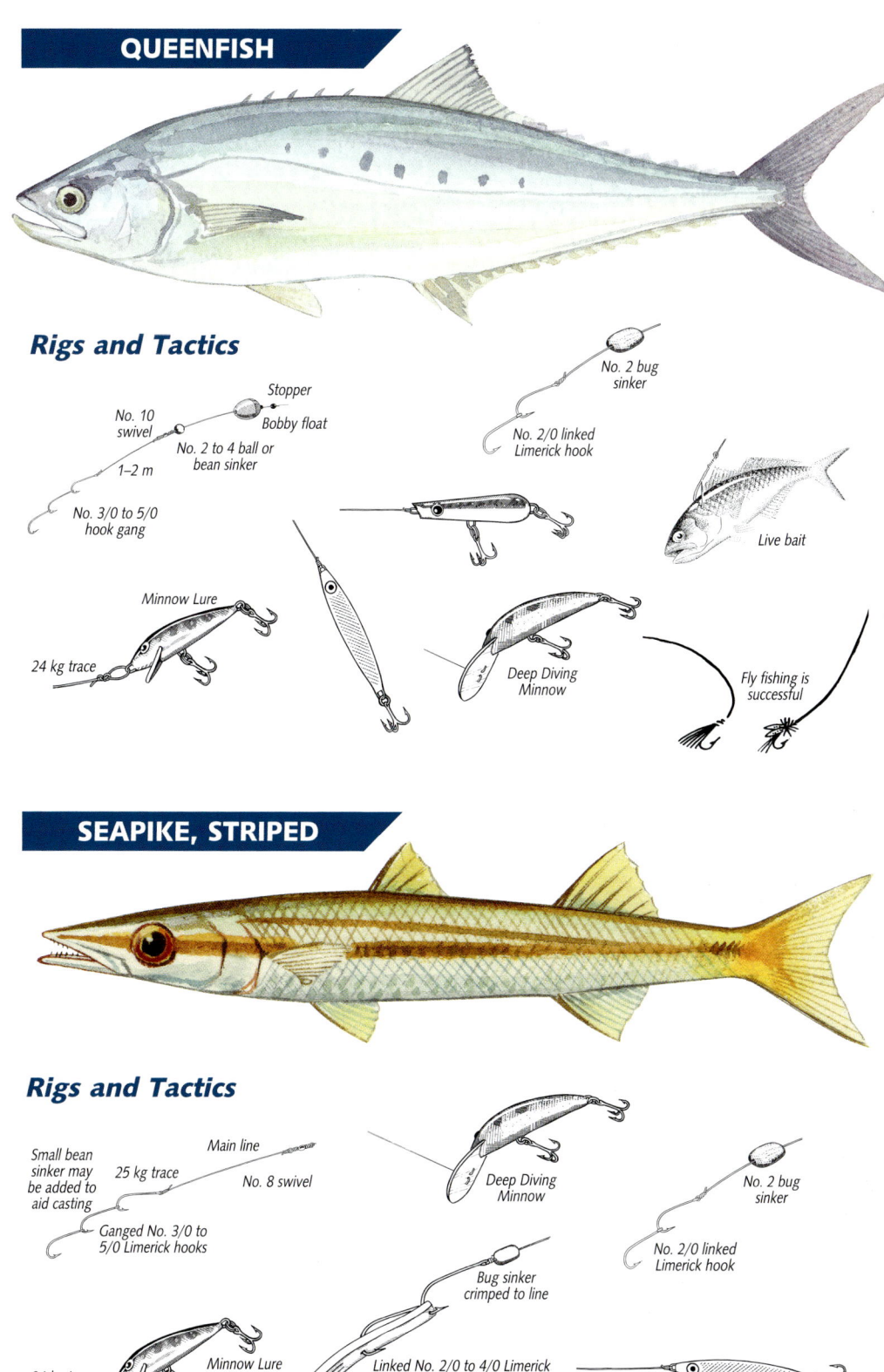

Rigs and Tactics

Stopper

No. 10 swivel

Bobby float

No. 2 to 4 ball or bean sinker

1–2 m

No. 3/0 to 5/0 hook gang

No. 2 bug sinker

No. 2/0 linked Limerick hook

Live bait

Minnow Lure

24 kg trace

Deep Diving Minnow

Fly fishing is successful

SEAPIKE, STRIPED

Rigs and Tactics

Small bean sinker may be added to aid casting

Main line

25 kg trace

No. 8 swivel

Ganged No. 3/0 to 5/0 Limerick hooks

Deep Diving Minnow

No. 2 bug sinker

No. 2/0 linked Limerick hook

Bug sinker crimped to line

24 kg trace

Minnow Lure

Linked No. 2/0 to 4/0 Limerick or Kendall Kirby hooks

Metal minnow lure

SALMON, AUSTRALIAN

Scientific name *Arripis trutta* (Eastern species), *Arripis truttacea* (Western species) Also known as Salmon, black back, cocky salmon, colonial salmon, kahawai. Salmon trout and bay trout, (juveniles).

Range There are now generally accepted to be two different species. The eastern species extends from Tweed Heads to Port Phillip Bay and including Tasmania, but is not common north of Sydney. The Western species extends from Kalbarri in Western Australia around the south coast to Lakes Entrance in Victoria, but is rare north of Yanchep lagoon. The range and abundance is linked to commercial netting and current strength on the east and west coast with strong southerly currents keeping the stocks further south. In some years, few salmon make it to the west coast or into NSW waters.

Description These 'salmon' species are not related to true trout and salmon in the family Salmonidae and are more closely related to the mullets. Both Australian salmon species are very similar, with the only difference being that the western species has fewer gill rakers and reaches a larger maximum size, 9 kg for western fish and 7 kg for eastern fish. In both cases, the larger fish are more commonly found at the northern end of the range as the fish undergo spawning migrations, reaching their northernmost points in late winter on the east coast and around Easter on the west coast. Very small salmon are often confused with Australian herring (tommy rough) but juvenile herring have black tips to the caudal fin and the body feels rough to a finger slid along the body, while the salmon feels smooth. The forked tail of adult salmon is dark, and the eye is generally yellow. The body is classically torpedo shaped and full of power. The head is quite large, and the mouth moderately large. There are distinctive brown dots or dashes along the dorsal surface although the larger specimens become dark across the back. The belly is silvery to white.

Fishing The Australian salmon is one of the best light tackle sportsfish in Australia. They are the best fighting fish taken from the beach, where their strong runs and spectacular leaps more than compensate for the average eating quality. Australian salmon form large schools as they move around the coasts, making them vulnerable to commercial fishing. There is little doubt that commercial fishing can affect local abundance and recreational fishing quality. These schools can provide spectacular fishing, but on occasions these schooling fish will not feed. Australian salmon are frequently caught on pilchards and cut baits, with belly fillets or baits with white skin attached doing better. Pipis, cockles and beach worms take many fish and can really surprise an unsuspecting whiting fisherman. In estuaries, salmon trout are often taken on whitebait, blue bait, prawns or squid. When Australian salmon are heavily fished, live bait will entice a strike when the freshest baits fail. The bite of the salmon is frequently quite fumbling and some patience is required before setting the hook. Australian salmon bite well on cast or trolled lures. Chrome spoons or slices, feather lures, surface poppers and minnow lures work well and are underutilised. Australian salmon will also take flies such as deceiver patterns for those who want real arm stretching action on light fly gear. Australian salmon are poorly regarded as food fish, with larger specimens becoming decidedly tough. The western species is better eating but all fish are improved if the strongly flavoured red muscle along the lateral line is cut out.

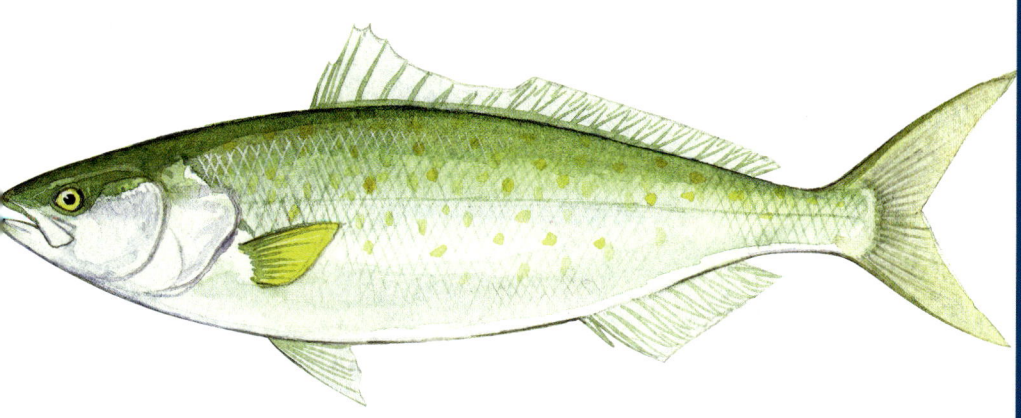

SALMON, AUSTRALIAN

Rigs and Tactics

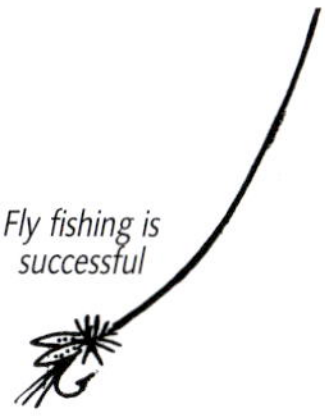
Fly fishing is successful

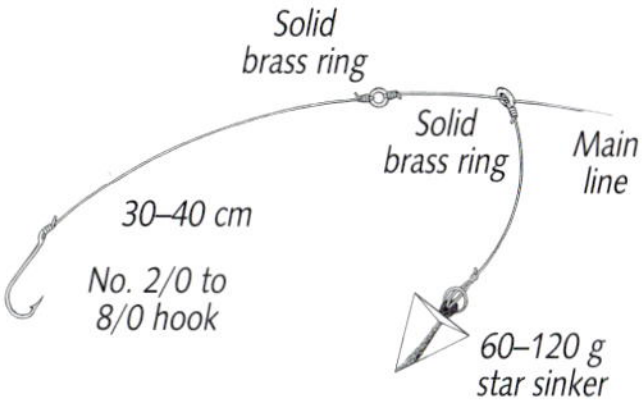
Solid brass ring
Solid brass ring
Main line
30–40 cm
No. 2/0 to 8/0 hook
60–120 g star sinker

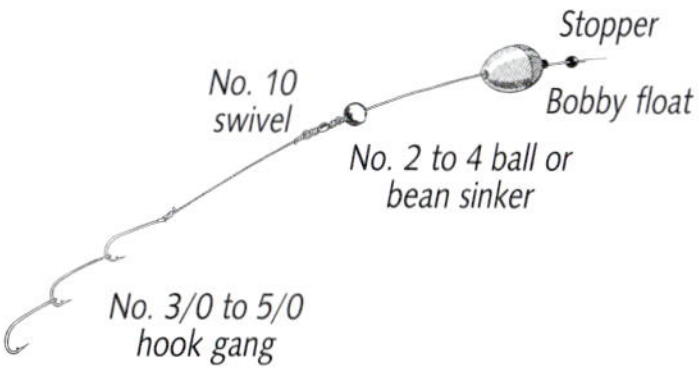
Stopper
No. 10 swivel
Bobby float
No. 2 to 4 ball or bean sinker
No. 3/0 to 5/0 hook gang

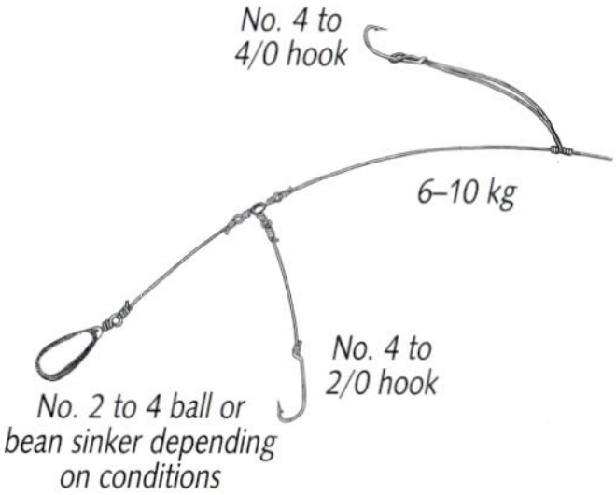
No. 4 to 4/0 hook
6–10 kg
No. 4 to 2/0 hook
No. 2 to 4 ball or bean sinker depending on conditions

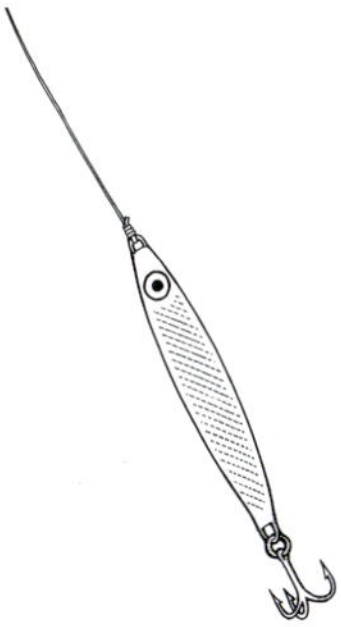

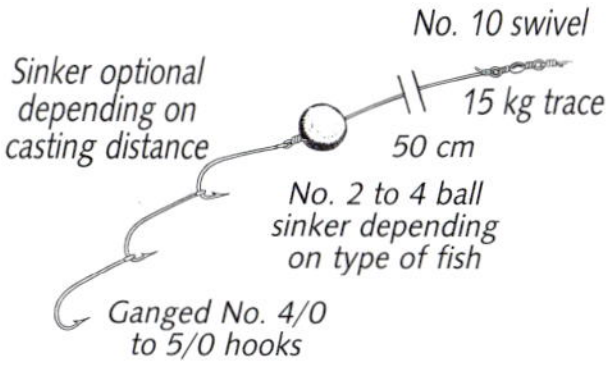
No. 10 swivel
Sinker optional depending on casting distance
15 kg trace
50 cm
No. 2 to 4 ball sinker depending on type of fish
Ganged No. 4/0 to 5/0 hooks

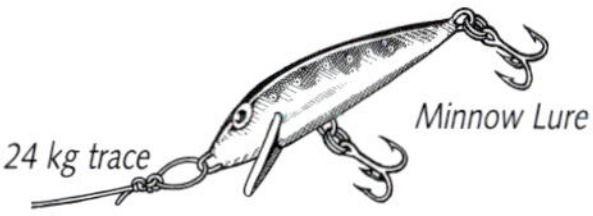
24 kg trace
Minnow Lure

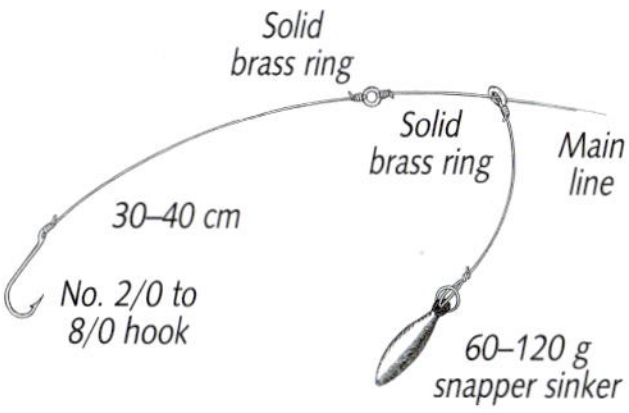
Solid brass ring
Solid brass ring
Main line
30–40 cm
No. 2/0 to 8/0 hook
60–120 g snapper sinker

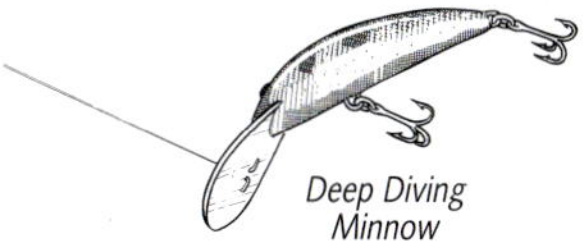
Deep Diving Minnow

SALMON, COOKTOWN

Scientific name *Eleutheronema tetradactylum.* Also known as Threadfin, giant threadfin, blue salmon, Rockhampton kingfish.

Range Port Hedland northwards and through tropical waters to around Hervey Bay in Queensland, although they are very rare this far south.

Description Even reliable reference books provide confusing information on the status of the various threadfin salmon species. The Cooktown salmon is the largest of these distinctive species which are easily identified by the unusual overshot upper jaw and absence of lips around a large mouth. The threadfin salmon species have an unusual body shape as the body is thickest through the second dorsal fin. The most obvious diagnostic feature is the divided pectoral fin with its separate, finger-like filaments. The Cooktown salmon has four separate, and shorter pectoral filaments as opposed to five in the threadfin salmon (see below). These fish are commonly found in estuaries, where they can range up to the tidal limit in creeks and rivers. They are also found close to shore, near jetties, in harbours or over coastal tidal mud or sand flats. The Cooktown salmon can reach 1.2 m and up to 18 kilograms.

Fishing The Cooktown salmon is often encountered while fishing for other tropical species such as barramundi or mangrove jacks as they frequent similar areas, although salmon are often found in turbid waters. The Cooktown salmon is less commonly taken on lures, although they will sometimes take bright lures. They prefer live or very fresh baits of prawn, crab, mullet or other fish, especially those with bright silver colour. When hooked, the Cooktown salmon is a spectacular aerialist, especially in shallow water and is highly regarded as a sportfish. Best fishing is at the edges of current lines, on the outside edges of mangroves or channels draining with the tide. Cooktown salmon are excellent eating and are regarded by many locals as being superior to barramundi. The flesh bruises easily and does not freeze well, but is superb fresh.

SALMON, THREADFIN

Scientific name *Polydactylus sheridani.* Also known as Blue threadfin, blue salmon, Burnett salmon, king salmon.

Range From the Kimberley region in Western Australia around the top end to around Hervey Bay in Queensland. Some reports have been received that this fish is occasionally taken as far south as Karratha.

Description The threadfin salmon is similar to the Cooktown salmon, but possesses 5 long, distinctive fingers on the lower edge of the pectoral fin. This species has a more pronounced blue colour and a long and relatively narrow caudal wrist. The threadfin salmon is common between 0.5 and around 3 kg with occasional specimens slightly larger. Another similar species, the Northern or striped threadfin salmon (*Polydactylus plebius*) is separated by its more prominent stripes and overall golden colour and five free filaments, of which the two uppermost are longest.

Fishing The threadfin salmon is a more common lure target, taking small barra lures, bright spoons, spinnerbaits and shiny minnow lures and saltwater flies. This species also prefers fresh bait with a white or silver sheen as well as prawns or crab baits. Although smaller, the threadfin salmon is a better target species as it is a more reliable bait or lure taker. The threadfin salmon is an excellent eating species which should be cleaned quickly and eaten fresh.

SALMON, COOKTOWN

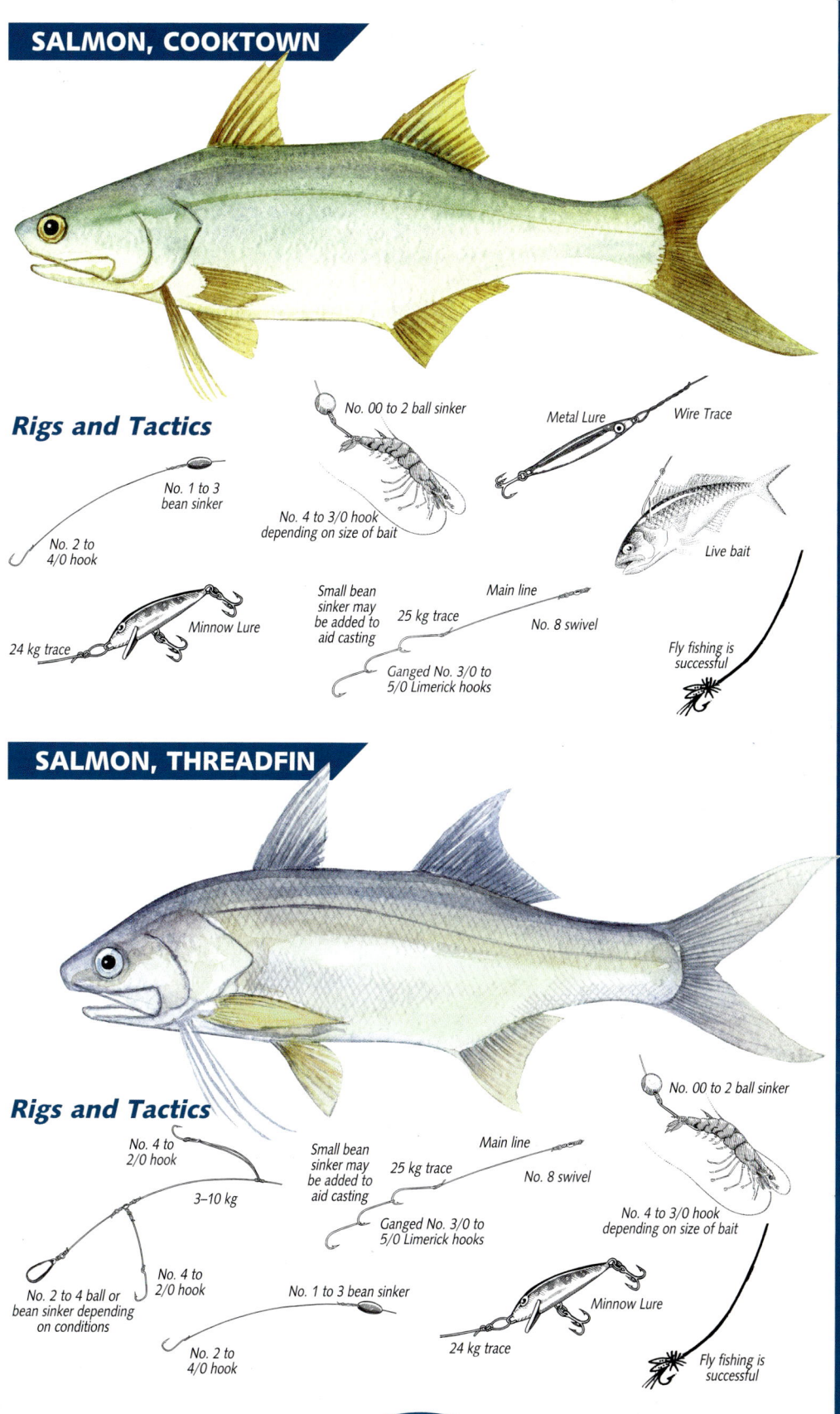

Rigs and Tactics

No. 00 to 2 ball sinker

Metal Lure

Wire Trace

No. 1 to 3
bean sinker

No. 2 to
4/0 hook

No. 4 to 3/0 hook
depending on size of bait

Live bait

24 kg trace

Minnow Lure

Small bean
sinker may
be added to
aid casting

Main line

25 kg trace

No. 8 swivel

Fly fishing is
successful

Ganged No. 3/0 to
5/0 Limerick hooks

SALMON, THREADFIN

Rigs and Tactics

No. 00 to 2 ball sinker

No. 4 to
2/0 hook

Small bean
sinker may
be added to
aid casting

Main line

25 kg trace

No. 8 swivel

3–10 kg

No. 4 to 3/0 hook
depending on size of bait

Ganged No. 3/0 to
5/0 Limerick hooks

No. 4 to
2/0 hook

No. 2 to 4 ball or
bean sinker depending
on conditions

No. 1 to 3 bean sinker

Minnow Lure

No. 2 to
4/0 hook

24 kg trace

Fly fishing is
successful

SOLDIERFISH

Scientific name *Gymnapistes marmoratus.* Also known as South Australian cobbler, devilfish

Range Fremantle southwards and along the south coast and including Tasmania as far north as Sydney NSW.

Description The soldierfish is similar in appearance to the related and similarly dangerous fortescue and bullrout. The soldierfish is readily identified by having scaleless skin. There is also a distinctive black stripe running back of the mouth upwards through the eye to the back of the head. The fins and body are blotched with darker irregular patches on a lighter background. The soldierfish reaches a maximum size of 23 cm, but juveniles can be taken in prawn drag nets. The soldierfish has 13 dorsal spines, all of which are poisonous. Pain is immediate and intense. First aid is for similar species, with hot but not scalding water recommended and medical attention sought if required.

Fishing The soldierfish is largely nocturnal and moves about the shallow coastal or tidal water freely searching for prawns, small crabs or small fish. Larger specimens can be taken on these baits as the large mouth can accommodate quite large hooks. This fish is not regarded as a food fish and extreme caution should be exercised while handling these fish.

SOLE, BLACK

Scientific name *Synaptura nigra.*

Range Southern Queensland through to Port Phillip Bay in Victoria

Description All the true soles in Australia are right-eyed. Their eyes migrate to the right side of their bodies as they develop when small juveniles. The similar lemon-tongue sole (*Paraplagusia unicolor*) is a left-eyed fish and has a diagnostic hook to the snout. The black sole is very round shaped and does not have a defined tail. The black sole prefers sandy or sandy-mud bottoms of coastal shallows and large estuaries and grows to a length of 35 centimetres.

Fishing The black sole is rarely taken by line fishers. It occasionally takes a bait of prawn, worm or pipi fished on light rigs. The black sole is most commonly taken by trawlers. All the soles are excellent eating and many are imported from overseas.

Rigs and Tactics

Not applicable as Soldierfish Fish are not recommended as an angling species

SOLE, BLACK

Rigs and Tactics

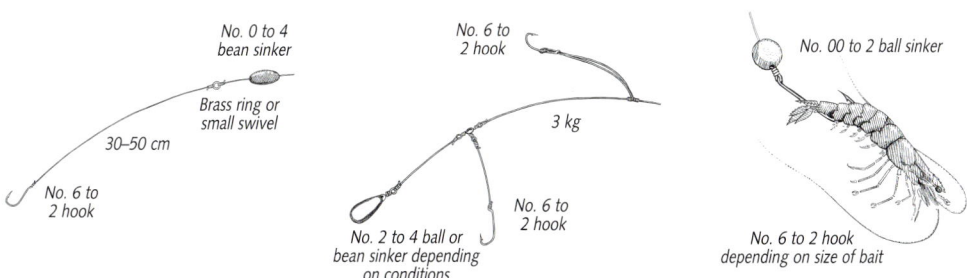

No. 0 to 4
bean sinker

Brass ring or
small swivel

30–50 cm

No. 6 to
2 hook

No. 6 to
2 hook

3 kg

No. 2 to 4 ball or
bean sinker depending
on conditions

No. 6 to
2 hook

No. 00 to 2 ball sinker

No. 6 to 2 hook
depending on size of bait

SPINEFOOT, BLACK

Scientific name *Siganus fuscescens* Also known as Happy moments, Stinging bream, Black trevally, mi-mi, pearl-spotted spinefoot, fuscous rabbitfish.

Range Fremantle in Western Australia and northern waters as far south as Eden in southern NSW.

Description The black spinefoot is a reasonably common schooling fish in coastal and estuarine waters, especially in northern NSW and southern Queensland and the coastal region around Perth in Western Australia. The black spinefoot is a dangerous fish with numerous poisonous spines in both the dorsal and anal fins. This array of sharp spines makes the handling of these fish difficult. A puncture wound can be treated with hot water to denature (cook) the protein. Ensure the water is not so hot as to burn the skin which adds other complications. The black spinefoot colours vary widely, but the seven anal spines is unusually high. The wrist of the tail is very narrow and the tail rapidly widens and is moderately forked. The mouth is quite small, which makes them difficult to hook.

Fishing The black spinefoot is frequently taken in prawn drag nets in estuaries, which add an extra challenge along with fortescue and bullrouts which also inflict painful wounds. The spinefoot is never a target species. They can be taken on baits of prawn, squid, octopus, pipi, and fish flesh. Long-shanked hooks will help to remove these fish without getting too near to the spines. As the spinefoot is a schooling fish, moving away is a good option. This species is marketed as black trevally and is fairly strong flavoured but makes acceptable eating.

STONEFISH

Scientific name *Synanceja horrida.* Also known as Estuarine stonefish, reef stonefish.

Range Shark Bay in Western Australia and tropical northern waters as far south as Moreton Bay in Southern Queensland.

Description Several authors describe two separate species, the estuarine stonefish and the reef stonefish (*Synanceja verrucosa*). These extremely well camouflaged species are separated by the habitat preference and the number of pectoral rays which is 16 in the estuarine species 18 or 19 for the reef stonefish. The estuarine stonefish reaches 47 cm and the reef species 35 centimetres. However, for all but taxonomists, counting stonefish pectoral rays is dangerous and highly unlikely. The stonefish has 13 extremely poisonous dorsal spines which can inject poison deeply into a wound and can lead to death.

Fishing The stonefish is never a target species and is rightly avoided at all costs. It is however, an effective ambush feeder of inshore reef or estuarine waters, often lying in extremely shallow water, where they can be trodden on. Sandshoes should be worn when walking on tropical reef tops or in tropical estuarine waters to provide some protection from stonefish, coral cuts and stingrays. Stonefish are particularly partial to small live baits, but they will also take prawns, crabs, and fish baits. They can also take slowly worked lures and flies. With stonefish, always cut off the hook and release the animal with no handling. If stung, immerse the wound in hot, but not scalding water. Seek hospitalisation immediately as morphine and medical supervision is likely to be required.

Rigs and Tactics

No. 1 to 3
bean sinker

No. 2 to
2/0 hook

No. 00
to 1 ball
sinker

No. 6 to 4
light gauge
fly hook

No. 2 to 5
ball sinker

20 cm
dropper

40–50 cm
dropper

No. 4 to 2/0 Long
Shank, Eastern Estuary or
Suicide hook depending
on species sought

STONEFISH

Rigs and Tactics

Not applicable as Stonefish are not recommended as an angling species

STRIPEY

Scientific name *Microcanthus strigatus* Also known as footballer

Range A disjointed distribution from Exmouth Gulf to Cape Leeuwin in Western Australia and from the Capricorn group in Queensland to Merimbula in NSW.

Description A small and colourful species reaching 16 cm that represents the first capture for many young recreational fishers. The stripey is found in small schools on shallow protected reefs and in embayments and harbours. They are common around jetties. The stripey is yellow with a number of prominent black stripes that run along the body and onto the head. The eye also has stripes through it. The forehead profile is distinctly concave and the mouth is quite small.

Fishing The stripey is colourful and is fished for mainly by kids or newcomers to the sport. They are unforgiving of bait quality and are persistent biters although their small mouths make them difficult to hook. They will readily take baits of fish, prawn, squid, liver, mince, beef heart, dough, pipi, worm or most baits. Can also be taken on bait jigs. The small size does not make these a rated food fish but they have been consumed by families to celebrate the entry of many children to their fishing careers.

TAILOR

Scientific name *Pomatomus saltatrix*. Also known as Tailer, chopper, bluefish (USA), elf (South Africa), skipjack.

Range Point Quobba in Western Australia and southern waters including Tasmania and as far north as Fraser Island in Queensland. Tailor are however, very rare along most of the south coast and Tasmania.

Description The tailor is a renowned predatory species best known for its relatively small but extremely sharp teeth. The tailor has a moderately forked tail, and a bluish to blue-green back which changes to more silvery and white on the belly. The eye can be yellow. The fins vary in colour but the tail fin is usually darker than the others. Juvenile tailor are found in estuaries and embayments. Larger tailor move to the beaches and inshore reefs at between 25 – 35 centimetres. Tailor undergo a spawning migration, finishing at Fraser Island in Queensland and possibly the Abrolhos Islands in Western Australia, although the largest fish are most commonly found in Shark Bay. Tailor can reach 10 kg with any fish over 5 kg being rightly claimed as a prize and fish over 1.5 kg being large. Tailor are voracious feeders, with individual fish gorging themselves before regurgitating to continue in a feeding frenzy.

Fishing Tailor are a highly prized species which readily takes a bait, fights hard and, if bled immediately after capture make fine eating. Tailor can be taken from boat or shore, on lure, fly or bait and by anglers of any skill level. The most common bait and rig would be a whole pilchard bait on a gang hook rig. In the surf and where casting distance is required, a sliding sinker rig works best, with a star or spoon sinker on a dropper trace doing well. In estuaries, from a boat, or in calmer surf, an unweighted or minimally weighted bait provides by far the best results. Tailor readily feed high in the water column and avidly attack a floating bait. Another rig which works well is to use a nearly filled plastic bubble to gain casting distance without rapidly sinking the bait. Tailor also bite well on whitebait, bluebait and cut flesh baits but they will also take prawn, squid, cuttlefish, mince, heart and other red meats. If using live baits, a small stinger hook near the tail will prevent the loss of successive baits to tailor. A wire trace is required with single hook rigs and small lures, but tailor almost always attack the offering from the back and bite offs are not that common with ganged hook rigs and minnow type lures. Tailor love chrome lures, jigs, spoons and minnow lures which are cast or trolled, especially into white water near rocks, reefs or bommies where tailor aggregate. Tailor will also take flies but their teeth badly knock around feathers. Tailor bite best at dusk and dawn. Tailor smoke very well and are fair eating when fresh which is improved if fish are immediately bled. The flesh of the tailor is fairly oily and bruises easily. Tailor makes a quality cut bait.

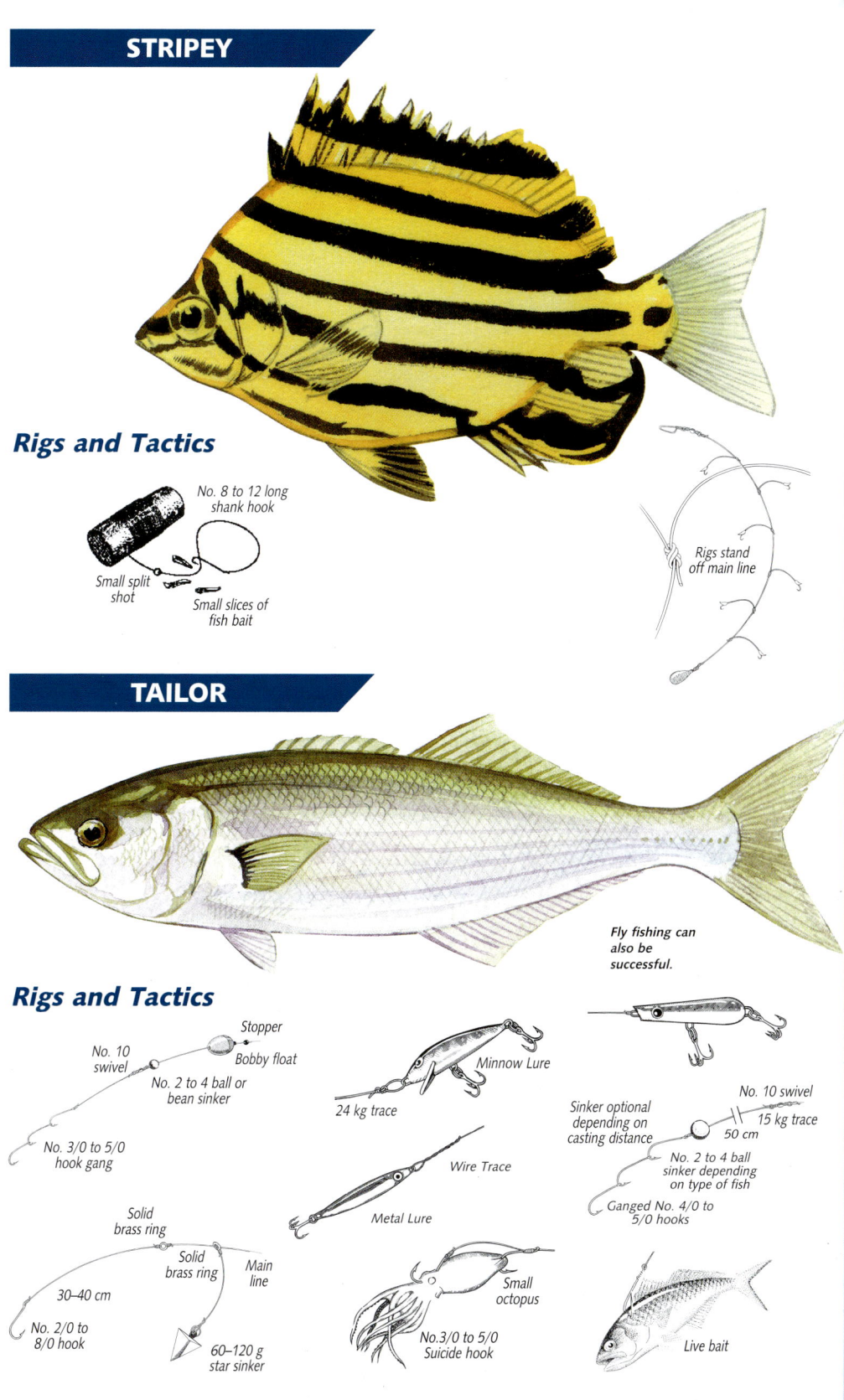

Rigs and Tactics

No. 8 to 12 long shank hook

Small split shot

Small slices of fish bait

Rigs stand off main line

TAILOR

Fly fishing can also be successful.

Rigs and Tactics

Stopper

No. 10 swivel

Bobby float

No. 2 to 4 ball or bean sinker

No. 3/0 to 5/0 hook gang

Minnow Lure

24 kg trace

No. 10 swivel

15 kg trace

Sinker optional depending on casting distance

50 cm

No. 2 to 4 ball sinker depending on type of fish

Ganged No. 4/0 to 5/0 hooks

Wire Trace

Metal Lure

Solid brass ring

Solid brass ring

Main line

30–40 cm

No. 2/0 to 8/0 hook

60–120 g star sinker

Small octopus

No.3/0 to 5/0 Suicide hook

Live bait

TARPON

Scientific name *Megalops cyprinoides.* Also known as Oxeye herring.

Range Onslow in Western Australia and northern waters around the east coast as far south as Sydney NSW.

Description The tarpon is most easily identified by the long trailing filament at the rear of the single dorsal fin. The eye is also very large as are the upper jaw bones. The tail is deeply forked and powerful. The scales are very large. Tarpon are commonly found in mangrove creeks, larger estuaries and bays. The tarpon can grow to 1.5 m and around 3.5 kilograms.

Fishing The tarpon will take dead fish bait but can be very finicky. They can sometimes be taken on small live baits. However, tarpon are a fantastic fighting fish and are a target species for lure and fly fishers. Most fish are taken on small white jigs or small chrome lures. They are also avid fly takers. The mouth of the tarpon is bony and hooks should be at their absolute sharpest to get a solid hookup that can survive the strong fight and aerial display of the tarpon. Tarpon are extremely bony and are considered poor eating. Care should be taken with handling to reduce scale loss and long term mortality of released fish.

TARWHINE

Scientific name *Rhabdosargus sarba.* Also known as Silver bream.

Range The tarwhine has a broken distribution, from Esperance to Shark Bay in Western Australia and from the Great Barrier Reef in northern Queensland to the Gippsland Lakes in Victoria.

Description The tarwhine is similar to the various bream species but differs in a few key areas. The tarwhine has a number of thin golden or brown stripes running the length of the otherwise silver body. The nose of the tarwhine is blunt and there are 11 or 12 anal rays whereas bream have 9 or fewer. The fins other than the dorsal fin are generally bright yellow or yellow-orange and the tarwhine has a black lining to its gut cavity. Tarwhine are common in inshore and estuarine areas and may be found on offshore reefs on occasions. Tarwhine form schools, especially in smaller sizes. Tarwhine can reach 80 cm and more than 3 kg but they are most commonly caught at a few hundred grams.

Fishing Tarwhine can be voracious feeders, taking a wide variety of foods. Tarwhine readily take cut flesh, bluebait, whitebait and parts of pilchard but many more are caught on prawn, pipi, worm, nipper or squid baits. Tarwhine are also occasionally taken on cabbage baits by luderick and drummer fishermen in NSW. While tarwhine bite very hard, their relatively small mouth and frequent small size makes them nuisance bait pickers in many instances. Use a smaller hook for better results, but don't let the fish run with the bait too far as they can easily become gut hooked. In estuaries or shallow waters, a light running ball sinker rig works best while off the rocks or in deeper water, use as little weight and as light a rig as you can get away with. Tarwhine fight well for their size. They also make very good eating although they can have an iodine taste if not bled immediately and the guts and black stomach lining removed as soon as possible.

Rigs and Tactics

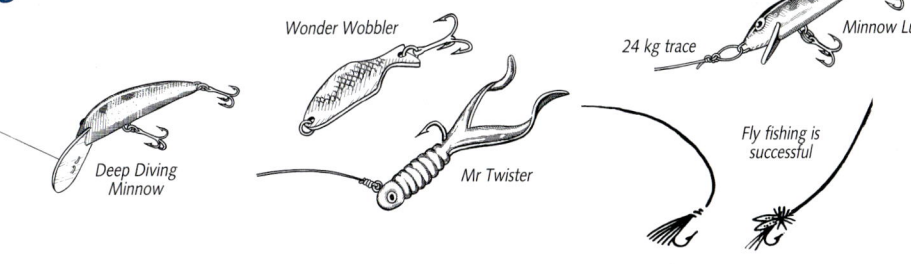

Wonder Wobbler

24 kg trace

Minnow Lure

Deep Diving Minnow

Mr Twister

Fly fishing is successful

TARWHINE

Rigs and Tactics

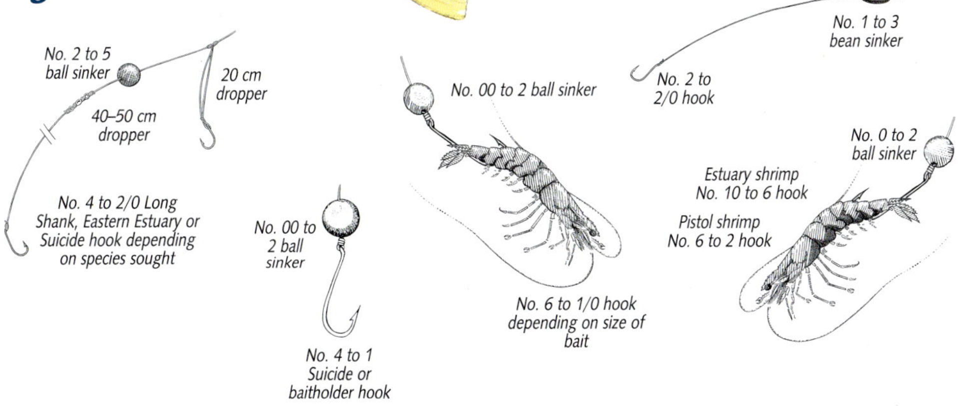

No. 1 to 3 bean sinker

No. 2 to 5 ball sinker

20 cm dropper

40–50 cm dropper

No. 00 to 2 ball sinker

No. 2 to 2/0 hook

No. 0 to 2 ball sinker

Estuary shrimp No. 10 to 6 hook

Pistol shrimp No. 6 to 2 hook

No. 4 to 2/0 Long Shank, Eastern Estuary or Suicide hook depending on species sought

No. 00 to 2 ball sinker

No. 6 to 1/0 hook depending on size of bait

No. 4 to 1 Suicide or baitholder hook

TOADFISH, COMMON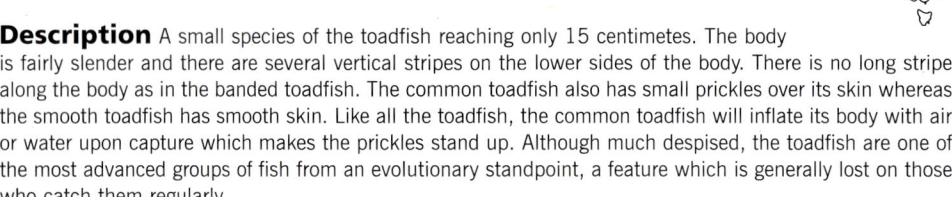

Scientific name *Tetractenos hamiltoni* Also known as blowie, toado

Range Townsville in Queensland and southwards to Merimbula in southern NSW.

Description A small species of the toadfish reaching only 15 centimetes. The body is fairly slender and there are several vertical stripes on the lower sides of the body. There is no long stripe along the body as in the banded toadfish. The common toadfish also has small prickles over its skin whereas the smooth toadfish has smooth skin. Like all the toadfish, the common toadfish will inflate its body with air or water upon capture which makes the prickles stand up. Although much despised, the toadfish are one of the most advanced groups of fish from an evolutionary standpoint, a feature which is generally lost on those who catch them regularly.

Fishing This small species is a well known bait stealer. Travelling in schools, the fused teeth enable any bait no matter how robust to be stripped. There are no specialist rigs for this species and only luderick anglers using green weed seem to be immune from their attentions when they are in the area. The common toadfish is highly toxic and must not be consumed or fed to pets under any circumstance. Because of this all toadfish should not be left anywhere where pets or wild animals can consume them as they will kill if not treated by trained professionals.

TOADFISH, SMOOTH

Scientific name *Tetractenos glaber* Also known as slimey toadfish, smooth blowie

Range Port Lincoln in South Australia and eastwards along the south coast including Tasmania and to Moreton Bay in southern Queensland.

Description A small species of toadfish growing to 16 centimetres. The smooth toadfish has all the common characteristics of the toadfish making it especially unloved among the fishes. There are the fused teeth which can bite through trace and make mincemeat of any bait in seconds and they have the toxic flesh and organs that makes them extremely dangerous. The smooth toadfish has smooth skin with no prickles even when inflated which at least makes their inflation upon capture less of a problem. The smooth toadfish has several large darker blotches along its upper body against its generally mottled background.

Fishing The smooth toadfish is not targeted by anglers and is avoided by all but the most raw novice or the extremely bored angler. The fused teeth and small mouth means that they can only be realistically taken on small long shanked hooks. All species of toadfish are highly poisonous and should never be consumed.

TOADFISH, WEEPING

Scientific name *Torquigener pleurogramma.* Also known as common blowfish, banded toadfish.

Range The banded toadfish is one of the most common species of toadfish with a wide but disjointed range from Coral Bay in Western Australia to Adelaide in South Australia and then Narooma in southern NSW to Hervey Bay in Queensland.

Description This is a fairly small species only reaching 22 cm and commonly found in sandy surf areas and around jetties and pylons where they are many children's first fish. The diagnostic feature is the single dark brown stripe down the side and up to six narrow dark bands which run downwards across the cheek and near the eye, giving the appearance of tear stains. Like all toadfish, the banded toadfish can inflate its abdomen with air or water and small rough spikelets are extended.

Fishing The weeping toadfish, in common with the other similar toadfish species can be caught on a variety of small baits, which can fit into the small mouth with its sharp fused teeth. This species has been known to give divers a painful nip and the teeth can cut through the line so a fairly small long shank hook is recommended, so new hooks are not constantly retied. While the weeping toadfish makes good sport for beginning anglers, they should never be kept and consumed or fed to domestic pets as there have been a number of fatalities, including humans. The toxins are strongest in the skin and internal organs, especially the liver.

TOADFISH, COMMON

Rigs and Tactics

Not applicable as Toadfish are not recommended as an angling species

TOADFISH, SMOOTH

Rigs and Tactics

Not applicable as Toadfish are not recommended as an angling species

TOADFISH, WEEPING

Rigs and Tactics

Not applicable as Toadfish are not recommended as an angling species

TREVALLY, BIGEYE

Scientific name *Caranx sexfasciatus*. Also known as Great trevally.

Range Margaret River in Western Australia and northwards through tropical waters and around the east coast as far south as Sydney in NSW but the bigeye trevally is more common in tropical waters.

Description Positive identification of all trevally species is particularly difficult. The bigeye trevally is best identified by the gelatinous covering to the rear of the relatively large eye. There are white tips to the dorsal and anal fins and a small black spot on the rear edge of the gill cover. The bigeye trevally's breast is fully scaled which separates it from the giant trevally. The soft dorsal fin of the bigeye trevally has 19 – 22 soft rays while the turrum, with which it is sometimes confused has 25 – 30 rays. Juvenile bigeye trevally prefer the tidal flats and can be quite common while larger fish patrol close to deep drop-offs especially those close to high tidal flows or near reef gaps. This is not a large species, reaching only 80 centimetres.

Fishing An avid lure taker, the bigeye trevally is fished near areas of fast water near reef gaps on the outgoing tide. Poppers work extremely well, with chrome slices, minnow lures and jigs also appealing to these strong fighters. Smaller fish, especially when in groups can be sight fished on tidal flats. Lures, a rapidly stripped fly or fresh bait, especially one that is kept moving will bring a strike and other fish also trying to get the lure. On a rising tide, these fish can often be on the inside of the reef edges or areas where break-offs are more common. Bigeye trevally readily take small live baits. Like all trevally, the fish should be bled and immediately iced. The removal of the red meat along the lateral line will make the taste more mild.

TREVALLY, BLUEFIN

Scientific name *Caranx melampygus* Also known as blue-finned trevally, spotted trevally

Range Exmouth Gulf in Western Australia and northwards through tropical waters and then as far south as Sydney in NSW.

Description Differentiating the various trevally species can be difficult even for trained taxonomists. However, the bluefin trevally exhibits several features that are readily identifiable to the average angler. The common name gives a clue to a diagnostic feature, with the prominent blue tail fin. The soft dorsal fin and anal fins as well as along the scutes which form along the tail end of the lateral line are also blue or bright blue. The transparent pectoral fin is elongated and extends to the commencement of the tail scutes. There are a number of small blue or dark spots on the upper body which may extend onto the head, but these spots are more numerous and never golden as in the thicklip trevally. The bluefin trevally is found on coastal reefs although larger specimens can be found along deeper reefs or adjacent slopes. The bluefin trevally can reach 1 metre which makes it a challenge on lighter gear near reefs.

Fishing The bluefin trevally is a typically hard fighting fish, turning side on and using all its resistance to get to some reef to break off the unwary angler. The bluefin trevally is taken on a variety of rigs, ranging from lures such as poppers, wobblers, minnow lures, soft plastics and fly gear to shallow, lightly rigged baits and standard reef bouncing paternoster rigs. The bluefin trevally will take a variety of baits including cut baits, whole fish, squid, prawns and live bait. The bluefin trevally is considered to be among the better trevally species to eat.

TREVALLY, BIGEYE

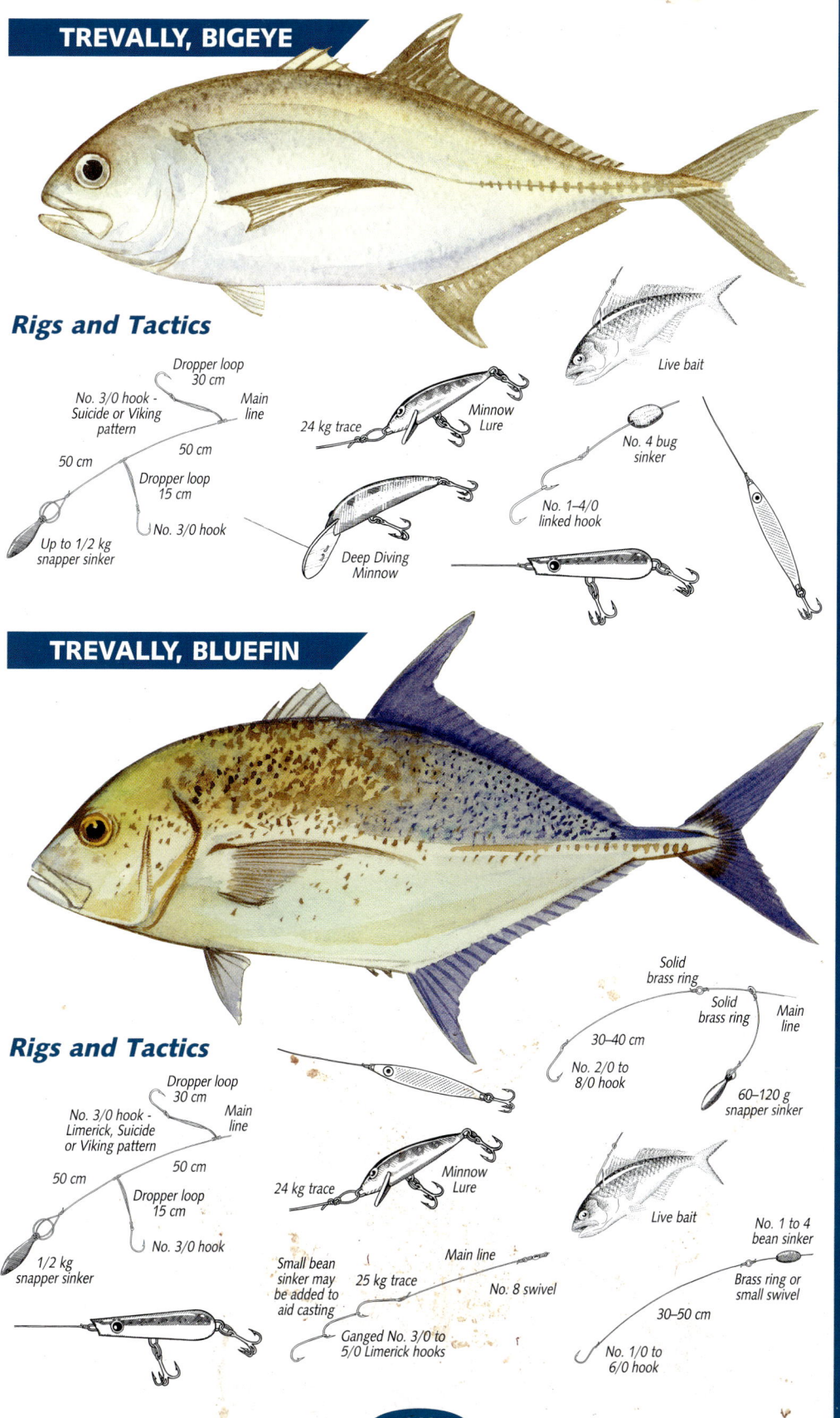

Rigs and Tactics

Live bait

Dropper loop
30 cm

No. 3/0 hook -
Suicide or Viking
pattern

Main
line

50 cm

24 kg trace

Minnow
Lure

No. 4 bug
sinker

50 cm

Dropper loop
15 cm

No. 3/0 hook

No. 1–4/0
linked hook

Up to 1/2 kg
snapper sinker

Deep Diving
Minnow

TREVALLY, BLUEFIN

Rigs and Tactics

Solid
brass ring

Solid
brass ring

Main
line

30–40 cm

No. 2/0 to
8/0 hook

60–120 g
snapper sinker

Dropper loop
30 cm

No. 3/0 hook -
Limerick, Suicide
or Viking pattern

Main
line

50 cm

24 kg trace

Minnow
Lure

Live bait

No. 1 to 4
bean sinker

50 cm

Dropper loop
15 cm

No. 3/0 hook

1/2 kg
snapper sinker

Small bean
sinker may
be added to
aid casting

25 kg trace

Main line

No. 8 swivel

Brass ring or
small swivel

30–50 cm

Ganged No. 3/0 to
5/0 Limerick hooks

No. 1/0 to
6/0 hook

TREVALLY, BRASSY

Scientific name *Caranx papuensis.* Also known as Papuan trevally.

Range Exmouth Gulf in Western Australia and tropical waters extending as far south as Sydney on the east coast.

Description The brassy trevally is a very similar species to the giant trevally and is often misdescribed in fishing publications. The brassy trevally is often in schools of similar sized fish on inshore tidal areas or reef edges where they they often ambush feed. The brassy trevally has a white rear border to the lower lobe of the tail fin and sometimes the rear of the anal fin which separates it from the giant trevally. Both dorsal fins are dusky coloured and other fins have a yellow tinge or are yellow. Very small dark or black spots are often found on the upper half of the body. The brassy tinge to the overall body colour gives rise to the common name. This species grows to around 80 cm, while the giant trevally can reach 1.7 metres.

Fishing The brassy trevally is an avid lure taker with a distinct preference for tidal flats or drop-offs near reef areas. Best lures include poppers, minnow lures, slices or spoons. Like all trevally, the brassy trevally gives a very strong and powerful fight. Gel spun line is considered important when trying to keep a determined trevally from a reef edge. Brassy trevally will also take flies, with large deceivers rapidly stripped in working best. It may be necessary to tease a school with a popper without hooks to improve the hookup rate on fly, but the fight on a fly rod is worth the effort. Brassy trevally will also take pilchard, cut flesh baits or large prawns, but prefer the bait moving. Therefore as little weight as you can get away with is preferred, as these fish will move to take the bait. Live baits are irresistible.

Small and medium brassy trevally make very good eating.

TREVALLY, GIANT

Scientific name *Caranx ignobilis.* Also known as Lowly trevally, barrier trevally.

Range Rottnest Island in Western Australia northwards including tropical waters and as far south as Sydney on the east coast.

Description The giant trevally is the largest of the trevally reaching 1.7 m in length and 60 kg which would be almost unstoppable on stand up fishing tackle. The steep profile of the head is typical of the giant trevally. There is also a small scale-less area on the ventral surface immediately in front of the ventral fins. A small patch of scales is generally found in the middle of this otherwise scale-less patch. There is no opercular (cheek) spot which is present on the bigeye trevally. As giant trevally increase in size, they form smaller schools with the largest fish frequently loners. Large fish also prefer deeper channels between large reefs while smaller fish are found on tidal flats or on the edges of shallower reefs.

Fishing Small giant trevally are one of the most challenging species for lure fishers in the tropics, with spinning near the edges of reefs, on drop-offs on tidal flats or sight fishing to individuals or small schools working well. Poppers are particularly attractive to these fish and can also be used as a teaser for fly fishers. Giant trevally also take minnow lures, large spoons and lead-headed jigs. Large giant trevally are most frequently taken on live baits. They will also take dead baits, including fresh dead baits, cut baits, pilchards or less frequently squid or large prawn baits. Giant trevally can be hooked when bottom bouncing with standard reef rigs for other species such as coral trout or various emperors, with arm stretching and tackle testing results. Top quality gear and gel spun lines are an advantage in landing these challenging fish. Small giant trevally are good eating but fish over 10 – 12 kg are poor tasting and are better released after a photograph to record the encounter.

TREVALLY, BRASSY

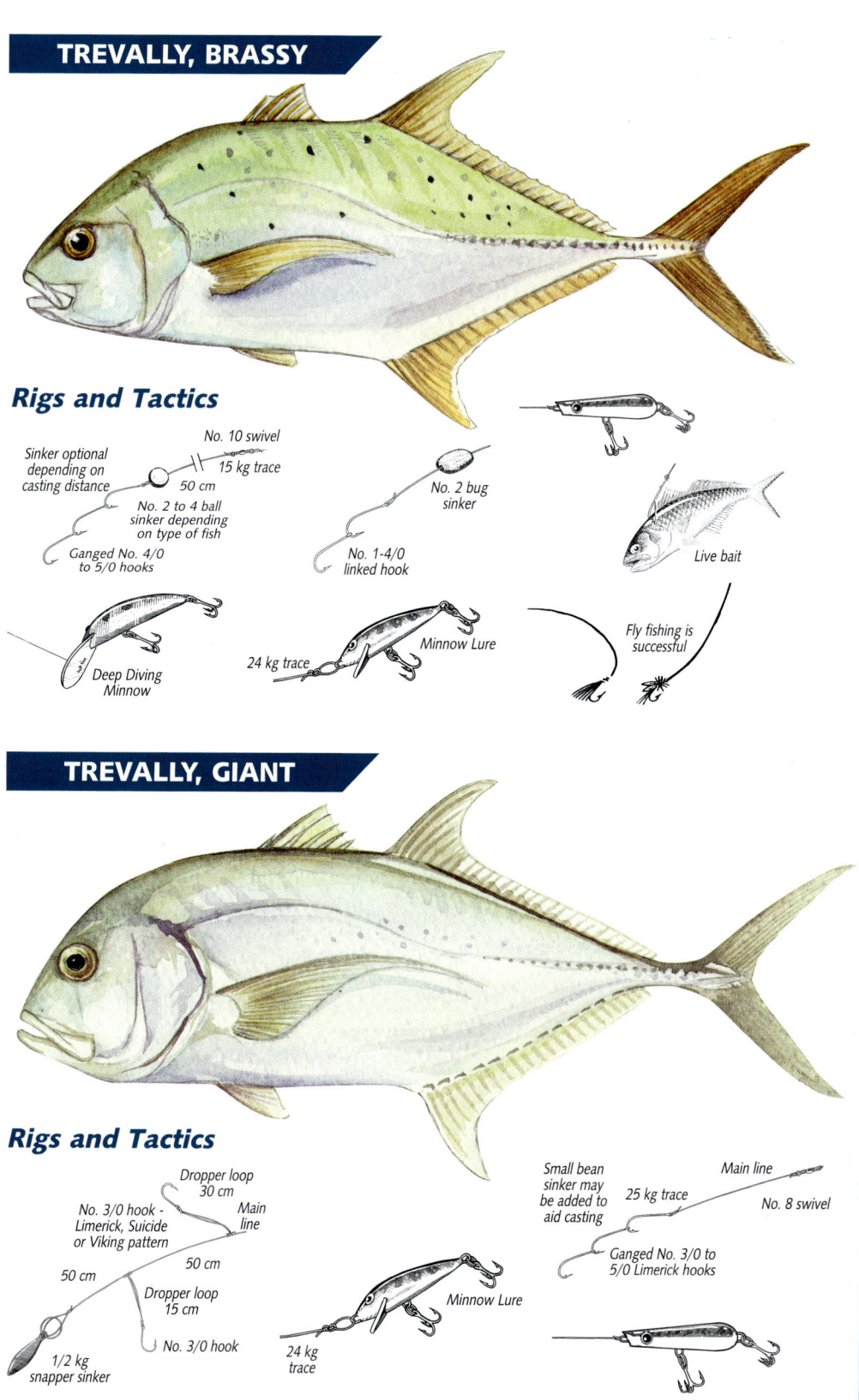

Rigs and Tactics

Sinker optional
depending on
casting distance

No. 10 swivel

15 kg trace

50 cm

No. 2 to 4 ball
sinker depending
on type of fish

Ganged No. 4/0
to 5/0 hooks

No. 2 bug
sinker

No. 1-4/0
linked hook

Live bait

Deep Diving
Minnow

24 kg trace

Minnow Lure

Fly fishing is
successful

TREVALLY, GIANT

Rigs and Tactics

Dropper loop
30 cm

No. 3/0 hook -
Limerick, Suicide
or Viking pattern

Main
line

50 cm

Dropper loop
15 cm

50 cm

No. 3/0 hook

1/2 kg
snapper sinker

Minnow Lure

24 kg
trace

Small bean
sinker may
be added to
aid casting

25 kg trace

Main line

No. 8 swivel

Ganged No. 3/0 to
5/0 Limerick hooks

TREVALLY, GOLDEN

Scientific name *Gnathanodon speciosus.*

Range A wide ranging species from Denmark on the south coast of Western Australia and the entire west coast, northern waters and as far south as Wollongong in NSW but most common in tropical waters.

Description The golden trevally is also a large species reaching 1.2 m and 37 kilograms. Juvenile golden trevally are striking and are often associated with large fish or sharks. They are a bright gold with vertical black stripes the first of which passes through the eye. Larger fish lose the distinctive stripes and the eye is quite small. These fish are often quite silvery when caught but flash yellow as they die and then are golden coloured, especially on the belly. A number of black spots are often present on the side, commonly near the tail but the number and size varies and they may not be present. The most obvious feature of this species is that they lack teeth.

Fishing Like many trevally, golden trevally form schools of similar sized fish, with smaller schools of larger fish. Large golden trevally are often taken trolling minnow lures in the vicinity of offshore reefs. Smaller fish are taken by shore based or small boat anglers either with lures including poppers, slices, spoons or minnow lures or less commonly on fly. Golden trevally take baits well, with prawns, pilchard, small fish or cut baits working well. Over sand, the baits can be weighted, but near reefs, lightly weighted or floating baits work better as the further any trevally moves from a reef to take a bait, the better the chances of landing it, as they fight very strongly and make use of any rocky outcrop. Golden trevally make very good eating, especially if bled and chilled immediately on capture.

TREVALLY, SILVER

Scientific name *Pseudocaranx dentex.* Also known as White trevally, skipjack trevally, skippy, trevally, blurter.

Range North-west Cape in Western Australia and southwards, along the entire south coast and Tasmania and as far north as south Queensland.

Description A common schooling fish of cooler waters, the silver trevally is found in inshore areas but may be found near offshore cover. Juveniles are often encountered in estuaries and bays but larger fish can also be found in these areas on occasions. The fins may be yellow and a narrow yellow stripe is often found on these fish but most fish are silver with a blue-green or darker blue, and dark bands may be present. The very similar sand trevally (*Pseudocaranx wrighti*) of central Western Australia only grows to around 800 g and has more prominent dark bands. The silver trevally can reach 1 m and more than 10 kg but fish of 2 kg are much more common and in most areas, a fish of 5 kg is noteworthy. The mouth is relatively small, finishing well in front of the start of the eye and the lips are rubbery. There is an obvious black spot on the rear edge of the opercular (cheek) bone.

Fishing The silver trevally can be present in almost plague proportions with areas like Port Stephens NSW famous for its 'blurter' runs. Like all trevally, they can be good sport, especially on light line. Silver trevally can be taken on small lures such as small spoons, leadhead jigs and small minnow lures. They can be coaxed to take flies, particularly when berley is used with a school of fish. While silver trevally can feed on the surface, they prefer to feed on or near sandy or gravel bottoms and lures presented close to the bottom do best. Silver trevally are a better bait proposition, taking baits such as half pilchard, bluebait, whitebait, cut fish baits, squid, prawn, crab, pipi, nipper or cunjevoi depending on the food found in the area fished. Silver trevally respond well to berley. Silver trevally can be taken on lines of 3 – 8 kg where they provide excellent sport. As they are a schooling fish which are not too prone to disperse if one fish escapes, persistence pays off with light line. Small silver trevally make excellent live baits, but size and bag limits must be followed. Silver trevally are fair eating, and must be bled on capture.

TREVALLY, GOLDEN

Rigs and Tactics

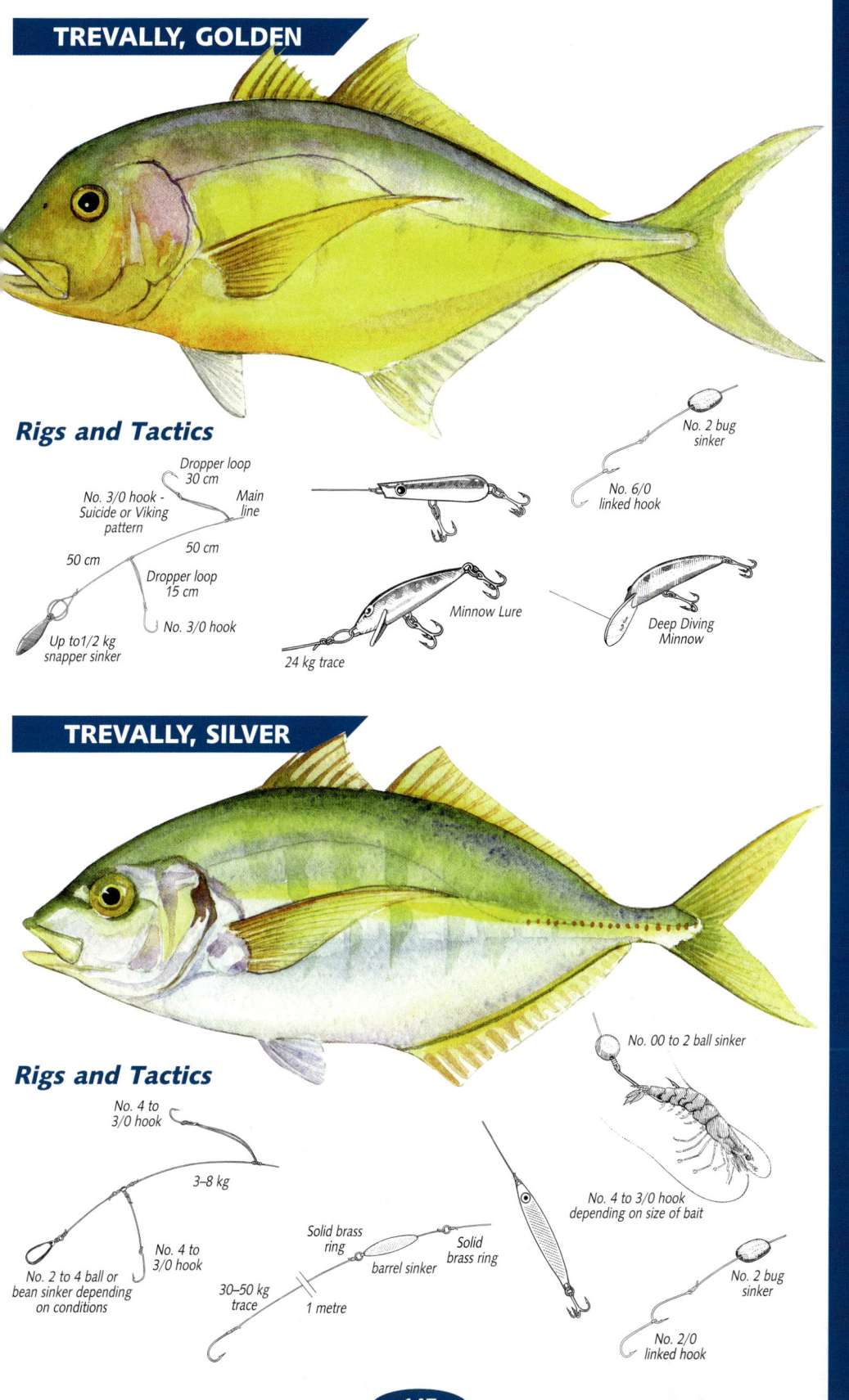

Dropper loop
30 cm

No. 3/0 hook -
Suicide or Viking
pattern

Main
line

50 cm

50 cm

Dropper loop
15 cm

No. 3/0 hook

Up to1/2 kg
snapper sinker

Minnow Lure

24 kg trace

Deep Diving
Minnow

No. 2 bug
sinker

No. 6/0
linked hook

TREVALLY, SILVER

Rigs and Tactics

No. 4 to
3/0 hook

3–8 kg

No. 4 to
3/0 hook

No. 2 to 4 ball or
bean sinker depending
on conditions

Solid brass
ring

barrel sinker

Solid
brass ring

30–50 kg
trace

1 metre

No. 00 to 2 ball sinker

No. 4 to 3/0 hook
depending on size of bait

No. 2 bug
sinker

No. 2/0
linked hook

TREVALLY, THICKLIP

Scientific name *Carangoides othogrammus* Also known as yellow-spot trevally, false bluefin trevally, island trevally, blue trevally

Range Fremantle in Western Australia and throughout northern waters around the top end as far south as Sydney in NSW.

Description The thicklip trevally has a slightly more rounded shape than the similar bluefin trevally. The scutes are less strongly developed than in many trevally species. The soft dorsal and anal fins are fairly scythe-like and the pectoral fin does not extend to the tail scutes. There are a small number of yellow or golden brown spots near the lateral line and towards the back end of the body. The fins may be bright blue to a dusky grey. There are bands of fine teeth in the mouth. Another diagnostic feature is the scaleless patches on the breast and at the base of the pectoral fin. The thicklip trevally reaches 70 centimetres. The thicklip trevally is found on inshore and offshore reefs and is better known for schooling in Queensland. Individuals from southern waters will travel with schools of other species of fish.

Fishing The thicklip trevally will occasionally rise to take lures, but is more commonly caught while drift fishing with live or cut baits near reefy ground. Standard paternoster rigs, or specific live bait rigs work well. A heavy line and strong trace is recommended to prevent even small fish from getting back to the reef. The thicklip trevally is considered to be good eating.

TRIPLE TAIL

Scientific name *Lobotes surinamensis.* Also known as Jumping cod.

Range Mandurah in Western Australia and northwards throughout tropical waters and around the east coast as far south as the Hawkesbury River in NSW.

Description The tripletail is a reasonably large predator of mangrove creeks, estuaries and inshore reefs which can reach 1 m and around 11 kg but is more common at smaller sizes. The most obvious feature is the elongated soft dorsal and anal fins which gives the resemblance of three tails. The base colour varies from yellow in small juveniles to chocolate brown with a silvery sheen and there may be grey mottling. The eye is relatively small and the mouth is also fairly small finishing in front of the eye.

Fishing The triple tail is a very strong fighter, with the surface area of the 'triple tails' providing significant leverage. The triple tail can also be a strong jumper. The triple tail is commonly found near drop-offs in mangrove creeks or near pylons, anchor chains or other structures in estuaries which they can use to advantage. Triple tails take lures well, particularly minnow lures, slices and jigs. They will also readily take fresh cut baits, pilchards or small live baits. These baits can either be drifted back near cover on lightly weighted rigs or cast to the base of cover with sufficient weight to anchor the bait to the bottom, even in moderate flows. The first rig is better suited to exploring wider areas and can also result in barramundi, mangrove jacks and threadfin salmon. The triple tail is excellent eating and many rate this species above barramundi.

TREVALLY, THICKLIP

Rigs and Tactics

Brass ring   Main line

100–200 g
barrel sinker

No. 6/0 to 9/0
hook Suicide or
Live Bait hook

Solid
brass ring

Solid
brass ring

Main
line

30–40 cm

No. 2/0 to
8/0 hook

60–120 g
snapper sinker

No.3/0 to 5/0
Suicide hook

Small
octopus

24 kg trace

Minnow Lure

Dropper loop
30 cm

No. 3/0 hook -
Limerick, Suicide
or Viking pattern

Main
line

50 cm

50 cm

Dropper loop
15 cm

No. 3/0 hook

1/2 kg
snapper sinker

Live bait

TRIPLE TAIL

Rigs and Tactics

No. 1 to 3
bean sinker

No. 2 to
3/0 hook

Deep Diving
Minnow

Dropper loop
30 cm

No. 3/0 hook -
Suicide or Viking
pattern

Main
line

50 cm

50 cm

Dropper loop
15 cm

No. 3/0 hook

1/2 kg
snapper sinker

24 kg trace

Minnow Lure

Live bait

TRUMPETER

Scientific name *Pelates quadrilineatus* Also known as four-lined trumpeter

Range Shark Bay in Western Australia and northwards through tropical waters and as far south as Narooma in NSW

Description A common bait stealing species of the estuaries and coastal bays. While it has a wide range, it is best known from NSW where it forms schools over weed and sand areas from the Sydney region northwards and disrupt bream, whiting and flathead fishing. The trumpeter has a more elongated nose than the striped trumpeter and there are four or five prominent stripes which run the length of the body. The mouth is relatively small, and as it only grows to 20 cm, this species is difficult to hook. A dark blotch behind the head and under the start of the dorsal fin is usually present.

Fishing The trumpeter is not generally targeted and isn't even highly regarded as a live bait. The trumpeter will take almost all baits but is more commonly associated with the picking of baits such as worm, pipi, prawn or mullet gut intended for other species. They are attracted to berley intended for bream and they can also be taken on bait jigs. While the trumpeter makes a good cut bait, their small size means that they are not targeted as a food fish.

TRUMPETER, STRIPED

Scientific name *Pelates sexlineatus*. Also known as Striped perch, striped grunter, trump.

Range Shark Bay in Western Australia southwards as far as Kangaroo Island in South Australia.

Description A small species reaching 32 cm and around 500 g, but more common at a bait stealing 25 centimetres. The striped trumpeter forms schools in coastal bays and estuaries over sand or weed bottom or near broken ground. The small mouth makes hooking difficult. The short head is quite rounded and there are around 5 – 6 lines running through the head and along the body. There may be a number of vertical blotches with one most prominent behind the head overlaying the stripes. The top stripes may be wavy.

Fishing While frequently considered a pest species, the striped trumpeter is a frequent early encounter for young anglers. The striped trumpeter will take most baits, but the small mouth and darting bites of a school means that a small long-shanked hook will improve catches. Baits of peeled prawns, cut flesh, blue bait, pipi, worms, or squid work well, with more robust baits such as squid recommended. Striped trumpeter make hardy and quality live baits. Striped trumpeter are not highly regarded as food fish but are often served to the family by proud young fishermen.

TURRUM

Scientific name *Carangoides fulvoguttatus*. Also known as Gold spotted trevally, yellow spotted trevally.

Range Augusta in Western Australia and northwards including tropical waters and as far south as Maroochydore in Queensland.

Description The turrum is a largely tropical species that may move further south during summer. It is found in inshore waters and around shallow and occasionally mid water reefs. A number of species are known as turrum, especially in Queensland, but the true turrum can be identified by a number of features. These include the complete lack of scales up to the base of the pectoral fin whereas the giant trevally has a small oval shaped patch of tiny scales in an otherwise large scaleless area of the breast. The second dorsal fin of the turrum has between 25 – 30 rays while the giant trevally has 18 – 21. The turrum differs from many other trevally in only having a band of fine teeth in each jaw. The turrum can reach 1.3 m and a weight of around 12 kilograms.

Fishing Many turrum are taken while trolling minnow lures near the edges of reefs, reef channels or other drop-offs. They will also rise to pusher type lures, slices, feathers and larger flies. Cast lures will also take fish. Turrum readily take live baits and are also taken on fresh whole fish, squid or cut-baits. Tackle needs to be strong. Small turrum are fair eating but larger fish are better returned to fight another day.

TRUMPETER

Rigs and Tactics

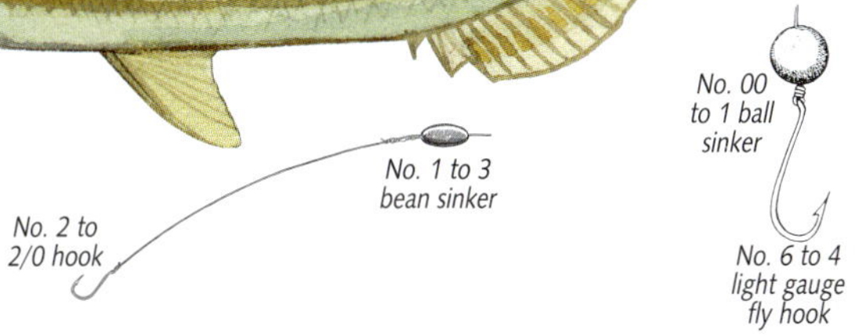

No. 1 to 3
bean sinker

No. 2 to
2/0 hook

No. 00
to 1 ball
sinker

No. 6 to 4
light gauge
fly hook

TRUMPETER, STRIPED

Rigs and Tactics

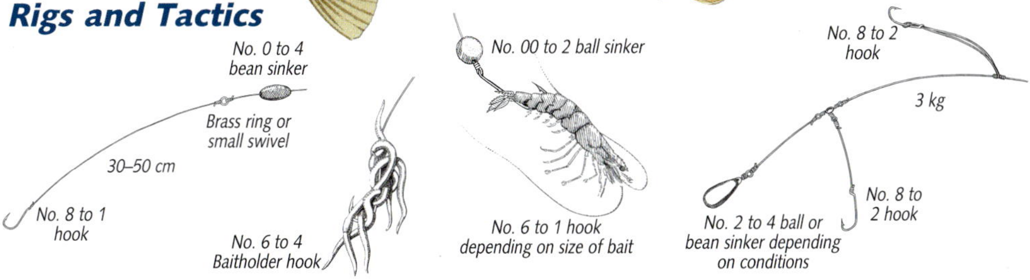

No. 0 to 4
bean sinker

Brass ring or
small swivel

30–50 cm

No. 8 to 1
hook

No. 6 to 4
Baitholder hook

No. 00 to 2 ball sinker

No. 6 to 1 hook
depending on size of bait

No. 8 to 2
hook

3 kg

No. 2 to 4 ball or
bean sinker depending
on conditions

No. 8 to
2 hook

TURRUM

Rigs and Tactics

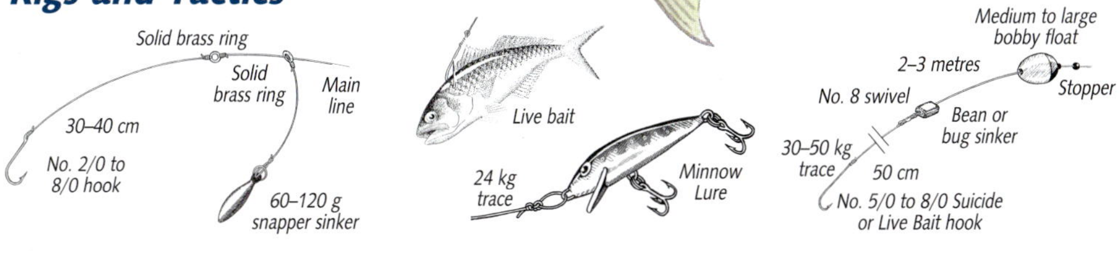

Solid brass ring

Solid
brass ring

Main
line

30–40 cm

No. 2/0 to
8/0 hook

60–120 g
snapper sinker

Live bait

24 kg
trace

Minnow
Lure

Medium to large
bobby float

2–3 metres

No. 8 swivel

Stopper

Bean or
bug sinker

30–50 kg
trace

50 cm

No. 5/0 to 8/0 Suicide
or Live Bait hook

WHITING, GRASS

Scientific name *Haletta semifasciata.* Also known as Rock whiting, blue rock whiting, weed whiting, stranger.

Range Fremantle in Western Australia and southern waters including Tasmania and as far north as Sydney, NSW.

Description Although the grass whiting vaguely resembles other whitings, this species is more closely related to the wrasses or parrotfish as it possesses fused teeth. It is a relatively common species which prefers seagrass habitats but may be found on nearby sand patches or shallow reefs. There is a single long dorsal fin compared with two dorsal fins for whiting. The grass whiting can reach 41 centimetres. There is vastly different colouring between males and females, with males a brighter bluish green with a black blotch towards the rear of the dorsal fin. Females and juveniles have pale greenish-brown backs which fade to brown after death. There is a distinctive blue blotch around the anus.

Fishing Grass whiting feed regularly on weed or kelp but can be taken with standard whiting rigs and baits. Light line and long-shanked hooks will help hook-ups as the grass whiting has a relatively small mouth. Best baits are beach or blood worms with peeled prawn, pipi, crabs and occasionally squid taking fish. Grass whiting can develop a weedy taste and fish should be bled and cleaned soon after capture.

WHITING, KING GEORGE

Scientific name *Sillaginodes punctata.* Also known as Spotted whiting, KG, KGW.

Range Dongara in Western Australia and southern waters, although rarely in eastern Tasmania and as far north as Jervis Bay but reasonably uncommon in NSW.

Description The King George whiting is the largest and most sought after whiting species in Australia reaching 67 cm and more than 2 kg, with the largest specimens found in oceanic waters. Juveniles spend time near sea grass beds inshore or in estuaries before moving to more open waters. King George whiting prefer sand patches near weed beds, gravel or broken reef country with water up to 10 m in depth being the most productive. King George whiting are readily identified by the typical whiting down-turned mouth and the distinctive dark brown or red-brown spots and broken dashes along the body.

Fishing The King George whiting is a magnificent and hard fighting whiting species. Smaller fish succumb most readily to baits of prawn, pipi, mussel, crab, nippers and worms. These baits are fished on light line with minimal weight near the edges of drop-offs or sand patches in sea grass beds or reef areas. Larger specimens, or fish taken in Western Australia are most frequently caught on blue sardines, whitebait or small cut baits. The largest King George whiting from South Australia and Western Australia are taken on reef fishing rigs intended for snapper or other species near reefs in depths up to 30 metres. Berley can work well, but can also attract bait pickers such as toads which are a nuisance. The best King George whiting experts adopt a mobile approach, fishing sometimes tiny sand patches near heavy cover and moving on if there are no bites in a few minutes. King George whiting are rarely taken on jigs, flies or other small lures generally intended for flathead or flounder. The King George whiting is magnificent eating, combining the meat quality of all whiting in a size large enough that generous boneless fillets can be obtained.

WHITING, GRASS

Male illustrated

Rigs and Tactics

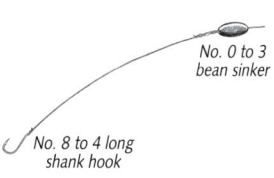

No. 0 to 3
bean sinker

No. 8 to 4 long
shank hook

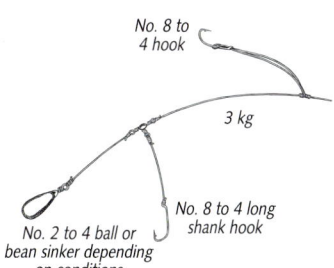

No. 8 to
4 hook

3 kg

No. 8 to 4 long
shank hook

No. 2 to 4 ball or
bean sinker depending
on conditions

WHITING, KING GEORGE

Rigs and Tactics

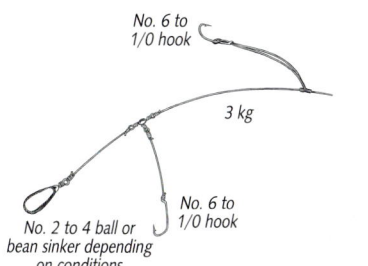

No. 6 to
1/0 hook

3 kg

No. 6 to
1/0 hook

No. 2 to 4 ball or
bean sinker depending
on conditions

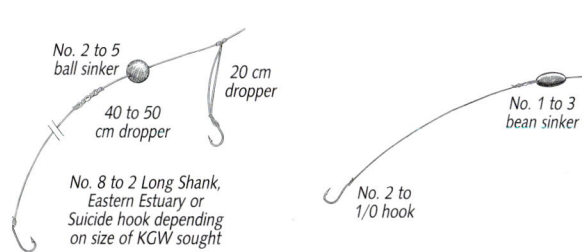

No. 2 to 5
ball sinker

20 cm
dropper

40 to 50
cm dropper

No. 8 to 2 Long Shank,
Eastern Estuary or
Suicide hook depending
on size of KGW sought

No. 1 to 3
bean sinker

No. 2 to
1/0 hook

WHITING, SAND

Scientific name *Sillago ciliata*. Also known as Silver whiting, summer whiting, blue nose whiting.

Range Cape York in Queensland and along the east coast as far south as eastern Tasmania and Lakes Entrance in Victoria.

Description The sand whiting is a common species of inshore and tidal sandy areas. The sand whiting can reach 47 cm and around a kilogram. It is readily identified by the lack of a silver stripe along the side and the dusky blotch at the base of the pectoral fin. Large sand whiting are sometimes confused with bonefish, but all whitings have two dorsal fins while the bonefish has one. A similar species, the yellow-finned whiting (also known as the Western sand whiting) (*Sillago schomburgkii*) reaches 42 cm but is only found from the Gulf of St Vincent in South Australia to Shark Bay in Western Australia. The yellow-finned whiting species lacks the dusky blotch at the base of the pectoral fin and is commonly taken on blue sardines, whitebait or small cut baits.

Fishing A scrappy little fighter which gives a good account of itself for its size. The sand whiting is a terrific light line quarry and fine tackle will greatly increase the number of strikes. Use the absolute minimum weight to either reach the bottom or to keep the bait from swinging wildly in current or wave wash. Sand whiting will take a moving bait and a slow retrieve will attract fish. A long trace behind a small ball sinker is the preferred rig. As whiting have a small mouth, a long shank hook around size 6 – 2 is recommended. Either putting red tubing or a few red beads above the hook works very well. The sand whiting feeds on nippers, pipis, prawns and especially beach, squirt or blood worms and all these make terrific baits. On a rising tide, sand whiting can be caught in very shallow water of only a few centimetres, while on a falling tide, fish the deeper edges of gutters or drop-offs but success is less assured. Sand whiting are a delicate, sweet flavoured fish often highly priced in restaurants but there can be a number of fine bones.

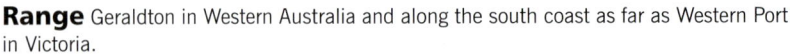

WHITING, SOUTHERN SCHOOL

Scientific name *Sillago bassensis* Also known as silver whiting

Range Geraldton in Western Australia and along the south coast as far as Western Port in Victoria.

Description The whitings can be extremely difficult to tell apart and the southern school whiting is one of the more difficult species to separate. The eastern school whiting (*Sillago flindersi*) only overlaps its range in Western Port in Victoria and is more heavily marked on the dorsal surface. The bars or streaks on the top of the southern school whiting may be very faint and a light orange or sandy brown colour. Under the water these streaks are very difficult to see. After death these bars may fade entirely giving a silver appearance. There is no spot at the base of the pectoral fin which separates the southern school whiting from all other similar species other than the yellow-fin whiting which has yellow to orange ventral fins. The southern school whiting is found on inshore sandy areas and will follow the tide onto sand flats and beaches. Although they are taken by recreational fishers in shallow waters, they can be taken on deeper sand bank and are trawled by commercial fishers to a depth of 55 metres. The southern school whiting can reach a very pleasing 36 centimetres.

Fishing The baits used to take whiting varies considerably from the east coast to the west coast. On the east coast, the best baits are squirt worms, blood worms, nippers or bass yabbies, prawn, pipi or cockles and occasionally squid. On the west coast, the best baits are bluebait, whitebait, pipi, prawn and squid. They are occasionally taken on small strips of flesh, especially if it is white belly meat rigged on small gangs of number 6 hooks. The rigs are best fished as light as possible and adding a few red beads or a piece of red tubing greatly assists the attractiveness of the bait. Whiting also prefer a moving bait so a cast and slow retrieve works best. Snags are not a problem as fishing is best on clean sand on a rising tide. The southern school whiting is excellent eating.

Rigs and Tactics

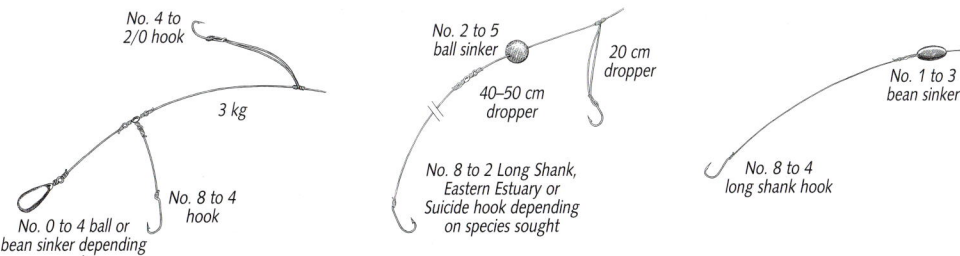

No. 4 to
2/0 hook

3 kg

No. 8 to 4
hook

No. 0 to 4 ball or
bean sinker depending
on conditions

No. 2 to 5
ball sinker

40–50 cm
dropper

20 cm
dropper

No. 8 to 2 Long Shank,
Eastern Estuary or
Suicide hook depending
on species sought

No. 1 to 3
bean sinker

No. 8 to 4
long shank hook

Rigs and Tactics

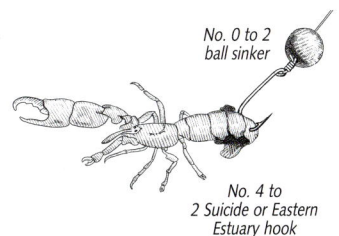

No. 1 to 3
bean sinker

No. 0 to 2
ball sinker

No. 4 to
2 Suicide or Eastern
Estuary hook

No. 00
to 1 ball
sinker

No. 6 to 4
light gauge
fly hook

No. 6 to
1 hook

No. 8 to 12 long
shank hook

Small split
shot

Small slices of
fish bait

WHITING, STOUT

Scientific name *Sillago robusta* Also known as yellow cheek whiting

Range Fremantle in Western Australia and northwards through tropical waters, although less common in the Northern Territory and to central NSW.

Description The stout whiting is a pale yellow on top and white below with a bright silvery band along the length of the fish separating these two zones. There is a bright yellow patch on the cheek and this species lacks the black spot at the base of the pectoral fin of many other whitings. There is nothing especially stout about this species which is more commonly encountered on offshore sandbanks in deeper water. The only exceptions are in Shark Bay and Moreton Bay where these fish can move into shallower water during winter when they mix with trumpeter whiting. The stout whiting grows to 30 cm but is most often seen in trawl catches at a much smaller size.

Fishing The stout whiting is a relatively small species which is found in quite deep water which makes their targeting rare. They are best taken on paternoster rigs drifted slowly over sand banks. Long traces on the bottom hook and a long shanked hook with red tubing will increase catches of stout whiting. Best baits are worms, pipi and prawn, but squid can work well in Western Australia. The stout whiting makes good eating.

WHITING, TRUMPETER

Scientific name *Sillago maculata*. Also known as Diver whiting, winter whiting, spotted whiting.

Range Geographe Bay in Western Australia and northwards through tropical waters and as far south as Narooma on the NSW south coast.

Description The trumpeter whiting is a common schooling fish with a preference for silty bottom or deeper gutters of bays and estuaries. The trumpeter whiting is more commonly taken during the cooler months, especially on the east coast. The trumpeter whiting reaches 30 centimetres. It is easily identified by having a series of irregular and disjointed brown blotches, spots or vertical marks. The similar eastern school whiting (*Sillago flindersi*) or southern school whiting (*Sillago bassensis*) both have unbroken vertical stripes. All of these species have a silver stripe which runs along the middle of the body.

Fishing The best catches of trumpeter whiting are made by drifting in a boat across drop-offs or deeper water until a school is located. The boat is anchored until the action slows and the drift recommenced. The fishing rig should be weighted just enough to keep contact with the bottom but moving with the drift. Best baits are beach, squirt or blood worms, nipper or small peeled prawn. Pipi, cockle, mussel or skinned squid also take fish. Trumpeter whiting in Western Australia will take blue sardines or whitebait. As these are a small fish, a small long-shanked hook in size 8 to 2 works best. Trumpeter whiting make excellent eating.

Rigs and Tactics

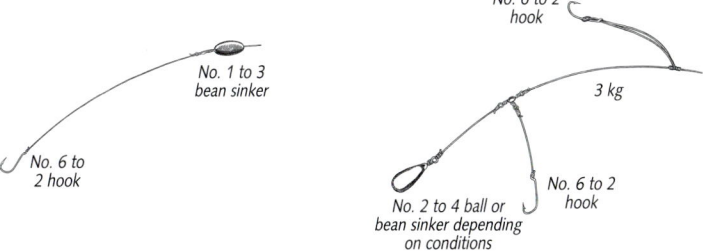

No. 1 to 3
bean sinker

No. 6 to
2 hook

No. 6 to 2
hook

3 kg

No. 6 to 2
hook

No. 2 to 4 ball or
bean sinker depending
on conditions

Rigs and Tactics

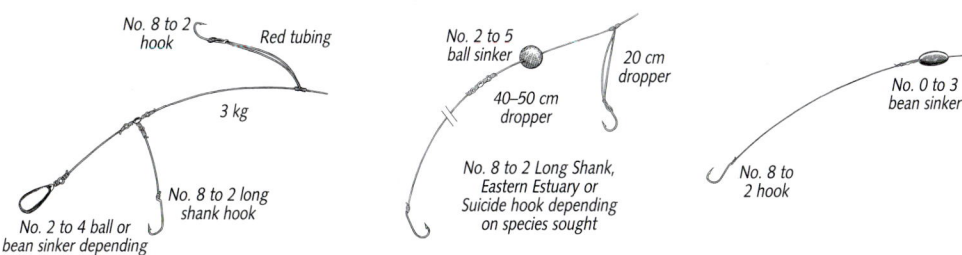

No. 8 to 2
hook

Red tubing

3 kg

No. 8 to 2 long
shank hook

No. 2 to 4 ball or
bean sinker depending
on conditions

No. 2 to 5
ball sinker

20 cm
dropper

40–50 cm
dropper

No. 8 to 2 Long Shank,
Eastern Estuary or
Suicide hook depending
on species sought

No. 8 to
2 hook

No. 0 to 3
bean sinker

WHITING, YELLOWFIN

Scientific name *Sillago schombergkii* Also known as western sand whiting, yellow-finned whiting

Range Shark Bay in Western Australia and southwards to the Gulf of St Vincent in South Australia

Description A similar species to the sand whiting but lacks the black spot at the base of the pectoral fin. The characteristic yellow to orange ventral and anal fins become less apparent in larger individuals. There is no obvious silver strip along the sides or any markings on the dorsal surface. Although the yellowfin whiting is found in South Australian waters it is most common on the west coast of Western Australia. It is found foraging in the estuaries and surf areas and can reach the most respectable size for a whiting of 42 centimetres. It is not uncommon at around 33 – 35 centimetres.

Fishing The excellent eating which this species provides makes it a worthwhile target for anglers. While they may be found in the estuaries, with the exception of the Peel-Harvey estuary, the best specimens are taken from ocean beaches. A light ball sinker and a bluebait or whitebait on small ganged hooks fished on a flick rod are highly recommended. When fishing for whiting, fishing at your feet first is good advice as many anglers cast way out behind the active feeding zone of this fish. They fish much better on a rising tide and can be in the sand wash area in only a few centimetres of water. Indeed, places where other anglers wade out to cast can help to attract yellowfin whiting. A slow retrieve works best.

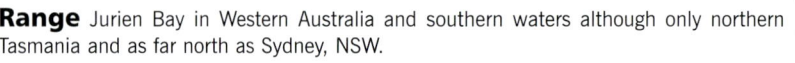

ZEBRA FISH

Scientific name *Girella zebra.* Also known as Stripey bream.

Range Jurien Bay in Western Australia and southern waters although only northern Tasmania and as far north as Sydney, NSW.

Description The zebra fish is a relatively common schooling fish of coastal reefs and surge zones of southern Australia. The common name is accurate for this close relative of the luderick and rock blackfish. The zebra fish reaches 54 cm but is most common from 400 g to 1.5 kilograms. The zebra fish is readily identified by the sloping forehead, small mouth and 8 – 10 vertical black bands which taper towards the belly. The fins may be dusky but are commonly yellow, especially the pectoral and tail fins.

Fishing Like luderick, zebra fish are largely herbivorous and can be taken on weed baits, with weed berley increasing strike rates. However, as these fish are relatively rare in NSW and weed fishing is really a NSW phenomenon, these fish are not generally taken in this manner. Most zebra fish are taken on peeled prawns, cunjevoi, cut crab, pipi, worms, mullet gut or bread intended for other fish. Berley with bread works well. These baits should either be fished under floats or with a small running sinker in the surge zone where bream, trevally or tailor can also be found. Zebra fish are a talking point if taken from a boat near weed or reef areas. Zebra fish should be bled and cleaned after capture as they can have a weed taint. However, in most instances, their flesh is similar to that of the luderick.

Rigs and Tactics

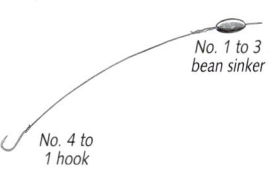

No. 1 to 3 bean sinker

No. 4 to 1 hook

No. 00 to 1 ball sinker

No. 6 to 4 light gauge fly hook

No. 2 bug sinker

No. 6 to 2 linked Limerick hook

ZEBRA FISH

Rigs and Tactics

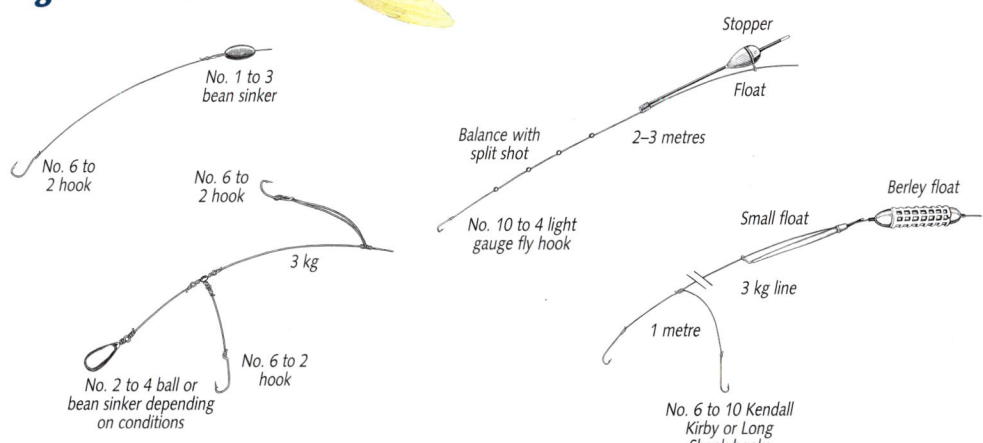

No. 1 to 3 bean sinker

No. 6 to 2 hook

No. 6 to 2 hook

3 kg

No. 2 to 4 ball or bean sinker depending on conditions

No. 6 to 2 hook

Stopper

Float

Balance with split shot

2–3 metres

No. 10 to 4 light gauge fly hook

Berley float

Small float

3 kg line

1 metre

No. 6 to 10 Kendall Kirby or Long Shank hooks

BASS, RED ☠

Scientific name *Lutjanus bohar* Also known as Two spot red snapper, kelp bream, kelp sea perch.

Range Ningaloo Reef northwards and tropical waters to Cape Moreton in southern Queensland.

Description The red bass is a strikingly coloured fish which can be almost bright orange to a deep brick red. The scales have a paler centre which gives an attractive dappled effect. There is a diagnostic deep groove or channel (often described as a pit) which runs from the nostrils to the front of the eye. The presence of this groove distinguishes the red bass from the similar mangrove jack where larger specimens are also caught on offshore reefs. The snout of the red bass is somewhat pointed. The tail fin is slightly indented and the ventral and anal fins may have a white margin. There is a moderate notch in the preopercular bone. Juvenile and sub-adult red bass have two or sometimes one silvery-white spots on the back, most prominent near the rear of the soft dorsal fin. The red bass can reach 13 kg and a length of 90 centimetres.

Fishing The red bass inhabits coral reefs, including sheltered lagoons and outer reefs, often adjacent to steep outer reef slopes. Juveniles and some adults can be caught near rocky headlands or near rocky drop-offs. The red bass is usually found singly, but it can be found in small schools, with larger fish showing more solitary tendencies. Red bass are taken with standard reef fishing gear and the standard reef paternoster rig. Best baits include fresh cut baits, squid, pilchard or other small whole fish. Live baits will attract any predatory reef fish, including red bass. Red bass are also taken on trolled lures intended for species like coral trout. The red bass fights extremely well and will try and bury the unwary angler into any nearby reef. The red bass is one of the worst offenders for ciguatera poisoning and should be returned immediately to the water, especially from Queensland waters.

BASS, SAND

Scientific name *Psammoperca waigiensis* Also known as Glass-eyed perch, jewel eye, dwarf palmer perch, reef barramundi.

Range Fremantle northwards through tropical waters to central Queensland.

Description The sand bass has one large flat spine at rear angle of preoperculum. Colour varies from light silvery grey to dark brown; eyes reddish. The lateral line extends onto the caudal fin. Inhabits rocky or coral reefs, frequently in weedy areas, usually in holes and crevices by day. This species can enter estuaries where it can be confused with juvenile barramundi. It can be separated from the barramundi in that the sand bass has granular teeth on the tongue, has a prominent lateral line and only reaches 47 cm but is more common at 30-35 centimetres. The sand bass forages on fishes and crustaceans at night.

Fishing The sand bass makes good eating, but does not reach the size of its more illustrious cousin the barramundi. Fishing for this species is best adjacent to rocky reefs. The large mouth of the sand bass means that it can be taken on baits intended for other species. The sand bass will take lures or jigs on occasion but they are more widely regarded as a bait species, with cut baits, squid and pilchards.

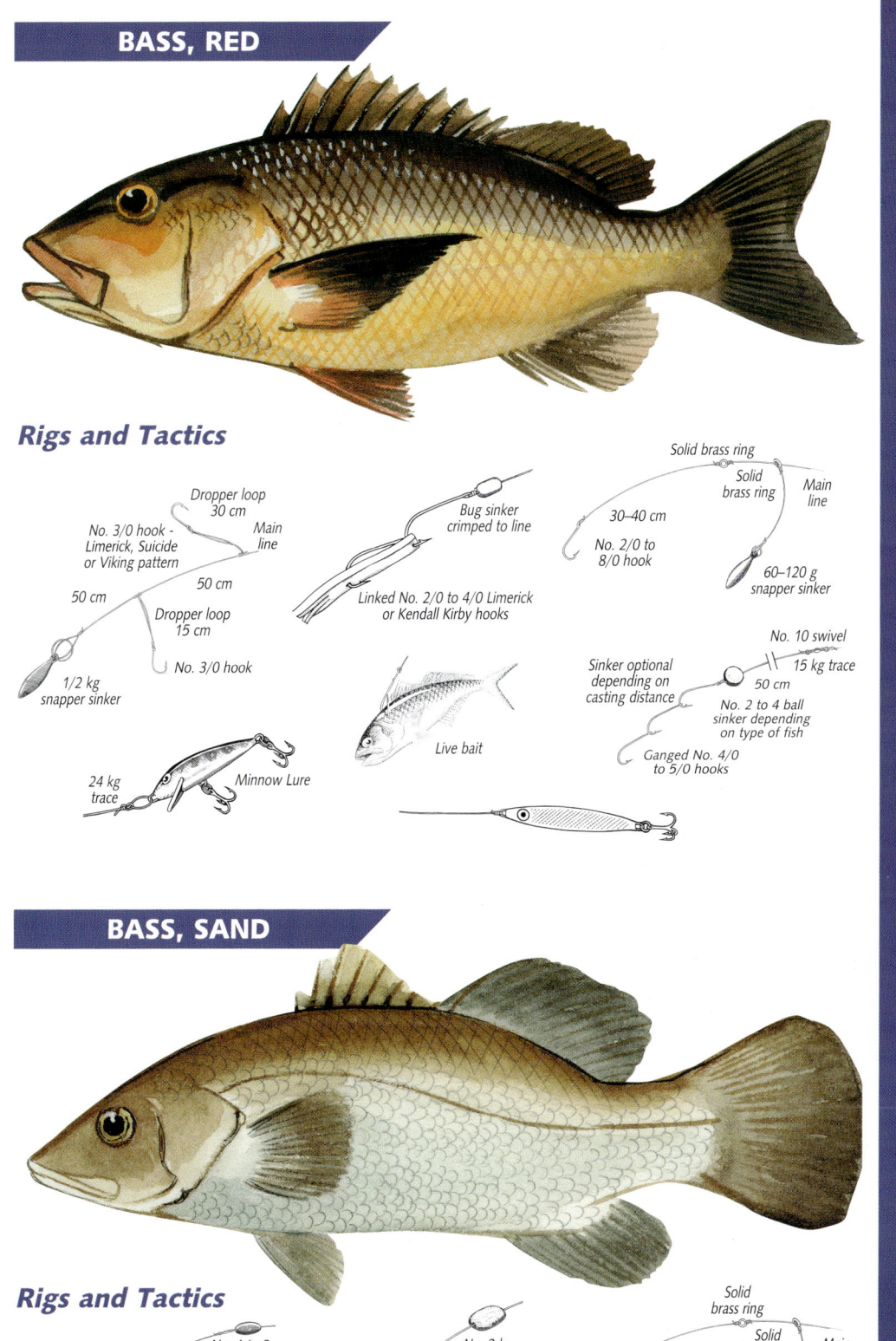

Rigs and Tactics

Dropper loop 30 cm

No. 3/0 hook - Limerick, Suicide or Viking pattern

Main line

50 cm

50 cm

Dropper loop 15 cm

No. 3/0 hook

1/2 kg snapper sinker

24 kg trace

Minnow Lure

Bug sinker crimped to line

Linked No. 2/0 to 4/0 Limerick or Kendall Kirby hooks

Live bait

Solid brass ring

Solid brass ring

Main line

30–40 cm

No. 2/0 to 8/0 hook

60–120 g snapper sinker

No. 10 swivel

15 kg trace

Sinker optional depending on casting distance

50 cm

No. 2 to 4 ball sinker depending on type of fish

Ganged No. 4/0 to 5/0 hooks

Rigs and Tactics

No. 1 to 3 bean sinker

No. 2 to 2/0 hook

No. 2 bug sinker

No. 2/0 linked Limerick hook

Solid brass ring

Solid brass ring

Main line

30 to 40 cm

No. 2/0 to 8/0 hook

60 to 120 g snapper sinker

BATFISH, HUMP-HEADED

Scientific name *Platax batavianus*. Also known as Humped batfish, batfish.

Range Found from Albany on the south coast of Western Australia around the top end to Sydney NSW on the east coast.

Description The hump headed batfish and the similar round-faced batfish, also known as tall-fin batfish (*Platax teira*) represent the largest of 10 species of batfish. The juveniles bear little resemblance to the adults. The hump-headed batfish has a distinctive black band over the head and including the eye. It is found in fairly deep water on open sandy substrates near large coral heads. The round-faced batfish has broad dusky vertical bands on its body and a black spot on its abdomen. Both species grow to around 4.5 kg and 60 centimetres.

Fishing Batfish are a reasonably common catch when fishing northern reef areas for coral trout and other similar species. Standard reef rigs and baits work well with a strong preference for fresh cut baits and large prawns. Batfish are not highly prized as food fish but smaller specimens make attractive aquarium fish.

BLUE DEVIL, EASTERN

Scientific name *Paraplesiops bleekeri*. Also known as Blue-Tipped longfin

Range Southern Queensland to Montague Island in southern NSW. Western blue devil from Cape Woolamai in Victoria and southern waters to the Abrolhos Islands in Western Australia.

Description A beautiful species much more common from Sydney to Ulladulla. Has been protected in NSW for many years as it can be inquisitive and was susceptible to spear fishing and aquarium trade harvest. The eastern blue devil can reach 40 cm. A dark coloured head is covered with peacock-blue spots. There are four black vertical bands over a white body and bright yellow tail wrist and part of the tail. The fins are long, often with bright blue fringes and some yellow highlights. Pectoral fin yellow. The western blue devil is also very distinctive and is separated by range and a frequently electric blue to blue/purple colouration, with even brighter coloured spots over the body and fins. It is often caught fishing inshore reefs, can reach 37 cm and is regarded as a food fish, although many consider them too beautiful to kill.

Fishing The eastern blue devil is protected and must be returned immediately to the water. They have quite a large mouth and can take fish or squid baits. However, the eastern blue devil is most highly prized by divers who marvel at their beauty.

BATFISH, HUMP HEADED

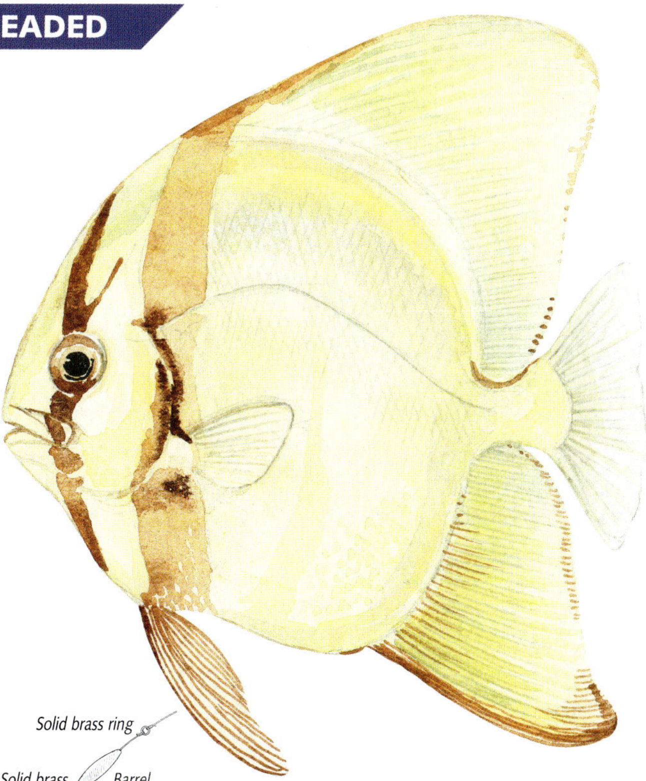

Rigs and Tactics

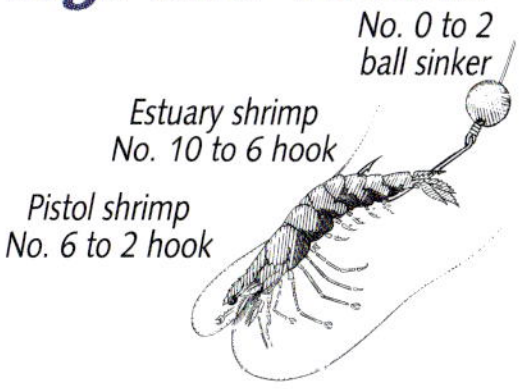
No. 0 to 2
ball sinker
Estuary shrimp
No. 10 to 6 hook
Pistol shrimp
No. 6 to 2 hook

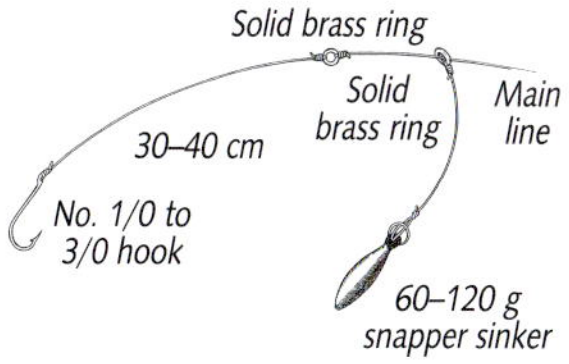
Solid brass ring
Solid
brass ring
Main
line
30–40 cm
No. 1/0 to
3/0 hook
60–120 g
snapper sinker

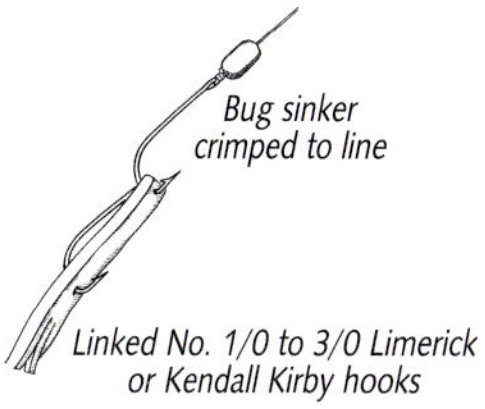
Bug sinker
crimped to line
Linked No. 1/0 to 3/0 Limerick
or Kendall Kirby hooks

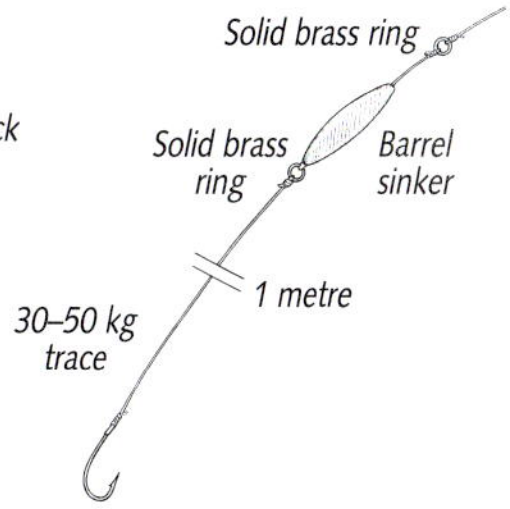
Solid brass ring
Solid brass
ring
Barrel
sinker
1 metre
30–50 kg
trace

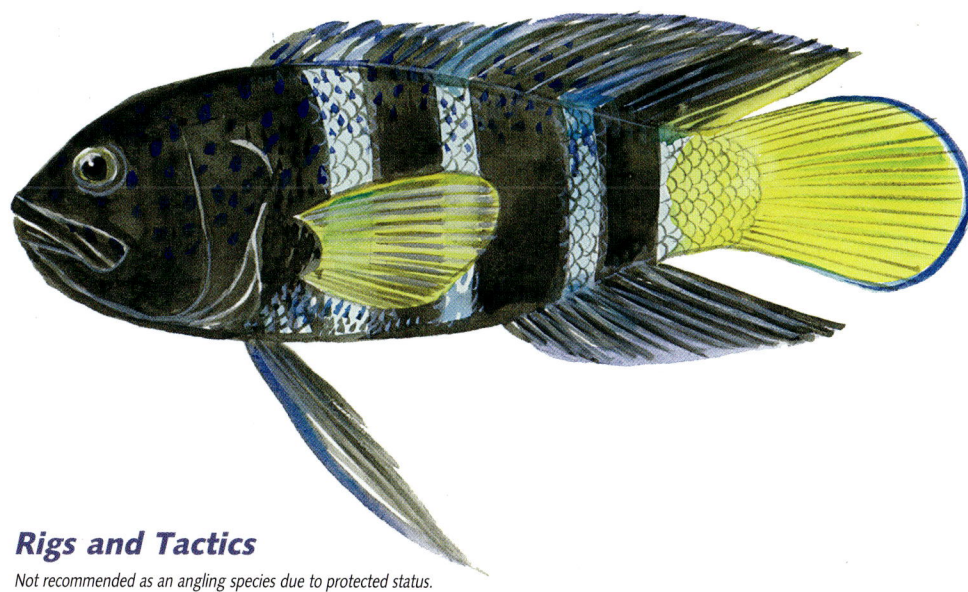

BLUE DEVIL, EASTERN

Rigs and Tactics

Not recommended as an angling species due to protected status.

BOARFISH, GIANT

Scientific name *Paristiopterus labiosus*. Also known as Boarfish

Range Walpole in Western Australia and southern waters, including Tasmania as far as Coffs Harbour in NSW. The brown-spotted boarfish (*Paristiopterus gallipavo*) is more common in South Australian waters.

Description The largest of the boarfish species reaching a metre and 12 kilograms. It is common on deep water reefs and is a common commercial species but can be caught from shallow water reefs which are close to deeper water. The dorsal fin of the giant boarfish is of similar height in adults. Juveniles have extended dorsal spines which become progressively smaller as the fish ages. There is a brown band that runs from the eye to the cheeks. The colouration is grey to brownish and may have lighter colours washed throughout. The mouth is large.

Fishing The giant boarfish is most often taken from deep water on heavy bottom bouncing tackle. It will take fish and squid baits and can be a welcome surprise when fishing inshore reefs near drop offs. The giant boarfish is considered to be excellent eating.

CHINAMAN FISH ☠

Scientific name *Symphorus nematophorus*. Also known as Threadfin sea perch (juveniles), galloper. Should not be confused with the Chinaman cod (*Epinephelus rivulatus*) which is a common and safe catch in northern Western Australia.

Range From Shark Bay in Western Australia and around the top end to Evans Head in northern NSW, but most common in tropical waters.

Description Juveniles look substantially different from adults with blue stripes on a yellow background and extended soft dorsal ray filaments. Fins are reddish pink. Adults lack extended filaments and are reddish with dark vertical bars. Adults have a stout body and a row of scales on the cheeks. The Chinaman fish also possesses a deep pit on the upper snout, immediately before the eyes.

Fishing Warning: This fish is a significant risk of containing ciguatera poisoning. Even though Western Australia has almost no ciguatera poisoning, this is one species which should be treated very carefully even there. A large, hard fighting fish taken in up to 50 metre depths while drift fishing tropical reef areas and edges. Reaches 80 cm and 17 kg, but should never be retained due to the risk of ciguatera poisoning.

COD, BARRAMUNDI

Scientific name *Cromileptes altivelis* Also known as polka dot cod, hump-backed cod, hump-backed rock cod.

Range Dirk Hartog Island off Shark Bay in Western Australia and north through tropical waters with juveniles found as far south as Sydney.

Description A truly spectacular species, especially for divers with its white or blotched body covered with black spots. Juveniles have fewer but larger black spots and can take on an almost pearlescent glow. Larger specimens can be the centrepiece of large public marine aquaria. The head of the barramundi cod resembles that of the barramundi in shape giving rise to the common name. There is also a noticeable hump to the back, which makes the head look much smaller than it is. The barramundi cod reaches 65 cm and 3.5 kilograms.

Fishing The barramundi cod is frequently taken by standard reef fishing rigs. They have a preference for reef caves or areas adjacent to them and may be susceptible to spearfishing. The barramundi cod can also be found in shallower reefs or even rock pools where they make a snorkelling expedition memorable. Baits include cut baits, squid and pilchards, with prawns also working well. Barramundi cod fight extremely hard, turning side on to the angler and making the most of their broad flanks. They will rise to take a trolled or cast lure and provide great sport and excellent eating. The barramundi cod has suffered a decline in Queensland where the live fish trade targets these fish and coral trout to get a top dollar in foreign restaurants.

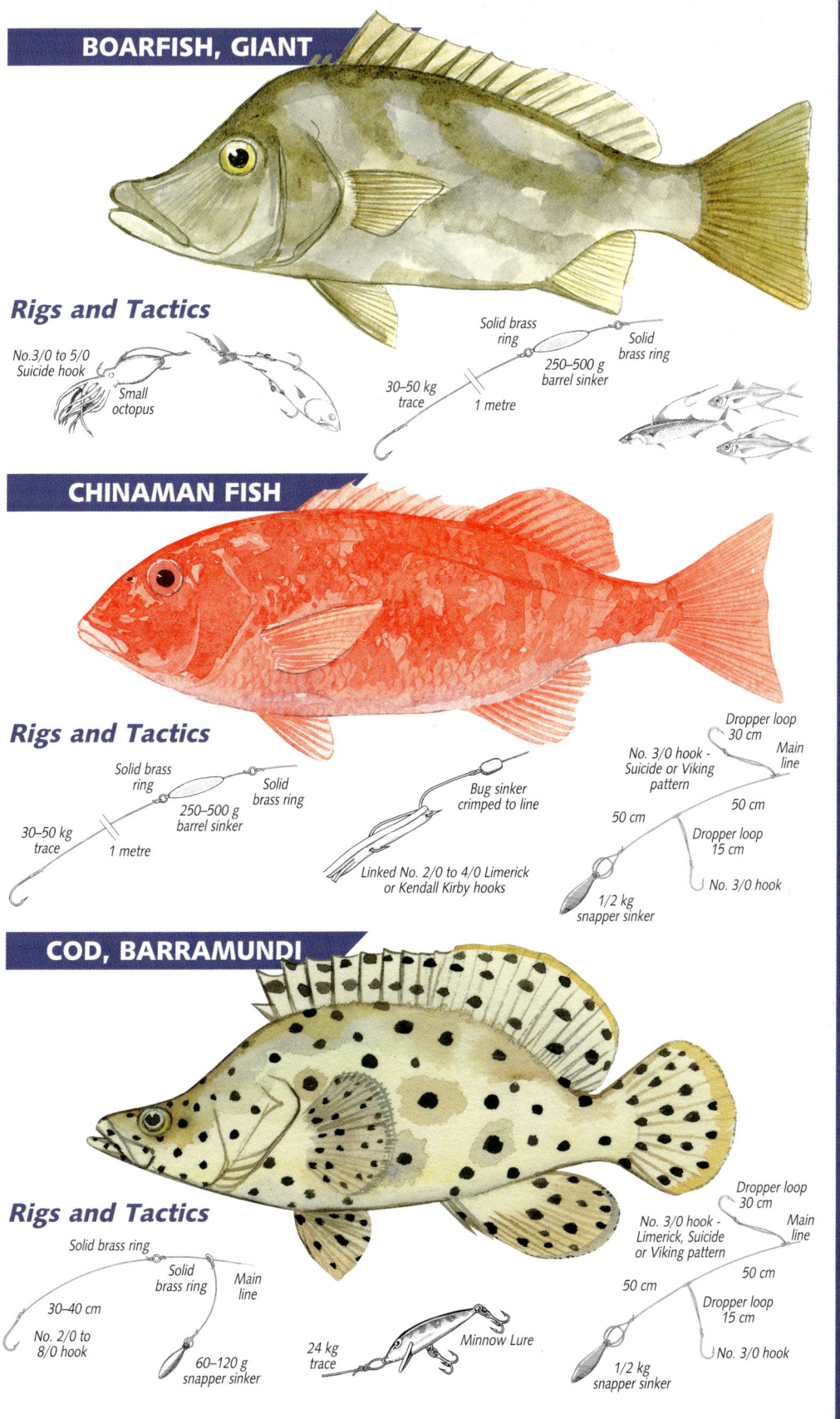

BOARFISH, GIANT

Rigs and Tactics

No.3/0 to 5/0
Suicide hook

Small
octopus

Solid brass
ring

Solid
brass ring

30–50 kg
trace

250–500 g
barrel sinker

1 metre

CHINAMAN FISH

Rigs and Tactics

Solid brass
ring

Solid
brass ring

30–50 kg
trace

250–500 g
barrel sinker

1 metre

Bug sinker
crimped to line

Linked No. 2/0 to 4/0 Limerick
or Kendall Kirby hooks

Dropper loop
30 cm

Main
line

No. 3/0 hook -
Suicide or Viking
pattern

50 cm

50 cm

Dropper loop
15 cm

1/2 kg
snapper sinker

No. 3/0 hook

COD, BARRAMUNDI

Rigs and Tactics

Solid brass ring

Solid
brass ring

Main
line

30–40 cm

No. 2/0 to
8/0 hook

60–120 g
snapper sinker

24 kg
trace

Minnow Lure

Dropper loop
30 cm

Main
line

No. 3/0 hook -
Limerick, Suicide
or Viking pattern

50 cm

50 cm

Dropper loop
15 cm

1/2 kg
snapper sinker

No. 3/0 hook

COD, BLACK

Scientific name *Epinephelus daemelii*. Also known as Saddled cod, saddled rock cod, saddletail cod.

Range On the Eastern coast as far south as Sydney, also Papua New Guinea and Lord Howe Island.

Description Found on offshore reefs, occasionally found in estuaries. Young fish are mottled grey with six vivid vertical bands. When fully grown they are capable of rapid colour changes, but retain a dark patch just above the tail. Grows to 45 kilograms.

Fishing Particularly susceptible to spearfishing especially if berleyed up and stocks are affected in NSW. Use standard reef fishing rigs with fish or squid bait. Smaller fish are excellent eating.

COD, BREAKSEA

Scientific name *Epinephelides armatus*. Also known as Black-arse cod, black arse, tiger cod.

Range Western Australia only from Albany to Shark Bay.

Description Relatively common inshore species often found around bommies and shallow reefs. Colour varies but can be brown to yellow with dusky black fins. The eye is a bright red and the anus is found in a large black spot, leading to the common names.

Fishing This species is commonly taken in mixed reef catches. Breaksea cod have a large mouth and will take large baits intended for other species. Standard reef paternoster rigs and baits work well with cut baits, prawn, pilchard and squid working well. Survival of released fis is gtraetly enhanced by using the release weight. This species is good eating.

COD, CHINAMAN

Scientific name *Epinephelus rivulatus* Also known as Chinaman rockcod, Charlie Court cod

Range Western Australia only, this species is most common from the Abrolhos Island to the Dampier Archipelago but can be found from Rottnest Island to the Kimberley coast.

Description A fairly small but attractive cod species with the fairly typical large mouth and long dorsal fin with lobed soft dorsal. The Chinaman cod can be distinguished by 4 or 5 prominent broad bars down the sides, although these can be very pale in specimens taken near sandy or broken bottoms. There are frequently white blotches on the head. The Chinaman rock is similar to the black-tipped rockcod, but lacks the distinctive black to reddish tips to the dorsal spines. The Chinaman cod reaches 45 cm and around 1.3 kg but is frequently caught at around 30 centimetres.

Fishing The Chinaman cod is a common table catch in the north-west of the state. The Chinaman cod is taken on standard reef rigs and baits of cut fish, pilchard, squid and octopus all taking fish. In places like Ningaloo Reef, the Chinaman cod is a common capture which makes pleasant eating and compensates for the times when north-west snapper and other more prized fish are less accommodating. Chinaman cod are most frequently taken from deeper reefs where the heavier lines and larger hooks tend to sandbag a reasonable fight.

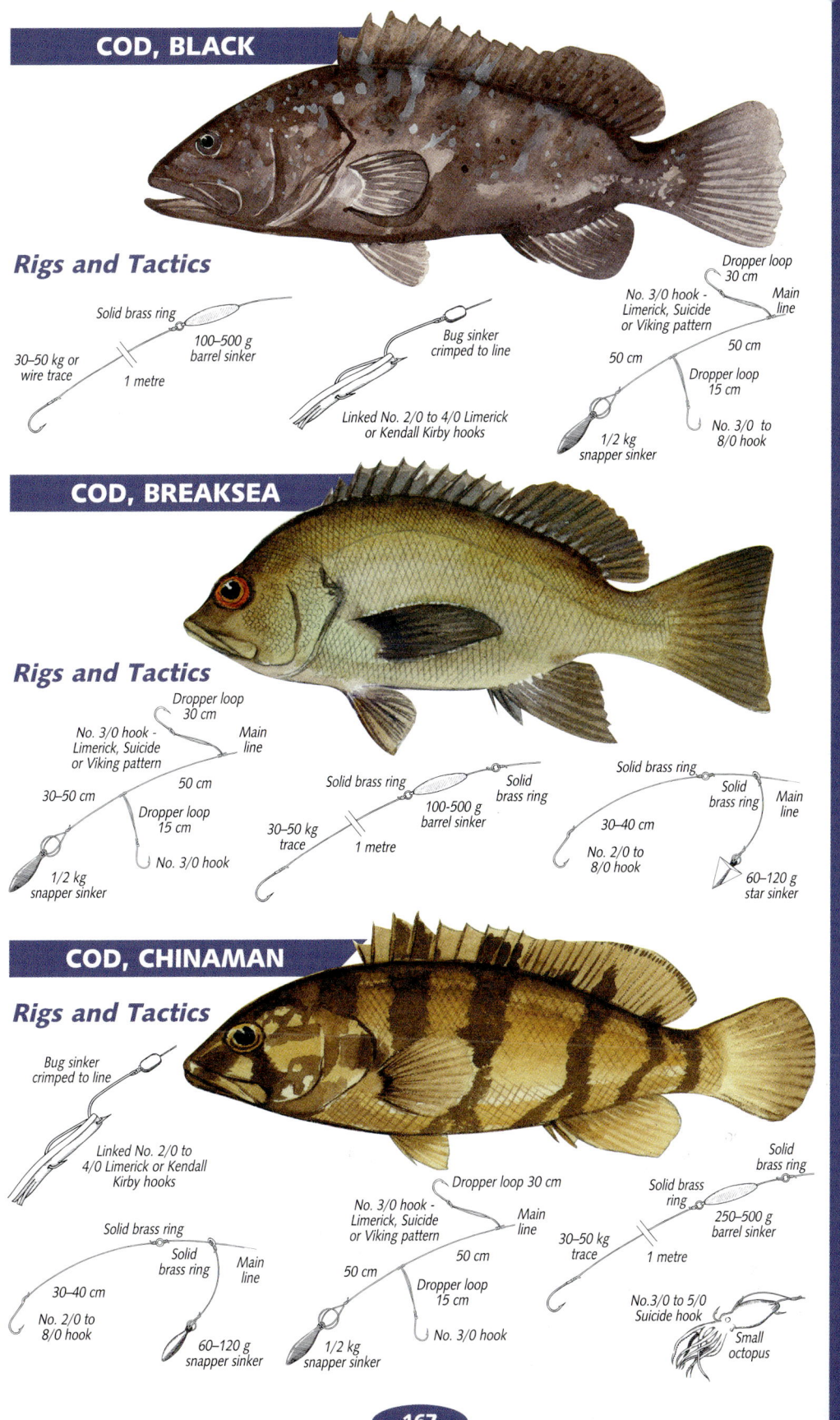

COD, BLACK

Rigs and Tactics

Solid brass ring
30–50 kg or wire trace
100–500 g barrel sinker
1 metre

Bug sinker crimped to line
Linked No. 2/0 to 4/0 Limerick or Kendall Kirby hooks

Dropper loop 30 cm
Main line
No. 3/0 hook - Limerick, Suicide or Viking pattern
50 cm
50 cm
Dropper loop 15 cm
1/2 kg snapper sinker
No. 3/0 to 8/0 hook

COD, BREAKSEA

Rigs and Tactics

Dropper loop 30 cm
No. 3/0 hook - Limerick, Suicide or Viking pattern
Main line
30–50 cm
50 cm
Dropper loop 15 cm
1/2 kg snapper sinker
No. 3/0 hook

Solid brass ring
Solid brass ring
100–500 g barrel sinker
30–50 kg trace
1 metre

Solid brass ring
Solid brass ring
Main line
30–40 cm
No. 2/0 to 8/0 hook
60–120 g star sinker

COD, CHINAMAN

Rigs and Tactics

Bug sinker crimped to line
Linked No. 2/0 to 4/0 Limerick or Kendall Kirby hooks

Solid brass ring
Solid brass ring
Main line
30–40 cm
No. 2/0 to 8/0 hook
60–120 g snapper sinker

Dropper loop 30 cm
No. 3/0 hook - Limerick, Suicide or Viking pattern
Main line
50 cm
Dropper loop 15 cm
1/2 kg snapper sinker
No. 3/0 hook

Solid brass ring
Solid brass ring
250–500 g barrel sinker
30–50 kg trace
1 metre
No.3/0 to 5/0 Suicide hook
Small octopus

COD, CORAL

Scientific name *Epinephelus corallicola*. Also known as Coral rockcod

Range Port Hedland in Western Australia and northern tropical waters around to Rockhampton, although juveniles may be found in estuaries further south.

Description A small member of the cod family, reaching 50 cm on the east coast and 31 cm on the west coast. The coral cod is identified by its grey or brown colour which is heavily blotched in darker brown and with small round black spots over the body and fins. There are three or four distinctive black marks on the upper back, frequently with another mark on the top of the wrist of the tail. The large mouth extends behind the back edge of the prominent eye. The coral cod inhabits shallow reefs and estuaries and may be found on mud or sand bottom near reefs.

Fishing The coral cod takes a variety of baits fished in reef country or near cover in tropical estuaries. Best baits include fresh fish baits, squid, octopus or small whole fish. As the coral cod is quite small, they are not often targeted but their large mouth means that they can take larger baits intended for other species. The coral cod can be taken infrequently on minnow lures and jigs. This species makes good eating.

COD, FLOWERY

Scientific name *Epinephelus fuscoguttatus* Also known as carpet cod, black rock-cod

Range Dampier archipelago in Western Australia and northwards through tropical waters to northern NSW around South West Rocks.

Description A heavy bodied cod species, the flowery cod generally has a fairly pale brown colour with darker chocolate brown 'flower' blotches on the sides. There are also numerous smaller spots over the body, including the stomach and the fins. The tail fin is heavily spotted and rounded while the spots on the ventral fins are an unusual feature of several closely related species. Juvenile flowery cod up to around 4 kg are often found in northern mangrove creeks. Adults are found on offshore reefs or on broken ground near reefs. This species can reach 90 cm while the small toothed cod reaches 63 centimetres.

Fishing In estuaries, juvenile flowery cod take a wide variety of baits and will take lures which are presented near them. They will take live or dead baits and provide good sport. On offshore reefs, larger specimens are taken on heavier, bottom reef fishing rigs. The flowery cod is highly regarded as a table fish presenting a thick fillet of white meat. Even large fish retain a high quality.

COD, POTATO

Scientific name *Epinephelus tukula*

Range Ningaloo Reef in Western Australia and northwards and throughout the Great Barrier Reef to central Queensland.

Description A large species reaching 1.4 m in length, the species has only recently been formally recognised. It was originally believed that the potato cod was a colour variation of the flowery cod or even the Queensland groper. This species is protected in Western Australia and Queensland. The potato cod can be identified by the large potato sized black blotches along its body. The head mat be covered with smaller blotches or dashed markings which may appear to radiate from the eye. In the water, the potato cod generally has a grey or off white background which makes the black blotches stand out. However, on capture, the potato cod may assume a darker overall colour and the blotches become much less apparent but can be seen with a careful examination. The potato cod has an undershot jaw and a straight forehead profile. The preopercular (inner cheekbone) is rounded and not notched which aids in identification. The potato cod is a residential species of mid-water reefs. They can appear tame but they can become aggressive when being hand fed by divers and those without gloves can risk cuts from the numerous small teeth.

Fishing As the potato cod is a protected species throughout most of its range, it is not a recommended angling species. Its large size and proximity to reefs makes this species a challenge for lighter lines. It is recommended that all potato cod be returned immediately to the water.

COD, CORAL

Rigs and Tactics

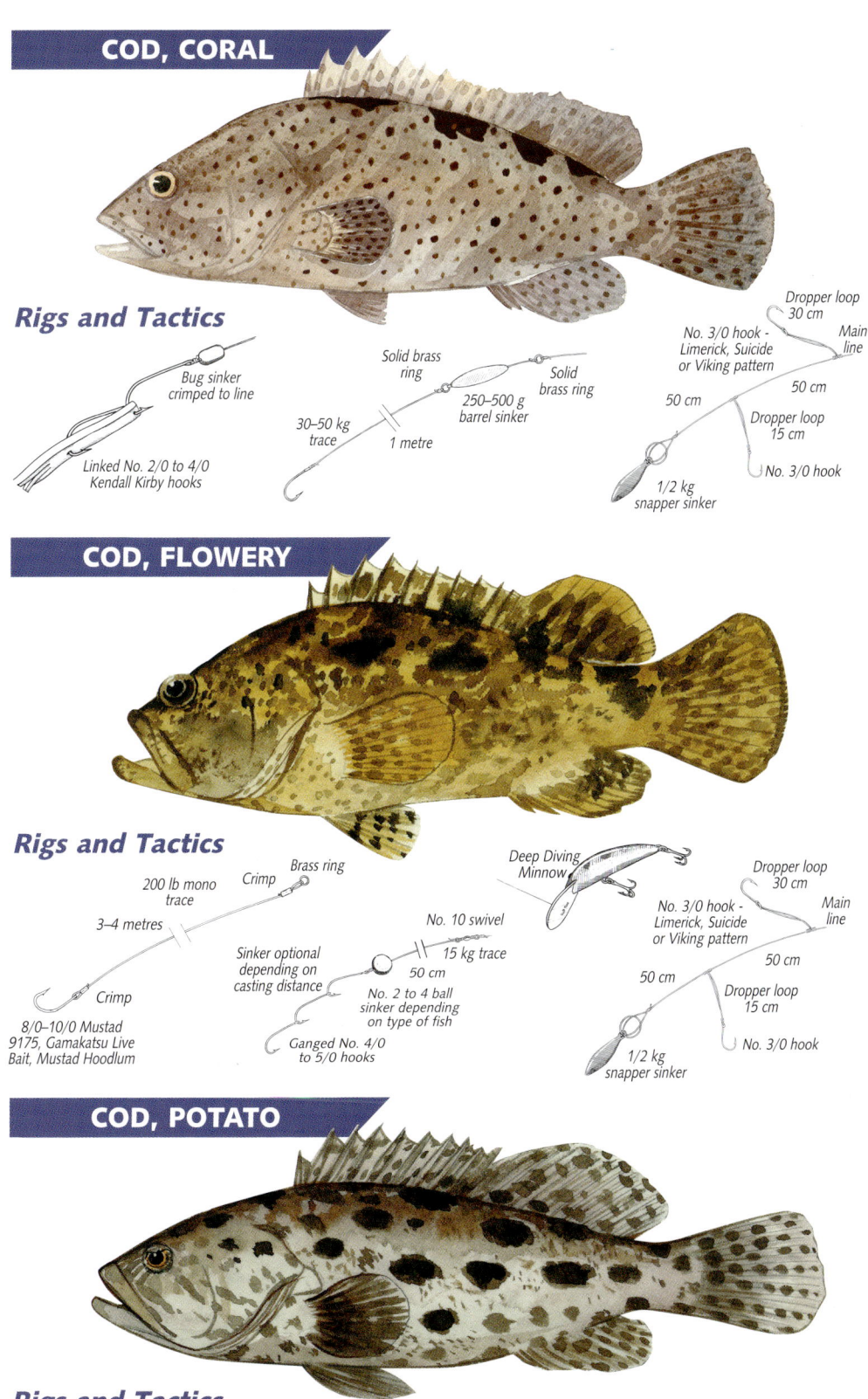

Bug sinker crimped to line

Linked No. 2/0 to 4/0 Kendall Kirby hooks

Solid brass ring

Solid brass ring

30–50 kg trace

250–500 g barrel sinker

1 metre

Dropper loop 30 cm

No. 3/0 hook - Limerick, Suicide or Viking pattern

Main line

50 cm

50 cm

Dropper loop 15 cm

No. 3/0 hook

1/2 kg snapper sinker

COD, FLOWERY

Rigs and Tactics

200 lb mono trace

Crimp

Brass ring

3–4 metres

Crimp

8/0–10/0 Mustad 9175, Gamakatsu Live Bait, Mustad Hoodlum

Sinker optional depending on casting distance

No. 10 swivel

15 kg trace

50 cm

No. 2 to 4 ball sinker depending on type of fish

Ganged No. 4/0 to 5/0 hooks

Deep Diving Minnow

Dropper loop 30 cm

No. 3/0 hook - Limerick, Suicide or Viking pattern

Main line

50 cm

50 cm

Dropper loop 15 cm

No. 3/0 hook

1/2 kg snapper sinker

COD, POTATO

Rigs and Tactics

Not recommended as an angling species due to protected status.

COD, VERMICULAR

Scientific name *Plectropomus oligocanthus* Also known as lined coral trout, vermicular trout

Range Abrolhos Islands in central Western Australia and northern waters as far south as central Queensland

Description The various coral trout species being coral trout, bar-cheek coral trout and vermicular cod are all easily confused. The vermicular cod tends to be more bright red or orange red, while coral trout can be a dark brick red. The vermicular cod has larger blue dots on its body and some are likely to be elongated dorsally. The spots on the head are fewer and larger than with the coral trout and are not elongated laterally as with the bar-cheek coral trout. The vermicular cod also has a higher soft part of the dorsal fin, but this characteristic is most useful when comparing another trout. The vermicular cod is found on off-shore reefs more commonly and reaches 56 cm in length whereas the coral trout reaches 75 cm and the bar-cheek coral trout 70 centimetres.

Fishing Like all the coral trouts, the vermicular cod is first rate eating. It is taken on standard reef fishing rigs. Its preference for coral reefs and strong first run makes heavier line more necessary as this species is definitely one for the table. The vermicular cod will also rise to take trolled lures and bait tipped jigs also work extremely well. Best baits include cut fish baits, pilchard, garfish, squid, octopus and large prawns.

DORY, JOHN

Scientific name *Zeus faber.* Also known as St Peter's fish, doorkeeper's fish, dory keparu (NZ).

Range From Cape Cuvier in Western Australia, around the southern part of the country, including Tasmania, to Bundaberg in southern Queensland.

Description An unusual fish with a large, upward pointing mouth which can be extended the length of its head. The John dory has a distinctive, prominent mark on each side, said to be made by the fingers of St Peter when he picked up this fish. The John dory has very fine scales compared with the mirror dory which has no scales. The elongated dorsal rays give a distinctive appearance. John dory are most common near mid to deepwater reefs from 10 to 80 m but can be found in deeper estuaries like the Hawkesbury River and Sydney Harbour in NSW. The John dory can reach 75 cm and 4 kg although they are commonly taken at around a kilogram.

Fishing The John dory is a poor fighter but it is absolutely delicious. The John dory is a common deep water trawl species in temperate waters but can be taken by anglers near deep reefs, wrecks and in deep estuaries such as the Hawkesbury. John dory greatly prefer live fish such as yellowtail for bait but can be caught on very fresh fillets.

DORY, MIRROR

Scientific name *Zenopsis nebulosus.* Also known as Trawl dory, deepwater dory, deepsea dory.

Range From the Pilbara in Western Australia around the southern part of Australia, including Tasmania to Southern Queensland.

Description The mirror dory is smaller than John dory, reaching 58 cm and 2.4 kilograms. The mirror dory is almost exclusively a deep water trawl species. It possesses a fainter fingerprint on its side. The forehead is distinctly convex and the anal fin has three spines as opposed to four in the John dory.

Fishing This excellent eating species is rarely taken by anglers as it prefers the deep waters of the Continental shelf. Occasionally encountered, the mirror dory also prefers live or extremely fresh baits and can be found near wrecks or deeper reefs.

COD, VERMICULAR

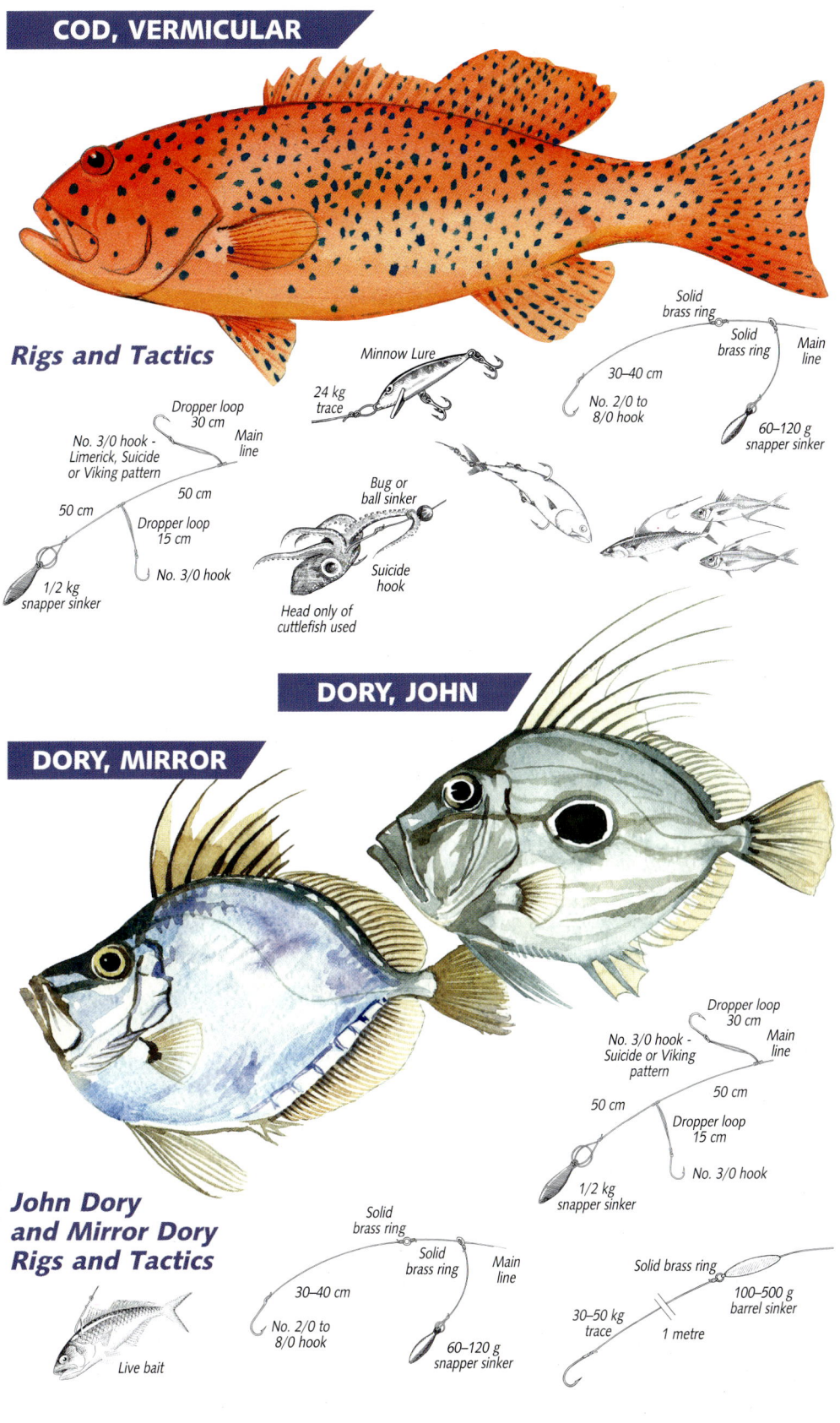

Rigs and Tactics

Minnow Lure

24 kg trace

Dropper loop 30 cm

Main line

No. 3/0 hook - Limerick, Suicide or Viking pattern

50 cm

50 cm

Dropper loop 15 cm

No. 3/0 hook

1/2 kg snapper sinker

Bug or ball sinker

Suicide hook

Head only of cuttlefish used

Solid brass ring

Solid brass ring

Main line

30–40 cm

No. 2/0 to 8/0 hook

60–120 g snapper sinker

DORY, JOHN

DORY, MIRROR

Dropper loop 30 cm

No. 3/0 hook - Suicide or Viking pattern

Main line

50 cm

50 cm

Dropper loop 15 cm

No. 3/0 hook

1/2 kg snapper sinker

John Dory and Mirror Dory Rigs and Tactics

Live bait

Solid brass ring

Solid brass ring

Main line

30–40 cm

No. 2/0 to 8/0 hook

60–120 g snapper sinker

Solid brass ring

100–500 g barrel sinker

30–50 kg trace

1 metre

DHUFISH

Scientific name *Glaucosoma hebraicum.* Also known as Westralian dhufish, jewfish, dhuie, jewie.

Range An icon of Western Australian fishing, found from Esperance to Shark Bay in Western Australia.

Description The dhufish is an attractive relative of the pearl perch, and is the most prized species for Western Australian boat anglers. The dhufish has a distinctive eye stripe. A dorsal ray, especially in males can be elongated. Juvenile dhufish have distinctive horizontal black stripes. It is found in depths of up to 40 m or so. Recent research indicates heavy mortality of fish taken in greater than 15 m or so due to brain embolism (bleeding) but using depth release sinkers or short lines to rapidly return the fish to depth is showing very positive results. Dhufish have a very large mouth and can take a big bait. Dhufish can reach 27 kg and every year a number of fish of 25 kg are taken.

Fishing Dhufish move closer inshore during summer months and very large fish can even be taken from beaches on occasion. Dhufish take baits fished on standard deep water two hook rigs. They take whole fish, squid, pilchard or live fish if available. Anglers drift lumps in waters from 10 – 40 m in depth for mixed bags with dhufish the most prized species. Taken from deep water, a big dhufish feels like the bottom, but the fight diminishes as the fish nears the surface. This fish is arguably the best eating species in Western Australia.

EEL, BLACK-BLOTCHED MORAY

Scientific name *Gymnothorax favagenatus.* Also known as Black-blotched moray, tessellated moray, coral eel, giraffe eel, knot-eel

Range Shark Bay in Western Australia and northern waters to the NSW border. Much more common on the Great Barrier reef.

Description A strikingly patterned reef moray with irregular black or chocolate brown blotches on a cream background. The front nostrils have moderate sized tubes. The back nostrils have no tubes and are in front of the eyes. The black-blotched moray can reach 2.5 metres but is generally regarded as a medium sized moray. It can be seen in shallow waters while walking on low tide. They can roam from their home, especially at night. The black-blotched moray is not overly aggressive and is unlikely to attack unless provoked. Of course what constitutes provocation to a moray eel is not something that you want to debate, especially while diving. All moray eels should be treated with caution, but they are an important, if territorial part of the reef community.

Fishing The black-blotched moray is not targeted while fishing, and should never be disturbed while diving. They are caught on baits, especially at night as little bait fishing is done in the tough reef country these eels prefer. When hooked, the black-blotched moray will try and regain its cave and the game is effectively over. If landed, they will wind themselves in knots, trying to dislodge the hook. If possible, cut the line close to the hook and get the eel back over the side as they can be nasty when angry on the deck of a small boat.

EEL, GREEN MORAY

Scientific name *Gymnothorax prasinus.* Also known as Green eel

Range Shark Bay in Western Australia and southern waters to the Gold Coast in Queensland and including northern Tasmania. Rare along south coast from eastern Victoria to near Esperance.

Description A strikingly coloured eel species reaching more than a metre in length. The body is coloured green, often an extremely bright hue due to a liberal coating of green slime. There may be orange or brown highlights and the head is frequently bright orange. One set of nostrils are near the mouth and have a long tube while the rear nostrils are on the top of the head behind the eyes and have short tubes. The nostrils and head pores are surrounded by black. The dorsal fin starts well in front of the gill opening. The mouth is large and the teeth are in a single row. The green moray is found on shallow coastal reefs but may range away from its home especially at night, when it is more active.

Fishing The green moray is a common and generally unwelcome catch when bottom fishing near rocks in temperate waters. They are more active at night and are quite aggressive, taking a wide range of baits including fish, prawns, squid and pipi. When hooked, the green moray will try and return to its home crevice. When landed, it writhes about, twisting up the line with thick, green gelatinous slime that gets everywhere. They have a sufficiently unpleasant disposition to nip at nearby fingers when unhooked. The green moray is not targeted and is not highly regarded for food. Their beauty is compromised by their mean attitude.

DHUFISH

Rigs and Tactics

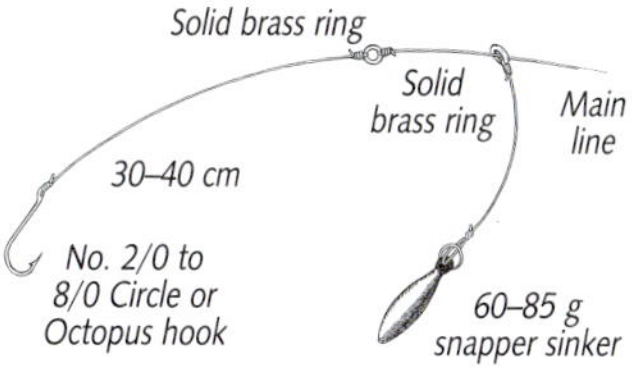

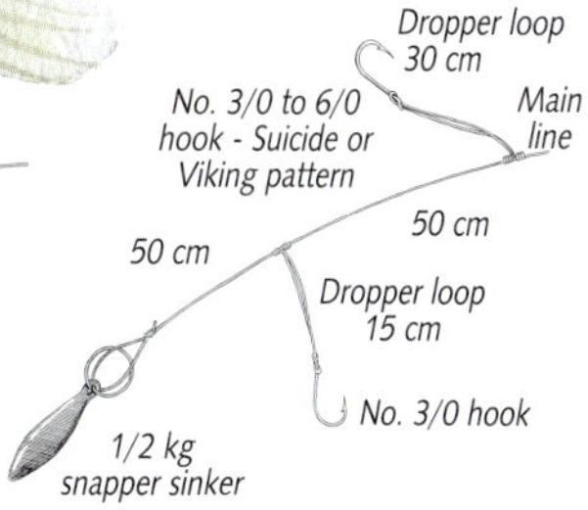

Solid brass ring

Solid brass ring

Main line

30–40 cm

No. 2/0 to 8/0 Circle or Octopus hook

60–85 g snapper sinker

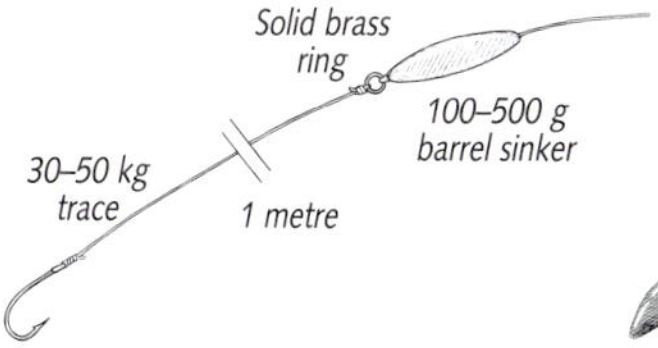

Solid brass ring

30–50 kg trace

1 metre

100–500 g barrel sinker

Dropper loop 30 cm

No. 3/0 to 6/0 hook - Suicide or Viking pattern

Main line

50 cm

50 cm

Dropper loop 15 cm

1/2 kg snapper sinker

No. 3/0 hook

EEL, BLACK-BLOTCHED MORAY

Rigs and Tactics

Not applicable as not recommended as an angling species

EEL, GREEN MORAY

Rigs and Tactics

Not applicable as not recommended as an angling species

EEL, SOUTHERN CONGER

Scientific name *Conger verreauxi*. Also known as Conger eel, common conger eel

Range Geraldton in Western Australia and southern waters including Tasmania and as far as the Gold Coast in southern Queensland

Description The largest of the conger eels from Australia which is found on shallow inshore rocky reefs to a depth of around 80 metres. The southern conger eel can reach two metres and around 25 kilograms. The southern conger eel can be distinguished by the large mouth with fleshy lips. There are two rows of teeth which are not normally used in attack, although a large conger eel caught in a lobster pot can be a daunting proposition. The tail ends in an obvious point and the colour is consistently dark or slate grey.

Fishing The southern conger eel is much more active at night and is more frequently encountered night fishing for snapper, mulloway or teraglin. While they can also be found on wrecks, they do not attract the notoriety or the food value of their larger European cousins. The southern conger eel will take a wide variety of baits and the large mouth means that even large live baits for mulloway can be taken. While conger eels are difficult to unhook, they are not as dangerous as some of the moray eels. They are much better eating than many believe and are excellent when smoked.

EMPEROR, BLUE SPOT

Scientific name *Lethrinus laticaudis*. Also known as grass emperor, grass sweetlip, coral bream, snapper bream, grey sweetlip, red-finned emperor, brown sweetlip.

Range Ningaloo Reef near Exmouth in Western Australia and tropical waters to southern Queensland.

Description The various species of spangled emperors are difficult to differentiate. Many of the species have different size limits and must be able to be separated to comply with various state fishing regulations. The blue spot emperor is a common capture in tropical waters and is often caught near weed beds. Juveniles in particular can be caught near beds of eel-grass (*Zostera sp.*). The blue lined emperor grows to an impressive 80cm, which is nearly as large as the spangled emperor. The species can be most easily separated by the blue spots on the cheeks, as opposed to blue bars on the spangled emperor. The blue spot emperor also has a whitish oblique bar behind the eye to the edge of the gill cover. When captured, the blue spot emperor will often have brown bars on the sides which fade after death.

Fishing While juveniles are frequently encountered in the larger estuaries with well established sea grass meadows, they are not generally a target species. They are taken in good numbers in Tin Can Bay in Queensland. Blue spot emperor are more commonly taken at larger sizes on offshore reefs where they can be taken with other species of the emperors. Standard reef fishing rigs will take this species in good numbers. Fresh bait, either fish flesh, squid or octopus is recommended. The blue spot emperor makes excellent eating.

EMPEROR, LONG NOSED

Scientific name *Lethrinus olivaceous*

Range Ningaloo Reef near Exmouth in Western Australia and northwards to central Queensland.

Description One of the largest species of emperor, reaching 10 kg and a metre in length. The long nosed emperor is easily distinguished by the long sloping head and the generally greenish colouration. The long nose becomes readily apparent when compared to other similar species. There is generally a red line on the lips of these fish and the dorsal fin may have red spots.

Fishing Standard reef fishing tackle and rigs will account for this hard fighting species. The long nosed emporer can be found on inshore or offshore reefs and its larger size can cause extra troubles for angling. High quality fresh baits and strong leaders are recommended for this species. Fish flesh, squid, octopus, pilchard or live baits account for the majority of these fish. The long nosed emperor is highly regarded as a food fish.

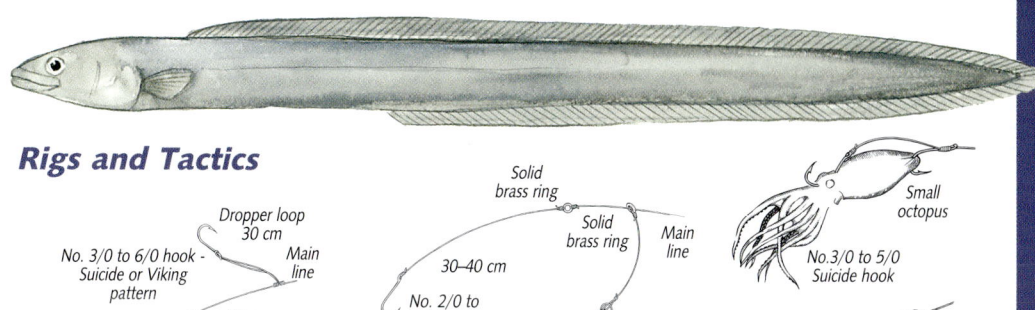

Rigs and Tactics

Dropper loop
30 cm

No. 3/0 to 6/0 hook -
Suicide or Viking
pattern

Main
line

50 cm

50 cm

Dropper loop
15 cm

1/2 kg
snapper sinker

No. 3/0 to 6/0 hook

Solid
brass ring

Solid
brass ring

Main
line

30–40 cm

No. 2/0 to
8/0 hook

60–120 g
snapper sinker

Live bait

Small
octopus

No. 3/0 to 5/0
Suicide hook

Bug sinker
crimped to line

Linked No. 2/0 to 4/0 Limerick
or Kendall Kirby hooks

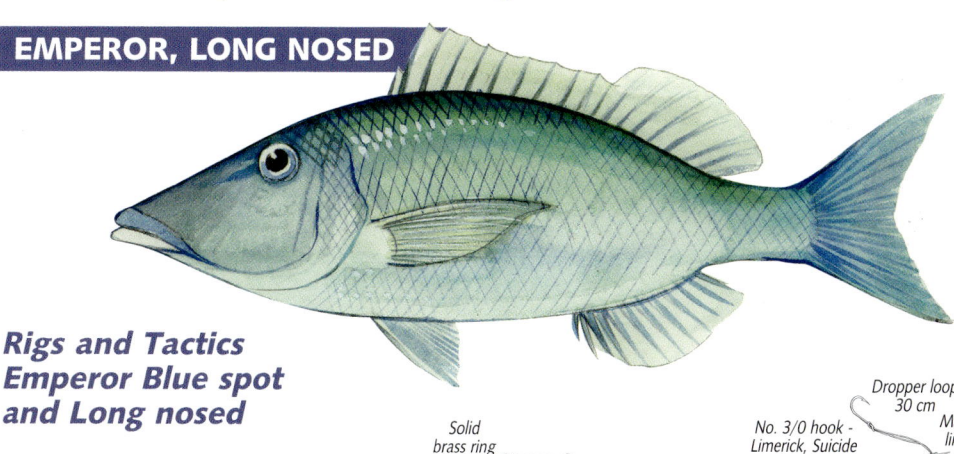

Rigs and Tactics
Emperor Blue spot
and Long nosed

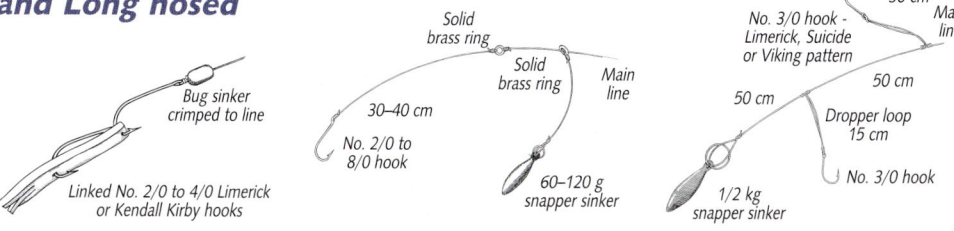

Bug sinker
crimped to line

Linked No. 2/0 to 4/0 Limerick
or Kendall Kirby hooks

Solid
brass ring

Solid
brass ring

Main
line

30–40 cm

No. 2/0 to
8/0 hook

60–120 g
snapper sinker

No. 3/0 hook -
Limerick, Suicide
or Viking pattern

Dropper loop
30 cm

Main
line

50 cm

50 cm

Dropper loop
15 cm

1/2 kg
snapper sinker

No. 3/0 hook

EMPEROR, RED

Scientific name *Lutjanus sebae*. Also known as Government bream, red kelp.

Range From Shark Bay northwards and around to Moreton Bay in southern Queensland, although specimens are occasionally taken further south.

Description A striking and highly prized reef fish. The red emperor is a schooling fish which means that fishing can be fast and furious, but this valuable species can be taken in large numbers in commercial fish traps and trawls. The red emperor changes appearance as it grows. Juveniles are known as Government bream as the three striking bands resemble a convict's broad arrow. This pattern fades with age and fish over 13 kg become a uniform scarlet or salmon pink. The reddish fins are narrowly edged with white. The cheeks are scaled and there is a deep notch in the lower edge of the pre-operculum (inner cheekbone).

Fishing Red emperor fight extremely well, even when taken from deeper waters where they are increasingly taken. The red emperor can reach 22 kg and more than a metre in length which increases their allure. Red emperor prefer moving water in channels near deeper reefs. As a result, they can be taken on drifts between reef patches in seemingly open ground. They tend to form schools of similar sized fish and are partial to cut fish baits, octopus, squid or pilchards. The red emperor is excellent eating even in the larger sizes and is considered safe from ciguatera.

EMPEROR, SPANGLED

Scientific name *Lethrinus nebulosus*. Also known as Nor-west snapper, Nor'wester, yellow sweetlip, sand snapper, sand bream.

Range Rottnest Island north and around the top end to Coffs Harbour in northern NSW.

Description A striking member of the sweetlip group. This species is easily identified by the blue spots on each scale and the blue bars on the cheek. This species can reach 86 cm and 6.5 kg and is considered very good eating.

Fishing The spangled emperor is generally taken adjacent to coral or rock reefs over gravel or sand bottoms. They frequent lagoons and coral cays and can be taken from the beach in Western Australia where there are reef patches nearby. They are particularly active at night. The spangled emperor can be taken with standard reef rigs, but as they are most common in water under 15 metres deep, lighter rigs and berley can bring these fish up into the open. Use cut fish, pilchards, squid, octopus, crab or prawn baits. Spangled emperor will take jigs or minnow lures either trolled or cast in areas near reefs where spangled emperor feed.

EMPEROR, SPOTCHEEK

Scientific name *Lethrinus rubrioperculatus*.

Range Ningaloo Reef in Western Australia and through tropical waters to central Queensland.

Description The spotcheek emperor reaches a length of 50 cm but only a weight of around 600 grams. This is a fairly light bodies species which is distinguished by its elongated shape with a fairly small head. It also has a red or brown blotch on the upper margin only of the outer gill cover. The spotcheek emperor is often confused with the purple-headed emperor (also known as the pink-eared emperor *Lethrinus lentjan*) but the latter species has a more robust form and a wider red margin to the gill cover, including to the lower edge.

Fishing The smaller size and mouth of the spotcheek emperor means that it needs smaller gear than that for the larger emperor species. The spotcheek emperor can be a nuisance at smaller sizes as it can be a bait picker and can travel in numbers. This species is taken on standard reef rigs using smaller hooks. Fresh cut bait, half a pilchard, a piece of squid or octopus or a piece of peeled prawn will take this species. The spotcheek emperor can also be taken on mud or softer bottom as well as the vicinity or reefs. It is taken in the trawl fisheries and appears on the market regularly where it causes some concern where it is often declared to be undersized spangled emperor. The spotcheek emperor is considered to be very good eating.

EMPEROR, RED

Rigs and Tactics

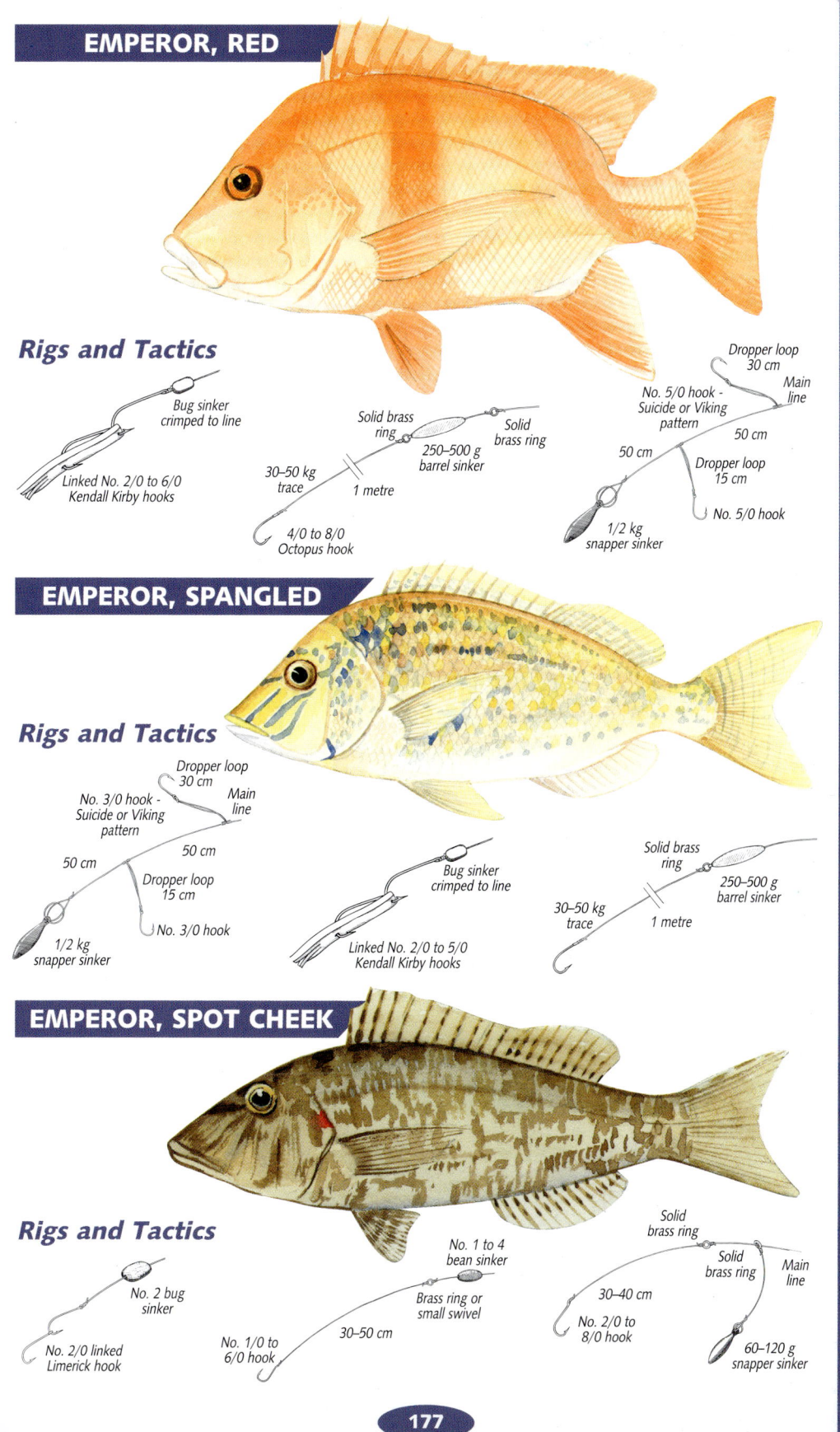

Bug sinker crimped to line

Linked No. 2/0 to 6/0 Kendall Kirby hooks

Solid brass ring

250–500 g barrel sinker

Solid brass ring

30–50 kg trace

1 metre

4/0 to 8/0 Octopus hook

Dropper loop 30 cm

Main line

No. 5/0 hook - Suicide or Viking pattern

50 cm

50 cm

Dropper loop 15 cm

1/2 kg snapper sinker

No. 5/0 hook

EMPEROR, SPANGLED

Rigs and Tactics

Dropper loop 30 cm

Main line

No. 3/0 hook - Suicide or Viking pattern

50 cm

50 cm

Dropper loop 15 cm

1/2 kg snapper sinker

No. 3/0 hook

Bug sinker crimped to line

Linked No. 2/0 to 5/0 Kendall Kirby hooks

Solid brass ring

250–500 g barrel sinker

30–50 kg trace

1 metre

EMPEROR, SPOT CHEEK

Rigs and Tactics

No. 2 bug sinker

No. 2/0 linked Limerick hook

No. 1 to 4 bean sinker

Brass ring or small swivel

No. 1/0 to 6/0 hook

30–50 cm

Solid brass ring

Solid brass ring

Main line

30–40 cm

No. 2/0 to 8/0 hook

60–120 g snapper sinker

EMPEROR, SWEETLIP

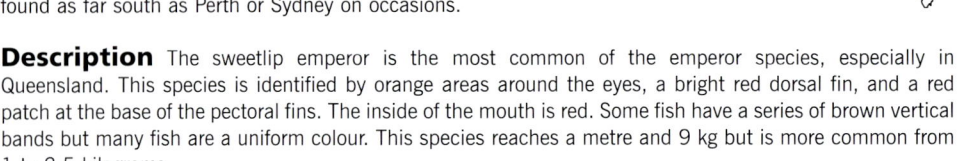

Scientific name *Lethrinus miniatus.* (formerly *Lethrinus chrysostomus*) Also known as Sweetlip, lipper, red-throat, trumpeter (Norfolk Island).

Range Abrolhos Islands around the top end to northern NSW around Evan Head but found as far south as Perth or Sydney on occasions.

Description The sweetlip emperor is the most common of the emperor species, especially in Queensland. This species is identified by orange areas around the eyes, a bright red dorsal fin, and a red patch at the base of the pectoral fins. The inside of the mouth is red. Some fish have a series of brown vertical bands but many fish are a uniform colour. This species reaches a metre and 9 kg but is more common from 1 to 2.5 kilograms.

Fishing Found in reef country, but frequently taken from areas between reefs, the sweetlip emperor can be berleyed up and large catches taken from the feeding school. The sweetlip emperor fights well and is able to dive to the bottom and break off an unwary angler. These fish respond well to oily fleshed baits such as pilchard or mackerel, but when feeding can be caught on most baits including cut baits, squid, octopus, prawn and crab. Sweetlip emperor are highly regarded food fish.

FOXFISH, WESTERN

Scientific name *Bodianus frenchii* Eastern foxfish *Bodianus sp.* Also known as Foxfish, Fox wrasse, crimson foxfish.

Range Kalbarri in Western Australia and southern waters as far as Port Lincoln in South Australia. The Eastern foxfish is found from southern Queensland and southwards along the east coast including eastern Victoria and the east coast of Tasmania.

Description A fairly common catch on offshore reefs in Western Australia, the western foxfish is very attractive fish which grows to 49 cm. It is an overall crimson or brick red colour with a lighter belly and a white chin. There are two large pale yellow or cream coloured blotches with the larger one near the centre of the dorsal fin and second smaller patch near the upper saddle of the tail. The eastern foxfish is separated by the range, and the two blotches are set further forward and are white. The first blotch is near the front of the dorsal fin and the second is near well in front of the tail, near the middle of the soft dorsal portion of the fin. Recent research by Murdoch University has indicated that the Western foxfish is extremely slow growing with many 'keeper' sized fish being between 30 and 50 years old. This has forced many anglers to take greater care with the humble foxfish.

Fishing The western foxfish is not specifically targeted but is a common by-catch when fishing for dhufish, snapper or red snapper. It is found in depths to 100 metres and can suffer from barotrauma. The use of a depth release device can greatly improve survival of released fish. The western foxfish does not have a large mouth but it can fit in many baits intended for larger fish. Baits of whole and cut fish, squid and octopus can be successful. Foxfish are considered good eating, if less highly regarded than the larger temperate reef species.

GOATFISH, BLACK-SPOT

Scientific name *Parupeneus spilurus* Also known as Red mullet.

Range From Rottnest Island in Western Australia around tropical waters to Sydney in NSW.

Description One of several distinctive goatfish species, the black-spot goatfish possesses two long white barbels attached to the lower jaw which are used to detect food on the bottom as a catfish uses its whiskers. This species has at least two dark stripes running the length of its body and a conspicuous black spot on top of the wrist of the tail. It can reach 1.3 kilograms.

Fishing A welcome catch when fishing for other species on shallow coastal reefs as it is one of the finest food fish available. They are found on sandy ground adjacent to reefs. Goatfish prefer their food on the bottom and will take all the usual fish, prawn and squid baits, although the relatively small mouth means that smaller hooks are recommended and caution should be taken not to set the hook too quickly. Goatfish are often taken on bait jigs that sink to the bottom as they are attracted to any berley which sinks past the baitfish.

EMPEROR, SWEETLIP

Rigs and Tactics

Sinker size varies with depth

Bug sinker crimped to line

Linked No. 2/0 to 5/0 Kendall Kirby hooks

Solid brass ring

250–500 g barrel sinker

30–50 kg trace

1 metre

Dropper loop 30 cm

No. 3/0 hook - Suicide or Viking pattern

Main line

50 cm

50 cm

Dropper loop 15 cm

No. 3/0 hook

1/2 kg snapper sinker

FOXFISH

Rigs and Tactics

Small octopus

No.3/0 to 5/0 Suicide hook

GOATFISH, BLACK-SPOT

Rigs and Tactics

No. 1 to 3 bean sinker

No. 2 to 2/0 hook

Solid brass ring

Solid brass ring

Main line

30–40 cm

No. 2/0 to 8/0 hook

60–120 g snapper sinker

No. 2 to 5 ball sinker

20 cm dropper

40–50 cm dropper

No. 4 to 2/0 Long Shank, Eastern Estuary or Suicide hook depending on species sought

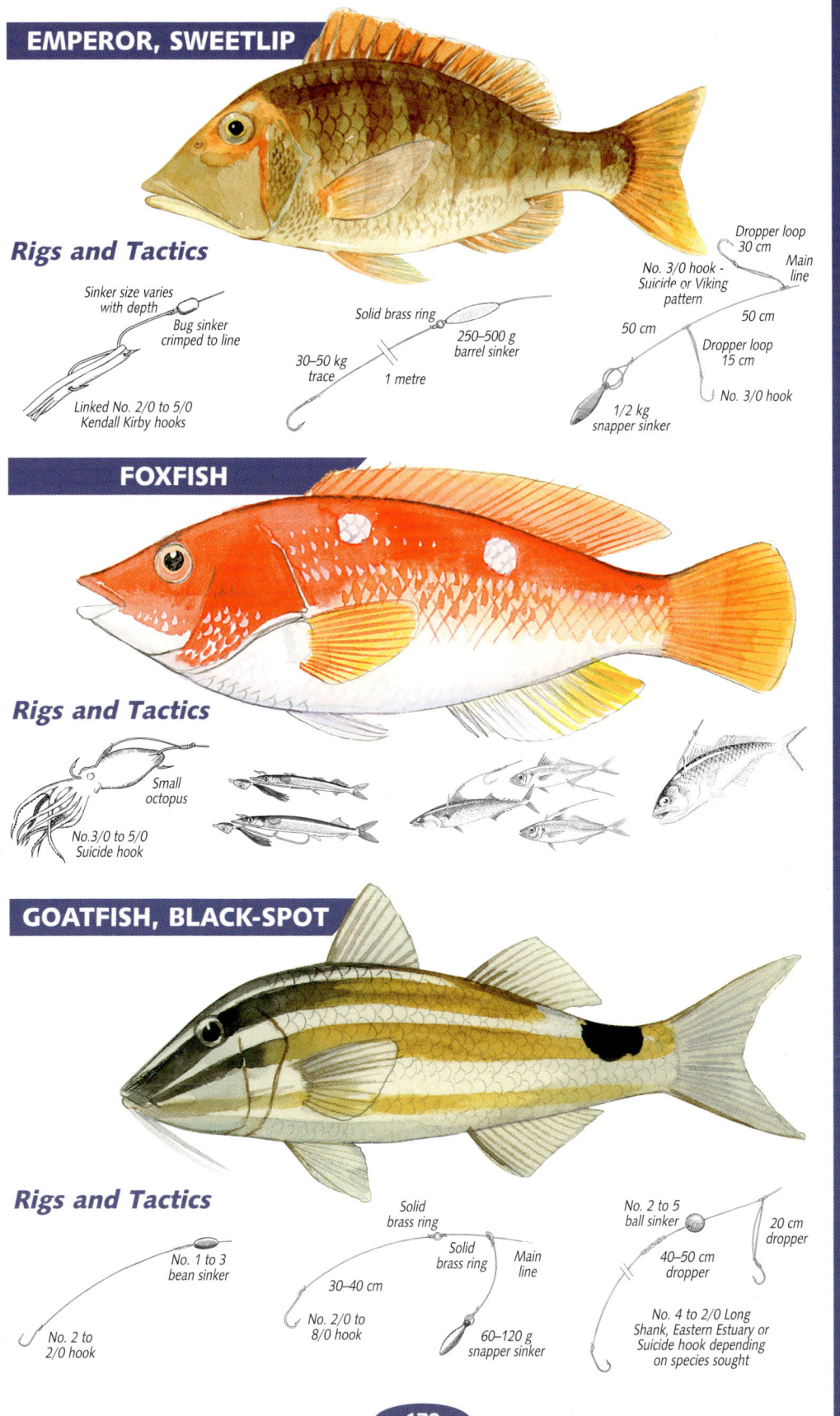

GOATFISH, BLUE-SPOTTED

Scientific name *Upeneichthys vlamingii* Also known as red mullet, black-striped goatfish, southern goatfish.

Range Jurien Bay in Western Australia and along the south coast to around Newcastle in NSW.

Description Like all the goatfish, there are two prominent white barbels on the lower part of the mouth. The blue-spotted goatfish can reach a respectable 42 cm and is commonly found on sand or weed areas near offshore reefs. The overall colouration can vary considerably, depending on the type of bottom the fish is taken from, with specimens ranging from bright red to a pale off-white. There is a darker stripe that runs along the side near the lateral line and which passes through the eye. There are blue lines along the snout which extend to the preoperculum.

Fishing The blue-spotted goatfish prefers shallow areas and can be found in larger bays and inlets of our southern waters. Their capture is a good sign that the drift has left the more productive reef areas and it is time to restart the drift. The mouth is fairly small but they can still be taken on fairly large hooks. They will take most baits, including those intended for King George whiting. Rigs can include standard reef rigs or lighter running sinker rigs. Although the blue-spotted goatfish is rarely specifically targeted, they make a welcome addition to mixed bags and are considered to be excellent eating.

GRENADIER

Scientific name *Macruronus novaezelandiae*. Also known as Blue hake, blue grenadier, whiptail, hoki.

Range A cooler water, mid depth species found from Cape Naturaliste in Western Australia and all southern waters including Tasmania to the south coast of NSW.

Description The grenadier is a long bronze-blue fish with a distinct lateral line, the second dorsal fin is low and reaches to the end of the tapered tail where it joins the also extended anal fin. Fins are purplish-blue. Commonly found in depths of 20 to 60 m, juveniles occur in southern bays and estuaries up to tidal influences. Adults reach 1.1 metres.

Fishing The grenadier is a common trawl species, especially in New Zealand where it is marketed as hoki fillets. The flesh is firm but is not as highly valued as many other species. Grenadier are taken while fishing for other species using standard bottom paternoster rigs. Grenadier readily take fish baits, squid and prawns. As with many deeper species, their fight is affected by the depth and heavier lines and sinkers commonly used.

GROPER, BALDCHIN

Scientific name *Chocrodon rubescens* Also known as Tusk-fish, baldie, bluebone.

Range This species is restricted to Western Australia, from Geographe Bay to Coral Bay. Other tusk-fish are found in tropical and sub-tropical waters and are large, typically brightly coloured reef species.

Description The baldchin groper is one of the largest tusk-fish species reaching 90 cm and 14 kilograms. All tusk-fish have prominent protruding, tusk-like teeth in both jaws. This species is easily identified by the white chin which is more prominent in males which are larger. The pectoral fin is yellow with a pale bluish base. The tusk-fish bones have a pale bluish colour, leading to one of their common names. This species is found on inshore reefs to a depth of 40 m, with smaller fish generally found in shallower waters.

Fishing An excellent fighting fish and one of Western Australia's premier eating fish, the baldchin groper is highly sought after. Baldchin groper are taken with standard reef fishing rigs and baits, although crabs can be particularly productive if available. Baldchin will also take prawns, octopus, squid, crabs and fish baits but there can be times when baldchin can be finicky feeders, so it pays to experiment with baits and rigs. Spearfishers can have a significant impact especially on small populations on isolated reefs.

GOATFISH, BLUE-SPOT

Rigs and Tactics

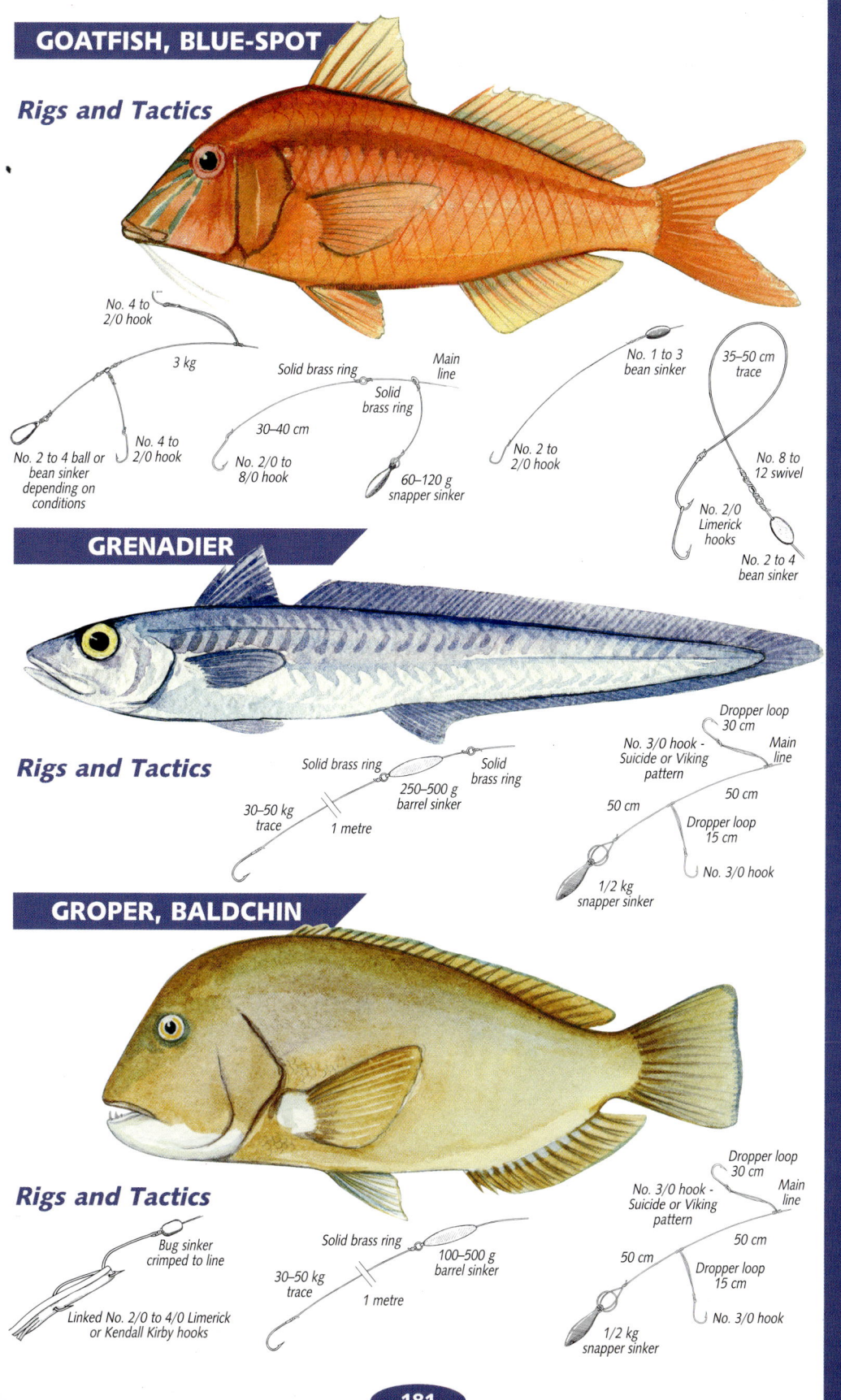

No. 4 to 2/0 hook

3 kg

No. 2 to 4 ball or bean sinker depending on conditions

No. 4 to 2/0 hook

Solid brass ring

Main line

Solid brass ring

30–40 cm

No. 2/0 to 8/0 hook

60–120 g snapper sinker

No. 1 to 3 bean sinker

35–50 cm trace

No. 2 to 2/0 hook

No. 8 to 12 swivel

No. 2/0 Limerick hooks

No. 2 to 4 bean sinker

GRENADIER

Rigs and Tactics

Solid brass ring

Solid brass ring

30–50 kg trace

1 metre

250–500 g barrel sinker

Dropper loop 30 cm

No. 3/0 hook - Suicide or Viking pattern

Main line

50 cm

50 cm

Dropper loop 15 cm

No. 3/0 hook

1/2 kg snapper sinker

GROPER, BALDCHIN

Rigs and Tactics

Bug sinker crimped to line

Linked No. 2/0 to 4/0 Limerick or Kendall Kirby hooks

Solid brass ring

30–50 kg trace

1 metre

100–500 g barrel sinker

Dropper loop 30 cm

No. 3/0 hook - Suicide or Viking pattern

Main line

50 cm

50 cm

Dropper loop 15 cm

No. 3/0 hook

1/2 kg snapper sinker

GROPER, EASTERN BLUE AND WESTERN BLUE

Scientific name *Achoerodus viridis* (Eastern blue groper) *Achoerodus gouldii* (Western blue groper) Also known as Red groper, brown groper (Actually female colouration of the Eastern blue groper), giant pigfish, blue tank.

Range The Eastern blue is found from Harvey Bay in southern Queensland to Wilson's Promontory in Victoria, while the Western Blue groper can be found from the Abrolhos Islands off Geraldton in Western Australia to west of Melbourne.

Description The second largest wrasse species (behind the hump-headed Maori wrasse), the Western blue groper is capable of reaching 1.6 m and 40 kilograms. The eastern blue groper can reach 20 kg but has been seriously over fished in many areas and fish of 2 to 10 kg are much more likely. The blue gropers are easily identified by their size, often brilliant colours, their fleshy lips, heavy scales and peg like teeth. Eastern blue groper prefer turbulent rocky shorelines or inshore bomboras. Western blue groper are found in similar areas, but the largest fish come off deep reefs of the south coast, or near remote islands of the Recherché Archipelago. Both species are curious and extremely susceptible to spearfishing. Female eastern blue groper are red or dirty brown and if the largest (blue) male from a group is taken, the largest female becomes a blue male and begins to grow larger. This phenomenon has not been recorded for the Western blue groper where most specimens are blue-green to a brilliant cobalt blue.

Fishing Blue groper present a real test for shore based anglers. They can be taken on cunjevoi, prawns and squid, fresh crabs, and especially the red crabs found in the intertidal areas of the east coast. Crabs are easily the best bait. Heavy rods and line and extra strong hooks are required for these hard, dirty fighters. A groper should not be given its head as it will bury you in the nearest cave or under any rock ledge. Western blue groper are more frequently taken by fishing the white water of offshore reefs with a boat. Small to medium blue groper are good eating, but large ones are dry and the flesh coarse. These are hardy fish which many anglers choose to return to the water, as their fight is their best and most memorable feature.

GROPER, QUEENSLAND

Scientific name *Epinephelus lanceolatus*. Also known as groper, giant groper, grouper.

Range Rottnest Island in Western Australia and northwards around the top end as far as Broughton Island in central NSW, with occasional specimens outside this range and larger specimens most common in northern Western Australia to the Great Barrier Reef.

Description A massive cod species, capable of reaching 2.7 m in length and nearly 300 kg in weight, if not taken by line fishing or spearfishing. The Queensland groper is one of the largest of all bony fishes. The Queensland groper prefers to live near coral reefs and rocky areas and can take up residence in large caves. This species can occasionally move into large estuaries and can be found near jetties or other cover. They can move south in summer on currents, sometimes surprising divers when they first encounter these fish. The size of the Queensland groper makes large specimens easy to identify. The tail is huge, rounded and powerful. The colour is dark grey or black and may have lighter coloured patches or blotches. The eye is relatively small, but the mouth is very large. The Queensland groper can be confused with the greasy or estuary cod, (*Epinephelus suillus*) when small, but the pre-operculum (first cheekbone) of the Queensland groper is rounded while in the greasy cod it is angular. The three spines near the back edge of the gill cover are obvious in the Queensland groper and the middle spine is closer to the lower spine.

Fishing The Queensland groper is an extremely strong fighter, which coupled with its large size makes them difficult to land in their larger sizes. The Queensland groper can be curious and is vulnerable to spearfishing. Given the size of the fish and its mouth, few baits were too large for a big Queensland groper, with large live baits working best. The Queensland groper is edible in smaller sizes up to around 25 kg, but the flesh is strongly flavoured. Above this size the fish is almost inedible. In many areas Queensland groper are rightly protected and they should be released immediately or left alone. They become important tourist attractions, although they have been known to help themselves to other line or spear caught fish.

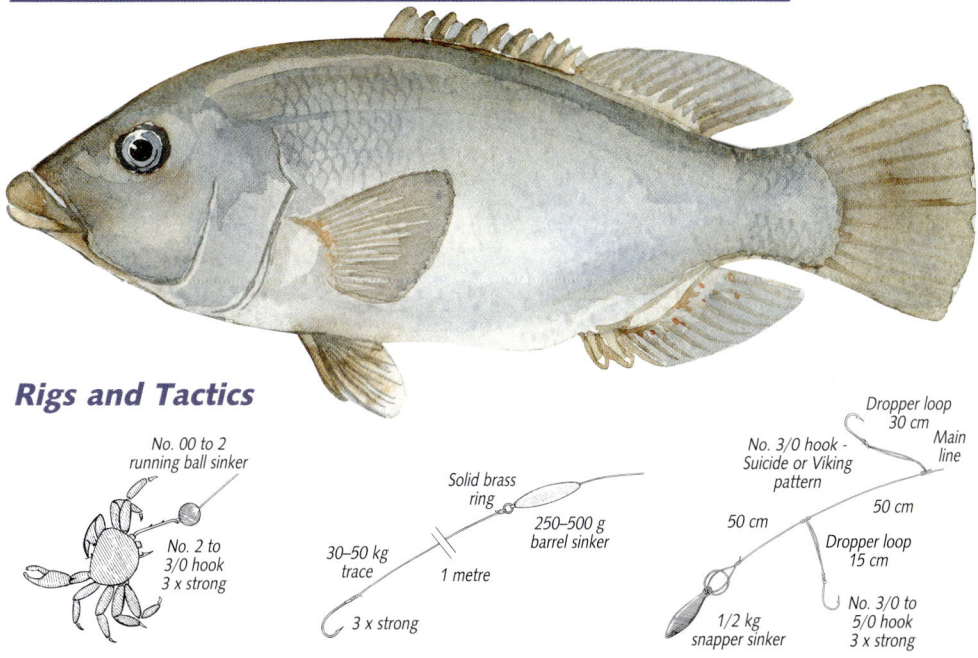

Rigs and Tactics

No. 00 to 2
running ball sinker

No. 2 to
3/0 hook
3 x strong

Solid brass
ring

250–500 g
barrel sinker

30–50 kg
trace

1 metre

3 x strong

Dropper loop
30 cm

No. 3/0 hook -
Suicide or Viking
pattern

Main
line

50 cm

50 cm

Dropper loop
15 cm

1/2 kg
snapper sinker

No. 3/0 to
5/0 hook
3 x strong

Rigs and Tactics

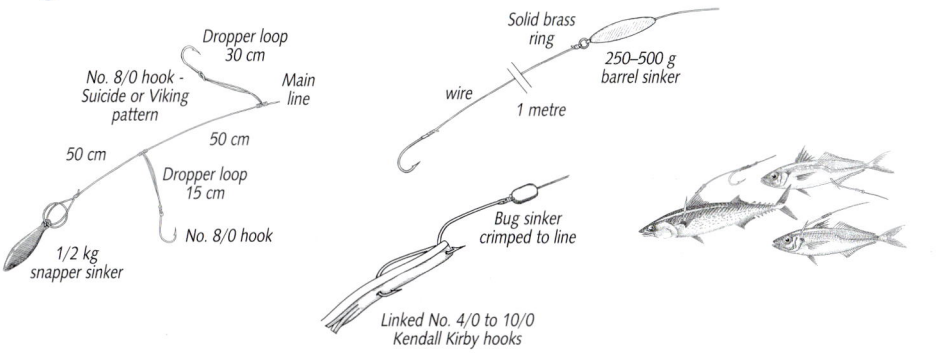

Dropper loop
30 cm

No. 8/0 hook -
Suicide or Viking
pattern

Main
line

50 cm

50 cm

Dropper loop
15 cm

1/2 kg
snapper sinker

No. 8/0 hook

Solid brass
ring

250–500 g
barrel sinker

wire

1 metre

Bug sinker
crimped to line

Linked No. 4/0 to 10/0
Kendall Kirby hooks

GURNARD, RED

Scientific name *Chelidonichthys kumu*. Also known as Gurnard, flying gurnard, latchet, kumu gurnard, kumukumu.

Range From Shark Bay in Western Australia, through southern waters including Tasmania and around the east coast as far north as the southern extremity of the Great Barrier Reef.

Description The red gurnard is a beautiful species with its large pectoral fins and brightly patterned ventral fins which are bright blue with a large black spot and scattered paler spots. The first three rays of the pectoral fin are free and act as 'fingers' for the detection of food in the sand. While the head is bony, it is smooth and the red gurnard lacks the bony horns of some other species. The red gurnard can reach 60 cm and more than 2 kg but is more common at 40 – 45 centimetres. It is commonly found from 80 m to the continental shelf but can be taken from shallower waters at times.

Fishing The red gurnard feeds on crabs, worms, molluscs and small fish and all these work for this species. The red gurnard is taken when fishing deeper waters for other species, being most prevalent on sand or broken ground near reefs and is generally taken on the bottom hook of a standard bottom drift rig. The fight is limited due to the depth which requires heavy lines and sinkers. The red gurnard is a highly regarded food fish.

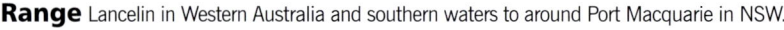

HAPUKU

Scientific name *Polyprion oxygeneios*.

Range Lancelin in Western Australia and southern waters to around Port Macquarie in NSW.

Description A very large species reaching 1.8 cm and 70 kilograms. It can be found occasionally in waters as shallow as 15 metres, and from 50 to 400 metres but is most common in 150 - 350 metre depths. This attractive fish is frequently slate grey to blue-grey and may tend towards dusky grey. The head and mouth is large and can take very big baits. The lower jaw is undershot which is diagnostic. The gill cover has a horizontal ridge which ends in a modest spine.

Fishing It is only in the last decade or so that anglers have been willing to chase hapuku in private boats as the depths they are found in involves considerable travel, favourable weather and specialised deep water gear. The use of braid line has made the task of getting a kilogram or more of weight and large hapuku back to the surface more realistic. Due to the extreme depths, most fish show considerable signs of barotrauma including popped eyes and protruding stomachs. Some charter boats are now targeting this species with some concern that they are vulnerable to over-exploitation at even modest fishing levels. Hapuku are frequently caught with other large species such as the bar cod and bass groper. Caught in shallow water, the hapuku puts up a strong fight. The fight in deeper water is sandbagged by the huge weights and heavy gear often used. The hapuku is caught by many commercial fishers and is considered to be one of the best cooler water fish to eat.

HARLEQUIN FISH

Scientific name *Othos dentex*. Also known as harlequin cod, Chinese lantern, tiger cod.

Range Jurien Bay in Western Australia and southwards to Victor Harbour in South Australia.

Description A truly stunning species which superficially resembles the coral trout of much more tropical waters but is a bit more long and slender. The harlequin fish can have blue spots on the head of variable shape which may extend to the chin. The overall colour can vary in a similar fashion to coral trout but is more commonly red or orange and much less frequently brick red. The harlequin fish has yellow or creamy yellow blotches on the lower sides of the fish. The tail is slightly convex whereas with the coral trout species the tail is either square or concave. These species do not overlap in range but can be confused if seen together in a fish shop. The harlequin fish inhabits coastal reefs in inshore waters. It is inquisitive and can be susceptible to spearfishing pressure. The harlequin fish can grow to 75 centimetres.

Fishing Standard reef fishing techniques rigs and baits will take harlequin fish. As they can be found in shallow reef areas, lighter sinkers and rigs work as well. The harlequin can be taken on squid, octopus, and pilchard or cut flesh baits. This species is considered very good eating and its bright colour and quality flesh means that it is considered a potential future aquaculture species.

GURNARD, RED

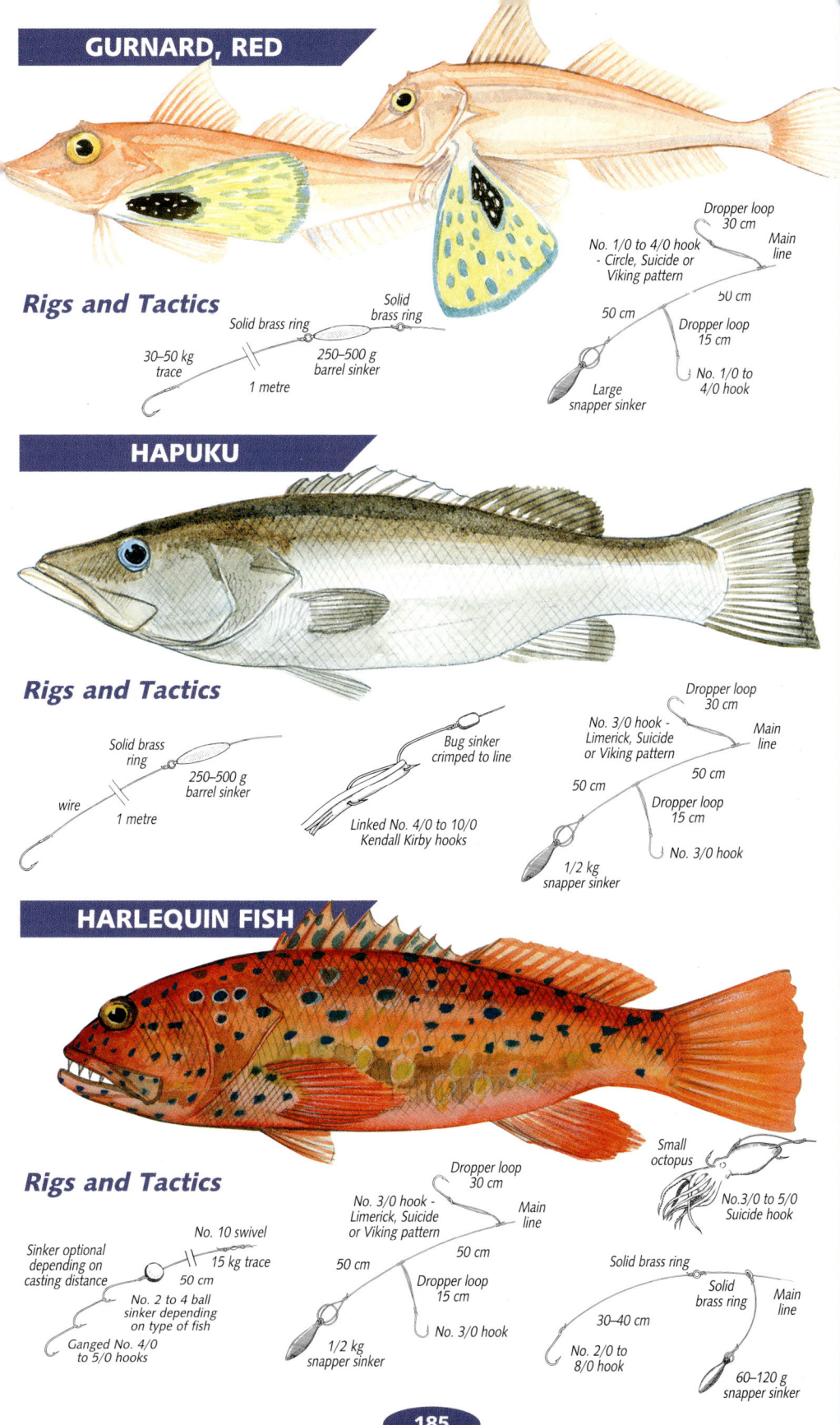

Rigs and Tactics

30–50 kg trace

Solid brass ring

1 metre

Solid brass ring

250–500 g barrel sinker

Dropper loop 30 cm

No. 1/0 to 4/0 hook - Circle, Suicide or Viking pattern

Main line

50 cm

50 cm

Dropper loop 15 cm

Large snapper sinker

No. 1/0 to 4/0 hook

HAPUKU

Rigs and Tactics

wire

Solid brass ring

1 metre

250–500 g barrel sinker

Bug sinker crimped to line

Linked No. 4/0 to 10/0 Kendall Kirby hooks

Dropper loop 30 cm

No. 3/0 hook - Limerick, Suicide or Viking pattern

Main line

50 cm

50 cm

Dropper loop 15 cm

1/2 kg snapper sinker

No. 3/0 hook

HARLEQUIN FISH

Rigs and Tactics

Sinker optional depending on casting distance

No. 10 swivel

15 kg trace

50 cm

No. 2 to 4 ball sinker depending on type of fish

Ganged No. 4/0 to 5/0 hooks

Dropper loop 30 cm

No. 3/0 hook - Limerick, Suicide or Viking pattern

Main line

50 cm

50 cm

Dropper loop 15 cm

1/2 kg snapper sinker

No. 3/0 hook

Small octopus

No.3/0 to 5/0 Suicide hook

Solid brass ring

Solid brass ring

Main line

30–40 cm

No. 2/0 to 8/0 hook

60–120 g snapper sinker

HUSSAR

Scientific name *Lutjanus adetii*. Also known as Yellow-banded seaperch.

Range Cape Moreton in Queensland and north as far as Rockhampton on the east coast only.

Description An attractive and distinctive sea-perch, the hussar reaches 50 cm. It is often bright pink and has a yellow stripe down the middle of the side from the gill cover to the tail. The dorsal fin has orange or pink stripes and the iris of the eye is yellow. Found on coral reefs, the hussar can form large schools and can be a nuisance bait stealer when in smaller sizes.

Fishing Standard reef rigs will take the hussar which is a common, if less prized capture when compared with the various emperor species. It has a large enough mouth to take most reef cut baits or squid, pilchards or large prawns even at its more common size of around 30 cm. The hussar is considered quite good eating and can be a saving grace for tropical offshore fishing trips.

JOBFISH, GREEN

Scientific name *Aprion virescens*. Also known as King snapper, jobfish, samurai salmon.

Range Ningaloo Reef in Western Australia around the top end to central Queensland.

Description The green jobfish has a torpedo-like body with a very large, deeply forked tail and is capable of reaching more than a metre and 15 kilograms. It has a dark green to blue-grey colour and diagnostic dark patches along the base of the dorsal fin. The green jobfish has prominent canine teeth in both jaws.

Fishing The green jobfish can be found in water from 10 to over 100 m in depth and around coral reefs and deep drop-offs. They have recently been subject to increasing commercial pressure due to their high regard as a food fish in south-east Asian markets, resulting in them becoming increasingly scarce in shallower waters. The jobfish is an active species which will attack trolled deep running lures on occasion. The fight of the jobfish, even in deep water can be memorable as they dive towards coral or rock to win freedom. Baits of whole or cut fish baits, squid and live baits work, along with vertically jigged lures.

JOBFISH, ROSY

Scientific name *Pristipomoides filamentosus*. Also known as Rosy snapper, crimson jobfish.

Range Point Quobba in Western Australia and tropical waters around to around Evans Head in northern NSW. It is recorded as being more common in southern Queensland waters and is anecdotally believed to be the 'king snapper' leading pink snapper schools around deeper waters.

Description A very attractive deeper water schooling species which can reach 100 cm in length. The rosy jobfish is most commonly found in depths from 80 - to more than 350 metres deep. The most obvious distinguishing feature from the other jobfish species is that the trailing edge of both the dorsal and anal fins is obviously extended and may reach almost to the start of the tail. The colouration is a rosy pink and may have olive hues. The scales have a bluish tinge to the edge.

Fishing In spite of the heavy rigs needed to fish the deeper waters the rosy jobfish prefers, their fight is strong and can be a real challenge. The rosy jobfish is a schooling fish and if bites stop, the drift should be quickly recommenced. A marker buoy is of great assistance, especially at night, when they are more active. The mouth is capable of taking standard reef fishing baits with fish, squid and prawns all working well. All the jobfish species are considered excellent eating.

HUSSAR

Rigs and Tactics

Small octopus

No.3/0 to 5/0 Suicide hook

Bug sinker crimped to line

Linked No. 4/0 to 10/0 Kendall Kirby hooks

Dropper loop 30 cm

No. 1/0 to 4/0 hook - Circle, Suicide or Viking pattern

Main line

50 cm

50 cm

Dropper loop 15 cm

No. 1/0 to 4/0 hook

Large snapper sinker

JOBFISH, GREEN

Rigs and Tactics

Small octopus

No.3/0 to 5/0 Suicide hook

Wire Trace

Metal Lure

No. 1/0 to 4/0 hook - Circle, Suicide or Viking pattern

Dropper loop 30 cm

Main line

50 cm

50 cm

Dropper loop 15 cm

No. 1/0 to 4/0 hook

Large snapper sinker

JOBFISH, ROSY

Rigs and Tactics

Small octopus

No.3/0 to 5/0 Suicide hook

No. 1/0 to 4/0 hook - Circle, Suicide or Viking pattern

Dropper loop 30 cm

Main line

50 cm

50 cm

Dropper loop 15 cm

No. 1/0 to 4/0 hook

Large snapper sinker

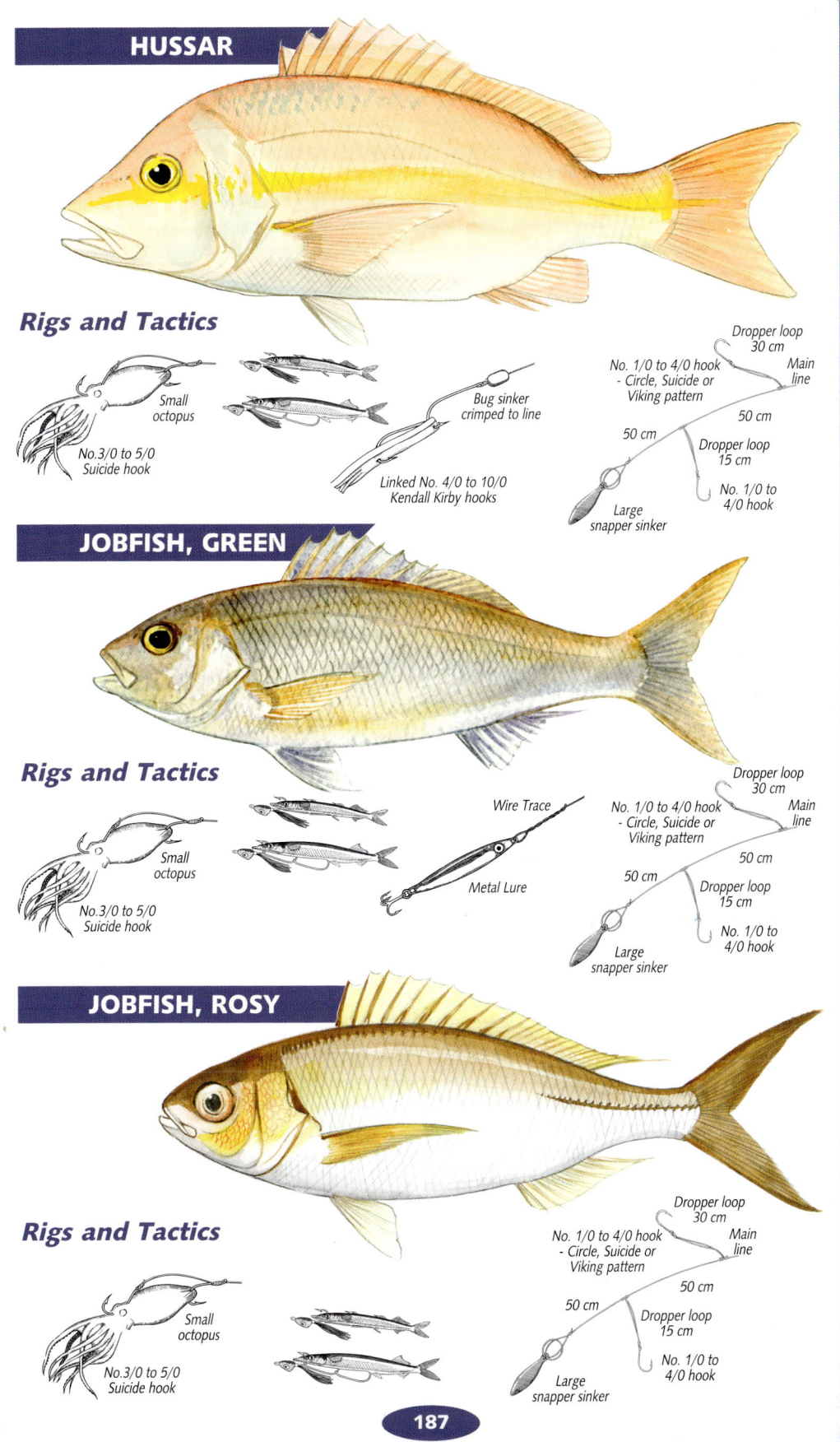

LEATHERJACKET, CHINAMAN

Scientific name *Nelusetta ayraudi*. Also known as Yellow leatherjacket.

Range North West Cape in Western Australia around southern water but excluding Tasmania to southern Queensland.

Description The extremely long head and long first dorsal and anal rays are diagnostic of the Chinaman leatherjacket. Females and juveniles are bright orange with red-orange fins, the males yellow or yellow-brown with yellow fins. This species can be found to depths of over 350 m but juveniles school seasonally in estuaries and coastal embayments. The Chinaman leatherjacket can reach over 70 cm and 3.5 kg making it one of the world's largets leatherjackets. It is often caught in inshore waters at 25 – 35 centimetres.

Fishing When schooling Chinaman leatherjacket can feed on almost anything. They will take prawns, squid, crabs, worms and cut baits. A wire trace or long shank hook can prevent bite-offs from the strong teeth. This species can move close to the surface and bite through lines fishing deeply, especially if a small bit of slime or weed catches on the line. This species is good eating when the skin is removed which is quite simple with the leatherjackets.

LEATHERJACKET, FANTAIL

Scientific name *Aluterus scriptus*. Also known as Scribbled leatherjacket.

Range Ningaloo Reef in Western Australia northwards around to northern NSW, although this species is recorded as being present in Sydney Harbour.

Description The largest of the leatherjackets, reaching a metre in length. It has an unusually large tail fin and unusually has a very fine dorsal spine which may be almost unnoticeable in larger specimens. The body is greenish yellow, covered with intense scribbling of deep blue lines and brown spots. This is an herbivorous species, grazing on algae which encrusts coral and tropical rocks.

Fishing This herbivorous species is most frequently taken by spearfishermen. They are occasionally taken while fishing for other species with prawn or squid baits, but the small mouth and extremely strong teeth can cut through hooks. This species is a very high risk from ciguatera and should not be consumed.

LING, ROCK

Scientific name *Genypterus tigerinus*. Also known as Tiger ling.

Range Albany in Western Australia and southern waters including Tasmania to southern NSW.

Description The body of the rock ling is pale grey to white and densely patterned in black. The dorsal and anal fins lack black bars which are found on the similar pink ling. The 'beard' is actually a modified ventral fin which is positioned under the chin. Easily separated from the beardie as the rock ling does not have a tail and the dorsal and anal fins meet at the end of the body. This species can be found to depths of 60 m and adults are found on rocky reefs and broken ground while juveniles are found inshore and in bays and estuaries.

Fishing Taken as part of mixed reef catches in cooler waters with standard reef paternoster rigs. The rock ling prefers fresh baits of cut and whole fish, squid and cuttlefish baits. This is an excellent food fish and a welcome bonus in a mixed bag.

LEATHERJACKET, CHINAMAN

Rigs and Tactics

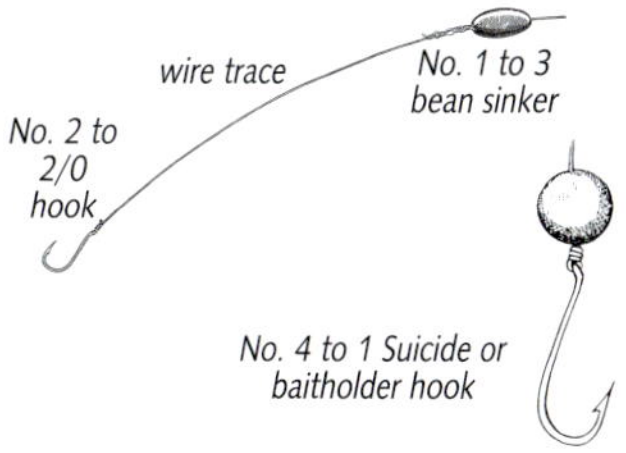

wire trace

No. 1 to 3
bean sinker

No. 2 to
2/0
hook

No. 00 to 2
ball sinker

No. 4 to 1 Suicide or
baitholder hook

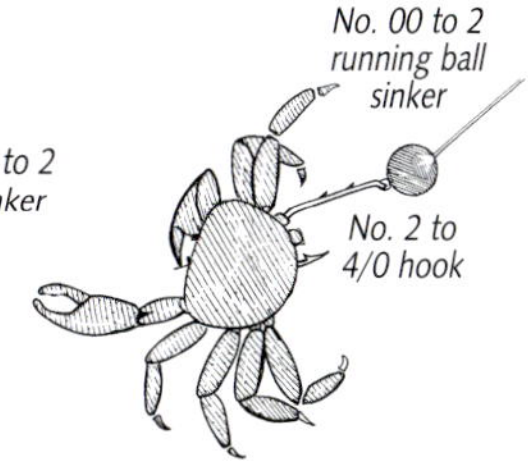

No. 00 to 2
running ball
sinker

No. 2 to
4/0 hook

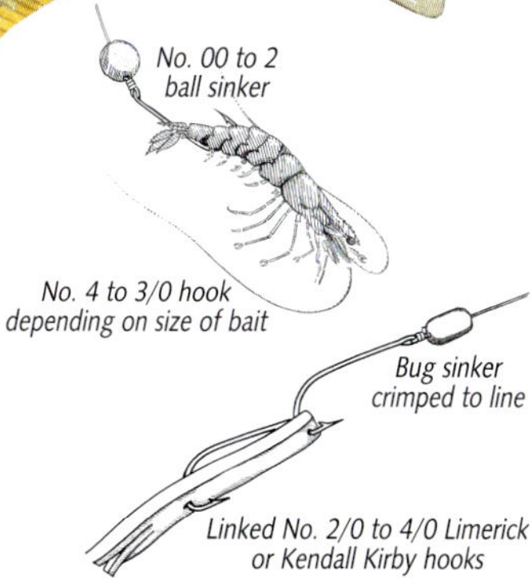

No. 00 to 2
ball sinker

No. 4 to 3/0 hook
depending on size of bait

Bug sinker
crimped to line

Linked No. 2/0 to 4/0 Limerick
or Kendall Kirby hooks

LEATHERJACKET, FANTAIL

LING, ROCK

Rigs and Tactics

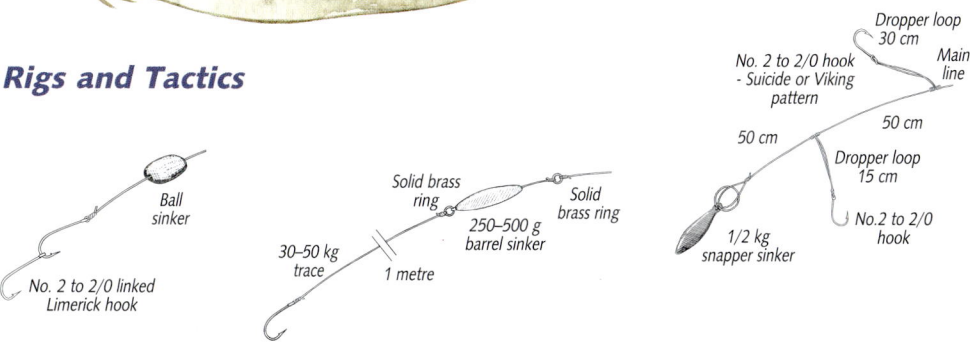

Ball
sinker

No. 2 to 2/0 linked
Limerick hook

30–50 kg
trace

1 metre

Solid brass
ring

250–500 g
barrel sinker

Solid
brass ring

No. 2 to 2/0 hook
- Suicide or Viking
pattern

50 cm

1/2 kg
snapper sinker

Dropper loop
30 cm

Main
line

50 cm

Dropper loop
15 cm

No.2 to 2/0
hook

MORWONG

Scientific name *Nemadactylus douglasii*. Also known as Grey morwong, silver morwong, blue morwong, common morwong, rubberlip, blubberlip, jackass, mowie, sea bream, porae (New Zealand).

Range Southern Queensland around Bundaberg southwards along the east coast to Melbourne and eastern Bass Strait and north-east Tasmania.

Description The morwong is a deep bodied fish with a relatively small mouth and prominent fleshy lips. The colour ranges from a pale grey to silver and to silvery blue. In common with other morwong, this species has several extended rays in each pectoral fin. Morwong can reach 70 cm and more than 4 kg, but is commonly caught at 1 – 2 kilograms. The morwong can be separated from the banded morwong and red morwong by their distinctive colourations and the queen snapper has distinctive gold lines on the head in large adults and gold stripes on smaller fish.

Fishing The morwong was once considered a poor second alternative to snapper, particularly in NSW, but increasingly scarce snapper numbers have elevated morwong as a more desirable species. Morwong feed on prawns, worms, squid, molluscs, fish flesh and other food which they encounter opportunistically. Best baits include fish flesh, prawns, squid and octopus tentacles. Baits are best presented on a traditional two hook paternoster rig, with sufficient weight to reach the bottom and bounce along the bottom on a slow drift. Morwong are often found in small loose schools so once fish are encountered, repeated drifts over the same area should continue to produce fish. If the current or wind is strong, a drogue or drift anchor will slow the drift and keep the baits in productive water which includes the edges of deep water reefs and drop-offs, with broken rock and gravel being particularly important. On occasions morwong can be taken over sand or mud bottoms, but a depth sounder is important to save time as fish feed more infrequently in these areas. Morwong are most commonly encountered from 30 to 200 m, but they are occasionally taken from shallower waters. They are an easy target for spearfishermen. The morwong is fair to good eating but can have a slight iodine taste, especially if fish have been grazing on weed which they occasionally do. Filleting helps improve the quality of the flesh.

MORWONG, RED

Scientific name *Cheilodactylus fuscus*. Also known as Five-fingers.

Range Southern Queensland from Bribie Island to southern NSW.

Description The red morwong possesses the typical extended lower rays of the pectoral fin and the prominent rubbery lips. This species is more common on inshore reefs or off rocky headlands. There is a distinctive red colouration on the upper body with several prominent white splotches and white bars near the tail. A red stripe runs through the eye. The red morwong reaches 45 cm and 3 kg but is more common around 1 kilogram.

Fishing This is a common species in spearfishing bags and is particularly vulnerable, resulting in a special bag limit in NSW long before this type of management came into more prominent use. The species is taken by line using fairly small baits of prawn, fish flesh and squid. As they are found in shallower waters, they are taken with other shallow water reef species including snapper, yellowfin bream and sweep. A light rig improves the hook-up rate for this fish. Red morwong are good eating but have been implicated in heavy metal contamination near sewerage outfalls and heavy consumption should be carefully considered.

MORWONG

Rigs and Tactics

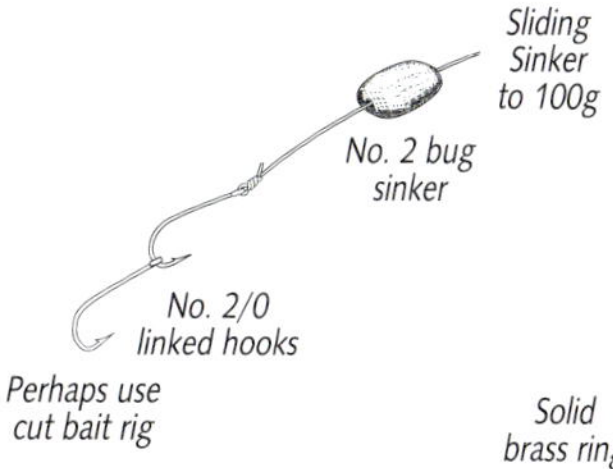

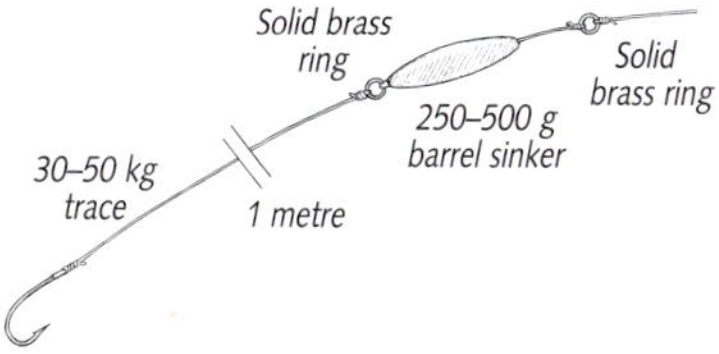

Sliding Sinker to 100g

No. 2 bug sinker

No. 2/0 linked hooks

Perhaps use cut bait rig

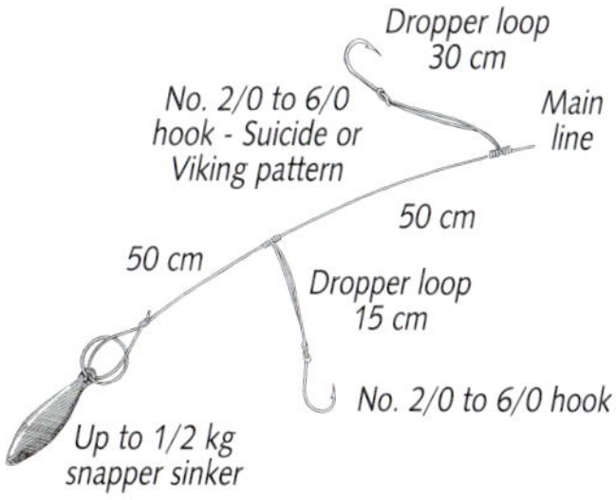

Dropper loop 30 cm

No. 2/0 to 6/0 hook - Suicide or Viking pattern

Main line

50 cm

50 cm

Dropper loop 15 cm

Up to 1/2 kg snapper sinker

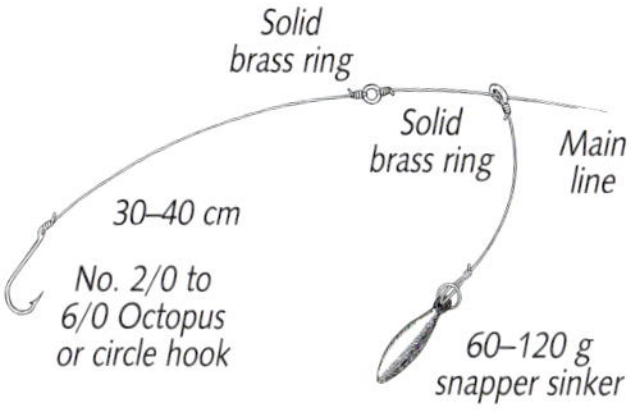

No. 2/0 to 6/0 hook

Solid brass ring

Solid brass ring

Main line

30–40 cm

No. 2/0 to 6/0 Octopus or circle hook

60–120 g snapper sinker

Solid brass ring

250–500 g barrel sinker

Solid brass ring

30–50 kg trace

1 metre

MORWONG, RED

Rigs and Tactics

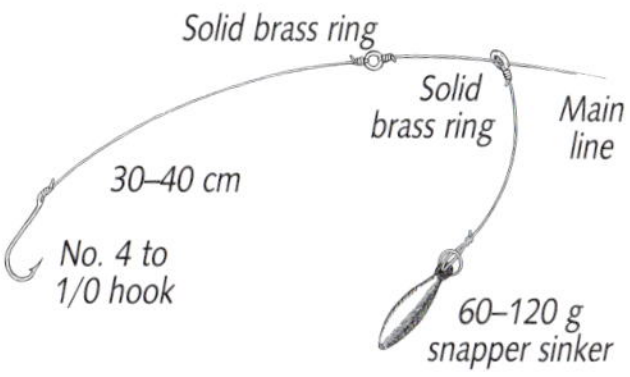

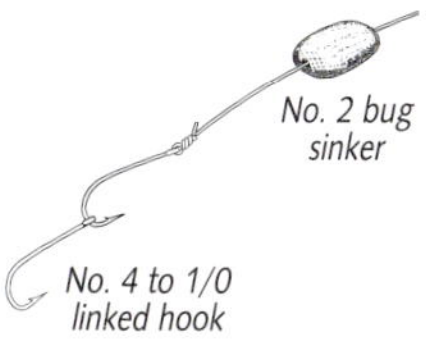

Solid brass ring

Solid brass ring

Main line

30–40 cm

No. 4 to 1/0 hook

60–120 g snapper sinker

No. 2 bug sinker

No. 4 to 1/0 linked hook

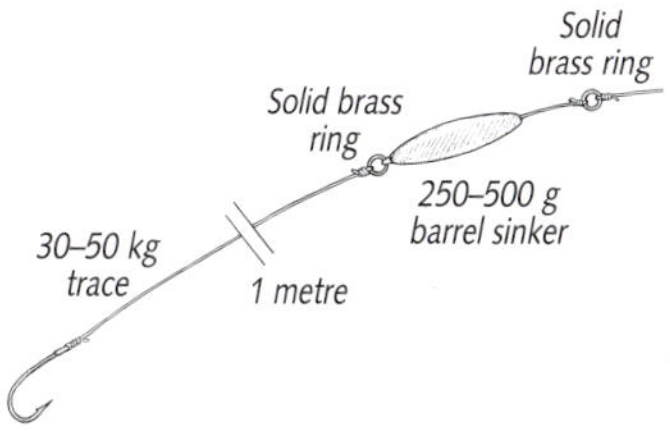

Solid brass ring

Solid brass ring

250–500 g barrel sinker

30–50 kg trace

1 metre

191

NANNYGAI

Scientific name *Centroberyx affinis*. Also known as Eastern nannygai, redfish.

Range A prolific east coast species ranging as far north as Moreton Bay in Queensland, but the nannygai is much more common from the Mid-North coast of NSW around to western Melbourne in Victoria including north-east Tasmania.

Description A pink to bright red or orange coloured fish, with large eyes, a large upturned mouth, a rounded snout and no pale fin margins. The nannygai is separated from other similar species such as the red snapper as it has 7 as opposed to 6 dorsal spines. The similar western nannygai is separated by its range (which commences around the South Australian/Victorian border to Shark Bay in Western Australia) and the western species has a yellow eye. While juveniles can school in estuaries and on inshore reefs, larger fish are found in larger schools in waters deeper than 25 m and out towards the edge of the continental shelf where they are a common trawl species. The nannygai is not a large fish, reaching around 45 centimetres.

Fishing The nannygai is often encountered when fishing deeper reefs for snapper and other deep water species. The large weights and relatively small size of nannygai means that they are less highly regarded than many other species. The large mouth and schooling nature of the nannygai means that large numbers can be caught, and on large baits. Standard snapper paternoster rigs with sufficient weight to drag bottom on a drift will take nannygai. Nannygai can be found near offshore reefs or near drop-offs over gravel or silt bottoms. Nannygai will take baits of fish, squid, octopus, crab, prawn and pilchard. When nannygai are biting freely, a fish can be caught on each hook on each drop and will often beat any snapper or other target species to the hook. Nannygai make good eating with firm white fillets. They are taken by trawlers in large quantities which are marketed as redfish.

NANNYGAI, SWALLOWTAIL

Scientific name *Centrobryx lineatus*. Also known as swallowtail.

Range Lancelin in Western Australia and along the south coast but not including Tasmania to Bermagui in southern NSW.

Description A common schooling deeper water reef species of the cooler southern ocean, the swallowtail nannygai can reach 43 centimetres. This species is most easily identified by the prominently forked tail fin which ends in an obvious point. The mouth is more prominently upturned and the swallowtail nannygai lacks the white stripe along the lateral line of the red snapper.

Fishing This species is taken commercially in large numbers and is highly prized by the market. When a school is encountered, large catches are possible and the fish are highly likely to be of a similar size. The swallowtail nannygai can be found on shallower reefs adjacent to deeper water in less than 10 m, but are much more common from 20 – 70 m deep. Their small size and deep water preference makes them a less than challenging sports fish. However, their large mouth means that they can be taken on larger hooks and baits intended for larger species. Standard reef rigs with the sinker weight tailored to fit the depth being fished are used. Best baits include squid, octopus and cut baits. These baits are preferred partly due to their ability to stand a few bites before a hook-up is made. Some anglers also wait until they think each hook has a fish before commencing the retrieve.

Rigs and Tactics

Dropper loop
30 cm

No. 3/0 hook -
Limerick, Suicide
or Viking pattern

Main
line

50 cm

50 cm

Dropper loop
15 cm

1/2 kg
snapper sinker

No. 3/0 hook

Solid
brass ring

Solid
brass ring

Main
line

30–40 cm

No. 2/0 to
8/0 hook

60 –120 g
snapper sinker

Solid brass
ring

100–500 g
barrel sinker

30–50 kg
trace

1 metre

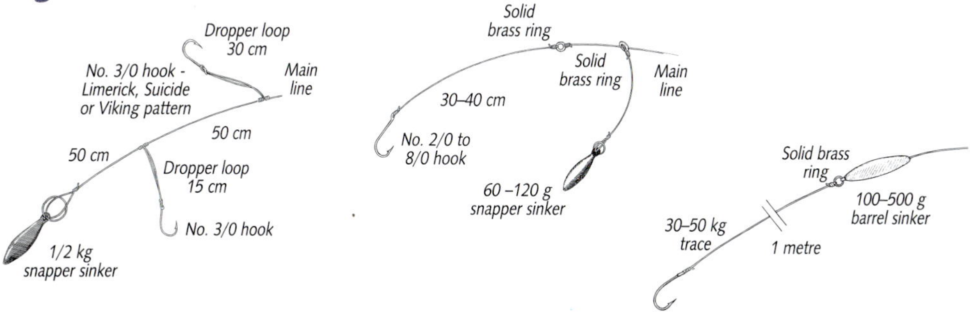

NANNYGAI, SWALLOWTAIL

Rigs and Tactics

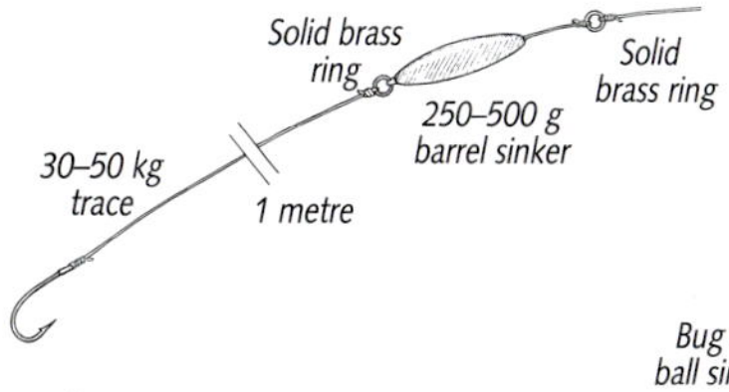

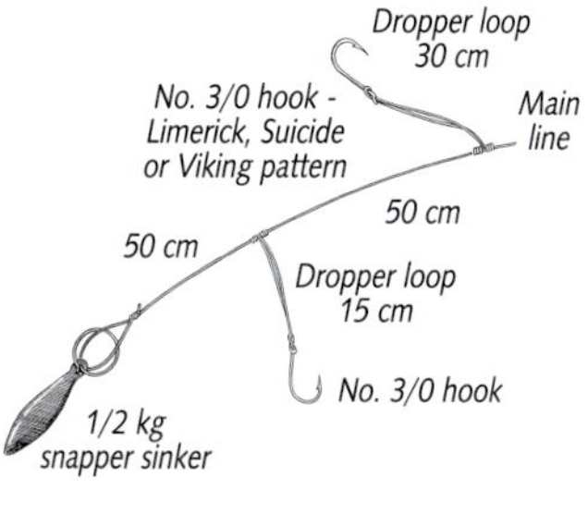

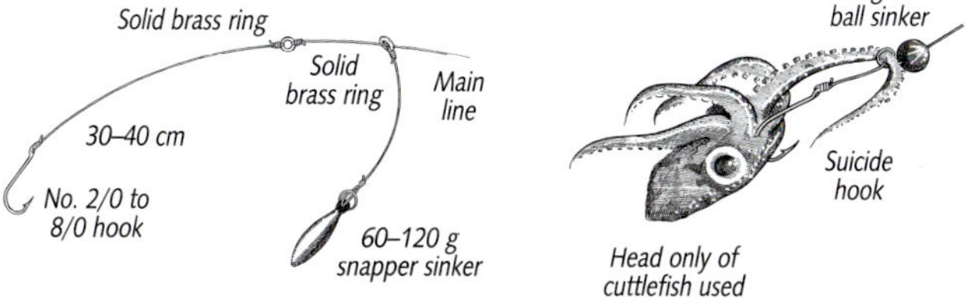

Dropper loop
30 cm

No. 3/0 hook -
Limerick, Suicide
or Viking pattern

Main
line

50 cm

50 cm

Dropper loop
15 cm

1/2 kg
snapper sinker

No. 3/0 hook

Solid brass
ring

250–500 g
barrel sinker

Solid
brass ring

30–50 kg
trace

1 metre

Solid brass ring

Solid
brass ring

Main
line

30–40 cm

No. 2/0 to
8/0 hook

60–120 g
snapper sinker

Bug or
ball sinker

Suicide
hook

Head only of
cuttlefish used

OLD WIFE

Scientific name *Enoplosus armatus.* Also known as Angelfish, moonlighter.

Range From Kalbarri in Western Australia and southern waters including Tasmania and around the east coast as far north as the Gold Coast in southern Queensland.

Description A deep bodied fish with a concave profile above the eyes. The Old Wife gets its name from the characteristic grinding of its teeth when caught, said to resemble the grumbling of an 'old wife'. The old wife has seven or eight black stripes on a white or silver-white background. Stripes extend to the fins. This fish can reach 800 g and around 30 centimetres. The old wife is usually found in pairs or small schools around reefs or weedy areas such as kelp forests or seagrass meadows. The old wife has two dorsal fins and this fish should be handled with care as the first dorsal spines and perhaps other spines are venomous. Puncture wounds should be immersed in hot but not scalding water to 'cook' or denature the proteins in the venom.

Fishing The old wife has a relatively small mouth and with its small size, is a 'picker' or bait stealer. The old wife will readily take prawns, worms, nippers, pipis and other smaller baits on small or long shank hooks fished near reefs or weed beds. They are often taken when fishing on bait grounds near these features. Although edible, the old wife is not a highly valued food fish.

PARROTFISH

Scientific name Family *Scaridae.*

Range A group of generally tropical species which are rarely found south of Shark Bay in Western Australia or the NSW-Queensland border, due in part to their close association with coral which they actively consume.

Description Closely related to the similarly colourful wrasses, but parrotfish have their teeth fused into strong beak-like plates. Sexes can have different colours and juveniles often have very different colours from adults. Some parrotfish can change sex when the largest male in a group is removed. Many parrotfish sleep in reef caves at night and can secrete a mucous envelope around their bodies while they rest. Sizes of parrotfish can range from the humphead parrotfish which can be up to 1.2 m to the more common green finned parrotfish which reaches 30 centimetres.

Fishing Parrotfish are almost never taken by line fishermen, but some species can be important spearfishing targets. The surf parrotfish can be herded into shallows and captured by hand in some Queensland reefs. The few parrotfish that are taken by line bite on prawn or worm baits intended for other species. Once hooked, the beak-like teeth can bite through lines and hooks. Parrotfish graze on live or dead corals or algae and can be important in the overall evolution of coral reefs. Parrotfish are highly regarded food fish but the bones are pale green which some find off-putting.

PERCH, MAGPIE

Scientific name *Cheilodactylus nigripes.* Also known as magpie morwong, black-striped morwong.

Range Albany in Western Australia and southern waters including northern Tasmania and along the east coast as far north as Nowra in NSW.

Description A distinctive species with a white overall colour with broad black and grey bands. The mouth is quite small and like most morwongs the pectoral fin is large and may be coloured. This species is separated from the similar crested morwong (*Cheilodactylus gibbosus*) by range as the crested morwong is found on the east coast from Newcastle to Bundaberg in Queensland and the first dorsal spine is obviously elongated while the fourth dorsal spine is longest in the magpie perch. The magpie perch is generally a shallow water reef dweller, although juveniles are found in deeper estuaries. This species prefers reef and weed margins and will venture onto sand to feed. The magpie perch reaches 40 cm and 2 kilograms.

Fishing The magpie perch is a more common spearfishing catch. The small mouth and its preference for feeding on small food make this a difficult species to take on line. Magpie perch can form loose aggregations. Magpie perch are incidentally taken while fishing with smaller rigs for other fish with baits of prawn, pipi, mussel and worm being best and squid and octopus also taking fish. Most anglers prefer to use larger hooks and baits and take a magpie perch if a hungry one happens along as they are good eating.

OLD WIFE

Rigs and Tactics

No. 10 to 4 hook

No. 1 to 3 bean sinker

No. 10 to 4 hook

3 kg

No. 10 to 4 hook

No. 2 to 4 ball or bean sinker depending on conditions

No. 00 to 2 ball sinker

No. 10 to 4 long shank hook depending on size of bait

PARROTFISH

Rigs and Tactics

No. 1 to 3 bean sinker

No. 8 to 4 hook

No. 00 to 2 ball sinker

No. 8 to 4 long shank hook depending on size of bait

PERCH, MAGPIE

Rigs and Tactics

No. 4 to 1/0 hook

No. 2 to 4 ball or bean sinker depending on conditions

3 kg

No. 4 to 1/0 hook

No. 1 to 3 bean sinker

No. 4 to 1/0 hook

No. 0 to 2 ball sinker

Estuary shrimp No. 10 to 6 hook

PERCH, PEARL

Scientific name *Glaucosoma scapulare.* Also known as Pearly, nannygai (Qld.).

Range Southern Queensland to NSW as far south as Newcastle but now very rare south of South West Rocks.

Description This is a handsome fish with a large eye and a large mouth. There is a small black spot at the base of the pectoral fin and a distinctive black flap of skin and bone near the top back edge of the gill cover. A similar species, the deepsea or northern dhufish (*Glaucosoma burgeri*) is found from Onslow north and lacks the distinctive flap on the gill cover, has a bright silvery appearance and can reach 2.5 kilograms. The pearl perch can reach 5 kg, but a fish over 3 kg is a quality fish.

Fishing This is widely regarded as one of the best, if not the best eating fish on the east coast. It was once found on mid depth reefs as far south as Newcastle, but commercial and recreational overfishing has pushed these fish further north and onto less heavily fished deep reefs in more than 50 m of water. Pearl perch are frequently taken in conjunction with snapper and other deep water reef species, although they bite most freely at dusk and dawn with early night being the next most productive time. Heavy weights are necessary to reach bottom where pearl perch are found. Best baits are fresh cut baits, squid or cuttlefish with pilchards being a reliable standby.

PIGFISH, BLACKSPOT

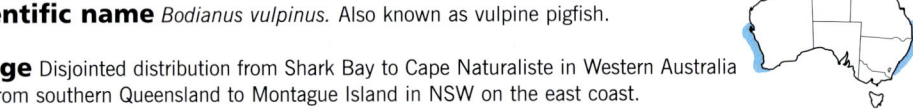

Scientific name *Bodianus vulpinus.* Also known as vulpine pigfish.

Range Disjointed distribution from Shark Bay to Cape Naturaliste in Western Australia and from southern Queensland to Montague Island in NSW on the east coast.

Description This species from the wrasse family, like many of its relative displays very different colouration between the male and female. The male is more brightly coloured, with bright red on the head and dorsal surface and a black blotch ringed by blue on the dorsal fin and a pale blotch below the dorsal fin near the tail. The female is a lighter orange tending to brick red with narrow darker stripes and sometimes blotches. The head is quite pointed and the eye prominent. The blackspot pigfish is found on rocky reefs in mid to deeper waters and can reach a respectable 60 centimetres.

Fishing The blackspot pigfish is frequently taken while drifting the deeper reefs for pink snapper, morwong and other larger species. The mouth is reasonably small and can be more difficult to hook on larger snapper rigs. Standard snapper rigs and baits take this species. The blackspot pigfish makes good eating.

ROCKCOD, MARBLED

Scientific name *Epinephelus maculatus.* Also known as Blackfin cod, spotty cod.

Range Abrolhos Islands in Western Australia and northwards through tropical waters to South West Rocks in NSW.

Description A pale brown fish covered with black spots fringed in brown. There is a large black patch at the front of the dorsal fin. A second and smaller black patch at the start of the soft dorsal. These black spots are separated by a lighter patch which may give a magpie type of colouration to the top of the body. The pectoral and anal fins are generally darker towards their edges.

Fishing The marbled rockcod is one of the mainstays of the Queensland tropical charter boat fleet and is regularly taken. It only grows to 50 cms but is more commonly encountered at around 30 - 35 cm. This species is taken near reefs on standard reef fishing rigs and baits, with pilchard, cut bait, squid, octopus, cuttlefish, and even prawns taking fish. The marbled rockcod is only regarded as average eating as the flesh can be quite strongly flavoured, but it is often proudly displayed as a memory of a day's charter fishing in the beautiful Great Barrier Reef.

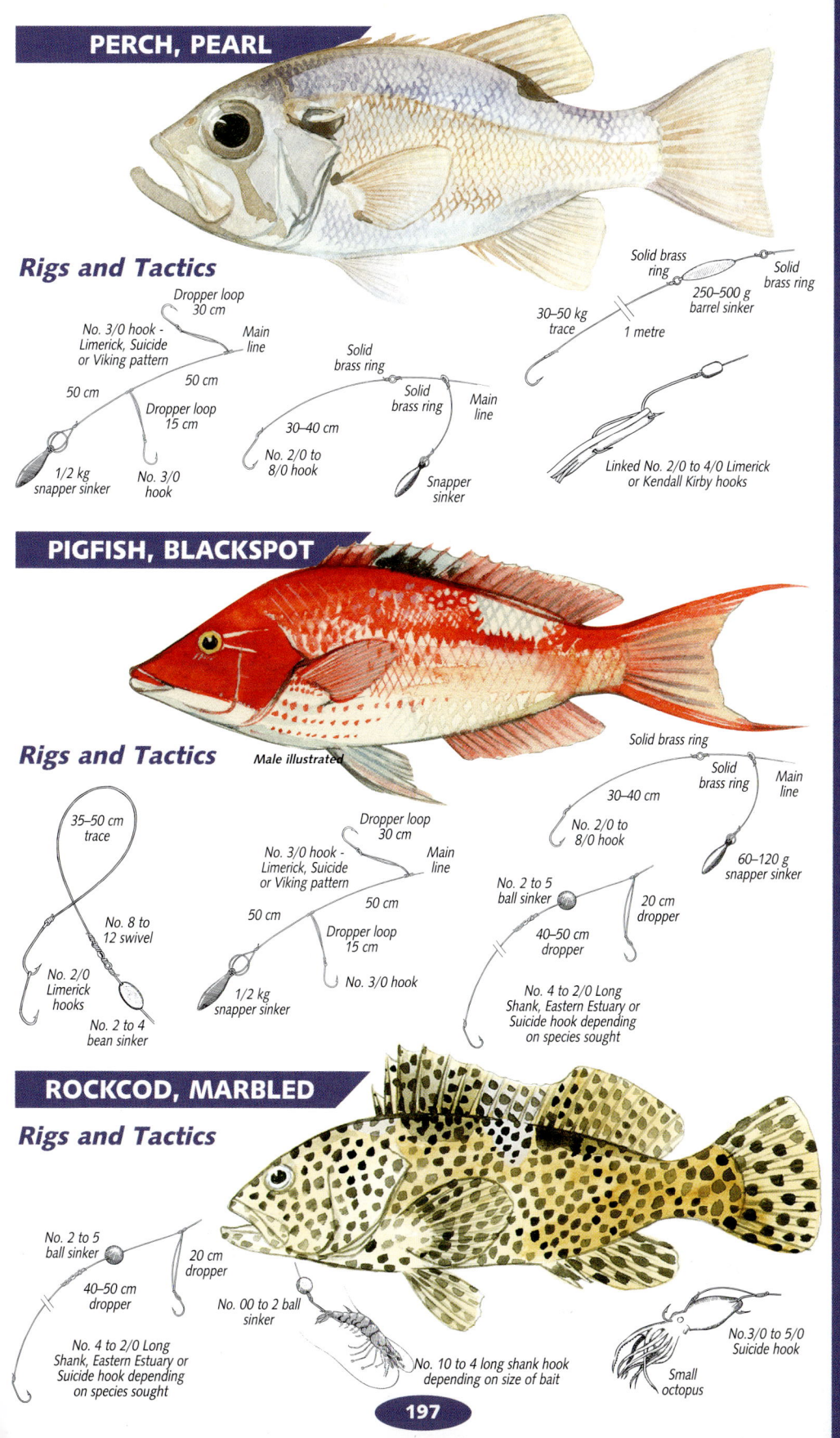

PERCH, PEARL

Rigs and Tactics

Dropper loop 30 cm

No. 3/0 hook - Limerick, Suicide or Viking pattern

Main line

50 cm

50 cm

Dropper loop 15 cm

1/2 kg snapper sinker

No. 3/0 hook

Solid brass ring

Solid brass ring

Main line

30–40 cm

No. 2/0 to 8/0 hook

Snapper sinker

Solid brass ring

250–500 g barrel sinker

Solid brass ring

30–50 kg trace

1 metre

Linked No. 2/0 to 4/0 Limerick or Kendall Kirby hooks

PIGFISH, BLACKSPOT

Rigs and Tactics   *Male illustrated*

35–50 cm trace

No. 8 to 12 swivel

No. 2/0 Limerick hooks

No. 2 to 4 bean sinker

Dropper loop 30 cm

No. 3/0 hook - Limerick, Suicide or Viking pattern

Main line

50 cm

Dropper loop 15 cm

1/2 kg snapper sinker

No. 3/0 hook

No. 2 to 5 ball sinker

40–50 cm dropper

20 cm dropper

No. 4 to 2/0 Long Shank, Eastern Estuary or Suicide hook depending on species sought

Solid brass ring

Solid brass ring

Main line

30–40 cm

No. 2/0 to 8/0 hook

60–120 g snapper sinker

ROCKCOD, MARBLED

Rigs and Tactics

No. 2 to 5 ball sinker

40–50 cm dropper

20 cm dropper

No. 4 to 2/0 Long Shank, Eastern Estuary or Suicide hook depending on species sought

No. 00 to 2 ball sinker

No. 10 to 4 long shank hook depending on size of bait

No.3/0 to 5/0 Suicide hook

Small octopus

ROCKCOD, PEACOCK

Scientific name *Cephalopholis argus*. Also known as Peacock cod.

Range Abrolhos Islands in Western Australia and tropical waters through to the southern end of the Great Barrier Reef.

Description A stunning medium sized cod species which grows to 50 cm. Adults have numerous peacock-blue spots with dark edges over the head body and fins. There are 5-6 bars generally present on the back part of the body as is a white patch around the pectoral fin. The soft dorsal, pectoral, ventral and tail fins are all bright purple. The body can be yellowish, to brown. The peacock rockcod is found around dead coral in quite shallow inshore reef areas. It is beautiful when seen by divers.

Fishing The peacock rockcod is very highly regarded as a food fish. They can be taken on a variety of whole, cut or live baits. They can also be taken on jigs and cast minnow lures.

ROCKCOD, TOMATO

Scientific name *Cephalopholis sonnerati*. Also known as Tomato cod, Orange-spotted cod.

Range Cape Cuvier in Western Australia northwards and tropical waters to Coffs harbour. Juveniles can be found further south.

Description The tomato rockcod can reach 65 cm and is found on or near coral and rock reefs. The frequently brightly coloured adults are often found in deeper water from 30 to 100 metres. Juveniles are more commonly found inshore. Juveniles are brown and may have bands. As the tomato rockcod grows, it develops orange spots which generally expand to dark red spots over a bright red base. Some fish, especially around Ningaloo Reef in Western Australia, have a brown form that may have white patches. The pectoral fins and the soft dorsal and anal fins are very rounded.

Fishing The tomato rockcod fits clearly the tropical maxim of red fish, good fish. It is considered excellent eating and has been known to be cut with a cookie cutter to make faux rock lobster. The tomato rockcod can be taken on a variety of baits and standard reef fishing rigs. They will take a variety of fish baits as well as squid and octopus. The mouth is not as large as many cod species, but can usually take a good sized hook. They can also be taken on white jigs, especially tipped with a piece of fish.

ROUGHY, ORANGE

Scientific name *Hoplostethus atlanticus*. Also known as Deepsea perch, sea perch, red roughy.

Range Sydney in NSW south to cooler waters, with greatest concentrations off Tasmania. Some populations found off southern Western Australia.

Description The orange roughy is a slow growing deep water fish species which forms large spawning aggregations near sea mounts where they have been over-harvested by commercial fishers in recent years. This is a deep bodied fish with a distinctive bright red to orange colour and a large upwardly pointing mouth. Orange roughy are found on the deeper edge of the continental shelf and so are not encountered by recreational anglers. However, they have high quality, white flaky flesh which is highly sought after and attains a top price. The management of this species provides a valuable lesson in taking a conservative approach to the development of any new fishery, as overexploitation became apparent shortly after spawning aggregations were identified and targetted near deep sea mounts. Ages for this species are now being challenged, but there is little doubt that they are very slow growing and long lived. Stock recovery will be a long and very difficult and challenging process.

Fishing This species is taken in huge numbers by deep water trawl methods and is not a recreational species except as a by-catch for the few who venture out to sea mounts and generally fish for hapuka with electric winches and very heavy sinkers. It makes an ideal purchase if the family wants fish and your own results have been less than satisfactory.

ROCKCOD, PEACOCK

Rigs and Tactics

Linked No. 2/0 to 4/0 Limerick
or Kendall Kirby hooks

No.3/0 to 5/0
Suicide hook

Small
octopus

Solid brass
ring

250–500 g
barrel sinker

Solid
brass ring

30–50 kg
trace

1 metre

ROCKCOD, TOMATO

Rigs and Tactics

Solid brass
ring

Solid
brass ring

250–500 g
barrel sinker

30–50 kg
trace

1 metre

No.3/0 to 5/0
Suicide hook

Small
octopus

ROUGHY, ORANGE

Rigs and Tactics

Dropper loop
30 cm

No. 3/0 hook -
Suicide or Viking
pattern

Gelspun
Super line

50 cm

50 cm

Dropper loop
15 cm

No. 3/0–7/0
hook

Large
snapper sinker

SEAPERCH, CRIMSON

Scientific name *Lutjanus erythropterus*. Also known as Small-mouth nannygai.

Range Onslow in Western Australia and northwards through tropical waters to the southern parts of the Great Barrier Reef in Queensland.

Description The crimson seaperch is very similar to the saddle-tailed seaperch which both grow to a similar maximum size of 100 cm and about 10 kilograms. The most obvious difference is that the head and mouth is much smaller in the crimson seaperch. The distance between the pre-operculum (front cheek bone) to the back of the eye and the front of the eye and the tip of the snout is roughly equal whereas the snout is obviously larger in the saddle-tailed seaperch. The head looks much more like a bream with the crimson seaperch while the saddle-tailed seaperch head looks much more like a mangrove jack. For the more technically minded, there are 9 or 10 scales above the lateral line in the crimson seaperch and 7 or 8 with the saddle-tailed seaperch. Both species can be found together near reefs or flat ground up to 100 metres in depth.

Fishing The fight of the crimson seaperch is very strong and can be a real challenge. The strong fight is rewarded with an excellent eating species which is highly prized. The crimson seaperch is taken on standard reef fishing paternoster rigs and baits of whole or cut fish, squid or prawns. Even though the mouth is smaller than the saddle-tailed seaperch, it can still take most standard reef fishing offerings. The crimson seaperch is a schooling fish but can be taken on relatively flat ground away from cover so attention to a depth sounder can help to find fish.

SEAPERCH, MAORI

Scientific name *Lutjanus rivulatus*. Also known as Scribbled seaperch, blubberlips seaperch.

Range Dampier Archipelago in Western Australia and tropical waters to around the Caloundra Reefs in southern Queensland. Juveniles may be found slightly further south.

Description An attractive seaperch species which grows to 75 cm and more than 6 kilograms. The Maori seaperch has a stocky build. The brown body may have olive or golden overtones. The head has bluish, narrow, short wavy lines that resemble the tattoo marks on a Maori warrior. The lips are thicker than in other seaperch species. The fins have a yellow or golden colour and the tail has a pronounced yellow rear edge. Juveniles have a white spot along the lateral line below the soft dorsal fin.

Fishing The fight of the Maori seaperch is typically very strong and can be a real challenge. The Maori seaperch is taken on standard reef fishing paternoster rigs and baits of whole or cut fish, squid or prawns. The Maori seaperch is found on reef country and may move from cover, especially as juveniles in depths of up to 100 metres. The Maori seaperch is an excellent eating species.

SEAPERCH, SADDLE-TAILED

Scientific name *Lutjanus malabaricus*. Also known as Large-mouth seaperch, Large-mouth nannygai, scarlet seaperch, Longman's seaperch.

Range Shark Bay in Western Australia and northwards to the southern end of the Great Barrier Reef.

Description The saddle-tailed seaperch is very similar to the crimson seaperch. It grows to a similar maximum size of 100 cm and about 10 kilograms. The most obvious difference is that the head and mouth is much larger in the saddle-tailed seaperch. The distance between the pre-operculum (front cheek bone) and the tip of the snout is longer in the saddle-tailed seaperch. The head looks similar to a mangrove jack. There are 7 or 8 scales above the lateral line with the saddle-tailed seaperch.

Fishing The saddle-tailed seaperch is a very hard fighting tropical reef species. Its fighting qualities are matched by its value as a food fish and is one of the highly regarded 'red' reef fish of the north. The saddle-tailed seaperch forms schools and is frequently caught along with the crimson seaperch. These fish can be found on trawl ground away from recognised structure and can be caught just when the drift is given up due to moving away from recognised structure. Standard reef fishing, multiple hook rigs baited with whole or cut fish, pilchards, squid or cuttlefish are most successful. Bait tipped jigs can also take these fish.

SEAPERCH, CRIMSON

Rigs and Tactics

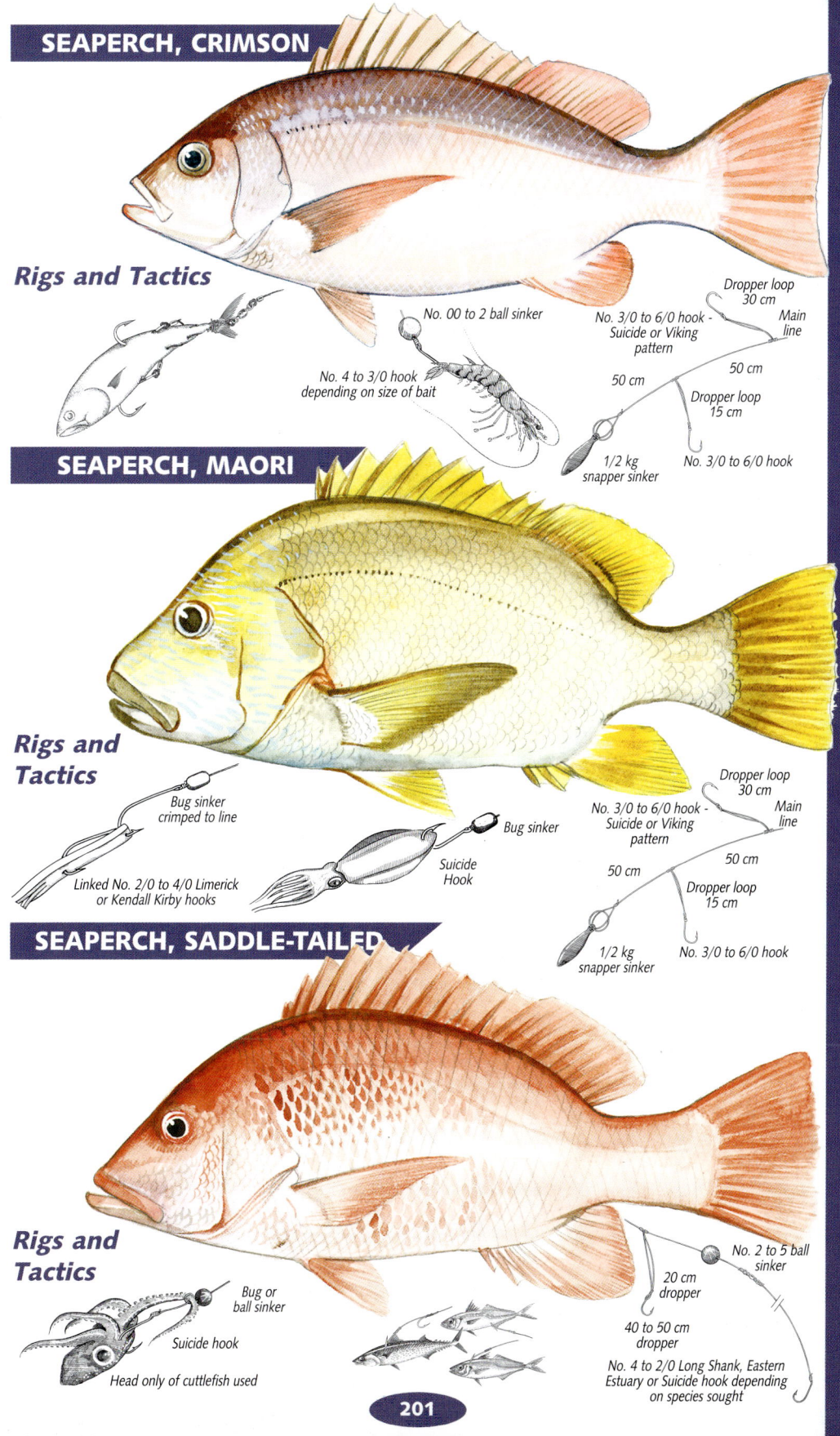

No. 00 to 2 ball sinker

No. 4 to 3/0 hook
depending on size of bait

Dropper loop
30 cm

Main
line

No. 3/0 to 6/0 hook -
Suicide or Viking
pattern

50 cm

50 cm

Dropper loop
15 cm

1/2 kg
snapper sinker

No. 3/0 to 6/0 hook

SEAPERCH, MAORI

Rigs and Tactics

Bug sinker
crimped to line

Linked No. 2/0 to 4/0 Limerick
or Kendall Kirby hooks

Bug sinker

Suicide
Hook

No. 3/0 to 6/0 hook -
Suicide or Viking
pattern

Dropper loop
30 cm

Main
line

50 cm

50 cm

Dropper loop
15 cm

1/2 kg
snapper sinker

No. 3/0 to 6/0 hook

SEAPERCH, SADDLE-TAILED

Rigs and Tactics

Bug or
ball sinker

Suicide hook

Head only of cuttlefish used

No. 2 to 5 ball
sinker

20 cm
dropper

40 to 50 cm
dropper

No. 4 to 2/0 Long Shank, Eastern
Estuary or Suicide hook depending
on species sought

SEAPERCH, STRIPEY

Scientific name *Lutjanus carponotatus*. Also known as Stripey, Spanish flag.

Range Shark Bay in Western Australia and northwards and through tropical waters to central Queensland.

Description A fairly small but attractive species which can reach 40 cm but is often seen at around 30 centimetres. The stripey seaperch has around 6 yellow or golden brown stripes which run along its body and which extend onto the head. The fins are all bright yellow but there is a diagnostic black spot at the base of the pectoral fin. The stripey seaperch is similar to the Moses perch (*Lutjanus russelli*) but lacks any black spot on the body and the stripes, while they may be pales are always present.

Fishing The stripey seaperch is an exciting an under-rated fish mainly due to its small size. The stripey seaperch will readily take a wide variety of lures and will form small schools to harass balled up baitfish. The stripey seaperch can be found in very shallow water so unweighted or very lightly weighted baits and rigs will work well, or they can be taken on mid depths reefs, but they show a decided preference for coral reefs. Although not highly regarded as a food fish and more often used as cut bait, the stripey seaperch makes quite good eating.

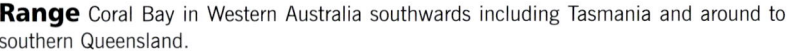

SERGEANT BAKER

Scientific name *Aulopus purpurissatus*.

Range Coral Bay in Western Australia southwards including Tasmania and around to southern Queensland.

Description A reasonably common fish of deeper coastal reefs and adjacent sandy patches, but can move into larger bays on occasion. Sergeant baker have a red, ruddy or rusty brown colour and a small adipose-like second dorsal fin. The longer first dorsal fin unusually does not have any spines, only soft rays and the second and third ray is elongated in male fish. The caudal fin is forked and the pectoral fins are large but the sergeant baker lacks the distinctive 'fingers' or bony head ridges of the gurnards. The sergeant baker reaches 70 cm in length and around 3 kg, but is more common at around 45 to 50 centimetres.

Fishing Sergeant baker are taken on standard bottom bouncing rigs adjacent to mid to deep water reefs. Sergeant baker prefer fresh fish fillets, pilchards, squid, octopus, prawn, or crab baits, but the large mouth does not prevent them from being taken on quite large live or dead baits. Sergeant baker can also be taken on bait tipped jigs. The flesh is white but only fair compared to other species like snapper or morwong taken from the same areas and can have a muddy taste.

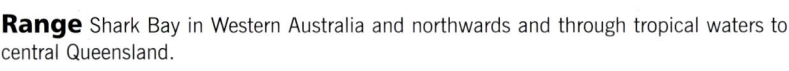

SNAPPER, LONG-SPINED

Scientific name *Argyrops spinifer*. Also known as frying pan snapper

Range Shark Bay in Western Australia and northwards and through tropical waters to central Queensland.

Description A very close relative of the pink snapper, the long-spined snapper is found in inshore waters, but is more commonly taken from deeper water trawl grounds. The long-spined snapper has a more rounded body shape leading to the frying pan snapper common name as they look ready made to fit a round fry pan. The other distinguishing feature are the much longer first three spines of the dorsal fin. The blue spots of this species are small and in the centre of the scales of freshly caught fish but can fade after death. The long-spined snapper can grow to 65 cm and more than 2 kg, but they are often caught in the trawl fishery at a much smaller size.

Fishing The long-spined snapper is found on deeper water reefs or on gravel bottoms adjacent to reefs where they can be taken by trawlers. They are a schooling fish and can be taken in good numbers when encountered but the deeper ground they prefer is not often targeted by recreational fishers. They are sometimes taken from 10 – 20 m especially where deep water is nearby, proving a pleasant surprise to anglers who wonder how a pink snapper could be so far out of its normal range. Standard deep reef paternoster rigs and baits for pink snapper will take the long-spined snapper, although they are often smaller and the mouth is smaller than the pink snapper. This species makes excellent eating when fresh.

SEAPERCH, STRIPEY

Rigs and Tactics

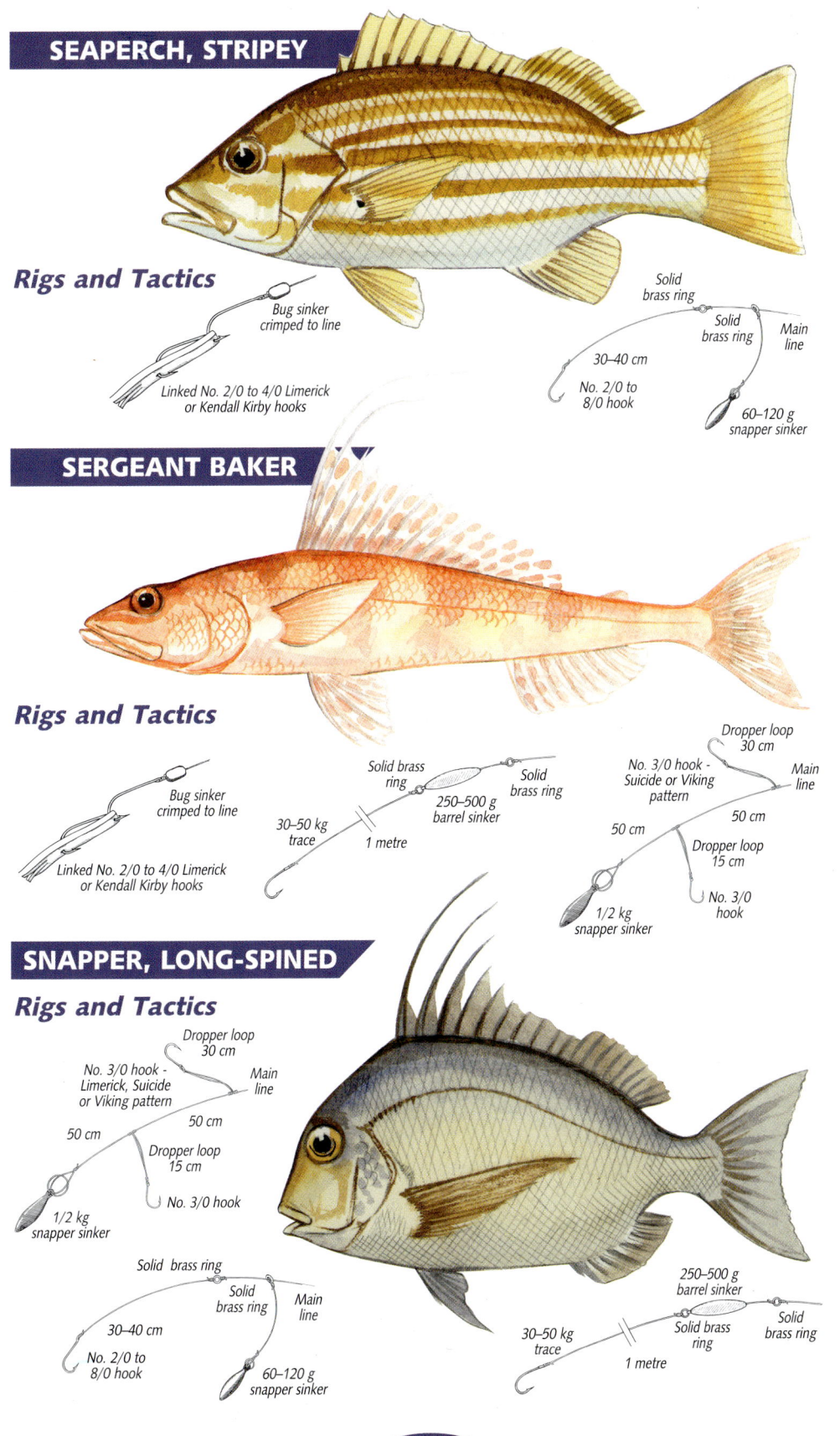

Bug sinker crimped to line

Linked No. 2/0 to 4/0 Limerick or Kendall Kirby hooks

Solid brass ring

Solid brass ring

Main line

30–40 cm

No. 2/0 to 8/0 hook

60–120 g snapper sinker

SERGEANT BAKER

Rigs and Tactics

Bug sinker crimped to line

Linked No. 2/0 to 4/0 Limerick or Kendall Kirby hooks

Solid brass ring

30–50 kg trace

1 metre

250–500 g barrel sinker

Solid brass ring

Dropper loop 30 cm

No. 3/0 hook - Suicide or Viking pattern

Main line

50 cm

50 cm

Dropper loop 15 cm

1/2 kg snapper sinker

No. 3/0 hook

SNAPPER, LONG-SPINED

Rigs and Tactics

Dropper loop 30 cm

No. 3/0 hook - Limerick, Suicide or Viking pattern

Main line

50 cm

50 cm

Dropper loop 15 cm

No. 3/0 hook

1/2 kg snapper sinker

Solid brass ring

Solid brass ring

Main line

30–40 cm

No. 2/0 to 8/0 hook

60–120 g snapper sinker

250–500 g barrel sinker

Solid brass ring

30–50 kg trace

Solid brass ring

1 metre

SNAPPER

Scientific name *Pagrus auratus.* (formerly *Chrysophrys auratus*) Also known as schnapper, Pink snapper and pinkie. With increasing size known as Cockney bream, red bream, squire, snapper and ultimately 'old man snapper' with the characteristic hump.

Range Snapper are common in southern waters and range from Coral Bay in Western Australia to the Capricorn Group in Queensland.

Description A truly stunning and highly sought after species, the snapper can have iridescent pink to burnished copper colouration with bright blue spots from the lateral line upwards which are brightest in younger fish. A hump on the head and nose area develops in some fish and is more likely in male fish. Snapper are relatively slow growing and mature at 29 to 35 cm and four to five years of age. Snapper numbers have been affected by both commercial and recreational overfishing. Prawn trawl by-catch and anglers gut hooking juvenile snapper in places like Botany Bay in NSW have contributed to the reduction in quality snapper fishing on the east coast in recent years. Recreational over-fishing in the eastern gulf of Shark Bay has affected one of the best snapper fisheries in Australia.

Fishing Snapper are traditionally taken on bottom paternoster rigs with the famous snapper lead. Snapper prefer the edges of reefs or broken ground and can be taken from the shore or as deep as 50 fathoms. Drifting over broken ground or drop-offs at the edges of reefs with just enough weight to bounce bottom will find fish and repeated drifts will pick up more fish. Like many reef species, snapper form schools of similar sized fish, with the size of the school decreasing with larger fish. In late winter on the east coast, snapper move inshore to feed on spawning cuttlefish and large fish can be taken from the rocks on cuttlefish baits. In Western Australia, snapper form large schools in winter in Shark Bay and around October in Cockburn Sound. Quality snapper can be taken by sinking a bait under a feeding school of tailor, salmon or small mackerel, feeding on uneaten baitfish. Good catches can also be made fishing washes at the backs of breaking reefs, frequently mixed with tailor, bream and other fish. Best baits for snapper are pilchard, bonito, squid, cuttlefish, octopus and yellowtail. Snapper respond well to berley and will rise in a berley trail to take lightly weighted or unweighted baits. In shallow waters, snapper are a magnificent fighting fish. Recent tagging research indicates that many snapper are residential, so letting fish go, or moving on to take other species means that the fish you leave are likely to be there at a later date. Snapper are also taken on leadhead or vertical jigs, especially tipped with a piece of fish or octopus. Snapper are taken while trolling, particularly around bommies or reef with minnow and feather lures working well. Like bream, snapper are being incresingly recognised as a lure taker. Snapper can be excellent eating, but do not freeze particularly well.

SNAPPER, QUEEN

Scientific name *Nemadactylus valenciennesi* Also known as southern blue morwong

Range Lancelin in Western Australia and southern waters to Port Phillip Bay in Victoria

Description A handsome representative of the morwong family, the queen snapper is often a rich blue colour. There are distinctive yellow lines on the face and around the eyes and there is usually a large black blotch in the middle of the side of the fish. The queen snapper has the extended rays of the pectoral fin like many of the morwongs. The tail fin is deeply forked. The queen snapper is found from inshore reefs to a depth of 240 m and has a preference for reef country.

Fishing The queen snapper is a beautiful and much prized catch for reef fishermen in cooler waters. They are taken from similar areas and with the same rigs as for pink snapper, although queen snapper are more often taken from the shallower reefs than pinkies. The queen snapper has a smaller mouth with the typical morwong lips and therefore slightly smaller hooks are recommended if queen snapper are the target species. Queen snapper are taken on squid, octopus, cut baits, pilchards, prawn or crab baits. The queen snapper is considered to be very good eating, especially from the cooler waters of the south coast. The queen snapper can reach one metre in length.

SNAPPER

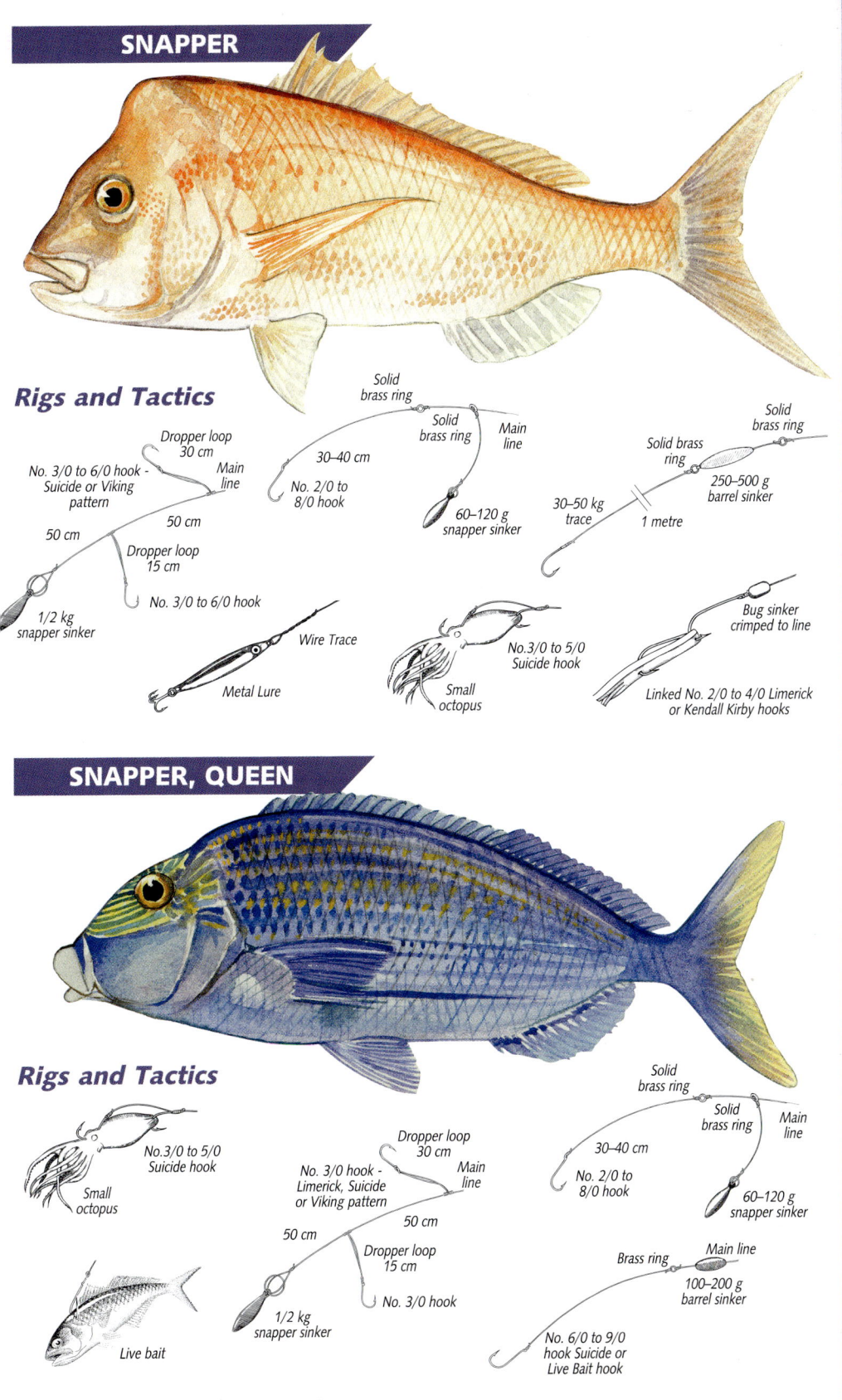

Rigs and Tactics

No. 3/0 to 6/0 hook -
Suicide or Viking
pattern

Dropper loop
30 cm

Main
line

50 cm

Dropper loop
15 cm

50 cm

1/2 kg
snapper sinker

No. 3/0 to 6/0 hook

Metal Lure

Wire Trace

Solid
brass ring

30–40 cm

No. 2/0 to
8/0 hook

Solid
brass ring

Main
line

60–120 g
snapper sinker

Small
octopus

No.3/0 to 5/0
Suicide hook

Solid brass
ring

Solid
brass ring

Main
line

30–50 kg
trace

1 metre

250–500 g
barrel sinker

Bug sinker
crimped to line

Linked No. 2/0 to 4/0 Limerick
or Kendall Kirby hooks

SNAPPER, QUEEN

Rigs and Tactics

No.3/0 to 5/0
Suicide hook

Small
octopus

Live bait

No. 3/0 hook -
Limerick, Suicide
or Viking pattern

Dropper loop
30 cm

Main
line

50 cm

Dropper loop
15 cm

50 cm

1/2 kg
snapper sinker

No. 3/0 hook

No. 6/0 to 9/0
hook Suicide or
Live Bait hook

Solid
brass ring

Solid
brass ring

Main
line

30–40 cm

No. 2/0 to
8/0 hook

60–120 g
snapper sinker

Brass ring

Main line

100–200 g
barrel sinker

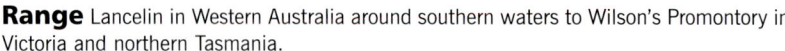
SNAPPER, RED

Scientific name *Centroberyx gerrardi.* Also known as Bight redfish.

Range Lancelin in Western Australia around southern waters to Wilson's Promontory in Victoria and northern Tasmania.

Description The red snapper is most commonly a species of deeper reefs in cooler southern waters which may range from shallow reefs to more than 300 metres. A handsome species very similar to the smaller nannygai but is able to be separated by having 6 dorsal fin spines versus 7 in the nannygai. The red snapper has a distinctive white line along the lateral line and white margins on the fins. The head is also less rounded than in the nannygai. The eye is generally red but can fade to red-silver after death. The red snapper can reach 66 cm, but is more common at 40 – 45 centimetres. It is found singly in larger sizes or in small groups when smaller.

Fishing A highly prized species of southern waters, the red snapper is much more active at night. The red snapper is most commonly caught drift fishing with standard deep water snapper rigs. The large mouth of the red snapper means that even small fish can be taken on large hooks. Best baits include prawns, squid and fresh cut baits. The red snapper is excellent eating.

SNOOK

Scientific name *Sphyraena novaehollandiae.* Also known as Short finned sea pike, sea pike, short finned barracuda.

Range Jurien Bay in Western Australia and southern waters, including Tasmania and around the east coast as far north as southern Queensland.

Description The snook is a very long and skinny southern relative of the barracuda. It is easily separated from the barracuda by its southern range and the first dorsal fin which commences well behind the end of the pectoral fin, while the first dorsal commences at the tip of the pectoral fin in barracuda. The snook is similar to the long finned sea pike but most easily separated by the snook's shorter anal fin, and its ventral fins which are set well behind the pectoral fin. The snook reaches 1.1 m and 5 kilograms.

Fishing The snook is relatively common in inshore cooler waters with a distinct preference for areas of weed or sand areas adjacent to weed or slight drop offs. The snook is an ambush feeder which may hunt in small packs, providing exciting fishing at times. Snook also favour regular haunts and may be found in identified hot-spots on a regular basis. Snook will take baits of whitebait, pilchard, bluebait, cut flesh or squid. Over shallow weed beds, lightly weighted or unweighted baits on single hooks or gang hook rigs work best and a gentle jigging action attracts additional strikes. Over deeper waters, or where snook may be holed up a small running sinker with a short trace to defend against the teeth will work well. Snook take lures and flies well. Best bets are silver or chrome spoons such as Tobys, or Wonder Wobblers. Feather jigs and small minnow lures also work well but the toothy mouth of the snook means that some fish can be lost to short strikes and lures and flies damaged. The snook makes good to excellent eating although the flesh is little soft and may bruise unless handled well.

SNAPPER, RED

Rigs and Tactics

Dropper loop
30 cm

No. 3/0 hook - Limerick, Suicide or Viking pattern

Main line

50 cm

50 cm

Dropper loop
15 cm

No. 3/0 hook

1/2 kg snapper sinker

Solid brass ring

Solid brass ring

Main line

30–40 cm

No. 1/0 to 4/0 hook

60–120 g snapper sinker

Bug sinker crimped to line

Linked No. 2/0 to 4/0 Limerick or Kendall Kirby hooks

Solid brass ring

Solid brass ring

250–500 g barrel sinker

1 metre

30–50 kg trace

SNOOK

Rigs and Tactics

Dropper loop
30 cm

No. 3/0 hook - Limerick, Suicide or Viking pattern

Main line

50 cm

50 cm

Dropper loop
15 cm

No. 3/0 hook

Smaller sinker for conditions

Wire Trace

Metal Lure

Small bean sinker may be added to aid casting

25 kg trace

Main line

No. 8 swivel

Ganged No. 3/0 to 5/0 Limerick hooks

Small octopus

No.3/0 to 5/0 Suicide hook

Wonder Wobbler

Mr Twister

24 kg trace

Minnow Lure

Fly fishing is successful

SWEEP, BANDED

Scientific name *Scorpis georgianus*. Also known as Striped sweep.

Range Kalbarri in Western Australia and southwards as far as Kangaroo Island in South Australia.

Description A handsome species of sweep with several prominent black bands running down the body and including the dorsal and anal fins but not the belly. The tail is also stronger and deeper, giving more power in the water. The banded sweep is most commonly found on coastal reefs and can form schools. It can reach a pleasing 45 cms.

Fishing The banded sweep can be taken on a wide variety of baits and rigs. They respond well to burley and are often a by-catch when fishing for silver trevally, whiting or herring. The best baits are cut flesh, prawn and squid, but the banded sweep can also be taken on small jigs. The banded sweep is considered good eating.

SWEEP, SEA

Scientific name *Scorpis aequipinnis*. Also known as Sweep.

Range Shark Bay in Western Australia and southern waters including Tasmania and the east coast as far north as Jervis Bay.

Description The sea sweep is a deep bodied fish quite common on deeper reefs of the south coast and south-west of Australia, but which can also be found inshore, especially in schools when young. The sea sweep is generally slate grey in colour. It may have two darker grey patches on the upper body above the back edge of the pectoral fin and also the back part of the dorsal fin. This species has a prominent lobe to the first dorsal ray whereas the similar silver sweep (*Scorpis lineolatus*) has a flat dorsal fin profile. The mouth extends to the middle of the eye in the sea sweep and only to the front edge of the eye in the silver sweep. The banded sweep (*Scorpis georgianus*) has prominent black bands, a lightly forked tail and is only found from Kangaroo Island in South Australia to Shark Bay in Western Australia.
The sea sweep can reach 61 cm and more than 3.5 kilograms.

Fishing In its smaller sizes, the sweep is frequently considered a pest. Its small mouth, schooling nature and fondness for picking baits intended for larger species has earned the sea sweep a poor reputation in some areas. However, in larger sizes sea sweep make good eating and are a welcome addition to mixed bags. As a rule, the larger fish are found in smaller groups and further offshore, with bait picking juveniles inshore. Sea sweep will take a variety of baits, with prawns, squid, cuttlefish and fresh cut fish baits working best. Smaller, long shank hooks will improve your hookup rate. If pickers are prominent, putting a smaller hook on a dropper above your standard snapper rigs will tell you the nature of the bait stealers. Small sea sweep make a hardy live bait for fish like kingfish or samsonfish.

Rigs and Tactics

No. 00 to 2 ball sinker

No. 4 to 3/0 hook depending on size of bait

No. 2 to 5 ball sinker

20 cm dropper

40–50 cm dropper

No 8 to 4 bait picker hooks

Bug sinker

Suicide Hook

Solid brass ring

Barrel sinker

1 metre

30–50 kg trace

Bug sinker crimped to line

Linked No. 2/0 to 4/0 Limerick or Kendall Kirby hooks

No. 6 to 1/0 Long Shank, Eastern Estuary or Suicide hook depending on species sought

SWEEP, SEA

Rigs and Tactics

No. 00 to 2 ball sinker

No. 4 to 3/0 hook depending on size of bait

No. 2 to 5 ball sinker

20 cm dropper

40–50 cm dropper

No 8 to 4 bait picker hooks

No. 6 to 1/0 hook

3 kg

No. 0 to 2 ball sinker

No. 4 to 2 Suicide or Eastern Estuary hook

No. 6 to 1/0 Long Shank, Eastern Estuary or Suicide hook depending on species sought

No. 2 to 4 ball or bean sinker depending on conditions

No. 6 to 1/0 hook

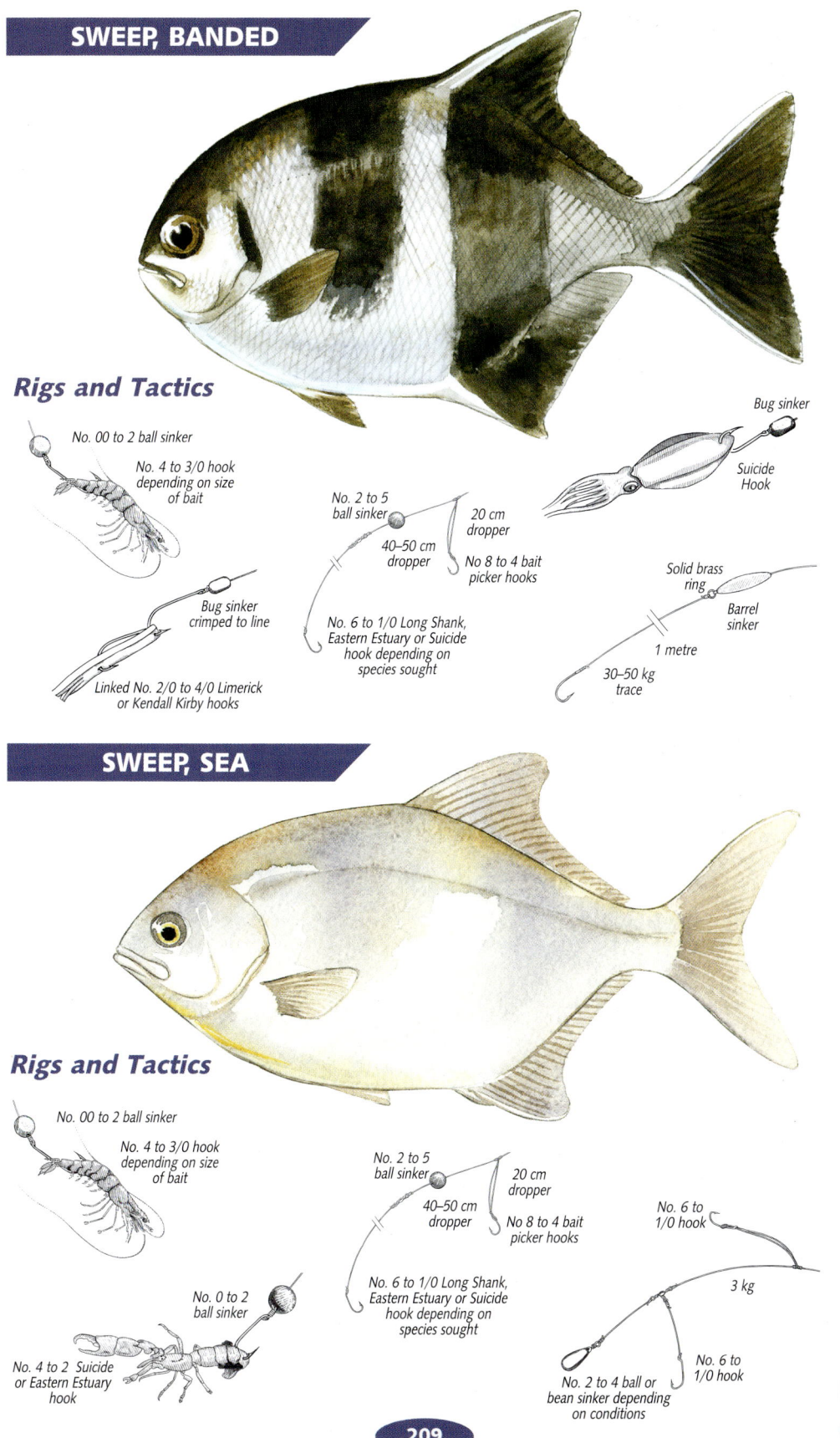

SWEETLIPS, GOLD-SPOTTED

Scientific name *Plectorhinchus flavomaculatus*. Also known as Painted sweetlip, netted morwong, gold-spot blubberlips.

Range Geographe Bay in Western Australia and northwards and around to the east coast as far south as Moruya in southern NSW.

Description The gold-spotted sweetlips is a largely tropical species which prefers protected reefs. The sweetlips are from the family Haemulidae as opposed to the group of species commonly called sweetlips which are in the family Lethrinidae which includes the emperors and north-west snappers. The gold-spotted sweetlips has many yellow spots on the body and fins and small yellow lines on the cheeks which are characteristic. The lips are large and prominent. The gold-spotted sweetlips reaches 60 centimetres.

Fishing This species is commonly caught by line and spear. However, the gold-spotted sweetlips frequently feeds on vegetation and individuals can taste weed tainted. As a result these fish should be bled and cleaned soon after capture. The gold-spotted sweetlips can be taken on prawn, squid, worms and fish baits. A smaller hook will get better results. Juveniles are often found inshore and large fish more frequently come from deeper water. The gold-spotted sweetlips can be fished on lighter line and the fight is strong but clean. Good catches can be made by casting baits up to coral outcrops or rocky lumps. The gold-spotted sweetlip is considered only fair eating.

SWEETLIPS, PAINTED

Scientific name *Diagramma labiosum*. Also known as Blackall, painted blubberlips, slate bream.

Range Rottnest Island in Western Australia and northwards through tropical waters and as far south as around Taree in NSW.

Description In spite of its colourful name, the painted sweetlips is one of the less colourful of the sweetlips. The painted sweetlips can be a bright bronze or silvery colour fresh from the water which fades to a dull grey after death. There may be scattered dark blotches over the cheeks and body. The lips are prominent but not obviously fleshy. Juveniles can have numerous spots or stripes. The dorsal fin is long. There is no separation between the spiny and soft dorsal fins which separates smaller fish from the similar Many-spotted sweetlips (*Plectorhincus chaetodontoides*) which has a much higher soft dorsal portion. There is a resemblance to the dusky morwong which is a southern species and the painted sweetlips has a normal sized pectoral fin compared to the prominent tendrils on the pectoral fin of the morwong family. Like the dusky morwong, the painted sweetlips is an easy target for beginning spearfishermen. It is particularly common in coral lagoons in the Great Barrier Reef and schools of several hundred fish can be found along the sandy edges of reef structure. It grows to 90 cm and 7 kilograms.

Fishing The painted sweetlips is not a discerning feeder, with schools moving over the bottom and sucking in sand, sediment and food and able to be seen from a distance in still waters. They will take fish baits, prawns, squid, worms and mussels. The fight is strong but that is the best feature. The painted sweetlips, while edible is considered poor fare compared with other reef species.

SWEETLIPS, GOLD SPOTTED

Rigs and Tactics

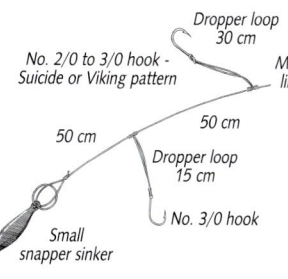

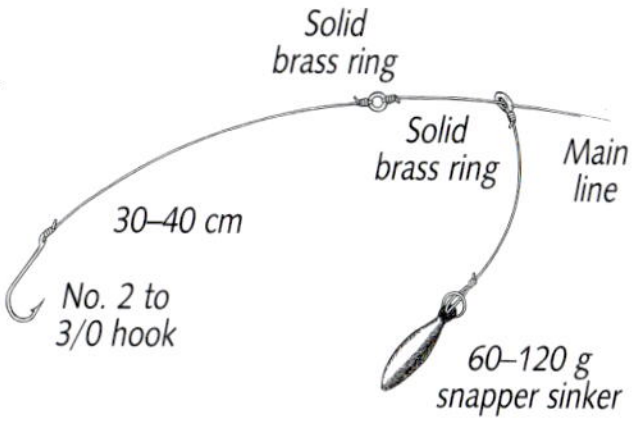

No. 2/0 to 3/0 hook - Suicide or Viking pattern

Dropper loop 30 cm

Main line

50 cm

50 cm

Dropper loop 15 cm

Small snapper sinker

No. 3/0 hook

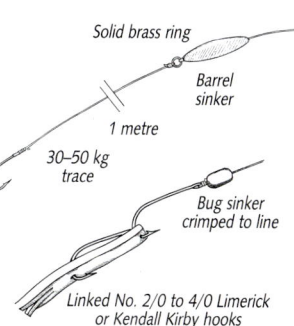

Solid brass ring

Barrel sinker

1 metre

30–50 kg trace

Bug sinker crimped to line

Linked No. 2/0 to 4/0 Limerick or Kendall Kirby hooks

Solid brass ring

Solid brass ring

Main line

30–40 cm

No. 2 to 3/0 hook

60–120 g snapper sinker

SWEETLIPS, PAINTED

Rigs and Tactics

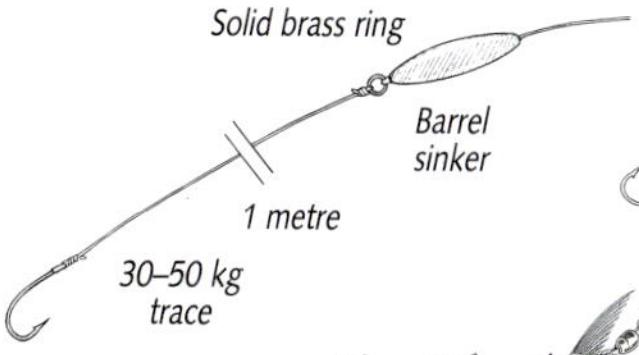

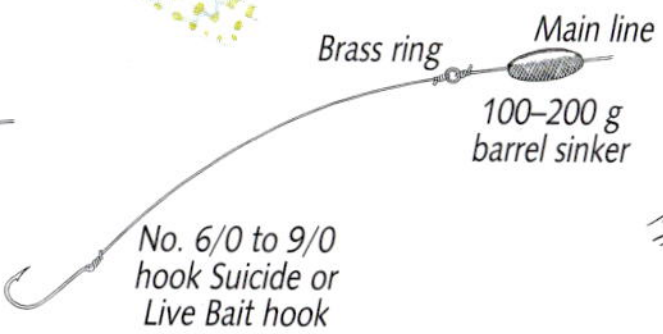

Solid brass ring

Barrel sinker

1 metre

30–50 kg trace

Brass ring

Main line

100–200 g barrel sinker

No. 6/0 to 9/0 hook Suicide or Live Bait hook

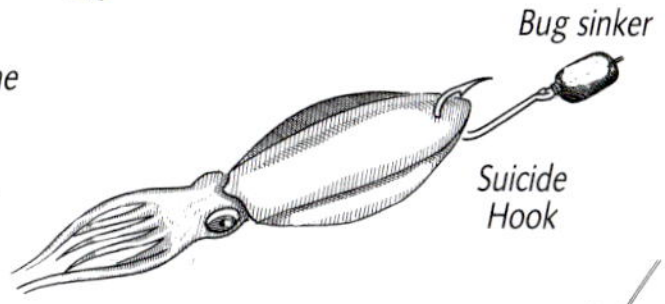

Bug sinker

Suicide Hook

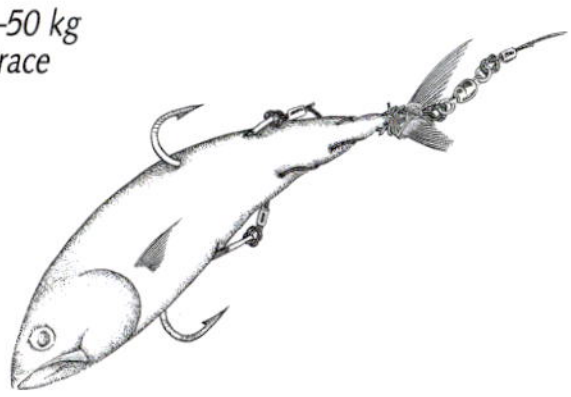

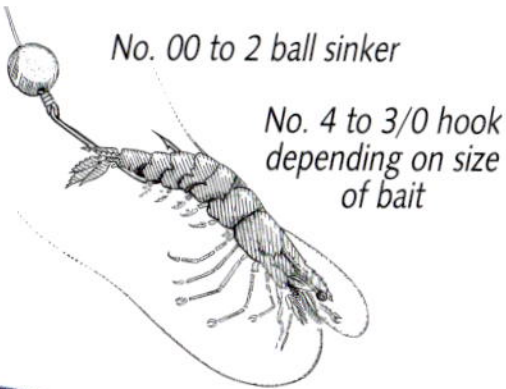

No. 00 to 2 ball sinker

No. 4 to 3/0 hook depending on size of bait

No. 6 to 4 Baitholder hook

TERAGLIN

Scientific name *Atractoscion aequidens*. Also known as Trag, trag-jew.

Range Double Island Point in Queensland to Montague Island in NSW.

Description The teraglin is very similar to the mulloway but can be separated by the shape of the tail, which is slightly concave (inwards curving) in the teraglin and convex (outward curving) in the mulloway. The inside of the teraglin's mouth is yellow or orange and this extends to the inside of the gill covers and occasionally to the lips. The anal fin is closer to the tail fin in the teraglin but this is only obvious when the two are seen together. The teraglin reaches a smaller size than mulloway, growing to up to a metre and 10 kg but any fish over 5 – 6 kg is considered large. The teraglin is found on offshore reefs and commonly forms schools which are smaller in number for larger fish.

Fishing The teraglin is commonly caught in depths of 20 to 80 m and over broken reef, although they can be found on the edge of larger deep reefs or on gravel bottom. Unlike mulloway, teraglin are rarely found inshore and not in estuaries. Teraglin are most common on the bottom but can be found in mid-water, especially when berley is used. Teraglin feed much more strongly at night and an area that produces nothing during the day can produce large catches of trag after dark. Teraglin bite best on small live baits or large strip baits with squid, cuttlefish, pilchard and large prawns also producing fish. Teraglin bite strongly and heavy lines are frequently used so that the fish are brought to boat quickly as a lost fish can often take the school with them. The school will often rise with hooked fish, enabling them to be taken in mid water. Common two hook snapper rigs are most commonly used for teraglin. As teraglin frequently school in the same areas, they are susceptible to over-fishing and only as many as are needed should be taken. Teraglin are excellent eating, with many rating them better quality than mulloway.

TOADFISH, GIANT

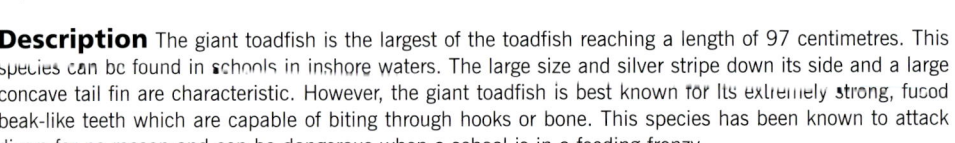

Scientific name *Lagocephalus scleratus*. Also known as silver toadfish, silver pufferfish, silver-cheeked toadfish, Northwest blowfish, Norwest blowie.

Range Near the Western Australia-South Australia border westwards and all northern waters and around the east coast as far south as Sydney but most common in more tropical waters.

Description The giant toadfish is the largest of the toadfish reaching a length of 97 centimetres. This species can be found in schools in inshore waters. The large size and silver stripe down its side and a large concave tail fin are characteristic. However, the giant toadfish is best known for its extremely strong, fused beak-like teeth which are capable of biting through hooks or bone. This species has been known to attack divers for no reason and can be dangerous when a school is in a feeding frenzy.

Fishing The giant toadfish is despised by anglers as it can steal baits and bite through hooks. In the water the giant toadfish can attack divers and if landed on a line can bite through a finger of the careless during unhooking. If a school of giant toadfish is encountered, it is best to leave the area. The prevalence of giant toadfish is a deterrent to the use of berley in many northern waters. As the giant toadfish is a schooling fish, catching one or getting several bite-offs is a sign to move locations. Like all toadfish, the giant toadfish is highly poisonous and should never be consumed.

TERAGLIN

Rigs and Tactics

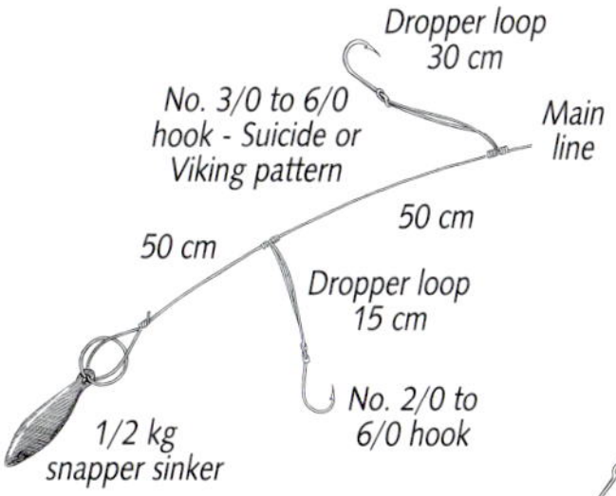

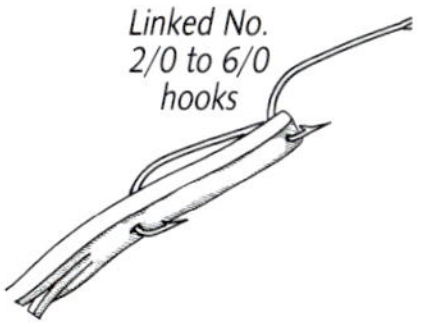

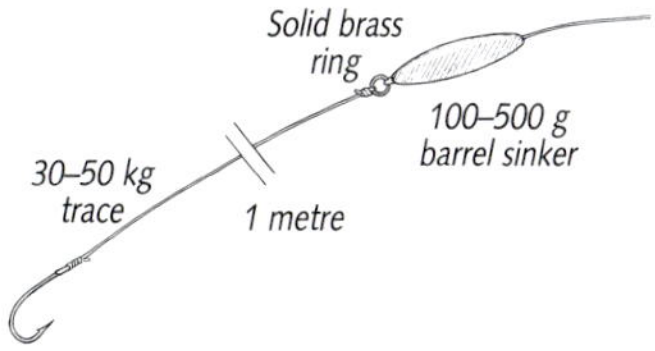

Dropper loop
30 cm

No. 3/0 to 6/0
hook - Suicide or
Viking pattern

Main
line

50 cm

50 cm

Dropper loop
15 cm

1/2 kg
snapper sinker

No. 2/0 to
6/0 hook

Linked No.
2/0 to 6/0
hooks

Solid
brass ring

Solid
brass ring

Solid
brass ring

Main
line

30–40 cm

No. 2/0 to
6/0 hook

60–120 g
snapper sinker

Solid brass
ring

100–500 g
barrel sinker

30–50 kg
trace

1 metre

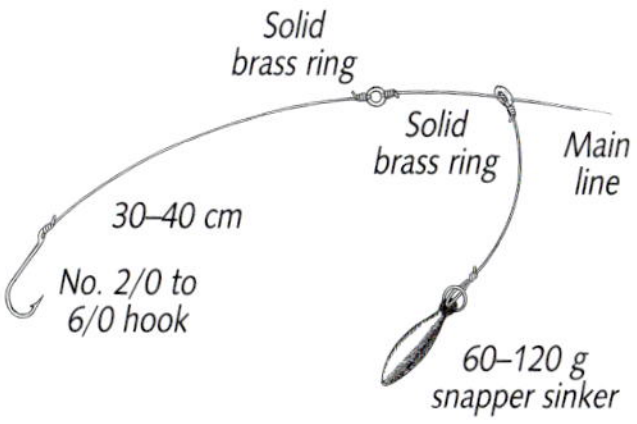

TOADFISH, GIANT

Rigs and Tactics

Not applicable as Giant Toadfish are not recommended as an angling species

TREVALLA, DEEP SEA

Scientific name *Hyperoglyphe antarctica.* Also known as Blue-eyed trevalla, blue eye cod, big eye, bluenose, medusa fish.

Range From central NSW southwards and including Tasmania as far west as near the South Australia Western Australia border.

Description The deep sea trevalla is a deeper water species which is taken in depths of up to 300 fathoms. It undergoes quite a dramatic change in form as it grows. Juveniles are often found associated with large jellyfish and have quite rounded fins which become angular, especially the tail of adults. Deep sea trevalla have a large deep blue eye with a golden ring. The large eye is typical of deeper predatory species. The mouth is large and this species is best separated from the similar but smaller warehou or the spotted trevalla (*Seriolella punctata*) by the more steeply sloping forehead and lack of spots in the deep sea trevalla. The deep sea trevalla reaches 1.4 metres and nearly 40 kilograms while the warehou grows to 76 cm and around 7 kilograms. The second dorsal of the deep sea trevalla is shorter and has 15 – 21 rays versus 25 or more for the other trevalla species.

Fishing Adult fish are found near the edge of the continental shelf or around deep sea mounts. A few are occasionally taken in waters of around 50 m when fishing for snapper or other deeper reef fish. A few dedicated specialists have been venturing out to the sea mounts off Wollongong and southern NSW to take bar cod, bass groper, hapuka and occasionally deep sea trevalla. However, there are very high fuel costs, a requirement for electric winches and no guarantee of a catch. Best baits are large cut baits on a multi-hook rig so that if a picker gets one bait there are other hooks because it is a long way up from the bottom. Weights of up to 2 kg are used to get the rigs to the bottom. The deep sea trevalla makes very good eating.

TREVALLY, BLACK

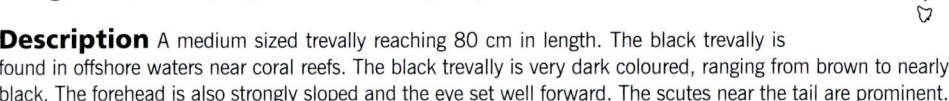

Scientific name *Caranx lugubris.* Also known as Dusky trevally.

Range Dampier Archipelago northwards through tropical waters to central Queensland.

Description A medium sized trevally reaching 80 cm in length. The black trevally is found in offshore waters near coral reefs. The black trevally is very dark coloured, ranging from brown to nearly black. The forehead is also strongly sloped and the eye set well forward. The scutes near the tail are prominent.

Fishing It is unusual not to see the flash of silver following the strong fight of a trevally but this species provides a darker 'colour' coming to the surface. It will take standard baits and rigs used for tropical reef fishing. Baits include fish and squid and the black trevally will also take jigs or metal lures fished more deeply. The flesh is of moderate quality.

TREVALLY, BLUDGER

Scientific name *Carangoides gymnostethus.* Also known as Bludger.

Range Coral Bay in Western Australia and tropical northern waters to southern Queensland.

Description The bludger trevally is found near inshore reefs or coral areas. It is similar to the turrum but the bludger trevally has no scales at all on its breast to the level of the pectoral fin. The eye is also lower in the face, close to the level of the pectoral fin. There may be small black spots on the flanks and a small black mark on the gill cover about level with the pectoral fin. The bludger trevally is a schooling fish that can reach 90 cm and 11 kilograms but is more commonly seen at 50 to 60 cm.

Fishing The bludger trevally got its name from commercial Spanish mackerel fishers who bemoaned the time wasted in catching this species which took baits trolled for more valuable mackerel. The bludger trevally will also take poppers and slice type lures. The bludger trevally is, like all trevally, a hard fighting fish that challenges the angler and tackle. It is of average eating quality with dark flesh. The bludger trevally had been traditionally used in north Queensland as bait and berley for reef species as they can be found in usual haunts, but this practice is rightly less common today.

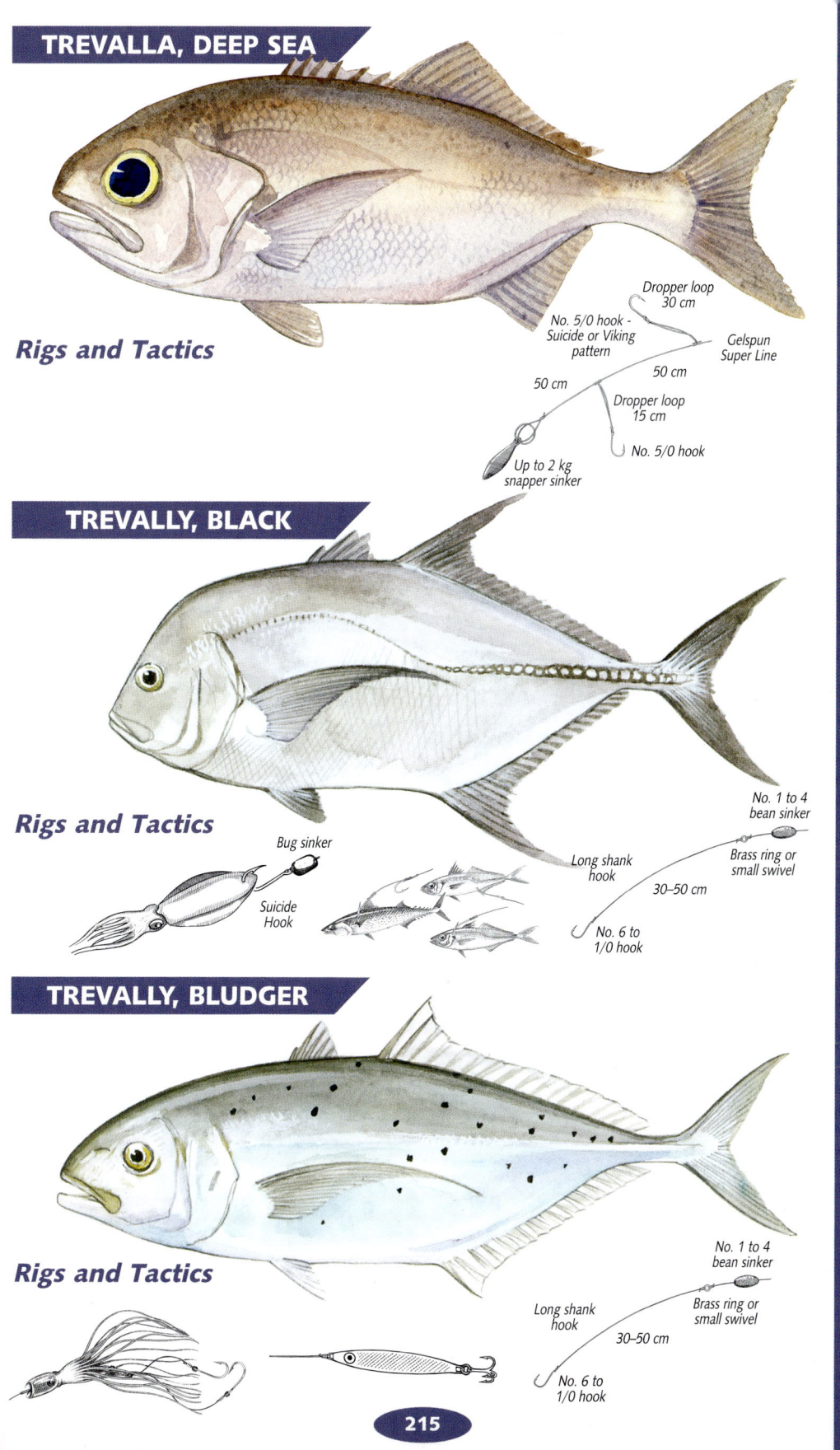

TREVALLA, DEEP SEA

Rigs and Tactics

Dropper loop
30 cm

No. 5/0 hook -
Suicide or Viking
pattern

Gelspun
Super Line

50 cm

50 cm

Dropper loop
15 cm

No. 5/0 hook

Up to 2 kg
snapper sinker

TREVALLY, BLACK

Rigs and Tactics

Bug sinker

Suicide
Hook

No. 1 to 4
bean sinker

Long shank
hook

Brass ring or
small swivel

30–50 cm

No. 6 to
1/0 hook

TREVALLY, BLUDGER

Rigs and Tactics

No. 1 to 4
bean sinker

Long shank
hook

Brass ring or
small swivel

30–50 cm

No. 6 to
1/0 hook

TREVALLY, DIAMOND

Scientific name *Alectis indicus.* Also known as Diamond-fish, mirror-fish, plumed trevally.

Range Shark Bay in Western Australia and tropical waters around to the northern NSW border.

Description A large and striking trevally species reaching 1.5 metres and about 12 kilograms. The diamond trevally has pearlescent scaleless skin in common with the similar pennant-fish (*Alectis ciliaris*). The diamond trevally has an almost vertical profile to the head which is more rounded in the pennant-fish and the gap between the mouth and eye is greater in the diamond trevally meaning that the pectoral fin is obviously lower than the eye. In both species, juveniles have majestic filaments from both the dorsal and anal spines. These long filaments are not likely to be present in mature fish, but the lack of scales is a clear indicator.

Fishing The diamond trevally is found on coastal reefs or harbour jetties. While it will take lures, it is more commonly taken with cut baits or squid intended for other reef species. It is a dogged fighter and the beautiful colours make a spectacular sight as they are brought to the boat on a sunny day. Standard reef rigs work well. The flesh is a little dark and is considered only average eating quality. Bleeding the fish and putting it immediately on ice improves the quality, but their beauty is their strongest feature.

TRIGGERFISH, STARRY

Scientific name *Abalistes stellaris.*

Range Jurien Bay in Western Australia and tropical waters and around the east coast as far south as Sydney.

Description The triggerfish are similar to the leatherjackets but differ in two obvious features. Triggerfish have three obvious dorsal spines in the first dorsal while leatherjackets have two of which the second is only rudimentary. Triggerfish also have obvious scales whereas leatherjackets have rough skin without obvious scales. The starry triggerfish is one of the largest triggerfish species, reaching 60 centimetres. It is the triggerfish most frequently taken by recreational anglers. The mouth is small in the large head. The colour is pale and the common name comes from three white blotches on the back and a scattering of white spots on the upper body. There are yellow spots on the lower body. There are two small trailing filaments on both lobes of the tail in adults.

Fishing This species is not a target species but is taken by line fishers, mainly in tropical reef areas. The small mouth means that small or long shanked hooks improve catch rates. Best baits are prawns, crab, squid or cut baits. Triggerfish are often regarded as a pest due to their ability to steal baits and avoid hook-ups. Triggerfish are reasonable eating but should be skinned.

TREVALLY, DIAMOND

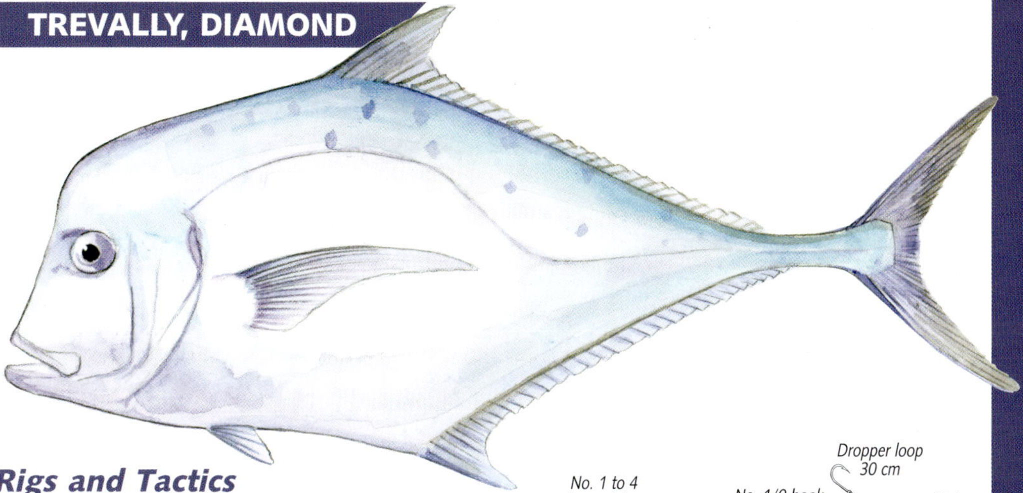

Rigs and Tactics

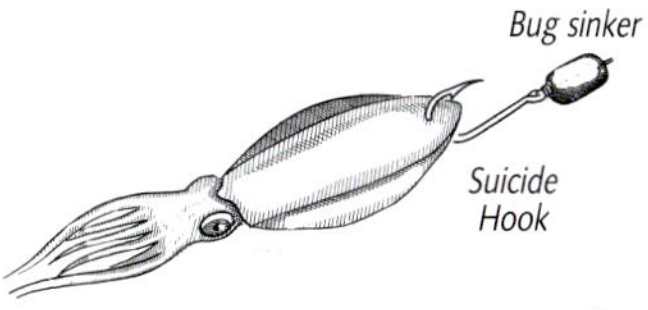

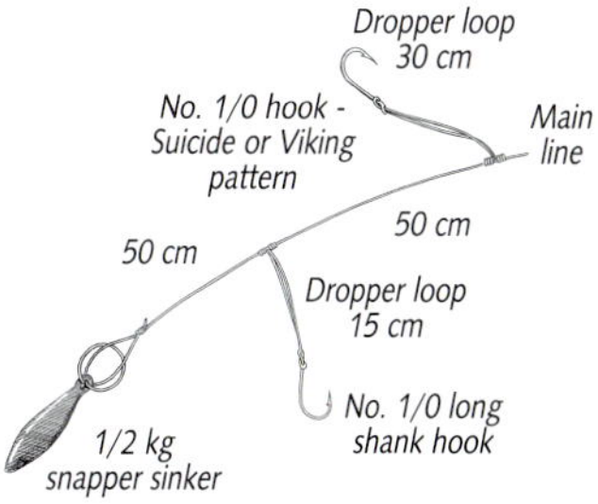

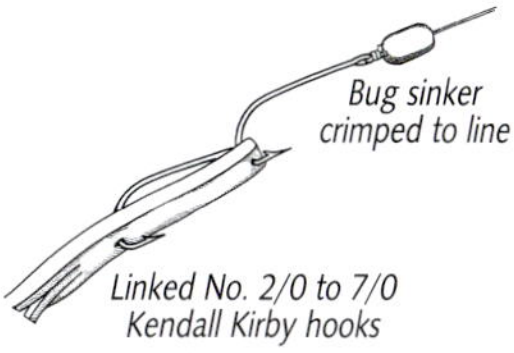

Bug sinker

Suicide Hook

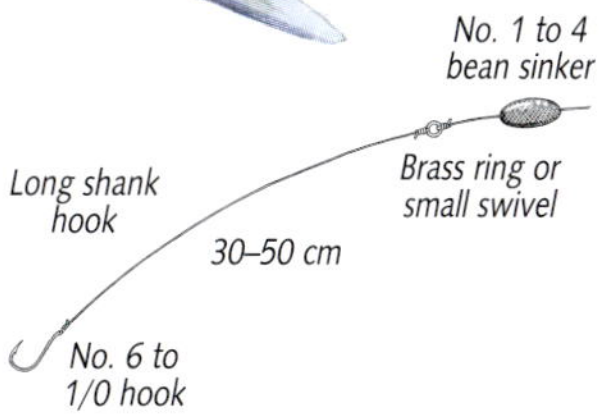

Bug sinker crimped to line

Linked No. 2/0 to 7/0 Kendall Kirby hooks

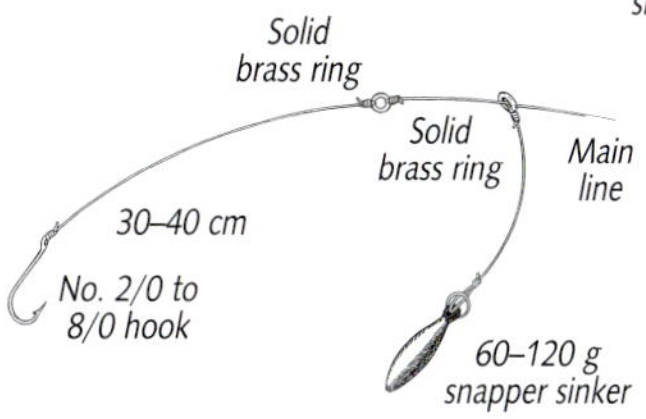

Long shank hook

30–50 cm

No. 6 to 1/0 hook

No. 1 to 4 bean sinker

Brass ring or small swivel

Solid brass ring

30–40 cm

No. 2/0 to 8/0 hook

Solid brass ring

Main line

60–120 g snapper sinker

Dropper loop 30 cm

No. 1/0 hook - Suicide or Viking pattern

Main line

50 cm

50 cm

Dropper loop 15 cm

1/2 kg snapper sinker

No. 1/0 long shank hook

TRIGGERFISH, STARRY

Rigs and Tactics

No. 00 to 2 ball sinker

No. 6 to 1/0 hook depending on size of bait

Long shank hook

30–50 cm

No. 6 to 1/0 hook

No. 1 to 4 bean sinker

Brass ring or small swivel

Dropper loop 30 cm

No. 1/0 hook - Suicide or Viking pattern

Main line

50 cm

50 cm

Dropper loop 15 cm

1/2 kg snapper sinker

No. 1/0 long shank hook

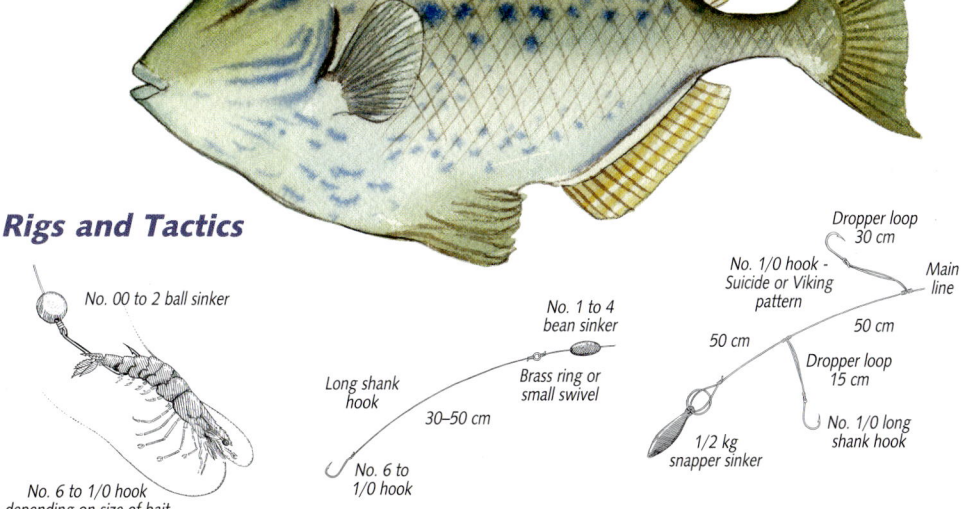

TROUT, BAR-CHEEKED CORAL

Scientific name *Plectropomus maculatus.* Also known as Bar-cheeked trout, coral cod.

Range Abrolhos Islands in Western Australia and tropical waters as far south as the southern extent of the Great Barrier Reef in Queensland.

Description The bar-cheeked coral trout can be as brilliantly coloured as the coral trout with which it is often confused. The bar-cheek coral trout is most easily separated by the blue spots on the head being elongated and not round as they are in coral trout. This species is smaller than the coral trout, reaching 70 cm and 6 kg but can be susceptible to overfishing and is generally taken at a smaller size. The bar-cheek coral trout has the same powerful tail which is used to good effect to bury anglers in reef country preferred by this species. It has a large mouth and sharp but widely spaced canine teeth. This species is trhe one usually taken in Western Australia.

Fishing This is undoubtedly one of the premier reef fish due to its brilliant appearance, hard fight near coral outcrops and excellent eating. The bar-cheek coral trout can be taken on bait, lure and fly. Trolled minnow lures and cast poppers, slices or jigs put near coral outcrops or channels between reefs can provide exciting sport. The proximity of sharp coral outcrops in many locations means that if the fish is given his head a break-off is certain. For this reason quality tackle and close attention, especially when trolling is required. The larger fish can be taken in deeper water. The bar-cheek coral trout can take large baits. Best baits are live baits, with whole fish and fresh fillets working well, and squid, prawn and crab taking fish. A trace can offer some protection during the fight. This species makes excellent eating.

TROUT, CORAL

Scientific name *Plectropomus leopardus.* Also known as Leopard cod, leopard trout, trout, blue-spot trout.

Range Dongara in Western Australia northwards around the top end to the southern extent of Queensland reefs.

Description The coral trout is frequently confused with other similar species, but the coral trout has numerous small and always round spots on the head and body. The colour varies but can be a brilliant red or red-orange or a brick red. The soft dorsal fin is rounded and the tail square cut which may have a blue edge. It has a large mouth and sharp but widely spaced canine teeth. The coral trout grows to over a metre and 20 kg, but can be over fished and is generally taken at a smaller size. Irresponsible overfishing for the live fish export trade in Queensland has had a big impact on coral trout numbers there.

Fishing This is undoubtedly one of the premier reef fish due to its brilliant appearance, hard fight near coral outcrops and excellent eating. Coral trout can be taken on bait, lure and fly but fishing is typified by a short battle of strength and will between the angler and the coral trout. Best lures include minnow lures which dive to different depths, as coral trout will readily move upwards to slam a lure. Poppers can take some large fish. Coral trout, like many of the cod which are found in similar areas, can take large baits, with live baits being best, followed by whole dead fish, fresh fillets, pilchards, prawns and squid. A trace can offer some protection during the fight. The frequent presence of numerous sharp coral outcrops in many locations and a strong fish like the coral trout means that if the fish is given his head a break-off is certain. Some of the largest coral trout are taken in deeper waters near less obvious cover, providing a welcome surprise for the lucky angler. Large coral trout have been implicated with ciguatera and some caution should be exercised with the largest fish, consuming a small portion initially otherwise this species provides a culinary delight.

TROUT, BAR CHEEKED CORAL

Rigs and Tactics

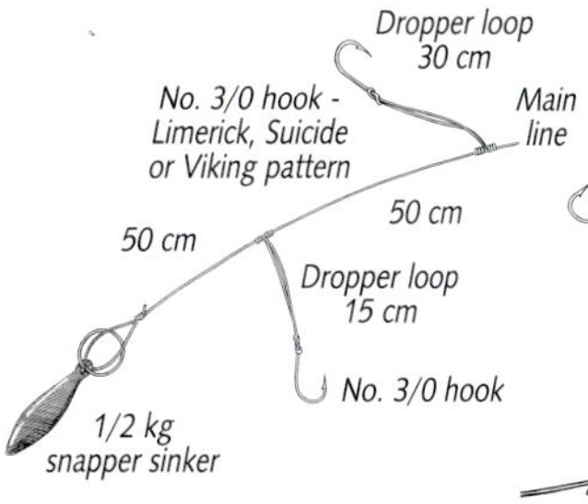

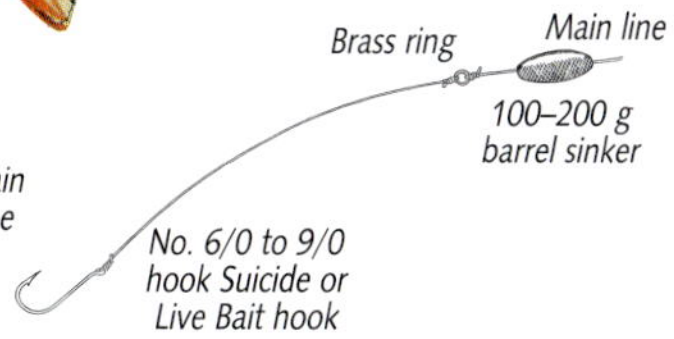

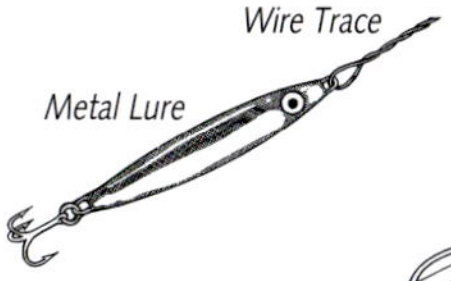

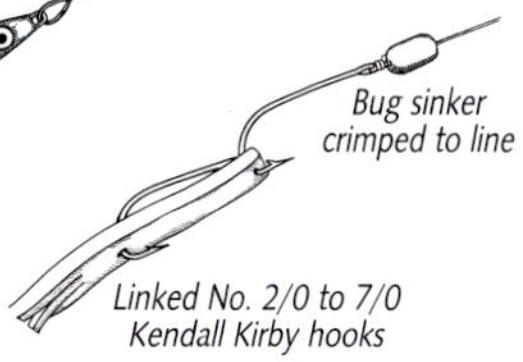

Dropper loop
30 cm

No. 3/0 hook -
Limerick, Suicide
or Viking pattern

Main line

50 cm

50 cm

Dropper loop
15 cm

No. 3/0 hook

1/2 kg
snapper sinker

Brass ring

Main line

100–200 g
barrel sinker

No. 6/0 to 9/0
hook Suicide or
Live Bait hook

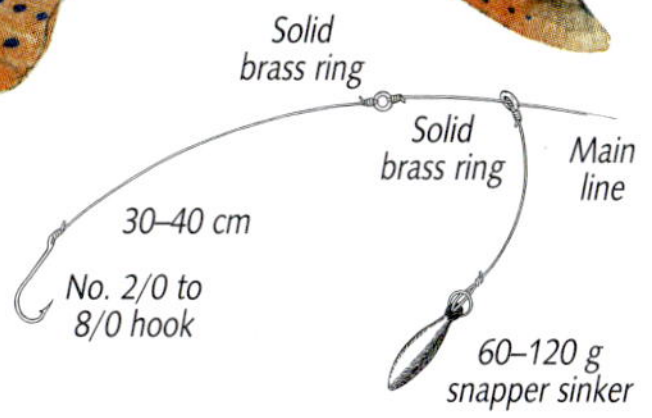

Minnow Lure

24 kg
trace

Solid
brass ring

Solid
brass ring

Main line

30–40 cm

No. 2/0 to
8/0 hook

60–120 g
snapper sinker

Wire Trace

Metal Lure

Bug sinker
crimped to line

Linked No. 2/0 to 7/0
Kendall Kirby hooks

TROUT, CORAL

Rigs and Tactics

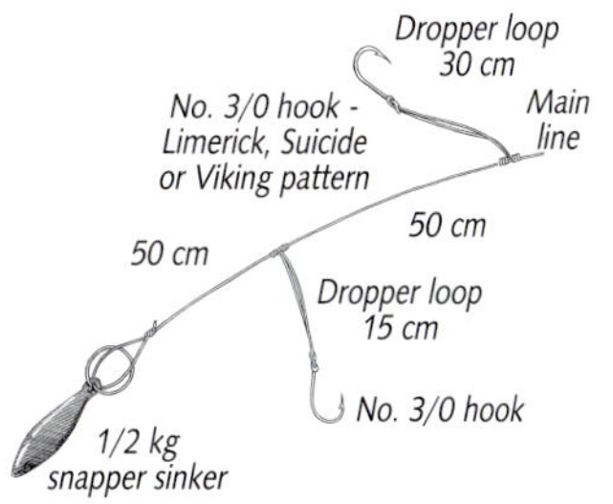

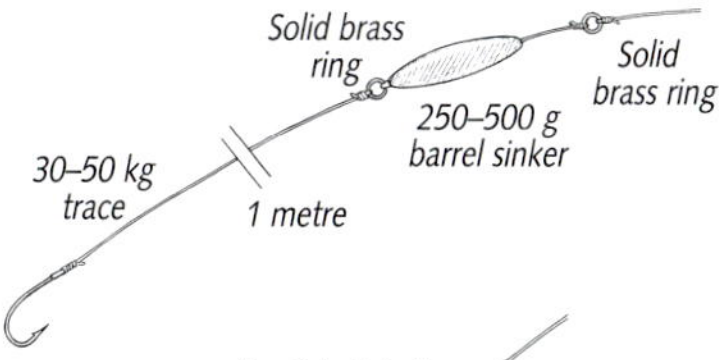

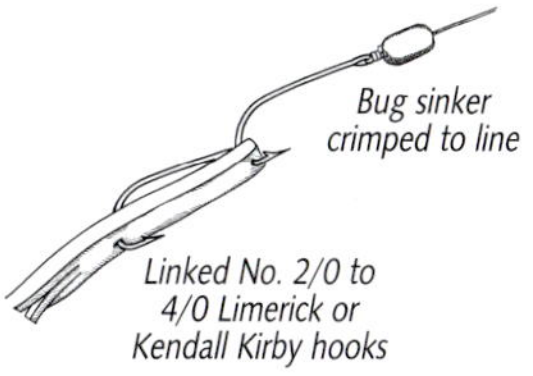

Dropper loop
30 cm

No. 3/0 hook -
Limerick, Suicide
or Viking pattern

Main line

50 cm

50 cm

Dropper loop
15 cm

No. 3/0 hook

1/2 kg
snapper sinker

Solid brass
ring

30–50 kg
trace

1 metre

250–500 g
barrel sinker

Solid
brass ring

Bug sinker
crimped to line

Linked No. 2/0 to
4/0 Limerick or
Kendall Kirby hooks

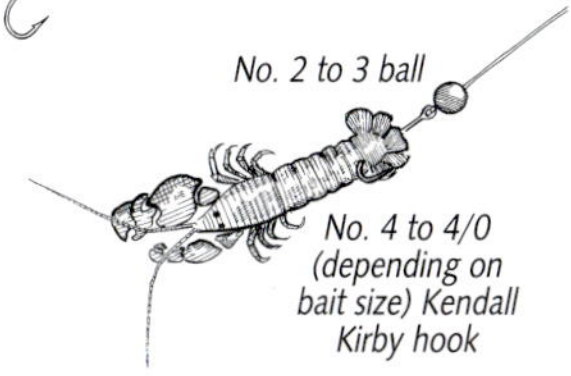

No. 2 to 3 ball

No. 4 to 4/0
(depending on
bait size) Kendall
Kirby hook

24 kg trace

Minnow Lure

TROUT, CORONATION

Scientific name *Variola louti* Also known as Lunar-tailed cod, fairy cod.

Range Shark Bay in Western Australia and around the top end as far south as Noosa Heads in southern Queensland.

Description The coronation trout is a beautiful fish which has vivid red or red-orange colouration flecked with yellow or red. The tail is distinctive with a sickle or lunar crescent shape and a distinctive yellow trailing edge. The cheeks and all the other fins are tinged with yellow on the trailing edge, especially the pectoral fins. The coronation trout is quite common on coral reefs, but may be found on deeper reefs to 100 metres. It grows to 80 cm and around 3 kilograms.

Fishing The coronation trout shares many features from an angling perspective with the coral trout, including a large mouth, aggressive nature, a strong lure taker and excellent eating. They can also have tapeworms in the guts which do not affect the eating quality of the fish. Coronation trout can be taken on lures such as minnows, jigs and chrome lures and flies. Live baits, dead baits and cut baits work best. A trace is an advantage, especially as coral trout can be taken from the same areas. As the coronation trout will move upwards to take a bait, less weight is necessary and a mobile approach, casting or drifting with the tide on reef edges or channels works well. The fight is strong, but the fish are not as big as coral trout and they can often be successfully extracted from the coral they frequent.

TRUMPETER, BASTARD

Scientific name *Latridopsis forsteri.* Also known as Moki, copper moki, silver trumpeter.

Range Robe in South Australia and eastwards including Tasmania and along the east coast as far north as Sydney.

Description The bastard trumpeter is a common species on inshore reefs especially in Tasmania and southern Victoria. This species can reach 65 cm and more than 4 kilograms. In smaller sizes, it forms schools but larger specimens are more solitary and can be found in waters beyond 30 fathoms. The mouth is small and set low down. The back and upper flanks are silvery-brown with a pattern of close-set slender yellow or white lines running along the body. The fins are brownish in colour and the edges of the pectoral, dorsal and the forked tail fin are black.

Fishing The bastard trumpeter is occasionally taken by anglers on baits of prawn, squid, cockles or worms. The small mouth means that a smaller, long-shanked hook will increase catches, as will berley. Standard snapper rigs with smaller hooks will take this fish. The bastard trumpeter is more frequently taken by spearfishermen. The bastard trumpeter is excellent eating.

TROUT, CORONATION

Rigs and Tactics

Dropper loop
30 cm
No. 3/0 hook -
Limerick, Suicide
or Viking pattern
Main
line
50 cm
50 cm
Dropper loop
15 cm
No. 3/0 hook
1/2 kg
snapper sinker

Solid
brass ring
Solid
brass ring
Main
line
30–40 cm
No. 2/0 to
8/0 hook
60–120 g
snapper sinker

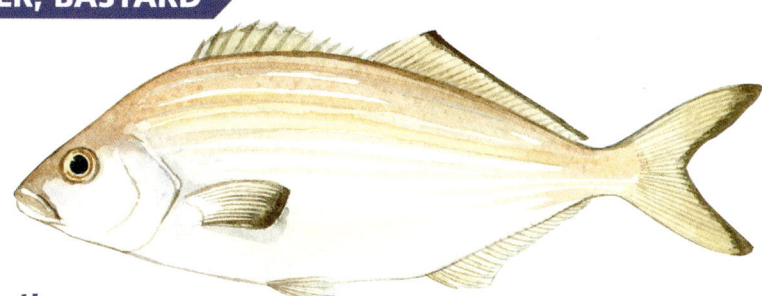

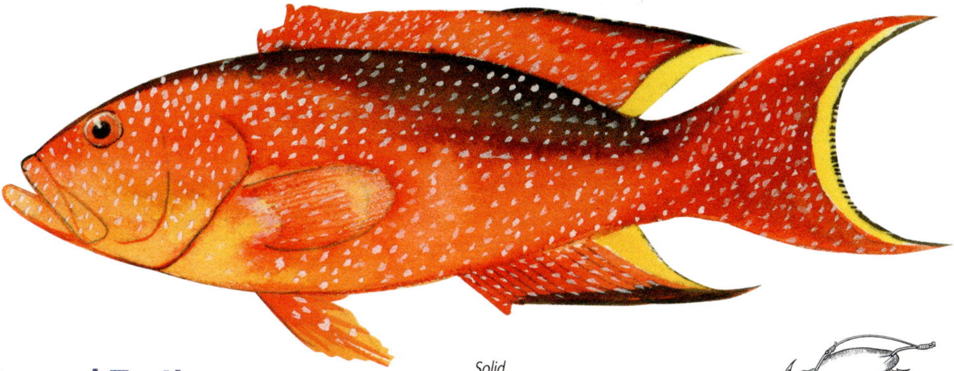

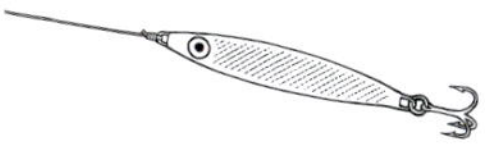

Small
octopus
No.3/0 to 5/0
Suicide hook

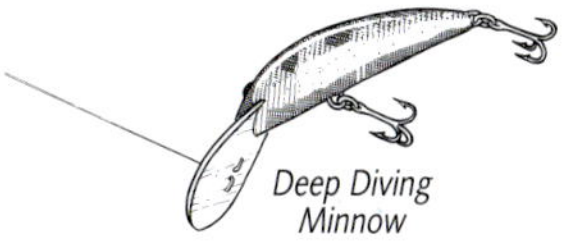

Deep Diving
Minnow

Brass ring
Main line
100–200 g
barrel sinker
No. 6/0 to 9/0
hook Suicide or
Live Bait hook

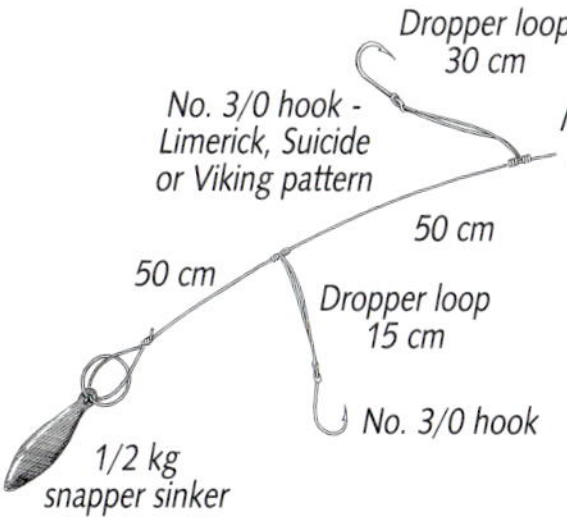

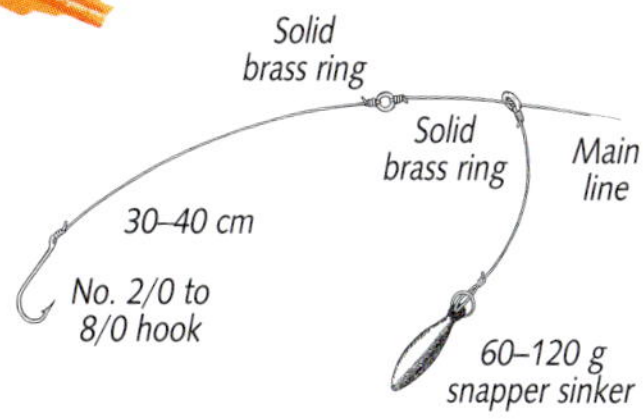

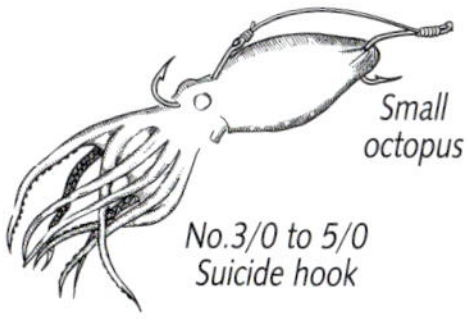

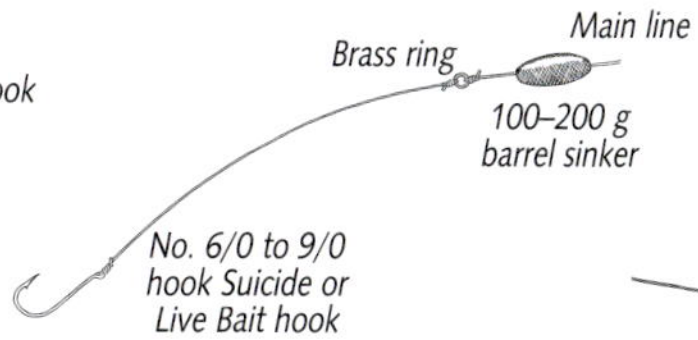

TRUMPETER, BASTARD

Rigs and Tactics

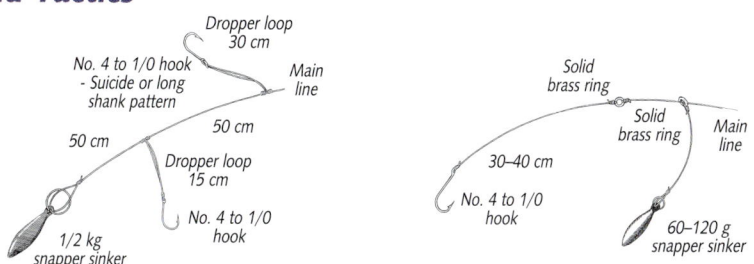

Dropper loop
30 cm
No. 4 to 1/0 hook
- Suicide or long
shank pattern
Main
line
50 cm
50 cm
Dropper loop
15 cm
No. 4 to 1/0
hook
1/2 kg
snapper sinker

Solid
brass ring
Solid
brass ring
Main
line
30–40 cm
No. 4 to 1/0
hook
60–120 g
snapper sinker

TRUMPETER, TASMANIAN

Scientific name *Latris lineata*. Also known as Striped trumpeter, common trumpeter, stripey, real trumpeter.

Range Albany in Western Australia and eastwards along the south coast including Tasmania and as far north as Montague Island in NSW and rarely as far north as Sydney.

Description The Tamanian trumpeter is is a medium to large species reaching 1.2 m and up to 25 kg, although the largest fish are found in deep waters. Overfishing has depleted stocks of the Tasmanian trumpeter on inshore reefs, where mainly juveniles are now found. The Tasmanian trumpeter has three distinctive brownish stripes along the sides. The Tasmanian trumpeter is easily separated from the similar morwongs as it lacks the extended 'fingers' on the pectoral fins. The fins are dusky and may have a yellow or reddish tinge. The mouth is large and the lips quite blubbery.

Fishing Fishing is with standard deep reef fishing rigs, with sufficient weight to get the bait to the bottom. Best baits are squid, prawns, octopus or cut fish baits. Pilchards and other small whole fish or live baits will also work well. Tasmanian trumpeter are occasionally taken on large lead head or vertical jigs, but tipping with squid increases strike rates. Smaller fish are likely to be encountered on inshore reefs and like many reef species, the smaller the size of the fish, the larger the school is likely to be. Working the edges of reefs when a school is located will bring good catches. The Tasmanian trumpeter is excellent eating and is rated as one of the best cool water reef species.

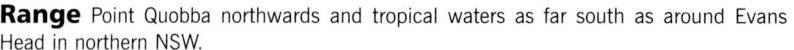

TUSKFISH, BLACK-SPOT

Scientific name *Choerodon schoenleinii* Also known as Blue parrot.

Range Point Quobba northwards and tropical waters as far south as around Evans Head in northern NSW.

Description A large tuskfish capable of reaching 15 kg and is found in sand and weed areas adjacent to coral reefs. The black-spot tuskfish is easily identified by the black spot which is found at the base of the middle of the dorsal fin. There is often a short, oblique purple bar set behind the eye and the tail is generally bright purple. The overall body colour is generally blue and the chin is blue-green or purple whereas in the blue tuskfish (*Choerodon cyanodus*) which is a smaller species, the chin is white or off-white.

Fishing The black-spot tuskfish has a strong preference for crab baits but can be taken on prawns, squid, pipi and worms. The black-spot tusk fish can often be observed and cast to, making presentation with lightly weighted baits less difficult, but they can be difficult to entice to strike on occasion. Because this species can move close inshore to graze on corals in a quest for larger food, they can be taken by spearfishermen. The black-spot tuskfish can be caught near deeper reefs where lightly fished and larger specimens are more likely. The black-spot tuskfish can be a challenging capture as they can cut off the unwary on nearby coral outcrops and is not easily brought to the boat. The black-spot tuskfish is excellent eating with firm white flesh.

TRUMPETER, TASMANIAN

Rigs and Tactics

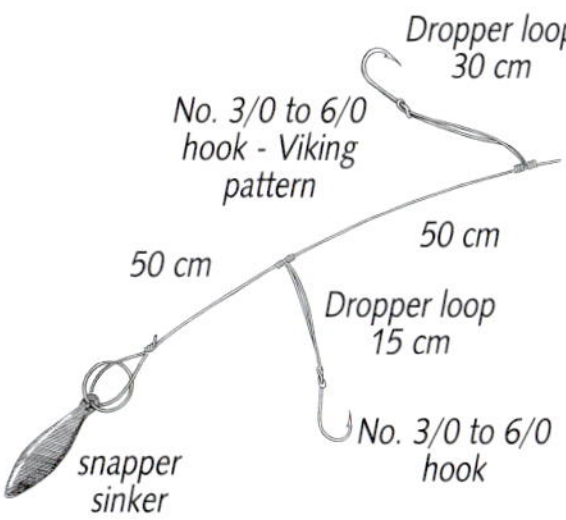

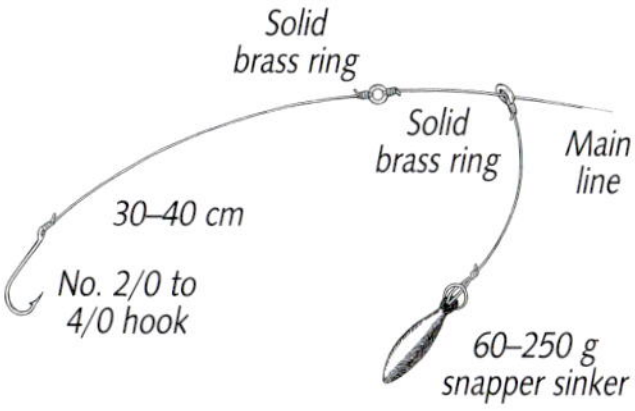

Dropper loop
30 cm

No. 3/0 to 6/0
hook - Viking
pattern

Main
line

50 cm

50 cm

Dropper loop
15 cm

snapper
sinker

No. 3/0 to 6/0
hook

Solid
brass ring

Solid
brass ring

Main
line

30–40 cm

No. 2/0 to
4/0 hook

60–250 g
snapper sinker

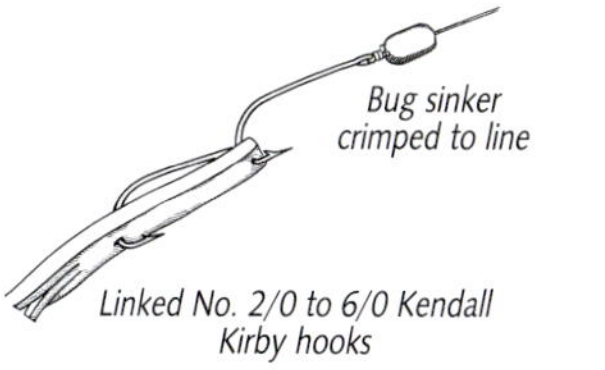

Bug sinker
crimped to line

Linked No. 2/0 to 6/0 Kendall
Kirby hooks

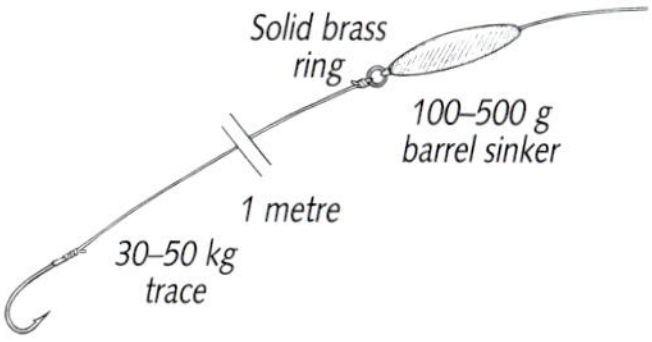

Solid brass
ring

100–500 g
barrel sinker

1 metre

30–50 kg
trace

TUSKFISH, BLACK-SPOT

Rigs and Tactics

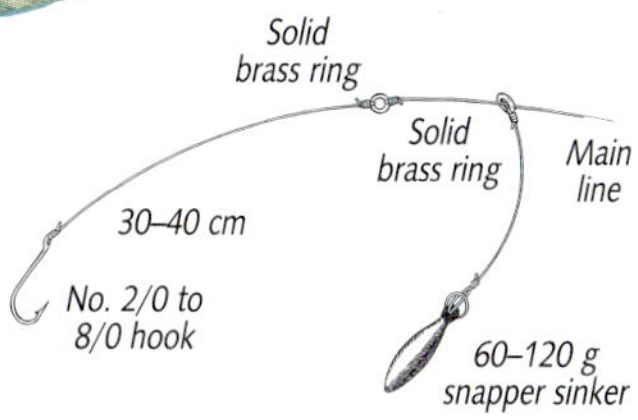

No. 00 to 2
running ball sinker

No. 2 to
4/0 hook

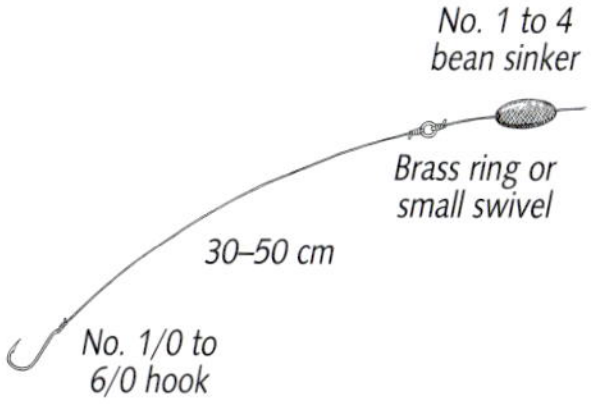

No. 1 to 4
bean sinker

Brass ring or
small swivel

30–50 cm

No. 1/0 to
6/0 hook

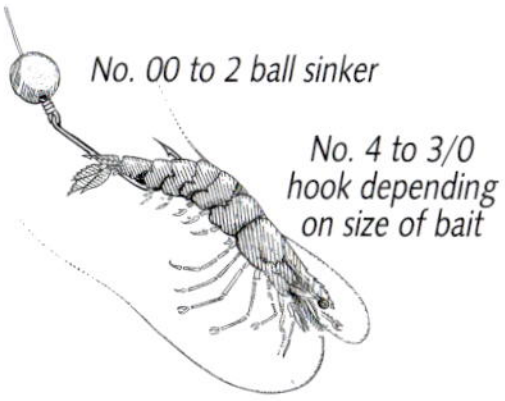

Solid
brass ring

Solid
brass ring

Main
line

30–40 cm

No. 2/0 to
8/0 hook

60–120 g
snapper sinker

No. 00 to 2 ball sinker

No. 4 to 3/0
hook depending
on size of bait

223

TUSKFISH, BLUE

Scientific name *Choerodon cyanodus.* Also known as blue-bone.

Range Exmouth Gulf in Western Australia and northwards through tropical waters to central Queensland.

Description A common species of inshore coral reefs, the blue tuskfish can reach 65 cm and 8 kilograms. The blue tuskfish also has the characteristic white chin of the baldchin groper but has a white spot on the back below the soft dorsal fin. The blue tuskfish also has brown scribbled markings on the tail. The upper and lower margins of the tail are also usually blue.

Fishing The blue tuskfish is most often taken on cut fish baits although like all tuskfish crab baits can take fish when all else fails. The blue tuskfish is also a quality target for lure fishers as they will hit minnow lures, jigs and even flies. They prefer to stay close to coral so make a challenge to light line fishers. The blue tuskfish is considered to be very good eating.

TUSKFISH, VENUS

Scientific name *Choerodon venustus.* Also known as Cockie.

Range Found only on the east coast from the northern Great Barrier reef as far south as northern NSW although occasional juveniles have been recorded as far south as Sydney.

Description The venus tuskfish is a fairly small species, reaching 5 kg but most commonly seen at around a kilogram. They are generally bright pink along the flanks, being darker above and paler on the belly. There are numerous small white or blue spots on the body and the fins and tail are splashed with blue as are the lips and chin. The venus tuskfish prefers shallow to mid depth reef country and is found very close to reefs where it feeds.

Fishing Venus tuskfish are generally taken while fishing for other reef species and can be taken on a variety of baits including prawns, crabs, whitebait, fresh cut baits and squid. Tackle needs to be fairly robust as even small fish can bury the angler in any nearby coral outcrops. The fight is strong and the first run needs to be stopped to avert a break-off. The venus tuskfish makes excellent eating and should be more highly regarded as a food fish than it is currently.

WAREHOU

Scientific name *Seriolella brama.* Also known as Silver warehou, blue warehou, snotty trevally, snot-nose trevalla, snot-gall, snotty.

Range South coast of NSW and southern waters including Tasmania and extending westwards into South Australian waters.

Description The warehou is a deep water schooling reef fish that can make inshore migrations, especially during winter. The warehou is especially common in Tasmanian and Victorian waters. The warehou grows to 7 kg with smaller specimens more likely to be encountered in the shallower waters more commonly fished by recreational anglers. The warehou is best identified by the rounded head and the dark patch behind the head and above the pectoral fin, but this fades with death. Warehou look similar to silver trevally but lack the scutes along the side near the tail. The warehou has a thick mucous coating and translucent nose area which gives rise to its less appetising common names like snotty.

Fishing Larger warehou are taken with heavy rigs fished on deep reefs. It requires heavy tackle and patience to find warehou. Many more fish are taken on inshore migrations when large schools of fish 0.5 – 1 kg can be taken in good numbers. Local information is invaluable in locating known hotspots and times of aggregation. Best baits include prawns, crabs, squid and cut flesh baits. When warehou are inshore, these baits are fished on fairly light multiple hook rigs. Warehou will occasionally take small lures but jigs tipped with bait and vertically jigged or bobbed near the bottom work better. Warehou are a common commercial catch which is gaining acceptance in the marketplace. The flesh is soft and does not freeze well. Warehou should be bled and cleaned soon after capture.

TUSKFISH, BLUE

Rigs and Tactics

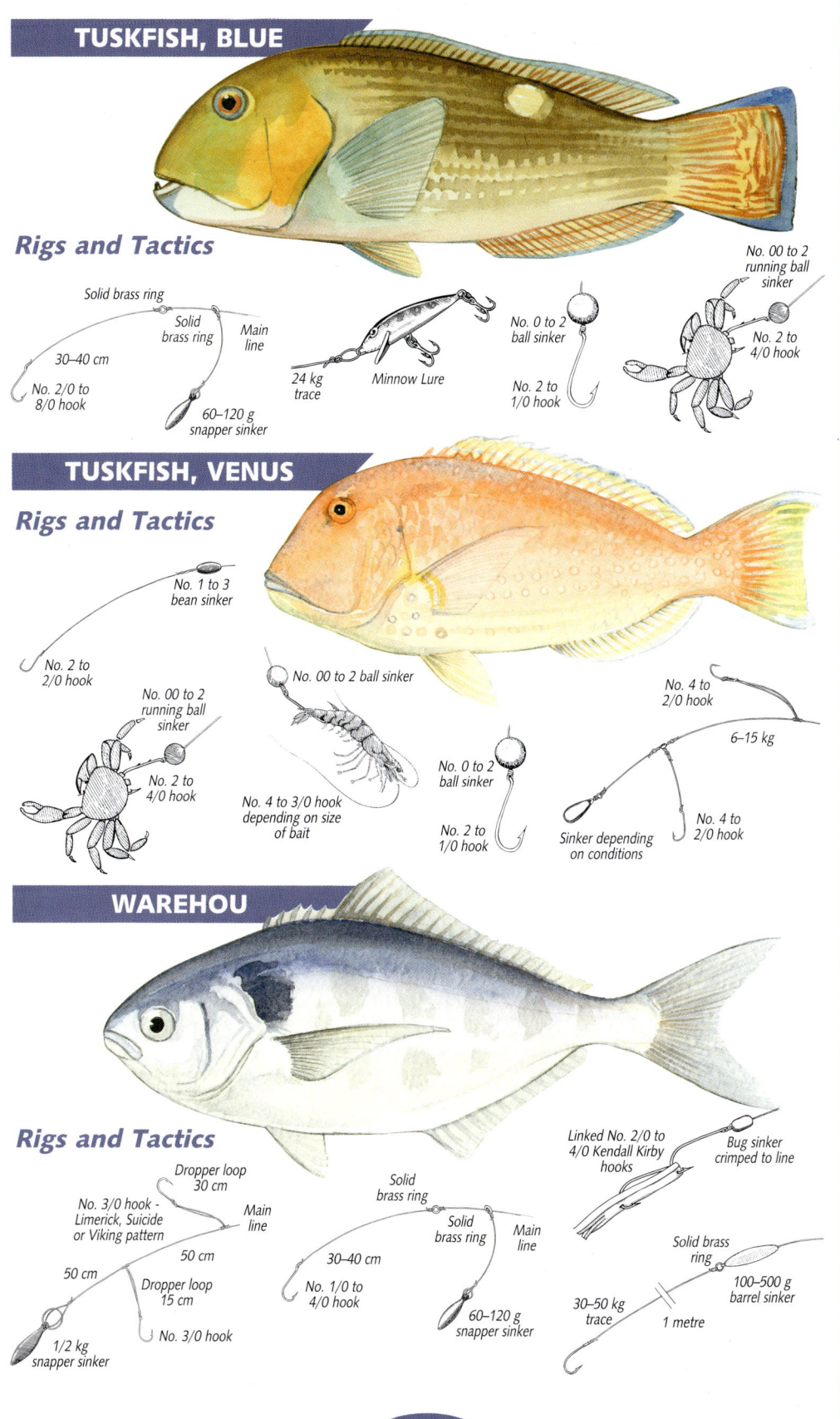

Solid brass ring

Solid brass ring

Main line

30–40 cm

No. 2/0 to 8/0 hook

60–120 g snapper sinker

24 kg trace

Minnow Lure

No. 0 to 2 ball sinker

No. 2 to 1/0 hook

No. 00 to 2 running ball sinker

No. 2 to 4/0 hook

TUSKFISH, VENUS

Rigs and Tactics

No. 1 to 3 bean sinker

No. 2 to 2/0 hook

No. 00 to 2 running ball sinker

No. 2 to 4/0 hook

No. 00 to 2 ball sinker

No. 4 to 3/0 hook depending on size of bait

No. 0 to 2 ball sinker

No. 2 to 1/0 hook

No. 4 to 2/0 hook

6–15 kg

Sinker depending on conditions

No. 4 to 2/0 hook

WAREHOU

Rigs and Tactics

Dropper loop 30 cm

No. 3/0 hook - Limerick, Suicide or Viking pattern

Main line

50 cm

50 cm

Dropper loop 15 cm

No. 3/0 hook

1/2 kg snapper sinker

Solid brass ring

Solid brass ring

Main line

30–40 cm

No. 1/0 to 4/0 hook

60–120 g snapper sinker

Linked No. 2/0 to 4/0 Kendall Kirby hooks

Bug sinker crimped to line

Solid brass ring

30–50 kg trace

1 metre

100–500 g barrel sinker

WIRRAH

Scientific name *Acanthistius ocellatus.* Also known as Eastern wirrah, wirrah cod, peppermint cod, meat wirrah, boot.

Range Gold Coast in southern Queensland and as far south as northern Tasmania.

Description The wirrah is common on exposed coastal reefs with juveniles found in tidal rock pools. The characteristic spots over the head and body of the wirrah are blue in the centre. There are 13 spines in the first dorsal fin and the fins are edged by blue-grey. The wirrah can reach 64 cm in length. The similar western wirrah (*Acanthistius serratus*) is found from Ceduna in South Australia to Kalbarri in Western Australia. This species reaches 50 cm and has no spots or few spots on the head, never with blue and obvious dark stripes behind the eye.

Fishing A large mouth makes this species easy prey for kids dangling baited hooks into rock pools. Wirrah will feed readily on most baits, preferring fresh cut baits, prawns, pilchard or virtually anything they can fit into their mouths. The wirrah is not targeted by serious anglers. The flesh is coarse, tough and flavourless, making the wirrah a 'mother-in-law' fish.

WRASSE

Scientific name Family *Labridae.*

Range Widely distributed large family of fishes, with many species found in tropical or temperate waters.

Description The wrasses are a large family most common in the tropics but with a number of species which extend into temperate waters. This group includes the wrasses, tusk fish, and blue and baldchin groper. Many wrasses have a fairly small mouth, rubbery lips and large teeth which may be green. The bones may be blue-green. Many wrasses are brightly coloured. The juveniles and adult males and females may be very differently coloured. Many wrasses also live in loose family groups with a single large male and several females. If the largest male is captured, the next largest female becomes a male. Most wrasses are found on or near reef country.

Fishing Most wrasses feed on animals found commonly on or near reefs. Some species use their large teeth to grind dead coral to get at the worms or molluscs living there. Many wrasse grow to less than 30 centimetres. Larger wrasses are dogged and dirty fighters who reward successful anglers and make good eating. Best baits for wrasses include prawns, worms, mussels, squid and fresh cut baits. Many wrasses are found right on reefs and catching some of the smaller species is often an indication that the drift is close to snaggy coral reefs.

WRASSE, WESTERN KING

Scientific name *Coris auricularis.* Also known as blushing wrasse, red wrasse, bloody wrasse.

Range Recherche Archipelago on the south coast of Western Australia and along the west coast as far as Coral Bay

Description The western king wrasse is a common and very attractive species found on inshore and offshore reefs and adjacent areas. The males and females are very distinctively coloured and were often claimed to be two different species. There is also a similar species, the eastern king wrasse (*Coris sandageri*) whose range is from Broughton Island to around the mouth of the Gippsland Lakes. Mature male western king wrasse have a distinctive green forehead, bright red cheeks and a red or red-orange body. The females are white with red or magenta stripes running the length of the body. There is a single wide stripe along the top of the body from the snout to the tail and passing through the eye. The pectoral fin is clear. The western king wrasse reaches 45 cm in length and possesses a fairly small mouth.

Fishing The western king wrasse is commonly taken by anglers fishing for pink snapper, dhufish, or spangled emperor in more northern waters. The small mouth and common occurrence of this fish gives it a poor reputation as a bait stealer as it will take all baits commonly used in reef fishing. Using a hook around 2/0 will increase catches of this species and other wrasse, but means a smaller bait is used and dhufish anglers in particular like a big bait for this prized fish. The western king wrasse is commonly used as a cut bait when fishing the reefs and is highly regarded. This species is less highly regarded for food, but they produce a fillet of firm white flesh that is much better quality than its reputation would suggest.

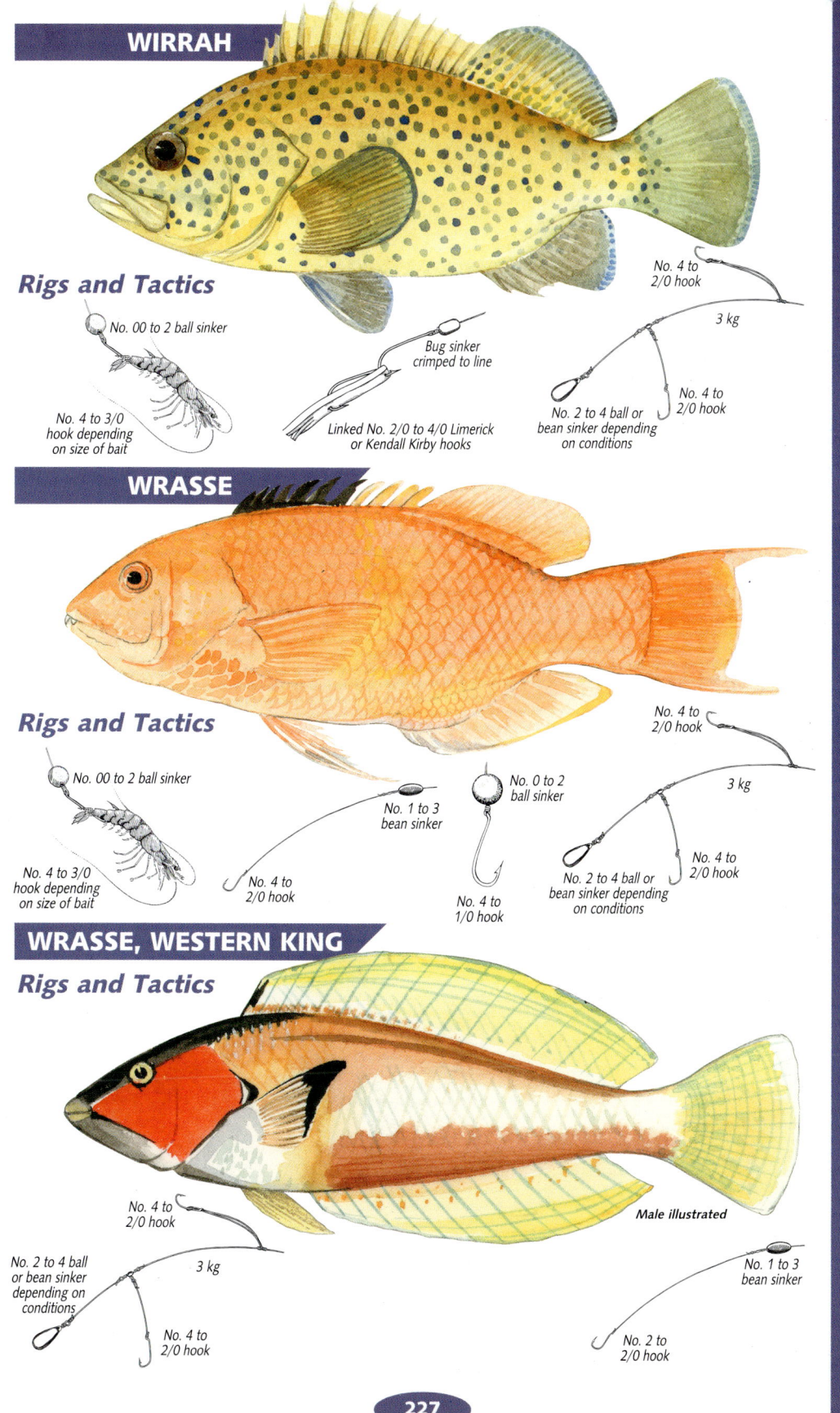

WIRRAH

Rigs and Tactics

No. 00 to 2 ball sinker

No. 4 to 3/0 hook depending on size of bait

Bug sinker crimped to line

Linked No. 2/0 to 4/0 Limerick or Kendall Kirby hooks

No. 4 to 2/0 hook

3 kg

No. 2 to 4 ball or bean sinker depending on conditions

No. 4 to 2/0 hook

WRASSE

Rigs and Tactics

No. 00 to 2 ball sinker

No. 4 to 3/0 hook depending on size of bait

No. 1 to 3 bean sinker

No. 4 to 2/0 hook

No. 0 to 2 ball sinker

No. 4 to 1/0 hook

No. 4 to 2/0 hook

3 kg

No. 2 to 4 ball or bean sinker depending on conditions

No. 4 to 2/0 hook

WRASSE, WESTERN KING

Rigs and Tactics

Male illustrated

No. 4 to 2/0 hook

No. 2 to 4 ball or bean sinker depending on conditions

3 kg

No. 4 to 2/0 hook

No. 1 to 3 bean sinker

No. 2 to 2/0 hook

WRASSE, HUMP-HEADED MAORI

Scientific name *Cheilinus undulatus.* Also known as Maori wrasse, giant Maori wrasse, double-headed maori wrasse, Napoleon wrasse.

Range Shark Bay in Western Australia and tropical waters and to central Queensland but this is essentially a tropical species.

Description The hump-headed Maori wrasse is the giant of the wrasses, capable of reaching 2.3 m and nearly 200 kilograms. The scales are extremely large and can be used as drink coasters from large fish. The scales are edged with cream which forms a series of wavy lines down the body. These lines match the wavy lines on the snout and the dorsal, anal and tail fins. Smaller fish can move in groups of 4 – 10 into coral reef bays to crush dead coral for the shellfish or worms which it contains with their peg-like teeth. Large fish develop a fleshy hump above and between the eyes.

Fishing The hump-headed Maori wrasse is totally protected in Western Australia and these magnificent animals should be released wherever possible. They are particularly prone to spearfishing. On a line, the hump-headed Maori wrasse pulls extremely strongly and will break off the unwary on nearby coral. Best baits are large prawns, crabs, mussels or squid. Due to the extremely large size of this fish, very heavy handlines, gloves and a strong back are most often used.

WRASSE, MAORI

Scientific name *Opthalmolepis lineolatus* Also known as southern Maori wrasse, Maori

Range The Maori wrasse has a disjointed distribution on the east and west coasts. The western population occurs from the Houtman-Abrolhos Islands in Western Australia and southwards to Kangaroo Island in South Australia. The eastern population is found from Byron Bay in NSW to Wilson's Promontory in Victoria.

Description An attractive wrasse which can reach 41 cm, but is more often encountered at a smaller, bait stealing size. This species is found on inshore, or more often offshore reefs throughout its range. The males and females are different in appearance. The males have a black stripe along the body below the mid line. While both sexes have a prominent orange brown top to the body, the male has a number of bright blue spots through this area. Both male and female Maori wrasse have a number of small blue stripes on the head. The belly is yellow or creamy yellow and is below a wide white stripe down the side of the fish.

Fishing The small mouth of this species and the fact that it occupies a similar area to more highly valued reef species such as snapper, morwong and dhufish means that the Maori wrasse is not highly regarded by anglers. The Maori wrasse can be taken on most baits, including on bait jigs when they are on inshore bait grounds. The Maori wrasse is generally used as a cut bait, but they make a quite acceptable live bait, being hardy and attractive to fish like Samson fish, kingfish and big snapper. The Maori wrasse is not generally targeted but is taken on standard reef fishing rigs. It is not generally regarded as a food fish but makes quite acceptable eating.

WRASSE, SENATOR

Scientific name *Pictilabrus laticlavius.* Also known as Senatorfish, purple banded wrasse.

Range Abrolhos Islands in Western Australia and southern waters including Tasmania and as far north as Byron Bay in northern NSW.

Description The senator wrasse is a common inhabitant of reef country or adjacent to beds of seaweed or kelp from just below the intertidal zone to 20 fathoms. The Senator wrasse can reach 33 cm and around 600 grams. Males and females have very different colouration, with males a striking bright green with two horizontal purple stripes that join near the tail. There is also a purple triangle which points down from the lower stripe to the start of the anal fin. Females are dull red. Females may also have a greenish tinge with a black spot usually present at the rear of the soft dorsal. During spawning, male Senator wrasse become very aggressive and may attack divers.

Fishing Senator wrasse are often encountered fishing near rough country and are a good sign that you are fishing close to dangerous kelp beds or rugged reef country. Senator wrasse are taken on baits or prawn, crab, squid or cut baits. The Senator wrasse makes good eating in larger specimens with firm white flesh.

WRASSE, HUMP HEADED MAORI

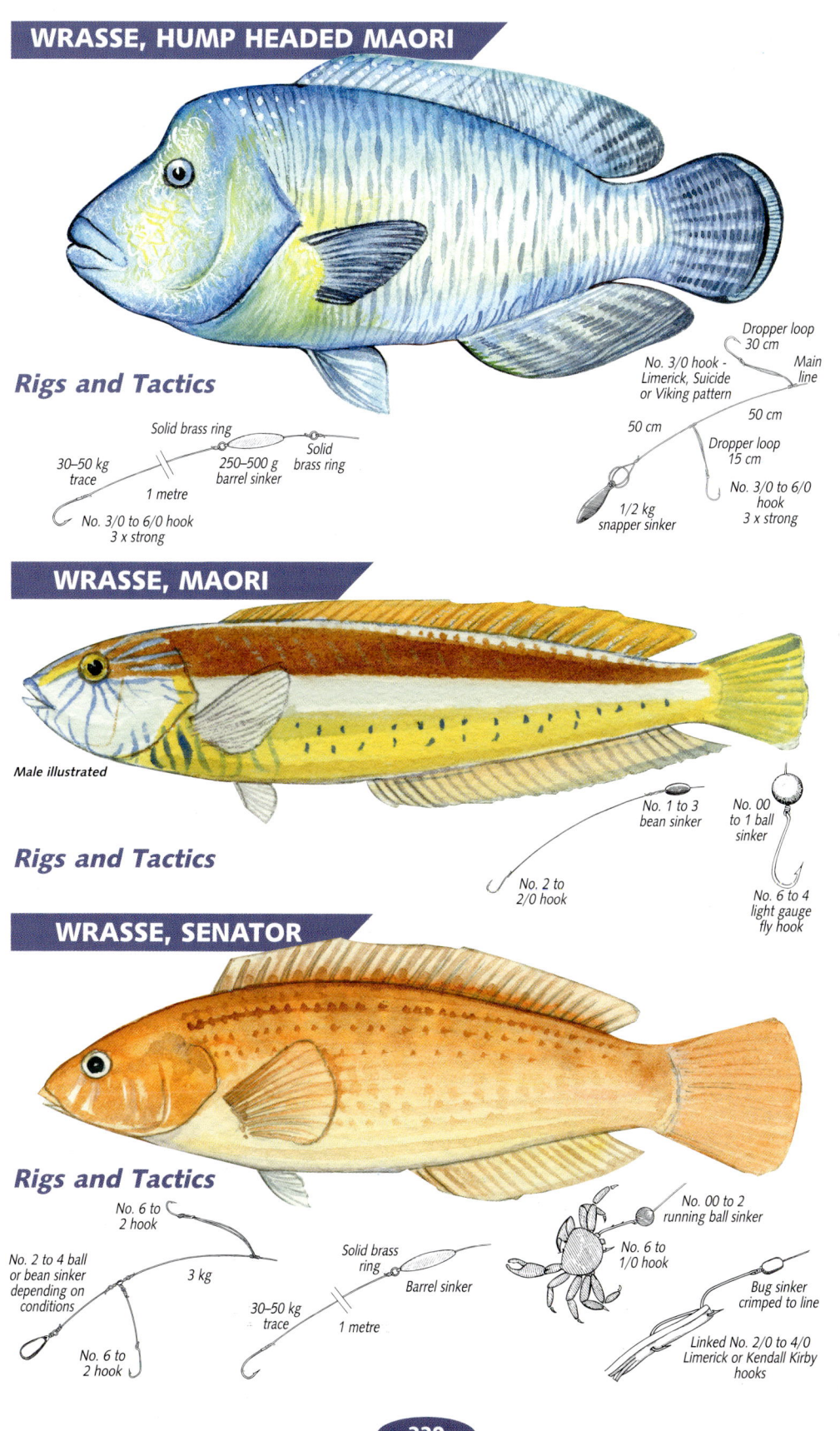

Rigs and Tactics

Solid brass ring

30–50 kg trace

250–500 g barrel sinker

Solid brass ring

1 metre

No. 3/0 to 6/0 hook 3 x strong

Dropper loop 30 cm

No. 3/0 hook - Limerick, Suicide or Viking pattern

Main line

50 cm

50 cm

Dropper loop 15 cm

1/2 kg snapper sinker

No. 3/0 to 6/0 hook 3 x strong

WRASSE, MAORI

Male illustrated

Rigs and Tactics

No. 1 to 3 bean sinker

No. 00 to 1 ball sinker

No. 2 to 2/0 hook

No. 6 to 4 light gauge fly hook

WRASSE, SENATOR

Rigs and Tactics

No. 6 to 2 hook

No. 2 to 4 ball or bean sinker depending on conditions

3 kg

No. 6 to 2 hook

Solid brass ring

30–50 kg trace

Barrel sinker

1 metre

No. 00 to 2 running ball sinker

No. 6 to 1/0 hook

Bug sinker crimped to line

Linked No. 2/0 to 4/0 Limerick or Kendall Kirby hooks

ALBACORE

Scientific name *Thunnus alalunga.* Also known as Tuna (Chicken of the sea).

Range Circum-Australia but common in waters well offshore of Australia's southern half, usually in schools.

Description A common species of offshore waters. Average size is 2 to 5 kg but can attain a weight of 30 kilograms. Adults are easily identified by the largest pectoral fin of all tunas, extending well behind the commencement of the second dorsal fin. Juveniles have smaller pectoral fins but the distinctive white rear border of the tail fin differentiates albacore from juvenile yellowfin or bigeye tuna.

Fishing A good light game fish which fights strongly and requires quality tackle. The albacore readily takes lures such as a feather, minnow or Konahead type lure trolled at around 6 knots. Albacore also take live bait drifted or fished under a bobby cork at a depth of 2.5 to 3 metres.
The albacore is excellent eating, with firm white flesh and a delicate texture.

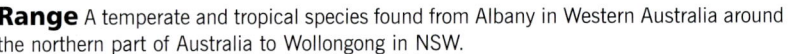

AMBERJACK

Scientific name *Seriola dumerili.*

Range A temperate and tropical species found from Albany in Western Australia around the northern part of Australia to Wollongong in NSW.

Description A relatively large, fast swimming species mainly found in offshore waters in the vicinity of reefs or drop-offs. Sometimes confused with yellowtail kingfish, the amberjack has a dark blue to olive tail fin whereas the kingfish has a yellow tail fin. The anal fin of the amberjack is darker in colour with a characteristic white edging. Differs from similar samson fish in having more rays in the dorsal fin (32 – 33) versus 23 – 25 for the samson fish. The samson fish also appears to have red teeth, due to blood engorged gums. The amberjack attains a weight of 36 kilograms.

Fishing A hard fighting fish which takes feather or minnow lures trolled near reefs and drop offs. Amberjacks will also take both live and dead bait fished in the vicinity of offshore reefs.
The amberjack makes good eating, although larger specimens tend to be dry and coarse textured.

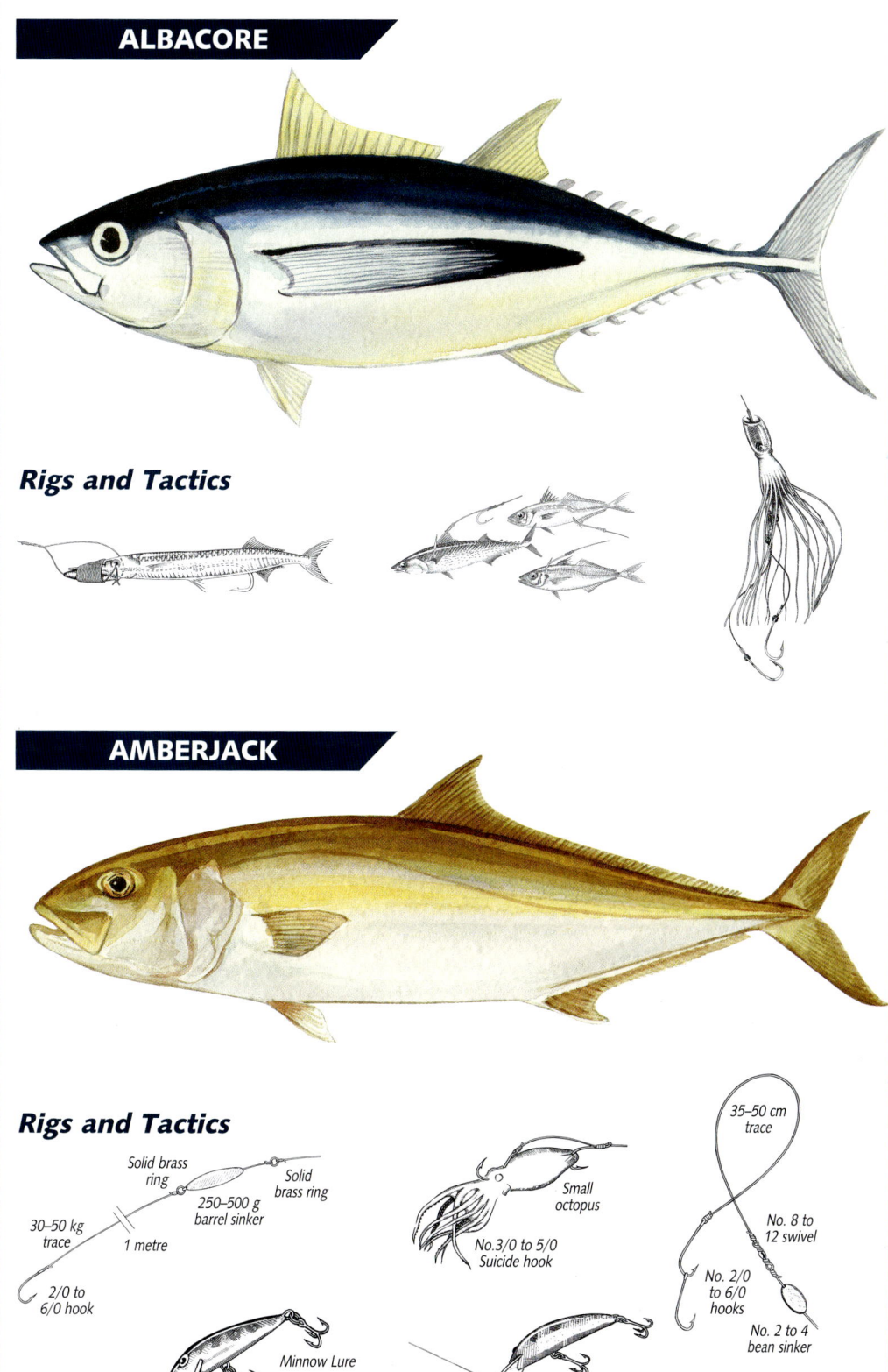

ALBACORE

Rigs and Tactics

AMBERJACK

Rigs and Tactics

Solid brass ring
Solid brass ring
250–500 g barrel sinker
30–50 kg trace
1 metre
2/0 to 6/0 hook

24 kg trace
Minnow Lure

Small octopus
No.3/0 to 5/0 Suicide hook

Deep Diving Minnow

35–50 cm trace
No. 8 to 12 swivel
No. 2/0 to 6/0 hooks
No. 2 to 4 bean sinker

BARRACOUTA

Scientific name *Thyrsites atun.* Also known as 'Couta, pickhandle, axehandle, occasionally by its South African name snoek.

Range Found from Shark Bay in Western Australia around the entire southern part of the country to northern NSW. Barracouta are a cold water species which are most common in waters of Tasmania, southern Victoria and South Australia to Cape Leeuwin in Western Australia. Barracouta are a good indicator of the presence of a cold water current. They are regarded as a pest in the northern part of their range due to significant parasitic infestation in the flesh which renders them inedible and the cold currents in which they are found put warmer water fish off the bite.

Description The barracouta is a member of the same family as gemfish (hake) which is a much deeper bodied fish. There is no resemblance to the more tropical barracuda. The barracouta has a very long first dorsal with a distinctive black patch near the leading edge and around 5 finlets on the caudal peduncle (the gemfish has 2 finlets). The colour is steely grey and the small scales are easily shed. The barracouta has three large teeth on its upper jaw. Grows to 4.5 kg and 1.3 m but commonly caught at 1 – 2 kilograms.

Fishing Barracouta can take a variety of baits and lures. They are frequently taken on chrome spoons or casting lures. Barracouta will also take minnow lures and feathers and soft plastics, but their teeth make short work of all but the most robust lures. A wire trace will help prevent bite offs of expensive lures and increase the catch rates with baits. Barracouta will take fish flesh, garfish or pilchard baits readily and while partial to live baits are difficult to hook due to a bony mouth and a habit of running with the bait across their jaws. Barracouta should be handled carefully due to their sharp teeth which also have an anticoagulant which makes any cuts bleed profusely. Barracouta are considered good eating from cooler water in the southern part of their range, especially Tasmania.

BARRACUDA

Scientific name *Sphyraena barracuda.* Also known as Great barracuda, giant barracuda, giant sea pike.

Range The barracuda is found from Albany in Western Australia around the top of Australia to southern Queensland, although it is much more common in tropical waters north of Shark Bay.

Description The most remarkable feature of the barracuda is its fearsome teeth. There are two pairs of enlarged canines on the upper jaw and one pair of enlarged canines on the lower jaw. There are other large, backward pointing teeth in both jaws. The body is long and cylindrical with approximately 18 grayish cross bands on the back above the lateral line. These bands on the back and the more heavy body differentiate the barracuda from the similar snook, which is generally found outside of the range of the barracuda. The barracuda reaches 1.8 m and nearly 25 kilograms.

Fishing The barracuda is rarely specifically targeted as the flesh is of poor quality and removing the hooks is difficult. The barracuda is also prone to ciguatera and should not be consumed except from Western Australian waters. Barracuda love trolled fish baits and will also readily hit minnow, feather and spoon lures. Wire is important, especially with bait. Larger barracuda are generally found near either offshore or inshore reefs. Small barracuda form schools and are more prevalent inshore or in estuaries.

BARRACOUTA

Rigs and Tactics

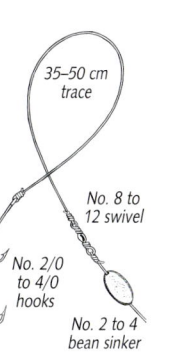

35–50 cm trace

No. 8 to 12 swivel

No. 2/0 to 4/0 hooks

No. 2 to 4 bean sinker

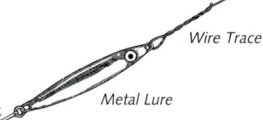

Stopper

No. 10 swivel

Bobby float

No. 2 to 4 ball or bean sinker

No. 3/0 to 5/0 hook gang

Sinker optional depending on casting distance

No. 10 swivel

15 kg trace

50 cm

No. 2 to 4 ball sinker depending on type of fish

Ganged No. 4/0 to 5/0 hooks

Small bean sinker may be added to aid casting

Main line

wire trace

No. 8 swivel

Ganged No. 3/0 to 5/0 hooks

Wire Trace

Metal Lure

Wonder Wobbler

Mr Twister

BARRACUDA

Rigs and Tactics

Small bean sinker may be added to aid casting

25 kg trace

Main line

No. 8 swivel

Ganged No. 3/0 to 5/0 Limerick hooks

Wire Trace

Metal Lure

Minnow Lure

24 kg trace

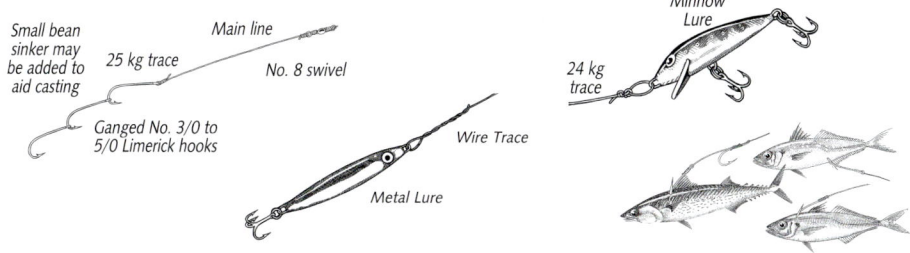

BONITO, AUSTRALIAN

Scientific name *Sarda australis*. Also known as Bonny, occasionally horse mackerel.

Range Gold Coast of Queensland down the East coast of Victoria and Tasmania

Description Commonly found in large schools on the coast of NSW. Easily distinguished from other tunas and bonito species by the presence of narrow horizontal stripes on the lower part of the body. Bonito also have a single row of small but distinct conical teeth. The Australian bonito can grow to 1 m and nearly 8 kg but is usually less than 3 – 4 kilograms.

Fishing An aggressive fish which takes lures well and is less discriminating than some of the smaller tuna species. Bonito can be taken on saltwater fly rapidly stripped through the school. Minnow lures, chrome slices and feather lures either trolled or quickly retrieved work very well. Bonito will take pilchard and other fish baits such as garfish and can be taken by cubing in a berley trail. While bonito make terrific live or cut bait, they are better eating than their reputation suggest, but are prone to bruising during their after capture struggles.

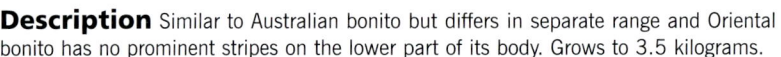

BONITO, ORIENTAL

Scientific name *Sarda orientalis*. Also known as Bonito.

Range Western Australia only, from Albany to Shark Bay.

Description Similar to Australian bonito but differs in separate range and Oriental bonito has no prominent stripes on the lower part of its body. Grows to 3.5 kilograms.

Fishing Similar methods for Australian bonito. Can be very common in inshore waters, giving a pleasant surprise to shore based casters fishing for tailor and herring. The Oriental bonito should be bled after capture and is only moderately regarded as a food fish.

BONITO, WATSON'S LEAPING

Scientific name *Cybiosarda elegans*. Also known as Leaping bonito.

Range An essentially tropical species from Geographe Bay (Dunsborough) in Western Australia along the western, northern and eastern coast to southern Queensland.

Description Watson's leaping bonito differs from other bonito as the colouring consists of a series of dusky grey broken lines and blotches above the lateral line and three grayish unbroken lines below the lateral line. It also has a significantly larger first dorsal fin than the other bonito. Reaches a size of approximately 2 kg and 54 centimetres.

Fishing During winter months the Watson's leaping bonito forms large schools which feed on aggregated baitfish. Schools can be found inshore or on occasions in estuaries. Can be taken on small chrome lures, Christmas tree lures, minnow lures and feather jigs. This species makes terrific cut bait or whole for game species and is better eating than its reputation suggests.

BONITO, AUSTRALIAN

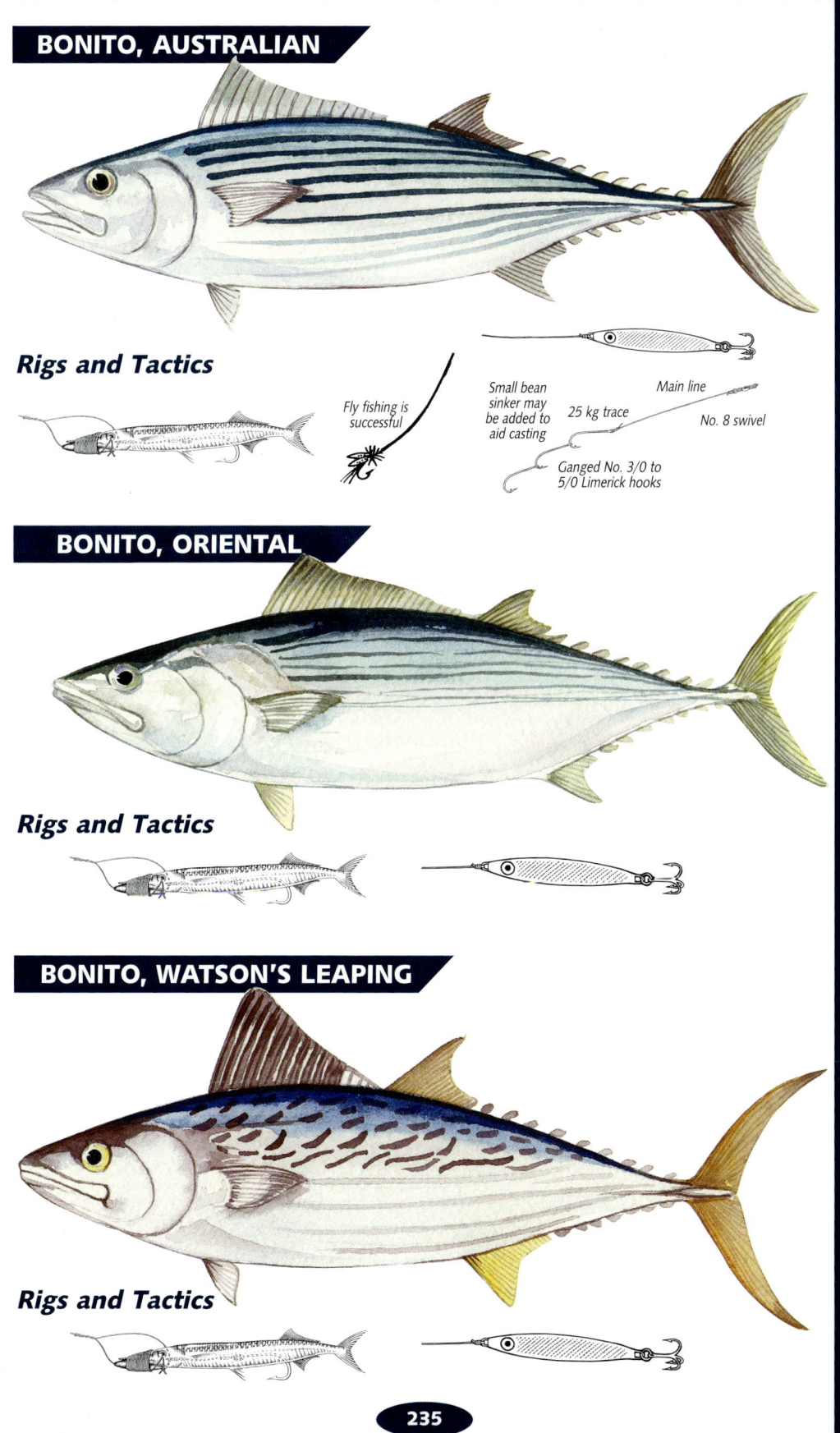

Rigs and Tactics

Fly fishing is successful

Small bean sinker may be added to aid casting

Main line

25 kg trace

No. 8 swivel

Ganged No. 3/0 to 5/0 Limerick hooks

BONITO, ORIENTAL

Rigs and Tactics

BONITO, WATSON'S LEAPING

Rigs and Tactics

COBIA

Scientific name *Rachycentron canadus*. Also known as Cobe, black kingfish, black king, crab-eater, sergeant fish, lemon fish.

Range Cape Naturaliste in Western Australia northwards, including sub-tropical and tropical waters around the top end to Sydney NSW.

Description A large pelagic species reaching over 2 m and 60 kilograms. Frequently mistaken initially for a shark in the water due to its high dorsal fin and large, dark pectoral fins. They have a relatively pointy head with the mouth at the middle of the front of the head. They have a white or creamy belly which tends to be darker around the anal fin region and a white stripe on their sides which may fade after death. They also have very short dorsal spines before the high soft dorsal fin. Other fins, except pelvic are dark and the overall colour is chocolate brown to black.

Fishing Cobia are generally encountered opportunistically. They congregate around structures such as wharves, bommies or reef tops and are renowned for traveling with manta rays and whale sharks. Many anglers chase manta rays to get a cast at these hard fighting, great tasting fish. Cobia will take a variety of baits including squid, crabs and cut or whole fish. While frequently fished to with unweighted or lightly weighted rigs, they will take baits off the bottom, especially on sand patches near reefs or jetties. They can be cast to with lures or flies but can be difficult to catch in some sight fishing situations.

KINGFISH, YELLOWTAIL

Scientific name *Seriola lalandi*. Also known as Kingie, yellowtail, hoodlum and bandit.

Range Shark Bay in Western Australia and southern waters through to central Queensland with good populations at Lord Howe and Norfolk Islands and New Zealand.

Description The yellowtail kingfish is a beautiful, powerful fish which has a large, deeply forked tail. The back and upper sides are dark, purply blue while the lower part of the body is white. These two distinctive colours are separated by a yellow band which varies in width and intensity from fish to fish. The tail is a bright yellow. This can be a large fish reaching 2 m and more than 50 kg although increasing commercial and recreational fishing is affecting the presence of large fish. Any yellowtail kingfish over 20 kg will be a memorable capture.

Fishing The yellowtail kingfish is a brutal, dirty fighter which will fully test the skill of the angler and the quality of their gear. The first run of a kingfish is straight towards the nearest bottom obstruction to cut off an unwary angler. Kingfish will take a wide variety of lures such as minnow lures, soft plastics and and flies. Vertical jigging with metail lures can be deadly at times. They will take a range of whole and cut fish baits, prawns, squid, octopus and cuttlefish but there are occasions when they can be finicky. At other times yellowtail kingfish will strike at bare hooks. Live bait is almost certain to attract a mad rush from any kingfish in the area. Kingfish were previously considered average eating, but they have been increasingly recognised as a quality fish, including as sashimi. Large fish are worse eating and can have worms in the flesh, especially from northern waters.

COBIA

Rigs and Tactics

Solid
brass ring

Solid
brass ring

Main
line

30–40 cm

No. 2/0 to
8/0 hook

60–120 g
snapper sinker

Medium to
large bobby
float

2–3 metres

No. 8 swivel

Stopper

Bean or
bug sinker

30–50 kg
trace

50 cm

No. 5/0 to
8/0 Suicide or
Live Bait hook

Bug sinker

Suicide
Hook

Solid brass
ring

Barrel sinker

30–50 kg
trace

1 metre

24 kg trace

Minnow Lure

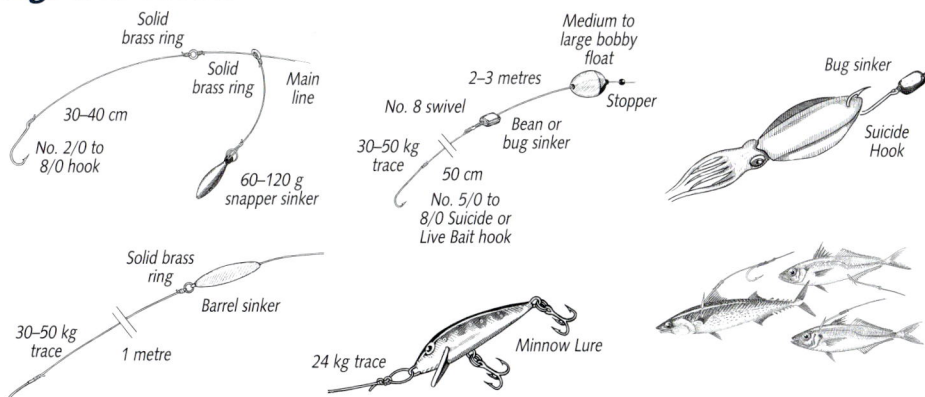

KINGFISH, YELLOWTAIL

Rigs and Tactics

No. 6
swivel

Stopper

Bobby
float

No. 2 to 4
ball or bean
sinker

No. 3/0 to 6/0
hook gang

Solid brass
ring

Solid
brass ring

250–500 g
barrel sinker

30–50 kg
trace

1 metre

24 kg trace

Minnow Lure

Small bean
sinker may
be added to
aid casting

25 kg trace

Main line

No. 8 swivel

Ganged No. 3/0
to 5/0 hooks

Fly fishing is
successful

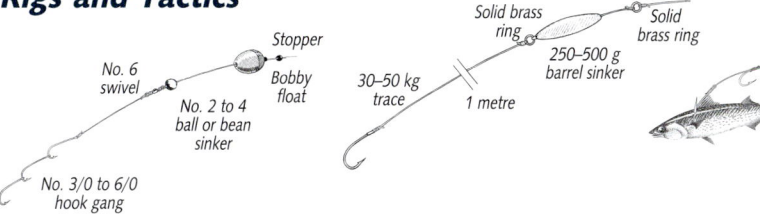

MACKEREL, BROAD-BARRED SPANISH

Scientific name *Scomberomorus semifasciatus.* Also known as Grey mackerel, tiger mackerel, broad barred mackerel.

Range Shark Bay northwards and around tropical waters to northern NSW.

Description A similar species to the more common and generally larger Spanish mackerel, they can be readily identified by the much larger soft dorsal and anal fins. The bars are much broader and fewer in number with live fish, but they fade significantly on death, giving rise to the marketing name of grey mackerel. The broad-barred Spanish mackerel reaches 1.2 m and 8 kg but is commonly caught at 1 – 3 kg from inshore waters or major embayments such as Tin Can Bay in Queensland.

Fishing Like its larger cousin, the broad-barred Spanish mackerel readily takes small minnow or chrome lures and whole or cut fish baits. Live baits work extremely well. This species fights well, particularly on light line but is not as highly regarded a food fish as the Spanish mackerel.

MACKEREL, FRIGATE

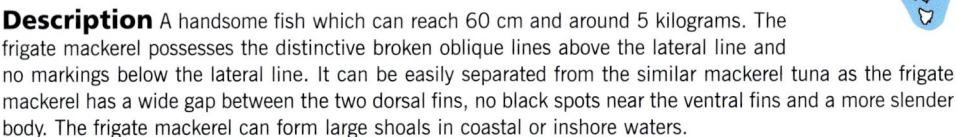

Scientific name *Auxis thazard.* Also known as Little tuna.

Range Circum-Australia but more common in sub-tropical or tropical waters.

Description A handsome fish which can reach 60 cm and around 5 kilograms. The frigate mackerel possesses the distinctive broken oblique lines above the lateral line and no markings below the lateral line. It can be easily separated from the similar mackerel tuna as the frigate mackerel has a wide gap between the two dorsal fins, no black spots near the ventral fins and a more slender body. The frigate mackerel can form large shoals in coastal or inshore waters.

Fishing The frigate mackerel will readily take quickly trolled silver or chrome lures. Christmas tree type lures work well trolled in a pattern. High speed spinning can work well. This species can be finicky at times, with large schools refusing all offerings, but on other occasions will strike savagely at any lure and will take trolled or cast dead baits. The frigate mackerel fights well for its size. It makes terrific bait, either trolled for billfish, or as cut bait for reef species. The frigate mackerel is not highly regarded as a food fish, but is suitable for sashimi or for poaching.

MACKEREL, QUEENSLAND SCHOOL

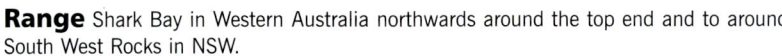

Scientific name *Scomberomorus queenslandicus* Also known as School mackerel, doggie mackerel, blotched mackerel, shiny mackerel.

Range Shark Bay in Western Australia northwards around the top end and to around South West Rocks in NSW.

Description The Queensland school mackerel is a schooling species which frequents inshore areas. The Queensland school mackerel can reach a metre in length and a weight of 12 kilograms. However they are commonly encountered from 1.5 to 4 kg, especially on the eastern seaboard. This species is easily identified by the large dark spots on the sides and the black then white areas on the first dorsal fin. The pectoral fin is also smaller and more pointed than in the broad-barred Spanish mackerel.

Fishing Schools of Queensland school mackerel can be berleyed close to the boat and taken with live or whole dead or fresh cut bait. These fish will take lures but can be finicky. Queensland school mackerel can patrol close to the shore and can be a surprise catch from tropical beaches or creek mouths, but they can bite off lures or baits intended for other species. The Queensland school mackerel is a top table fish if filleted.

MACKEREL, BROAD-BARRED SPANISH

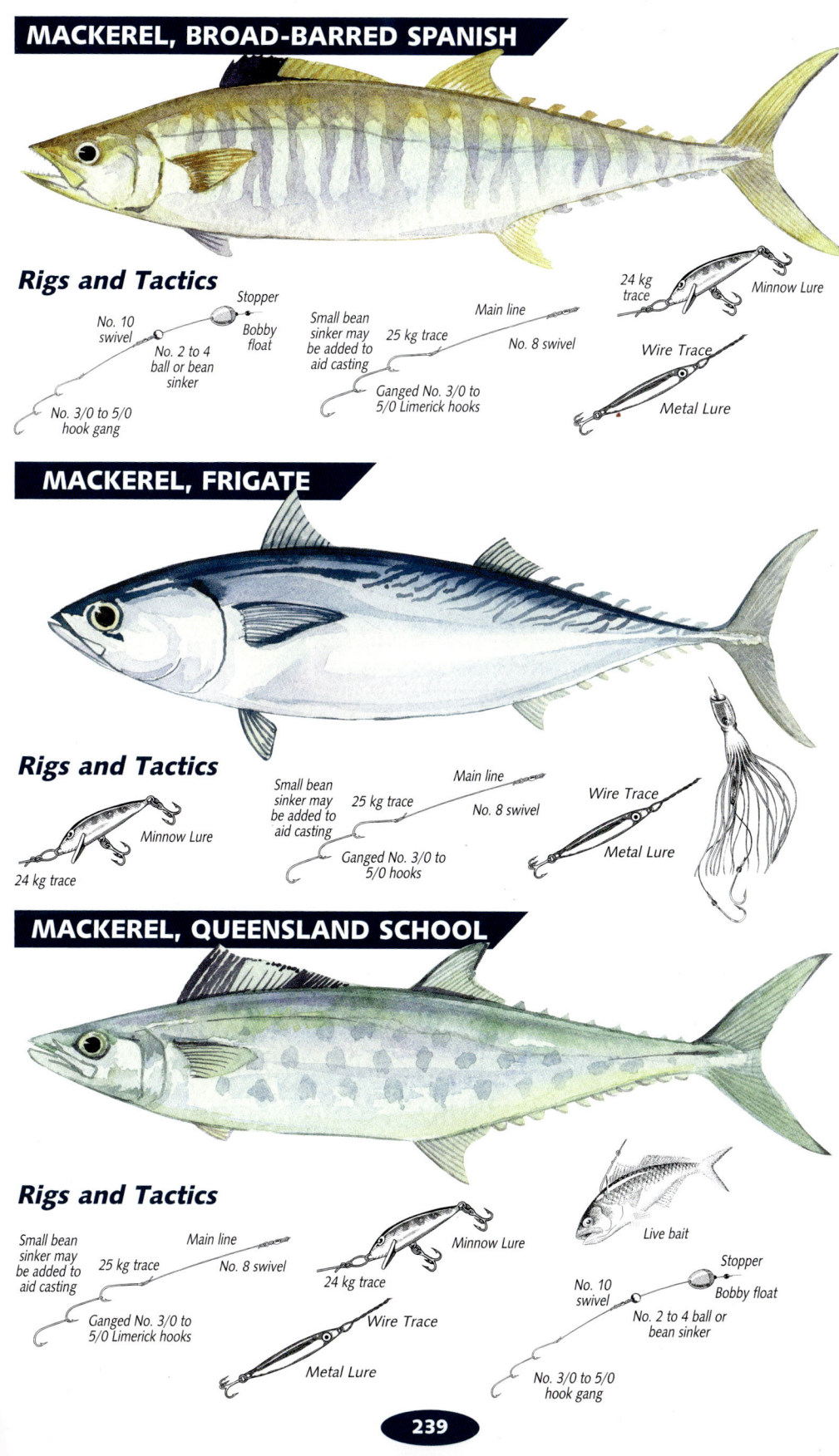

Rigs and Tactics

No. 10 swivel

No. 2 to 4 ball or bean sinker

Stopper

Bobby float

No. 3/0 to 5/0 hook gang

Small bean sinker may be added to aid casting

25 kg trace

Main line

No. 8 swivel

Ganged No. 3/0 to 5/0 Limerick hooks

24 kg trace

Minnow Lure

Wire Trace

Metal Lure

MACKEREL, FRIGATE

Rigs and Tactics

Minnow Lure

24 kg trace

Small bean sinker may be added to aid casting

25 kg trace

Main line

No. 8 swivel

Ganged No. 3/0 to 5/0 hooks

Wire Trace

Metal Lure

MACKEREL, QUEENSLAND SCHOOL

Rigs and Tactics

Small bean sinker may be added to aid casting

25 kg trace

Main line

No. 8 swivel

Ganged No. 3/0 to 5/0 Limerick hooks

Minnow Lure

24 kg trace

Wire Trace

Metal Lure

Live bait

Stopper

Bobby float

No. 10 swivel

No. 2 to 4 ball or bean sinker

No. 3/0 to 5/0 hook gang

239

MACKEREL, SHARK

Scientific name *Grammatorcynus bicarinatus*. Also known as Scaly mackerel, large-scaled tunny, salmon mackerel.

Range Geographe Bay in Western Australia around tropical waters and into central NSW around Newcastle.

Description A sought after fish found on shallow reef areas throughout its range. This species has a distinguishing double lateral line which divides at the pectoral fin and joins again at the tail base. The belly displays dark spots and the eye is relatively small, especially compared to the similar double lined (or scad) mackerel. The scales of the shark mackerel come away in large sheets. The name shark mackerel comes from a distinctive ammonia smell (shark-like) when the fish is cleaned but which disappears with cooking. The shark mackerel can reach 1.3 m and 11 kilograms.

Fishing Shark mackerel are good lure prospects, rising to take minnow or spoon type lure where they put up a determined surface based fight. Shark mackerel are also taken on drifted whole or cut fish baits and live baits, although shark mackerel are not the general target species with live baits in tropical waters. The shark mackerel makes reasonable eating but the quality is improved by skinning the fillets.

MACKEREL, SPANISH

Scientific name *Scomberomorus commerson*. Also known as Narrow-barred Spanish mackerel, blue mackerel, tanguigue, Spaniard, seer, seerfish.

Range Mandurah in Western Australia northwards and around the top end and as far south as Bermagui in southern NSW.

Description The Spanish mackerel is a highly sought after and valued species capable of reaching 2.35 m and 42 kilograms. It is commonly taken from 5 – 15 kilograms. Smaller fish travel in pods of similar sized fish. The Spanish mackerel is similar to the wahoo but has fewer dorsal spines (15 – 18 versus 23 – 27) in a shorter dorsal fin. The upper jaw of the Spanish mackerel has an obvious external bone which extends to at least the middle of the eye, while in the wahoo there is no obvious bone and the upper jaw extends to the front edge of the eye. The Spanish mackerel is found in coastal waters, frequently in the vicinity of reefs.

Fishing Spanish mackerel will aggressively take trolled lures and baits. Minnow lures, spoons and feathered lures run at 5 – 7 knots work best, while trolled garfish, slimy mackerel or other fish at 3 – 5 knots will take good catches. Spanish mackerel will also take drifted live, whole or cut baits. Land based fishermen drift large baits under balloons to take large fish. A wire trace can be an effective counter to the sharp teeth of the Spanish mackerel. The Spanish mackerel is an excellent sport fish, particularly on light line, as it runs strongly and occasionally jumps in its attempts to escape. Spanish mackerel can actively feed at different depths, so lures and baits which target a wide range will more quickly locate fish. The Spanish mackerel is a highly regarded food fish, but does not freeze particularly well, especially if cut into steaks. The quality is much better when the fish is filleted.

MACKEREL, SPOTTED

Scientific name *Scomberomorus munroi*. Also known as Australian spotted mackerel, spotted Spanish mackerel, Japanese spotted mackerel, schoolie.

Range Abrolhos Islands in Western Australia northward and around the top end and into NSW, sometimes reaching as far south as Sydney.

Description The spotted mackerel is smaller than the Spanish mackerel but the fight and eating qualities are at least equal to their more illustrious cousins. The spotted mackerel can reach over one metre and more than 10 kg which makes it a worthwhile light tackle target. The spotted mackerel is more commonly encountered from 2 to 6 kilograms. It can be identified by the broad band of dark spots along the middle of each side. The inside of the pectoral fin is dark blue or black. The first dorsal fin is blue with a dusky blotch on the front section.

Fishing This species is most common in summer when it follows warmer currents which extend down the east and west coasts. It takes pilchard and garfish baits well either drifted or slow trolled. Spotted mackerel take smaller live baits readily. They are frequently taken on larger lures intended for Spanish mackerel, but are good propositions with slightly smaller Rapala or Laser type minnows or spoons. The spotted mackerel is excellent eating, but should be bled and kept on ice for optimum quality.

MACKEREL, SHARK

Rigs and Tactics

Small bean sinker may be added to aid casting

25 kg trace

Main line

No. 8 swivel

Ganged No. 3/0 to 5/0 hooks

24 kg trace

Minnow Lure

Wire Trace

Metal Lure

Live bait

Medium to large bobby float

2–3 metres

Stopper

No. 8 swivel

Bean or bug sinker

30–50 kg trace

50 cm

No. 5/0 to 8/0 Suicide or Live Bait hook

MACKEREL, SPANISH

Rigs and Tactics

Small bean sinker may be added to aid casting

25 kg trace

Main line

No. 8 swivel

Ganged No. 3/0 to 5/0 hooks

24 kg trace

Minnow Lure

No. 10 swivel

Stopper

Bobby float

No. 2 to 4 ball or bean sinker

No. 3/0 to 5/0 hook gang

Wire Trace

Metal Lure

Live bait

MACKEREL, SPOTTED

Rigs and Tactics

Small bean sinker may be added to aid casting

25 kg trace

Main line

No. 8 swivel

Ganged No. 3/0 to 5/0 Limerick hooks

Wire Trace

Metal Lure

24 kg trace

Minnow Lure

Live bait

No. 10 swivel

Stopper

Bobby float

No. 2 to 4 ball or bean sinker

No. 3/0 to 5/0 hook gang

MAHI MAHI

Scientific name *Coryphaena hippurus.* Also known as Dolphin, dolphin fish, common dolphinfish, dorado.

Range Geographe Bay in Western Australia and northwards through warmer temperate and tropical waters to Bermagui in NSW.

Description The mahi mahi is one of the most beautiful fish in the ocean when lit up, with bright yellow to blue colouration and brilliant blue flecks over most of the body and fins. The fantastic colours fade to a washed out grey after death. Mature male or 'bull' mahi mahi have a prominent high forehead and tend to be more brightly coloured. Females have a more streamlined head profile. The species is easily recognised in photographs due to its shape and brilliant colours. Other diagnostic features include the very long dorsal and anal fins and the deeply veed tail. Mahi mahi are arguably the fastest growing species in the ocean, growing as much as a centimetre a day when food is plentiful. Mahi mahi can reach 2 m and more than 20 kg but are frequently taken in Australia from 2 to 10 kilograms. In Western Australia, mahi mahi are first found in oceanic waters at less than a kilogram and within five months, those that have not been caught are more than 10 kilograms.

Fishing A brilliant blue water angling species which presents a spectacular sight as a lit up mahi mahi rises to take a trolled lure or bait. Mahi mahi are renowned residents around floating debris and Fish Aggregating Devices (FAD's) are now set in many areas to attract this and other pelagic species. Hundreds of mahi mahi can be concentrated around a floating log. These fish can be picked up by trolling or casting close to the debris with minnow, feather jigs or pusher type lures such as from Pakula. As fishing pressure increases, cut bait or whole fish and ultimately live bait are needed to take fish. An unweighted large peeled prawn drifted back to the school can take fish when all else fails. The mahi mahi provides a strong and spectacular fight, mixing dogged runs with leaps. They are a reliable light tackle standby in many parts of the world when blue water gamefishing is slow. Mahi mahi make excellent eating but should be bled and chilled immediately after the special photographs are taken. The flesh does not freeze well so only enough for immediate needs should be taken. The extremely fast growth rate and thumping which accompanies landing means that the mahi mahi bruises easily and can suffer post harvest trauma so should be released very carefully.

MARLIN, BLACK

Scientific name *Makaira indica.* Also known as Giant black marlin, silver marlin.

Range Circum-Australia, but only spasmodically recorded from the south coast. Prefers tropical waters and moves further south in summer and early autumn with warmer currents.

Description A magnificent blue water billfish capable of reaching a length of nearly 5 m and 850 kilograms. The black marlin is readily distinguished by its rigid pectoral fins which cannot be laid next to body in any black marlin and are completely rigid in all fish over 50 kg. In this fairly heavy bodied fish, the start of the second dorsal is forward to the start of the second anal fin. Black marlin are most commonly found in blue water, with many fish moving southwards with the warmer currents. Black marlin are found near current lines and where baitfish aggregations are prevalent.

Fishing The black marlin is widely recognised as the most highly prized gamefishing species. The most famous fishing ground is off Cairns, where the future of grander marlin (over 1000 pounds) has been enhanced by the almost exclusive use of tag and release fishing and the recent establishment of this species as recreational only in Australia's 200 mile Exclusive Economic Zone. Black marlin are targeted by gamefishermen along most of the east and west coasts. Black marlin are caught on trolled live and dead bait or less frequently on bait fished from a stationery boat. Marlin are also taken on trolled lures which consist of a hard moulded plastic or resin head and soft plastic skirt which travels just at or below the surface and leaves a bubble trail. Black marlin are a fast swimming pelagic species which are trolled at speeds between six and ten knots. A few marlin are caught by land based game fishermen, but only where deep, clean water comes close to shore. Marlin have a bony mouth and bill which can make setting and holding the hook difficult. When hooked, a marlin will often jump spectacularly in an effort to throw the hook and many fish are lost near the boat through the hook pulling out. Catching marlin requires patience, skill and a bit of luck. The capture of a large marlin requires perfectly maintained tackle and teamwork from all involved. They are not regarded as a food fish and almost all recreationally landed fish are released.

MAHI MAHI

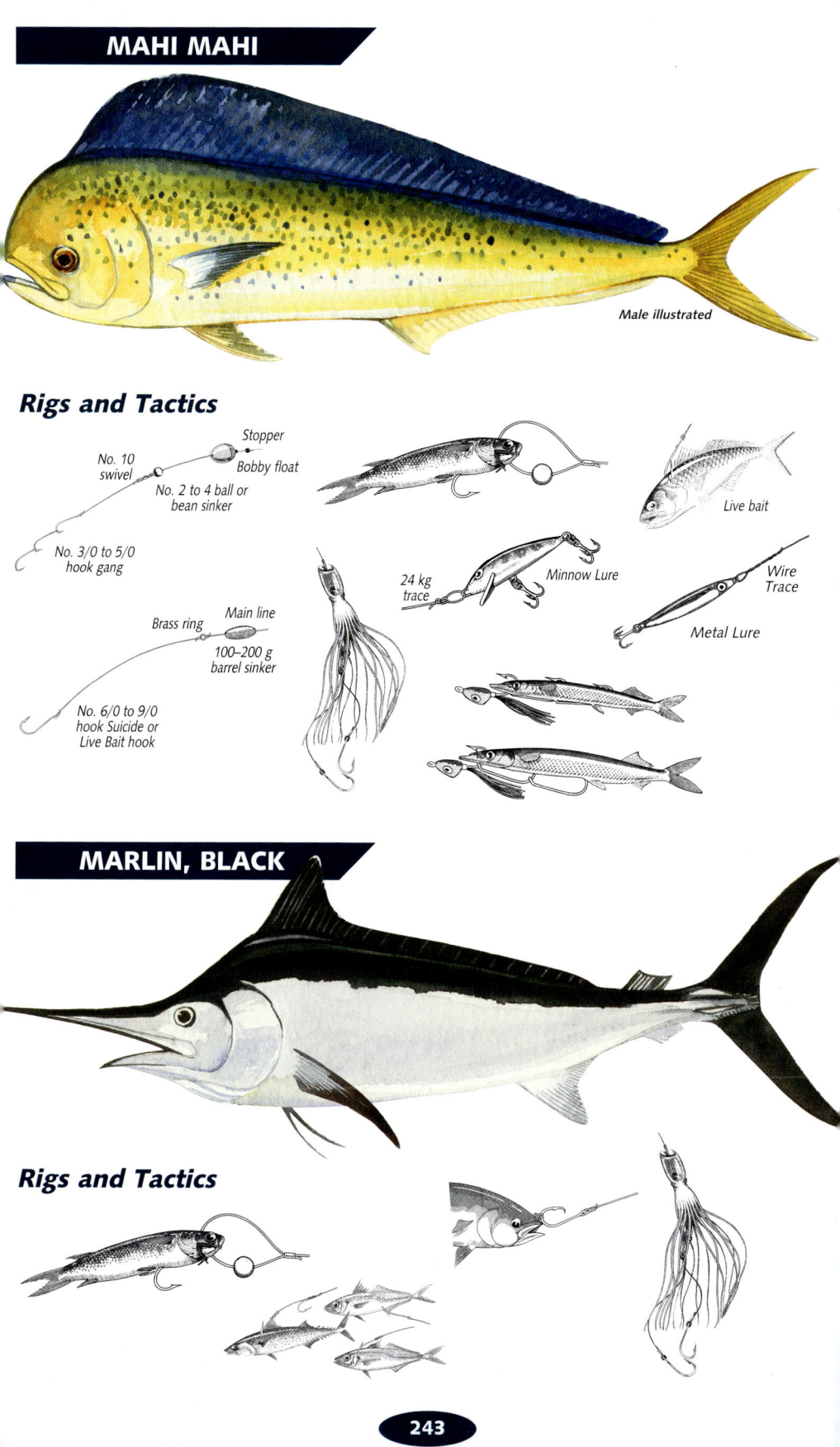

Male illustrated

Rigs and Tactics

No. 10 swivel

Stopper

Bobby float

No. 2 to 4 ball or bean sinker

No. 3/0 to 5/0 hook gang

Brass ring

Main line

100–200 g barrel sinker

No. 6/0 to 9/0 hook Suicide or Live Bait hook

Live bait

24 kg trace

Minnow Lure

Wire Trace

Metal Lure

MARLIN, BLACK

Rigs and Tactics

MARLIN, BLUE

Scientific name *Makaira mazara*. Also known as Indo-pacific blue marlin, Pacific blue marlin, beakie.

Range Albany in Western Australia and northern waters around the east coast to Mallacoota in Victoria but blue marlin are rarely found in water cooler than 20 degrees Celsius.

Description The blue marlin is one of the largest marlin, recorded as reaching a maximum weight of over 1100 kg, although specimens in Australia are less than 300 kilograms. While alive the fins and tail of the blue marlin are electric blue. The blue marlin can be separated from the black marlin by the lighter stripes on the side and the fact that the pectoral is flexible and can be laid flat in the blue marlin. The blue marlin can be separated from the striped marlin by the lower dorsal fin and the start of the second dorsal fin is behind the start of the second anal fin. The lateral line does not generally show in adults but is a distinctive chain which is apparent when scales or skin is removed.

Fishing The blue marlin is an open ocean species most commonly found along the Continental shelf, above deeper canyons and along current lines in deeper water. They can also be found by trolling around oceanic debris. Blue marlin will take trolled hard and soft plastic lures or trolled live or dead baits. Blue marlin can be taken by drifting or at anchor with live or dead baits, although this method is not generally used in Australia as fish are not common enough for a concentrated approach to be successful. The blue marlin is a tough, strong fighter whose first run may spool an unwary angler or inexperienced skipper. The blue marlin can be a spectacular jumper, but often fights deeply. When jumping the blue marlin will spin or suddenly reverse direction which can break the line. The blue marlin is not eaten, not just because of the poor quality of the flesh which is not highly regarded but because of the enormous value which gamefishermen place on these magnificent animals. Consequently, all but very few blue marlin are tagged and released. The recent national decision to prohibit the retention of all black and blue marlin by commercial fishers in Australian waters should lead to benefits to recreational fishermen.

MARLIN, STRIPED

Scientific name *Tetrapturus audax*. Also known as Striper, stripey.

Range Cape Naturaliste in Western Australia northwards and around the east coast as far south as northern Tasmania. The striped marlin prefers water temperatures of 20 – 26 degrees so is most common on the main east and west coasts.

Description The striped marlin is more compressed than the other more cylindrical marlin species. The striped marlin reaches a smaller maximum size than the black and blue marlin at 250 kg, with Australian specimens encountered to over 150 kilograms. The striped marlin has striking cobalt blue or lavender stripes which fade to a fair degree after death. The first three rays in the high first dorsal are of similar height. The 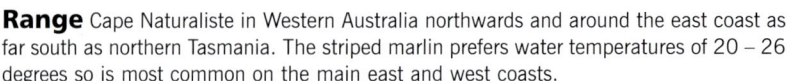striped marlin also has a single lateral line which may not be readily visible but which is raised and can be felt. The pectoral fin is longer than the body depth and can fold against the body. The tail appears squared of at the end of the top and bottom lobe.

Fishing The striped marlin can be taken at slower trolling speeds than blue and black marlin and can be an exciting catch on minnow and other lures trolled for Spanish mackerel. Striped marlin will also take traditional hard and soft plastic lures for other high speed pelagics. They can be found closer inshore, shadowing baitfish schools, and are often taken in conjunction with tuna species, especially by commercial longliners. Striped marlin are fished for with trolled live or dead baits and strip baits, particularly with plastic squids. As striped marlin are often found around baitfish schools, they are fished for with cast or drifted live baits either near worked bait fish or to cruising fish. When hooked, the striped marlin is a tenacious fighter which is a real challenge on lighter lines. They display long runs and can dive deep and tail walk across the surface. The striped marlin is excellent eating, particularly for sashimi and is therefore often retained by commercial fishing boats as it attracts a good price.

MARLIN, BLUE

Rigs and Tactics

MARLIN, STRIPED

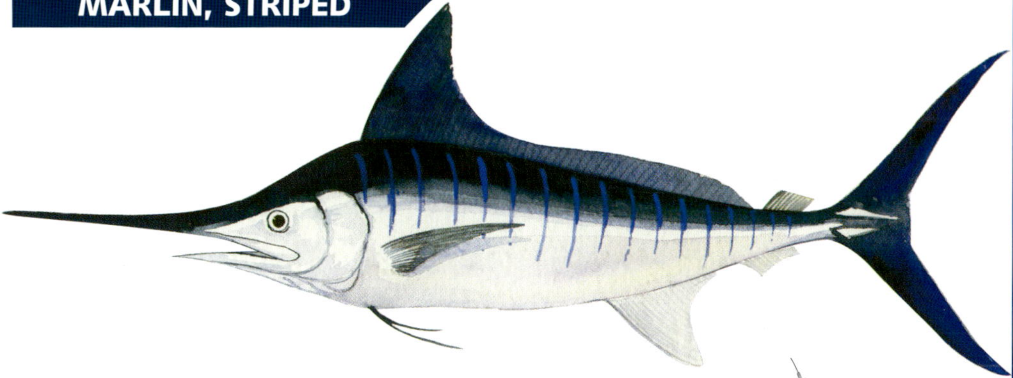

Rigs and Tactics

RAINBOW RUNNER

Scientific name *Elegatis bipunnulata*. Also known as Rainbow yellowtail, runner.

Range Rottnest Island in Western Australia and through tropical waters around to Bermagui in NSW.

Description The rainbow runner is a long powerful fish, similar in appearance to the yellowtail kingfish. However, the rainbow runner has a smaller mouth and obvious small finlets just in front of the tail but behind the dorsal and anal fins. The yellow tail is very deeply forked. The rainbow runner is strikingly coloured, with a deep blue or purple back and a silver belly. There are two to four lengthwise bands of alternating yellow and electric blue near the lateral line giving the fish an appealing appearance. Rainbow runners are schooling fish in all but the largest sizes, which can be more than a metre and more than 7 kilograms. Rainbow runners prefer warm open ocean waters, but are occasionally taken adjacent to deeper water reefs or ledges.

Fishing Most rainbow runners are taken incidentally while trolling small or medium sized minnow or feather lures for mackerel, bonito, tuna and other smaller pelagics. Like other oceanic pelagic species, the rainbow runner feeds mainly in surface or mid waters on small fish and squid. Rainbow runners can also accompany large sharks or rays similar to cobia. If a school of rainbow runners is located, using unweighted or very lightly weighted cut baits or pilchards, garfish or similar whole baits gets the best results. Berley will keep the fish near the boat. They will also take cast lures or flies. The rainbow runner puts up a strong fight with a long first run, but unlike kingfish they will not try to bury the angler by diving straight down. The rainbow runner is fair to good eating, similar to small kingfish, although the flesh is a little darker. Small rainbow runners are among the best live or dead baits trolled for billfish or fished for large sharks.

REMORA

Scientific name *Remora remora* Also known as short suckerfish, suckerfish

Range Around Australia but more common in tropical seas

Description A most unusual species easily identified by the prominent sucker disc on the top of the head which is actually modified dorsal spines. The remora will swim with or attach itself to larger predators such as sharks, manta rays mackerel and even boats or more rarely surprised swimmers. The remoras are more likely to follow a boat if the fish that they were associated with are taken. Remoras can remain attached to a large fish even if it is quickly brought on board. This species reaches 45 cm in length and differs from the slender suckerfish (*Echeneis naucrates*) which can reach 1 m and has a more slender body shape. The slender suckerfish is not found on the south coast and also has a few wide stripes. The remora is generally a consistent brownish-black to mid grey in colour. The remora is less frequently seen swimming alone but they are quite effective foragers in their own right. Remoras were reputedly used by aborigines for catching turtles, allowing a tethered remora to attach to a turtle that could then be retrieved.

Fishing The remora is occasionally taken on baits fished around larger fish. They can be taken by anglers fishing for cobia near manta rays, if there are no cobia to grab the larger baits and they can be a nuisance when following the boat, taking baits as they are dropped into the water. Given their pelagic nature, lightly weighted rigs work well and a variety of baits such as fish, prawns, squid and octopus will take these fish. Even though their appearance is somewhat intimidating, the remora provides a high quality fillet.

RAINBOW RUNNER

Rigs and Tactics

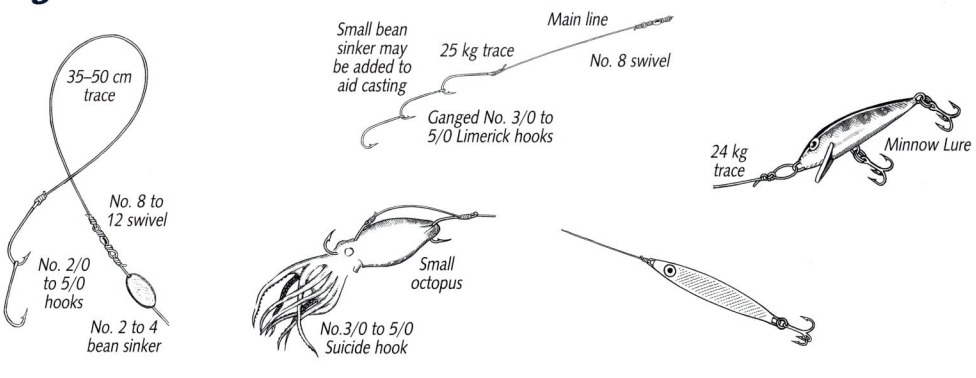

35–50 cm trace

No. 8 to 12 swivel

No. 2/0 to 5/0 hooks

No. 2 to 4 bean sinker

Small bean sinker may be added to aid casting

Main line

25 kg trace

No. 8 swivel

Ganged No. 3/0 to 5/0 Limerick hooks

Small octopus

No. 3/0 to 5/0 Suicide hook

24 kg trace

Minnow Lure

REMORA

Rigs and Tactics

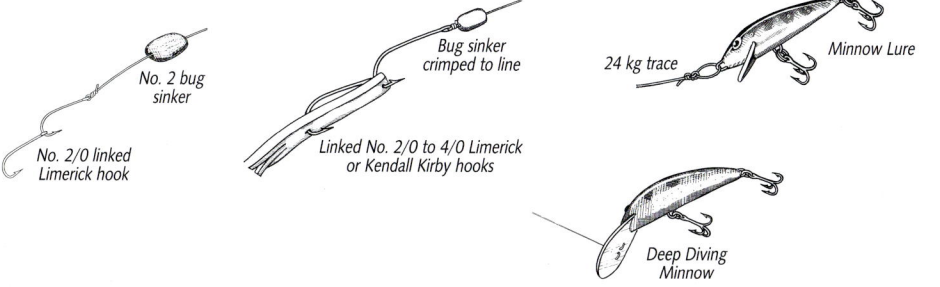

No. 2 bug sinker

No. 2/0 linked Limerick hook

Bug sinker crimped to line

Linked No. 2/0 to 4/0 Limerick or Kendall Kirby hooks

24 kg trace

Minnow Lure

Deep Diving Minnow

SAILFISH, INDO-PACIFIC

Scientific name *Istiophorus platypterus*. Also known as Pacific sailfish, bayonet fish, sailfish.

Range Cape Leeuwin in southern Western Australia and tropical waters around the east coast as far south as Port Stephens in NSW.

Description The Indo-Pacific sailfish is most easily recognised by the prominent sail-like dorsal fin which forms the basis of the common name. The dorsal fin when lowered, fits into a groove. The shorter median dorsal rays are still longer than the body is deep. The characteristic upper jaw spear is slender and more than twice the length of the lower jaw. The ventral rays are very long and extend almost to the anus. The body and sail are spotted with dark and light blue. Stripes on the side may darken after death. Indo-Pacific sailfish can reach 120 kg, but any fish over 45 kg is a proud capture.

Fishing The Indo-Pacific sailfish is a spectacular fish renowned for its spectacular leaps and strong surface runs. The sailfish is one of the smaller billfish but is highly prized, especially as a light line target. Sailfish can be taken by trolling live or dead baits of mullet, mackerel, garfish, rainbow runner or other common medium sized bait fish. Baits enhanced with plastic or feather skirts seem to take more fish. Many fish are taken on lures, including pusher or doorknob type lures or even minnow lures. Sailfish are becoming increasingly targeted with fly gear, as the use of teaser baits or lures can bring lit up sailfish within casting range and their spectacular fight makes them one of the ultimate targets for fly fishing aficionados. Indo-Pacific sailfish are occasionally taken from rocky headlands adjacent to deeper water on drifted live baits or spincasting with baits or lures. Sailfish can travel in small pods and multiple hookups are possible, challenging the skills of all involved. The best sailfishing grounds are undoubtedly off Exmouth, Karratha and Broome in Western Australia, where even fairly small boats can encounter sailfish during peak periods. Sailfish flesh is palatable but not highly regarded and these days all but the record fish are returned to the water, although there are relatively low tag return rates to date.

SAMSON FISH

Scientific name *Seriola hippos*. Also known as Sambo, samson, sea kingfish.

Range Shark Bay in Western Australia to Yorke Peninsula in South Australia then disjointed distribution from around Bribie Island in southern Queensland to Montague Island in NSW.

Description A large and powerful fish capable of reaching 1.8 m and more than 50 kg in weight. Similar in appearance to the closely related yellowtail kingfish, but the samson fish is a much cleaner fighter which does not usually bury the angler on any available reef. The samson fish is best separated by counting the second dorsal rays which has 23 – 25 as opposed to 31 or over for yellowtail kingfish. The 16 – 17 anal rays on the samson fish distinguish this species from the amberjack which has 19 or more anal rays and 29 to 35 second dorsal rays. The samson fish also has a more rounded forehead which is more pronounced in younger fish. The flesh surrounding the teeth in both jaws in the samson fish is often but not always engorged with blood, giving the tooth patches a red appearance. The colour varies but the samson fish can often have distinct vertical blotches which, while fading with age, are not found in the other similar species.

Fishing A real challenge on light gear as skillful handling can present some extremely large fish due to their relatively clean, strong fight. Samson fish can be taken at all depths from nearshore waters to around 60 fathoms. They can be found near sand patches, around reefs or seagrass and can take whiting, garfish or other small fish from surprised anglers. Best baits are live fish, whole fresh dead fish, fillets, pilchard, octopus, squid or crabs. Samson fish can be taken on deep vertical fished jigs and rarely on trolled lures. Small samson fish make good eating, but large fish over 15 kg are best returned to fight another day. Large fish in particular can be infected with a parasite which causes the flesh to virtually disintegrate on cooking. The aggregations near Rottnest island in WA provides unbelievable sport fishing on jigs over summer. Tagged fish have been recaptured is Esperance less than a month later- which is truly remarkable.

SAILFISH, INDO-PACIFIC

Rigs and Tactics

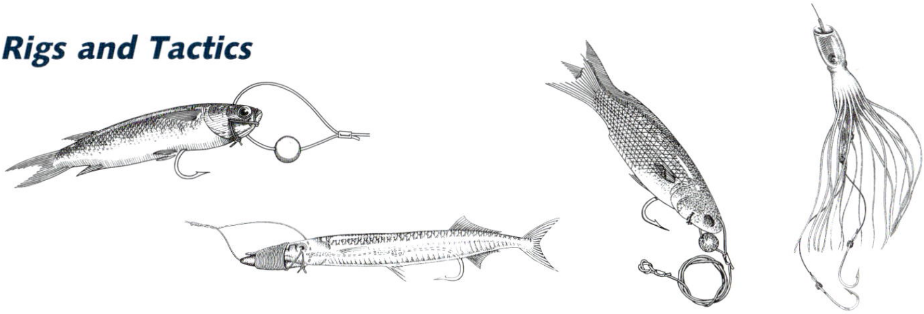

SAMSON FISH

Rigs and Tactics

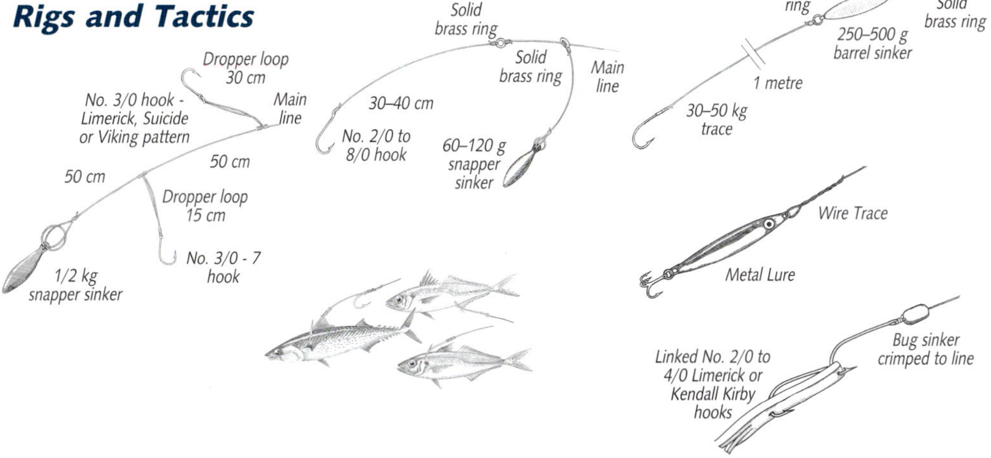

Dropper loop
30 cm

No. 3/0 hook -
Limerick, Suicide
or Viking pattern

Main
line

50 cm

50 cm

Dropper loop
15 cm

No. 3/0 - 7
hook

1/2 kg
snapper sinker

Solid
brass ring

30–40 cm

Solid
brass ring

No. 2/0 to
8/0 hook

60–120 g
snapper
sinker

Main
line

Solid brass
ring

250–500 g
barrel sinker

Solid
brass ring

1 metre

30–50 kg
trace

Wire Trace

Metal Lure

Linked No. 2/0 to
4/0 Limerick or
Kendall Kirby
hooks

Bug sinker
crimped to line

SPEARFISH, PACIFIC SHORTBILL

Scientific name *Tetrapturus angustirostiris*. Also known as Shortbill spearfish.

Range The Pacific shortbill swordfish is quite rare in Australian waters. The range is presumed to be from Cape Leeuwin in Western Australia and northern waters as far south as around Montague Island in southern NSW.

Description The Pacific shortbill spearfish is a long slender species readily identified by the fact that the upper jaw is only marginally longer than the lower jaw. The other distinct feature is the wide separation between the anus and the anal fin. In other billfish the anal fin commences near the anus. The Pacific shortbill spearfish reaches 2 m in length.

Fishing The Pacific shortbill spearfish is a rare capture in Australian waters. They will take trolled lures intended for other billfish species. They are an incidental but welcome catch in warmer waters. The Pacific shortbill spearfish exhibits slashing jumps and long runs, but they are often outgunned on the heavy tackle intended for larger marlin. This species is only kept for record purposes.

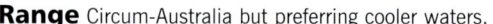

SUNFISH

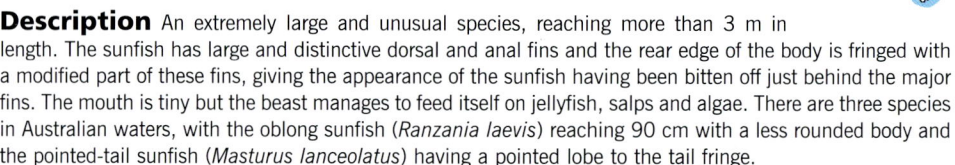

Scientific name *Mola ramsayi*. Also known as Southern sunfish, short sunfish, southern ocean sunfish, Ramsay's ocean sunfish.

Range Circum-Australia but preferring cooler waters.

Description An extremely large and unusual species, reaching more than 3 m in length. The sunfish has large and distinctive dorsal and anal fins and the rear edge of the body is fringed with a modified part of these fins, giving the appearance of the sunfish having been bitten off just behind the major fins. The mouth is tiny but the beast manages to feed itself on jellyfish, salps and algae. There are three species in Australian waters, with the oblong sunfish (*Ranzania laevis*) reaching 90 cm with a less rounded body and the pointed-tail sunfish (*Masturus lanceolatus*) having a pointed lobe to the tail fringe.

Fishing The sunfish is not taken by recreational anglers, but can be seen on the surface, with the dorsal fin cutting the surface as a shark would. Sunfish can be washed ashore after storms and they can be hit by boats as they loll about on the surface. The sunfish is poor eating.

SWORDFISH, BROADBILL

Scientific name *Xiphias gladius*. Also known as Broadbill, swordfish.

Range Circum-Australia but preferring cooler, temperate waters

Description The broadbill swordfish is easily recognised by a long, broad, flattened sword, a single fleshy keel along the caudal peduncle (tail wrist) and the absence of ventral fins. The broadbill swordfish also has a prominent eye, suited to predation at great depths which these fish can frequent. The broadbill can reach more than 500 kg in Chilean waters, and specimens over 300 kg have been taken in Australian waters by commercial longliners. Only a few small broadbill swordfish have been taken by recreational anglers in Australia.

Fishing The broadbill is regarded as the ultimate challenge by gamefishermen. The few Australian broadbill have been taken at 10 to 90 m depths by drifting at night near the edge of the Continental Shelf with squid baits fitted with cyalume light sticks. However, extreme patience and perseverance are required to actually land one of these hard fighting fish, with baits set at a variety of depths and a keen eye required for international shipping coming too close during the night. In other parts of the world broadbill swordfish can be taken trolling live or dead baits or even casting baits to sighted fish, although they are very rarely sighted at the surface in Australia. The broadbill swordfish is considered excellent eating and is highly sought after by commercial fishermen, although large specimens can have large quantities of mercury.

SPEARFISH, PACIFIC SHORTBILL

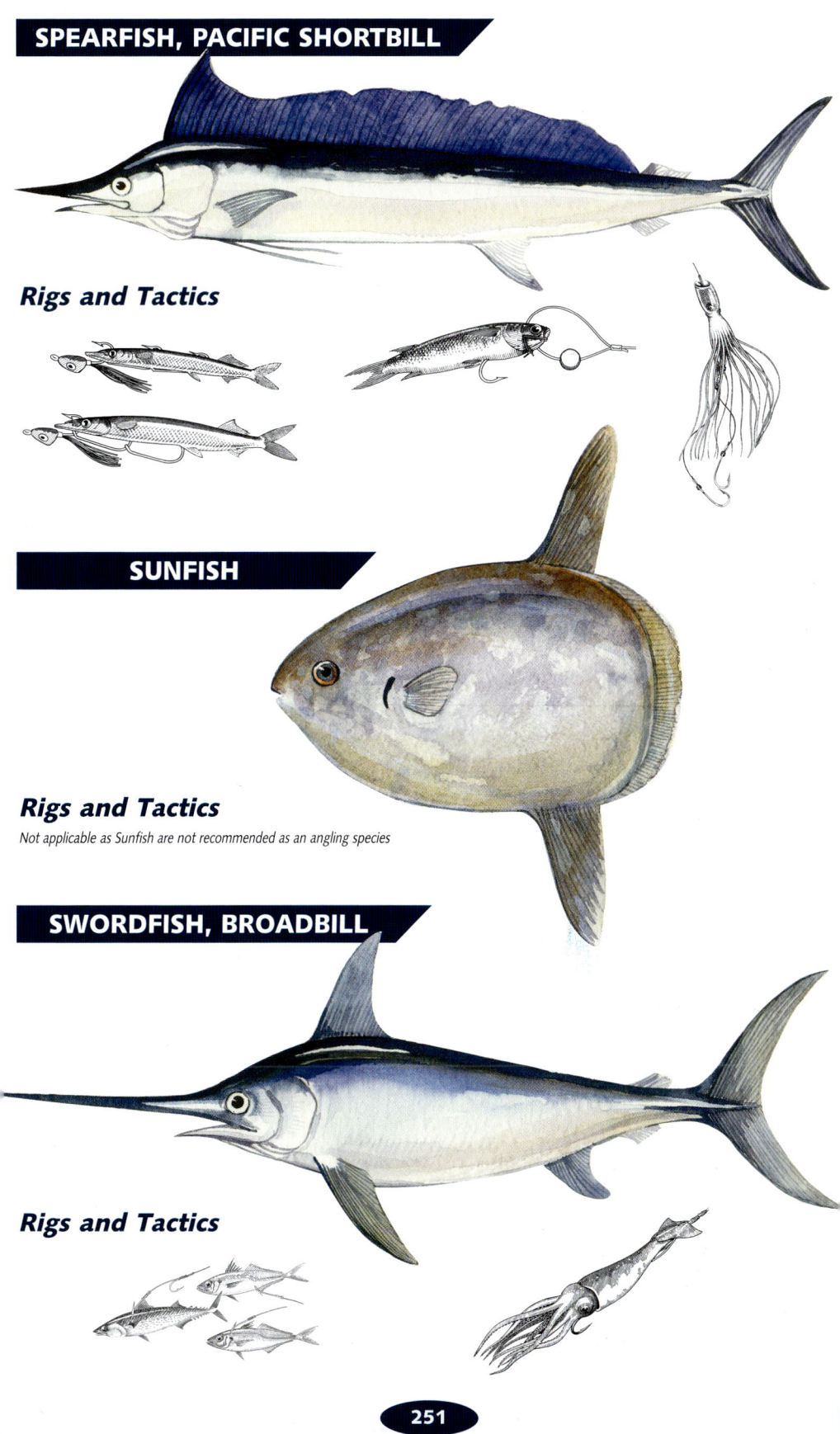

Rigs and Tactics

SUNFISH

Rigs and Tactics

Not applicable as Sunfish are not recommended as an angling species

SWORDFISH, BROADBILL

Rigs and Tactics

TUNA, BIGEYE

Scientific name *Thunnus obesus.*

Range Most of Australia except Tasmania, but more common in warmer waters and moving further south in summer. Most commonly from around Albany in Western Australia and northern waters as far south as Montague Island in NSW.

Description The eye is large and the bigeye tuna is quite heavy set. The anal and second dorsal fin lobes, although elongated are not obviously extended. The pectoral fin extends to the commencement of the second dorsal lobe which readily separates this species from the bluefins with shorter pectoral fins and the albacore with its extremely long pectoral fin. Small bigeye tuna are often confused with small yellowfin tuna which do not have the obvious sickle-like anal and second dorsal fins. In small bigeye tuna the eye is larger, the liver is prominently striated (with ridges and grooves) and they do not have whitish bars across the body. A prominent keel near the tail base is located between two smaller keels with the bigeye. The bigeye favours offshore waters and is commonly taken by longlining off the Continental Shelf, although juveniles can be taken in inshore waters. It can reach 2.35 m in length and nearly 200 kg, but Australian specimens are generally smaller than 40 – 50 kilograms.

Fishing The bigeye tuna is regarded as one of the most prized gamefish, with its dogged fight and deep circling forcing the angler to fight for every centimetre of line. The bigeye tuna can be taken while trolling lures such as minnow, pusher or squid trolling lures or lures like the Halco Trembler. Trolling baits such as garfish, slimey mackerel, small striped tuna or other fish works well. Larger bigeye are taken fishing with large live or whole dead baits in bluewater, either in known feeding areas or patiently fished deeper. Bigeye tuna will also respond to berley and cubing can take these fish. Lines should fit the size of the fish and tackle must be first rate to withstand the punishment of these fish. Large bigeye tuna bring the highest price for sashimi with good reason. Small fish make excellent sashimi right on the boat and many fishermen carry soy and wasabi sauce for an immediate feast. Bigeye tuna are also excellent cooked in a variety of recipes.

TUNA, DOG-TOOTH

Scientific name *Gymnosarda unicolor.* Also known as Dog-tooth, lizard-mouth tuna, white tuna, scaleless tuna.

Range Onslow in Western Australia and through tropical waters as far south as around Rockhampton in Queensland. The species is more common off the north-east near the Great Barrier Reef.

Description The dog-tooth tuna can reach 150 cm and a record weight of 130 kilograms. In Australia, this tropical water speedster is more commonly caught from 2 to 40 kg with some fish between 50 to 60 kg to really test the angler. The dog-tooth tuna is most commonly found in clear deep water at the edges of outer reefs, deep drop-offs and reef passages. The dog-tooth tuna is easily identified by its large conical teeth. Although related to the bonitos, the dog-tooth tuna does not have any stripes on its back or flanks. The dog-tooth is also scale-less except for a small patch under the pectoral fins. The lateral line is prominent and wavy which is unusual.

Fishing Like many species, dog-tooth tuna form schools of similar sized fish, with larger fish becoming increasingly solitary. The dog-tooth tuna is an aggressive predator which can be susceptible to overfishing. They will take a variety of fish baits, squid, octopus and large crabs. As dog-tooth tuna are a deeper water fish, lures which run deeply or are fished on downriggers near deep drop-offs take the most fish. Minnow or spoon type lures work best. Although they will take pusher and squid type lures, but their teeth can damage plastic skirts. Dog-tooth tuna can be taken on slow trolled baits of small mackerel, garfish or other fish but catches are improved if the baits are weighted or trolled very slowly at greater depth than for marlin or other tuna. Live baits either slow trolled or fished quite deeply, but above the bottom, work very well.
The dog-tooth tuna makes excellent eating and has pinkish-white flesh.

TUNA, BIGEYE

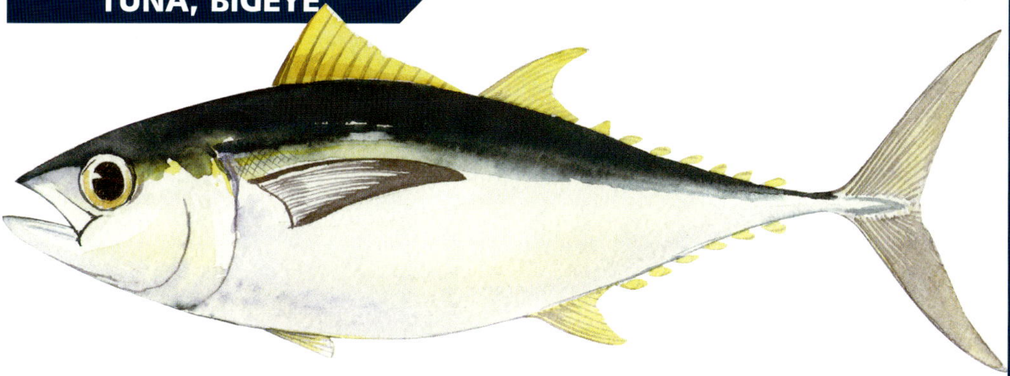

Rigs and Tactics

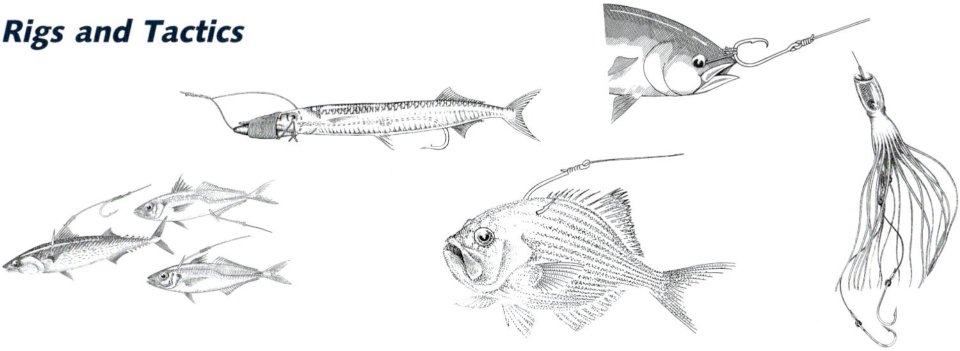

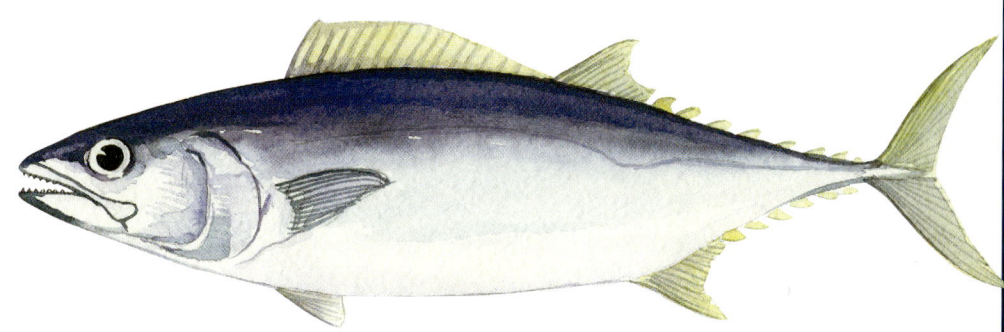

TUNA, DOG-TOOTH

Rigs and Tactics

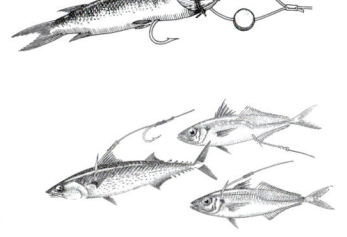

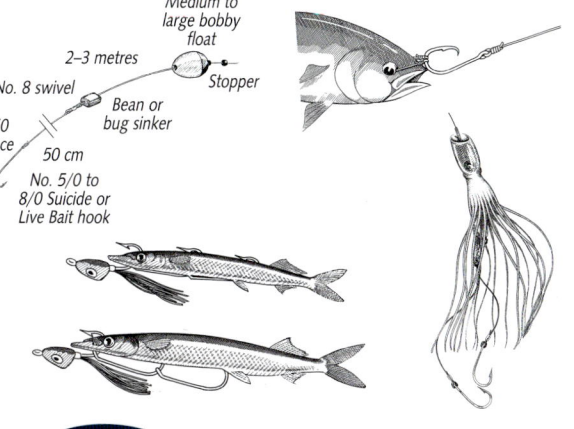

Medium to large bobby float
2–3 metres
Stopper
No. 8 swivel
Bean or bug sinker
30–50 kg trace
50 cm
No. 5/0 to 8/0 Suicide or Live Bait hook

TUNA, LONGTAIL

Scientific name *Thunnus tonggol*. Also known as Northern bluefin tuna, northern blue.

Range Geographe Bay in Western Australia and northwards including tropical waters and as far south on the east coast as Eden in southern NSW.

Description The name longtail comes from the light build to the rear half of this species, giving a narrow tail wrist and a slender outline. The pectoral fin is very short and finishes well in front of the start of the second dorsal fin which readily separates the species from yellowfin and bigeye tuna. This species is much more common in tropical waters but can migrate southwards in summer.

Fishing In tropical waters, small longtails can form vast schools like mackerel tuna or bonito. These schools move rapidly and fish can be caught by casting lures or trolling lures or baits near the edge of the feeding school. Minnow lures, lead slugs or Christmas tree lures, feather jigs, spoons and flies all work well with larger fish preferring larger lures and a faster retrieve. Longtail prefer inshore waters and although most are taken by anglers in boats, longtail are a highly prized land based game species. Specialised gear with live baits below large floats or balloons or high speed spinning can bring these speedsters to the rocks. As with all rock based fishing, special care should be taken of wave conditions, especially when landing large fish. Longtail love live baits fished from boats and cubing (berleying with tuna flesh and feeding unweighted cubes into the trail, one with a hook) can work well once a school is located. Longtail tuna are red fleshed and of lower quality than many species, but it is greatly improved with immediate bleeding.

TUNA, MACKEREL

Scientific name *Euthynnus affinis*. Also known as Jack mackerel, little tuna, kawa-kawa.

Range Cape Leeuwin in Western Australia northwards and throughout northern waters as far south as Merimbula in NSW.

Description The mackerel tuna is a highly prized lightweight game species which is caught in inshore waters or larger bays, harbours and large estuarine systems as well as offshore islands or larger reefs. The mackerel tuna can reach 1 m in length and 12 kg but is much more common at 2 – 8 kilograms. The mackerel tuna has prominent wavy green lines in the rear portion of the body above the midline. The mackerel tuna is similar to the frigate mackerel but the first dorsal of the mackerel tuna reaches almost to the second dorsal while the frigate mackerel's first dorsal is short and widely separated from the second dorsal fin. The mackerel tuna has two to five dark spots above the ventral fin and more prominent teeth than the frigate mackerel which also only reaches 58 cm in length.

Fishing The mackerel tuna is a schooling fish which feeds heavily on pilchards, herrings, whitebait, anchovies, squid and occasionally krill. However, even when a feeding school is located, they can be very selective and difficult to entice to strike. Mackerel tuna are mainly taken on fast trolled or high speed retrieved lures such as plastic skirted lures, Christmas tree lures, minnow lures, plastic squids, lead jigs and feather lures and spoons. The mackerel tuna will take live baits, fresh dead baits either cast and retrieved, trolled or fished under a float. They will more rarely take cut baits. Mackerel tuna are a frequent catch of high speed land based game fishermen. Mackerel tuna have dark and sinewy meat which is best steamed and served with sauces or used as berley or cut bait.

TUNA, LONGTAIL

Rigs and Tactics

Medium to
large bobby
float

2–3 metres

Stopper

No. 8 swivel

Bean or
bug sinker

30–50 kg
trace

50 cm

No. 5/0 to
8/0 Suicide or
Live Bait hook

Wire Trace

Metal Lure

TUNA, MACKEREL

Rigs and Tactics

TUNA, SOUTHERN BLUEFIN

Scientific name *Thunnus maccoyii.* Also known as SBT, southern blue, bluefin, bluey, tunny.

Range A cool water species more common in southern waters but the only identified breeding area is off the north-west coast of Western Australia in International waters where they have been heavily exploited. The range is from the North-west coast of Western Australia and southwards along the south coast including Tasmania and as far as Montague Island in southern NSW. Larger fish are found near the Victoria/NSW border, but commercial over-exploitation has severely reduced the number of large fish found off the south-east.

Description The southern bluefin tuna is a heavily built and very highly prized species which prefers open oceanic waters, especially in larger sizes. The southern bluefin tuna can grow to greater than 150 kg but is most commonly caught well below this size. Small southern bluefin can be found in inshore waters and weigh from 3 – 25 kg, with the average size generally increasing as you move eastwards along the southern coast. Southern bluefin tuna have been overexploited by commercial fishing operations, especially on the high seas. The commercial overexploitation has lead to the development of extensive aquaculture, based around Port Lincoln to on-grow these fish; a process which previously occurred naturally before overfishing of juveniles removed larger adults from the south-east. Southern bluefin tuna can be identified by their heavy bodies, and the short pectoral fins which do not extend to the second dorsal. The dorsal and anal lobes are also short as opposed to the yellowfin with its scythe-like lobes in larger fish. The finlets at the rear of the body are edged with black and the caudal keels on the wrist of the tail are conspicuously yellow, especially in the sizes normally encountered by recreational fishers.

Fishing The southern bluefin tuna schools at all sizes although the larger fish form much smaller schools. Small fish can move close to shore if deeper water is nearby and can be taken by land based gamefishers. Most southern bluefin tuna are taken on trolled lures, with rubber squids, pushers and other gamefishing lures working well. They will also take minnow lures, feathers, slices and large lead slugs. They can be taken on fly. Southern bluefin tuna like offshore debris and can be taken with mahi-mahi around floating logs, shipping containers or other large flotsam in bluewater areas. The southern bluefin tuna can be taken on cast lures, but they can often hang at depth and downriggers can be productive, especially when a sounder indicates fish holding at a specific depth. Southern bluefin tuna are less frequently taken on baits, although they can be taken on trolled baits, live baits or dead baits including cubes, especially if used with berley. Deep fished live baits or whole squid can take larger fish, but local knowledge is necessary as there is lots of water between the larger fish. The Southern bluefin tuna is a highly prized gamefish species which fights hard and is a considerable challenge on lighter tackle. The southern bluefin tuna has rich dark meat which is highly prized for sashimi. These fish are much improved by being bled and chilled soon after capture.

Rigs and Tactics

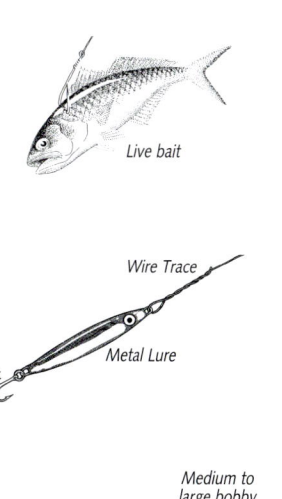

Live bait

Wire Trace

Metal Lure

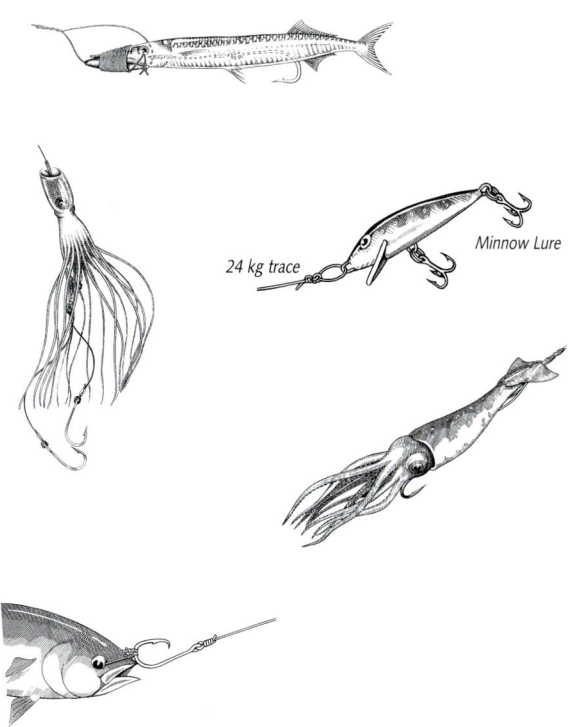

24 kg trace

Minnow Lure

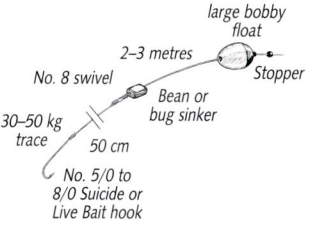

Medium to
large bobby
float

2–3 metres

No. 8 swivel

Stopper

Bean or
bug sinker

30–50 kg
trace

50 cm

No. 5/0 to
8/0 Suicide or
Live Bait hook

TUNA, YELLOWFIN

Scientific name *Thunnus albacares.* Also known as Allison tuna, yellowfin or 'fin, ahi.

Range Circum-Australia but less common along the south coast and Tasmania.

Description The yellowfin tuna is a beautiful, powerful and challenging species which prefers warmer currents but may move inshore where deep water comes close to the coast. This species can be taken from shore in southern NSW in summer where they provide an extraordinary battle for those with the specialised tackle, patience and skill to tackle them. The yellowfin tuna is easily separated from other tunas by the scythe-like dorsal and anal lobes in adult fish. The pectoral fin is long and extends to the commencement of the second dorsal fin. Small yellowfin have short dorsal and anal lobes, but have whitish bars down the sides which may disappear after death. The liver of yellowfin tuna is smooth as opposed to the ridged liver of the bigeye. The caudal keels (ridges) on the wrist of the tail are also dusky and never yellow as in the southern bluefin tuna. Yellowfin tuna can reach more than 200 kg in other parts of the world, but in Australia fish over 100 kg are magnificent and most fish are between 2 and 50 kilograms.

Fishing Yellowfin tuna form schools at all sizes but fish over 40 kg are more likely to be travelling alone. Yellowfin tuna are a dogged and extremely challenging fish to catch, frequently diving deeply and circling under the boat, forcing the angler to pull against the broad sides of the fish every centimetre of the way to the boat. Smaller yellowfin are frequently taken on cast, or more likely trolled lures. Best lures include plastic squids, pusher lures, slices, minnow lures and feathers. Yellowfin will take flies, but berley and/or teaser lures to bring the fish to the back of the boat will greatly increase hook-ups. Landing the fish on fly gear is another matter altogether. Medium and large yellowfin may be taken on lures, but in some locations they are difficult to take with this method. Live baits either trolled or fished near clean current lines will entice strikes from larger fish. Big yellowfin will take live baits up to 5 kilograms. Yellowfin respond well to berley. Feeding cubes of tuna or cut pilchards into a berley trail can bring fish right to the transom. Putting a hook into a cube can bring a real test of gear as a large yellowfin tuna on short line tests the drag, rod and angler to the limit. The yellowfin is rated with albacore as the best tuna for cooking. For sashimi, the yellowfin is generally regarded behind bigeye and southern bluefin tuna, but a fat specimen is world class eating. Bleeding and chilling the fish greatly improves the quality.

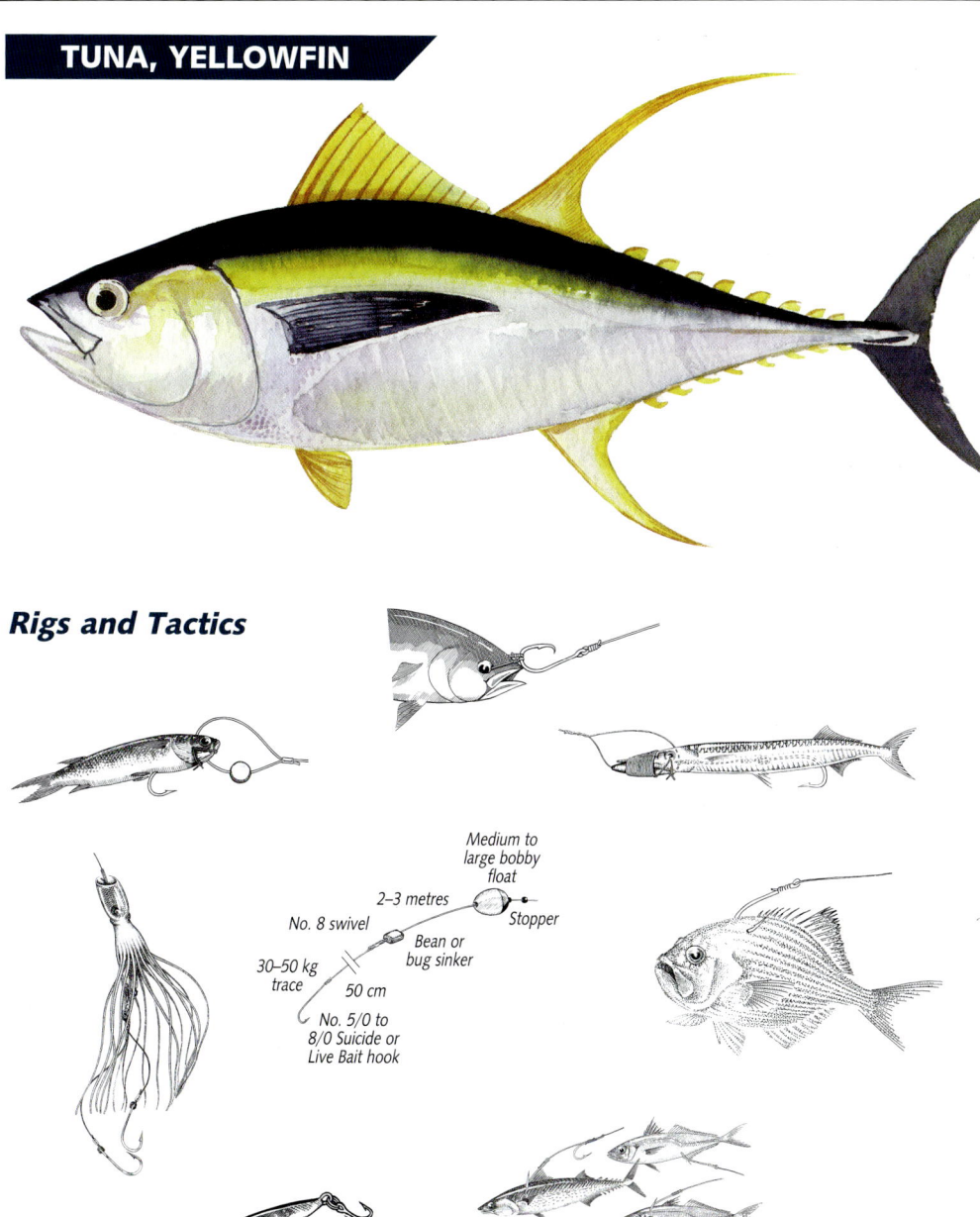

Rigs and Tactics

Medium to large bobby float

2–3 metres

Stopper

No. 8 swivel

Bean or bug sinker

30–50 kg trace

50 cm

No. 5/0 to 8/0 Suicide or Live Bait hook

24 kg trace

Minnow Lure

TUNA, STRIPED

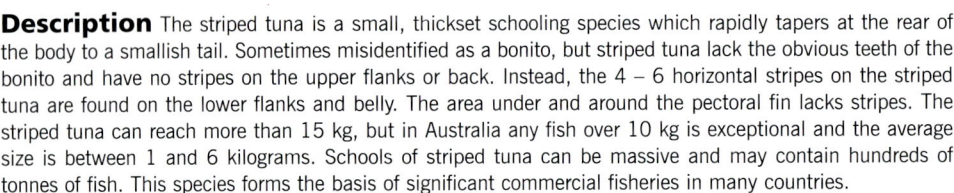

Scientific name *Katsuwonis pelamis*. Also known as Skipjack, skipjack tuna, stripey, aku.

Range Circum-Australia but more common in temperate waters between 17 – 25 degrees Celsius.

Description The striped tuna is a small, thickset schooling species which rapidly tapers at the rear of the body to a smallish tail. Sometimes misidentified as a bonito, but striped tuna lack the obvious teeth of the bonito and have no stripes on the upper flanks or back. Instead, the 4 – 6 horizontal stripes on the striped tuna are found on the lower flanks and belly. The area under and around the pectoral fin lacks stripes. The striped tuna can reach more than 15 kg, but in Australia any fish over 10 kg is exceptional and the average size is between 1 and 6 kilograms. Schools of striped tuna can be massive and may contain hundreds of tonnes of fish. This species forms the basis of significant commercial fisheries in many countries.

Fishing Striped tuna are mainly taken on lures trolled or cast from boats, deep shores or jetties which extend to deeper water. Many striped tuna are taken on heavy cord lines and Smiths jigs to be used as bait or berley. Striped tuna provide excellent sport on lighter lines as they are very hard fighting speedsters. Most bright lures which work well at around 5 knots will take striped tuna, with Christmas tree style lures working well. Slices, slug lures, feather jigs, small poppers and medium sized flies also take good numbers of fish, although striped tuna can be finicky about size and action type of lures at times. Striped tuna can be taken on pilchards, cut baits or squid, especially if a berley trail excites the fish. Larger fish can take small live baits. Striped tuna have very dark red meat which is quite strongly flavoured but is suitable for smoking, salting and canning. If bled and chilled immediately they are fair eating. However, striped tuna are excellent live baits for large pelagics and their cut flesh makes a first rate bait or berley where their oil rich red flesh attracts most species.

WAHOO

Scientific name *Acanthocybium solandri*. Also known as Ono, 'hoo.

Range Kalbarri in Western Australia and all northern waters and as far south as Montague Island in southern NSW.

Description The wahoo is a long and sleek pelagic species which is capable of very fast movement in the water. Most wahoo in Australian waters are between 8 and 30 kg but they can reach 65 kilograms. The wahoo is a solitary open water species which can be identified by the long and higher dorsal fin of approximately even height. The dorsal fin starts behind the commencement of the pectoral fin while with the Spanish mackerel it commences at the leading edge of the pectoral. The head is longer and more pointed with the wahoo and the trailing edge of the tail fin is vertical compared to the forked tail of the other mackerels. The wahoo has a number of prominent zebra-like vertical stripes along the body but these are less noticeable in some especially larger specimens and fade considerably after death.

Fishing The wahoo favours offshore blue water and temperatures between 21 and 30 degrees Celsius. Wahoo are frequently found near the surface and can be found above deep reef drop-offs and offshore reef pinnacles. Many wahoo are taken on trolled lures such as squids, pusher or Konahead type lures, bibless minnows, feather jigs or large slices. Wahoo can take lures trolled faster than for most tuna species. The teeth of wahoo can severely damage rubber skirts and wooden lures. Wahoo are criticised by many marlin trollers for their habit of coming behind a perfectly swimming bait and chopping off the tail immediately behind the hook. Wahoo can be taken on a variety of skip or swimming baits. A wire trace is an advantage, but many wahoo are hooked lightly due to their tailing tendency on baits or lures. Wahoo are seldom specifically targeted in Australia but are a welcome catch when hooked due to their blistering runs and frequent direction changes during the fight. Wahoo are excellent eating. Parasites which are commonly found in the wahoo's gut do not affect the taste or quality of the flesh.

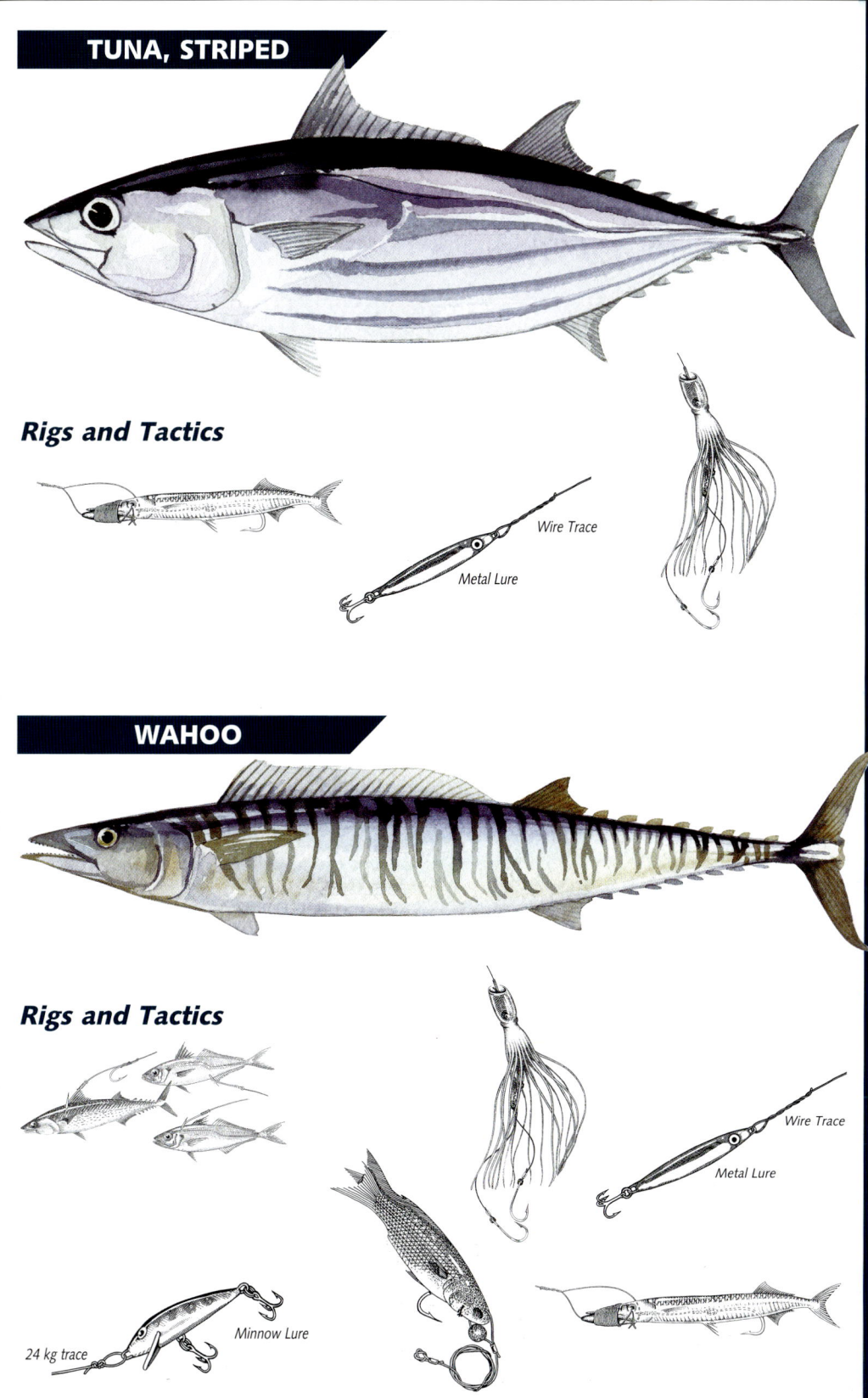

TUNA, STRIPED

Rigs and Tactics

Wire Trace

Metal Lure

WAHOO

Rigs and Tactics

Wire Trace

Metal Lure

24 kg trace

Minnow Lure

CALAMARI, SOUTHERN

Scientific name *Sepioteuthis australis* Also known as calamari, calamari squid, southern squid.

Range Shark Bay in Western Australia and southern waters including Tasmania as far north as southern Queensland.

Description A moderate sized and lightly framed squid with smooth skin that reaches up to 50 cm in length. The fins extend along the entire length of the body, forming a diamond shape. Like most squid, there are eight arms and two extendable feeding tentacles, however the arms and tips of the feeding tentacles have suckers with a horny teethed rim which can grip very well when handling the southern calamari. The colour patterns are generally yellow-green to orange but can vary rapidly while chasing bait, being handled or in a bucket of water. There are often three or four dark bars across the upper or lower surfaces of the body. The shell or 'pen' is almost transparent and quite thin as opposed to the heavy shell of the cuttlefish. The southern calamari is common in shallow inshore waters, often in sand habitats and seagrass meadows. It is more active at night but can also be regularly caught during the day. Smaller calamari form small schools and largest specimens tend to be solitary. They are attracted to lights. Their main defences are jetting away from danger and ink squirting but they also camouflage well amongst weed. The southern calamari can eject its ink quite a distance and always seems to have just that little bit left for when you try and unhook it. Most anglers allow the squid to squirt several times before bringing them on board, but boating a recently hooked squid on board was a way to repay family members who had cast aspersions on angling ability. The ink washes out and is prized as part of a pasta sauce.

Fishing Calamari are one of the species that inspires celebration of Australia's multicultural history. Once despised or used solely as bait, many anglers target little else and rate them above many of the smaller finfish that are also found in similar areas. The southern calamari is delightful eating and fresh caught ones that are ringed and very quickly cooked in a batter of two parts flour and one part salt and one part pepper are divine. Southern calamari will take most fish baits and can be a nuisance, attacking live baits set for other species. They can be frustrating to hook on a gang hook rig, but a bait rigged on a squid jig will get you a quality feed. The special cloth covered squid jigs work extremely well and everyone has a favourite colour or pattern. A better quality squid jig will catch more squid. A slow jerky retrieve will work best. While a small live southern calamari makes an excellent bait and larger ones make a great bottom bait, this is a waste of such a great meal.

CRAB, BLUE SWIMMER

Scientific name *Portunus pelagicus.* Also known as Blue manna crab, blue swimmer, blue crab, sand crab, bluey.

Range The blue swimmer crab is the only decapod crustacean with a distribution around the entire Australian continent although it is more common in temperate waters.

Description The blue swimmer crab is an extremely attractive lightly bodied crab with finely textured and very sweet meat. The claws are long and tinged in blue, white or purple. There are no obvious spots on the back of the carapace. They are most commonly found in lower reaches of estuaries. There are obvious points or spikes at the widest point of the body. Queensland and Western Australia measure the blue swimmer crab across the carapace while in NSW the length of the body from between the eyes to the back of the body is used. The belly is white. Males have a narrow pointed flap at the back of the carapace, while in females the flap is broader and may have eggs attached.

Fishing Blue swimmer crabs are caught with witches hat nets or two hoop drop nets baited with fish or meat. Care should be used when using spleen as bait as it takes a very long time to break down in the water. Witches hat nets are illegal in some states and there are mesh size restrictions so check with the relevant authorities before fishing. In Western Australia blue swimmer crabs can be taken by divers with a scoop net, but taking anything with scuba is prohibited in most parts of Australia. Blue swimmer crabs are sometimes taken on baited lines, although they will usually release the bait near the surface, but a scoop net can catch these tasty crustaceans. Blue swimmer crabs are excellent eating and rated by many as their favourite crustacean.

CALAMARI, SOUTHERN

Rigs and Tactics

Live bait

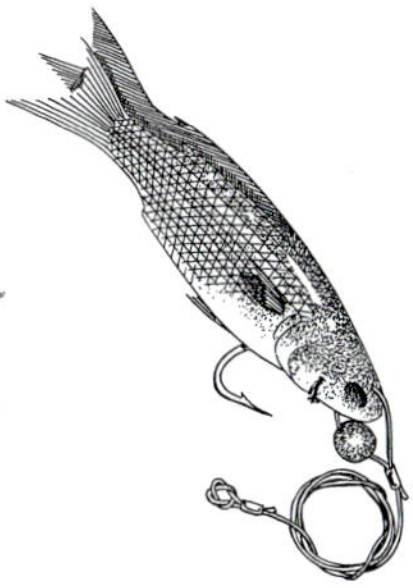

CRAB, BLUE SWIMMER

Rigs and Tactics

Use baited witches hat or two hoop drop nets.

CRAB, MUD

Scientific name *Scylla serrata*. Also known as Mangrove crab, muddie, brown mud crab, black mud crab.

Range Kalbarri in Western Australia and tropical waters to southern NSW. Most common from Exmouth to the Hawkesbury River near Sydney.

Description A heavy bodied and heavy clawed crab species which is commonly found near mud banks or flats and mangroves. The body is olive, brown or black and the gripping pegs on the inside of the claws are frequently orange or beige. A very similar species, the green mud crab is found in cleaner water in Western Australia. It is very difficult to differentiate from the more common mud crab other than it is smaller in size, is olive or olive-green in colour and is found in cleaner 'green' water whereas the brown mud crab is found in nearshore tidal and 'brown' water. Mud crabs are much more common in Queensland and the Northern Territory where mangroves and fertile mud flats are more common.

Fishing Mud crabs can be found in burrows at low tide, frequently in mud banks near mangroves. They move out over the flats as the tide rises. Mud crabs can be caught with a blunt hook in their burrows in some places. This can be a dirty and challenging method as a large and unhappy mud crab looks for something to latch onto upon being removed from its burrow. Mud crabs can severely damage or destroy a witches hat net or hoop drop net. In some areas they are taken in traps, but regulations vary and should be checked. Female mud crabs are protected in Queensland, but the reason is historical much more than biological for this regulation. On capture, the claws of a mud crab are generally tied with twine which involves skill, bravado and dexterity with bare toes and large mud crabs. The mud crab is considered excellent eating which is reflected in the high price to purchase this species. Chili mud crab is one of Queensland's delicacies.

CRAB, SAND

Scientific name *Portunus ovalipes*. Also known as Red-spot crab, surf crab, nicky crab

Range From Rottnest Island in Western Australia and southern waters including Tasmania, up to Wide Bay in Queensland.

Description A medium sized crab, often found in shallow waters of surf beaches and estuaries. The body is cream or light brown coloured with two distinctive red or maroon spots near the rear of the carapace. A similar species is found from deeper water in Queensland, known as the red-spot crab which has three red spots surrounded by a white fringe.

Fishing The sand crab is commonly brought to the surge zone in the surf after having grabbed hold of a meat, fish or even squid bait and trying to eat it. The sand crab will often burrow into the sand. The sand crab can be a by-catch when using drop nets for blue swimmer crabs in places such as Geographe Bay in Western Australia, but they are rarely targeted. They are sometimes found in fish shops as commercial beach seiners can take them in reasonable quantities at times. The sand crab is considered quite good eating, but is often small enough to make getting the meat a reasonable task.

CRAB, SOLDIER

Scientific name *Myctiris longicarpus*. Also known as blue army crab

Range southern Queensland to southern NSW

Description A small and attractive crab of about 25 - 30 mm that emerges in huge numbers from estuarine sand flats, especially those near mangroves. This crab is small with a beautiful sky blue shell. The legs are cream with maroon or light brown leg joints. The soldier crab is very round in shape and the claws are relatively small.

Fishing At low tide, soldier crabs can be easily gathered by following the legions of crabs that scurry across the flats. Even when approached, they burrow shallowly into the sand and can be dug out easily. They are often taken in small numbers when pumping for nippers. Soldier crabs are used for bream bait and for whiting in estuaries but are less effective than nippers which are often found in similar areas. The soldier crab is an important part of the estuarine ecology and makes a low tide visit to the flats memorable. They can easily be over-exploited so only small numbers should be taken or local requirements followed.

CRAB, MUD

Rigs and Tactics
Use baited nets or traps.

CRAB, SAND

CRAB, SOLDIER

CUTTLEFISH

Scientific name *Sepia apama*. Also known as giant cuttlefish, Australian cuttlefish

Range Ningaloo in Western Australia and southern waters including some parts of Tasmania as far as Port Jackson in NSW.

Description The cuttlefish species most common in southern Australian waters is one of the world's largest species reaching 5 kilograms and 60 cm main body length. The cuttlefish is easily separated from other cephalopods because of the thickness and size of the shell. This shell is the cuttlebone which delights budgies the world over and is often found washed up on beaches after a storm. The cuttlefish feeds on small fish, crabs or prawns by shooting out two tentacles which are normally carried in small pouches near the eyes. The cuttlefish also possesses excellent camouflage. Cuttlefish can be found in depths of up to 50 metres and can move into inshore waters to breed, in winter, where they can be tracked by predatory fish such as snapper.

Fishing Cuttlefish can be taken with squid jigs, but they are less commonly specifically targeted. They are also more easily taken on fish baits and can be an interesting by-catch when bottom bouncing in cooler waters. The cuttlefish possesses the same inking capability as the squids but when in jumbo sizes can eject lots of ink a long way - don't say you haven't been warned! The cuttlefish makes excellent bait but is slightly less highly regarded for food than the squid as large cuttlefish can tend to be tougher and require more careful preparation and skinning.

LIMPET

Scientific name *Family Littorinidae*. Also known as cling shells.

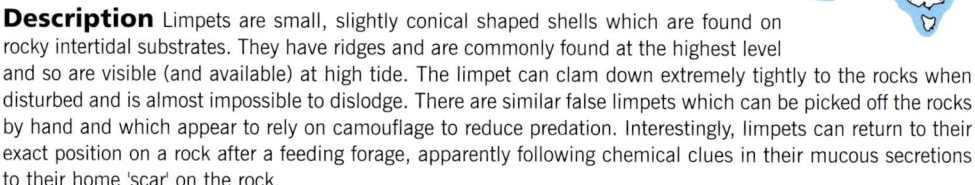

Range Various species of limpets are found around Australia.

Description Limpets are small, slightly conical shaped shells which are found on rocky intertidal substrates. They have ridges and are commonly found at the highest level and so are visible (and available) at high tide. The limpet can clam down extremely tightly to the rocks when disturbed and is almost impossible to dislodge. There are similar false limpets which can be picked off the rocks by hand and which appear to rely on camouflage to reduce predation. Interestingly, limpets can return to their exact position on a rock after a feeding forage, apparently following chemical clues in their mucous secretions to their home 'scar' on the rock.

Fishing Limpets are viewed as the bait of last resort. On the positive side they are tough and withstand pickers but they are not highly prized and can often soak for long periods with little action. There are times when limpets make reasonable bait for bream and trevally but there are generally better baits available.

MUSSEL, BLUE

Scientific name *Mytilus edulis*. Also known as Sea mussel, mussel.

Range Mindarie in Western Australia and southern waters including Tasmania as far as Forster in NSW.

Description A relatively small mussel species which grows to about 12 cm. The shell is purplish black and the inside of the shell is bluish white. They are wedge shaped and can have a small 'beard' which helps them to attach to substrates such as bridges, jetties and rocks to a depth of up to 10 metres. The blue mussel likes areas of high water movement but needs more than 15 parts per thousand (about half normal sea water to survive)

Fishing The blue mussel is harvested by hand from areas where they are common and used as bait for bream, whiting and other estuary species. The meat is fairly small and any picker present will remove the bait. Others crush up mussels and use the shells and bits of meat as an excellent burley, but care should be taken not to be too vigorous as this is the food that attracts many fish to the area in the first place. The blue mussel forms part of an extensive aquaculture industry and good catches of fish can be taken in the vicinity. They are excellent eating, with chili mussels one of Perth's specialty dishes. Blue mussels taken from waters with pollution or heavy boat traffic should not be consumed as they can have a petrol 'taint' or could harbour harmful bacteria. They are quite cheap to buy anyway.

CUTTLEFISH

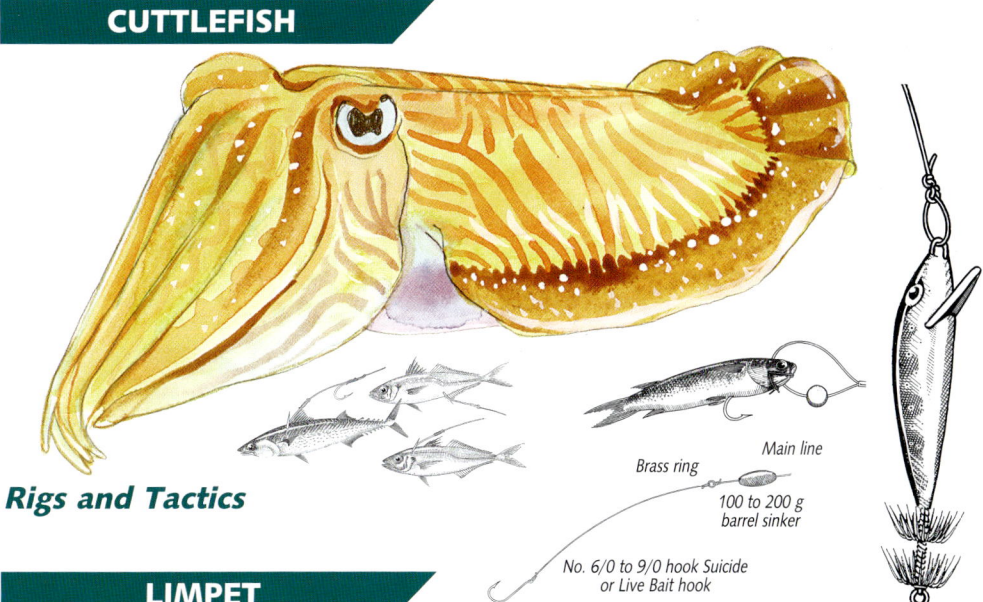

Rigs and Tactics

Brass ring

Main line

100 to 200 g
barrel sinker

No. 6/0 to 9/0 hook Suicide
or Live Bait hook

LIMPET

MUSSEL, BLUE

OCTOPUS, GLOOMY

Scientific name *Octopus tetricus.* Also known as Occy, inshore octopus.

Range This species is distributed from Exmouth Gulf to Albany in Western Australia and from Brisbane to Eden on the east coast. The similar southern octopus (*Octopus australis*) is found from Sydney southwards to west of Ceduna and including the north and east coasts of Tasmania.

Description The gloomy octopus is one of the larger species reaching 80 cm total length and a weight of 3 kilograms. The gloomy octopus differs from other octopus in having long arms which differ in length. The southern octopus reaches a smaller size and has arms of similar length. The octopus is very intelligent but is a much maligned animal, despised by rock lobster fishers and simply viewed as icky by many. The small, blue-ringed octopus (*Hapalochlaena spp.*) looks benign at rest with the usual brown camouflage but it can be readily identified by the small electric blue rings which become very bright when disturbed. The beak is right under the animal and only a true idiot or very young child would find themselves with a bitable piece of themselves near the mouth of an angry blue-ringed octopus. However the bite is extremely poisonous. Octopus live for two years and die after mating. The females are much larger and the gloomy octopus can produce around 150,000 eggs which are laid over several nights before passing away and turning into snapper bait.

Fishing The octopus is caught less frequently than squid, but will latch onto bottom baits near their hides. They are much more active at night. Octopus will take most baits and can consume an enormous number of rock lobster if left in the pot. Octopus make an excellent bait. Skinning the octopus seems to make it more visible and improves it as a bait. Octopus is regarded as an excellent food, but should be skinned and can become extremely tough and chewy if not cooked either extremely slowly at low heat, or extremely quickly at high heat.

PRAWN, EASTERN KING

Scientific name *Penaeus plebejus.* Also known as king prawn, giant prawn.

Range Cairns in Queensland and southwards as far as Lakes Entrance in Victoria

Description A large species which can reach 30 cm in length. The body is flesh coloured, the legs can be reddish in colour and the tail fan can be blue tinged or bright blue in colour. The similar Western king prawn (*Penaeus latisculatus*) ranges from north Queensland to south of Perth in Western Australia has blue legs.

Fishing Most Eastern king prawns are taken in commercial nets in deep waters. Juveniles are taken from Moreton Bay in southern Queensland and other southern estuaries and may be scooped or drag netted from these areas when moving to the offshore grounds on the dark of the moon. Some western king prawns are taken at night by scuba divers in the Swan River, where the large size and dexterity needed makes an unusual challenge. All king prawn species are excellent eating and expensive to purchase and as a result are rarely used for bait.

PRAWN, RIVER

Scientific name *Metapenaeus macleayi.* Also known as bait prawn, white river prawn.

Range Bundaberg in Queensland to Eden in NSW.

Description The shell is relatively smooth, the shell lightly sprinkled with very small brown dots on a translucent background. The spike on the tail has four large lateral spines and the head spike or rostrum curves upwards for the end half. The river prawn grows to about 17 cm but is commonly seen at around 10 cm.

Fishing The river prawn forms the basis of significant recreational and commercial fisheries. During the summer darks of the moon, river prawns make their way from estuaries to oceanic waters to breed. They are taken in scoop nets with a lantern either wading the shallows or from a boat positioned near the channel edge. River prawns are also taken in small drag nets run near the weed beds or sandy flats. They can be taken at all times other than the full moon. Luminescent plankton can make drag netting almost impossible, but it is an enjoyable way to spend an evening and get a feed of tasty prawns. While river prawns are excellent eating, they are also excellent live baits for bream, bass, trevally and mulloway.

OCTOPUS, GLOOMY

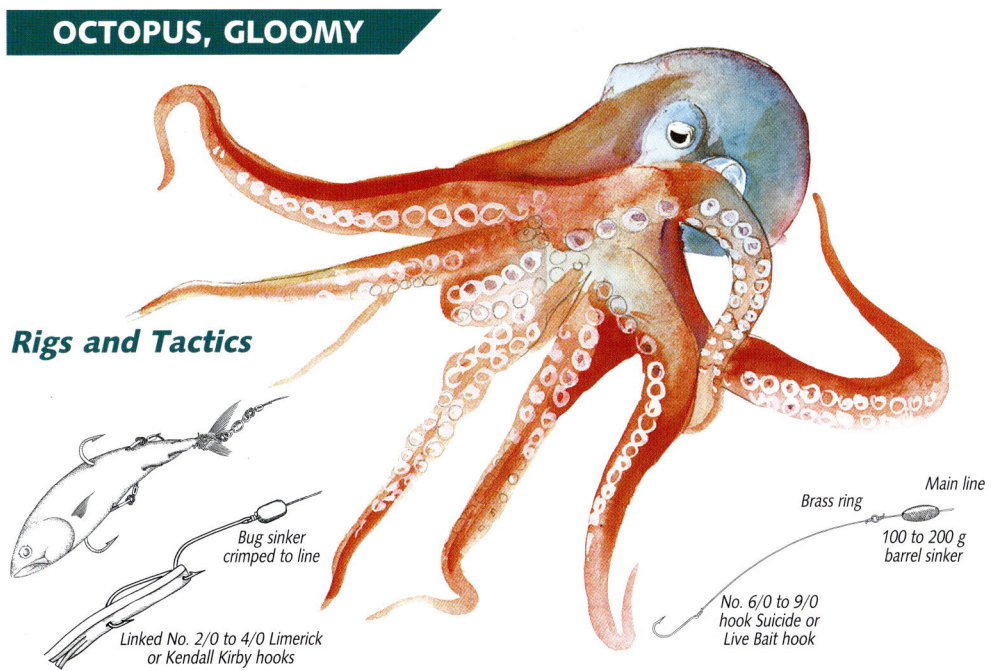

Rigs and Tactics

Bug sinker
crimped to line

Linked No. 2/0 to 4/0 Limerick
or Kendall Kirby hooks

Main line

Brass ring

100 to 200 g
barrel sinker

No. 6/0 to 9/0
hook Suicide or
Live Bait hook

PRAWN, EASTERN KING

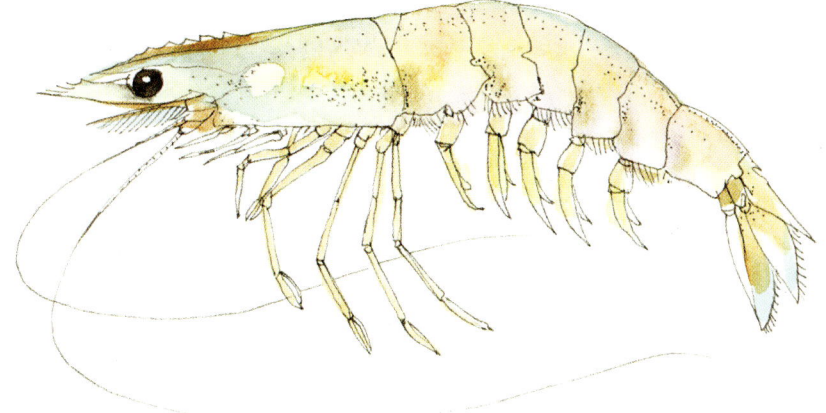

PRAWN, RIVER

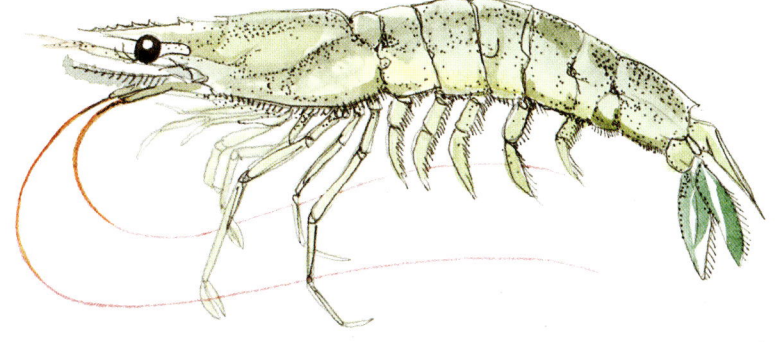

ROCK LOBSTER, EASTERN

Scientific name *Jasus verreauxi*. Also known as Eastern crayfish, spiny lobster.

Range Tweed Heads in northern NSW and southwards to Port McDonnell South Australia, including Tasmania.

Description A large species of rock lobster reaching up to 26 cm carapace length and a weight of 8 kilograms. It can live up to 20 years and is found in nearshore waters to deeper reefs. The eastern rock lobster has a green body with orange, orange-brown or brick red legs and most of the tail fan. The main body segments are smooth and importantly the eastern rock lobster lacks horns at the front of the head. The eastern rock lobster is found near the intertidal zone, often need weed and rocky caves where it shelters. They move offshore in winter. In the 1950's, large quantities of eastern rock lobsters were caught by trawling which impacted on the stocks to an extent that is only just now recovering. The tight restrictions on commercial operations has improved the productivity and profitability of the commercial fishery in NSW.

Fishing The eastern rock lobster can be taken by diving, but the use of compressed air or implements such as a cray loop or blunt hook is carefully regulated and illegal in many jurisdictions. The size limits and prohibition on taking females with eggs are important management tools. Similarly, the design and number of pots which may be used to take rock lobsters is carefully regulated and is closely policed to control dedicated illegal operations. The pot should be baited with oily fish such as tuna heads and the pots pulled the next day. The length of rope used should be long enough for the float to be visible, but not so long as to create a navigation hazard. Care should be taken when setting pots near popular recreational fishing spots as it can greatly affect the enjoyment of many people if they regularly become snagged on a pot rope. While the regulations may be quite complicated, the rewards from catching your own eastern rock lobster are worth the effort as they are a luxury item to purchase. The eastern rock lobster is considered by many to be the best eating species.

ROCK LOBSTER, ORNATE

Scientific name *Panulirus ornatus*. Also known as Tropical rock lobster, ornate cray, painted cray, painted rock lobster.

Range Kalbarri in Western Australia and tropical waters, including Torres Straits Islands as far south as central Queensland.

Description A striking and brightly coloured tropical species which can reach 15cm carapace length. There are several tropical rock lobster species which can appear similar and are often generally referred to as painted crays. The true painted rock lobster (*Panulirus versicolor*) can appear very similar but tends to be less brightly coloured, with muted greens and green-reds (leading to its Western Australian common name of green rock lobster). The painted rock lobster has distinct long stripes on the legs whereas in the ornate rock lobster the legs have distinct rings and blotches. The back (carapace) of the ornate rock lobster can be bright blue, blue-green or have reddish overtones. The ornate rock lobster forms the basis of a significant commercial fishery in north Queensland and the Torres Straits.

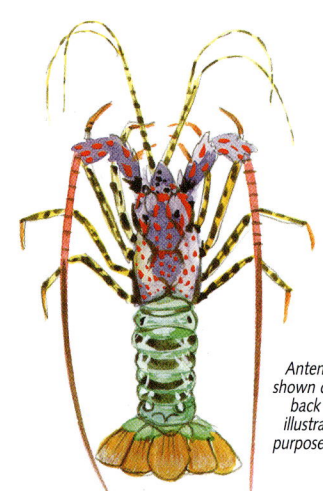

Fishing The ornate rock lobster is not taken in pots. The antennae sit strait out from the body and prevents the lobster from entering the narrow openings of conventional lobster pots. As a consequence, they are taken by diving under the various forms of control in the different jurisdictions. The ornate rock lobster can also be taken off reef tops at night during neap tides by looking in small rock pools, but bag limits should be carefully adhered to as these rock lobsters are very vulnerable to over-exploitation. The ornate rock lobster, while considered to be good eating, can be tough and less flavoursome than southern species and so is not heavily targeted by recreational fishers.

Antennae shown draw back for illustration purpose only

ROCK LOBSTER, SOUTHERN

Scientific name *Jasus edwardsii*. Also known as southern crayfish.

Range From about Jurien in Western Australia and southern waters including Tasmania as far as southern NSW, but much more common along the entire southern coastline.

Description A large and striking rock lobster species which has a rough tail shell and two prominent horns beside the eyes but they do not project past the front of the head. The southern rock lobster can reach 23 cm carapace length. The colour of the southern rock lobster is uniform and is often a shade of dark red.

Fishing The southern rock lobster can be taken by diving or by baited pots. They can range in depth from the intertidal zone to 200 m and can also have an offshore migration. The southern rock lobster is very highly prized for its eating quality and forms the basis of a very large export commercial fishery along the southern shores.

ROCK LOBSTER, WESTERN

Scientific name *Panulirus cygnus*. Also known as Western crayfish, cray and depending on stage of moult 'white' or 'red' rock lobster.

Range Western Australian only from Exmouth to Walpole, but commercial densities are from Shark Bay to Augusta.

Description The Western rock lobster forms the most valuable single species commercial fishery in Australia, with an average harvest of approximately 10.5 million kilograms able to be sustainably harvested each year, with a further 500,000 kilograms of recreationally caught rock lobsters. The Western rock lobster has a rough tail section and the two prominent horns extend past the eyes and the front of the head. They can reach a carapace size of around 16 cm but the fishery more commonly targets a carapace size between 76 and 85 mm. Each year between November and January large numbers of pale orange or light red coloured, recently-moulted juveniles (known as 'whites') migrate from inshore reefs to the deeper reefs offshore. This migration, called the 'whites' run, is the time of most intensive recreational fishing. The recreational fishery is concentrated inside 20 metres deep. Later in the season, adult and non-migrating lobsters are known as 'reds' and form the catch between February and 30 June.

Fishing The Western rock lobster fishery provides the best opportunity for recreational fishers to catch their own rock lobsters. Early in the season, divers, who may also use compressed air, regularly take their bag limit of 8 lobsters. Potting with two allowed pots can also yield excellent catches and this fishery provides the basis of many Christmas dinners on the West Coast. All western rock lobsters taken by recreational fishers must have the central part of the tail fan clipped to prevent black market sales. A license is required and it pays to read the fine print carefully as West Australians jealously regard this as the best managed fishery in the world and want its quality to remain. The western rock lobster makes excellent eating and freezes very well.

SEA URCHIN, PURPLE

Scientific name *Heliocidaris erythrogramma*. Also known as Sea eggs, kina.

Range There are many different types of sea urchins which are known as echinoderms. The purple sea urchin is found from Shark Bay in Western Australia and southern waters including Tasmania to Caloundra in southern Queensland.

Description Sea urchins are closely related to starfish and sea cucumbers. They move about with tube feet, have a hard external shell usually covered with spines of some description and have the mouth on the underside. The purple sea urchin is important as it forms the basis of a small commercial fishery and is most highly prized by recreational fishers. This species has many spines, with primary spines between 10 and 25 mm long with sharp points while the secondary spines have more blunt tips. The spine colour is generally a deep reddish purple or purple/black with the main shell often a more dirty brown. The purple sea urchin is found in depth of up to 15 metres and in exposed areas concentrates in crevasses where their spines penetrate even the most cautious rock hopper at some time! The purple sea urchin is more common where abalone or rock lobster numbers are low are they are predated upon by these animals.

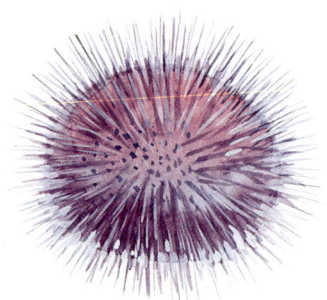

Fishing Sea urchins are taken for their roe which is highly prized as food, especially by Pacific Island and Asian people. The big orange roe can be up to 50% of the space inside the shell or they can be disappointingly small. Unfortunately, the only way to determine the size of the roe is to kill the animal, although technology is being developed to 'scan' the urchin before killing it. To people who do not value the roe, their removal is a blessing as they are a hazard when walking across reef tops, but they are an important part of the habitat and the harvest of urchins is now controlled. Another important point is that not all urchins are created equal and the purple and black varieties by far the best. Some people burley with sea urchins, but this generally only attracts every rubbish fish for miles.

WORM, BEACH

Scientific name *Australonuphis teres*. Also known as Giant beach worm, kingworm, stumpy.

Range South Australia and eastwards as far as southern Queensland but not including Tasmania.

Description There are a variety of beach worm species that go by the colourful names of slimy, pinky, stripey, wiry, white-head wiry and green. They are all part of the genus *Australonuphis sp.* (giant and slimy) and *Onuphis sp.* (others). The beach worms live in the intertidal zone of medium energy beaches. They are extremely strong burrowers and come to the surface to feed on meat or weed. They grab the offering with their head tentacles and arch themselves to tear off a small piece to consume. The giant beach worm can reach nearly 180 cm in length and has a distinctive white head. The common names help to distinguish the other species and finding a good beach wormer in operation will provide many clues about their habits and what is locally prolific.

Fishing Beach worms are among the best baits for surf and estuary fishing. They will take everything from whiting to mulloway and Australian salmon also take them with relish, but they will attract any fish in the area. Catching beach worms is a special skill that some never master. A large bait of fish (the traditional bait is a stingray) is put into a stocking and either tied to the wrist or to a long stick. It is washed in the surge zone and the heads of the beach worms pop up to 'taste' the water. A small finger bait, usually a pipi or firm flesh is then presented to the worm which latches on. When the worm arches to tear off a piece, the fingers or special worming pliers grab the worm. You then dig down about 15 centimetres and grab the body and pull out the worm. Even if you are good enough to grab the worm, pulling straight up is likely to take only the top few centimeters (which can grow back). This sounds easy and many can make it look simple, but many is the time when a big swell has hit just as you go to catch the worm, but it is great fun and the quality of the bait makes the adventure worth the effort.

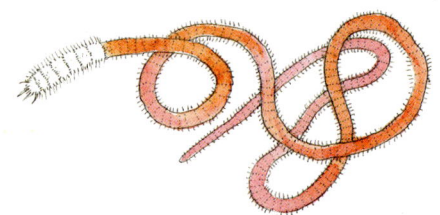

WORM, BLOOD

Scientific name *Marphysa sanguinea*. Also known as Mud worm, wriggler worm, bristle worm.

Range Australia wide but most common from Perth to southern Queensland.

Description A dark red or brownish red worm that makes its home in the mud, muddy sand or weed of intertidal areas around Australia. They can also be found under rocks in the same areas. The blood worm has a marked purple sheen when it is rinsed after capture and if broken, exudes a considerable amount of 'blood', hence the common name. The blood worm has been recorded at about a 90 cm in length but is most commonly seen at 15 to 20 cm. The blood worm has a pair of sharp jaws which can give a painful bite and they will attack other worms harvested at the same time.

Fishing Blood worms make an excellent bait for all estuarine species and can be the most effective bait for whiting and bream at times. They do attract pickers and are extremely expensive to buy from bait shops where they are probably preserved and less effective. The most important attribute for getting blood worms is a pitchfork or similar device and a strong back. A reduced sense of smell can also be an advantage. Blood worms are gathered at low tide on muddy flats by sifting through the dug up mud. They are also found around weed, but digging in weed is rightly prohibited in most areas. The worms need to be put into damp ribbon weed or they will cut each other up - they also toughen up in the weed and make a better bait.

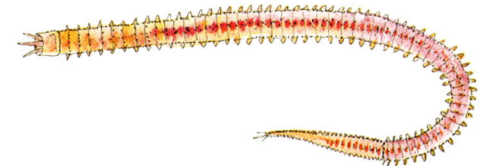

WORM, SQUIRT

Scientific name *Australonereis ehlersi*. Also known as Sand worm, pump worm, rag worm.

Range Australia wide, but most commonly harvested on the east coast.

Description A relatively small worm reaching about 6 cm in length. The squirt worm is found on intertidal sand or sandy mud flats in estuaries in similar habitats to nippers and soldier crabs. They can be located by finding the fine paper-like 'tube' that is actually sand gummed up from mucous as the worms eat. This tube can extend a centimeter or so from the bottom. The squirt worm lives in a tube which has both a front and back entrance. The worm itself is fairly thin and can break apart fairly easily. They do have a reasonable set of jaws but this is rarely enough to bite the fingers. Squirt worms are sand or red coloured.

Fishing Squirt worms make excellent bait especially for whiting, bream, flathead and luderick in estuaries. As they are fairly fine they are often used whole and as any fish around will happily eat them, you can go through many baits. Fishing the shallow flats on a rising tide will give whiting an advantage but some can be tiny. Squirt worms can be dug but this is very hard work. Generally the tube is located and a bait or yabby pump is placed over the hole. Rather than sucking like for nippers, air is blown into the hole and the worm 'squirts' from the other entrance onto the sand where it can be easily picked up.

ANCHOVY

Scientific name *Engraulis australis.* Also known as Anchovy, frogmouth pilchard, froggie, Australian anchovy.

Range From Shark Bay in Western Australia and around the entire southern part of Australia and Tasmania to the Capricorn group in Queensland.

Description The anchovy is a common bait species which schools in coastal bays and mouths of estuaries and offshore. The pointed fleshy snout and extremely large mouth are characteristic. Grows to 15 cm and is frequently seen smaller in bait shops.

Fishing A very good bait for fish like flathead and bream. Rig on a single hook or a gang of No 4 to No 1 hooks. Anchovies can be a little soft so they need some care for maximum effectiveness, but the oils which add flavour on pizza also help make this a top bait.

COCKLE

Scientific name *Katelysia spp.* and *Anadara spp.* Also known as blood cockle.

Range southern parts of Australia from Albany in Western Australia to central NSW

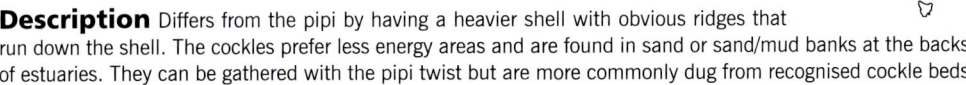

Description Differs from the pipi by having a heavier shell with obvious ridges that run down the shell. The cockles prefer less energy areas and are found in sand or sand/mud banks at the backs of estuaries. They can be gathered with the pipi twist but are more commonly dug from recognised cockle beds with a fork or gathered at the absolute bottom of the tide when they may be moving.

Fishing Cockles make an excellent bait for bream, whiting, Australian salmon and other species. They must be shelled and the shells make an excellent berley. The cockle should be hooked through the muscular foot to stay on the hook better. Some anglers use bait elastic to help keep the bait on if there are pickers around. Cockles are also excellent eating if cleaned of sand and lightly steamed.

CRAB, BLACK ROCK

Scientific name *Leptograpsus variegatus* Also known as swift-footed rock crab, steelback crab.

Range Southern Australia and along the south coast.

Description The most commonly seen rock crab of temperate Australia but one that can be difficult to catch. The black rock crab varies from a uniform dark olive-green to purple to almost completely black. It is found generally just below or just above the tide line and will scurry away when threatened. They can grow to around 10 cm across the carapace.

Fishing The black rock crab is seen as a poor substitute to the red rock crab. It can be difficult to catch and does not have the same appeal to groper, bream, snapper and other crab loving species.

CRAB, RED ROCK

Scientific name *Plagusia chabrus* Also known as bait crab, red crab.

Range Lancelin in Western Australia and throughout southern waters to around Newcastle in NSW.

Description The crab is red to brick red and may have white tips to the claws. There is a dense covering of hair on the body and legs. The red rock crab can reach 12 cm across the carapace. The red rock crab is found near the bottom of the intertidal zone where it forages near seaweed and shelters at the base of weed, among the cunjevoi or in rock crevasses.

Fishing The red rock crab is gathered at low tide when there is a very low swell by walking along the lower tidal area and feeling at the base of seaweed fronds or along crevasses. Some care must be taken as the same crevasses can harbour the dangerous blue-ringed octopus. Although these crabs can be difficult to gather, they are easily the best bait for groper and big bream will be tempted on a half of crab when nothing else works. The crabs should be hooked through the leg socket after the leg is removed and used as berley. Depending on the size of the crab it is fished whole, as a half or in quarters.

CUNJEVOI

Scientific name *Pyura stolonifera* Also known as sea squirt, conjevoi, conjeboy, cunjeboi, cunje.

Range Southern Queensland to around Geelong in Victoria.

Description This is the animal that surprises people when walking on rocks at low tide and getting squirted by water up their legs or onto their face. The cunjevoi is an unusual animal, being born as a larvae with a notochord or primitive backbone, before becoming attached to the rocks and growing its brown leathery coat. Cunjevoi grow in colonies and form their own ecosystem around them, from the absolute bottom of the lowest tide to above the half mean tide on exposed rocks. The cunjevoi feeds through two siphons in the upper surface that appear as a raised, cross shaped 'mouth'. One opening is the entrance for food, the other expels water that has been filtered. The animal which lives inside the tough fibrous skin or test inside of the cunjevoi is a rich brick red or purplish colour and the gonads can be bright orange.

Fishing Cunjevoi need to be gathered at low tide. The largest and longest cunjevoi do not make the best bait and ones that are around 5 cm in diameter and around 5 – 7 cm high are the best. The cunjevoi is cut from the rocks with a sharp knife by inserting the blade and twisting it around. The finger is then inserted along the skin and the two siphons slid out with firm pressure. The cunjevoi will them slide from its skin. The shell makes good berley. The bait is generally cut in half for larger baits and the hook is inserted into the siphon which is much tougher than the rest of the cunje. Baits from tall cunje should be trimmed at the bottom as extra soft parts of the bait merely provide additional food for the pickers. Cunjevoi makes an excellent bait for black drummer and will take some exceptional bream from the rocks. Luderick are occasionally taken on cunje and silver trevally and tarwhine love it as well. Unfortunately every picker, wrasse and gobbleguts in the ocean also loves cunjevoi and these can be a nuisance. However, a really large drummer taken from the wash on cunjevoi makes up for the inconvenience of feeling the dreaded taps of the pickers. Cunjevoi is either used on a hook with a small ball sinker straight to the hook and fished in the white water (where many rigs can be lost), or fished under a float with a similar but much heavier rig as for luderick. Rules now protect Cunjevoi from over harvest.

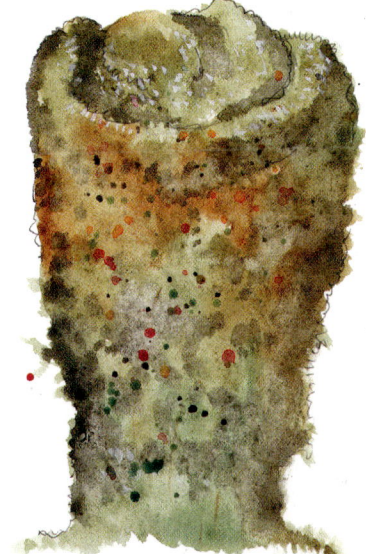

FLYING FISH

Scientific name *Cheilopogon pinnatibarbatus* (Great flying fish, tailfin flying fish, large flying fish) *Hirundichthys rondeletii* (Rondelet's flying fish, blackwing flying fish) and others. Also known as Flying fish, common flying fish.

Range Flying fish are generally a tropical or sub-tropical pelagic species of ocean and coastal waters. However, Rondelet's flying fish can be found around Tasmania and into the southern ocean and another species can be found in Western Australia as far south as Albany.

Description The extremely large and over-developed pectoral fins mean that these fish are easily identified. The ventral fins are also enlarged and aid in stabilising the flying fish while gliding to escape predators. They range from a maximum size of 23 cm for Rondelet's flying fish to 43 cm for the great flying fish.

Fishing Flying fish feed on plankton and are only taken by recreational anglers when they accidentally fly into a boat. They are however, excellent whole bait for other pelagic predators. Their beautiful gliding is one of the highlights of boat trips where flying fish are common.

GARFISH, RIVER

Scientific name *Hyporhamphus regularis*. Also known as Gardie, beakie, needle gar, splinter gar, lakes garfish.

Range Gladstone in Central Queensland to Lakes Entrance in Victoria. Also found in Western Australia from Bunbury to Kalbarri, which may be a sub-species.

Description The river garfish is similar in appearance to the sea garfish, but the body is slightly more stout and the silver stripe is not so prominent. The river gar also has quite large scales which are obvious when they become dislodged with handling. The beak is generally dull coloured except for the red or orange tip. The upper jaw is broader than it is long. River garfish reach 35 centimetres.

Fishing As for sea gar, but maggots are a particularly favoured bait in many areas. River gar are not as

highly regarded as food as sea gar and need to be scaled before consumption. They are a fantastic bait for tailor, mulloway and other pelagic species.

GARFISH, SEA

Scientific name *Hyporhamphus australis*. Also known as Beakie, gardie, ballyhoo, eastern garfish. Young specimens called pencil gar.

Range Found from Moreton Bay in Queensland south to Eden in NSW and including Lord Howe and Norfolk Islands.

Description The sea garfish is an attractive slender fish with a brilliant silver stripe down the side and fine delicate scales. The lower jaw is long and is bright red or orange, particularly at the tip. The upper jaw is triangular and always longer than it is broad. The sea gar grows to 45 centimetres. The sea gar is an inhabitant of open waters except in the early summer months when aggregations enter bays and estuaries for spawning.

Fishing Sea garfish are an important bait species for tailor, salmon and all pelagics including billfish (Garfish are called Ballyhoo in game fishing books). They are excellent eating as the bones are fine and can be broken up by 'rolling' the garfish with a bottle before cooking. Sea garfish can be taken by fishing with dough, maggot, prawn piece or a small piece of squid on a number 12 long shank hook, suspended under a light float or quill. Berleying with pollard and pilchard oil will help to keep a feeding school near the boat. A good trick is to live bait with a garfish while fishing for them, as large

predators can often move into a berley trail, especially when fishing in bays.

GARFISH, SNUBNOSE

Scientific name *Arrhamphus sclerolepis.* Also known as Snubbie, short-bill.

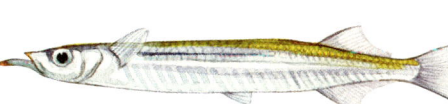

Range Generally a tropical species, from Carnarvon in Western Australia and northern waters to northern NSW estuaries.

Description The snubnose garfish differs from other garfish in that the lower jaw is only about one fifth of the length of the head. The lower jaw has a prominent red tip. This is an inshore species sometimes found in the lower freshwater reaches of river, tidal rivers and estuaries. It reaches 38 centimetres.

Fishing As for the sea garfish, however, the shorter beak makes a long shank hook less necessary for the snubnose gar. This species is excellent eating and also makes a fantastic live or dead bait.

GARFISH, SOUTHERN SEA

Scientific name *Hyporhamphus melanochir.* Also known as South Australian garfish.

Range Lancelin in Western Australia and southern waters including Tasmania to Eden in NSW.

Description A similar species to the sea garfish but differing by range and this species is more common in estuaries or near shore seagrass areas. The southern sea garfish reaches 50 cm and the anal fin starts below the front of the dorsal fin. The silver stripe on the side is particularly prominent.

Fishing A common and enjoyable species to catch over or adjacent to seagrass meadows where mixed bags of Tommy rough, King George whiting and squid can be taken from the same pollard and pilchard oil berley trail. The southern sea garfish makes excellent eating.

GOBY

Scientific name Family *Gobiidae.* Many common names for various species.

Range The largest family of fishes with some 1800 species ranging from oceanic to freshwater environments and the tropics to cool fresh water.

Description Mainly small species, including one which reaches maturity at 12 mm. Gobies have no lateral line, two clearly separate dorsal fins and the pelvic fins are joined to form a sucker disc. This group includes the mud skippers of tropical areas which can be found clinging to mangroves or hopping over mud at low tide.

Fishing These are generally forage species which are rarely targeted but several species can make reasonable bait.

HARDYHEAD

Scientific name Family *Atherinidae.* Also known as Whitebait.

Range Found throughout Australia in estuaries, bays and inshore waters. Several species such as the flyspeck hardyhead are found in fresh water.

Description The hardyheads are small forage species reaching a maximum size of 17 cm, but commonly found from 5 to 12 centimetres. They have large tough scales for their size, two separate dorsal fins and a bony head. Marine species are light coloured with a prominent silver stripe along the side. The pectoral fin is placed very high on the body.

Fishing These are generally marketed as whitebait or hardyheads and are excellent bait for all fish eating species. They are a bit tougher on the hook than bluebait and pilchards. Hardyheads can be caught with fine mesh dip nets or cast nets (where legal) in many estuaries where they form vast schools and can be berleyed with pollard or bread.

HERRING, SOUTHERN

Scientific name *Herklotsichthys castelnaui* Also known as striped herring, estuary herring, pilcher

Range Central Queensland to southern NSW near the Victorian border.

Description A small fairly rounded bait species which forms large schools offshore in winter in southern Queensland and smaller schools can be found in the estuaries in late summer and autumn. Freshes can push them near the mouths of estuaries where they are preyed upon by fish such as tailor, mulloway and flathead. These herrings have a large eye, large upturned mouth and a deeply forked tail which has dusky tips. The dorsal fin is quite short and lacks the extended filament of the hairback herring (*Nematalosa come*) of more tropical waters. The southern herring has three or more faint gold stripes along the upper sides. The similar spotted herring (*Herklotsichthys koningsbergeri*) has a series of small black spots in a single or double line along the side.

Fishing The southern herring is netted in large quantities and makes a good bait for many species. Strips of herring makes an excellent bait for bream and flathead and they make an acceptable live bait although they can lose their scales on handling. Southern herring can be taken on bait jigs, especially when berleyed up with bran and pilchard oil. They can be taken on dough and on a small piece of prawn or squid on a small long shanked hook or as a sweetener on a bait jig rig. If possible, don't handle the fish until they are ready to be used as bait This herring species is quite bony and its small size makes it a challenge for eating.

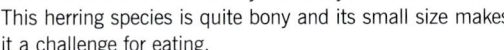

MACKEREL, HORSE

Scientific name *Trachurus declivis.* Also known as Jack mackerel, scad, cowanyoung, greenback scad.

Range Cooler and temperate waters from Shark Bay in Western Australia to around Bundaberg in Queensland. This species is particularly prolific around Tasmania.

Description The horse mackerel is a more open water schooling species which is easily confused with the similar yellowtail. The horse mackerel lacks the definitive yellow coloured tail and has more than 74 bony scutes (scales) along the lateral line close to the tail. This species can reach a maximum size of 60 cm but are more often encountered at around 30 – 45 centimetres. Horse mackerel can form vast schools out to the continental shelf in depths of over 300 metres.

Fishing Horse mackerel can move inshore in small schools or groups of 20 or so fish. They will take reasonably large baits intended for other species, including half pilchards, blue bait, white bait, prawns, squid and most other baits. Horse mackerel can be taken on bait jigs and will take small wobblers and lures such as Tassie Devils. Like yellowtail, berley with potato peelings brings on a fierce bite, but can cause these fish to regurgitate when kept in live bait tanks. When this happens, the water should be regularly changed. Horse mackerel fight very well for their size and are regrettably less highly regarded as they should be as a sport fish. Horse mackerel have a strong fishy taste which means that they are generally used for pet food or fertiliser when taken commercially. The oily flesh makes them a fantastic cut bait and their hardy nature and larger size is the reason why the horse mackerel is highly valued as a live bait.

MACKEREL, SLIMY

Scientific name *Scomber australasicus.* Also known as Blue mackerel, spotted chub mackerel, slimies.

Range Recorded from all Australian waters and also found in Japan, but is much more common in temperate waters in the southern half of Australia.

Description A relatively small species, reaching 65 cm and 2 kg but which is most often encountered at 25 – 35 centimetres. The slimy mackerel has wavy bars on its back, spots on its side and 5 – 6 finlets behind both the dorsal and anal fins. It can be separated from the jack or horse mackerel as it lacks the bony scutes along the rear of the lateral line. Slimy mackerel travel in schools which can enter bays and some larger estuaries. The slimy mackerel is an extremely important forage species with many pelagic species attracted to feed on slimies. The decimation of pilchard stocks by virus has made slimies even more important. Proposals to increase commercial slimy mackerel exploitation has angered recreational fishers as the impact on local fishing quality is likely to be severe.

Fishing The slimy mackerel is often taken for granted, taken in quantity for live bait with the use of bait jigs on recognised bait grounds. Slimy mackerel is also a first class cut bait as the oily flesh is attractive to many species. Slimy mackerel react well to berley and in many areas great fun can be had on slimies mixed with Australian herring, garfish and tailor or juvenile Australian salmon. The slimy mackerel is not highly regarded as food as it has a strong fishy taste, but they are popular in some Mediterranean cooking which values the stronger fish flavour.

MUD SKIPPER

Scientific name *Periopthalmus argentiventralis* Also known as mud hopper

Range Carnarvon in Western Australia and northwards through tropical waters to around Moreton Bay in Queensland but is rare this far south.

Description A very unusual species which is often seen at low tide among the exposed mangroves foraging for small crabs, shrimps or stranded fish well above the high tide mark. The mud skipper has an expanded gill chamber which it can fill with water to survive while it 'walks' on its enlarged pectoral fins across the mud flats. When disturbed, the mud skipper uses its tail to move or skip quickly across the flats. The mud skipper can get to 27 cm but many are seen at 8 – 15 centimetres. Their eyes protrude obviously above the head and the first dorsal fin is high and sail like. The mud skipper is well camouflaged for its mangrove mud flats environment and is brown to chocolate. The dorsal fin has a single prominent black stripe and the outer margins may be tinged with red.

Fishing The mud skipper is very rarely taken by line fishing due to its size. They are often taken in throw nets when fishing for mullet and can be used as live bait. They are good at finding cover and snagging the angler and there are better live baits. This species is a joy to watch in its natural environment and is a curiosity and a special part of tropical mangrove creeks.

NIPPER

Scientific name *Callianassa australiensis* Also known as Bass yabbie, ghost nipper, yabbie, burrowing shrimp, lobby, pink yabby, pink nipper.

Range Eastern coastline from central Queensland to eastern Victoria.

Description A fairly small delicate looking crustacean that lives in holes around 60 cm deep on the sandflats of estuaries. The male nipper has a much enlarged claw which can give quite a painful nip and when removed from the nipper, the muscles contract which makes the claw more difficult to remove. The female has a less well developed large claw and may carry up to 2000 eggs in a cluster under the abdomen. The nipper is generally white or cream and may appear translucent. The eggs may give the abdomen a bright orange appearance before they are laid. The nipper can grow to around 6 cm but are more commonly seen at around 3 centimetres.

Fishing The nipper is gathered at the bottom half of the tide on the sand flats with the aid of a bait or yabby pump. The angler looks for holes that have a build up of fresh sand around the opening or where there is water movement out of the hole. Each nipper hole can have up to three openings so the actual numbers of nippers can be less than the holes would indicate. The pump is inserted into the sand near an active hole and two to three pumps are made. These can be made onto the nearby sand, or if in deeper water, into a special sieve that has foam around it to keep it floating. Nippers are placed into a bucket which should be changed every

hour or two. Any unwanted nippers should be put back into the water where they can easily burrow back into the sand. Take only as many nippers as needed for the session so that the grounds do not become depleted. Nippers make excellent bait for all estuary species including bream, flathead, luderick, trevally, tarwhine, big mullet. Even tailor will readily hit a nipper, likely causing a bite-off. Gathering nippers is great fun for the family and makes a real adventure out of estuary fishing.

PILCHARD

Scientific name *Sardinops sagax neopilchardus.* Also known as Sardine, mulie, blue pilchard, Australian pilchard, blue bait, bloater (NZ).

Range While generally a cooler water species, its range extends from Kalbarri in Western Australia and sourthern waters including Tasmania to around Bribie Island in Queensland, a range which has been confirmed by massive pilchard deaths caused by a herpes virus in 1995 and 1998.

Description The pilchard is a common schooling forage species of cooler waters taken in large numbers for fishing bait, pet food, aquaculture food and increasingly as a food fish. The pilchard feeds on plankton, using its fairly large mouth and dense gill rakers to filter food. While the pilchard can reach 23 cm, it is commonly used as bait at between 12 and 20 centimetres. The pilchard is very well known to nearly every angler in Australia as the best stand-by bait available. The pilchard has a line of small black spots along the middle part of the body, where the deep blue back changes to the silver belly. The smaller blue sprat (*Spratelloides robustus*) which is sold as blue sardine or bluebait has a smaller mouth, lacks the black spots on the sides and only reaches 10 centimetres.

Fishing The pilchard is only taken by commercial fishermen in purse seine or less commonly in beach seine nets. This species was subject to devastating fish kills in 1995 and again in 1998/99 caused by a virus of unknown source. The pilchard is used in nearly all fishing situations where its oily flesh acts as an excellent attractor of fish. Most pilchards are fished on a linked gang of hooks, although the practice of using a treble hook 'stinger' cannot be encouraged, as many juvenile fish are killed during handling and unhooking. The pilchard is fairly soft bodied, so when fish like tailor hit, the rest of the bait acts as its own berley, keeping the

school interested. The pilchard can be toughened by soaking in brine or sprinkling with salt, which is especially attractive to some reef fish such as snapper, but is less attractive to fish which must have fresh bait such as mulloway. Individually snap frozen pilchards are also better from a freshness and durability perspective.

PIPI

Scientific name *Plebidonax deltoides.* Also known as ugarie, cockle, goolwa cockle, Coorang cockle, clam.

Range Southern Queensland and southwards and along the south coast as far as the northern limits of the Coorong in South Australia. Although it is not reported in Western Australia, I have seen a very similar species in Geographe Bay.

Description A fairly large bivalve mollusc growing to 7.5 cm across the shell. They have a triangular shell without the obvious circular ridges of the true cockle. The pipi is found in the intertidal area of oceanic beaches where they can be gathered in fairly large numbers on a dropping tide.

Fishing The pipi can be gathered with a fork in the sand in the wash zone at the bottom of the tide. However, the most common method is to use the pipi twist. Stand in the wash zone and twist both feet together to wriggle into the sand. Pipis will be felt with the toes and can be flicked up when the water won't wash them too far down the beach. Pipis will be no deeper than say ankle deep and a roving approach works well. When pipis are found they are generally in the same depth band along the beach. Some people claim to be able to feel an indent in the sand where a pipi is found, but I have never found this. Pipis can also be gathered by hand at the very bottom of neap tides when they seem to wash to the bottom of the tidal zone. Care should be taken not to over harvest pipis as excessive catches and black marketing them for bait has led to bag limits in NSW. Pipis are an excellent bait for all surf species from whiting to school mulloway. Australian salmon have a special fondness for pipi. The hook should be placed in the foot so that it stays of the hook. Pipis are actually much under-rated for their eating qualities, but they should be purged or rinsed as they can contain a fair bit of sand which adds an unwelcome crunch to the pipi dish.

PRAWN, SCHOOL

Scientific name *Metapenaeus spp.* Also known as bait prawn, schoolie, western school prawn, york prawn, bay prawn, endeavour prawn, greasyback prawn, greentail prawn, green prawn, river prawn, white river prawn.

Range One or other of the school prawn species is found throughout Australia.

Description The term school prawn is used to describe a variety of smaller prawn species, many of which are packaged and sold as bait for recreational fishing. The true school prawn, can reach 17 cm and makes a quality meal, but they are harvested by small prawn trawlers in Queensland, NSW and Victoria. The shell is smooth and the rostrum, or head spike is upward pointing which makes it more of a weapon when you are foraging in a bait bag for your next offering. The body has a number of small spots but few anglers would inspect their bait to this degree.

Fishing This is the archetypal bait for recreational fishers. It must be remembered that the source of this bait is from inshore or estuarine trawlers which also have a high (but reducing with technology) by-catch of important recreational species. The conundrum is that recreational anglers expect high quality bait and so must accept that there will be some by-catch damage, although management can reduce any significant impact. Recreational fishers can gather their own school prawns with a drag or scissors net (where legal) or with a scoop net and a tilly lamp, especially during the dark of the moon in summer. Small numbers of school prawns can be taken by scooping at the edges of weed beds during the day, although school prawns can burrow in sand during the day. There is probably no better live bait in our estuaries than a live school prawn, if the angler can forego their excellent flavour when cooked and eaten. Unfortunately, every fish in the estuary will eat a live prawn and pickers can attack valuable baits. A live prawn fished under a float near snags is unbelievably successful for bass in the east or black bream in the west.

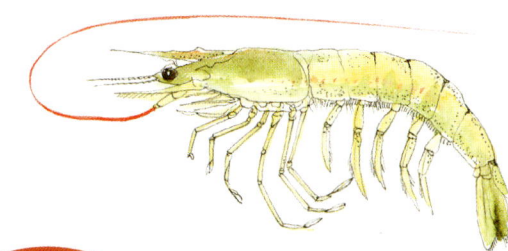

RAZORFISH

Scientific name *Solen correctus* Also known as Chinaman's fingernail.

Range World wide, but a most important bait species in South Australia.

Description An unusual bivalve mollusc, whose narrow shell is known as the Chinaman's fingernail. The razorfish lives on sheltered ocean beaches or in estuaries usually only a few centimetres below the surface but when disturbed, can burrow through the sand much more quickly than a man can dig. The razor fish burrows with its prominent muscular foot which is yellow and is larger than the shells. The razorfish is sometimes confused with the razor clam (*Pinna menkei*) which is a large triangular shelled mollusc that grows in sandy or muddy estuaries and mangrove areas and which can cut the feet of the unwary wader.

Fishing The razorfish is an excellent bait for King George whiting and other whiting species. It is gathered either by digging with a spade which is hard work as disturbed razorfish will dive out of range, or by using a wire hook forced down the burrows and then dragging the animal out. The razorfish is extremely common in the Gulf of St Vincent and Spencer Gulf and along the Eyre Peninsula in South Australia.

SARDINE

Scientific name *Amblygaster leiogaster*. Also known as Blue sardine, blue sprat, bluebait.

Range Dampier Archipelago in Western Australia and around the southern coast but not including Tasmania and as far as the Gold Coast in southern Queensland.

Description The sardine is a small schooling species reaching only 10 cm which often shelters near shallow reefs in large numbers. Apart from its size, this species is distinguished by it smaller eye and black horseshoe shaped mark near the base of the tail.

Fishing This is a plankton feeder that is never caught by angling methods. The sardine is one of the most under-rated baits, possessing the oily flesh of the larger pilchard, but in a size better suited to species like bream, Australian herring, small Australian salmon and chopper tailor. Sardines can be threaded on a larger hook, or preferably fished on gangs of No 2 or 1 hooks.

SAURIE

Scientific name *Scomberesox saurus*. Also known as King gar, Saury, Billfish, Skipper

Range Jurien Bay in Western Australia and around southern waters including Tasmania to Jervis Bay in NSW.

Description The saurie is a garfish relative easily distinguished by two short, slender but toothless jaws and 6 to 7 finlets behind both the dorsal and anal fins. This species is frequently found in offshore waters, skipping across the wake of passing boats. Saury schools can enter large coastal bays during summer.

Fishing The saurie is an excellent trolling bait for large pelagic species although it is rarely available, except through fish shops at certain times. This is not a target recreational angling species.

SILVER BIDDY

Scientific name *Gerres subfasciatus* Also known as roach, silverbiddy, common silverbelly, blacktip silverbelly, ovate silverbelly.

Range Albany and northwards throughout Western Australia. Reports are unconfirmed from the Northern Territory, but found throughout Queensland waters and southwards to Port Hacking in NSW.

Description A common forage species found in coastal bays and estuaries throughout its range. The quite small mouth of the silver biddy is in the middle of the small head. The eye is quite large and the fins are translucent. The front of the dorsal fin has a prominent black blotch. The silver biddy differs from the southern silverbelly (*Parequula melbournensis*) which is found in southern waters and only overlaps in range from Rottnest Island to Albany in Western Australia and lacks the black spot on the dorsal fin. The southern silverbelly is also more rounded in body shape and the eye appears even larger.

Fishing The silver biddy is most often taken in cast nets in tropical waters where it is highly valued as a live bait for species such as flathead, snapper and mackerel. They can be attracted by berley and taken in throw nets or with bait jigs. The silver biddy is not highly regarded as a food fish.

SPRAT

Scientific name *Spratelloides robustus.* Also known as Blue sprat, bluebait, blue sardine.

Range Dampier Archipelago in Western Australia and southern waters but less common in Tasmania, and up the east coast as far as Southern Queensland.

Description A small schooling species common around inshore reefs, the sprat reaches 10 cm in length. The sprat is most easily identified by a black horseshoe shaped mark at the base of the tail fin abd has no spots. The sprat is bluish green on the back which differentiates it from the sandy, translucent colour of the similar sized whitebait.

Fishing The sprat is not taken by recreational anglers but is an excellent and frequently under-rated bait for many species. The bluebait can be fished on a single hook or on a gang of small linked hooks in number 1 – 4 in a scaled down version of the ganged hook rig used with pilchards.

WHIPTAIL

Scientific name *Pentapodus paradiseus.* Also known as Paradise whiptail, blue-faced whiptail, paradise-fish, rainbow.

Range Around Darwin in Northern Territory and eastwards with juveniles as far south as Sydney Harbour, although this species is more prevalent north from northern NSW.

Description A strikingly beautiful fish, which only reaches around 23 centimetres. The nose is brilliantly striped with blue and gold or yellow horizontal stripes which extend to around the beginning of the eye. There is a long lateral yellow stripe along the midline, with a gold-brown stripe running below. There is also a yellow stripe running from the back of the mouth to the lower edge of the pectoral fin and a bright blue stripe along the base of the dorsal fin. This species gets its name from the elongated upper lobe of the yellow or pink-yellow tail fin. There is also a prominent black spot at the base of the tail fin. This small fish can form quite large schools in large estuaries or near inshore weedy reefs.

Fishing The whiptail is highly regarded as a baitfish either fished dead or as a cut bait for bottom species such as snapper or fished as a hardy live bait for Spanish mackerel, tuna and other tropical pelagics. Once a school is located, they can be caught on lightly weighted rigs with small hooks baited with worms, prawns, squid or fresh flesh.

WHITEBAIT

Scientific name *Hyperlophus vittatus.* Also known as Sandy sprat, glassy, white pilchard.

Range Kalbarri in Western Australia and southern waters except Tasmania as far as southern Queensland.

Description The whitebait is a schooling forage species common in coastal bays, off beaches and in the mouths of estuaries. The whitebait can be separated from the hardyheads which are often marketed as whitebait by the single dorsal fin while hardyheads have two dorsal fins. The whitebait reaches 10 cm in length and is often available at 6 – 9 centimetres.

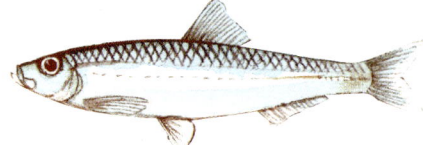

Fishing The whitebait is an excellent bait species which stays on the hook better than the softer bluebait. Whitebait is best fished on a gang of smaller number 6 to 1 hooks depending on the size of the baits.

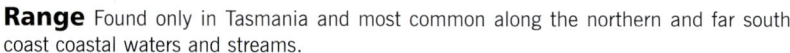

WHITEBAIT, TASMANIAN

Scientific name *Lovettia sealii.*

Range Found only in Tasmania and most common along the northern and far south coast coastal waters and streams.

Description The Tasmanian whitebait is a small species reaching less than 8 cm and commonly seen at around 6 centimetres. It is fished for as it migrates upstream out of estuaries. Another species, the jollytail or common trout minnow (*Galaxias maculatus*) is also sold as small transparent whitebait but the Tasmanian whitebait has a more restricted range, an adipose fin and a more concave tail.

Fishing A common and important forage species, the adults of which are favourites as bait for sea run trout. Juveniles are fished in special nets.

YELLOWTAIL

Scientific name *Trahurus novaezelandiae.* Also known as Yellowtail scad, scad, yakka, bung, chow.

Range Point Quobba in Western Australia and all southern waters, although relatively uncommon in Tasmania and as far north as Bribie Island in southern Queensland.

Description The yellowtail is a common schooling forage fish of inshore estuaries, bays or inshore oceanic waters. The yellowtail reaches 33 cm but is most commonly encountered at between 18 and 25 centimetres. Larger fish are almost certainly cowanyoung (also called horse mackerel or jack mackerel *Trachurus declivis*). Yellowtail have scutes (large scales along the lateral line) which extend from the back of the head whereas similar southern mackerel-scad (*Decapterus muroadsi*) or Russell mackerel-scad (*Decapterus russelli*) only have scutes at the rear of the body.

Fishing Gear can be as basic as a handline with 4 kg line and a size 12 long-shanked hook. One or no split shot completes the rig. Yellowtail will take most baits, but the most common baits are small pieces of cut bait, prawn, squid, mince meat, heart or mullet roe. Yellowtail respond very well to berley, with bran, pollard or commercial berleys working well. Many yellowtail are now taken on commercial bait jigs, either fished lightly weighted or vertically jigged with a larger sinker, but there are restrictions on the number of hooks in most states. Yellowtail make very good whole dead baits with fairly oily flesh, but they are arguably the best live bait

available. The common name yakka comes from the work that yellowtail put in as a very hardy live bait. Yellowtail should be lightly hooked in the back and either fished under a float or drift fished for all manner of larger fish. Yellowtail make acceptable eating but there are a number of small bones.

BIBLIOGRAPHY

The following publications have been of assistance in compiling this book and may provide additional reference.

Allen, G (1997). Marine Fishes of Tropical Australia and South-East Asia. Western Australian Museum. Perth. 292 pp.

Allen, G (1989). Freshwater Fishes of Australia. TFH Publications. Sydney. 240 pp.

Allen, G.R., Swainston, R. (1995). The marine fishes of north-western Australia. Western Australian Museum, Perth. 201 pp.

Goadby, P. (1996). Billfishing. The quest for marlin, swordfish, spearfish and sailfish. Harper-Collins, Sydney. 208 pp.

Grant, E.M. (1982). Guide to fishes. Wilke Printers, Brisbane. 896 pp.

Grant, E.M. (1987). Grant's fishes of Australia. EM Grant Pty Ltd, Brisbane. 480 pp.

Hutchins, B and Swainston, R. (1986). Sea Fishes of Southern Australia. Swainston Publishing, Perth. 180 pp.

Hutchins, B., Thompson, B. (1995). The marine and estuarine fishes of south-western Australia. A field guide for anglers and divers. Western Australian Museum, Perth. 103 pp.

Kailola, P et al (1993). Australian Fish Resources. Inprint Limited. Brisbane. 422 pp.

Kuiter, R.H. (1996). Guide to sea fishes of Australia. New Holland Publishers, Sydney. 433 pp.

Marshall, F (1969). Bait for Saltwater Fishing in Australia and New Zealand. Angus and Robertson. Sydney. 109 pp.

McDowall, R. M. (1996). Freshwater fishes of south-eastern Australia, 2nd Edition. Reed Books, 247 pp.

Merrick, J.R., Schmida, G.E. (1984). Australian freshwater fishes. Griffin Press, Netley SA. 409 pp.

Starling, S. (1986). The Australian fishing book. Reed Books, Sydney. 512 pp.

Yearsley, G, Last, P and Ward, D (1999). Australian Seafood Domestic Species. Courtney Colour Graphics. Melbourne. 461 pp.

Special thanks go to Dr Stephen Newman of Fisheries WA for his assistance in his own time to review the scientific names and other information in this book. Any errors are entirely the fault of the author and are unintentional.

ABOUT THE AUTHOR

Frank Prokop comes from a long line of Frank Prokops who fish. Frank was born in Detroit, Michigan in 1960 where he learned to catch the various American species and developed his love of freshwater fishing. Frank, his parents and five brothers and sisters moved to Australia in 1973, settling in Wollongong.

Frank started work at the Narrandera Inland Fisheries Research Station in 1984, working on trout cod and Macquarie perch research and native species production. Following a stint at the Grafton Research Station and as a National Parks ranger in the Hunter Valley, Frank became Australia's first specialist recreational fisheries manager with NSW Fisheries in 1989. In 1992, Frank settled in Perth, Western Australia where he worked for Fisheries WA until 1998 when he was appointed as Executive Director of Recfishwest, the lobby group for recreational fishers in WA.

With the support and help of Rod Harrison, Frank Prokop began writing on fishing in 1984 and his work has been published in *Fishing World* and *Freshwater Fishing* magazines. Frank has pioneered the jig flicking fishing method and has now writen about a dozen books on fishing.

Frank holds a science degree and a Master of Business Administration, which prove he has the pain threshold necessary to write a book of this type. In his spare time, Frank maintains an interest in basketball, having been a Board member for the Perth Wildcats and Basketball Western Australia, and is currently with the WA Sports Federation.

Frank enjoys the lifestyle and saltwater fishing of Perth where he lives with his wife Sonja and children, Frank and Natasha, but he misses the freshwater fishing available on the East Coast.

INDEX